Browning's Youth

Six Early Impressions of Robert Browning. *"Posterity will pronounce me a puzzle in that respect, no two transcripts of my respectable features being alike."*

Top right: Robert Browning (the poet), as late as 1830s. Probable pencil sketch by Robert Browning Sr.

Bottom right: Robert Browning, ca. 1835. Engraving by John Sartain of Beard sketch (or Armytage engraving).

Bottom left: Robert Browning—Portrait of the Artist Being Lifted into a Boat, ca. 1835-1840. Pencil cartoon self-portrait.

Top left: Robert Browning, July 4-7, 1837. Pencil drawing by Count Amédée de Ripert-Monclar.

Bottom left: Supposed Early Portrait of Robert Browning, ca. 1820s. Pencil sketch by Robert Browning Sr.

Right: Robert Browning, ca. 1835. Engraving by James Charles Armytage of a sketch by Beard.

Browning's Youth

John Maynard

Harvard University Press
Cambridge, Massachusetts
London, England
1977

Copyright © 1977 by the President and Fellows of Harvard College
All rights reserved
Printed in the United States of America
Publication of this book has been aided by a grant from the Andrew W. Mellon Foundation

Library of Congress Cataloging in Publication Data
Maynard, John, 1941-
Browning's youth.
Includes bibliographical references and index.
1.   Browning, Robert, 1812-1889—Biography—Youth.
I.   Title.
PR4232.M3   821'.8 [B]   76-16555
ISBN 0-674-08441-1

Preface

Along with his poetry the life of Robert Browning has continued, since his death, to hold interest for a substantial number of readers. His enormous vitality, his assertion of the fullest individuality even while he strove for the broadest view of humanity, his overflowing creative abundance, and his insistence on moral purpose and action could not fail to exert a personal attraction coincident with, but not identical to, the attractions of his literary work. Above all the central event of his personal life, his marriage to Elizabeth Barrett, continues, through endless rehearsals and across every form of sentimental distortion and appropriation, to exercise the legitimate attraction of a great tale of decisive human choice. Since the time in the late nineteenth century when Browning societies and clubs began to appear both in England and America in the mistaken hope that there might be found in the poet the old certainty of faith that was being lost in the complexities of the modern age, Browning's life has been told and retold, praised, scrutinized, or debunked, but never long ignored. With regularity, or perhaps even with increasing frequency, popular studies of Browning or studies of the life of Elizabeth Barrett in which he figures as a second major character have kept the story of his life before the public; and, now and then, a dramatic adaption of biography stirs up interest in yet another version of a living Robert and Elizabeth.

Nor has all study of Browning's life been by any means mere potboiling upon the surface of a popular curiosity. Serious creative talents, Edmund Gosse, William Sharp (Fiona Macleod, the romancer), G. K. Chesterton, Edward Dowden, Betty Miller, and, most recently, Maisie Ward have meditated at length on the artistic and personal success story that his life appears to offer. Even Virginia Woolf was once inspired to try her hand at a study of the Browning circle from the vantage point of Flush, Elizabeth's faithful spaniel. Behind such interpretive approaches, major full studies—the *Life and Letters* by Browning's friend, Mrs. Sutherland Orr (still important as something close to a primary source), the detailed history by Hall Griffin and H. C. Minchin, and the most recent critical and biographical study by William Irvine and Park Honan (authoritative on Browning's later years in London), as well as a number of articles and a good deal of professional editing of the seemingly endless mass of Browning letters—show no lack of serious scholarly attention to his life and poetic career.

In such a plenum of biographical activity a new work should be explicit about its claims to additional space. This study is an attempt to treat comprehensively the background to Browning's life in his family and early environment and the slow emergence of his own interests and motivations in his first creative efforts and in his education. It brings together whatever information survives, published or in manuscript, that can shed light on the poet's dimly known and hardly recorded youth. No student of life—far less Browning himself in his own most effective character studies—can remain totally faithful to his oft-quoted dictum "my stress lay on the incidents in the development of a soul: little else is worth knowing." But in focusing necessarily on the objective and often external facts of Browning's early life, I have tried as much as possible to discern in their configuration the larger patterns of a poet's inner development toward his ultimate creative and intellectual faculties.

The result will not interest the reader who looks for another restatement of the story and the romance of Browning's life. Rather, it addresses itself to those who wish to understand Browning's mature complexity by comprehending the diverse strands and combinations of experience and learning that went into the making of his personality as man and poet. By this, I in no way wish to argue the dubious concept of environmental determinism: that a poet can be understood as the sum of his parts. For no human being, least of all for a man of creating genius, is it possible merely to tally up the contexts and influences on a biographer's calculator and come up with the certified measure of the man. On the contrary, my aim has been to avoid the simplifying mechanisms by which studies of the youths of creative people can distort and dehumanize our view of the development of an artist. My premise, if I were to formulate a practical approach abstractly, is that we must take seriously the context and content of a child's and young adult's development as a hugely varied process of interaction between the past available to him and his own growing values and self-direction. In such a view, each person is a unique combination of environmental and traditional values all molded and made new by his particular energies and capacities and by the personal needs that shape his development. Understanding an artist's past in this way should provide not simpler explanations of his abilities, by which he may be reduced in our minds or dismissed out of hand, but a more humble awareness of the richness of his inheritance from the past and the possibilities opening to him in his maturity. A full examination of the total range of forces working to create an adult human out of the unformed stuff of infancy should stand as a critique of all simplifying systems that attempt to reduce development to one set of explanations, whether those of unconscious psychological forces, intellectual development by a logical process of ideas, environmental or educational determinism, or the more usual arbitrary postulation of leading characteristics through a series of untrustworthy anecdotes. In exploring some of the complex ways in which Browning developed out of the conditions of his family life, out of the artistic ideas to which he was exposed, or out of the educational and literary traditions available to him, I intend to free him from the misuses of the past that result from simplified focus and partial knowledge and, wherever possible, to shed light from his past on facets of his mature achievement which have been overlooked or underestimated. I have, in the same aim, tried to be as explicit as possible, even at the risk of much documentation, about my own sources and about the many lacunae in our knowledge of this period in his life.

Finally, a word about the organization of this study may be indulged. Usually a biographer is able to choose between following a strictly chronological arrangement of his materials and imposing his own topical order on them. But in looking at Browning's earliest years I was forced, because of the lack of specific records of his life, to focus separately on the different aspects of his experience rather than to follow a chronological scheme that could be at best only vague and fragmentary. In doing this my primary concern has been to provide a picture of Browning's experience in his first twenty to twenty-two years when he was most fully immersed in his home environment. I have not hesitated, however, to bring in information from the entire period of Browning's life down to his marriage in 1846, when I felt that it would help to illuminate the general nature of his early environment and of the milieu from which he came. In describing the Browning family I have thus drawn upon incidents that took place at the later Hatcham residence as well as at the Camberwell homes in which Browning actually spent his earlier years. In discussing the set, a group with which Browning was primarily associated in his twenties, or in looking at his friendship in the 1830s with the Frenchman, Ripert-Monclar, I have likewise deliberately focused upon episodes from a somewhat later period of Browning's life because they seemed to me naturally related to the subject of his early environment. With a similar aim, I have not hesitated, in discussing Browning's early poetry and intellectual development, to point up continuities between his early interests and his mature art and opinions. A biographer must live, with Sidney's historian, in the mere brazen world of fact, not in the golden world of the time-warping poet or stream of consciousness novelist; consequently, in taking these liberties, I have been as explicit as possible about dates.

I have used the notes to provide the summaries of sources and basic information about subjects and people discussed that are otherwise unavailable for this period of Browning's life. They are there, in the back, for those who wish to consult them. Those who relish genealogical charts and detailed information on the families of the great will find what they seek in Appendix A, where others may with impunity overlook them.

ACKNOWLEDGMENTS

When the Browning family possessions were mercilessly put up on the block at Sotheby & Company in 1913 and thence dispersed throughout the world, all that was mortal of Browning's literary life was doomed to rest, if at all, in pieces and fragments, and students of the poet were condemned to wander eternally from library to library like moaning restless shades. In my intermittent journeying over the past nine years I have accumulated a large debt for permission to look at Browning materials, to quote from materials in collections, and for many other kindnesses. I am very grateful to the authorities and staffs of the following institutions who have been, without exception, most generous: the Alexander Turnbull Library, Wellington, New Zealand, especially Mrs. Heather Blakeley; the Armstrong Browning Library, Baylor University, especially Dr. Jack Herring, Director, and Mrs. Betty Coley, Librarian; also Mr. Craig Turner for helpful information and for generously allowing me to draw upon his M.A. thesis on Cyrus Mason; Balliol College, Oxford, especially Mr. E. V. Quinn, Librarian; the Governor and Company of the Bank of England, for generously providing photographs, and especially Mr. E. M. Kelly and Miss Turner of the Archives Section; the Beinecke Rare Book and Manuscript Library, Yale University, especially Miss Marjorie Gray Wynne, Research Librarian; the Berg Collection and the New York Public Library, especially the late Dr. John Gordan; the Bodleian Library, Oxford; the Boston Public Library; the British Library; the British Library of Political and Economic Science, London School of Economics; the Camberwell District Registry Office; Cambridge University, especially Miss H. E. Peek, Keeper of the Archives and S. C. Aston, Bursar of St Catharine's College; Cheshunt College, Cambridge, especially President J. E. Newport who also helped me obtain friendly assistance from Dr. J. C. Q. Binfield of the University of Sheffield and the Rev. Dr. Stephen C. Orchard of Trinity Church, Sutton; the Public Library, Cheshunt, especially Mr. Jack Edwards; Columbia University Library; the Fitzwilliam Museum; the Houghton Library, Harvard University; the Humanities Research Center of the University of Texas; the London Borough of Lambeth Library, especially Miss M. Y. Williams of the Minet Public Library; the London Borough of Lewisham Library, especially Mrs. Joan Read of the Manor House Branch; the London Borough of Southwark Library, especially Miss Boast of the Newington District Library; the Henry E. Huntington Library; the National Library of Scotland; the National Portrait Gallery, especially Mr. Richard Ormond, Assistant Keeper; the New Register House, Edinburgh; the Pierpont Morgan Library; the Public Record Office, Chancery Lane; the Robert Browning Fellowship Hall, Walworth and the hospitable keepers, Mr. and Mrs. Wallace; the Scripps College Library; the South London Art Gallery, especially Mr. Kenneth Sharpe, the Director; the South Place Ethical Society, especially the Manager Miss Robyn Miles; the University of Chicago Library; University College London, especially Mrs. Mary Lightbown and the staff of the D. M. S. Watson Library; the Victoria and Albert Museum, South Kensington; the Wellesley College Library, especially Dr. Eleanor Nicholes, Special Collections Librarian, and Mrs. S. C. Godfrey. The editors and staff of the Harvard University Press, who frown at more particular acknowledgment of my gratitude, have been extremely helpful.

Professors Jerome H. Buckley and John Clive of Harvard University supervised this work in its early stages and provided many helpful comments and suggestions. My debt to both of them, as my mentors in nineteenth-century studies and as kind friends, is great and ever-growing. I wish to express my thanks to the following individuals who have also provided exceptional help with this work: Professor Richard D. Altick, for reading the study and making helpful suggestions for improvements; Professor Kingsbury Badger, for suggestions and personal kindness; Mrs. Elaine Baly, for generously putting family records and her own extensive genealogical investigations at my disposal; Professor Warner Barnes, for scholarly help and personal kindness during my visit to the University of Texas; Mrs. Nora Collings, for kindly answering my inquiries about family traditions; Mrs. Dorothy Gwyther, for furnishing me copies of her Browning items and for friendly answers to my inquiries; Dr. and Mrs. Jack Herring, for scholarly and personal kindnesses, which made my long task at the Armstrong Browning Library rewarding and extremely pleasant; Professor Park Honan, for kind suggestions; the late Elvan Kintner, for letting me see the new edition of the letters of Robert and Elizabeth before publication; Mr. John G. Murray for generously granting me permission to reproduce works of the Brownings protected by his copyright; Professor William S. Peterson for permission to reprint in slightly different form an article published in *Browning Institute Studies;* Professor Richard Purdy, for very kindly opening his exceptional personal collection to me. Finally, I cannot leave off the names of Professors Douglas Bush, David Kalstone, and the late Reuben Brower, all of whom offered examples of humane literary scholarship and provided personal encouragement when it was badly needed.

This work would not have been possible without the generous assistance of a year's research grant from the National Endowment for the Humanities, a travel grant from the American Philosophical Society, and a summer grant from the Canaday Humanities Fund, Harvard University. The Harvard English Department also kindly helped defray costs for research in England in the early stages of this work.

My wife, Florence Michelson Maynard, and my parents, A. Rogers and Olive Maynard, know my gratitude for so many little kindnesses in this work which amount to a large debt over the years.

Contents

Part One
Early Environment

Part Two
The Development of
a Poetic Nature: First Steps

Part Three
Education

Appendixes

Illustrations

15

S. Yates 1826

Part One
Early Environment

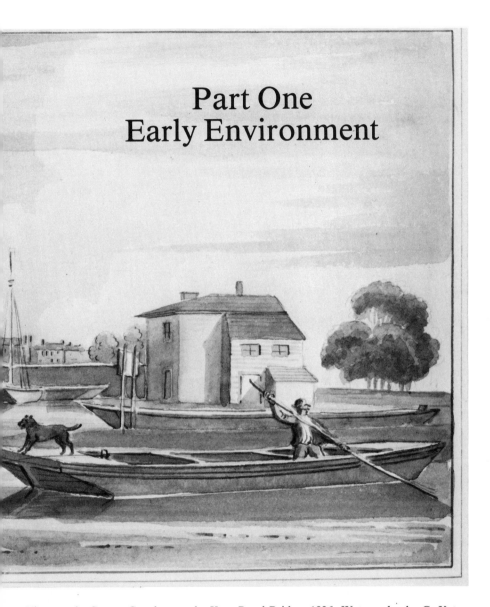

View on the Surrey Canal, near the Kent Road Bridge, 1826. Water color by G. Yates.

I
Introduction:
Seeing Young Browning Plain

Robert Browning was born in suburban Camberwell, outside London, on May 7, 1812. A good deal is known about the circumstances of his childhood and adolescence, but until the early 1830s, when a few letters that have been preserved begin to offer occasional glimpses into his doings and thoughts, there is little but the most general information available about the external events of his life, far less about the internal development of his personality and poetic genius. In fact, there are very few written records from the time that mention the young Browning directly. Church register entries of his birth and the baptism of June 14 of the same year,[1] the family Bible and some books with transcriptions or markings, his father's correspondence about his enrollment at the new London University and his name on the rolls, and two letters from Sarah Flower, later author of "Nearer, My God, to Thee," mentioning her young friend, are virtually all that are available before the 1830s. Of his boyhood poetry only a few occasional couplets and two short poems—remarkable for a boy of fourteen but imitative in conception and not very revealing—have survived.

This scarcity of evidence is partly mere accident but also in part the result of a deliberate effort to destroy and conceal everything relating to the poet's youth. The offender—as we must now think of him, though he felt he was justly defending his rights to privacy—was none other than the poet himself, a man who might praise in the abstract the idea of studying incidents in the development of a soul but protected and hid his own history and consciousness with the care of a mother hen brooding over her precious eggs. His known ravages included over one hundred early poems in addition to his entire first boyhood volume and a family correspondence piled high enough to occupy him a week in sorting and burning.[2] When someone did try to get at a part of his personal history, he was liable to respond with extravagant indignation. "What I suffer," he fulminated over a request for information about his married life, "in feeling the hands of these black-guards (for I forgot to say, *another* man has been making similar applications to friends)—what I undergo with their paws in my very bowels, you can guess & God knows!"[3] His injunction, which he made good even for future biographers by wholesale slaughter of letters and manuscripts, was blunt and clear: "Be assured that all such interferences with the sacredness of the grave are abominable."[4]

With the same defensive stance Browning in his poems, as every reader of his fine sonnet "House" well knows, deliberately refused to unlock his heart. Insisting with tedious iteration that his works should be considered "so many utterances of so many imaginary persons, not mine," he shied away from all personal revelation. Not one of his poems, in any strict sense, can be considered as a memoir or autobiography. In the very few poems, such as "May and Death" or the late and delightful "Development," in which he does speak directly of his boyhood, the account is limited to an isolated episode or reminiscence, and he gives us no assurance that he is not creating from the materials of memory a "fancy portrait" of earlier times, from fact creating a poetic fancy.[5] Browning's earliest published work, a first-born for which he was long unwilling to acknowledge paternity, the short narrative poem, *Pauline* (1833), was given the subtitle *A Fragment of a Confession* and has often been claimed as an exception to, or rather an early indiscretion from, his usual scruples over autobiography. In part that is true as he himself virtually admitted.[6] The poem does offer some glimpses into his early life beneath the shallow mask of the speaker: into his childhood reading, his love of nature, his education, his early attempts at poetry, and his intellectual and religious doubts in adolescence. Yet the whole presents not a detailed biographical history but merely a schematic view of some of the main elements in his growth as he interpreted them in earliest manhood. Although it is the most important single aid to understanding his growth and development, it remains more a confession than an autobiography. It reveals more about Browning at the time when he wrote it than about his earlier experiences and thoughts. Much the same must be said about a work from the other end of his career, the *Parleyings with Certain People of Importance in their Day* (1887). It has been dignified by the description, "the autobiography of a mind," but it is rather a series of essays on subjects dear to the aged writer.[7] Although Browning anchors his opinions in "parleyings," that is imaginary conversations (or monologues) with writers familiar to him in youth or early life, he offers in the poems only a few scraps of information about his early experience—far less a history of the growth of his opinions or an account, in Wordsworth's sense, of the growth of a poet's mind. A choice, often deliberately eccentric, of seven authors out of the thousands he read, the *Parleyings* do not even present a reliable record of the works most important to him in early reading.

In addition to these limited sources, what little other information there is about his early life comes largely from reminiscences by Browning and his sister that have been picked up and repeated by various friends and biographers or found among their correspondence. With the exception of an occasional rare reference to his childhood in Browning's letters before marriage, these are generally the recollections of forty or fifty years later, and taken together, they offer less a history of the growth of a poet's mind than a series of disjointed and none too consistent family anecdotes. In one we see the young child, just at the point of lisping into speech, endearing himself to his mother: "A pitty baze, mama," as his mother's fine Brussels lace veil goes up in flames. We hear also of complaints registered at the local dame school to which he was sent that Master Browning's remarkable progress in his studies was leading to the neglect of the other pupils. Evidently there was a terse diary entry by Browning when he was about seven or eight: "Married two wives this morning." Other stories tell of his symbolic exorcism of a fit of homesickness when he first went to school as a weekly boarder; of his horror at the fable of the lion who was kicked to death by an ass; of early rhymes on the subject of taking medicine and of still earlier attempts at painting in lead pencil and black currant jam juice.[8] To these stories may be added a few reminiscences by acquaintances or relatives. For instance, a gentleman recalled, more than sixty years later, seeing the Brownings in church; a certain cousin Cyrus Mason, himself a good deal younger than the poet, put together a strange book of reminiscences and family gossip in his old age in Australia, and a few others left some impressions, but their recollections were equally fortuitous and incomprehensive.

Pleasant as such anecdotes often are, illuminating as they occasionally appear to be, they are obviously dubious aids in drawing any fully credible picture of Browning as a boy or adolescent. The family stories, in particular, could be matched by similar tales in most families and were obviously shaped by the normal processes of imagination and selection involved in all hindsight over the youths of the later famous. Nor does it even appear likely that these anecdotes have the virtue of offering typical or representative vignettes from the countless moments of childhood and adolescence. Taken together such recollections and the few available documents certainly do not provide a coherent idea of the character of Browning as a boy or of his earliest development.

When we try to look directly at the boy Browning, or even at the adolescent or young man of twenty or twenty-two, through the limited information we have, we attain at best only a few general impressions and become aware of even greater difficulties. There can be no doubt, for instance, that Browning was almost from babyhood a boy of very quick, even exceptional intelligence and varied talent. Anecdotes stress his cleverness, active imagination, and liveliness, and there are records of truly precocious, if imitative, displays of artistic and literary talent. All stories agree in giving him a restless, even rather nervous energy, almost as a biological trait that was projected into every situation throughout his life. We can be fairly sure that he was on the whole assertive and even at times rather given to showing off, both traits naturally encouraged by his position as admired first child in his family. At the same time, with an almost innate love of music and a strong bond with his family, he seems to have had a balancing sensitivity and a capacity for strong feeling when once moved.

Such impressions give us some idea of what kind of boy it was who later grew into a poet, but only an excessively sensitive imagination can make out of them a picture of the poet in embryo or deny that such qualities might equally have been the biological basis of any number of diverse adult personalities. Nor is a great deal added by the one visual impression of his boyhood appearance: Browning's recollection, confirmed by his sister, that he was born "supremely passionate—so I was born with light yellow hair."[9] The passionate temperament persisted; but as he grew older his hair darkened into a brown verging on black, which he let grow in adolescence and early manhood in a long, flowing, romantic style. The contrast between the hair and his bright gray eyes, almost pale, white complexion, and rather fine features set on a thin body of modest stature made him seem in later adolescence a romantic, even striking, youth.[10] As he becomes a young adult, some clearer sense of a distinct personality thus begins to emerge; and it is confirmed by letters that give us a picture of a clever, even too clever and slightly affected, young man by the time he first begins to attract some notice in London literary society. Yet, even for this later period, lack of information and the naturally unformed nature of youth renders any simple or single-faceted portrait suspect. If he appears as something of a romantic adolescent challenging the assumptions of his society and family, he certainly does not fit in any sense our modern idea of youth in full revolt and alienation. Although he may appear a clever young man about town in his early manhood, he remains simultaneously very much an earnest, serious, and quite idealistic young person. There is simply not enough evidence to make it possible to assert which sides of his personality were the most prominent. Browning the young man, like many talented young people who have not yet settled their way in life, seems indeed to have had less a single organized personality than a large number of potential qualities and abilities all floating in suspension in his still somewhat undefined character.

Speaking in later life, Browning remarked to a friend that portraits and drawings of him seemed to reveal not one personality but a variety: "Posterity will pronounce me a puzzle in that respect, no two transcripts of my respectable features being alike."[11] This effect is most apparent in his earliest portraits, which only complicate our problem. Two sketches by his father (one not certainly of Browning) do seem to confirm written reports of his attractive, romantic appearance but are rather too simplified and idealized to give a very clear impression of personality.[12] Two other, probably somewhat later portraits of 1835 and 1837, give quite different and also mutually contradictory impressions.[13] One is the well-known and often-reproduced J. C. Armytage engraving of a pen sketch by Beard (1835), and the other is a pencil sketch by Browning's French friend Ripert-Monclar

(1837). The Monclar drawing shows a sophisticated, almost rakish young gentleman with sharp attractive features. The Beard drawing, as Robert and Elizabeth often complained to each other and their friends, spread a foolish image of Browning as rather pretty, excessively genteel, and, in Browning's opinion, supercilious in the manner of a fine ladies' sales clerk. Both show the long dark hair and fine features with a prominent, slightly turned down aquiline nose, but otherwise they portray totally different personalities.

A more objective verbal description entered on a Russian visa issued to Browning in 1834 is even less helpful. It indicates that the young British gentleman was of medium height (about five feet, eight), with dark brown hair and eyebrows, gray eyes, oval face, rounded chin, and "moderate" (or average-sized) forehead and mouth. The space in which special features could be noted is left blank.[14] Even descriptions left by friends of Browning in his twenties give a similarly vague or confused impression and leave us wondering sometimes whether the confusion was theirs or Browning's or some combination of the two. One young lady found him merely a "plain-looking boy" while another recalled him as something quite exotic, even "a trifle of a dandy."[15] Carlyle saw at least *three* young Robert Brownings. He recalled his first meeting with Browning, probably in the later 1830s, in almost antithetical anecdotes. To Moncure Conway and William Allingham he remembered meeting a "beautiful youth" with "simple speech and manners," "a modest youth, with a good strong face and a head of dark hair."[16] To Browning himself he earlier confessed a very different impression: being "anything but favorably impressed" by Browning's smart green riding coat which suggested "proclivities for the turf and scamphood."[17] At another time this Rembrandt of Victorian prose was painting Browning in yet a third pose: "a neat dainty little fellow, speaking in the Cockney quiz-dialect"; "a dainty Leigh-Huntish kind of fellow, with much ingenuity, vivacity and Cockney gracefulness."[18]

If Browning thus appeared literally as something of a chameleon poet even as late as the 1830s and 1840s, the opening consideration in looking at his earlier years must be to acknowledge the limits of our knowledge—limits resulting both from the dearth of reliable biographic evidence and from the difficulty of fixing the flowing uncertainties and vague possibilities of youth in the inflexible mold of straightforward description. This is not to imply that his youth remains merely unrecorded and unknown, even less that there is, as some have wished to see, some deeper gothic story of multiple personality beneath the normal vacillations and complexity of an intelligent and sensitive young person. Compared to what is generally known about the early years of eminent persons in other ages, the external events of Browning's young life—his birth date, the places he lived, the schools he attended—are quite fully known. We can certainly see, if we survey the entire period of his early years, the steady, if not always trouble-free, development of an adult personality ready by the 1830s to try the extraordinarily difficult task of finding his own form of expression and organization in poetry. But because of the limited specific records, only a few dubious

instances or some vague and general summaries may be given of the growing boy's day-to-day or even year-to-year activities. We may imagine the
flow of aspirations, interests, and enthusiasms, the endless stream of discoveries, new ideas, and thoughts that made up his immediate existence.
But we are barred from obtaining any detailed sense of how they fitted
together over time or any exact idea of their nature. Nor is it generally possible, as it often is in looking at his later life, to draw definite conclusions
concerning his personality or full state of mind at any particular point in his
early development.

On the other hand, if we cannot know exactly what the young Browning was at any point in his development, we can at least come to understand
the forces that were working upon him and helping to shape, in complex
interaction with his natural temperament and abilities, his ultimate interests
and development. Fortunately there is a good deal of general information
available, from Browning's later letters, from memoirs of his family and
friends, from his father's various sketchbooks and notebooks, or from contemporary illustrations and prints, concerning the general conditions and
circumstances of his family and early home environment. In the absence of
much more direct knowledge about his youth it is at least possible to recon-
struct from such sources some picture of the society and culture in which he
grew up. Unable to see the young Browning himself very clearly, we may at
least get some impression of the kind of world he looked out upon. We can
get some indication, too, of the kinds of influences exerted upon him during
those years and of the possibilities opened to him by his childhood environment, especially for the growth of his imagination and poetic abilities.

With this background understanding of the context and premises of
Browning's early life, we may turn in the second and third parts of this
study to look in more detail at the later period of Browning's youth for
which *Pauline* and other records give us some vague chronology of his
growth. Here in at least two large areas of his creative and intellectual development, some direction is already apparent, and we have enough information to trace broadly the slow emergence of Browning's own personal aims
and interests. In his early attempts at artistic expression, which culminate in
the production of *Pauline,* he is at least beginning to grapple with the problems of the proper role of the poet and of the nature and function of art that
will be central to his mature poetic development. In the long and somewhat
erratic process of his education he can be seen slowly developing, in reaction
to the ideas of knowledge prevalent in his society, his own vision of the
humanities and a personal understanding of man's past achievement upon
which his own work will build. Although we may not be able to obtain
either a full history of his early life or a complete picture of his interests,
enthusiasms, or personal qualities, we can at least realize some idea of the
major formative influences that worked upon Browning in his youth and
gain some insight into the earliest development of his sense of a vocation as
a student of mankind and as a poet.

II
Camberwell and New Cross

During the entire period of Browning's childhood and adolescence his family lived in Camberwell, then a village or small town located about two and a half miles south of the London Bridge. In late 1840 they moved east to the nearby town of New Cross at the three mile bar on the Kent Road, where Browning lived with them until 1846 when he eloped with Elizabeth Barrett. Browning was twenty-eight when he moved to New Cross, no longer a boy or student but a grown man boarding at home. But his life and circumstances in both Camberwell and New Cross were generally so similar and the villages themselves so much a part of the same kind of social and cultural pattern that they may be looked at together.

Although only a short distance from their giant neighbor, London, both villages, undistinguished for any particular qualities, had maintained throughout the eighteenth century their age-old sleepy existence as quiet farming communities. In both villages, and indeed in the nearby and very similar villages of Dulwich (famed for its old boarding school), Peckham, and Walworth, older buildings, still existing in Browning's time but today known only from prints or illustrations, suggest the traditionally modest and generally rustic character of the area. The parish church of Camberwell, the Church of St. Giles, for instance, unlike its present large and pretentious successor in ersatz Gothic, was a small, unassuming structure—"an antient gothic building of rough stones, with an embattled tower; on which is a cupola of wood, with a bell and weathercock."[1] In one print from the early nineteenth century we can see a forecourt with a rustic fence, two children lounging within, and some chickens pecking around the yard.[2] Another well-known old building, preserved now only in prints of the time, was the Rosemary Branch, an inn not far from the Brownings' several homes at Camberwell. It was a two-story structure built out in a rambling,

Map of the Parish of St. Giles, Camberwell, 1842. By J. Dewhirst. *The Brownings' three houses in Camberwell were on Southampton Street. The site of the third, Hanover Cottage, is probably that marked "Hanover Cots."*

The Rosemary Branch. By H. Prosser. *Landmark sporting inn near the Brownings' Camberwell houses: an "establishment which had no suburban rival."*

View of London from Camberwell, 1797. Engraving by W. Knight of a painting by E. Dayes. *"A view of the First City of the World"—from the tranquillity of a rural suburb.*

The New Phoenix Brewery, ca. 1925. Water color by Guy Miller. *Probably the home of Browning's cousins, the Silverthornes, in No⋅ːh Terrace or Portland Place.*

comfortable way, famed as a respectable pleasure haunt with extensive sporting grounds, and proclaimed as an "establishment which had no suburban rival."[3] At both Dulwich and Camberwell, rough-built old windmills were still a prominent part of the landscape.[4]

The entire area had a serene and rural aspect that today would be incredible for a location so close to the center of a large city. A map of 1763 shows the entire Camberwell-New Cross district as completely separate from London with only a few clusters of buildings around the crossroads, where villages were located, and miles of open area, punctuated only by an occasional estate or gentleman's farm or villa.[5] Camberwell Grove, a long hill or rise south of St. Giles Church, was for eighteenth-century printmakers, as it later was for the young Browning, a favorite vantage point. Prints show us, with almost startling incongruity, a lazy scene of cows grazing in long sloping meadows with "a view of the first city in the world," rising in many towers and a cluster of masts as a not very distant background.[6]

Social life, too, and the composition of local society were not greatly changed in essentials during the eighteenth century from what they had been for centuries before. Changes in religious outlook, manners, or customs had, no doubt, over long periods of time worked variations in the character and temper of the people. Yet occupations and labor, the division of power and authority, and the physical conditions of life were on the whole much the same as they had been for centuries. There were some few large owners: lords, or squires and gentlemen, men such as Lord Thurlow whose stately three-story Georgian country house, Knight's Hill Farm, is shown in a print of about 1800.[7] Less affluent and influential, but still among the few who might write themselves down "Gent.," was the small number of professional men—ministers, fellows at the college at Dulwich, a few wealthy merchants or an occasional man of eminence, such as Sir Christopher Wren, who had settled there.[8] In the villages, in Camberwell, New Cross, Dulwich, or Peckham, there were, in addition, a small number of true villagers: shop keepers, an innkeeper or two, one or two village or church officials, various craftsmen and perhaps a local producer such as Browning's Uncle Silverthorne the Camberwell brewer. But on the flat Thames riverbed meadows leading from Camberwell toward London and on the grassy, up and down hilly region between Camberwell and Dulwich and around New Cross, the staple and by far the most important industry in the eighteenth century was, as it had always been, agriculture and dairy farming.

Whatever changes of fashion or thought might slowly percolate in from the nearby city, the structure of life in the village remained fundamentally unchanged and, despite the nearness to London, the area maintained its independent and rural character into the nineteenth century. By the time of Browning's birth in 1812, and even earlier, however, it was clear that the character and populace of these villages were beginning to undergo a very substantial change. At first it was simply a matter of a relative increase in the number of gentlemen's country seats in the area. But even the term *villa,* which came to be used for these country houses, indicated that the change was something new, a new kind of people moving into the area rather than just an increase in the number of persons among the landed class.[9]

By the time of the publication of Macaulay's *History of England* in 1848, the emergence of a new suburban civilization and way of life—now an obvious fact to us—was sufficiently clear for a man like Macaulay, in close touch with the development of middle-class nineteenth-century England in all its aspects, to comprehend what had happened. Comparing London in 1685 with the London of his own day, Macaulay provides a useful, if somewhat roseate, picture of the kind of society that was evolving in the Camberwell area just before and during Browning's early life:

> The town [London in 1685] did not, as now, fade by imperceptible degrees into the country. No long avenues of villas, embowered in lilacs and laburnums, extended from the great center of wealth and civilization almost to the boundaries of Middlesex and far into the heart of Kent and Surrey . . . The whole character of the City has since that time, undergone a complete change. At present the bankers, the merchants, and the chief shopkeepers repair thither on six mornings of every week for the transaction of business; but they reside in other quarters of the metropolis, or at suburban country-seats surrounded by shrubberies and flower gardens . . . The City is no longer regarded by the wealthiest traders with that attachment which every man naturally feels for his home. It is no longer associated in their minds with domestic affections and endearments. The fireside, the nursery, the social table, the quiet bed are not there.[10]

For whatever reasons—and no doubt strong among them would be the continuing growth of London, the development of a larger clerical and managerial class, better transportation into the city, and a new taste for garden and country life and domestic ease—a large number of new settlers, men whose professional or financial ties were with the larger London area and not with the local region, was visibly changing the rural and village character of the area. Even as early as 1823 when Browning was only eleven years old, a map of London shows a great proliferation of new buildings. Substantial three-story brick dwellings were built all along the old main roads connecting Camberwell to neighboring Walworth or Peckham usually in fashionable row "terraces" set back from the road. Smaller, trim "cottages," semidetached or independent with gardens in front and behind, were slowly filling in the former area of open fields between the main roads —now a familiar pattern but not so then, when the expansion of the city had usually proceeded by the creation of new city blocks adjacent to open fields.[11] Although most of the older buildings of Camberwell or New Cross would remain for another thirty to forty years, and although large stretches of open meadow or hill still persisted during all the period of Browning's residence there, the overall change worked by this influx of new inhabitants in the character of the district was so great as to suggest an entirely new way of conceiving of the area. "Your letter," wrote one of Browning's youthful friends to another in 1874, "was as fresh gushing and as good naturedly exaggerated in tone as in the past years when we used to stray together in the suburban shades of Camberwell."[12] No longer the pejorative term that it had been in earlier times, when it had connoted a lawless, brothel-and-scribbler-infested area at the outskirts of the city proper, *suburban* had become the descriptive term for a new kind of life and society.

A water color of a *View on the Surrey Canal, near the Kent Road Bridge,*[13] dated 1826 and depicting a place not far from the street in which the Browning family lived, shows a very placid canal scene with two swans floating gracefully on the untroubled water. The picture includes a view of the Kent road itself and shows a number of well ordered and substantial houses with open, flat meadows and light, delicate trees behind. On the canal there is a small barge being drawn on a rope by a man on the tow path while a dog barks happily on the deck. Over the fine arched stone bridge a coach drawn on by handsome horses hurries toward London while the four outriders in the back look over the pleasant scene. Taken as a whole, the picture presents almost an epitome of the values and concerns of the society in which Browning grew up: the love of a calm, serene, natural world, ordered almost into one larger garden; the taste for graceful but solid dwellings set out within the garden world; and within this idyllic world, an insistence, nonetheless, upon the value of labor and efficiency, not as opposed concepts but as part of the quest for a complete harmony and natural order. In all other accounts or pictures of the area the same general tendencies are apparent. Even the facades of buildings show placid, even at times stately, Georgian and Regency country architecture with a simple grace in the repeated use of arches along the fronts of buildings. But along with the new order brought in by the new building is a persistent respect for the natural environment, now often closed in and bordered by fences or walls, yet still left to assert itself in full trees, high hedges, and verdant meadows. In every picture of the area, artists transmit the vision of their society by insisting upon seeing men and buildings not in isolation but in close relation to the picturesque natural environment.

Along with the influx of new, well ordered terraces and cottages, many new institutions developed while smaller, old ones began to expand. Not far from the old church of St. Giles at Camberwell, a stylish New Church of St. George in the Greek manner with a high steeple was built near the Surrey Canal. Throughout the area there was a proliferation of churches representing the entire range of Protestant sects, including the York Street Congregational Church at Walworth, which Browning's family attended, and the Camden Episcopal Chapel at Camberwell where Browning and his sister were in the habit of going on Sunday evenings. Many new schools—including a charity school with the proud plaque posted on the front, "Supported by Voluntary Subscriptions," a large and surprisingly attractive new workhouse, even a Friendly Society Asylum for Poor Women Who Have Seen Better Days—began to appear.[14] In the eighteenth century large holders, such as a certain Dr. Lettsom, had drawn up careful plans for their estates and added improvements: a green house, a library, a Shakespeare walk or a Sybil temple in their fields.[15] Now it was the efforts of a group of men, in fact the voluntary work of most of the society, that was ordering not an estate but an entire community.

Lettsom had foreseen the development of Camberwell as a place that would "combine neighborhood and friendship, thereby to ensure the reciprocal enjoyment of rational gratification."[16] His sentiment remained the cooperative ideal for the growing community in the early nineteenth century. Indeed, this was Pickwick country, where reasonable eighteenth-century ideals seemed to live on into the more complicated nineteenth century, and it is not surprising to find that the benevolent Mr. Pickwick himself retired to nearby Dulwich at the end of his adventures. There, with a miniature conservatory, a study with pictures, easy chairs, and "books out of number," with a lawn in front, and a garden behind, and a cheerful "window opening upon a pleasant lawn and commanding a pretty landscape, dotted here and there with little houses almost hidden by the trees," Pickwick was, of course, a model citizen.[17]

About the kind of people, other than Pickwick, who lived in the area where Browning grew up it is, however, dangerous to generalize. No doubt many were, as Macaulay implies, very substantial merchants, City people, and other "opulent families" living in circumstances on their country villas that would have seemed comfortable even to landed gentlemen.[18] Such, for instance, were the spacious dwelling and grounds at Herne Hill about a mile from Camberwell, where Ruskin grew up, and which he described so charmingly in *Praeterita*. But at Walworth, Camberwell, or Peckham, it is clear that many families, like Browning's own, lived in rather more modest, if decidedly comfortable circumstances. The father of one of Browning's friends, Joseph Arnould, was a doctor. Another friend, Alfred Domett, came from a line of naval men; his father, who lived a short way up Camberwell Grove, was a shipowner and kept a small yacht. Another neighbor at Camberwell, John Relfe, with whom Browning studied music, was a musician in ordinary to his Majesty but made his living by giving music lessons at Camberwell and in London. Perhaps the occupations of Browning's own relations were themselves most typical of the area. Both his grandfather, who lived at first at Camberwell, and his father were employees of the Bank of England. His uncle Reuben, who lived near the Browning family at New Cross, had a similar position with the House of Rothschild. What was common to most of the suburban residents was their lack of any clearly defined position in the traditional social life of Camberwell. No longer content with the long standing position of the merchant and business classes as a separate urban burgher class, owners, managers, clerks, London professional people, and various unpropertied men of special talents began to create a separate society in which they might assume, in a modest way commensurate with their more limited means, many of the traditional privileges of the landed or aristocratic classes. Not only was every small landholder's or renter's house his castle and his well-cultivated plot in back his estate and gardens, but there were even signs of a tendency toward the democratization of some of the special prerogatives of the upper classes. Unlike a son of a peer, Browning was not trained in boyhood in the dubious art of the shoot. But, like other residents of Camberwell or Dulwich, he did have the then unique opportunity of enjoying at the new Dulwich Picture Gallery—the first public art gallery in London—firsthand acquaintance with as fine a collection of paintings as that in any aristocratic house.

This spectacle, for modest as the events were, such it is, of a new society and a new way of life in the process of formation evokes a sense of open possibilities and even of new freedom. Outside Camberwell, and with surprisingly little immediate impact on local life and the local imagination, the greater changes and wilder social optimism touched off in the French Revolution had flared up and, at least for a while, burned themselves out. But here, if infinitely more modest, was change that seemed destined to last. If no open revolution or sudden secular millennium, here at least was real improvement in the simple ways in which nineteenth-century England would be ready to see it: increased and more widespread prosperity and greater room for individual effort and advancement. Optimism and even everyday freedom was reflected in the evident pride of the residents in their new churches and institutions, in their care of gardens and houses, in their reliance on voluntary subscriptions—even in their concern for education and the arts. For individuals, too, there was a degree of real freedom and opportunity, which would not usually be found, for all the Victorian trumpeting about the efficacy of self-help, in most sections of nineteenth-century England. With their education and social background, suburban men of limited means, like Browning's neighbor Benjamin Jowett or his friends Arnould and Domett, or—for that matter—Browning himself, could go on to hold very influential positions in society. Jowett became the eminent Master of Balliol College; Arnould, an acknowledged expert on marine law and a judge at Bombay; Domett, Prime Minister of New Zealand. Here quietly, but here if anywhere, the dominant movement of English society in the early nineteenth century toward middle-class prosperity and middle-class democracy appeared in its most positive and attractive form.

Change and freedom from traditional social structures could also, however, make this new suburban society peculiarly susceptible to insularity, mediocrity, petty moralism, and social decay. "You are right about that New Zealand life—Camberwell with a dash of the Coal-Hole is the very living portraiture of the whole thing . . . 'tis the effigy of the place in its totality of seediness, stale tobaccoism, & attorney clerkdom,'' Arnould wrote Domett, who was then in New Zealand.[19] With a twist of perspective the "suburban shades" could lose their idyllic quality and become merely a stale and poor compromise between country and city life; pleasant, hilly New Cross could become "this Thulé of a suburb,'' as Browning termed it in a pique over its isolation.[20] A vital variety of religion could degenerate easily into sectarian shrillness, as a plaque on the Grove Chapel in Camberwell still testifies: built, "for the preaching of the Gospel of God's Grace to Sinners as revealed by Inspired Scripture & witnessed to by the English Reformation.''

That Camberwell and the area around it also nurtured their share of Mrs. Grundys is at least suggested by an anecdote of Browning's babyhood. We are told of a certain old crone, unhappily known as Aunt Betsy, who was in the habit of visiting Browning's mother, evidently for tea and gossip. One day she made a usual old-maidish and contemptuous reference to a local Lover's Walk and, so the story goes, so angered the young Browning that he dashed in nude to her in the drawing room in protest.[21]

In the long run, the forces of dullness and narrow conformity, allied with uncontrolled, unimaginative middle and late Victorian building and a gradual movement of richer residents further away from London along railway lines, prevailed in the Camberwell-New Cross area. Although the town's official historian could exclaim over what was happening—"It reads like a Romance when we recall how great have been the changes within the brief space of one life''[22]—Matthew Arnold, looking in 1871 for a deplorable example of the middle-class faith in machinery, could find no better choice than Camberwell. "Your middle-class man thinks it the highest pitch of development and civilization when his letters are carried twelve times a day from Islington to Camberwell . . . and if railway trains run to and from them every quarter of an hour. He thinks it is nothing that the trains only carry him from an illiberal, dismal life at Islington to an illiberal, dismal life at Camberwell; and the letters only tell him that such is the life there.''[23] When Browning himself, probably about the same time, returned to look at his childhood home in a spirit more of nostalgia than of criticism, it was the brute fact of change that struck him: "he could not recognize the place.''[24] Today, though the type of civilization that Camberwell represented has become, for better or worse, almost the dominant one in modern countries, Camberwell and New Cross have largely disappeared in the form in which Browning knew them. In fact, much of Camberwell itself has recently been built over for the second time—this time with large council housing developments.

III
Family

What does remain, though the early nineteenth-century civilization at Camberwell and New Cross exists no longer, is the impact of a society and culture upon the persons who lived within it. In Browning's case many of the tendencies generally apparent in the larger society were present in the specific circumstances of his family life. And it was the future poet's good fortune to benefit largely from what was best in this new society, its opportunity and individual freedom, while escaping many, if not all, of its more narrowing middle-class influences. Through the peculiarly attractive, though in many ways quite peculiar, circumstances of his family life, he was made heir to the best legacy of the most active social and cultural forces of his day.

A great deal has been written about Browning's ultimate roots outside of this society. Attempts have been made to locate his poetic powers in a variety of real or mythical family antecedents ranging from more local, sturdy English yeomen and Scots gentlefolk to more distant German Jews, French Creoles, and West Indian mulattos. From all that is known about Browning's ancestors the more mysterious origins, which have at times been given to him, are false conjectures inspired by rather patronizing, "enlightened" attitudes among some early Browningites.[1] But, more generally, the concern with distant genealogical origins leads to a mythic view of a person's background and serves to obscure the realities of the immediate social and cultural ethos. In Browning's case, everything that we can find out about his ancestors only seems to lead back to the special society of suburban Camberwell from which he started out in life.

This is not to say that his family had no sense of family or of a family history. The Brownings, the poet included, liked to pretend to trace their ancestry back to a knight of Falstaff's time who took Henry V across to

France.[2] With more plausibility but equal lack of proof, he and the family believed themselves related to an heroic Captain Michael (or Michaiah) Browning, who perished as he broke through the boom across Lough Foyle at the siege of Londonderry in the seventeenth century.[3] On his own authority his grandfather had taken up a crest from a Browning family with the stern motto "sola virtute fac" and Browning would in later life follow this in abbreviated form with a less crotchety, "virtute."[4] Such family vanities were, however, not the mark of a family enmeshed in its own traditions but of a rising family which looked to a mythical past to spur its members on beyond their more immediate and less inspiring ancestors. There was a great deal of family pride among the Brownings, but it was pride in what members of the family could do not in any hereditary honors they carried into life from the past. "There is a tradition in his family," Elizabeth Barrett explained to her sister, "that 'a Browning can fail in nothing.' "[5]

Although Browning and his family, like many ordinary and otherwise scrupulously truthful people, chose to focus on this general great idea of a Browning rather than on their recent past, some real justification for this belief in family success can be found both in the poet's immediate Browning predecessors and in the other families that contributed to his existence. In all that we know of his background, there is a similar pattern of relative, if not extraordinary success, and of increasing comfort and security. Whatever mythical pasts they might invoke, his recent ancestors were all clearly part of the larger development of an expanding and rising managerial and entrepreneurial class, which fed into villages like Camberwell. Although they came from widely different parts of the world—maternal grandparents from Scotland, paternal grandparents from nearby Dorsetshire and distant St. Kitts in the English West Indies—they had a similar freedom in their middle station in life and had similar aspirations to better themselves. Neither truly a part of the traditional ruling classes of gentry or aristocracy, nor, like the great majority of English people, entirely rooted in a local region and in the routine of manual labor, they indicate that Browning's real roots were not in a particular region or a special past but in the middle class that created places like Camberwell and that was to play such a significant, even dominating, role in nineteenth-century England.

The most obvious example of the family ability to rise in the world was also the one which would have been most certainly before Browning's eyes as he grew up, his prosperous paternal grandfather, named, like his son and grandson, Robert Browning. Born in 1749,[6] this Robert Browning had grown up in the country village of East Woodyates in Dorsetshire, southwest of London, where first his great-uncle and subsequently his father operated the Woodyates Inn. Whatever occupation his grandfather (Browning's great-great-grandfather), also Robert Browning, had he was clearly a respected citizen of Woodyates and the parish of Pentridge and his brother and son became increasingly more important as their inn prospered. The poet's grandfather was given an education good enough to qualify him for an appointment at London in the Bank of England, a choice, semiprofessional position that was obtained for him through the influence of the family's aristocratic landlord. A beginning clerk at twenty just up from the provinces, by the age of thirty-four in 1784 he had risen to the highest position in the giant, quasi-governmental institution that mere talent could expect to command: a principal clerkship of one of the divisions. With time he drew a salary of £561, an amount in that time which easily placed him in buying power, if not in hereditary dignity, among the comfortable gentry. To that prestigious position, tantamount to being head of one governmental office, he added the pomp of an appointment as lieutenant in the Honourable Artillery Company and a record of actual service in defense of the bank during the Gordon Riots. His grandfather had been plain Robert Browning, his father, Mr. Browning in parish records; he and his son and grandson would be Robert Browning, Esquire, an acknowledgment of their new status as gentlemen among the middle classes.

With his rapid success in the Bank, Browning's grandfather was able to marry at age twenty-nine into a prosperous colonial family named Tittle,[7] a family that had started out as leather workers in the West Indies and quickly risen to be substantial plantation owners. Margaret Tittle, whom he married, was, as far as records suggest, the daughter of a clergyman who had founded, in his abundant and self-interested secular activities, the family holdings on the island of St. Kitts. Although there is no evidence of the French or African Creole blood that has been attributed to her, her portrait by Wright of Derby shows a very handsome, dark-haired lady. They settled in suburban Battersea, where Browning's father was born, and moved to Camberwell in 1784. After the death of his first wife in 1789, he married Jane Smith, a well-connected woman of twenty-three from Chelsea, and had the vigor, beginning after forty-five, to sire nine more children before he died in 1833 at the ripe, if gout-stricken, age of eighty-four.

There can be little doubt of the cleverness or ambition of Browning's grandfather; but he apparently paid willingly a price in personality and human relations for his success. Even at the office he was something of an ill-tempered bully who was called down for the language he used to his staff.[8] One of his grandsons, Browning's cousin Cyrus Mason, who wrote a long manuscript account of the family in his old age in Australia, recalled the "importance and what I must term, the pompous characteristics of the prosperous 'cit.' " His "arrogant city manner"[9] found something of a match in his second wife whom Cyrus recalls with inexplicable fondness, sitting "in state" at the window in her old age, immaculately dressed and on the lookout for something shocking enough to rouse her to her characteristic activity: a censorious head shaking that set the strings of her widow's cap jangling in disapprobation. At successive houses at Chelsea, Peckham, and Islington in the north of London, they established a solidly proper household, which impressed and rather intimidated Cyrus. "No veneering there. The massive tables and sideboards seemed as much fixtures as the fireplace;

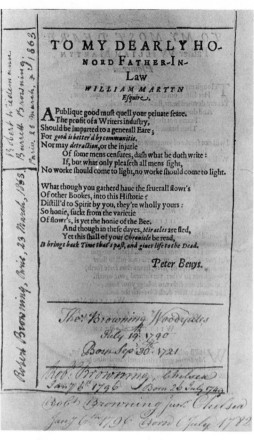

Above left: Autographs of Five Generations of Brownings. Dedication page of William Martyn, *The Historie, and Lives, of Twentie Kings of England* (1615). *Signatures of Thomas Browning, great-grandfather of the poet; Robert Browning, grandfather; Robert Browning Sr.; the poet; and his son, Robert Wiedeman(n) Browning.*

Above right: Margaret Tittle, Paternal Grandmother of Robert Browning, ca. 1778-1789. Painting by Wright of Derby. *The portrait that was taken down by the second Mrs. Browning, only to reappear in the home of Robert Browning Sr.*

Below right: Tom Bowling's Advice—on Employment at the Bank of England. Cartoon by Robert Browning Sr. *"Why— the Bank will never do for you—no more than you'll do for the Bank—I'm told they drink nothing but Small beer—& are obliged to put on a clean shirt every other Sunday!—Pugh-pugh! you'd better go to Sea again!"*

the grandparents' portraits . . . always had an effect upon my young nerves . . . their eyes from the canvas followed my every movement.''[10] His grandson the poet seems not to have been similarly intimidated, for the family story was rather that he made the old gentleman himself nervous by his liveliness near his gouty leg. But there is little in this background that would seem to encourage the development of a poet in the family. Margaret Tittle's portrait did capture her resting her hand genteelly on a copy of Thomson's *Seasons,* and there may have been some serious interest in literature on her part. Outside of a copy of Quarles's *Emblems* and an odd *Scots Poems Wrote by Tugenious before 1600*[11] in dialect, her husband's few known books show little literary interest. More revealing is *The Young Gentlemen and Ladies' Monitor,* a collection of polite readings aimed at helping to "Eradicate Vulgar Prejudices and Rusticity of Manners," a work with an obvious utility to a country boy on the make in the metropolis.

Although we are told that he only read *Tom Jones* and the Bible,[12] the other books known to be his, most with his "Rob. Browning" stamped on them, suggest he was sophisticated in the narrow but demanding culture of Bible, religious tract, and sermon and that he may even have had something of an old-fashioned scholarly bent. With the puritanical emphasis often found even within the Church of England in the middle classes, he possessed works of seventeenth-century theology and piety with titles such as *The Spiritual Chymist, Precious Remedies against Satan's Devices,* or *Joseph and his Mistresse, the Faithfulnesse of the One and the Unfaithfulnesse of the Other, Laid Downe in Five Sermons.* His name was also listed as a subscriber to a translation of a curious work that greatly interested his grandson, the *Travels of Rabbi Benjamin, Son of Jonah of Tudela.* If he showed little promise of becoming a fountainhead for poetry, he may have been the conduit for the sober, almost rabbinical, scholarly streak that came out so strongly in his son and grandson. One recollection of him by Browning suggests that he may also have passed along a taste for old murder cases: because of the closeness to his name, Elizabeth Brownrigg, hanged in 1767 as the torturer and killer of an apprentice, was still very much in his mind when he talked to his grandson in the 1820s or early 1830s.[13]

Whatever suppressed tendencies for developing personal interests and a personal view of life may have existed within the prosperous and pompous bosom of this Robert Browning, his son, Robert Browning the father of the poet, must appear more a sport than a scion.[14] While the poet's grandfather clearly put worldly success first, his father appears, in his very first important action in life, to have made a decisive break with the rigid, worldly, responsible values of the respectable middle class in general and of his father in particular. At the age of twenty, and no doubt with the full encouragement of his father, he was sent out to the West Indies where his mother's family had plantation holdings on the island of St. Kitts. As he was already the beneficiary of a small independent income from relatives on his mother's side, it may be assumed that he had a real claim to a part in his mother's holdings.[15] But the condition of these good, possibly even great, expectations was clearly that he should live in St. Kitts, take an active part in management of the family plantations, and, as he soon found upon arrival, participate implicitly in the slave system upon which the colonial economy was founded. Instead, something in him stood up and said no to the entire arrangement when he saw it in operation, and, as Browning told Elizabeth, he "conceived such a hatred to the slave-system in the West Indies . . . that he relinquished every prospect,—supported himself, while there, in some other capacity, and came back, while yet a boy, to his father's profound astonishment and rage."[16] This unworldly act of conscience provoked a formal break between father and son. Browning's grandfather demanded and received full repayment of all the expenses he had incurred for Browning's father from babyhood on; years later, he went out of his way to warn an uncle of his son's fiancée "that his niece 'would be thrown away on a man so evidently born to be hanged' ! "[17] That formal break, however, only exposed the gap in sympathy and viewpoint between the two generations of Brownings that had been growing all along. The son, it appeared, who no doubt rejected St. Kitts as much for its provinciality and isolation as for its immorality,[18] had interests both as a scholar and also as quite a promising artist, which were not dreamed of in his father's philosophy of life.

His temperament, like that of his shy, rather reclusive sister Margaret Morris Browning, one year his junior, seems to have been affected by the loss of his mother at age seven and by a childhood spent in what was thereafter probably a very cold household. Not that his father was ungenerous according to his own lights. Education to him was clearly a good thing, as long as it served the ultimate end of advancing his son toward the colonial squire's role planned for him. He was sent, probably at some expense, to a progressive classical school, kept by a Reverend A. Bell at Cheshunt, north of London, that prepared "Young Gentlemen . . . in the Latin, French and English Languages."[19] One of his classmates was his son's future benefactor, the prosperous West Indian gentleman and poet, John Kenyon, who, like most of his friends, went on to university. The school gave Browning's father the knowledge of classical languages of a scholar of his day. His natural bent led him to memorize the first book of the *Iliad* and to distinguish himself by organizing play battles from Homer among the other schoolboys: battles—"with mock sword, and slate, our mimic shield, / Hector or Ajax, overfought each field"[20]—which remained in Kenyon's memory all his life. His love of learning and his emerging talents as an artist were evidently encouraged by a less pompous older Browning, his Uncle Reuben (not the poet's uncle of the same name) who had come up to London after his brother, followed him into the bank, and settled in Camberwell. Cousin Mason[21] retails a family tradition that Reuben took Browning's father under his wing and gave him the friendship and encouragement he wasn't receiving at home. Reuben's wife was inclined toward some version of what Mason calls "Methodism." Reuben's stepson would later be affiliated with the same Congregational Church the poet's family attended;[22] and it may be that Methodism was actually Congregationalism from the first. Reuben followed his wife's religion, making his influence on the poet's father, who would eventually follow his own wife into Congregationalism, doubly subversive. Indeed it may have been through Reuben's circle that the poet's father became introduced to his Congregational wife.

When the poet's grandfather remarried, his son, who was almost twelve years old, came quickly into conflict with his twenty-three-year-old stepmother and was probably driven further into dependence on Reuben and conflict with his father. Margaret Tittle's portrait was too attractive to compete with Jane Smith in her own house and was put away, to reappear years later in her son's house in a place of honor. Browning's father thought seriously "of devoting himself to art, for which he had many qualifications and abundant love,"[23] but was coldly discouraged by a father who refused even to look at his first picture.[24] A later attempt to go to university, even at his own expense, was vetoed because of opposition from the jealous second wife.

The ultimate result of the failure of sympathy and comprehension on the part of the father and growing defiance on the part of the son that culminated in the quarrel over the position at St. Kitts, can only seem a bit of an anticlimax: "the quarrel with his father,—who married again and continued to hate him till a few years before his death,—induced him to go at once and consume his life after a fashion he always detested."[25] That is, on November 10, 1803, he too, nominated by a Bank director for whom he had worked in St. Kitts after leaving the plantation, was effortlessly appointed to a clerkship at the Bank of England.[26] At the time, he may have felt that this was an act of self-destructive retribution. In practice, it turned out to be the foundation stone of an agreeable and comfortable way of life. After a lonely period of years in lodgings[27] he married a respectable, churchgoing woman of Scottish background on February 19, 1811, settled in a cottage at Camberwell, and proceeded to raise a family, one boy and one girl, amid circumstances of domestic tranquillity. Eventually even the rift with the father scarred over. His family came to know their pompous old grandfather before his death.[28] The widow Jane Smith Browning settled near the stepson with whom she had once competed (as did the Masons),[29] and Browning's father was acknowledged, despite family sniping at his and his children's individualistic ways, as head of the Browning clan.

The apparent non sequitur in this transition from rebellion to an untroubled, conventional life is worth dwelling on, for it illustrates the particular circumstances of Browning's home life. In fact, the paradox is more apparent than real, for Browning's father was hardly such a young rebel in the eyes of the rest of his society and especially of those close to his own age, as he came to appear to his father. Wilberforce was already leading a very respectable crusade against the slave trade; and even in Camberwell Dr. Lettsom, the wealthy owner of Grove Hill, was renowned for having liberated his slaves in youth, "a singular instance of fortitude, virtue, and humanity."[30] Likewise, an interest in literature and art was, for many residents of the Camberwell area, not a mark of damnation but an indication of fitness for civilized society.

The kind of life Browning's father settled into after his initial confrontation with his father was in reality neither a radical break with the past nor a capitulation to the narrow ambitions of his father. Instead, he managed a calm and apparently easy resolution of the two. For nearly fifty years he traveled daily from Camberwell or New Cross into London to the Bank and performed his duties there very adequately. Rebellion settled down to small jokes at the expense of the clean-shirt gentility required by a clerkship; it was certainly not strong enough to endanger the serene occupation of a position rather close to a sinecure.[31] The chief accountant described him as "a very honourable character," and he was far more of a favorite at the Bank than his more successful father. At his retirement he was granted a "handsome" pension at two-thirds salary.[32] Yet he showed little willingness to put in the extra effort and interest required of the more important officials, and he never rose to a position equal to that of his more ambitious father.[33] For all his diligence he was impractical, even improvident enough to leave his daughter at his death without the benefit of the widow's fund that he had dutifully maintained for half a century. "With his usual simplicity and utter ignorance of worldly matters,"[34] he misunderstood the arrangement by which the pension could be reassigned to her! His true life was obviously not at the Bank but in the Camberwell or New Cross households. Above all, it was in his passion for rare books, his devotion to eclectic scholarship, and his love of drawing. The energy devoted to these avocations was such that he hardly ever failed to leave a lasting impression upon people who knew him. From his diligent scouring of book stalls throughout London, his library grew so large that once, when the family was moving, a neighbor decided he must be a bookseller.[35] Eventually at New Cross virtually the entire third floor of the house was given over to his books. At the same time, while he gave up all serious pursuit of art as a profession when he entered the Bank, he continued all his life to make sketches and satirical cartoons. Many of the cartoons, generally done in ink and wash, have captions and tell a story. Some of the sketches reveal great talent and fine feeling for composition in groups of men or natural scenes.

For all his indulgence, as Browning's grandfather might have termed it, in personal eccentricities, neither his enthusiasm for books nor drawing isolated Robert Browning Sr. from the society around him. He was generous in lending and giving his books, and he must have made many friends—such as the Frederick Locker-Lampson, who wrote warmly of him to Browning after his death[36]—through his interest in old books and prints. As for his drawings, their raison d'être seems to have been as much social as artistic. They were "generally knocked off in the evening, at the request of some guest," his grandson recalled.[37] The daughter of his friend Earles added:

"The sketches . . . were made on rough slips of paper which younger children were careful to have ready against his visits—made during the course of family chat going on round him, or while my brother was singing; and they represent imaginary (and very queer) persons repeating and commenting on the news of the day—the 'Nincum tax' which old ladies coming to take up their dividends at the bank can't be made to understand and so on— other series are full of the family news or jokes current at the time."[38] Above all, whatever frustrations and regrets he may have had over his early life and choice of career were subsumed under an unfailing good humor. Mason remembered him as a man whose appearance suggested the quiet serenity of John Wesley and whose countenance bore habitually "a sort of sedate cheerfulness, as if enjoying a pleasant little chat with himself."[39]

Although he had rebelled against his father and the kind of ambition he represented, he was far from being a rebel or even a Bohemian outcast from the middle-class world of talented, relatively free individuals that made up the Camberwell society. If anything, the dark-haired, blue-eyed, Roman-nosed,[40] reserved, and rather absentminded person seemed to take on the prerogatives of a semiretired gentleman. Even a regular clerk at the Bank had a status similar to an officer of government or a civil service employee.[41] With his education, his small inheritance from his mother's family, and his father's secure position behind him, he was—in an age when insecurity was far more the rule than the exception—relatively free from anxiety, relatively comfortable, and, his daily dues to society paid at the Bank, essentially an eccentric independent gentleman free to please his curiosity and taste.

The path in Browning's mother's life that led her to the placidity of married existence at Camberwell was less traumatic and is far less well documented than that of his father. Sarah Anna Wiedemann was born June 13, 1772 at Sea-Gait House in Dundee, Scotland, the substantial residence of her family for two generations, and baptized into the Church of Scotland.[42] She must have enjoyed a comfortable and fairly cultivated middle-class way of life. Her grandfather, William Wiedemann, probably a Dutchman by birth though often referred to as a German, had found a good living through his association with the Dundee Sugar House. Her father, also William Wiedemann, was called a mariner in a Dundee register of deeds, probably meaning that he was a merchant who managed his own ship. He seems to have been a person of gentlemanly cultivation, a draftsman of talent and a lover of music.[43] Unlike that of her future husband, her family was apparently a warm and friendly one. After her death, Browning preserved the name Wiedemann (as Wiedeman) in his son's name in memory of "her own father and mother, whom she loved so much."[44] When her father sold Sea-Gait House in 1787, it is likely, though not certain, that her mother, née Sarah Revell, was dead. Then or later (but certainly sometime before 1806 when her name appeared in a list of members of a Congregational Church) her family, or possibly only her sister Christiana and herself, moved south

The Immediate Family of the Poet: Father, Mother, Sister (*page 30*).

Robert Browning Sr., ca. 1860. By Sarianna Browning (his daughter, sister of the poet).

Robert Browning Sr., ca: 1810-1820. Portrait miniature, artist unknown. *In the high-necked costume of the Regency period.*

Sarah Anna Browning (Mother of the Poet), ca. 1826. Caricature by Robert Browning Sr. *The only likeness of the poet's mother—comic and teasing.*

Sarianna Browning (Sister of the Poet), ca. 1826. Sketch probably by Robert Browning Sr., possibly by the poet.

S. Browning Es^{qre}, ca. 1835-1840. Caricature study of his sister Sarianna by Robert Browning.

View of the London and Croydon Railway from the Deep Cutting Made through the Hill at New Cross. Engraving by E. Duncan. *The three-story building is probably the New Cross house of the Browning family.*

to London. Very likely they settled at Peckham or at Camberwell where Christiana married a local brewer, William Silverthorne. It is also likely that Sarah Anna was living at Camberwell with an uncle at the time of her marriage.[45]

The little that we know suggests that she was well on her way to becoming a pleasant old maid, rather preoccupied with religion and perhaps somewhat shy and foreign as a Scotswoman in London. She was thirty-eight at her marriage in February 1811, and she had probably already taken on the plain, rather blunt and certainly unexceptional appearance her husband gave her in a not unsympathetic caricature sketch of the 1820s, the only picture of her we have.[46] Nor is it likely that she in her turn was bowled over or swept off her feet by the shy, studious, and somewhat naive and strange bank clerk who was to be the poet's father. Even nearly forty years later, when he courted a somewhat worldly widow von Muller after his wife's death, Browning's father wooed and won by his affectionate character and serious conversation rather than by any more sexual graces.[47] He must have been far more earnest and shy at age twenty-nine. He was, indeed, ten years younger than his wife. There is even a family story that he was found on his wedding day playing like a boy at dissecting a duck rather than looking to his duties.[48] (If true, and it probably isn't, it might seem a telling indictment of the lack of sex education at the time.)

Whatever problems there may have been seem to have been overcome, or at least submerged, by good will and affectionate tempers on both sides. Two people, whom one can easily imagine rather lonely, undirected single persons, became a happy, seemingly very conventional, and really rather odd couple. For Sarah Anna, old enough to have become fairly sure of her capabilities on her own, the marriage to the quiet, younger man gave her a domestic life that was singularly democratic: quite free from the disbalanced predominance of the husband as lord and master that is often thought of as typical in nineteenth-century marital relations. As long as he was indulged in his pet hobbies, her husband even seems to have been willing to let her play the larger part in directing their relation. Years later, after his wife's death, in his senile affair with the widow von Muller he was to be batted almost without will of his own between the attractions and wiles of the widow and the scruples of his daughter and son. In the end he was called "dotard" in open court in a breach of promise suit and was forced by an adverse judgment to take up residence abroad.[49] Later friends had the impression that he was totally dependent in practical matters upon his daughter during his declining years. But senility only accentuated what was there from the beginning. Cousin Cyrus Mason, looking for something to criticize in his relatives, found not the Victorian stereotype of the dominated woman but the history of an exploited man. Ignoring the large measure of contentment that his uncle found in his life of hobbies, Mason saw him as a mere convenience to his family, a kind of mechanical man wound up and sent off to the bank daily to support the sweet life of his wife and daughter. Mason makes much of his walking to work and of the poor expedient for rainy days: "in his simple way he would tell me that he had been ordered to ride to town and given the money for a third class ticket," a mode of traveling, Mason felt, that "but ill-accorded with the social position of the elderly gentleman dressed in black clothes, standing at my side, for I knew that the Robert Browning establishment at New Cross was maintained in some style with my Uncle's salary."[50]

More sympathetically than Mason or Betty Miller, who sees both father and son as psychologically dependent on the mother figure of the family, we can perceive that Browning's father agreed to give his wife predominant say in the household affairs and manner of living in return for the freedom to pursue his serious hobbies without being forced into some alien social role. The man who changed restaurants when he was forced by a waiter to choose his dish,[51] and who seemed, at least in old age, indifferent enough to his own concerns to worry family friends that he might let himself slip into unkempt scruffiness if his daughter weren't around to care for him,[52] was pleased to have his mind and attention freed for the things he considered important. At times his hobbies and absentmindedness may have been a trial to his wife. Mason claims there were even complaints about his messy drawing habits.[53] But she also had advantages that no wife of a domineering Edward Barrett could have: a chance to develop her own style of life, freedom to follow her own interests without being held to social standards dictated by her husband's ambitions, opportunity to grow by taking on much of the serious responsibility for bringing up her children.

She was probably less well educated than her husband and certainly less bookish and intellectual in her interests. Mason is no doubt correct in seeing her as the one primarily concerned with "household punctillios" and the external forms of gentility.[54] But if some of her free energy went into establishing the Brownings in faultless gentlemanly respectability (and consequently free from the patronizing authority of her husband's more ambitious father), she had, or developed, a larger mental freedom from the excesses of Podsnapery. If she acquiesced in her husband's strangely split life, she never tried to make him conform to the usual notions of the time of what a man should be like and, unlike Ruskin's mother, she seems to have had no desire to force her son into some socially successful career. She too, like her husband, found in her married existence at Camberwell and New Cross a way of life that let her bloom in her personal individuality, if not, like him, sprout into exotic growths of eccentricity. She took a strong interest in music and was known as a fine pianist. She continued her independent association with her own church and eventually brought Browning's father into it. She was a devoted gardener and a student of wild life and nature. Despite her age, she had, after an initial miscarriage,[55] two children, Robert and his sister, Sarianna, and ultimately received from both not only warm affection but serious admiration.

At least in her later years before her death in 1849, she lived as a semi-invalid, always threatened by attacks of acutely painful neuralgia. The son of a family friend recalled seeing her "bowed with pain" and scarcely able to talk to anyone as she and Browning's father took a slow walk.[56] In his letters to Elizabeth Barrett, Browning speaks repeatedly of her sickness; and we hear of her "suffering sadly" or referred to as "the dear invalid."[57] Yet even in her old age she remained very much involved in the life of her family and in her own interests.

In the few records that we have of the Browning household at various residences in Camberwell and at New Cross there appears much the same union of social conventionality and personal and intellectual freedom that is apparent in Browning's parents' lives. None of the three residences the Brownings occupied between 1811 and 1840 on Southampton Street in Camberwell nor their later house further southeast from London near the new railway line at Hatcham, New Cross survived the onslaught of lines of two-story row houses in the later nineteenth century. About the Camberwell houses there is so little specific information that they all seem to blur into one. Only the third, Hanover Cottage, even had a specific name.[58] Concerning the first and second, both near the then open Cottage Green, indeed really nothing is known, except that the first was somewhat old. The impressions that survive of Hanover Cottage, where the family lived from 1824 until 1840, are similarly vague, though the newly built, semidetached Cottage was at least substantial enough to have a name. Browning's sister recalled it as having no other particularly outstanding features.[59]

At the two later Camberwell houses there were evidently stables. Hanover Cottage certainly had one, located at the end of a long garden on the next road. In addition to the garden behind we know that there were trees in front of the Cottage. From a few remaining older houses in the area we can guess that all the Camberwell houses were probably neat, two-story dwellings with arched lower windows balancing a center door. They were certainly not pretentious homes but large enough for Browning to have a room to himself in the 1830s when he began writing in earnest. The households were substanial enough to include a pageboy—who plays Hector in Browning's poem "Development"—and probably other servants.[60]

The New Cross house, to which the family moved in 1840 and which was really in the smaller village of Hatcham, was something more special. Here the family realized the style of life to which it had always aspired. Despite the railway cutting for the London and Croydon line adjacent to the Brownings' land, despite the beginnings of suburban terrace development in Hatcham, this was still a country community. The family's new residence, which Browning once rather unhelpfully compared to a goose-pie, was located off the Old Kent Road at the end of a lane going up Telegraph Hill.[61] It was a larger three-story dwelling, formerly a farmhouse. It had a good-sized garden with a holly hedge and Browning's favorite chestnut tree, as well as a pleasant pond nearby. Further on, there was a wicket gate (for which members of the family had a key) opening into an orchard and fields sloping up the Surrey hills through bleating lambs to a magnificent outlook on London.[62] We hear also of an attached stable and coach house and a day gardener. The gardener's duties included caring for Browning's favorite horse York, actually the possession of the elder Browning's half-brother, Reuben, who lived nearby at Albert Terrace on the Old Kent Road with his mother, the widow Jane Browning. Inside there was room on the third floor not only for the elder Browning's library of some six thousand volumes but also for a small study for Browning himself in a room—so tradition had it—once the secret chapel of a Roman Catholic family.

"If we are poor," wrote Browning to Elizabeth Barrett, telling her of his father's selfless decision against his own prospects in the West Indies, "it is to my father's infinite glory."[63] His statement was echoed by one biographer: "For the Brownings were poor."[64] In fact, though nothing in the Browning household speaks of affluence, of carriages, elaborate entertainment, or expensive furnishings, there is still less indication of any kind of poverty or straitened circumstances. In an age when thirty-eight pounds a year would be considered an extravagant income for a laborer, Browning's father's income, which amounted to roughly three hundred pounds at his retirement, though in no sense large, certainly placed the Brownings among the relatively comfortable. And there was some additional income from the father's aunt and uncle.[65] Mason repeatedly recalled the household as "well-kept," "genteel," "well-appointed," and even as maintained "in some style."[66] Occasional glimpses of the Browning's everyday life reinforce the overall impression of a comfortable, regular, middle-class existence. A letter of Robert's dated "Saturday morning—6½" and ending "Think for me, and let me breakfast," suggests the family rose early, no doubt because Mr. Browning, like John Ruskin's father, had a distance to go to work.[67] "Out comes the sun, in comes the 'Times' and eleven strikes," another letter tells us, and the triple harmony of nature, parish church, and the great voice of worldly affairs is revealing.[68] So too—in the absence of any firsthand picture of the household—are some surviving objects: a stolid and upright inlaid mantel clock, more handsome and practical than elegant, or a Thomas Dexter silver teapot "on four scrolled feet with chased floral pattern" that must have often been among the best things set out for visitors or special occasions.[69]

Such fragments suggest, however, only one side of the Browning home life: its comfort, its placidity, and its outward conventionality. Even very conventional life in Camberwell or New Cross allowed for a good degree of independence and freedom from outside interference in the details of life. Like their entire community, the family lived in close relationship to the civilized natural world around them. Animals, too, were much in evidence: Browning's pony at Camberwell, the horse at New Cross, a cat (imagined as Helen of Troy in the poem, "Development"), at least two dogs; and these must have been part of a larger pattern of easy-going freedom in everyday activities. More important for Browning was the atmosphere of tolerance and encouragement for artistic and intellectual growth and independence, in which both he and his sister were allowed to follow their own interests. A piano had an important place in their household; even at 6:30 A.M. Browning speaks of hearing music coming up to his room: "M[other?] is playing very beautifully."[70]

Cousin Cyrus Mason, smitten with mingled feelings of envy and inferiority, found the household "genteelly dreary" and its occupants, in their concern with cultivation, "constantly self-absorbed" and "enveloped in a misty pride."[71] To more welcome visitors the family seemed both warm and lively. To Browning's friends, especially, they were hospitable and open. "Let him but come back and come here," they send in Browning's letter to Alfred Domett, who had gone to New Zealand.[72] Even when Browning himself had left with Elizabeth for Italy, his friend Joseph Arnould continued to seek out the company of the family. He and his wife, he wrote Browning, had been out at New Cross and had had "a most delightful evening there . . . one of the old evenings."[73]

Sarianna Browning, two years younger than her brother, was a particularly good friend to many of Browning's acquaintances in the 1830s and 1840s and was often invited to come along with him on visits or to entertainments.[74] A plain but intelligent, sensible, and sensitive girl with the family talent for drawing, Sarianna took a sympathetic and helpful interest in her brother's poetic career. For years she served as copyist—"my amanuensis in those days," Browning later recalled.[75] She shared with Browning the secret of the anonymously published *Pauline*, and she continued to take an active interest in his work and career all her life.[76] With something of the talents of that more famous sister to a poet, Dorothy Wordsworth, Sarianna was also encourager and sounding board for her brother.

All that we know of her suggests that she had a great respect for her mother and modeled herself upon her, perhaps somewhat to the detriment of her own development. Mason portrays her as a somewhat precious, churchgoing young lady with her servant walking behind carrying her books for her.[77] There is no doubt that she became something of a petty snob. Friends of the family recalled her attempts to turn her father away from the subject of his occupation at the Bank by ineffectual looks or more successful digs at his toes.[78] But along with such "petty vanities" she had rather great talents, which only found expression in private life or indirectly through her brother. Even as a schoolgirl she made a lasting impression on her Italian tutor as "ben fornito d'intelletto."[79] Later observers remarked on her common sense, her shrewd face, and the "wit and tact that appeared more French than English."[80] She proved her good sense, like her brother, by holding out against the spiritualist craze in the 1850s, to which Elizabeth Barrett succumbed. In return Elizabeth half deplored and half respected her "admirable sense and excessive scepticism."[81] She had a wide taste for literature, enjoying works as varied as the comic verse of Thomas Hood and the novels of Tolstoy, which she read in French in old age.[82] She was a great walker, a gardener, and, like the rest of the family, a tremendous lover of animals of all sorts. Most of all she excelled as a raconteuse. Here some of the family literary talent showed itself. A friend of Browning's praised her as "marvellously clever, such fine clear animal spirits, talks much & well."[83] Other friends remembered her as "quite a character," delightful and humorous.[84] "It was as good as reading a page from an old novel to hear her narrate an anecdote," and her power of "vivid realization" seemed extraordinary, so much so that she even appeared ready to lie down herself to illustrate the principal event when she told the story—which her brother also tells in *La Saisiaz*—of finding a friend suddenly dead.[85]

Such critical sense and imaginative talents obviously made her an important intellectual companion to Browning and indeed, with the exception of about twenty years in the middle of their lives, "Dearest Sis" was his closest confidante throughout his life. Although contemporaries universally extolled her devotion, first to her sick mother, then to her widower father, throughout her life to her brother, and finally to her nephew, as a stalwart, dutiful, "ministry of love," we may wonder whether she didn't suppress her own instincts and even some of her own talents in her "old Trojan" devotion to brother and family.[86] She was short, not beautiful, and spoke with an impediment that turned Robert into Wobert.[87] Her brother was certain, however, that she could have married had she not devoted herself instead to her family.[88] Certainly in her youth she could interest men. Browning's French friend, Ripert-Monclar, dwells especially on her "fraîche" attractions in his journal. He was especially taken by her jet black eyes and ebony hair set off to advantage against her white skin. He found her both "charmante" and "spirituelle" and approved her ladylike skills in drawing and on the piano.[89] Despite such good ordinary qualities, it would seem that the extraordinary talents of her brother to some degree overwhelmed her and left her living more through his friends and activities than through her own. She could speak in old age of "feeling through the experience of my brother who was part of myself."[90] Relatives even hinted vaguely at major sacrifices she had made to benefit him.[91] Certainly she made the very real sacrifice of endlessly copying his works in her fine hand, and perhaps there was an even greater sacrifice of imagination and sympathy in her deep concern for his literary trials and successes. In his youth and early manhood Browning no doubt fell easily into depending upon her help and interest and, in an innocent way, into exploiting her for his own growth. Later, he began to realize his debt to her for this and the even greater debt of caring for both their parents while he made his own life with Elizabeth. Even as he was repaying her to some extent by supporting her after their father's death, he kept accumulating more debts. She helped him with the practical side of his life and even took on an informal role as censor of his writings to protect him from his occasional fits of temper.[92]

Her choices in life were ultimately her own responsibility and perhaps more generally the responsibility of a society that could praise and encourage clever women but not provide them with substantial roles in their own right. If the only rewards she sought were those of playing an important part in the purely private life of her family and of feeling a vicarious pleasure in her brother's success, she certainly had the satisfaction of living within a family that gave her full encouragement in developing her mind and abilities. Within the limits she imposed upon her activities, she was able to live a varied and intellectually stimulating existence. For Browning she was a part, if too often a part taken for granted, of the generally supportive family life that he enjoyed, a life that combined intellectual and imaginative vitality with kindness and mutual sympathy. Cousin Mason might find the Brownings too inwardly turned and apparently precious; others might praise dutifulness and family piety as if conventional and rather meaningless duties and responsibilities were the only things that kept them together. Browning's friend Domett, who knew the family well, saw the real sources of strength, in mutual affection and shared interests, which bonded the family together. "Altogether," he recalled, "father, mother, only son and only daughter formed a most suited, harmonious and intellectual family, as appeared to me."[93] The testimony of Browning's father, when he had just lost his wife and become a grandfather at nearly the same time, is even more convincing. "I can truly say," he wrote to Robert and Elizabeth about their new son, "with sincere gratitude to Almighty God whilst I write it, that if it shall prove as great a comfort to you as yourself and Sarianna have ever been to me, it will be the greatest blessing heaven could have bestowed upon you."[94]

The environment of suburban Camberwell and New Cross, and the temper of Browning's family thus combined to offer to the young Browning, always in placid and fairly limited circumstances, a rather large degree of freedom to develop according to his inclinations and interests. If anything, Browning was somewhat spoiled. Carlyle, who came to visit him at Hatcham, remarked from the "trim" of Browning's little room that "he was the very apple of their [his parents'] eyes."[95] Browning himself admitted to Elizabeth Barrett: "When did I once fail to get whatever I had set my heart upon?—as I ask myself sometimes, with a strange fear."[96] Then he added in a later letter to her: "I have been 'spoiled' in this world."[97] If Browning was spoiled, however, it was less by material gifts—a pony in boyhood, fancy books from his father, or a "trim" room—than by encouragement and practical aid in his education and early career as a poet. Fees for weekly boarding school; special tutors in music, French, and Italian; a one-hundred pound bond to enable him to register at The London University; and later expenses for two trips to Italy were all paid willingly by Browning's fond parents. So too were the printers' bills for volume after volume of poems—*Paracelsus, Sordello,* and eight numbers of *Bells and Pomegranates*—by an author too unknown or poorly regarded to pay his own expenses. On top of this they provided year after year of lodging at home until his marriage at thirty-four, while he struggled to make his way as a poet.

Above all, there was the "spoiling" of unfailing sympathy and interest from his entire family. Not only was his sister, like the sensible sister of the young poet Paul Desforges, whom Browning described affectionately years later in *The Two Poets of Croisic* (1878), a constant and helpful aid to him. His parents showed a continued concern, if not always enthusiasm, for his work. His father, with no doubt some fond lapse of critical judgment, exclaimed over one of his earliest poems "remarkably beautiful—and had I not seen it in his own handwriting I never would have believed it to have been the production of a child."[98] When the secret of *Pauline's* authorship was revealed, Browning's parents joined with him in scanning the reviews and rejoiced at the favorable review by Allan Cunningham in the influential *Athenaeum*. Browning recalled years later that the review "gratified me and my people far beyond what will ever be the fortune of criticism now."[99] His first flush of literary success with *Paracelsus* and the production of *Strafford* before age twenty-five left his parents obviously delighted and a bit amazed at their own prodigy. His mother kept proof sheets of *Paracelsus* as a literary memento from the new man of letters.[100] His proud father allowed himself to be towed backstage after the first night of *Strafford* and given a chance to shake hands with his son's famous actor-friend, Macready.[101]

Later, as early success yielded to the trials of *Sordello* and the long struggle to capture (or recapture) an audience, his father's enthusiasm waned for a period. To his friend Mr. Earles, Browning Sr. brought a copy of the long, obscure *Sordello*, in which his own annotations struggled through only the first dozen or so pages, and presented it with the comment, so tradition has it: "Mr. Earles, my son sends you his last poem—perhaps you can make head or tail of it but I confess I can't."[102] Browning's friend Domett even recalled in later years a time "when he would not 'believe in you' unlike Khadija in Mahomet."[103] If enthusiasm flagged for a time while Browning struggled to find his poetic voice (or voices), sympathy and support seem never to have dried up. Whatever their private doubts about the wisdom of his actions, his family was willing to give him the means to go ahead as long as he was himself still convinced. By 1846 the situation had evidently changed considerably, for we find Browning telling Elizabeth, "At night he [Browning Sr.] sits studying my works—illustrating them (I will bring you drawings to make you laugh)—and *yesterday* I picked up a crumpled bit of paper . . 'his notion of what a criticism on this last number [of *Bells and Pomegranates*] ought to be,—none, that have appeared, satisfying him!' "[104] A year later, Browning's father even showed a doting pride in his son. Applying for a reader's ticket to the British Museum, he asked that the usual letters of reference be dispensed with in his case, trusting, "that the circumstances of my having been 44 years in the Bank and being the father of R. Browning, Author of Paracelsus, will be deemed sufficient" (they weren't).[105]

Although his parents' attitude toward his work fluctuated, the free, even permissive, nature of his family and social environment never changed. The Mrs. Grundys, in the shape of some gossiping, envious, and somewhat puritanical relatives were ready to raise eyebrows at his upbringing, his later involvement with the theater, or his intellectual and social independence.[106] Mr. Clayton, his minister, and Mr. Ready, his schoolmaster, were there, as we shall see, as the formal representatives of society's claim to control the development of the individual, ready to rebuke Browning, as Clayton may have done in church, if he flouted their authority. But with his immediate family securely behind him, such forces could generally be ignored or bypassed. At the most, the modest price paid for his freedom would be charges of ignoring kinsfolk, some feelings of guilt over teenage religious apostasy, and subterfuges for enduring school routine. The overall impression that we have of his home life is of a remarkable degree of freedom and encouragement: remarkable especially in an age when childhood was, for so many persons from John Stuart Mill to Samuel Butler, at best a time of dull restraint, at worst a long agony of repression and enforced tasks. During his courtship Browning came to comprehend the dominance of Elizabeth Barrett's father, Edward Barrett, over a household of grown children, and he could only exclaim in amazement at the difference from his own home life. His comment is a tribute to the unfailing kindness and encouragement he received from his parents throughout his early years. "The likelihood is, I over frighten myself for you, by the involuntary contrast with those here—you allude to them—if I went with this letter downstairs and said simply 'I want this taken to the direction tonight—and am unwell and unable to go, will you take it now?' my father would not say a word,—or rather would say a dozen cheerful absurdities about his 'wanting a walk,' 'just having been wishing to go out' etc."[107] Later in the correspondence with Elizabeth he acknowledged their generosity—a generosity composed of trust and freedom even more than of personal kindness and material support—even more explicitly. "Since I was a child I never looked for the least or greatest thing within the compass of their means to give, but given it was,—nor for liberty but it was conceded, nor confidence but it was bestowed."[108]

Other writers, indeed most people in Browning's time or today, might envy such a secure, warm, and open childhood environment. From our perspective the impossible security, the ease and freedom for endless cultivation, seem almost idyllic, part of some half-real, if solidly respectable, scholar-gypsy existence. But open opportunities and seemingly limitless possibilities of self-cultivation do not relieve children from the strain of living. On bright individuals, opportunities can impose their own strenuous demands. Cyrus Mason repeatedly asserts that Browning was a made poet, dedicated and trained to his profession from the day of his birth.[109] In fact, such breeding or psychological coercion was the farthest thing from the dynamics of the Browning family. But it is logical to suspect that, in unstated, even unconscious ways, strong demands, or at least heavy challenges were placed before the growing boy along with freedom and opportunity: challenges the more weighty for being there for him to discover and take up for himself rather than thrust upon him by pushing parents.

Most apparently there was the challenge posed by the unresolved tension between the different ambitions of two generations of Robert Brownings before him, a challenge implicit even in the particularly kind treatment that the Brownings gave their child in reaction against the grandfather's unkindness. The banker grandfather had gone on, after his relative ill success with his eldest son, to mold the offspring of his less exotic second wife into a large and mostly respectable Victorian family of bankers and maiden schoolteachers.[110] But the eldest son, conforming in outward ways to the values of his father, challenging them daily in the freedom of his home life, continued quietly, while he cheerfully stifled his own ambitions to be an artist, to keep open the rift in the family which once he had opened widely in his youth. To his younger half-brothers, especially the talented Reuben and William Shergold Browning, his cultivation and scholarship set an alternative standard of excellence and offered a different set of values by which to live. Ultimately, both of them settled on a similar life of compromise, combining success as bankers with private interest in scholarship and the arts.[111]

After the death of the grandfather in 1833, Browning's father, for all his simplicity and eccentricity, was accepted as titular head of the Browning family. In his various complaints about the poet's indifference to kinsfolk, what Cyrus Mason inadvertently makes very clear is that the young Browning, eldest son of the eldest son, was even more naturally looked upon as the legitimate heir to the leadership of the family. Mason's odd annoyance with the poet, evidently acceded to with some feeling by some of the other members of Jane Smith Browning's family (but by no means all), did not stem primarily, as one would imagine, from jealousy at the special treatment and training made available to him by his parents. Mason emphasizes that kinsfolk were only too anxious (as indeed kind Uncle Reuben or Aunt Silverthorne, on the mother's side, certainly were) to contribute to further the education and career of "young Robert." What especially embittered some relations was rather that the poet, thus prepared, should choose in mature life not to involve himself overmuch with the Browning clan and not to become the center and leader of family life.

Mason makes explicit a comparison, which must have been implicit in the larger family and clear enough to the boy himself: that between the grandson and his forceful and imposing grandfather. Recalling Browning as he first knew him in the vigor of early manhood, Mason can only explain the differences between the vigorous son and the docile father by constant comparison between Browning and the departed patriarch of the family. To Mason it was merely a matter of the hot temper and strong will of the grandfather—"ebullition of the Robert Browning temper"—emerging virtually as a biological trait in the grandson.[112] But to Browning's growing under-standing the awareness that he was by rights the heir to the vigorous, highly successful, and rather antipathetic, gouty old City man of affairs was en-tirely more complicated. Unlike the father, who had chosen, seemingly of necessity, a life of compromise and self-abnegation, the grandson might expect to fulfill the great expectations of the Browning family, to rise, to become someone in the greater world. At the same time, persuaded of the justice of his father's cause against the narrow, worldly grandfather and brought up to the fullest cultivation of his own talents, Browning would naturally not aspire to rise to be some greater functionary of the Bank of England. Only by succeeding in a field of endeavor above and beyond the ambitions of a City man, might he fulfill the expectations of his liberal up-bringing and at the same time decisively settle the old issue between his father and his grandfather.

In one gesture in the family, which linked grandfather and grandson—both Robert Brownings and both with initials, R. B.—the dilemma seems almost symbolically projected. From the brother of his first wife, Margaret Tittle, Browning's grandfather had inherited a pair of cuff links. Although the story was confused and had probably become exaggerated in the telling, apparently this Great-Uncle Tittle had died a violent death at the hands of his slaves and the cuff links had been taken from his body. Browning's grandfather inscribed them proudly with his own initials. Then, as Brow-ning recalled it, years later they were "taken out of the nightgown in which he [the grandfather] died, and given to me, not my father."[113] His father, who had rejected outright the inheritance in St. Kitts and settled for a quiet, uneventful life, was naturally skipped over in this token of greater family lineage. For the inheriting grandson, the problem of putting on the grand-father's strength and activity without accepting the dubious legacy of ex-ploitation and mere worldly ambition, which had been so much a part of the lives of his grandfather and other vigorous ancestors from all sides of his family, would be a very real one.

Some such logic of complicated and crossed motivations was no doubt present in the quiet easy home life of the Brownings, leading the young boy to feel that he must pay the wages of freedom some day by some more than ordinary exertion. Although some of his contemporaries and even his biog-rapher Betty Miller saw in the freedom and indulgence of Browning's fam-ily life a shocking encouragement of irresponsibility, even laziness, there is good reason to suspect that just the opposite was true. The freedom of his opportunities combined with the particular circumstances of his family life sometimes overburdened him with the responsibility of success. Even in old age he would be bothered by the debt he felt he owed for his freedom and would continue to see his own career as somehow a rectification and justifi-cation of his father's compromise. "It would have been quite unpardonable in my case," he told Hiram Corson, "not to have done my best. My dear father put me in a condition most favorable for the best work I was capable of . . . My good father sacrificed a fortune to his convictions. He could not bear with slavery and left India [*sic*: for West Indies] and accepted a humble bank office in London. He secured for me all the ease and comfort that a literary man needs to do good work. It would have been shameful if I had not done my best to realize his expectations of me.''[114]

It is also worth noticing that there were certain limits imposed upon his opportunities by the very positive circumstances of his early life. Perhaps necessarily, such a situation deprived him of some experiences even while it gave others. Above all, it put him at one remove from the lives and concerns of great numbers of his countrymen. Browning would never be indifferent to the very less fortunate lives of the majority of his age. But his lack of firsthand experience of the poverty-stricken lives of the London poor or of the grinding routine to which the new industrial proletariat in the North were beginning to be exposed, would keep doors closed to him that were opened to a Dickens, a Mrs. Gaskell, or, later, to a D. H. Lawrence by their very different environment and experience. Not that life in Camberwell left Browning in a state of blissful ignorance about the realities of the world. The remnants of the older English society still existing along with the newer middle-class life in Camberwell gave him the opportunity to experience at first hand something of the complexity of traditional village and country culture. He would evoke again and again in his poetry the lower-class world of the older rural and village England with good humor but essential realism. He certainly had opportunities enough to view the very different worlds and ways of life in nearby London before he was very old. Yet the lives of the urban poor and the industrial workers remained for him, as for other Camberwell residents, something outside his own personal experience: a reality as distant observation, or statistics, or as a social problem, but not a reality in his own life, not something that would demand from him imaginative expression.

In a sense, it was the very forces of change and development that had placed Browning and his family in a position of unwonted security and freedom that also kept them from full experience of their less beneficent workings. England, Disraeli would declare in the famous phrase in *Sybil*, was becoming a country divided into two nations, the rich and the poor. And it was not the age-old differences in affluence but the increasing division and isolation of classes that was remarkable. If birth and growth in Camberwell placed Browning invisibly but surely in one of the two emerging nations and cut him off as surely from full experience of the impact of the nineteenth century on the working classes, in other ways his early circumstances put him in a uniquely central position in the development of the mind and outlook of his time. Not only was the general freedom and openness of his early life a key that would unlock a range of opportunities rarely available in his society, but, as we shall see, even the specific influences exerted on him before he began as a young adult to develop his own version of reality gave him an intuitive understanding of many of the diverse and sometimes conflicting forces forming the culture and intellect of his time.

IV
Self-Consciousness

The mature Robert Browning, self-styled "writer of plays," creator in his monologues of a world of "imaginary persons" not himself, is not commonly associated with intense or morbid self-consciousness. In most of his poetry, as he made clear in the sonnet "House," he emphatically refused to unlock his heart with the key of verse. He made all his characters talk about themselves but hardly ever spoke directly about himself. Even to his close friends he appeared more as a benevolent, good-humored man of the world than as a person of intense sensibility.

Yet it was precisely the poet's intense self-consciousness that most disturbed John Stuart Mill, when he read Browning's first published poem *Pauline*. In his well-known comments, written at the end of a review copy he had inspected, he complained, "The writer seems to me possessed with a more intense and morbid self-consciousness than I ever knew in any sane human being."[1] The remark was not surprising, nor even original. In the poem Browning had himself called attention to this quality. With a degree of adolescent bravado he had his poet-speaker confess, "I strip my mind bare," and what he found in first and central place was this:

I am made up of an intensest life,
Of a most clear idea of consciousness
Of self.

Of course Browning soon became ashamed of his first published poem and turned away from a confessional style of writing altogether. He did not, however, repudiate his early claim to an especially intense self-consciousness. He read Mill's comment, when the review copy was returned to him, and though he quarreled with many of Mill's comments, he did not deny

Mill's general assertion. On the contrary, twelve years later he even bragged to Elizabeth Barrett about that part of Mill's criticism. "Then, I had a certain faculty of self-consciousness, years, years ago, at which John Mill wondered, and which ought to be improved by this time, if constant use helps at all."[2] For all his reticence, in his mature poetry a sense of unique and vivid consciousness remained with him as a hidden, even mysterious center of poetic power: that "inner power" which he once attempted to explain to Elizabeth by the metaphor of a lighthouse over the Mediterranean: the light "ever revolving in a dark gallery, bright and alive," which leaps out suddenly "from the one narrow chink, and then goes on with the blind wall between it and you."[3]

Under the liberal, expansive conditions of Browning's home life, it is hardly difficult to conceive that he should have developed such a strong sense of personal independence and self-awareness. But to determine more explicitly what Browning meant by self-consciousness, and to try to trace its origins back to particular causes in his youth and boyhood is a much more complicated undertaking. In one sense, self-consciousness has no biographic origins. It is simply the necessary condition of human existence, the principal "I am conscious of myself, therefore I am" that preceded, or is the same thing as, "I think, therefore I am."[4] In another sense, the more common sense which Browning chose rather to ignore in Mill's comment, it is an embarrassed preoccupation with oneself, a focus on the problems of one's own identity to the exclusion of external reality. But Browning's sense of special powers of self-consciousness, a development that Mill could find unhealthy and hardly sane, really fits neither of these definitions. There is no doubt that in *Pauline*, as in his earliest letters, Browning appears, as Mill sensed, a very self-preoccupied, socially self-conscious, young man.[5] If Browning was awkwardly self-conscious in the ordinary manner of bright adolescents and young men, he was nonetheless trying in *Pauline* to express a deeper quality of awareness, a state of felt internal vitality in mind and emotion that was far more fundamental to his personality than the mere self-preoccupation of youth. What Browning was aware of appears to have been essentially a particular psychological quality or a special quality of consciousness itself, an unusually strong sense of his own being as a thing separate from that of others and a peculiar predilection for introspection and for reworking external experience in internal meditation.

That some such quality is by nature particularly strong in certain individuals is no doubt true; that a poet—even one who wrote so little poetry about himself—should be born with this kind of accentuated self-consciousness seems very likely. It is also true, however, that this kind of self-consciousness is in large part a matter of cultivation. While it leads to a sense of the individual's separation from society, it is itself a form of culture, more strongly emphasized in some periods of history and less so in others. For all Mill's horror at the immature, confessional self-consciousness of the poet who reveals himself in *Pauline*, the age in which Browning grew up was, of course, one in which self-awareness, the cultivation of fine sentiments in isolation, a habit of contemplation and introspection were far from disreputable or uncommon. In some ways, as Carlyle indeed noted with alarm in his signal essay "Signs of the Times," the overall temper of the age was largely mechanical and external. Yet even by the time of Browning's birth, strong counterforces were present in many sections of English society and were generating a new interest in inner, personal experience and awareness. In literature, even before Browning's birth, the first generation of major Romantics, Blake, Scott, Wordsworth, and Coleridge, had of course been placing a new and strong stress upon feeling and individual cultivation apart from society. They were followed soon afterward by Byron, whose *Childe Harold's Pilgrimage* first began to appear, in fact, in the year of Browning's birth, and then by Keats and Shelley, Lamb, Hazlitt, and De Quincey, and their lesser contemporaries: all—though often in quite different ways— asserting the primacy of the individual mind and consciousness over the power of society or the collective wisdom of the past.

Browning was an early lover of Byron. He quite certainly knew Coleridge's and Wordsworth's poetry at an early age.[6] Later in youth he read Keats and Shelley and no doubt he was influenced by many other writers, such as his favorite Christopher Smart,[7] who provided examples of acute self-awareness and inner sensibility. But although we hear of his early love for Wordsworth or of his enthusiasm on first discovering Shelley and Keats, we do not hear of any sudden conversion, such as that which Mill reports in his *Autobiography,* from preoccupation with external things to a new interest in cultivating an inner sensibility. The taproot of his self-consciousness, though no doubt fed and stimulated by the diverse forces of romantic literature and feeling at work in his age, appears rather to extend deep into his earliest experience, into his upbringing in a private, very domestic and somewhat inwardly turned household, into the evangelical religious atmosphere of his early family life, and into his childhood immersion in the natural world around suburban Camberwell.

1 Domestic Life

"(And my mother loves me just as much more as must of necessity be—),"[8] Browning hastened to assure Elizabeth after describing his father's kindness. It was not, as it might appear, a duteous afterthought, but simply a recognition of the affection that evidently existed between himself and his mother from boyhood up. Given our twentieth-century preoccupation with the abnormal or harmful effects of parental affection—a preoccupation perhaps unavoidable when rapid changes in social and cultural behavior make reasonable and sympathetic communication between different generations strained and difficult—it is tempting to infer from the affection between Browning and his mother and from the fact that Browning lived at home until the age of thirty-four, that he was tied, in a morbid and unhealthy way, to his mother's apron strings.[9] For the affection between them there is ample evidence. Browning himself spoke of his mother in after years with—we are told in the dialect of dutiful biography—"tremulous emotion," as "a divine woman."[10] Browning's friend Domett noted in 1878 "how affectionate he was towards her," and recalled that in their early acquaintance he saw Browning, who had thrown a roll of music across the room and was afraid he had struck her, run "to her to apologise and caress her, though I think she had not felt it."[11] Elizabeth, writing home to Browning's family after she and Browning had taken up residence in Italy, assured them especially of Browning's love for his mother: "Robert is so anxious about her always. How deeply and tenderly he loves her and all of you."[12] After his mother's death in 1849 she wrote repeatedly of Robert's deep affliction and "passionate love for her." "My husband has been in the deepest anguish . . . He has loved his mother as such passionate natures only can love, and I never saw a man so bowed down in the extremity of sorrow—never."[13] Even when allowance is made for the tendency to overstate Browning's filial tenderness in an age when this was generally considered as unquestionably a virtue, it is clear that a very close attachment must have existed between Browning and his mother.

What there is no evidence for, however, is that this relationship, any more than Browning's affectionate ties with his father and sister, became a constricting, emotionally dominating influence, or that it prevented his growth to maturity as a person or as a writer. Browning did, after little more than a week of living in London while he attended classes at the new London University, beat a retreat to his home where, though he finished out the year at the university, he remained until his marriage eighteen years later. But at the time he was only sixteen. In an age when people generally married later than they do today, and when prolonged residence at home was by no means uncommon, Browning may be forgiven for preferring the pleasant company, the books and quiet, the country environment of his family's home to a student lodging house in London. In the years that followed, rather than limiting himself to the local concerns of his family circle, he seriously pursued his chosen occupation as a writer. He developed a wide social and literary acquaintance in London. When he finally resolved to marry Elizabeth Barrett and left with her to set up life in Italy, it was with the full sympathy and approval of all members of his family.[14]

Although Browning may be exonerated from the charge of oedipal fixation and spared the attacks of those who bend the insights of psychology to the old aims of polemical abuse, there is also no doubt that his mother exercised a very strong influence, perhaps the strongest influence, upon his growth and character.[15] She died before there was sufficient public interest in Browning to lead anyone to inquire about his mother. Perhaps, too, because her life, unlike her husband's, was lived almost completely within her domestic sphere, there are very few records of her. Alfred Domett, who did know her, amusingly, but not very usefully, recalled that she had "the *squarest* head and forehead I almost ever saw in a human being, putting me in mind, absurdly enough no doubt of a tea-chest or tea-caddy.''[16] The squareness is confirmed by the one caricature sketch of her by her husband, but it offers little by way of character revelation.[17] Browning's French friend Ripert-Monclar, who might have told us much, merely remarks to his journal on her "bonté parfaite."[18] As we have seen, both her marriage to a quiet, scholarly man and the circumstances of the family life at Camberwell and New Cross gave her, if not a free life by the standards of the modern professional woman, at least a large degree of personal independence and the freedom to order her own thinking and her own way of living. Residing outside of London and away from the business life of her husband, she pursued a quiet, ordered way of life, very much centered upon her family and household activities: obviously not an unusual pattern, but less common then, when the life of the average woman was bound up far more directly with the occupation of her husband. Not having to work in the fields, or in a factory, or keep a shop, or do put-out work at home, she was, by the standards of the day, a woman of leisure, a gentlewoman if not a person of fashion or a lady of social position.

The few references to her daily activities are hardly surprising: she is working in her garden at Camberwell or New Cross, going out for a walk with her small son, entertaining a visitor for tea, nursing Robert through a sickness, or playing the piano: some very few of thousands of household activities or family concerns, but probably not untypical.

The picture appears quite ordinary; yet on those who did come to know her she seems to have made a strong and decided impression. Carlyle, who met her when he visited Browning at New Cross, spoke of her in a frequently quoted phrase as the "true type of a Scottish gentlewoman," from him a phrase more meaningful and emphatic than it might seem. Browning's friend, Arnould, who kept up his friendship with Browning's family even after the poet went to Italy, wrote at his mother's death of "her whom to know was to love."[19] John Kenyon, prominent literary man and later Browning's benefactor, is said to have declared, "that such as she had no need to go to heaven, because they made it wherever they were.[20] Even Elizabeth Barrett, who never actually met her, speaks of "her angelic nature" or of "that pure and tender spirit."[21] Such testimonials may smack somewhat of courteous overstatement, but they do suggest that Mrs. Browning was neither a mere "matter-of-fact" hausfrau nor the emotionally dominating matriarch that she has sometimes been called.[22] Nor was she, despite the allusions to heavens on earth and "angelic" natures, merely the passive angel in the house serving, like some later Victorian women, an ideal thrust upon her without any personal choice of a style of life. What she does seem to have been was an individual with a personality and sense of identity strong enough to leave a lasting impression on those who knew her and on the members of her family. If she was a woman of the Camberwell society in taking on the career of mother and homemaker, she brought a force of vitality and imagination to her work which was quite uncommon. Particular incidents show her stamping her personality upon the events of her household, events perhaps insignificant in themselves but made interesting by her interest and her way of working them up imaginatively. A big apple on a tree against the garden wall at New Cross thus becomes a thing of remarkable interest: "a gigantic apple," Browning wrote to Elizabeth, "which my mother had set her heart on showing a cousin of mine who is learned in fruits and trees."[23] As Browning and his mother discuss this everyday object it turns into almost a sensate thing. She decides to let it hang—"The next day or two would do its cheeks good"—and the incident itself becomes a small drama, as, despite Browning's amused warnings, she leaves it just one day too long and it falls, "bruised in the dirt, a sad wreck."

The same kind of application of consciousness is apparent in another incident, concerning an equally ordinary subject, a fierce, somewhat ill-tempered, bulldog given to Browning.[24] Instead of just a nasty dog, he becomes a special creature, one who only obeys Browning's mother, who has a great fierceness for all other creatures save Browning and his mother, but who, at her command, would violate his own nature and passively put up with the scratches of the family cat: trivial tales and probably exaggerated but examples of the personal presence that she registered in her domestic world.

What should strike us in such stories, if we are not blinded by the way in which our century has often been forced to link a good thing, honesty, with a bad thing, alienation and failure of communication between individuals, is the picture they present of two generations in full communication with each other within a family: making contact in their perceptions and imaginations even in minor everyday matters. To her children Mrs. Browning was thus a model not of passive angelic good nature but of a forthright and active approach to experience. Sarianna, who learned from her a similar power of telling a story with "vivid realization" spoke of her in later life not only as a strong personality but as a person of "immense courage,"[25] a strong and unusual statement to make about a nineteenth-century housewife. Her own conversation often included tales in which her mother figured as the principal subject.

To his complaints about Browning's treatment of kinsfolk, Cousin Cyrus Mason added one that no doubt carried more force at the end of the Victorian era when he was writing than it would now: that Browning showed no "knowledge of the meaning of the word domesticity."[26] Mason's complaint implies, quite correctly, that the mature Browning was not willing to elevate the values of ordinary middle-class home life into the essential concerns of life. He criticized Harriet Martineau to Elizabeth for doing just that: making fetishes out of the ingredients of cottage life rather than taking them merely as the setting for life.[27] His poems, whether portraying Andrea del Sarto's special domestic arrangements or the corrupting paternal solicitude of the solicitor-father Hyacinthus de Archangelis in *The Ring and the Book* (whose idea of justice is anything tht serves his own "dear domestic ties'') often warn of the danger in the domestic trap, a danger inherent in any partial good when it is treated as an ultimate one.

In another sense Browning's early life and his relationship to his mother gave him a very strong domestic ideal, one focused not on forms but on the essential privateness of domestic culture. Speaking of their own very withdrawn early years of marriage in 1847, Elizabeth told a friend that Robert "has seen a good deal of the world . . . always hating it, as he says, & yearning for the 'garden of cucumbers' to which he has come now.''[28] What is attractive in a garden of cucumbers is, of course, not so much the cucumbers, but the fact that they are one's own cucumbers, that the garden allows a person to have a private existence in which he is more truly himself and at ease with himself. Browning would never be content only with a private life, even when the garden had Elizabeth (as well as cucumbers) in it. Far less could he live an entirely public life. Even in the red-letter days of dining out in his later life in London, he insisted upon maintaining a balancing private world, partly open to his family and a few close friends, partly closed entirely in the private garden of the mind. Like other writers of his time, George Eliot or Tennyson for instance, Browning often seems to be excessively protective about his personal privacy, excessive even when account is taken of the enormous amount of public scrutiny to which he was subjected because of his wife's highly emotional devotees and, later, because of his own growing reputation. In part, the reason for such sensitivity was not a personal but a social one, for his society was exceptionally unwilling to hear about a person's private life and treated ordinary private matters as scandals when they were made public. But sensitivity was not only a social stance, a conventional protective armor to wear in his society. It was also a more serious defensive posture, a means of shielding personal values that might be lost in public life.

In this second sense, as something positive which existed only in protection from the larger public world, the private, domestic life had become for the generation of writers before Browning, and to some extent for society as a whole, a locus, even a kind of metaphor, for a range of values and an area of experience. For Wordsworth and Coleridge a domestic life in some country cottage offered something like the more traditional pastoral ideal of a retreat into a world of simpler forms and more direct communication. To Coleridge, for instance, awareness of the possibility of affection in a domestic retreat is the precondition of his poetry and in a sense the subject of most of his best conversational poems. Conversely, his private life's failure, the awareness of a "coarse domestic Life" that kept him from developing a deeper range of feeling and sympathy, lay behind his sense of failed imaginative powers in the ode "Dejection."[29] Wordsworth's most important experiences were, of course, those of solitude, but he insisted throughout the *Prelude* that an intimate family or personal relationship, with his sister Dorothy or with Coleridge, was a necessary context for his more personal moments of self-consciousness. So too, despite their varied and complicated domestic arrangements both Bryon and Shelley held up in their poetry an ideal of love and communication in retreat from the world: the idyll of Juan and Haidee in *Don Juan* or the strangely unepic conclusion of *Prometheus Unbound,* in which Asia and Prometheus are reunited in a domestic epiphany of free flowing love. In each case domesticity, a protected place in which the individual could develop feelings of sympathy and love and a fuller sense of his conscious existence than he could in the greater world of what Coleridge calls the "loveless ever-anxious crowd," was the condition of an opening of the inner self.

From the secluded, inwardly turned life of his family and the close relationship between mother and children, Browning developed a similar sense of private inner cultivation. In his early poems the theme of domesticity was a common one, and like his romantic predecessors—as well as his contemporary Dickens—he verged on sentimentality in his celebration of the love-charged home world presided over by the beloved female figure. Michal in *Paracelsus*, the beloved mate of Paracelsus' friend Festus, is such a figure and never fails to arouse in the Promethean scholar an awareness of the side of human life he is missing, that of simple happiness and assured love. We need not go as far as Betty Miller, who sees her explicitly as a study of Mrs. Browning, to realize that the portrait obviously embodies many of the values Browning associated with his mother. In 1837, standing godfather at the christening of the first child of some friends, Browning wrote a poem called "A Forest Thought" in their family album.[30] Such an occasion brought him to an even more explicit formulation of an ideal of domestic love. Although his metaphor, comparing the father and mother to two giant trees and their son to a seedling, is a bit strained, the conclusion, in which Browning expresses his wish that they may live in "a charmed retreat" free from outer turmoil, is revealing. Speaking in the same metaphor of "glancing squirrels' summer love, / And the brood-song of the cushat-dove!" he hopes that they may be able to cultivate in domestic retreat a charmed world of peace and love. There is little doubt where Browning found the model for this symbolic picture. When his mother died he recalled his own early domestic retreat with emotional, even sentimental vividness. "He says it would break his heart," Elizabeth wrote, "to see his mother's roses over the wall, and the place where she used to lay her scissors and gloves."[31] He recalled even such small details so strongly because they were a part of his own most important early experience of communication with another person.

Sentimentality, the distorting perception of feeling indulged for its own sake, is an obvious danger from such an early environment. Not only is there the temptation not to move beyond the first, close relationship with the parents to form new relationships with others, but for the writer, there is the more real danger of presenting a jejune, overly emotional view of life in which feeling takes the place of mind instead of complementing it. Browning was less burdened with sentimentality than many writers of his age, but it was a problem for him and remains one for readers who can't believe men die of conflicting passions alone (as they can in early Browning) or who can't see the greatness of *Pippa Passes* because they are offended by its frequently excessive richness of sentiment. Had the home world of his mother been merely one of peace and love, the effect might have been on the whole even negative, emotionality or a Pollyanna sickish sweetness of outlook. The domestic retreat that Mrs. Browning provided for her children was not merely a place of positive emotions but also a place of intelligence and imagination. In communicating with her, Browning began to learn to perceive his world fully and intensely. For him, as for the Romantics, the concentration and protectiveness of domestic life was not the end in itself but the means to developing a fuller self-awareness and a more intense consciousness. Eventually, as would most women as well as men of our day, he would find such a world in itself too constrained, too limited in the range of experience it offered, to satisfy fully all his energies and curiosities. Yet it was a necessary beginning, and the quality of his mother's imagination and vital consciousness was such that it allowed his mind, following hers, to begin to grow upward into more than average awareness.

2 Evangelical Religion

In another area of experience, in particular, the influence of Mrs. Browning seems to have had an especially decisive effect upon the awakening consciousness of her son: that of religious feeling.

When, in an episode in the long courtship by mail between Browning and Elizabeth, Elizabeth "confessed" that she was to be numbered in religion, among "those schismatiques of Amsterdam" Donne talks of, Browning, always the opportunist in the affair, fired back: "Can it be you, my own you past putting away, *you* are a schismatic and frequenter of Independent Dissenting Chapels? And you confess this to *me*—whose father and mother went this morning to the very Independent Chapel where they took me, all those years back, to be baptized—and where they heard, this morning, a sermon preached by the very minister who officiated on that other occasion!"[32] The Independent Chapel in question was the Locks Fields Chapel, or, as it came to be called, the York Street Congregational Church, at Walworth, about a mile from the Browning home, just off the main way to the Elephant and Castle. The minister was a George Clayton. Browning's credentials as a schismatic were, however, less obvious than he implies. His father's family were members of the Church of England (his grandmother was the daughter of a clergyman in the Church). In the 1830s Browning and his sister also attended evening services at Camden Chapel, a separate offshoot from the parish church of St. Giles on the Peckham Road near their uncle's brewery, in order to hear the more "eloquent and earnest" sermons of Henry Melvill, which John Ruskin also highly approved.[33] If Clayton's Independent Chapel was nonetheless the family church, there can be no doubt that this was because of the influence of Browning's mother, already a member there before marriage. About 1820, her husband, raised in the

"Where they took me, all those years back, to be baptized—and where they heard, this morning, a sermon preached by the very minister who officiated on that other occasion."

Upper right: The York Street Congregational Church, Walworth, ca. 1928. Photo. *The Browning family's church—built 1790, with the pompous and prosperous façade still as they knew it.*

Lower right: The Reverend George Clayton— the Browning Family's Minister. Engraving.

Bottom: Entry of Robert Browning's Birth and Baptism. Register of Baptisms, Locks Fields Walworth (York Street Congregational Church). *Recording the birth May 7 and baptism June 14, 1812, signed by George Clayton.*

Church of England, followed her and officially joined the York Street Congregation.[34]

In this affiliation, however, there is little ground for the suggestion of narrow dissenting background with which Browning is often stereotyped. As a Scotswoman, as Chesterton pointed out, Browning's mother came from a country where doctrinal Calvinism and intellectual and social attainments were in no sense opposed.[35] To be a "Scottish gentlewoman" was naturally to be Puritan in religion. When, sometime after 1787, she and her sister left Dundee and came to Camberwell, it was equally natural that she should join the Congregational Church as the nearest local equivalent to the National Church of Scotland (Presbyterian). Nor, as Browning's humorous and urbane reference to Dissenters suggests, was this church—the Independent Church of Milton, Cromwell, and the New England Puritans—to be strictly identified with more fundamentalist or working-class Dissenter churches such as the one Browning would portray in *Christmas-Eve and Easter-Day* (1850). The term Browning himself uses to characterize his mother's church and religion is "evangelical," and this could apply equally well to Congregationalists or Low-Church members of the Church of England.[36] Clayton's father, John Clayton, also a Congregational minister in London, had in fact been trained by the famous Evangelical patroness, the Countess of Huntingdon, to be a preacher in the Church of England and had only become Congregationalist when he found orthodox ordination unobtainable.[37]

Camberwell in the early nineteenth century was united as a community —and also splintered into many subcommunities—by an almost universal interest in religion and preaching. Sects were constantly being formed and reformed; new ministers of talent found this area a challenging and often rewarding theater in which to exhibit their powers of rhetoric and persuasion. With more than twenty different churches and sects in the Camberwell area alone, there is no doubt that the Brownings, in choosing to go into Walworth regularly for services, were making some kind of choice, not merely following family precedent or convention. George Clayton, who has been characterized as combining "the characters of a saint, a dancing master, and an orthodox eighteenth-century theologian in about equal proportions," was in fact neither saint, nor fool, nor unthinkingly orthodox.[38] In the first decades of the nineteenth century he was still a young man, and he was probably, before Melvill's advent, the best educated and most solid thinker of the divines in the area.[39] His church professed "the views of doctrinal truth which for the sake of distinction are called Calvinistic."[40] Like many of his American contemporaries he was, however, far from a fire-and-brimstone Calvinist preacher. His was the largest congregation among the Dissenters in Walworth. It included many prosperous merchants and middle-class people who paid for the privilege of the better pews.[41] In keeping with his conception of his dignity, he drove to the trim and graceful new Georgian church in a gown and bands and had himself ushered in by a footman in white gloves. Rather than fulminating against the Babylonian whore, he spoke decently, though critically, of the Catholic Church and decorously referred to the Virgin as "this most distinguished female."[42] Nor, as has been implied, was he puritanically hostile to polite literature. Clayton had a good literary classical education and a command of French.[43] His wife, who was evidently his intellectual superior, was an indefatigable reader of good books: Wordsworth as well as Plato, Seneca, Milton, and Jonathan Edwards. She was something of a bluestocking leader in the local intellectual life as well as in the church charities.[44] A manuscript which appeared when the Browning family collections were sold, even suggests that Clayton himself had sometimes felt another calling. The manuscript contained original verse compositions (albeit on religious subjects) stylishly entitled "Horae Claytonae, No. 5" and apparently shared with certain of his more cultivated parishioners.[45]

Despite such unwonted efflorescence into poetry, Clayton was normally, as even an admirer asserted, one of those "minds that live in steadfast godly prose."[46] Although he was able to turn pretty phrases well enough to get a large number of his sermons, mostly funeral tributes, into print, his message was, at the most, fervid, not inspired. Most often the manner itself, unctuous and winning,[47] was more prominent than the message. While Clayton drew new members yearly and had to enlarge his church every five or ten years, he did not find endless new wealth of insight to offer his parishioners, though he dutifully refused to reuse old sermons. From his long sermons, worked out methodically week after week on the pulpit system of three headings and a conclusion, Browning could not have failed to receive some general understanding of religious ideas and doctrines. But the Walworth church probably had most influence merely in setting patterns and habits of religious devotion and concern. All four Brownings were regular attenders and sat habitually, in the best of the modest seats, at the far end of a long, semicircular gallery, which curved back close to Clayton's pulpit. With some romantic elaboration of memory a former member of the congregation recalled the family at church: the "noble faces" of the parents, Sarianna "whose countenance was a combination of both their noblenesses and sweetnesses"; and, at the far corner and at the right hand of his minister, the future poet: "the most wonderful face in the whole congregation,—pale somewhat mysterious,—and shaded with black flowing hair."[48]

The Brownings also participated in the religious life of the church in other ways. Both children were baptized there by Clayton, who took keener pleasure in this than in any other ministerial function. Mrs. Browning joined her family to the great mistaken missionary efforts of the English churches militant of the nineteenth century by regular contributions at the church. Later Sarianna was a sponsor of Clayton's charity and Sunday school projects.[49] Yet the impression remains that for these latter-day Puritans it was more the idea of going to church than the functions of the church itself that was important. When Tennyson wanted to give a picture of holiness to counter the temptations of rationalism and nihilism in "The Two Voices," he painted not a family *in* church but one going *to* church, and the focus rested revealingly on the family, not the church, as the center of the religious life. For Browning, certainly, even churchgoing was mainly accessory to the more important religious influences in his family and home life, especially those exerted by his mother. In later life he spoke well of Clayton primarily because he associated him with the values favored by his mother. When he had his own son baptized in Florence in 1849 it was shortly after his mother's death and he confessed in a letter to his sister that he had been "thinking over nothing else, these last three months, than Mama and all about her, and catching at any little fancy of finding something which it would have pleased her I should do."[50] In this light he was pleased with finding a service like Clayton's at a French Evangelical Protestant Church: "Very simple and evangelical—just the same as at Mr. Clayton's, except that there is a form of prayer and service. I saw the minister, a very simple, good and sincere man apparently."

The word *evangelical* was apt as a general term for his mother's religion. What little we know of Sarah Anna's religious beliefs suggests that she was greatly affected by the moral and spiritual awakening of her day, which is often loosely termed evangelical: a movement of feeling and religious and moral sentiment more widely, if more vaguely, active in nineteenth-century English life than the specific Evangelical movement within the Church of England. Partly this was a matter of sharing in the evangelizing movements of missionary work. Partly it was an emphasis upon knowledge of the Gospel as the basis of Christianity. Although Browning's father gave him a variety of books on many subjects, his mother's known gifts consisted of two Bibles (one given as a parting present in 1834 when he joined an embassy mission to Russia) and a *Concordance to the Scriptures*.[51] No doubt regular Bible reading was a basic and central fact of family life, though hopefully the ritual of reading was less formal than that in John Ruskin's family where, lists of begetters and begotten and all, the book was read rigorously from cover to cover and then begun again immediately.

Even more fundamental to her religion was Mrs. Browning's concern with living the moral Christian life, in effect with bringing the standards of her religion and morality to bear on ordinary life in the world. In this she was at one with evangelical leaders as diverse as the father of Methodism, John Wesley, and the Church of England Evangelical crusader, Wilberforce. It was in this sense, too, that Clayton, like his father and brothers, styled himself more often as an evangelical preacher than as a Congregationalist.[52] Although he spoke to one particular sect and supported their particular beliefs, he saw his main role as that of an evangelist in the larger movement that was awakening a new religious and moral sensibility in English life. It was this role as an apostle of sweetness that Browning continued to respect in Clayton long after he had ceased to respect his religious authority or intellectual light. What pleased Browning later in the French minister in Florence was what Clayton and his mother's religion most stressed: simplicity, in the sense of directness or unworldliness, moral concern, and sincerity or earnestness. Such values, embodied by both father and mother and implied in the life they lived and in the beliefs they espoused, became focused almost as a center of moral consciousness and left their lasting impression on Browning's outlook and character.

Beyond this general focus it is difficult to know more specifically the content of religious discussion at the Brownings. In reading the few religious books that have known associations with Mrs. Browning, with her daughter, or with Clayton, however, it is hard not to remark on a similarity in outlook to Browning's own later religious presuppositions and attitudes. While they offer no specific sources for Browning's ideas or for his more doctrinaire poems on religious subjects, they do suggest that many of the attitudes taken by turn-of-the-century enthusiasts to be a special Browning philosophy were really only the commonplaces of the late puritanical and evangelical ethos in which Browning was raised.

Elisha Coles's *A Practical Discourse of Effectual Calling and of Perseverance* (London, 1677), for example, a book signed "Sarah Anna Wiedemann" in a florid hand and identified, "(My mother's maiden name) / Robert Browning. June 4, '73,"[53] reminds us that, as with American Protestants of the time, the Calvinist theology was still the cornerstone of Mrs. Browning's creed. Far from the contemptible work it is assumed to be by Betty Miller, it is a serious English attempt to grapple with the difficulties of the Calvinist theology. Like his contemporaries in America, the English schoolteacher and lexicographer Coles proposed a theology of the covenant in which he attempted to maintain the Calvinistic supreme authority of God while yet giving the religious man a reasonable assurance of salvation. As Perry Miller stated it, "Antinomians expected God's grace to do all, Arminians attributed everything to our consent. The covenant theology held to both the grace and the consent, to the decree of God and the full responsibility of man, to assurance in spite of sin and morality in spite of assurance."[54] In practice, Coles took the lenient view that all who are believers are among the elect and that all the elect will come to believe. Such a compromise theology can be criticized for weakening the force of Calvinism by seeming to seek a legal relationship with the Divinity. From a different perspective it can be said—and it is really saying the same thing—that it humanized the older Puritanism, offering assurance, as Coles's treatise does,[55] that the nature of God is in accord with our best human ideas of morality and justice. Browning himself would stigmatize the atrocity of a different view of God in "Johannes Agricola in Meditation" in the middle 1830s. And in the system of Calvinism the development of some such theological scaffolding was a very significant step toward a more tolerant and more worldly viewpoint. Within the Calvinist emphasis upon the essential religious situation of independent man facing God without any intermediary institution, it allowed man a reasonable idea of his position in the moral universe without excessive anxiety as to his ultimate fate. The main focus could then turn, as it did with people like the Brownings, from the after-state of the soul to man's present moral state.

Another book of Mrs. Browning's, an anonymous, *Spiritual Gleanings, or Select Essays with Scripture Mottoes* (London, 1808),[56] suggests the direction such thinking was likely to take. Supposedly basing the argument on scripture alone, the author actually proposes a kind of metaphysical outline concerning the uses of the world to the soul which will come to ultimate perfection out of the world. In this pre-Browning Society exposition of the Browning philosophy of the imperfect, this world has its use as a field for the development of the "life of righteousness which the soul begins here, and perfects hereafter."[57] The mark of the saved person is not immediate perfection but a sense of moral struggle, even an awareness of present imperfections: "It is nowhere written in the Scriptures that, in the present scene, the saints attain perfection;—no, they 'follow after and pass toward the mark'; but they are in the midst of temptation and liable to fall . . . nevertheless, there is a consciousness of imperfection, there is a desire to live holy,—there is a voice within imploring divine assistance."[58] In a broader view, as in the spectacle of the many different kinds of men in Browning's mature dramatic monologues, the world thus consists of innumerable souls working, more or less successfully, to develop their moral and religious selves. All men are understood and evaluated in relation to their individual struggles toward the perfection of the Divinity. There is no institutional hierarchy but rather a democracy of more and less fulfilled individuals: a constellation of stars: "each shines, tho different in brightness, yet expressing its own holiness: each has a place."[59]

There is no need to assert that Browning remembered—if he had read at all—this particular work when he spoke of the significance of aspiration and imperfection or when he began to conceive of a poetry that let each man give voice to his personal state as best he could. As truisms of the religious outlook in which he was brought up, such attitudes and perspectives on man were simply in the air, just as very different metaphysical outlooks were common heritages in the Middle Ages or in Shakespeare's time. The ideal of moral aspiration, summarized, virtually epitomized, by the injunction that the author of the *Gleanings* appends to the first chapter—"Work whilst it is called To-day; for the night cometh, wherein no man can work"—this ideal would be a commonplace, if also a deeply held truth for the entire early Victorian generation that grew up under the wave of evangelical religious sentiment.

By the same token, there is no reason to look for any one locus for a complementary thrust in the religious life in which his mother raised him, the aspiration toward moral self-awareness and religious self-consciousness. It is natural for Browning to speak, as he does in a letter to W. C. Macready in 1841, of going through a period of renewed spiritual self-consciousness:

"the old rubbing of eyes and unfolding of arms in me—a wake-up bodily and spiritual.[60] Emphasis in his family's religion would have been placed upon the periodic need to renew and advance the inner religious life. Although the Brownings did not give themselves to the more emotional forms of religious revival, they certainly looked upon the religious life as primarily a matter of attaining to moments of heightened awareness and emotional conviction, to those times when, as Coles puts it, consciousness of God's goodness "melts the heart of those in Covenant with God" and the man is raised closer to his ultimate spiritual perfection.[61]

In this enterprise special importance was given to the business of self-examination. The minister raised one's thoughts by his preaching; Bible reading recalled the truths of religion; prayer prepared the heart. But the proof of all would come in the self-evaluation and self-realization of the individual when alone in meditation. The *Spiritual Gleanings* suggests that meditation focus on images from the Bible and nature, for instance on the beauty of the rainbow and on the promise in Revelation that there will be "a rainbow round about the throne, in sight like unto an emerald."[62] Unlike the traditions of meditation in the Renaissance, however, primary stress fell not on attaining to vision or a movement of emotion to God but on enhancing self-consciousness in itself as a way to better realize the divine soul within.

Another book from the Brownings' library, an anonymous Village Pastor's *Advice to a Young Christian on the Importance of Aiming at an Elevated Standard of Piety* (Religious Tract Society, 1831), gives some idea of what was generally expected. It is inscribed on a flyleaf, "Miss Browning, / from / the Rev^d.\ G. Clayton / with best wishes, / on the 7th of Jany. / 1832."[63] For the writer the aim of meditation is to attain an "Assurance of salvation, or even a well-grounded, uniform, and scriptural hope . . . a blessing which is not attained by a superficial and infrequent self-examination."[64] The examination is to be largely an evaluation of the individual's moral worth and spiritual elevation. "Our self-examination . . . respects our state of feelings, and our external conduct. Has the former partaken of the spirit of Christ? Has the latter corresponded with his precepts?"[65] Such meditation does not raise all the terror or anxiety of the Puritan's fevers over his election or damnation; but it does suggest an atmosphere of almost hothouse introspection. Self-interrogation becomes a kind of muckraking of the consciousness: " 'Did I wrestle? Did I agonize? Was my frame of mind sluggish and cold? . . . Had I a deep sense of my unworthiness? . . . Have I detected and suppressed the first risings of secret iniquity? . . . Have I spoken a word of warning or exhortation to any person this day?' "[66] From Clayton's own diary, an intimate record kept throughout his life and amounting to some two thousand self-conscious pages, it is clear that he made such inner inspection a very serious part of his religion. Again and again he took time off from his ever prospering work as a very popular minister in a major London parish to probe his psyche into renewed spiritual palpitation. "How is it with thee, O my soul? Hast thou made any progress in the divine life?" he wrote one year. And another year found him almost despairing at a view of his own inner landscape. "When I lift up the veil from my heart, I am sickened and discouraged by a view of the abominations which disclose themselves. What a chamber of imagery! What a cage of unclean birds! What a sink of sin!"[67]

It is tempting but probably useless to speculate whether the *Advice to a Young Christian*, given to his sister at the beginning of the year in which he would write *Pauline*, had any specific influence on Browning's own religious meditations in that poem. In any case, the general atmosphere of moral soul-searching, no doubt exaggerated in Clayton by his exemplary role as pastor, certainly lies behind Browning's own overly introspective book. If *Pauline* is also a good deal more, it is at the least a work of moral and spiritual self-evaluation. The speaker in *Pauline* scrutinizes the state of his soul, past and present; he rakes up his faults and also reassures himself of his fundamental religious convictions and his yearning for God and higher perfection. Finally he reaffirms his central conviction in Christ (if also in Shelley). Even the resolve in *Pauline* to agonize less in the future, to "look within no more," is not a turning against religious self-examination but an expected fruit of it, the turning to a healthy moral life involved in the work of the world. For the very religion that played such a large part in stirring up a high degree of self-consciousness simultaneously placed the greatest premium on a committed, outer-directed life. Even when in his later works Browning would turn from looking within to looking out at the consciousness and consciences of others, he in no way was turning his back on the habits of self-examination of his religious upbringing. In the dramatic monologue he would find a vehicle for subjecting each of his characters to the most penetrating and yet most empathetic scrutiny, that of the individual's own self-examination. Although the persuasive or rhetorical function of the speech is sometimes predominant, in the best monologues it is most often the process of self-revelation—or the distortions of partial revelation—that is the primary subject of the monologue. What was initially for Browning a personal process becomes dramatically universalized.

His mother's evangelical religion thus exposed Browning to certain general attitudes and concerns that would exercise an influence on him all his life. There is, of course, much that can be criticized in this influence even where, as in Browning's experience, the worst aspects of the evangelical tradition—moral busybodying or joyless Sabbatarianism—were not much present. Strong as it might be in sincerity, in moral energy, and even in serious hard thinking, the evangelical tradition tended, even at its best, to neglect or minimize equally worthwhile areas of experience: the intellectual play and openness to enriching experience that Matthew Arnold found so notably lacking at Camberwell at a later date; the passion for genuine art and for the creative labor of art that Ruskin felt was so wanting as he looked out from Herne Hill onto the new suburban civilization that had developed there; perhaps, above all, the sense of humor and perspective that keep self-awareness from becoming morbid or precious self-preoccupation. Against the narrower side of this religious tradition Browning fortunately felt the tug, both from father and mother, of other less earnest, more broadening influences. In the upshot the young Browning, probably without any very clear understanding of his own motives, soon rebelled against and rejected much that was limiting or constricting in his mother's religion. The boy who had been, as he himself recalled, "passionately religious" in infancy began to move away from his mother's influence.[68] As he grew older he became openly bored and restless through Clayton's long, newspaper-like prayers filled with church events and local happenings. According to the aged memory of a former church member, he even gnawed the mahogany tops of the pews.[69]

Eventually, he was even found, as we know from a letter from Sarah Flower to W. J. Fox written when Browning was fifteen, actively questioning the grounds of Christian belief. Sarah, who later recovered sufficiently to reaffirm her faith in "Nearer, My God, to Thee," wrote pathetically: "My mind has been wandering a long time, and now it seems to have lost sight of that only invulnerable hold against the assaults of this warring world, a firm belief in the genuineness of the Scriptures . . . It was in answering Robert Browning that my mind refused to bring forward argument, turned recreant and sided with the enemy."[70] We distort this twice-told incident if we make Browning into the enemy, a Mephistophelean or even Cloughian figure mercilessly destroying the faith of a helpless innocent daughter of God. The enemy was Satan himself, or skepticism. Sarah was seven years Browning's elder, far from ignorant or uneducated, and herself from a liberal, open-minded, Christian background. Rather than a victim of the boy's advanced opinions, she represented herself, in the only evidence that exists of the incident, as a spiritual adviser who fell into unexpected difficulties. "Seeking to give light to others, my own gloomy state became too settled to admit of doubt." The fact that Browning, who carried on a sentimental friendship with Sarah and her sister Eliza, the musician, should have thus spent his time in earnest debate over subjects of religious faith only reinforces the general impression we have of the serious, rather unwordly religious milieu in which he grew up.

Still, even at fifteen he was clearly moving into a period of serious doubt. Various influences, not only Voltaire and some of Shelley's writing but also an increasing exposure to worlds of thought and experience that seemed somehow left out in the excessively moral and pietistic vision of evangelical Protestantism, served to draw him further away from full involvement in his mother's religion and church. After a long period of doubts, open skepticism, and vacillations, *Pauline* may seem to signal some return to earlier religious paths. Yet it would not lead him into the kind of simple commitment to one church and one creed that his mother possessed.

He might look for something similar to his own experience when he came to baptize or educate his own son, but he never became a regular churchgoer and church member after the plan of his mother. In *Christmas-Eve and Easter-Day* (1850) he casts himself as a religious eclectic who feels he must choose among churches and settles on the rude simplicity of a demotic Dissenters' chapel (nothing like the starched propriety of York Street) over Rome or German rationalistic religion. In real life he was more often the eclectic, independent Christian who never would choose a specific church but sampled one minister or another to see what he might have to offer. In his later years in London the tradition of regular family attendance at church was left to his sister Sarianna. When she returned home, their butler reported, Browning "would discuss and argue with her at lunch about points in the sermon."[71]

If Browning's religious upbringing failed to make him into an exemplary member of the Congregational community, its general effect upon his character and sentiments was permanent and fundamental. The deeper working of the evangelical sentiment of the early nineteenth century was, as George Eliot comprehensively described it in *Scenes From Clerical Life,* at the level of basic personality and attitude toward life.

> Evangelicalism had brought into palpable existence and operation . . . that idea of duty, that recognition of something to be lived for beyond the mere satisfaction of self, which is to the moral life what the addition of a great central ganglion is to animal life . . . Whatever might be the weaknesses of the ladies who pruned the luxuriance of their lace and ribbons, cut out garments for the poor, distributed tracts, quoted Scripture, and defined the true Gospel, they had learned this—that there was a divine work to be done in life, a rule of goodness higher than the opinion of their neighbours; and if the notion of a heaven in reserve for themselves was a little too prominent, yet the theory of fitness for that heaven consisted in purity of heart, in Christ-like compassion, in the subduing of selfish desires.[72]

However much wider knowledge and greater sophistication might add to these simple qualities, the values embodied in his mother's evangelical religion, like her domestic values, became a part of the future poet's consciousness. As ideals of unworldly goodness, they were there to be drawn upon, to a greater or lesser degree, when he set out in later life to portray a positive character, a Pippa or a Pompilia, or even more complex characters, such as the Pope in *The Ring and the Book,* whose essential goodness and sincerity have been educated by reading, thinking, and wide experience. The values were there, too, as we have seen, as a general moral outlook on the universe, a view that stressed the reality of imperfection at the same time that it urged the necessity of growth and development. Above all, such religious and moral values, with their strong stress upon moral self-awareness and a vital, inner religious life, must also have played a large part in developing the special sense of self-consciousness that the author of *Pauline* professed.

3 Nature

It would be an impossible task even if much, rather than the little we have, were known about Browning's youth, to divide up the development of his consciousness into neat packages of experience each carefully labeled and clearly distinguished from the next. At best "domestic affections" or "evangelical religious feelings" merely provide imprecise, general descriptions of what are in fact very complicated clusters of attitudes, values, and emotions, all changing and developing over time. Similarly, Browning's feeling for nature or interest in the natural world is not a discrete, simply definable state of emotion or characteristic of personality but a complex association of attitudes and feelings.

For Browning interest in nature very likely also began in large part through the influence of his mother. There has been a tendency among Browning's biographers to oppose the religious influence of Sarah Anna to his teenage interest in Shelley.[73] If the young Shelley's atheistic teachings alone are considered, there is obvious truth in this. In larger perspective, however, her influence is not generally opposed to the romantic influences of the age in which Browning grew up and of which Shelley is one outstanding example. Although, like Coleridge's "pensive Sarah," she no doubt did disapprove of the rationalistic and libertarian attitudes present in some aspects of the larger movement of romanticism, she would have had little objection to the stress on true feelings, sincerity, and the reality of subjective experience that was a hallmark of romanticism and evangelicalism alike. Least of all would she have had reason to complain of the preoccupation with nature so prevalent in the early nineteenth century. Among the very few books known certainly to be hers it is not surprising to find William Cowper's *The Task* with the later addition, "(My mother's Book, R. B.)"[74] Of all poems of the eighteenth century this low-pitched, somewhat quizzical and even pathetic work by a poet himself closely associated with the leaders of the Evangelical religious movement, most nearly approaches the direct, sincere expression and the immediate involvement in nature of Wordsworth or Coleridge. According to William Sharp, a biographer not entirely to be trusted in details that formed attractive anecdotes, Mrs. Browning "inclined to the Romanticists" against her husband's liking for Pope.[75] If so, she may even have read the earlier Romantics and been the person who introduced Browning to them sometime in childhood. From a late comment by Browning it would seem likely that his mother at least shared with him a liking for Burns: "When you conjecture that I 'must needs love Burns,'—I answer that I have some Scottish blood in my veins,—my Mother's blood, that is to say."[76]

Whatever acquaintance she had with romantic poetry and whatever corresponding sympathy she felt for the spreading interest in natural scenery and outdoors reality that it encouraged, her own interest in nature was far from a mere literary or fashionable, parlor-bred enthusiasm. Although she kept a rather conventional household, she established her own unique and quite unconventional relationship with the natural world outside her house, a relationship that brought her closer to the elemental vitality of living things and life's basic processes than might be expected in the rather decorous world of Camberwell middle-class society. She was a devoted gardener, working outside at her roses so regularly that both Browning and Cyrus Mason remembered her by this occupation. By growing vegetables and fruits she gave the family a sense of contact with the traditional cycle of nature despite their nearness to the city. When he heard that Dickens, the master chronicler of the oppressive, inescapable unnature of London, was sick, Browning naturally sent some homegrown apples. And he seemed almost to be speaking from one of Dickens's distant and impossible worlds of country content and natural growth rather than from a few miles distance: "May I offer you two or three?—no more, because the Scripture blessing of the good man in 'his basket and his store' has only been half-accomplished with us here."[77]

More surprising than her liking for gardening was Mrs. Browning's undisguised fondness for all kinds of living things. Along with "her immense courage" it was "her love of animals" that Sarianna still recalled with admiration when she spoke of her to friends in her own old age.[78] Of her remarkable sympathy with natural creatures we are told, to add to the interesting if none too credible family story of Robert's bulldog, that "she would lure the butterflies in the garden to her, and the domestic animals obeyed her as if they reasoned."[79] Browning himself could recall how tenderly she sewed up and nursed a wounded cat that he brought home to her.[80] With her began a trait in the Browning family that lasted for at least two generations. No one who knew Sarianna failed to comment on her love for animals and their reciprocal interest in her. The same passion was more grotesquely obvious in Browning's son who, along with four dogs, Japanese nightingales, choughs, and other things, even kept a fine boa constrictor as a favored pet.[81]

"Robert's love of animals comes from her,"[82] Browning's sister asserted and certainly Browning's own boyhood involvement with nature began by his following his mother's interest—decidedly odd for a woman of his time—in the variety of creatures, domestic and wild, "nice" and not so "nice" that nature spread before him in Camberwell for his curiosity—what Browning himself termed "my odd liking for 'vermin.'"[83] Leaving aside horses and his various household pets, dogs like the Rapp drawn by Browning's father or the "good cat" Sarianna remembered from New Cross,[84] his more unspeakable specimens included two lady birds in a box labeled, "Animals found surviving in the depths of a severe winter," owls, monkeys, magpies, hedgehogs, an eagle, and a couple of large snakes—all these alive! And

he often brought them home to give to his mother who, we are told, was genuinely pleased to receive them.[85] Browning, it is also alleged, once refused
to take his medicine until his mother found him a delectable little speckled
frog among the strawberry beds, which she did, holding a delicate parasol
over her head. Around Browning, as around his mother, faintly credible
stories of human magnetism toward animals have clung: most notably, the
account of the favorite toad at New Cross which would come out from his
hole under a rose tree at a fixed signal from Browning, parade behind him,
let him tickle his head, and look at him with a "loving glance of the soft full
eyes."[86] But perhaps skepticism is out of place here: even in later life Browning kept not only a pet owl but some geese, sometimes called Quarterly and
Edinburgh, who followed him with great affection. And at least this later
tale, in light of Konrad Lorenz' studies of imprinting in geese, we can now
readily believe.

Certainly as important for the development of Browning's personality
as his enthusiasm for all kinds of animals, was his gradual exploration of
the more truly wild and natural areas still close to suburban Camberwell or
New Cross. For real country was still readily attainable and clearly captured
Browning's greatest interest. When, in 1845, he visited his friend R. H.
Horne in Millfield Lane, Hampstead Heath, "in the very lane Keats loved
so much," he reported his impression of the Heath area to Elizabeth: "I can
testify it is green and silent, with pleasant openings on the grounds and
ponds, thro' the old trees that line it." It was pleasant but his preference
was clearly for open natural landscape such as he could find behind his
house at New Cross: "But the hills here are far more open and wild and hill-
like,—not with the eternal clump of evergreens and thatched summer
house—to say nothing of the 'invisible railing' miserably visible everywhere."[87] The same preference for true country rather than cultivated suburban landscape is apparent in Browning's choice of outdoor haunts and
roaming places in boyhood or adolescence. In Camberwell or Peckham, villages of Browning's boyhood closest to London, there were trees, greenery,
and open areas. Although wild nature was gradually being supplanted by
human habitations and well kept gardens, there was still country enough to
raise country difficulties at the end of the century: not only from too many
"Camberwell beauty" butterflies but from sparrows, pole cats, and even
roaming hogs.[88] Even in the 1820s and 1830s in the adjacent towns farther
to the south Browning could still find large areas of farmland or open country and woods, where, in Ruskin's phrase for one of these—a certain Goose
Green located between Dulwich and New Cross—"rural Barbarism" still
prevailed.

From Camberwell Browning might walk over to Nun's Head (or Nunhead Hill), a queer outcropping from which the undulating country hills
sloped off in all directions. Here on at least one occasion Browning was
joined by his father, who would sometimes read to him as they walked up
the rough, country hill.[89] Although he may have preferred Pope's poetry

*Country Spots near the Brownings' Homes
in Camberwell and New Cross.*

Nunhead Green, 1832. Water color by H. Prosser.   *A favorite country walk—
where Robert Browning Sr., on at least one occasion, read to Browning from Dryden.*

View of the Gipsy-House, in Norwood, Surrey. Engraving.   *Rough country
where Browning and his cousin James Silverthorne liked to ramble.*

over the Romantics', his father appreciated natural scenery sufficiently to leave among his more usual art some sensitive, lyrical impressions of country views.[90] At other times, Browning might be joined by his sister. She recalled taking long walks in the country in early youth, and even in their old age she would often join her brother for rambles up to six hours long.[91] More often he might enjoy alone "a green half-hour's walk over the fields," still open, rural country in his youth, from Southampton Street to the rustic village of Dulwich.[92] At Dulwich he would sometimes, like Mr. Pickwick, enjoy "a walk about the pleasant neighborhood on a fine day" or stop to visit the truly excellent collection of paintings left to the school there as the Dulwich Gallery; but about a mile further on were the favorite resorts, the College Wood and Norwood.

Here, no more than five or six miles from London, Browning might have been in Wordsworth's isolated Lake Country or Coleridge's favorite Somerset. He was, though probably unknowingly, rambling through the same haunts that Byron, as a youth, had roamed not very long before when he studied at a private school in Dulwich. Huge, fine elms interspersed with smaller oaks left the ground beneath dark with occasional bright spots where the sun broke through. Now and then a rustic woods cottage with heavy stone chimneys smoking up into the branches might break the wildness of the scene;[93] or Browning might have observed the Gypsy community's encampment, long a famous sight in Norwood, now removed to Dulwich Wood.[94] In his rambles here, as he tells us in his poem "May and Death" (published 1857), he sometimes had the company of his cousin James Silverthorne, whose death in 1852 made him sadly recall the pleasures of "sweet sights and sounds" of May days spent in the woods, and "the warm Moon-births and the long evening-ends." Even as an adult Browning must often have sought out the woods for solitude and reflection. We are told that the poem, *Pippa Passes*—or at least the central situation in it— was conceived during a walk in the College Wood.[95] William Sharp (again a dubious authority) claims further that the description Browning makes the fifteen-year old Luigi speak, as he looks back on the supernal experiences of his short life, was drawn from Browning's own intense response to the apparition of a double rainbow.[96] Luigi's splendid description, combining romantic fullness of emotional coloring with a Shakespearian pomp of language, suggests in any case the strength of Browning's feeling for nature, a feeling that by the time of *Pippa Passes* he already places in character rather than presents as his own lyrical response:

> God must be glad one loves his world so much—
> I can give news of earth to all the dead
> Who ask me:—last year's sunsets and great stars
> That had a right to come first and see ebb
> The crimson wave that drifts the sun away—
> Those crescent moons with notched and burning rims

That strengthened into sharp fire and stood
Impatient of the azure—and that day
In March a double rainbow stopped the storm—
May's warm, slow, yellow moonlit summer nights—
Gone are they—but I have them in my soul!

Like Luigi—indeed like the Wordsworth of "Tintern Abbey" or *The Prelude*—Browning may have seen such experiences as already things of the past, part of the first, full and unconscious experience of self in nature. Yet what was first sensed and felt at that level has become part of his more complicated mature self, ready thus to be recreated consciously in his poetry.

Even when Browning did not go as far as the isolated Dulwich Wood, he could escape up a lane from the Camberwell parish church to Grove Hill where new buildings were only just appearing. Still attractive even today, the Grove was the showpiece of Camberwell: "Camberwell's fair grove and verdant brow, / The loveliest Surrey's swelling hills can show," an eighteenth-century enthusiast called it.[97] Its glory was the tremendous view of the London basin to the North: "the extensive peopled vale, / From ancient Lambeth's west extreme, / Beside the Thames' bending stream, / To Limehouse glittering in the evening beam."[98] Here was a setting where the individual might begin to sense, beyond his immediate pleasure in the natural scenery, some consciousness of his part in the complexity and enormity of human life spread out below him. Perhaps it was here, as has been suggested, that Browning made many of his early impossibly grand plans, such as the enormous dramatic scheme into which he claimed he intended to fit *Pauline*.[99] Perhaps it was also here that some of his more realizable ambitions had their beginnings in his sense of inner power and personal awareness.

Later, at less settled New Cross, open country really began at the end of the family garden and Browning spoke often in his letters of the wild Surrey hills, especially the present Telegraph Hill where he loved to walk. Once through the garden gate he could lock out all the world. "What say you to coming here next Wednesday?" he wrote Domett with a sophisticated enthusiasm for country life that superimposed Virgil's bucolic countryside on the outskirts of nineteenth-century London, "Our little hills are stiff and springy underfoot with the frozen grass—and you crunch the thin white ice on the holes the cattle have made—hedge & tree are glazed bright with rime —(to speak bucolically)."[100] At another time of year a friend was invited to defy city life and all its stir and trouble for meditation on settled things. "Come here, under my chestnut-tree, over the pond, by the cow house, under the garden-wall—'I hope here be truths!' ''[101] Wordsworth, to whom the country where Browning lived was once pointed out, might scoff at the pretension of such mounds—mere "rises" to his northern eyes—to the title of hills.[102] Elizabeth Barrett, living in nearby London, was more surprised that such rural things should exist so close to the city. "So you really have *hills* at New Cross, & not hills by courtesy?"[103] Even from the room in which he wrote at New Cross, Browning could hear the lambs in the open country and look out on a scene of thick natural growth and activity: "lilacs, hawthorn, plum-trees all in bud,—elders in leaf, rose-bushes with great red shoots; thrushes, white-throats, hedge sparrows in full song."[104]

In all the rural or wooded resorts of his early years, Browning's primary interest seems to have been neither in classifying or obtaining a practical understanding of nature nor in sensing in or through nature intimations of some moral or metaphysical order. His concern was rather to perceive and experience immediately the vitality he felt actually present in the natural world. For instance, he might lie down at Grove Hill, William Sharp reported, "beside a hedge, or deep in meadow grasses, or under a tree . . . and there give himself up so absolutely to the life of the moment that even the shy birds would alight close by and sometimes venturesomely poise themselves on suspicious wings for a brief space upon his recumbent body. I have heard him say that his faculty of observation at that time would not have appeared despicable to a Seminole or an Iroquois: he saw and watched everything."[105] Such talk sounds somewhat like the old Indian bragging about his powers when he was a young brave, but the general recollection of his total involvement in the immediate world around him is striking and suggests the way in which his mind would open in awareness to outside life. An even better idea of the kind of experience Browning found in his rambles is suggested by a vivid and forceful, if none too well organized passage, or rather series of passages, in *Pauline*. Browning begins by boasting of his ability actually to live through his imagination the very life of the creatures and objects he finds in nature.

> I can live all the life of plants, and gaze
> Drowsily on the bees that flit and play,
> Or bare my breast for sunbeams which will kill,
> Or open in the night of sounds, to look
> For the dim stars; I can mount with the bird
> Leaping airily his pyramid of leaves
> And twisted boughs of some tall mountain tree,
> Or rise cheerfully springing to the heavens
> Or like a fish breathe in the morning air
> In the misty sun-warm water.

Then, with the courage of this fairly bold assertion, he tells his imaginary audience, the patient Pauline, "fly with me" (if she can) and starts off on a long, disjointed description of nature: day, night, in "the very heart of the woods," on "the hill-top level with the air," then careening "Down the hill! Stop—a clump of trees," then "little smoking cots, mid fields and banks," finally ending at "Hedgerows for me." The whole is a magnificent tour de force that doesn't quite come off; but in the process Browning gives

us an almost complete tour of his boyhood haunts. Even more interesting is
the evidence this poem, written at twenty, provides of the significance for
him of such experiences. For Browning sees them explicitly as exercises of
consciousness, "ces élans de l'ame [*sic*]," as he himself puts it through the
cryptic note in French attached to the end and signed "Pauline": springings
upward or out of the soul.

The passages in *Sordello* (1840) that speak of the dubious hero's youth,
spent in the isolated beauty of nature at Goito, cannot be assumed to give us
any necessary parallel to Browning's own youthful experience in Camberwell. Yet inasmuch as they were probably written only a year or two after
Pauline, the general approach to experience in nature does amplify the more
personal and lyrical descriptions of *Pauline*.[106] Sordello's prelude, lived
alone "amid his wild-wood sights" where he is imaginative master of all he
surveys, allows him the fullest development of his poetic and fanciful powers. The process is finally important less for the love of nature that it
induces in Sordello than for its part in bringing him consciousness of his
own inner faculties. Like the class of poets Browning describes, who go beyond mere lyrical rapture in nature, Sordello—and no doubt Sordello's
author—is one of those who finds in external beauty increasing revelation
of inner power:

> Proclaims each new revealment born a twin
> With a distinctest consciousness within
> Referring still the quality, now first
> Revealed, to their own soul.

For Browning, as for romantic poets as distinct as Wordsworth and
Shelley, Coleridge and Keats, exploration out into the natural world provided a means also for exploration, or even creation, of inner awareness and
self-consciousness. The process can be understood as parallel to the complicated, almost paradoxical one analyzed by Geoffrey Hartman in his fine
study of Wordsworth and frequently described in a general way by Wordsworth himself.[107] In the early experience there is merely a going out into
nature as an external thing to be explored and understood. Over long periods of time, powers of perception and imagination are brought unconsciously into use in the process of solitary exploration. As they develop,
there is eventually a further movement away from perception of nature to
perception of self, as the explorer begins to realize that his intense experience has been as much the result of what has been going on within his mind
as of what has been going on outside in nature. In the end, external activity
becomes most important in its internal effect, the development of a consciousness which is continually aware of its own powers.

Years after *Pauline,* sickened at an exhibition of painstaking but second-rate works of art, Browning could exclaim, probably thinking of the
hedges in the lanes at New Cross: "This short minute of life our one chance,

an eternity on either side! and a man does not walk whistling and ruddy by the side of hawthorn hedges in spring, but shuts himself up and comes out after a dozen years with 'Titian's Daughter' and, there, gone is his life, let somebody else try!''[108] Experience in the natural world was for him, as for a romantic predecessor such as Wordsworth, not only a pleasure—a rosebud to pluck while ye may—but a means to life or consciousness itself and a large part of that sense of "an intensest life, / Of a most clear idea of consciousness" which Browning enunciated in *Pauline.*

"It's one thing to say pretty things about swallows, roses, autumn &c," Browning wrote thirty years after *Pauline,* commenting on Maurice de Guérin's *Remains,* "and another to look an inch into men's hearts."[109] Of Byron, he wrote, "if he were in earnest and preferred being with the sea to associating with mankind, he would do well to stay with the sea's population."[110] Such comments, and the fact that Browning, unlike Wordsworth, does not habitually draw upon experience in nature as a means to talking about man's consciousness, might seem to suggest that Browning rejected in his maturity his youthful concern with nature. In fact, he did come to take less (though only relatively less) interest in directly experiencing the natural world, and he did, like many of the Romantics themselves, and like his anguished Sordello, who left Goito to try to come to terms with the life of his time, come to value love of man over love of nature. Yet the sense of conscious vitality, which Browning discovered in part through his boyhood rambles and experiences, instead of dying out with maturity, remained a firm and fundamental element in his personality. His ability, as well, to sympathize imaginatively with living beings outside of himself and to enter into other consciousnesses, grew rather than dried up in his mature years. "What a fine fellow our English water-eft is; *'Triton paludis Linnaei,'* " Browning could still exclaim with humorous rapture in 1845, "*e come guizza* [how it darts] (*that* you can't say in another language; cannot preserve the little in-and-out motion along with the straightforwardness!)—I always loved all those wild creatures God '*sets up for themselves*' so independently of us, so successfully, with their strange happy minute inch of a candle, as it were, to light them."[111] Except for some few fine poems of landscape such as "De Gustibus," or the queerly humorous piece "Sibrandus Schafnaburgensis," in which Browning exults in the riot of eft and snail life that has overcome the dry pages of a poor pedant's book he stuck outside in a tree, Browning has few poems after *Pauline* that immediately reflect, in the first person form of romantic nature poems, his sense of the vitality of nature. However, the way in which a man or woman in his dramatic monologues sees and responds to nature is often used to characterize and define personality. The Englishman in Italy, for instance, exulting in describing the vitality and complexity of the southern Italian coast, is revealing the way in which a person may open to the challenge and excitement of new experience. Whereas David in "Saul" sings of the beauty of nature as God's banquet before man, the good of earth that foretells the greater good of heaven, Caliban, without any less vividness, sees only the predatory underworld of nature's vitality. Both, it may perhaps be said, seem to Browning preferable to the fictive, if rich filament of false apprehension which a character such as Andrea del Sarto casts over nature, sealing himself in the metaphorical vision he imposes on the world.[112]

Nature may be only fitfully, not as in Wordsworth, habitually, the subject of his poems. Still, Browning's lifelong interest in exploring the nature of consciousness itself at least in part began in his own experience with nature's ministry in calling forth in him an early and acute sense of self-awareness. After hearing a minister preach at flowery length on the beauties of nature, Browning is reported to have remarked incisively that this was all very interesting but he would have preferred to have heard not a description of nature but an account of "the impression made by nature" on him.[113] In the same way, interesting as Browning's occasional descriptions of nature are, it is nature's effect on him—its part in the development of his nature more than his ultimate views of nature—that is most significant. Even when he wrote poetry, as he often did, without any reference at all to nature or scenery, the sympathy he learned for independent beings set up for themselves and the sense of self-awareness he found in nature remained with him. They helped him to realize in imagination, and then to portray in speech, a sense of the consciousness living strongly or weakly within all men, even burning brightly in characters like the Duke in "My Last Duchess" or the Bishop of "The Bishop Orders his Tomb at St. Praxed's Church" with whom he could have little moral sympathy.

No doubt many factors besides domestic life, evangelical religion, or experience in nature contributed to Browning's awareness of an "intensest life" of consciousness within and to his belief in the reality and importance of subjective experience. Browning himself speaks in *Pauline*, for instance, of the special stimulation his consciousness received from early reading, "alone with wisest ancient books, / All halo-girt with fancies of my own." In reading such works he would come, as he did in his experiences in nature, to live a life outside his life: "I myself went with the tale." Later the experience of reading Shelley, of whom he speaks with such strong feeling in *Pauline,* not to mention hundreds of other writers, must have once again served to reinforce his sense of inner, vital self-consciousness. Perhaps many other kinds of experience could be cited as well. In the absence of any full account from Browning of the growth of his mind, this look at some aspects of his early environment that appear to have especially called forth an answering inner awareness may serve to sketch out one large aspect of his personality, a kind of center of feeling or consciousness upon which his later experience and understanding of men and society might grow.

One does not need to be a Samuel Johnson or even an Irving Babbitt to see the difficulties to which such cultivation exposed Browning. Like the

Romantics before him, and like his contemporary, Tennyson, he risked riding isolation and self-involvement into the lost land of simple narcissism, in which consciousness of self is not a means to apprehending life but an escape from it. A more practical problem would be that he would stand the risk all his life of becoming so involved in the perceptions and schemes, the opinions and arguments of his own full, inner life, that he would find it impossible to make them clearly manifest to others. Such hyper-self-consciousness is indeed both the subject and problem of his most painfully meditated and least well-received work, *Sordello*, a poem that anticipates many of the problems writers have felt themselves confronted with in our even more self-conscious, and self-preoccupied century. There was a danger too in his closeness to his mother: not the danger of repressive religious moralism that Betty Miller felt she saw. This Browning was able, far more than most Victorians, to laugh away, preserving from his mother's religion only what seemed necessary in his own view of man's condition. However, there was the danger, whatever the specific beliefs, of excessive concern and of too much earnestness even in good things. In religion it could lead to the embarrassed anxiety for certainty reflected both in the overly complex analysis of modern choice in *Christmas-Eve and Easter-Day* and in the too direct pronouncements of the later more doctrinaire poems. In morality it could lead him at times to make impossible demands on himself, as in the overly responsible, overly concerned role of father he forced upon himself after Elizabeth's death. Or it could make him, especially in his early years in London, too ready to take offense when he felt his personal honor and worth were at stake. In his work, it could make him at worst too punctilious, too labored, and overly refined, as if poetry should be produced as a moral duty. "I am greatly afraid you overwork that brain of yours—which is absurd, besides a shame," his friend Domett wrote in 1846, "for a thing of such fine material is not for drudgery, even at Poetry."[114] What Domett recommended, a little healthy "lethargy or at least *vacancy*," often proved the best stimulus to Browning's finest poetry.

With all these pitfalls it is nonetheless hard to imagine that Browning could have developed into a significant poet at all without such a vigorous early cultivation in self-awareness. The poet in his time, as in ours, found no given point of view or preshaped values that he could strive to express in a going and accepted form. Like other modern poets, Browning faced the nearly impossible problem of creating both the subject and the form of his poetry. Mere novelty or individual eccentricity could, of course, fail as certainly as attempts to continue outmoded traditions, to keep step (in Eliot's metaphor) to the beat of an antique drum. But without an ability to find within himself a center of consciousness, a world from which to start to make a new creation of poetry, he would have been absolutely lost. Unlike most of the major poets of the generation active when he was growing up, Browning would move deliberately away from the strategy of the Romantics, which placed the poet himself, as creator and universal man, as a consciousness at the center of his work. Yet throughout his career Browning's position would be that of a romantic who has developed beyond romantic self-portrayal. As he worked away from the direct self-involvement of his early work he would come to substitute the many voices and many personalities and perspectives of his characters for his own. Still, the world of his poetry remained, in a far more real sense than it would for poets working in a preexisting tradition, the world of his own consciousness. Whereas many of the Romantics moved on from their personal experience to generalize about the capacities of the human mind which they saw exercised within themselves, Browning would work from his own special self-awareness to a more general vision of a world made up of millions of independent minds and beings, each set up with his own individual consciousness and his own more or less perceptive and honest perspective on life.

Important as Browning's enthusiasm for the Romantics was—especially for Byron and Shelley—he found in them, as we shall see, not a sudden revelation of the concerns of the great English Romantics but catalysts who helped give a first form to much of his previous experience. For Browning was not only heir to the Romantics but also a poet who independently discovered in his own early life the central romantic preoccupation with self-consciousness and individuality and who then progressed in his own way back from this discovery toward a revised general vision of man. Why he developed as he did has a great deal to do with the additional and very different influences on his mind and personality.

V
Objectivity

Had the influences outlined above been the only, or even the predominating ones in the suburban society and culture in which Browning grew up, he would have developed into a very different man and poet. Perhaps, like Wordsworth, he might have used his poetic powers to portray to an age, increasingly removed from a life of simple domestic affections and involvement in nature, the enduring value of the kinds of simple, natural feeling from which they were largely cutting themselves off. Or, like George Eliot, he might have decided to leave his childhood environment and join the life of his own age, only to be haunted at times by the remembrance of what seemed a more expansive, less troubled life, in which communication and feeling flowed more freely.

Although Browning experienced much of the inner subjective cultivation that a sensitive child of his age might have found in village or country life, he had roots through his childhood experience that reached deeply into the London, the England, and even the Europe of his day. Even before he began, as a young adult, regularly to frequent London and to take part in social and literary life, Browning had opportunities around his suburban homes, through the astounding store of general information possessed by his father, through his group of friends, and through his family's business and social connections in London and abroad, to come to know a variety of men and a wide range of the forms of human society. Such knowledge and experience, experience especially of men, of society, of social life, and of the ways of the everyday world, suggest almost a different life from that isolated individual one of domestic concentration and rambles in nature. As a balance to Browning's other experience, it brought not a more intense feeling of identity and self-consciousness but a kind of basic objectivity, even the beginning of a sophisticated understanding of men and the different forms by which their lives are, or have been, ordered.

1 Quirky Types

In exploring the world of human life outside of the immediate family circle, Browning appears at first to have followed, perhaps even unconsciously, his father's lead as surely as in other areas of experience he looked to his mother's example. Chesterton, in a finely drawn mis-characterization of Browning's father, remarked, "Numerous accomplishments of the lighter kind, such as drawing and painting in water colours, he possessed; and his feeling for many kinds of literature was fastidious and exact. But the whole was absolutely redolent of the polite severity of the eighteenth century."[1] The interests of Robert Browning Sr. were to a large extent those of the eighteenth century, but it was to the more boisterous, broadly drawn eighteenth century of Hogarth or Smollett, not that of fastidious etchings and polite watercolors, that he looked for artistic models. His most serious instincts as an artist in fact linked him consciously to the classic realists, especially the Dutch genre painters of the Haarlem school—Brouwer, Ostade, Jan Steen, and the similar, if lesser Teniers the younger and Gerard Dou. "Brouwer, Ostade, Teniers," Browning noted with a touch of exasperation, "he would turn from the Sistine altar-piece to these."[2] While living a life as spotless as Brouwer's was checkered, he followed the master in his attempt to catch the life of street and tavern directly and vigorously. The Corkran sisters, who knew the elder Browning in old age in Paris, recalled how he would go out with sketch book and pencil on the lookout for any detail of life that he could strike off in his rapid sketches. He particularly loved to paint "groups of working men that used to assemble & drink their glass of wine outside the *barrière* of the Arc de Triomphe or of one of the Customs leading into Paris."[3] Art was for him, as in a somewhat similar way it would be for his son's Italian realist, Fra Lippo Lippi, a means for catching the living substance of others' lives. The drawings of this sort, a few of which have survived,[4] are obviously hurried, but deft and sympathetic. They suggest a clear focus, if from a somewhat shy outsider's perspective, on the realities of man's everyday life, a focus in both manner and subject similar to that which his masters had originally helped bring into European art.

In his most serious art Browning's father thus accepted a simple realism as aim. However, most of his sketches, the quick impromptu ones he did in pen or pen and wash to amuse his family or friends, suggest a more stylized and more immediate tradition, that of English caricature. Most often it was his favorite Hogarth,[5] and, more broadly, the whole tradition of English caricature running from Hogarth to Rowlandson, with its exaggerated, microscopic realism and its common sense, comic, social emphasis, which his art emulated. And it was this tradition which largely determined his manner of observing and commenting on the human scene around him in Camberwell, New Cross, or London. The effect of the father's caricature or cartoon method (for he used both) is to focus attention almost exclusively upon the variety of human personalities and character-types, especially upon the quirky kinds of low characters or eccentric gentlemen who have long been almost proverbially a part of the London scene. Life, as he found it in walks around London or as it came to him for business at the Bank,[6] was a grand quarry to be endlessly worked; and the rough material taken out was as incessantly hewn into simple, immediately apprehensible cartoon forms. One cartoon indeed suggests in fun that this was his habitual way of looking at other people. Entitled "The Unprotected Female," it shows a charmless, haggard crone, who can have had little to fear from all but the most hardened assailant, turning on a man who has been following her. "Pray, fellow! what do you mean by following me in this manner? I wish, sir, if you have nothing to say to me, you would just take another direction." To which the man, perhaps the artist himself: "Madam, I humbly beg your pardon, but the fact is I'm a caricaturist by profession, and your face is a treasure to me."[7]

Typically this professional caricaturist and amateur banker worked by building up a character-type in a few broad strokes, then adding an appropriate caption below. At one sitting, drawings might center on one subject and an imagined situation or they might tell some kind of tale. As, in a usual series, one after another character-type has his say, whether the theme is a comment on a play, a dialogue on the search for a lost diamond, or a discussion of a strange fellow who had put up at the Green Lion Inn, the viewer begins to feel, as Keats perceived he felt in a room full of people, a variety of identities pressing in upon him. One series, for example, concerns a collection of sharpsters who are pictured plotting at an inn to relieve a certain poor bumpkin, one Harry Clodpole, of his hard-earned funds at cards.[8] They play him on at first by letting him win. Then while Harry is out for a minute they reveal their intentions in one after another vignette of cunning, maliciousness, or rank hypocrisy. To their surprise, Harry Clodpole never comes back and it is finally reported that these unpleasant gentlemen have fallen for one of the world's oldest confidence games at the hands of a master, who has skipped out with his early winnings: hardly a surprising or very original ending. But it is not the story but the understanding of human nature and the human scene that makes the sketches interesting. Many of the series, of which quite a few are still preserved, focus, like this one, on grotesque, unpleasant forms of human nature. However, if the vision is satiric, showing up with abnormal clarity and emphasis men's common and ordinary limitations, it is far from misanthropic. Indeed, the small, puppet-show world into which the sketches bring us so vividly is essentially a comic one. In another series, for instance, we are informed that Mr. Scott is about to tell a ghost story.[9] Then, for a seemingly endless number of frames, person after person, pronounced personality after pronounced personality, has

Left: Genre Scene. Drawing by Robert Browning Sr. *An example of serious work in a Dutch-English realist tradition.*

Above: Locke's Philosophy (Bad Pun), ca. 1835-1840. Cartoon by Robert Browning (the poet). *"I was a young wonder (as are eleven out of the dozen of us) at drawing."*

Above: Suspicion—With a Consciousness of Guilt. Character study by Robert Browning Sr. *"Each face obedient to its passion's law, / Each passion clear proclaimed without a tongue." ("Pictor Ignotus")*

Far left, below: Doctor Humbug, the Great Phrenologist. Cartoon by Robert Browning Sr. *"& the first who applied that science to pecuniary purposes."*

Near left: The Little Master Brought Home (Baby Reform to Papa Bull), 1832. Political cartoon by Robert Browning Sr. *Comment on the passage of the Reform Bill: "There Master Bull—there, your own little Darling Master Reform—as like his Papa as 2 peas—See the little dear, he's pulling you by the Ear already—well, Mrs. has had a bad time of it—but I hope Your Honour won't forget the Nurse!"*

The Camberwell Fair and Richardson the Showman of the Fair.

Top: View at Camberwell Fair Showing Richardson's Theater, ca. 1820. Engraving from the time. *"Disgusting and demoralising scenes"; "concentrated essence of vice, folly and buffoonery."*

Above left: Tom Smith as Macbeth—Scene from Richardson's Theater. Cartoon by Robert Browning Sr. *"Tom)—Is this a Bayonet that I see before me? Richardson)—a Dagger—you fool you—a Dagger—."*

Above right: The Showman Richardson on Kean. Cartoon by Robert Browning Sr. *"Filch, Sir—Why Kean offered his Services in that character—But No No—I confin'd him to Richard—& made a Man of him—."*

his or her say on the matter. By the time, in the final frame, we are informed that it is too late for Scott's long awaited tale, we have had a kaleidoscopic whirl of possible opinions and attitudes. Alone, each may have its force and may throw us toward its linear perspective on the subject and toward the bias of the speaker's personality. Together, they force us to acknowledge the comedy of human self-seriousness as a universal absurdity in which all play their part. They ask us to hold up particular opinons and theories for evaluation against the permanent and more fundamental realities of man's nature and of his social existence.

Although his medium was visual, his intention was, no less than that of Alexander Pope in his poetry, to understand the hidden springs of human nature in portraying it. Caricature allowed him to focus on the details of expression through exaggeration and this in turn made it possible for him to type character or states of feeling with precision. He would even perform exercises in the anatomy of expression. One sketch, for example, is titled, with minute refinement, "Suspicion—with a consciousness of guilt," and actually manages to give quite a convincing visual register of such a complicated psychological state.[10] From another, a sheet of exercises, it is clear that he was consciously using his art to develop a method for evaluating character. Working from an ostensibly scientific text of physiognomy, he has drawn two heads side by side to analyze the difference between "Intellect, Strength & Courage" in one and "Weakness & Timidity" in the other.[11] His annotations point out how minute differences in details, a knit, concentrated eyebrow against an uncontrolled wide-open arch, tell us that one person is "prompt" and "predacious," the other, timid. "Each face," as his son will have his "Pictor Ignotus" (1845) define such an art, "obedient to its passion's law, / Each passion clear proclaimed without a tongue." A book that Browning's father gave to him in 1837, a nineteenth-century edition of Theophrastus' *Characters*[12] with modern caricature engravings much like his own to illustrate the different character types defined by the Greek philosopher, suggests that the father may even have thought of his art as the visual part of a science of mankind. Markings in the book, probably by both father and son, follow the remarks in the notes and the preface of the nineteenth-century translator, Francis Howell, as he attempts to refine the general Theophrastian character-types by linking them to specific physical classifications. The aim, to create "a comprehensive and scientific Natural History of Man,"[13] may seem a will-o'-the-wisp, though one that has distinguished company in the Renaissance conception of the humors, or in the modern Freudian classifications (not to mention those of astrology). But whether the elder Browning's studies were really serious efforts toward a science of character, or, as seems more likely, merely another serious hobby, the focus of his attention was clearly on his fellow man and on man in society.

A similar focus is apparent in another professional hobby of the elder Browning. "He would be constantly telling to me and to my younger sister

Mary, who was his favorite, and whom he always called 'little Pigtails,' thrilling tales of lawless actions . . . I remember the dramatic way in which he would relate the lurid history of the Mannings. How the unfortunate victim had been lured, how his grave had been dug in the kitchen, and how he had been felled by a blow from behind.''[14] This recollection of one of the Corkran girls makes it sound as if Browning's father, like many readers of thrillers in his time and since, gratified a good deal of the bolder instincts that were repressed into a quiet life of commuting, clerking, and family, by his passionate interest in murders. Very likely he did. But this quiet, unassuming, gentle person by day spent his nights not as Mr. Hyde or Jack the Ripper but in equally quiet armchair inquisitions over corpses and murder cases long cold. Perhaps he once indulged his curiosity to the extent of coming in late for work on the morning of the Mannings' execution. (It is said that he was late only this once in his life because of the enormous crowd, but I think we may without unfairness claim to know better. The place of execution was not in his normal path.)[15] Normally his curiosity was more psychological than pathological: he had "a detective's interest in crimes and criminals" and pondered endlessly not over the gory details themselves but over the complex motivations of the principals, making detailed charts to back up his assertions and taking an interest in the principles of circumstantial evidence.[16] As with his successors, Conan Doyle or his more deeply psychological son in *The Ring and the Book* or *Red Cotton Night-Cap Country,* he may even strike some people as too motivated by curiosity and not enough bothered by the brutality of the facts upon which he exercised it. His aim was to go beneath the general facts and find the particulars of motivation that could explain conduct. Much as in his pen and ink caricatures he looked for visual clues to enable him to strike off men's exteriors, in probing their mental contours he tried to grasp at the principal springs that made them move and tick. In both cases his clarity may seem finally to grow from too much detachment, even from too secure an idea of the various types of men who exist in society and from too certain opinions as to the conduct to be expected from each.

The son himself was similarly capable of taking too much pride in his self-assumed role as psychologizer of everyone and his self-appointed function as subtle prober of every mental state. He could fall, as he did in his attack on Alfred Austin in *Pacchiarotto,* into poetic caricature as boldly outlined and grossly drawn as anything his more even-tempered father ever turned out in his drawings. That Browning was indeed early influenced by the kind of curious focus on man and society which his father embodied is strongly suggested by a group of drawings labeled by Browning's father "Sketches by R. Browning, author of Paracelsus, etc., when a child,"[17] and described as "spirited and rather grotesque, being obviously much influenced by his father's caricatures." The subjects of these youthful efforts by Browning—"I was a young wonder (as are eleven out of the dozen of us) at drawing"[18]—are much like those of his father and in themselves constitute a little caricature cross-section of society: a quack, a man on horseback who has lost his wig, a man attacked by a bird, two men playing violins, men singing, a clergyman reading prayers.[19] At school, a fellow student recalled, "he was fond of making pen and ink caricatures which he did very cleverly."[20] Even in the 1830s, when he had clearly chosen between writing and art, Browning would amuse himself as he sat staring at his desk by turning off rapid caricature puns essentially in his father's style only with greater emphasis upon word play.[21]

The father delighted in children and offered them, in an easygoing form of peripatetic instruction, a ceaseless flow of information and observation as he proceeded on his walks.[22] There were not only learned readings from Dryden on excursions up Nun's Head but also casual trips to local sights and amusements, during which Browning picked up unconsciously his father's habits of analysis and quick eye for significant detail. For instance, father and son went together to Cross's zoo, first at Exeter Change in London and then after 1831 nearer home at the Surrey Zoological Gardens. The boy was naturally first impressed by the animals—a lion that he would recall for a splendid description in "The Glove" and a dying elephant that he would remember vividly all his life.[23] His father called his attention to what was less obvious but really more interesting: the human menagerie watched watching the animals. One of a series of cartoons on the zoological gardens shows a motherly creature warmly cooing over one of the cuter specimens: "Oh, the sweet pretty little creature—well I never saw a Rhinoceros before."[24] The poet, who would eventually turn from nature to man, had an obvious, literal precedent here, and from innumerable walks and expeditions, the influence of the father in shaping the direction of his son's observation must have been very considerable.

Browning thus first learned to look at mankind through the eyes of his father. But in the Camberwell of his youth he also had abundant opportunity to meet on his own a broad variety of human character and personality. With the slow growth of a suburban, largely middle-class society in Camberwell or New Cross, there was no doubt some tendency toward a more homogeneous social life, with less place for the variety of odd types that resulted from special trades or ways of life. Middle-class standards of morality and proper conduct probably tended as well to discourage ebullient or aberrant behavior. Tradition has it that:

All the maides in Camberwell
May daunce on an Egge-shell
For ther are none maydes in that well.[25]

However, this picture of lusty village life hardly squares with what we know of Sarah Anna and Sarianna Browning—and these ladies were probably not uniquely chaste.

Still there were occasions when Browning could see more of unaccommodated man than the normal decorum of suburban society might permit. For one thing, there was "that fearful nuisance . . . this abomination," that farrago of "disgusting and demoralising scenes," the Camberwell Fair.[26] Complaints were frequently registered about the "concentrated essence of vice, folly and buffoonery" that tended "to contaminate the youth of the district and annoy the more staid and respectable residents."[27] Nonetheless, the age-old Camberwell Fair continued to take place yearly on the Green, August 18-21, until 1855. In truth, a print of the Fair hardly shows such a vision of sin as such complaints might suggest.[28] There are trim booths set up in a circle with a flag raised above much as it was in the Elizabethan theatres. Down below, a rather staid, respectable crowd with ladies in bonnets or carrying parasols mill about looking at the various exhibits. Evidently things were different at night; and it is true that the main feature was a huge Anchor Tavern. In any case, the Fair with its strange show people and its appeal to all classes provided young Browning with a rich opportunity to get to know his fellow men.

Better yet, at the Fairs Browning still had a chance to see the well-famed, if none too artful, theatrical performances of John Richardson's itinerant troupe. Among the assortment of actors and roles in a selection of plays that ran from Shakespeare to *The Warlock of the Glen,* Richardson himself was perhaps the most interesting character. A man who had begun life as a menial worker, built up a famous and successful traveling company, given a start to actors as important as Edmund Kean and Saville Faucit, and died worth twenty thousand pounds, Richardson himself insisted upon wearing a seedy black coat, red waistcoat, corduroy breeches, and worsted stockings, and made his only home in a caravan.[29] Browning's father evidently took a great interest in Richardson for he or a reference to him appears in a number of his cartoons.[30] His pleasure in Richardson's odd gusto is suggested by one series showing a certain Tom Smith as Macbeth: "Tom)—Is this a Bayonet that I see before me? Richardson)—a Dagger—you fool you—a Dagger—." Browning too seems to have been fascinated by this living remnant of an earlier, more virile and fustian age of the drama and recalled in later years how "when, at the Fair in my young days, Richardson the show man, at any crisis of his tragedy found the action halt, he set the blue fire burning, and ended the scene with éclat."[31]

When the Fair was finally done in by concerned citizens in the 1850s, John Ruskin proclaimed not progress but the deadly triumph of "our precious gentilities here at Camberwell" and saw the next step in this "Camberwellishness" would be to " 'obviate the necessity' of Punch" and translate all children's books into the mode of modern insipidity.[32] Browning himself (as indeed Ruskin too) would take his social place normally not among the disreputable fair people but among the staid householders, and in his poems after Elizabeth's death he would even use the idea of the householder—the responsible, self-disciplined Victorian citizen—as a metaphor for himself and for the self generally. Still, to him the responsibility of the householder included the knowledge of life and its various good and bad possibilities, not a feeble isolation from all vitality for fear of the bad that might be mixed with it. The theme is one that he takes up seriously, if none too lucidly, in *Fifine at the Fair* (1872) in which Don Juan, a self-styled householder, argues with his wife for the necessity of swimming in the mixed sea of life as the moral condition of human existence. The setting is another village fair, that of Saint Gille in Pornic, France rather than St. Giles, Camberwell. It is not difficult to imagine, however, that both setting and subject may have first impressed themselves on him in the excitement of the annual fair. At the end of *Fifine* Don Juan apparently sinks in his own metaphorical sea as he succumbs to the one-shilling attractions of the performer Fifine. Despite his protagonist's casuistical hypocrisy, Browning does not discredit his message: the moral necessity of engaging in the complexities of life. Indeed, as often in his career, merely in writing such a poem he was challenging a prudish public to look with open eyes upon the realities of their lives. Having learned about mankind through pre-Victorian institutions like the Fair without becoming himself one of the youths permanently "contaminated" by such knowledge, he would be all his life unwilling to restrict the subjects of his poetry—really his interest in the complexity of human life—to the standards of later prudish Camberwellishness.

Other traditional manifestations during the year in Camberwell may equally have provided Browning with special opportunities to take in the types and humors of different people and ways of life. The geologist, Joseph Prestwich, remembered Guy Fawkes Day, "religiously kept by us boys," as second only to the Camberwell Fair for excitement. Sticks were gathered at Norwood and the poor scapegoat guy was roasted on a huge bonfire, "to the accompaniment of many squibs and crackers."[33] Browning must often have mixed in the crowd around the great bonfire and listened to the variety of talk and chatter. "I heard a woman," he recalled, "singing at a bon-fire Guy Faux night when I was a boy—Following the Queen of the Gypsies, O!"[34] This "one intelligible line" from an overheard folk song left so lasting an impression that Browning later built upon it his entire tale of "The Flight of the Duchess" (1845), the romantic story of a lady who leaves the Duke her husband to join the Gypsies. Browning might not choose to run off with the Gypsies himself (only with Elizabeth), but his early contact with the open ways of folk social life allowed him to criticize what was narrow and life-denying in some kinds of householdry, whether that of some of his too Camberwellish neighbors, that of the burghers of Hamelin, or even that of the Duchess's Duke, or the Duke of Ferrara.

A less pleasant picture of human nature, of course, could be seen on other holidays. Election day in Browning's boyhood still followed the seedy, gin-drenched, traditions of the eighteenth century and, if we can even half believe the satirical picture presented in a cartoon of the time, "Citizen T——rn——y drawn by the Populace through the Borough to the Grove house [a large country tavern] at Camberwell,"[35] Browning would have had ample chance to study a grotesque and corporate display of grosser human passions and expressions. From his father's cartoons it is clear that he, certainly, and probably his son with him, took a ready interest in political events and opinions. Browning's father was a political cartoonist with a difference. His frequent cartoons on political subjects were perceptions rather than persuasions. His focus was not on presenting an opinion but on understanding man as a political animal. He delighted in politics as a field in which he could play with different views and set opinions and motives against each other for comparison. His quick eye and pen caught and objectified the ridiculous if very ordinary situations of those in the tangle of politics. In one sketch a dumb, happy fellow reveals only too clearly his interest: "Cheap Bread! Cheap Beer! & Squire Loggenton for ever!" In another, entitled "My first address," a skinny nobody undergoes the perplexity and self-alienation of suddenly being a somebody—but no longer himself. Placards proclaim "Scroggins and Independ'ce" "Scroggins for ever,"[36] while in the interests of politics poor bewildered Scroggins prepares to give himself wholly to such dubious immortality. Again and again he would be suggesting to his son that he should look behind opinions to the character and situation of the individual who holds them—a lesson graphically made in a cartoon, "Difference of Opinion," where a worker comments on political philosophy: "Our foreman says we must have a King—now I prefer a republic."[37]

Although Browning had little firsthand experience of the lives of the abject poor in London's slums, he still had everyday opportunities, outside of holidays and political occasions, to become acquainted with the workaday humanity of ordinary laborers. There was even a tough section of town, Bowyer Lane, commemorated in a cartoon by the father in which a barefooted and menacing local champion warns, "Take care what you say against Bowyer Lane."[38] His pen likewise picked up workmen—Irish bricklayers waiting to be hired—lounging and talking around St. George's church.[39] Like him, his son soon acquired the knack for catching the illuminating detail in such ordinary scenes. Looking for an analogy to Elizabeth Barrett's claim that love is fortified by the marriage bond, Browning seized upon an amusing conversation he once heard in the street: "a labourer talking with his friends about '*wishes*'—and this one wished, if he might get his wish, 'to have a nine gallon cask of strong ale set running that minute and his own mouth be *tied* under it'—the exquisiteness of the delight was to be in the security upon security,—the being 'tied.' ''[40] Elizabeth may have found the parallel something less than flattering, but the story itself suggests how even a very ordinary conversation, overheard in passing, could become a means of insight into human character and psychology.

Despite their shared interests and perceptions, at his best Browning, unlike his father, did not create a directly caricatural art out of his insight into the quirky traits of ordinary characters. In 1843, after reading *Martin Chuzzlewit,* Browning in fact strongly criticized Dickens for doing just that:

"Uproarious and (I think) disgusting, in his Pecksniffs and (what Strafford said of the Parliament) 'that generation of odd names and natures.' "[41] The criticism is unfair. Dickens is far more than a caricaturist and purveyor of human oddities, and Browning himself constantly turned to odd names and natures as subjects for his poems. However, except in a few ill-tempered attacks on his critics, he did not use true caricature in his poetry. Nor were his subjects, like his father's, from everyday life, as he first came to know it at Camberwell. Yet there is an obvious broad parallel between the father's caricature art, with its countless studies of individual men and women, and the son's mature development of the dramatic monologue.[42] Certainly the same interest as the father's in the quirky traits that make up character is apparent in countless poems by the son. Everywhere in the son's poems there is also a similar concern with uncovering and exposing the true workings of human psychology and institutions. Perhaps it is more than just a curiosity that Browning's father tried his own hand, both in drawings and poetry, at a number of the subjects on which his son wrote. There is, for instance, a cartoon series of "Sludge, the Medium" as well as an independent, and rather clever poetic version of the Pied Piper story called "Hamelin" by Browning Sr.[43] A few of his son's poems, the more direct dramatic ones of the 1840s, stimulated him to do illustrations—some so fine that Elizabeth even suggested Browning publish them with his poems.[44] Where they attempt the same subject, Browning's treatment is far more complicated and technically far more complex. Similarly, the father is much better at illustrating the grotesque and comic descriptions in poems like "The Pied Piper" or "The Flight of the Duchess," where his illustrations of the Piper or the old crone are superb, than he is at more subtle effects such as those in "Soliloquy of the Spanish Cloister." Evidently he was not much interested in even trying drawings for the more serious poems. However, the pleasure both father and son took in poking their walking sticks into the trickery of the Yankee Medium, Sludge, or the queer old legend of the Pied Piper serves as another indication of Browning's large debt to his father for helping him open his eyes upon the human scene.

2 *An Encyclopedic Outlook*

The life he met on the streets or at public gatherings at Camberwell might have given Browning his first glimpses into the variety of human character and activities. Within his house a much broader, if not always as vivid or immediate scene of human life was opening up. The Browning home was crammed with books. In fact, in their smaller Camberwell houses Browning's tolerant mother must sometimes have wondered whether she and her children would at last be driven by them into the street. As obviously, books dominated the mental space of the home. Browning Sr. was the collector and scholar of the house, but all members of the family were great readers and discussion of books and reading was a large part of family life.

There was a great deal to discuss: books for every interest and books on virtually every subject. There were books on music, books discoursing on art, rare books (such as the 1568 Bible—"Not in the Duke of Sussex collection," Browning's father proudly told him),[45] books on magic and necromancy, books in Latin, Greek, French, Spanish, Italian, Hebrew, books on Roman history, on the Junius controversy, the works of Plato, of Voltaire, a book purporting to be the *Original Letters of Sir John Falstaff and His Friends,*[46] six thousand books and more, we are told, and growing every day as the elder Browning's curiosity went poking into some unexplored corner of learning and came home with a small, proud addition. Limited funds and his own interests as a reader made Mr. Browning's collection more a book reader's than a book buyer's, with emphasis on interesting titles and wide distribution rather than on fancy bindings and costly editions. Standard works, classical or English literature, or reference volumes like the *Biographie Universelle* or Johnson's *Dictionary* were balanced by a wide selection, lovingly chosen, of curious volumes and out-of-the-way learning. Shakespeare, Horace, Epictetus, Corneille, Plutarch, Suetonius, and Bolingbroke stood cheek to jowl with Agrippa's *De Scientiis*, the Latin letters of the famed fifteenth-century Cardinal Bembo, Plaisted's *Journal from Calcutta in Bengal, by Sea, to Busserah, The Cabinet Dictionary* (of upholsterer's and cabinetmaker's terms) or *An Epitome of Logic* by an unknown J. Collard writing under the anonym N. Dralloc.[47]

Even more prodigious than the range of the library was that of the librarian, who indeed expressed surprise that Archbishop Whately had never heard of Collard's work and perhaps expected every man of education to share his passions in his conquests as a bookman.[48] A quiet humble scholar, he was also persistent and unflagging in his pursuit of books and knowledge. When Browning visited the Grand Chartreuse years after his father's death, he remarked on seeing the "handsome library" that his father would have been entirely content with the life there "(all but the lathe-turning)."[49] Mr. Browning's scholarly habits were very much those of a contented studious monk, working lovingly and patiently over volume after volume with the quiet intensity of a true scholiast. Year after year, work after work passed through the deliberate hands of this self-contented scholar until his son, trying to put some order into the "dead weight" of "old tomes" that he inherited, could only cry out in despair, "Oh that *hellou librorum* [devourer of books] my father, best of men, most indefatigable of book-digesters!"[50]

With this process of digestion ceaselessly adding fiber and substance to his very considerable knowledge, he was able, in the words of Browning's Uncle Reuben, to serve as a "wonderful store of information" to his son. He was a competent classicist who had learned, we are told, the first book of the *Iliad* and all the odes of Horace by heart at school.[51] His special interest in the classics, apart from his favorite Homer, was in the Augustan Age and throughout most of his life he compiled notes for "a sort of biographical novel," of which a one hundred and four page "Memoirs of the Roman Poet Horace" was probably only a part, on the literary figures contemporary with Virgil and Horace.[52] He read, as well as Hebrew, Greek, and Latin, French, Spanish, and Italian. Even in old age he could respond to an inquiry by his son concerning church history with "a regular book of researches, and a narrative of his own, exhausting the subject."[53] Reuben also credited him with knowledge of "all political combinations of parties." One of his pet subjects was the complicated skein of intrigue wound about the knotty Junius question,[54] and another, his grandson recalled, was the French Revolution: "He knew every detail which could be known."[55] In truth, there were few realms of learning or philology into which this "extraordinarily learned and able man"[56] had not made at least an exploratory foray that he could report to his son.

From time to time this famous reader would work at one specific problem or another until he might seem a professional scholar preparing a piece of detailed research. One favorite interest, for instance, was the science or comparative history of military fortifications, for which he drew up careful illustrative drawings showing means of defense and attack.[57] Another was an "Index to the Persons Mentioned in the Works of Horace," a work of immense painstaking.[58] He had a leaning toward catalogues and compendia of information, especially toward the kind of historical summaries provided by genealogies, which he would often sketch out along with reading notes. His greatest interest in genealogy led to sustained work on a complete genealogy of the Old Testament, which he called the "Nomenclator." Done in careful fine lettering (on the back of an old account book brought home from the Bank) with a system of circles and diamonds to indicate male or female lineages, the work extends some ninety four closely written pages in the smallest, Baylor manuscript.[59] The scholarship—and other versions are almost four hundred pages—is a monument to industry and little else. It is the kind of thing one can imagine George Eliot's Mr. Casaubon taking up had he ever completed his key to mythologies. Quaint even in its time, it now seems a rather ludicrous enterprise, neither a contribution to religion nor to historical scholarship but a work of pure philology untainted by an idea. Mr. Browning took it seriously enough to offer it to publishers, and his son and daughter-in-law kindly, if unavailingly, did what they could to puff it into print.

Such special projects again make us think of the cloistered monk. However, his predominant scholarly passions were even closer to the universal ones of the eighteenth-century encyclopedists. All together, his surviving books and notes give the impression that he was less interested in particular problems, even specific historical periods, than in a general mastery of all history and all events. On whatever book he fell, he bound in extra pages at the back and added careful comments and meticulous marginalia to give a profile of the author and work, to correct errors, or to list cross references to other works on the subject.[60] From scraps which remain from this banquet of learning, we may infer that he was endlessly recording and codifying the information he had gleaned, perhaps in preparation for some ever receding grand synthesis. There is a notebook dating from 1810 on the subject of Cesare Borgia and Italian history.[61] More than fifty years later the compilation was still going on, and a surviving workbook ranges from notes on Denholm's *History of Glasgow*—for information on the clergy in the thirteenth century—to Ranke on the *Popes of Rome*.[62] Thus busy everywhere in his reading, he seems to have been working toward some ultimate and unimaginable goal, an encyclopedic grasp of all knowledge, the sum of all the books he could find.

However naive his lifelong enterprise may now seem, this book and knowledge devouring man most obviously communicated to his son a sense of how real this immaterial world of learning was to him. In effect, he connected the immediate world that Browning saw around him at Camberwell with an endless world of fact reaching out in time and place. With something of the obliviousness of an eighteenth-century world historiographer to the uniqueness of different periods and cultures, he made events of the past and places far away a part of the world before him. If anything, his library, his constant purchases, the endless reading and discussions, this life was more real to him than the quiet suburban actuality. His half-brother Reuben noted that he seemed to know by heart the contents of all the bookstores in London. Certainly in his own library he was master supreme of all he surveyed: "Not infrequently, when a conversation at his table had reference to any particular subject, has he quietly left the room and in the dark, from a thousand volumes in his library, brought two or three illustrations of the point under discussion."[63] Even in the dark—for he knew this world of books as familiarly as the real world he studied around him in Camberwell or London.

From him Browning came to think of learning and scholarship as a normal part of his daily life and to consider the other worlds of time and place that books kept alive as a natural, even inevitable part of his conscious existence. Better than any child's encyclopedia or book of knowledge, the father was an unflagging and very human and agreeable fountain of general information. Any child near him was brought suddenly into the thick of an endless discussion of all ages led by a man who was always ready to translate it into terms accessible to a child. The man who courted an ordinary widow after his wife's death by learned discussions of Strauss on the Christian religion would take up the most erudite subjects with a child with no sense of incongruity and would find ways, by delighting, to bring them home.[64] This "wonderful child's friend," as his son would later call him, could soothe the most savage fact-bristling subject—even anatomy—into pleasant comic rhymes and games.[65] He loved to have an audience with whom to share bits of learning. Alice Corkran recalled long rambles in Paris while he turned every statue and street name back into an historical reality, ending up as surely lost in the Paris of the present as he was securely at home in its history.[66] Or the past might come even more vividly alive as he drew out scenes of history or geography or turned dull genealogical roots into living trees of history, "wonders of complicated boughs, each bearing little tablets with portraits of the persons described."[67]

Of course, such a natural teacher succeeded in delighting by making history into something closer to storybook tales. It would be wrong to suppose that the awareness of the past that he gave his son was either very accurate or insightful. But he did open up a world; and stimulated by his father's enthusiasm, Browning evidently continued to explore the reaches of history and historical anecdote in his own early reading. This, at least, is the impression that remains from the very little we know of Browning's childhood reading. As with most children, romance and fiction naturally commanded his first allegiance. But the interests generated by his father as naturally led him into works in which story and history mingled pleasure and objective knowledge. In fact, the poet who would devote much of his best ability to turning historical fact into literature began his own reading in history by just the reverse process: gleaning his knowledge of the world as it was from reports in historical works that were little better than fables.

Such a work was the *Wonders of the Little World* (1678) by the curious English divine, Nathaniel Wanley. A large, strange book, written not in Latin but in seventeenth-century English and filled with a huge variety of anecdotes and sensational facts gathered from dusty corners of scholarship, it would naturally attract a curious young reader. To judge by his frequent inspiration from it and his familiar later references to the work, it seems likely, as Griffin and Minchin have argued, that this was early favorite reading.[68] Wanley professed to be answering Bacon's call in the *Advancement of Learning* for a kind of encyclopedia of man, showing, "out of the faithful reports of History," the heights to which individual men have attained in all fields.[69] In fact, he went not to man's nature but to bookish knowledge—primarily classical authors—used indiscriminately and entirely uncritically, so that fact and fable lie together as in a medieval history. His focus also slipped from stress on man's high achievements to more than equal concentration on the depths or freakish extremities of his nature. The result is a hodgepodge of historical anecdote and gossip, sometimes extraordinary, sometimes downright marvelous, now and then prurient or disgusting. Prodigies of love, of vice, of envy, of pygmy or giant size, if also of excellence and virtue, fill the pages and gratify basic, if none too refined, curiosities in all readers. More serious sections attempt, without any coherent historical frame, to survey various classes of men, painters, church fathers, emperors, or to make a naive analysis of different practices and conventions in different cultures.

In such a childish and good-natured compendium of fact and fiction Browning could view only isolated frames of history, not any continuous picture of the working of history or any clear definition of life and mores in other times. Like the more scholarly but rather similarly organized enterprise of his father, a work like Wanley's would, however, have the effect of showing the young Browning the vastness and richness of the world open to the scholar and reader. Romans, Greeks, Italians of the sixteenth century, ancients, moderns, Chinese, Persians, or Russians, all were mere grist for the compiler's explorative, if uncritical mind. Here was a panorama of humanity in all ages and inklings of possible ways of life beyond anything he could know directly in his age. In Wanley and in similar works of historical anecdote there was, as with his father, at least the same uncompromising focus on man as the greatest wonder of the world and on his infinite variety and essential unity. Again as with his father, the naiveté was in many ways an advantage. The very childishness of Wanley's work made it appeal when more serious works would have only bored. His method of popularizing history by reducing it to sensational details, not too different from the father's habitual use of caricature, made his work a storehouse of vivid incident and fable that would continue to feed Browning's imagination throughout his life, most fruitfully when an old story in Wanley suggested the idea of "The Pied Piper." Here was a model, if a simple and naive one, for bringing alive in literature the past by focusing on the particular experience of one individual. However, from this kind of reading it would be a long and slow process before he could develop a clear sense of the difference between mere tale spinning and fact, and an even longer way to what his father himself essentially lacked, a conception of the different patterns of culture and ideas that distinguish life in one time or place from life in another.

We can only guess the many other byways into which his early reading in his father's library took him. Sometime after his Latin was good enough, he took an interest in a similarly curious and otherwise second-rate miscellany, which his father gave to him as a present,[70] Otto Melander's *Jocoseria* (1597). A better work was the English Jeremy Collier's *Great Historical, Geographical, Genealogical and Poetical Dictionary* (1701), which Browning claimed to have read right through as a "boy," though boy should probably be interpreted as closer to sixteen than six.[71] This enormous and quite comprehensive work, though quite out of date by the nineteenth century, was certainly an adult and serious compendium of information. Collier had freely edited and added to a translation of the French Louis Moreri's *Grand Dictionnaire historique,* a massive compilation remembered as the predecessor of modern encyclopedias. If it was, like Wanley's, primarily an omnium-gatherum of information culled from none too trustworthy "best authors," Moreri and Collier's work was quite unlike Wanley's in criticizing and evaluating all that was presented and in beginning to organize the huge mass of information into classes and categories. It offered not merely a confused heap of the wonders of the world but knowledge in an organized form: brief articles on significant persons and major countries and places; thumbnail evaluations of major thinkers, artists, and their work; even serious attempts at comparative description of religious sects or cultural practices. In the massive work (two hefty volumes and a *Supple-*

ment nearly as large), which Collier boasted was "rather a Library than a Book," Browning had virtually a guide to what he might find in his father's library. From the tantalizing articles on subjects like Paracelsus or the Druses, Browning may have even caught the first spark that led him on to further reading and finally to his own mature imaginative use of historical detail.[72] With a command of French in his teens, he could begin also to browse in a more up-to-date survey of human experience, the *Biographie Universelle* (1822), which we know he consulted in his work in the 1830s.

When Browning later spoke of his father's library it was as a place where really anything might turn up: for instance, the first English religious novel, which he sent to a friend as "a curiosity and a very unpleasant one," and compared to a strange, thorny fish hung up at a fishmongers among the ordinary varieties: "Not that such a prodigy is to be eaten by any means, but to show *what* the 'vast sea's entral' can produce on occasion."[73] Here he might fish to contentment and come up with a surprise, a fine catch or a mere old shoe of learning; but at least he was picking up the scholar's sense of the vastness of life and experience packed away amid the dust and old print. We may be sure that many other, unrecorded, works of description or history among his father's thousands of odd volumes caught young Browning's interest intensely, just as one day a queer, old volume at Florence would supremely captivate him. That later discovery was one made by the prepared mind, a mind which could seize from the dusty text a living scene as real as the world before him because understood in equal complexity and depth. Although no such revelations followed his childhood enthusiasms, he was at least developing a superficial sense of a greater world beyond that of his local time and place, and this sense of the expanse of knowledge, when once acquired, was not likely to be lost in later life.

In his amateur encyclopedic aims and in the direction he gave to his son's early interest and reading, Browning's father reveals rather dramatically the limitations of more serious thinkers, from Diderot to Jeromy Bentham or Dickens's Thomas Gradgrind, who confused great knowledge with a great accumulation of information. Still, in this tradition of enlightenment through breadth there were very definite virtues as well as weaknesses in critical and historical perspective. More important than the specific knowledge that Browning may have picked up from his father and his father's library were the attitudes that were implicit in his father's unending scholarly pursuits and that were present to his son almost as an unconscious influence in his own learning and reading. When his father died, Robert told his son that the chaplain who read the service, a friend of the elder Browning, said he "had been always struck with his humility and goodness, as well as his acquirements."[74] His father's personal and moral qualities very much directed his interests and acquirements. Intellectually humble almost to the point of self-abnegation, he embodied the spirit of toleration and open-mindedness in common-sense eighteenth-century English thought at its best. Not that he had no convictions himself. His son asserted quite rightly that he was an "unhesitating" believer in Christianity.[75] His faith was a placid one, however, that began and ended in a conviction of God's love and that took as its primary creed goodness, benevolence, and morality. Unconcerned as to whether he worshipped in the Church of England of his own family or in the Independent Church of his wife, he endorsed the general views common to all Christian sects. He once copied out and very evidently accepted the simple basic creed of a Dr. Armstrong, whose farewell sermon from Philippians he heard in Paris: "Finally Brethren Whatsoever things are true . . . Whatsoever things are honest . . . just . . . pure . . . lovely . . . of good report. If there be any Virtue, and If there by any praise, Think on these things."[76] In a marginal note to a book which dwelt upon the coming hell fires he put his belief even more succinctly: "But a good life will prevent even the apprehension of all these terrors & it is not very difficult to be good and humane."[77] Without needing the arguments of Paley's *Evidences,* he had a general faith that the world revealed its creator and, like his son in "A Death in the Desert," he relied upon the goodness of the creator for the authenticity of the biblical accounts.[78]

A person leading a life based on humble reverence, benevolence, and trust in goodness often strikes others, as Browning's father invariably did impress those who have left any record of him, as both loveable and rather weak. Trusting in the best and doing his humble work toward it, he lacked any strong will to shape things to his own vision and aims. Hence the rather pedantic, futile quality of his attempts at sustained work on his own. But the weakness is also in some ways a decided strength. His very willingness to take his stand as a humble, merely human observer, tolerant of others' differences from him, also set him in an ideal position for seeing clearly what was merely human in the pretensions of others. If he was not always able to comprehend fully the special qualities that made a man or an entire culture different from him, he was able to see their ordinary humanity with extraordinary lucidity and, where warranted, with critical sharpness. Whether commenting on the distant past or on the phenomena of his own day, his strength lay in his ability to set all men against a common human standard. Nor was his yardstick as unrefined in its gradations as that of many universalist or enlightenment historians who, with Voltaire, saw mankind as mostly motivated by knavery or wily priest-craft.

Against the pretensions of those who used special knowledge or a professional office to claim a privilege over their fellow men he could be quietly devastating. He was totally immune to all kinds of quackery, whatever the scientific guise in which it might be packaged. A cartoon at the Boston Public Library shows a doctor spouting out: "The organs of every sense are double," and the low-keyed rejoinder: "(Pray, Dr does your science include *common* sense)."[79] One of many comments on the nineteenth-century rage for phrenological analysis of character shows a practitioner pointing learnedly to a diagrammed head. The caption might fit many a faddist doctor in any age: "Doctor Humbug, the great Phrenologist—& the first who applied that science to pecuniary purposes."[80] The specialist quack is seen for what he is, merely human or even a bit less. But the human standard can also be a source of positive value. Another spoof of craniology judges this would-be science by seeing whether it is good enough for man at his best: "Here is the Cranium of Dr Johnson. Here you see the Rambler. Here you see the Idler—here you see the Dictionary—here you see Rasselas & Irene."[81]

More legitimate crafts receive the same low-keyed scrutiny. His cartoons again and again ridicule the tedium and stupidity of much of the legal process—a subject that his son would turn to with a vengeance in *The Ring and the Book*. Like Dickens, he must have spent some time in the courts doing sketches and enduring the machinery of the law. One sketch, at least, of a lawyer going full force, speaks eloquently of firsthand experience: "Now, my Lord, comes the gist of my argument."[82] Clearly he had been talking for hours! The elder Browning's own simple piety gave him, similarly, a touchstone for evaluating what was merely human in the practitioners of religion. A preacher more pleased with himself than pleased to serve his faith is thus castigated, "Highly poetical!—got the bump of oratory in the highest perfection—would preach an audience of 7000 to sleep in an hour & three quarters."[83]

The same quality of observation, applied indifferently to every object, familiar or great, current or historical, gave him an unusual ability to distance himself from issues of politics or ideology and to see them simultaneously from the differing views of the various partisans without himself becoming greatly involved. He couldn't help playing with political ideas, and in the process he usually succeeded in rescuing them from the realm of abstraction and placing them in perspective against the humankind they were intended to serve. One cartoon, entitled "The Political Adviser," has a funny old pedant on a stool speaking the ideas, if not the language, of Montesquieu: "But for Francis—take care how you blend the legislative with the Executive."[84] As in his son's monologues, though with more flippancy, ideas were to him counters to be jiggled and toyed with and finally played off against the character of the person who espoused them. Many of his cartoons are, in fact, exercises in applied specious reasoning, essentially intellectual caricatures. For instance, one shows us rather broadly the skewed thinking that underlies conservative radicalism. It even seems to foresee some of the absurdities in Disraeli's Young England movement of the 1840s: "I assure you gentlemen—nobody has the cause of reform more at Heart than Mr. Tory & what's more my friend Tory is a Radical from principle—nor would he have advocated the cause of Negro slavery if somebody hadn't told him those fellows never read Cobbett's register."[85] His own sympathies were probably slightly toward Whig or later liberal positions, but his satire ranges broadly from Tory to Radical. A cartoon aimed at the latter shows a rough rogue declaring his principles: "I live in Fox alley & I vote for Cobbett."[86] His only work that ever obtained the circulation that many deserved, a comment on the greatest issue of his day, the Reform

Bill of 1832, takes a surprisingly objective and neutral view of an event that greatly agitated his contemporaries. Parodying Brougham's statement to the house of Lords, "I have, my Lords, passed the Bill," he has him report to John Bull: "I've passed the Bill—Johnny!" And John Bull replies with more subtlety and perspicuity than he was wont to:

A pretty pass you've brought it to
This Bill—*will* pass—or won't:
'Tis Revolution if you do—
Rebellion if you don't.[87]

The sketch was evidently passed around the Bank and possibly was even shown to Sir Robert Peel. Another has the little Master Reform brought home to Papa Bull by the nurse (the Whigs): "See the little dear, he's pulling you by the Ear already—Well, Mrs. has had a bad time of it—but I hope Your Honour won't forget the Nurse!"[88] Other drawings on the Bill take a similarly shrewd detached look at arguments for rotten boroughs ("so respectable a borough as Hogs-Norton") or for the supposed utility of bribery in the old regime.[89]

The perspective is not that of a contemporary of the events but of a detached historian. In Paris, after his retirement, when he could devote all his time to his scholarship, Robert Browning Sr. even seemed to lose a sense of the difference between his world and the world of his books. Henriette Corkran, commenting on his absentminded preoccupation with books, felt "the present no longer existed for old Mr. Browning. He was unconscious of time, or of what society or the world expected of him."[90] His involvement in the past gave him an extraordinary sense of detachment in viewing the present. Both past and present were seen, in effect, from one universal and unchanging perspective. Just as he looked at the present with the detachment of an historian, so he would treat distant historical personages or events with the same familiarity and irreverence that he applied to the events of his own time. A series of cartoons, drawing on his studies of the early history of France, enumerates a few monarchs of some stature, then dismisses the remainder and their hundreds of years of history with the gesture of a man exasperated by the foibles of a set of men he has come to know only too well: "Indeed the rest of these kings are hardly worth mentioning . . . a parcel of idle fellows."[91] Browning's father could hardly fail to offer a kind of intellectual model to his son. What was important in his example was not so much his dutiful scholarship and wide-ranging historical and contemporary curiosity as his way of looking at human events. Above all, he represented a disinterested detachment that placed what he studied in a clear and objective light and he exemplified a consistent way of evaluating all subjects by a common human standard.

Of course, had Browning fils been willing simply to apprentice himself to the work of Browning père neither of them might ever have been heard of. In his approach to history or contemporary affairs the son was to be, as in all things, more forceful and more personally involved. His first political creed, a secular millenarianism modeled after that of Shelley, would lead him to turn his back on the past entirely. Later, if he would recreate the past with a greater sense than his father of the differences between past and present, he would also insist far more on using the past for the interests and aims of the present. A far greater poet of history than Tennyson with a much greater interest in bringing the past alive in his poetry, he would still agree with Tennyson's contention that there must be "a frame—something modern" in a poem set in the past to make it more than an antique period piece.[92] Like his father Browning could be a quiet observer and detached ironist, as he is in the devastating poems on intolerance, "Holy-Cross Day" or "The Heretic's Tragedy. A Middle-Age Interlude" (1855). Yet even here, and certainly far more in some of his other poems set in the past, Browning is a shaper and interpreter of history, not merely a detached and amused observer. His father's universal interest and objective observation became in his hands a tool rather than the end in itself.

Still, it was a tool that shaped the user as well as his materials. However much the young Browning might yearn to fill a religious or prophetic role as a poet, however much he would aspire to the status of sage or seer throughout his life, he had at base his father's pervasive sense of common humanity on which to rely. When he could not make his beliefs and philosophy clear as abstract metaphysics in *Sordello* or his late discursive poems, he could always revert to a more secure, more familiar world of men and women, living or dead, and explore their fate, as his father had, not by generalization but in specifics. And when more earnest, more committed stances failed, he could always fall back on the detached playfulness and genial comic outlook that was his father's habitual mode.

Above all, his father's enlightenment range of curiosity and breadth of historical vision forced Browning, sometimes despite his more earnest instincts, to confront man's situation from an individual, and hence modern, standpoint. With such an early exposure to the world of knowledge, in a spirit of tolerance and critical skepticism, Browning would never be able to lose himself in the frustrating, impossible quest for a single sufficient idea or a single simple tradition that might explain away the complexity of the modern world. Nor did he, like many of his contemporaries, have to spend much of his creative energy in the effort to free himself from the blinders of a narrow or provincial background. The true sophistication of a complex understanding of man in different times and places might still be a thing of his own distant future. But his early life in an ambience of endlessly curious, impartial scholarship at least set an ideal of knowledge for him. Dimly the greater aim of a deep understanding of the chameleon but not entirely unknowable nature of man himself as understood through his different manifestations in history was being implanted along with the fragments and curiosities that his father was constantly turning up. The father provided the essential beginning; it would be up to Browning in his maturity to take the further and harder steps, where his father did not venture, beyond mere sympathetic detachment to a full vision of man's nature.

3 Our Set

His father's habit of observing carefully the affairs around him and of inquiring ever more deeply into the larger world of history and learning thus opened to Browning a wide perspective on human life and society. Present life or the societies of the past could seem to the son, as they did to the father, all engrossing theaters of humanity and the people on view the dramatis personae of the most interesting performance imaginable.

Still, the elder Browning, if quiet and somewhat modest in his ways, was essentially a sociable though not a clubbable man. His independence and distance were never so great as to remove him from life itself and turn him into a mere reclusive looker-on. As he grew into a young man, Browning learned like his father to combine detachment and perceptivity with friendship and social life. As he explored the social life outside of his family circle his interest naturally centered on his own acquaintances and friends. With his peers, around Camberwell and other similar suburbs of London, he developed common values and social ideals, which would give him a secure sense of relation to the men of his generation even while he continued to assert his right to a fresh and independent vision of all men. Especially in the little group that called itself the set, we can see clearly many of the social and intellectual values that Browning shared with the progressive middle class of his age.

Unfortunately, about Browning's very earliest friends in his childhood and even during his adolescence little, indeed almost nothing, is known. No doubt there were various schoolfellows and chums over the years, boys like a certain improbably named William Shakespeare Williams, "one of the cleverest boys he had ever known," Browning averred, though he was recalled only because he later availed himself of old time's remembrance to put the touch on his old friend, the prosperous poet.[93] Only his early friendship with his cousins, George, John, and James Silverthorne, sons of his mother's sister and the local brewer who lived only a short distance from the Brownings' various residences at Camberwell, seems to have had permanence enough to leave any anecdotes or records. All three have been cast, with no sense of any incongruity, as "gifted musicians" and as "wild youths."[94] Jim, the boy with whom Browning sometimes explored the Dulwich Woods, was a particular friend, though three years Browning's senior. Especially during Browning's late teens, he seems to have been a frequent companion. If to enjoy rambles in the woods or reading Shelley (he was the person who first gave Browning a volume of Shelley's poems)[95] were marks of wildness in those days then Browning and his cousin were wild youths. Together they explored the new freedom opening up with the beginning of adult life. Jim had aspirations to become an artist.[96] Although such aspirations ill suited his later career at the family brewery and probably contributed to its eventual failure in his hands, they made him an ideal companion with whom Browning could share his ideas and dreams about art and poetry. We hear of their walking home late from nights at the theater—possibly from Richmond where Browning saw Kean in *Richard III*[97]—and can imagine their warm discussions and rehashings of what they had heard and seen.

From the little that is known of their pursuits, their wildness seems to have consisted only in a natural desire to explore what they could of the world and the people in it. Browning recollected a night at the opera with his "cousin," almost certainly Silverthorne. The picture we have is of two young enthusiasts with a sophisticated eye for the amusing aspects of human character. They had gone to hear *Fidelio*, in the first season of German Opera, and Browning recalled how they scrambled up to the gallery, "in order to get the best of the last chorus,—get its oneness which you do." They took a great delight in the music, but even greater pleasure in a certain "mild greatfaced white haired red cheeked German," whose whole body, as Browning vividly recalled, "broke out in billow, heaved and swayed in the perfection of his delight, hands, head, feet, all tossing and striving to utter what possessed him."[98]

There can be little doubt of the warmth of Browning's attachment to his cousin from their early walks "arm in arm" till 1846 when, except for Elizabeth's maid, Silverthorne was the only witness of Browning's marriage, and on until Browning's affectionate poem on his early death in 1852, "May and Death" (published 1857). Just because of the closeness of their affection and the strength of the old friendship and family ties, however, the companionship between Browning and his cousin seems to have been largely an unconscious sharing of experiences and interests that each might have pursued independently. Perhaps it was some such recognition of the larger indifference of their companionship to the growth of his own personality and understanding that Browning struggled awkwardly to express to Elizabeth: "I never was without good, kind, generous friends and lovers, so they say—so they were and are—perhaps they came at the wrong time—I never wanted them,—though that makes no difference in my gratitude, I trust—but I know myself."[99]

Without slighting the value of their affection or kindness or denying his own high regard for them, Browning probably felt something of the same larger indifference for the only other known friends that he made apart from literary and social London. These friends, among whom the closest to Browning were perhaps Christopher Dowson, Alfred Domett, and Joseph Arnould, not only shared with Browning much of his experience and interests during the 1830s and early 1840s but formed, along with a number of other persons, a small society with its own distinctive values and attitudes. He later would lose contact with most of the individuals in this group. As an influence entirely outside of his family circle but still focused upon the early suburban environment of his youth, the group or set, as they styled it, was important in offering to Browning a way of conceiving of his relation to other men. Far more than the friends he would make in London literary society, the members of the set were his contemporaries, persons from similar backgrounds with whom he could share and develop, consciously or unconsciously, basic social and personal values. The set provided a kind of theater for the development and expression of a common intellectual and artistic culture.

In later years Chris Dowson, writing to his brother Joseph, recalled "our 'set' . . . which, I consider, consists of Arnould, Alfred [Domett], Browning, Pritchard and ourselves. How are they all dispersed! Never, I fear to be reunited in this world."[100] Actually the set cannot be defined quite so simply or easily. As a loose society or association of friends existing over many years, its activities varied as the lives of its members changed. Even the membership of the group changed greatly as old members died or moved away and new ones were brought in. At first, probably from sometime around the late 1820s or early 1830s to the early 1840s, gatherings were held at the family home of two of the members, Frederick and William Curling Young. Then the set, consisting only of men, was almost exclusively a club or society for discussion or debate on literary, philosophical, or scientific topics: "the little 'Debating Society' that met regularly at our house," as the Youngs' sister recalled.[101] Accordingly they called their meetings colloquials, gatherings for talk, rather than colloquies to suggest the friendly informal nature of the discussions.

It was during this earlier period that Browning was evidently most actively involved in the group. Later, as many of the founding members drifted out of reach of the meetings and those who remained became largely settled, middle-aged family men, the set or colloquial became mainly a club that met half-yearly for dinners at various London or suburban inns, "the British Coffee-house in Cockspur Street—The old British," or "The old Artichoke at Blackwall—with a bow window projecting over the Thames—a forest of masts the foreground and Shooter's Hill the distance."[102] These meetings had already the overtones of commemoration of past times. "We have gathered together lately the remains of the fine old Colloquial," Joseph Arnould wrote to Alfred Domett in New Zealand.[103] And Browning added, speaking of a later meeting: "You were 'in our flowing cups freshly remembered.' "[104] Wives were invited too—"a sprinkling of ladies"—and later meetings served mostly as reunions of old friends. Then Browning's departure for Italy with Elizabeth and the death of Chris Dowson in 1848 put an end to the meetings entirely. "The old Colloquials don't meet now," Arnould later informed Domett, "in fact never since poor dear Chris Dowson's death did it fairly hold up its head."[105]

Over fifteen or twenty years, and with many changes in membership, what continuity the set had came from an unquestioned belief on the part of all the members in the value of society, especially of social communication and association. Again and again letters from the time speak simply of the pleasures of good company: "I can hardly fancy a pleasanter or merrier party," Arnould wrote to Domett. "Such small talk as we used to have," Browning wrote in another letter to New Zealand, "the true charm of which —there, there!"[106]

> If from society we learn to live
> 'Tis solitude should teach us how to die[107]

wrote a certain Captain Pritchard, member of the set, quoting Byron's *Childe Harold* in a moment of depression during an illness (not fatal after all), and the sentiment, or at least the first half of the couplet, might stand for the spirit of the set as a whole: that human fellowship is itself one of the great goods of life to be enjoyed while it can be. Society was a decided good, too, for the chance it gave members to come to know personally and in some depth a variety of human beings. "You have mixed with men of all kinds—you have an open heart & a penetrating eye," Arnould wrote to Domett, urging him to write a kind of prose *Canterbury Tales* for the nineteenth century. "Believe me, there is nothing like the bold, flexible, masterly line of Dryden or Byron. Chaucer, Shakespeare and he who wrote Don Juan are our three highest masters of the highest school of art, that namely whose object is universal man."[108] In some such spirit, though perhaps not with identical literary tastes, the members of the set seem to have taken a frank pleasure in the variety of personalities, backgrounds, and interests that they offered to each other. Throughout its varied history the set served this desire by bringing together men of ability and intelligence from a broad range of professions.

Chris and Joe Dowson, both good friends of Browning, lived at Limehouse, out east from London along the north side of the Thames, in what was then a suburban village.[109] Despite a family itch for literature—an itch that would only find full gratification two generations later in Chris's grandson, the decadent poet Ernest Dowson—both brothers made their livings in businesses connected with the shipping trade at Limehouse and nearby Poplar. Chris inherited the family Bridge Dock at Limehouse, a comfortable old place with a view of the shining gray water outside where business was done amid old maps, prints of sailing ships, and an old ship's figurehead.[110] Joe Dowson, the younger son, was in a separate copper business and his partner was another member of the set, Fred (later Sir Frederick) Young. To complicate business and friendship further, Chris also shared a separate venture with Fred in Ship's Biscuit Bakers. Fred's father was a shipbuilder as well, and became, as a member of Parliament, a spokesman for the shipping industry in general. He was also active in the New Zealand Company, a massive enterprise for colonization. Through his interest, his other son, still another member of the set, William Curling Young—"high-minded" but impetuous—eventually emigrated to New Zealand only to be drowned during a surveying expedition in 1842.[111] In the early 1830s it was in this milieu of shipping and exploration, at the Young's family home in Church Row, Limehouse, a comfortable residence with a fine view across the flat and open riverbed fields, that the set generally met.

Closely related to these ship-outfitting, seafaring and distant-land-colonizing members, men typical of the enterprising expansive tendencies of early Victorian England but men, too, of cultivation and intellectual ability, was Browning's especially close, though somewhat later, friend, Alfred Domett. In fact, he was distantly related to the Youngs through his mother, and his father, Captain Domett, was also in shipping.[112] Perhaps from his father, who began life as a midshipman in the Navy and continued in later years to be so attached to the sea that his family claimed he was not born but "came up out of the sea one fine morning 'like Oannes the FishGod of the Chaldeans,' "[113] Domett inherited a certain restless taste for travel and experience of the world. A sketch by the artist George Lance, himself a distant member of the set, casts Domett as a romantic, handsome traveler with a dark wide-brimmed hat shadowing his face.[114] When Browning himself tried his hand at a "fancy portrait" in his poem "Waring" (1842) he, too, heavily colored his picture with the tones of romance. As Waring, Domett becomes almost a personification of the wandering spirit, a man who "gave us all the slip, chose land-travel or seafaring, / Boots and chest or staff and scrip," and thereafter was seen "with great grass hat, and kerchief black" by a British traveler in the Tyrrhenian Sea—but only for a moment as his light vessel turned away and "went off, as with a bound, / Into the rose and golden half / O' the sky." In fact as well as fancy, though he tried for a while to settle down to a career in law after early travels in America and Italy, Domett did give his friends the slip and set off for New Zealand with the aim of joining his cousin William C. Young. However he found there a rather unromantic practical life as a colonizer, administrator, and for a time, prime minister. "Of a passionate, fiery nature; full of suppressed energy . . . no dreamer, no waverer, but a fiery resolute man of action, capable of making his weight felt and his will prevail,"[115] Tom Arnold, Matthew's brother, concluded when he met him in New Zealand. Still, for all his restlessness and practical activity he found time for a second career as a poet, publishing early *Poems* in 1833, occasional periodical pieces, and a longer poem, *Venice*, in 1839. His bid for fame as a poet, the fourteen-thousand line New Zealand romance epic *Ranolf and Amohia* (1872) has, needless to say, not made his name a household word, but it did attain some estimation in its day.[116]

Despite a maternal grandfather in shipping, Browning himself was so ignorant of sea life that Domett's brother Edward, who was at school with him, had to teach him how to pronounce the word *bow* as a nautical term.[117] He must have had a brisk exposure in the set to the vigorous British shipping and nautical tradition, then in its pride of power and anecdote, as well as to the commercial expansive spirit closely allied to it. One member, Captain James Pritchard, the "dear old Pritchard" of whom Browning often speaks in his letters to Domett, was simply a warm and friendly old tar. Chris Dowson's daughter recalled his visits to her father's house. "He used to arrive laden with presents, a little white haired sailor with a squint who told delightful stories of adventure."[118] He was a person worth knowing: odd—"that singular little man"—and independent—"he never let anyone know where he lived"—he was also extremely fond of the persons in the set and, though well on in years, "was a great admirer of the girls."[119] Pritchard was by no means the chief luminary of the set, but he was in many ways its presiding spirit. Although scarcity of information of any kind about Browning in the 1820s and early 1830s makes it difficult to determine exactly how he came to know the members of the set, Pritchard seems to have been the catalyst. He knew Browning as early as 1829 and was possibly an old friend of both the Browning and Dowson families. He is mentioned in an early letter from Browning to Chris, and he had probably first introduced Browning to the Dowsons.[120] Through them Browning could then have come to know the others who formed the informal club.[121] Once having brought them together, he helped to keep the set together as a group by his warm concern for the members. "I saw Pritchard yesterday, full of this New Zealand news—always hoping and believing in you," Browning wrote to Domett, reminding him of a friendship that ignored all differences of age or generation.[122] The picture that Pritchard's message evokes of old and young joined together in fellowship and friendship, is one of the most attractive aspects of the set.

Despite some overrepresentation by sailors and adventurers, there were, besides Browning, a number of persons from other professions. Dr. James Blundell, a doctor rich as Croesus, whose famous lectures on midwifery and physiology at Guy's Hospital Browning attended around 1829 to satisfy his curiosity, was evidently a sometime visitor with his cousin Pritchard. At least once, in the later years of periodic dinners, he was elevated to the status of "fine old Blundell" as "the munificent donor of the feast."[123] More often his nephew Bezer Blundell—"a possible Sidney tyring to squeeze himself into the 'clothes' of an attorney"—would join the colloquials where the exuberance—"sprightly as a lark"[124]—that later landed him in jail helped spur on discussions.

Another lawyer, Joseph Arnould, three years Browning's junior, took his law more seriously: the "most honourable course of exertion, which the first country in the world presents to her citizens."[125] For years he ground away on a work on marine insurance—"a long & dreary task"—by which he finally made a name in his profession and became Sir Joseph Arnould and judge of the Supreme Court of Bombay.[126] But his career belies the nature of the man. Lawyer's lawyer though he may have been, he was a person, as his letters to Browning and Domett still testify, of great personal charm and wide intellectual and artistic interests.[127] At Oxford he won, like the young Tennyson of a few years earlier at Cambridge, a prize for a poem.

Despite his increasing involvement in law, he could still sprout wings on the publication of Browning's fine but hardly recognized *Dramatic Lyrics* (1842) to draft quite a good, if somewhat outdated, verse epistle.[128] (His later verses as Poet Laureate to the Legal Home Circuit, including lines on the retirement of the lord chief justice were less creditable.) For some time before his marriage in 1841 he was on the books as a fellow of his college at Oxford. Thereafter he kept up an interest in literature, published with Browning's assistance a learned article on Rabelais, and covertly contributed leaders to the radical press.[129] In later years he lived what he considered a modestly bohemian existence, choosing his friends among "actors, actresses and authors who come to drink coffee, chat and enjoy some good music in our little house."[130] Although he came from Camberwell, where his father was a doctor,[131] Arnould evidently, like his own early friend Domett, first met Browning through the set. He and his wife Maria later became particularly close friends of Browning and his family, and he served for years as a trustee to Browning's marriage settlement.[132]

Among the doctors, lawyers, men of affairs, and shipmen there were, besides Browning himself—"our poet" as Arnould called him—some full-time artists: Field Talfourd, younger brother of the lawyer-dramatist T. N. Talfourd and in later years portraitist of both the Brownings: not a consistent "comer," but close enough to the group to recall "the old 'set' " when he was a "handsome old man."[133] George Lance, disciple of Haydon and already winning his place among the foremost still life painters of his age as the master detailer of the bounty of the earth and the carnage of the hunt, was another occasional member, though not well known to Browning.[134] Scholarship, too, was represented professionally for a while by Benjamin Jowett, later the famous Master of Balliol College, translator of Plato, and liberal contributor to *Essays and Reviews.* Here again, however, though his presence suggests the level of urbanity of the set, there is little evidence that Browning himself knew him, though he would become a close friend years later.[135]

There were other members, well liked but now hazy figures, such as the Bakers of Limehouse or the Oldfields of Champion Hill, Camberwell, both families related to Domett, or sometime members like George Parker Bidder, "calculating Bidder wondrous the boy Bidder of some 30 yr. back," a childhood friend probably introduced by Arnould to the group: a man in close touch with the spirit of the age, "one of our first Railway engineers now floated up by the spring tide of the Iron mania into a notability of the day."[136] But the names of even Browning's closest acquaintances among the set are hard enough to keep in mind; and what is most significant about the group's make-up is clear enough from the members whom we can still see fairly distinctly. It provided for Browning as for all the members an opportunity to come to know a number of persons of very different professions and interests, and to come to know them through close conversation and association, as separate and complicated persons.

Our Set.

Far left: Joseph Arnould. Painting by Middleton. *Expert on marine insurance, sometime poet and essayist, lover of philosophy, affectionate friend of Browning and his family.*

Near left: Alfred Domett, ca. 1830-1840. Sketch self-portrait. *Traveler, poet, New Zealand politician, Browning's "Waring" and his "warm & rather violent advocate & champion."*

Above: Earliest Extant Letter of Robert Browning: to Christopher Dowson, Jr., Member of the Set, ca. 1832. *Chris Dowson: inheritor of the family Bridge Dock, lover of the theater, a trifler, "highly sensitive & nervous," full of "quips and cracks."*

Membership in the set introduced Browning to a wide variety of talented and intelligent men of his time, young and old, practical, learned, or artistic. What was perhaps even more significant, it allowed him to participate in a common culture and a common set of interests. At a time in his life when he was just beginning to make his first tentative ventures into the far more complicated society of literary London, the set, composed largely of persons like himself from the new suburban areas of London, offered to Browning a smaller, more meaningful and cohesive society in which to develop his interests and try out his powers of thought and expression.

In a letter of 1845 to Domett in New Zealand, Arnould speaks of "enjoying a great treat": an evening spent with Browning and his London literary friends, the poet B. W. Procter and *Athenaeum* critic H. F. Chorley. Nonetheless, recalling the old days of the set, he was left with a sense of loss and found himself wishing Domett had been present to mix his "more practical sense with our more bookish theoric & London gossip; not that we have not good talk excellent talk on these occasions but not what Samuel Johnson wd call discussion, not such thorough sifting into the very heart of things as used to delight our more boisterous, but more joyous colloquies of old."[137]

Regrettably, there was no Boswell present at the early "meets" to bring back for us from memory the actual texture of the discussion or the play of personalities and interests between the members. No doubt we would probably have a good deal that was different both in subject and tone from the conversations of Johnson's little club. From the recollections we do have of the colloquials, especially in the 1830s, it appears that there *was* often discussion such as might have pleased Johnson himself: consideration of serious subjects and ideas in a spirit of real interest. Arnould's wife, Maria, recalling evenings spent with Domett, speaks of the "full earnestness and interest" of the conversation.[138] And though the term *earnestness,* used too often in the nineteenth century to cover sins of inflexibility and lack of humor, has become somewhat debased in the subsequent reaction, it still conveys something of what Johnson would have approved in the discussions of these friends: the belief that ideas and discussions are finally important in the lives of those involved.

Such a concern naturally must have led to treatment of fairly heavy topics. Years later, Fred and William Young's sister Emma recalled the colloquial almost as a debating society. Her brother liked her to be in the drawing room, "on the evenings when these young men used to come in for Tea, after their Debates." The serious topics of the debates are perhaps suggested by her exclamation: "What an interesting set they were, Poets in Embryo, Philosophers, Scientific—Literary all."[139] History and politics must have been common subjects of discussion. We hear, for instance, of Frederick Young and the lawyer Bezer Blundell deep in reading Greek history together at Blundell's law chambers.[140] Although a surprisingly large number of the group were destined to be involved in the development of the Victorian British Empire, Arnould in India and the Youngs and Domett in New Zealand, they saw themselves as liberals, colonizers, and free traders, not as nationalist imperialists. William Curling Young, a person of talent and ability as a writer, even wrote a strong book on the question of imperialism in China, during the buildup of irrational sentiment in the 1830s prior to the Opium War. Ironically, the war rapidly succeeded in bringing about his pacifist suggestion, that Britain should seek only trade, not control, of China by establishing an offshore trading colony. His argument in the book, which he presented to Browning,[141] is more humane and enlightened than the disguised imperialism of his day. He insists that trade should not be forced upon nations but merely offered in peace, and throughout he asserts that British dealing with foreign countries must be based on a sympathetic understanding and toleration of their peoples' different national characters and habits.

Enlightened views don't inoculate a person against the ambiguities of historical action. In New Zealand Domett might demonstrate his cousin's liberal interest in other peoples by spare time work on the South Seas epic in which the customs of the native Maoris are sypathetically described. In practice, he found himself a leader of the party that took a tough stand against the natives and an exponent of the policy, patently illogical in a country where few settlers could be counted on to share Domett's own sense of justice, that Maoris should be fully subjected to English power and law. Still, if colonial life placed Domett in a situation where normal English standards of right were apt to end him in the wrong, there is little doubt that the members of the group were, by the standards of the time and in their own land, progressive in their views. During the early 1840s feeling ran high for the repeal of the Corn Laws, and Arnould reported that Chris Dowson, always somewhat mercurial in temper, had been moved to "deeper and more agonizing paroxysms of scorn and contempt than can be at all compatible with his comfortable digestion. He has far outspat all his former venom upon the luckless heads of honourable friend after honourable friend, and outslavered all his former slavering of the illustrious Duke."[142]

Although both Domett and Arnould were university men who subscribed to the Church of England, they were close enough to Browning's opinions that they had at least some common outlook on religious questions. Both friends, and very likely the others in the group, took a dim view of the Tractarian movement in the Church and of Newman's influence. Generally tolerant and open-minded, they grew nervous and somewhat unjust on that subject because they saw the developments in the High Church toward sacramentalism and authority as political events that threatened a return to a closed world of repression. Although they formed no party or single sect, they yet spoke with the assurance of shared assumptions. Domett especially praised "The Laboratory" ("a nut for Young England") and "The Confessional" ("a sugar plum for the Puseyites") when he read *Dramatic Romances and Lyrics* (1845) and called on Browning for more of the same. "That Puseyism—for God's sake give it some graphic digs in the wind . . . from time to time."[143] Browning himself spoke of another poem in the volume as "just the thing for the time—what with the Oxford business."[144]

On matters of religion or politics discussion might assume a common ground. On other subjects the aim was rather to expand and exercise their intelligence by debate and free speculation. When Joseph Arnould was present, no doubt the discussion often turned to philosophy: for this pleasant, rather cultivated and delicate looking person maintained throughout his long practical career in law a fresh interest in the larger metaphysical and ethical questions that stand behind the practice but are generally put away with other university memories when a career is taken up.[145] It is not surprising to hear of Domett and Arnould reading Plato's *Phaedo* together attentively during Christmas term break in 1833.[146] It is another matter, and an indication of the kind of interest that Arnould still looked for from an old member of the set, to find, in one of his pleasant letters to the Brownings in Italy, the suggestion that he and Robert start up a philosophical correspondence on the ideas of Fichte. "If you knew the pleasure your letters give me, I should not ask this in vain. I should so like you to give me the benefit of your thoughts on such great subjects as that of the Progress of the Race as developed after Fichte's theory . . . [it] would be an infinite refreshment to my mind if you would condescend occasionally to hold commune with it on such points & then too I think our letters, having some worthier end than mere gossip might be more frequent."[147]

"Worthier ends" were not in the colloquials, as they certainly weren't in Arnould's own life, only a matter of earnest and serious discussions. "*Literary* all—& so light & lively!" Miss Young added to her description of the colloquials. And intellectual play and fun seems to have been as much a staple of their discussions as more serious inquiry. The attractive lord of such unearnest misrule was doubtless Chris Dowson, a person who, from all that we know of him, often seems to call up the combined playfulness and pathos of Charles Lamb. Members of the group often remarked on "his highly sensitive & nervous temperament," and his habitual "quips & cracks." "When last he dined with us," Arnould reports, "he was at as high a pitch as ever."[148] The spirit of fun and gentle mockery that he evoked seems to have been one of his great attractions to Browning, who in the first letter we have to Dowson, falls into a playfully affected manner in turning down an invitation, "which I cannot bring myself to decline, and which I can as little venture to accept." Then he as playfully breaks through—"cutting the pathetic"—and admits simply that he has been sick.[149] With Domett, who himself came from a "bright, unconventional" household, Dowson must have often joined in dubious and highly animated verbal tiffs, thrown "into fevers" by Domett's combativeness.[150] By about 1846 it was clear that Chris was suffering from tuberculosis and his recollection—with Domett now in New Zealand and Browning established in Italy—of the old days of the set is a moving combination of warm sentiment and balancing good humor.

"How are they all dispersed! Never, I fear to be reunited in this world. 'Oh! could those days (as Charles Lamb says) but come again.' Yet it is foolish to indulge in such vain wishes, rather let us be thankful we have once enjoyed them."[151]

Dowson's passion was for the theater and his conversation was as consistently spiced and flavored with the parlance of plays and the "London boards" as Captain Pritchard's must have been with ships and the sea. Browning spoke of him, "as vigilant of theatrical polity as ever," and took the trouble to write him a long detailed letter in 1844 about his own dramatic work.[152] Even in his long final sickness Dowson wasn't able to resist the theatrical view of life and spoke of himself aspiring only to "an engagement as 'walking gentleman,' " and deriving "consolation from having played better parts in better days."[153] Nor was interest in the theater confined to Dowson. At times the set as a whole seems to have been as much a club of theatrical enthusiasts, if not performers, as a discussion group. Joe Dowson recalled "being *one* of the 'clappers,' " at the first performance of Browning's *Strafford,* and probably a good number of the set were there cheering him on.[154] Later we hear that one large gathering adjourned after dinner at the British Coffeehouse in Cockspur Street, and went "all together to the play."[155]

Literature of all kinds was a favorite subject for discussion. Arnould, the university prize poet and sometime journalist, Domett, a poet in his own right, Joe Dowson, "literary & a character,"[156] Fred Young, who prided himself on his contributions in later years "on various subjects to the columns of 'The Thunderer,' "[157] William Curling Young, who asked Browning to be sure to send copies of his poems out to New Zealand: these men, and probably most of the other members of the set, found in literature their chosen avocation. Conversation must have ranged, to judge from the interests of the different members, over the entire field of literature both ancient and modern. Perhaps it touched especially on the masters of ten or twenty years before: Arnould's favorite Byron or Domett's Shelley and the literary events of their own day.[158] In the correspondence of Arnould and Browning with Domett in New Zealand, Carlyle was a frequent topic, Tennyson and Dickens noted as rising stars, Macaulay, Bulwer-Lytton, and a host of lesser lights mentioned in passing. Domett even recalled debates over the merits of the poetesses and minor poets of the day, with Browning sympathetically defending even Mrs. Hemans, Laman Blanchard, "LEL [Letitia E. Landon] & God knows who."[159] The level of discussion in the early years is hard to determine, but if Arnould's shrewd and sophisticated comments in his later letters are any indication, they may have been not only spirited but well informed. In any case the set must have provided for the young Browning a forum in which to put forward his own ideas on literature where he could compare them with those of others, become aware of the limitations and inadequacies of his own knowledge, and come to understand many of the common interests of his day.

"They had a journal too," recalled Miss Young, and this, in a varia-

tion on the periodical essay titles of the eighteenth century, was called the
Trifler. This was clearly an amateur effort, published monthly in only about
ten pages and then probably only for the set and their relations. It began in
the winter of 1834-1835 and seems not to have lasted for any considerable
time. Like many such ventures since the days of Addison and Steele, it consisted, to judge from the two surviving issues inscribed by the editor to
Browning, of a mixed lot of poetry, essays, letters, and other comment.[160]
Enthusiasm for the venture must have been high among the set for at least a
while. There is a story of Browning's visiting Joe Dowson at the offices of
Young Dowson and finding him "walking to and fro" worrying not over
the copper business but over some verses for the next edition.[161]

Like the set itself, the editor (or editors, for the two first editions have
leaders signed differently, the first "E," the second "J") took trifling with
sufficient seriousness and ceremony. Under the portentous motto, "Pleased
with a trifle," in the first issue, the editor defines a new Victorian ideal for
the periodical essay, a kind of muscular do-nothingism that lightly insists on
seeing life steadily and whole. Rather than languish yearning after some
"darling object" that can't be, the trifler accepts reality as he finds it and
concentrates all his unseriousness on finding what is interesting in whatever
he happens to see. He is "an ever animated witness . . . though seldom vio-
lently excited, he is always interested; his sources of pleasure are every where
available." The ideal, like that of the set itself, is sophistication without
egotism or cynicism. In the other surviving issue, the number for February
1835, the other editor offers a model for the trifling philosophy by showing
us how to content ourselves, when in a coffee house, over newspaper adver-
tisements, when the rest of the paper is expropriated by someone else. A
woman who seeks a Swiss maid offers the trifler much food for reflection.
Quite above such affectations himself, he sees this desire for imported help
as the result of one or another disbalancing enthusiasm: "Perhaps the lady
was a rigid Protestant of the Nanty Ewart school, fearful of having her religion taken from her," or perhaps she was a "sentimentalist" for Swiss
scenery.

The idea behind the *Trifler*, which was obviously much influenced by
the social and moral perspective of its eighteenth-century predecessors, was
thus similar to that in much of the Victorian fiction and social comment of a
slightly later time, for instance in the sketches and novels of Thackeray: an
ideal of worldly, good-humored, perceptive, and objective observation of
life and character. To judge from the work that we have of the triflers in the
set, this ideal proved on the whole more successful for life than for literature. Analyzing the affections of others, the contributors have their own
young men's pretentiousness. An epistolary tale, "Travers Templeton to
Horace Seymour, Esq.," (No. 1) about the foolish imagination of a jealous
bridegroom-to-be, only reminds the reader by contrast how extraordinary
Jane Austen's talents are at this kind of social and psychological description. Worse are two poems, a trivial, "To a Lady Who Had Worked Me a

Watch Chain" (No. 1) and a travel poem, "The Rhone," which alludes to Byron and Rousseau but lacks the spirit of the one and the perceptivity of the other. Even an "Epigram" (No. 1), which should probably be ascribed to Browning himself, another slam at his old schoolmaster, Thomas Ready whom he had elsewhere ridiculed in biting verse, is only more clever, not more mature.[162]

Another contribution by Browning, also obviously the work of a young man, "Some Strictures on a Late Article in the 'Trifler,' in a letter to the author thereof" (No. 2), shows how willing Browning was to accept the trifler view of things as a part of the group of friends.[163] The article is only not typical in one essential way: it is a work of stunning if still uncontrolled powers of rhetoric and intellect. His reply was elicited by a very heavy-handed lucubration in the previous issue which really violated the spirit of the set's forum by its moral weight and turgid tone. In a spirit of paradox and intellectual teasing, Browning catches up his adversary in a whirlwind of argument and case making. Taking his stand on every possible ground of argument, metaphysical, moral, and natural, or from a range of literary or moral authorities, he almost bullyingly devastates the small house put up so laboriously on such a conventional site by the previous writer. His method in this praise-of-folly madness is to take on the different pompous voices suited to the serious use of these arguments, dropping in here and there an obvious guffaw to tip his readers off in case they need it. If the result is a great display of talents rather than great literature, it does suggest the wide range of knowledge assumed by the set: Browning speaks familiarly of Quarles, Luther, Swift's Gulliver, Rousseau ("the impassioned Jean Jacques"), Anacreon, and Shelley ("the sweet poet of our days") as well as of his personal favorites Donne and "the subtle Mandeville"—two obvious sources of inspiration for this argumentative work. The text is sprinkled with Greek and Latin and ends with a Latin translation of Schiller done by the Swiss-German Füglistaller. Browning is comfortable with the language of the metaphysician, the ethical philosopher, the lawyer, the doctor, or other specialists, all turned to demonstrating what debts a man must have. To quell his opponent he calls up "here a sophist urgent on their [the debts'] venerable standing, there a moralist voluble on their magnitude,—over thy shoulder a poet rendering more formidable the sum total in flourishes of red-ink, —under thy nose a spruce humanist jotting down an unexpected demand on any the most trifling appropriation thou mayst meditate." Like the proper trifler, he is at home with all men and can speak the language of each. Browning's tour de force also indicates how much emphasis the triflers placed upon the kind of intellectual and verbal play involved in argumentative case making. The entire case against the earlier author depends upon word play —ordinary financial debt compared to dying as paying the "debt" of nature or to the social contract as a debtor's relation to society. It also depends upon complicated logical and metaphorical comparisons between unlike things. "All moralists have concurred in considering this our mortal sojourn as indeed an uninterrupted state of debt, and the world our dwelling-place as represented by nothing so aptly as by an inn, wherein those who lodge most commodiously have in perspective a proportionate score to reduce, and those who fare least delicately, but an insignificant shot to discharge.'' Browning confesses he has an ''itch of proselytizing'' that leads him to such pains to convert his adversary. However, the essay suggests, as it ends with Browning taking off for a walk in the park when he is sure that the bailiffs waiting to collect *his* debts have given up, that the spirit of trifling encouraged by the set tended rather to broaden the mind to view things from many perspectives than to narrow it in fervid advocacy of particular opinions.

Clever as Browning's prose is, it remains an anomaly in the generally dull stuff of the *Trifler* and in his career as a poet. We should go very wrong if we looked in this literary concoction of young friends for a serious literary coterie. Although nothing of permanence grew out of the literary attempt of the set, the ultimate importance for Browning's literary development through his involvement in the group should not be minimized. For Browning, who in the later period of the set was also coming to know many of the foremost writers and literary persons of the time, such company was valuable precisely because, while saturated in literature, it was not, in the restrictive sense, merely literary. For all the members' literary ambitions, and despite Domett's independent standing as a serious, if minor, poet, the set brought Browning in contact not so much with a society of fellow writers as with a representative group of potential readers of the best sort: respectful of literary tradition, but in touch with the moving forces and events of their own age; serious and thoughtful, yet also bright, witty, and playful.

They seem, too, to have taken a serious interest in the work and career of ''our poet.'' Browning sent old Captain Pritchard a copy of *Strafford*, and he thought enough of the literary sympathy and discernment of even such a casual comer as Bezer Blundell to give him a copy of some of his work.[164] At another time he spoke of a friendly letter from Dowson—''a piece of himself, so kind is it''—on his much criticized *Sordello*.[165] Domett, who styled himself, ''your warm & *rather violent* advocate & champion,'' wrote a biting poem against a criticism of *Pippa Passes,* in which Browning, by contrast to his beetle-like earth-bound critics, is portrayed as an imperial eagle of verse dallying with the sun.[166] He crammed the margins of his copies of his friend's early works with comments that reveal close reading and serious reflection.[167] Arnould's warm praise in the verse epistle he sent to Browning in 1842 expressing ''the tumult of delight which your most noble Dramatic Lyrics have given me'' stands as one of the earliest recognitions of the real stature of this volume.[168] Nor was the set merely a group of clappers for their personal friend. Domett and Arnould both provided practical critiques of individual volumes or poems and repeated expressions of concern at his tendency to obscurity and his failures of communication. ''Now this,'' Browning told Arnould, in referring to a criticism Domett sent him, ''is what one wants; how few men there are who will give you this.''[169] What he found only carping and unhelpful in a hostile review he would take as a valuable lesson from a group of disinterested persons, on whose sympathy and good will he surely could count. With perhaps even too much candor, Domett wrote in 1845 scolding Browning for his obscurity and blaming it upon his too reclusive life and brooding intellectuality. By the time his letter arrived from New Zealand the comment was a bit out of date, but not the remedy prescribed by this self-appointed doctor: "more exercise, more Arnould, and more cold water." Such friends, who could help him make the necessary and impossibly difficult link between life and art, were uniquely valuable even at the cost of some busybodying advice. "Arnould writes with everflowing kindness about you—he is certainly a prince," Domett added in the same letter. "I wish he said that you were oftener with him. His society is good for body & soul: The health of both in him is contagious."[170] Few writers have been lucky enough to have such sympathetic and intelligent friends cheering them on from the sidelines and giving them at least some idea of what an audience might be at its best.

Although the set held together in one way or another till Chris Dowson's death in 1848 and although Browning's close friendship with Domett and Arnould flourished in the late 1830s and the 1840s, Browning's involvement in the group is naturally associated with his early years before he began in earnest to pursue a literary career in London. Not only was the set as a whole more active, and Browning's participation in it greater in the early 1830s but also, at that period, before he became involved with new, more professionally literary friends in London, the little society must have seemed more important and had a greater impact upon him than in later years. As a group centered almost entirely in the similar suburban towns of Camberwell and Limehouse, the set is linked more closely to the social environment of Browning's childhood than to the larger society in which he later made friends and acquaintances. Through a man like Captain Pritchard the group might look back toward an older English society of stalwart characters and good cheer, such as Browning celebrated in his poem, "Here's to Nelson's Memory" ("Nationality in Drinks") where he raises a glass of English beer to the hero of Trafalgar. But most of the younger men, setting out on such different careers as law, colonial administration, engineering, painting, literature, or business, shared a common background of childhood in the villages of suburban London. Despite the wide range of professions and interests they represented, there is a larger similarity in the lives of most of the members. Young men, like Browning, of education and talent but not of wealth, most of the members moved from the limited environment of their childhood into the larger Victorian society, where their abilities brought them into positions of prominence and power. Browning's acquaintance with the set in some degree served to put him in touch not so much with society in general as with the ablest young men of his own background and social position. And this was a group turned as decidedly to modern life and modern experience as some social groups in England were turned toward the past. It gave Browning a natural sense of an audience facing, like himself, an open world in which values and beliefs were to be worked out by the individual rather than merely inherited from a class interest or traditional class assumptions. That the set and his own family really was nonetheless a class, what in popular Marxism would be termed the bourgeois intelligentsia, also no doubt limited the range of Browning's response to the condition of his time. Partaking in the set in the optimism of a clever group of men, who would find little real opposition in Victorian England to their serious efforts to advance themselves, Browning would be somewhat too ready to accept the liberal ideal of the career open to talents as a solution for the problems of men of all classes rather than as merely a justice for a particular class in a particular time. If the association with friends in the set did little more than his family had done to put him in touch with the modern situation of the industrial poor and of other groups who would find the coming age merely perpetuating old social injustices or inventing new ones, it did connect him with major realities of his age: with the men and progressive ideas that would shape Victorian society. Imagining himself speaking to them by his poetry, he would be speaking essentially to the same persons most modern poetry since his time has addressed: the people of intelligence and education who find themselves, in their values and attitudes to experience, in an impermanent and open-ended situation which they must learn to understand in new, appropriate terms rather than by those supplied by past authority or tradition. As an approach to this new world, participation in the set did help, in addition, to fix and objectify some general social attitudes that Browning would maintain throughout his life: belief in the value of discussion and of forthright communication between men of all ages and occupations; a predilection both for earnest and serious exploration of philosophical, religious, or moral issues and for bright, playful, and spirited discussion; and a love of literature and the arts not as an isolated and unsocial amusement but as the joint possession and culture of able persons of all interests and professions.

4 *Family Cosmopolitanism*

To enumerate all the experiences or influences that contributed to Browning's understanding of man's life in society and helped to develop his own social values would be as tedious and impossible as to trace all the factors that brought out his special sense of identity or self-consciousness. One other aspect of his early experience, however, was so directly important in Browning's growth to an objective sense of social reality and cultural life that it needs to be looked at separately. This is the rather unusual cosmopolitan flavor that family business connections and cultural interests alike gave to Browning's experience. It was a cosmopolitanism that was, of course, more obvious in the Browning of later years, the long-time resident of Italy, prosperous and often mistaken for a businessman or banker, a man of the world who could impress even the tough-minded critic John Gibson Lockhart as being, in an oft-quoted though dubious testimonial, very unlike "a damned literary man."[171] The roots of this aspect of his personality reach, however, down into his early background and experience, into his childhood family life, and into the formative period before he began to be a regular part of London literary and social life in the later 1830s and 1840s.

Unlike traditional small towns or villages, Camberwell and New Cross, for all the distinctiveness of their suburban life, were by their very nature not isolated or self-contained societies but communities that opened out onto the much larger world of London, and London itself, long the disproportionate metropolis of all of Britain and growing quickly into its later Victorian position as the greatest city of Europe, opened further, by a thousand passages of politics or commerce, onto all of England and the world.

Until Browning began to take his own part in the life of London, his connection with this larger world was of course primarily through his family's business affairs in London. Although not an important official, Browning's father, even as a clerk in the Bank of England, had daily contact with the affairs of one of the most important national and international organizations in England. From boyhood, Browning would have had some sense, however vague, of the larger workings of government and business in nineteenth-century Britain. His father, as Browning himself concluded in a tribute to him at the time of his death, hardly knew, "what vanity or ambition or the love of money or social influence meant," and he clearly tried to bring as little of the Bank and its far-flung affairs home with him as was compatible with doing his job.[172] Browning, however, was not merely the son of one recalcitrant clerk; he was born into a whole family connected with banks and international finance. Even had his father never mentioned his profession he would have heard a good deal about business and the ways of the world from his other relatives.

Robert Browning the grandfather, truly a man of substance in the financial world of the City, came in later years to some working understanding with his (to him) no-account son and sometimes consented to see his family. Through him, Browning probably came to know something of the aims and manners of the City. He was more familiar with his uncles, the half-brothers of his father, Reuben and William Shergold Browning. Both men, through the influence of Browning's grandfather, had positions with the House of Rothschild, already a firm of European dimensions and of enormous importance in international finance and politics. Both combined their father's serious concern with banking and finance with the more humane and scholarly interests of their older half brother. William Shergold Browning served in Rothschild's Paris office from 1824 to 1845. He managed at the same time to establish a modest literary reputation as the author of a *History of the Huguenots,* two historical novels or fictionalized histories, and a collection of miscellaneous essays, poems, and tales. For years, too, he contributed articles to the *Gentleman's Magazine,* and he knew many of the French historians and academicians of his day.

Reuben Browning had a position in the London office of Rothschild's at New Court. Unlike Browning's father, he took his profession quite seriously and came in time to be an authority on financial affairs. He published a number of books under such titles as *The Finances of Great Britain Considered,* or *Reflections on the Currency.* Some long and technical letters preserved in the British Library show that he was well enough esteemed by the 1850s for Gladstone himself to appeal to him concerning the advisability of a new government annuity. For all his competence in his profession he was, unlike his own more rigid father, a man of broad culture and learning. In this he seems to have followed his half-brother—twenty-one years his elder—upon whom he looked with "regard and admiration," almost as a second father.[173]

With both uncles Browning was on friendly, even close terms, and their influence, especially the examples they offered of different ways of life were particularly important to him. Just as the older Reuben, brother of Browning's grandfather, had helped and encouraged Browning's father, and Browning's father, in turn, had acted as a friendly older brother to William and Reuben, so they took a special interest in their talented young nephew. Of the two, William was somewhat less close to Browning only because he lived in Paris from Browning's twelfth year on. Yet Browning knew him well enough to speak of him as a favorite uncle. No doubt he was often home on business or vacation and then saw his nephew. At least once, in 1837, he entertained Browning in Paris, introducing him, in Cousin Cyrus Mason's pompous language, to "congenial society."[174] Although Cyrus tried here to uncover yet another smouldering family grievance against him for mistreatment of kinsfolk, Browning seems in fact to have maintained a very friendly relation with this uncle, even to the point of honoring him by keeping a plaster bust of him after his death.[175] Nothing in William's life or writing suggests that he was a man of genius, but he was, like so many of Browning's close relatives, a person of considerable talent and accomplishment. In many ways his influence on Browning would simply reinforce that of Browning's father. Linguist and antiquary, he too was a prodigious amateur scholar and regular poker into the odd corners of history.[176] He never lost an opportunity of inspecting old ruins or tombs, and he speaks in one of his novels with romantic enthusiasm of the antiquarian temperament that is in "constant communion with the men of other days."[177] Yet even aside from his greater enthusiasm for business, he was in far greater touch with his times than was his elder brother. In Paris he came to know and mix with important men of the intellectual and political world. His historical study of the Huguenots, though outdated today, was a work of considerable scholarship and intellectual detachment on a subject still quite controversial: the right of French Protestants to full religious liberty.[178] Even his novels, though now unread and never reprinted in his time, show him to have been quite up on contemporary literary fashions. *Hoel Morvan* (1844), a not unreadable novel in three volumes about the times of Henry the Fifth, follows obviously on the vogue for the historical novel initiated by Walter Scott. Although he creates a sprawling plot, William is interesting in his analysis of political motives and he has a genuine ability to capture a wide world of experience. He gives life to a Hollywood-style range of characters from two different cultures, French and English, and from virtually every social class, from Falstaffian gangs to churchmen and royalty. Like his greater contemporaries in the Victorian novel, he seems a man of the world speaking to us from a wide and open knowledge of life.

Perhaps more important to Browning than anything William wrote was the mere fact that he actually finished what he wrote and really did publish. When Reuben set out to write a memoir of Browning's father he could find no more fitting motto than one from Gray's "Elegy": "Full many a gem of purest ray serene."[179] With all his reading and knowledge, with all his talent and leisure time Browning's father seemed to have no need to be other than a self-pleasing scribbler, publicly mute and happily inglorious. William is today no less unknown, but he at least took an active part in the intellectual and literary life of his day. To Browning he was, if no model of literary excellence, "a bookmaking man," someone at the least forcefully engaged in the business at which Browning would spend his life.[180] To his nephew he talked about his problems with publishers and probably offered practical suggestions as well as intellectual encouragement. Browning sent him copies of his works and he in turn gave public testimony of his support for his young relative.[181] Mediocre but kind "Lines Addressed to the Author of 'Paracelsus' on hearing of the success of 'Strafford' " in a book of occasional efforts, *Leisure Hours* (1841), celebrated Browning's success in *Paracelsus* and *Strafford:*

> With joy we heard the praise your talent earned,
> When *Paracelsus* opened on our view;
> The germ of sterling genius was discerned—
> And by *The Earl of Strafford* we have learned,
> The augury was just—the judgment true.

The judgment seems, indeed, premature. How many uncles would be ready to proclaim their nephews geniuses in public? Later, in *Hoel Morvan,* he even went so far as to use quotations from *Paracelsus* twice as mottoes for chapters, placing Browning in the company of Scott, Byron, Shakespeare, Homer, Pope, and Shelley.[182]

To this fortunate nephew, Uncle Reuben was equally supportive and a good deal more accessible. In the early 1840s he even lived with his mother in Albert Terrace close by the Brownings, but all through Browning's early life he was close enough for frequent visits. Only nine years older than Browning, he was as much an older brother as an uncle and a natural person for Browning to model himself upon. Like William, he also integrated unworldly bookishness with an active participation in the life of his time. At his death a friend eulogized him for just this mixture of qualities. "He had the soul of a gentleman, and the temperament of a philosopher. In the midst of practical pursuits, he never lost sight of the highest aims; and moving in the world, he preserved the purity of his nature intact."[183] Indeed, anyone who troubles to dig out his polemics on financial subjects will find not dull technical treatises but eloquent pleas in which bank acts and interest percents stand next to citations from Aristotle, Plato, Lycurgus, Bishop Berkeley, or Locke. He seems to have had virtually as wide a general knowledge as Browning's father, with whom he loved to discuss historical matters over dinner. He knew Latin, Greek, French, Spanish, Portuguese, and German: Latin so well that an inscription he did for an inkstand given by the clerks to a daughter of the Rothschilds attracted the admiration of Disraeli;[184] French so casually that William would sometimes write him in French from the Paris office of Rothschild's. He also shared the family talent at painting.[185] Like William, he nonetheless never retreated from the world into his reading and hobbies. His work at Rothschild's brought him into contact with an international world of men of affairs and intellect. His daughter recalled that he frequently entertained French visitors. Because he spoke French like a native, he probably served as his firm's official host.[186] His financial writings, both under his own name and in letters to the *Daily Telegraph* under the anonym of Brutus Brittanicus, were as much political acts as works of technical study. He attacked the endowment of privilege by the government and, identifying himself with the reform movement generated by the Corn Law agitation of the 1840s, tried to get at some of the reasons why rigid adherence to a gold standard tended to aggravate the severity of periodic depressions in the economy.

If he was finally no Keynes, he had much of Keynes's breadth of interest and experience. During the 1820s and 1830s when he was still a young man finding his way in his own career, he seems to have fulfilled many of his ambitions toward literature and the arts by supporting his nephew. Like William, he no doubt gave Browning the helpful impression that he could not only enjoy intellectual and literary talents but actually find public expression, even perhaps recognition, for them. Indeed, he seems to have somewhat spoiled Browning. Even usually dyspeptic Cousin Cyrus calls him "our ever generous cousin Reuben." Browning himself, in 1858, named him without exaggeration "the kindest and best friend to me this many a long day."[187] From him came gifts of books—a translation of Horace's *Odes* by Christopher Smart (possibly a sympathetic aid from a former schoolboy to a neophyte) and later a fancy edition of Epictetus also inscribed, "the gift of his Uncle, Reuben Browning," and printed on silk pages.[188] After 1840, Reuben's "good horse York," stabled at the Brownings at New Cross, was left to Browning to exercise and generally treat as his own: to canter furiously, dreaming of rides from Aix to Ghent and only succeeding in startling poor Cousin Cyrus. On dim authority, Cyrus even asserts that Reuben provided money for Browning's honeymoon voyage to

Italy with Elizabeth.[189] Certainly Browning drew very heavily on Reuben's kindness throughout his life, if not also on his bank account, for he used him extensively as a personal banker and a financial counselor.[190]

Reuben's greatest aid was his generosity of spirit. He was a frequent visitor and companion to Browning—so much so that Browning ascribed his tendency to loud talking as "a trick caught from having often to talk with a deaf relative of mine," namely Reuben, whose hearing had been damaged from early life by an accident with a cricket ball.[191] A good-tempered man with a kind and agreeable expression, Reuben would drop by Browning's study—in fact does so in the midst of one letter to Elizabeth[192]—for chats about literature or general conversation. He and Browning had or developed a great number of interests in common. According to family tradition, Reuben not only had a passion for literature and the classics but even shared the Browning family's enthusiasm for the world of insects, animals, and plants.[193] Reuben was indeed something of an enthusiast for anything that caught his imagination. We can well imagine that his talk would have helped stimulate his nephew to think and aspire beyond the self-contented world he knew at home. In 1858, writing as a longtime resident of Italy, Browning recalled to his England-bound uncle the dreams of travel they had shared long before and which he, at least, had fulfilled: "I often think of your idea of going to Rome for one day only to see (I believe) St. Peter's, & the Coliseum & Pantheon."[194]

In even more important ways the nephew seems to have succeeded in living out the daydreams of his uncle. Reuben had a "terrific sense of fun," and a love for making friendly caricatures of friends and acquaintances.[195] He seems to have had a natural, if never more than amateur, love for entertainment and the theater. "He was extremely witty and often by himself entertained large company by his humorous tales, anecdotes and songs, imitating in a measure the mono-polylogues of the elder Charles Mathews whom he greatly admired."[196] Very likely his enthusiasm for objective theatrical entertainment helped to stimulate his nephew's interest in the drama and had a great deal to do with his serious ambition for a theatrical career. Charles Mathews's career as a comedian and entertainer was at its height in the 1820s, and it would seem likely that Reuben's interest in the theater was also strongest at that time, when he was still in his twenties. His example would certainly have reinforced the interest Browning took in school theatricals and independent reading in drama. Moreover, the uncle's lifelong enthusiasm for Mathews, and specifically for Mathews's "monopolylogues," suggests that his influence may have been working indirectly even in Browning's ultimate movement toward a dramatic form something short of full drama. For Mathews's forte as an actor was impersonation, mimicry, and parody.[197] Although he played over four hundred regular dramatic parts in his lifetime, his greatest success—and one which made him almost as famous in his time as a great tragedian like Edmund Kean—was in the revue-like "At Homes" of the 1820s. In these "comic annuals," put together loosely around some simple organizing theme, such as a description of Mathews's trip to America or a memorandum of folks he knew about London, Mathews would put on an incredibly varied one-man show. He would tell anecdotes, sing songs, recite poetry, and, above all, offer a remarkable series of very different, full characterizations or caricatures complete with rapid change of costume and makeup. The monopolylogues—mono-*polly*-logues, as Hood called them—were merely the distilled principle of Mathews's mastery at parroting. In a single skit he would take on as many as six characters, giving the impression not of a one-man show but of a society of diverse individuals. Although it is hard to strike a new spark into the outlines of the performances that have been printed and preserved, those who knew Mathews found him not merely a fine mimic but an actor who could bring alive the patterns of thought and feeling of an imagined character and create not merely a type but a believable individual.

In his enthusiasm for Mathews and for the kind of character-making Mathews might inspire, Reuben would naturally have offered his nephew an objective focus on a variety of personalities and characters similar to that in his father's cartoon series. Only, here the model was even closer, though by no means a simple parallel, to the dramatic monologue form Browning would ultimately settle on for his work. Browning claimed that a dramatic idea even lay behind the confessional poem *Pauline. Pauline* was to be the first in a series of poems that would be presented as so many creations by so many different persons—"a foolish plan . . . which had for its object the enabling me to assume and realize I know not how many different characters."[198] This idea, closer to a conception of a series of impersonations than to the dramatic monologue form, suggests that something like the work of Mathews may have been Browning's first inspiration for dramatic creation —a bridge from the monologue confession to the true dramatic monologue.

Reuben was a producing writer on financial matters; but he was still only a would-be writer of imaginative works. At Baylor there is even an amusing, if somewhat strange story of a Rothschild's (?) bank clerk named Cher who has died and now reports back to earth via the new celestial telegraph system on his court case before the pearly gates, and a letter of Browning's speaks of other stories, probably his.[199] He was certainly pleased and proud to have a relative who was a serious full-time writer and he gave Browning all the encouragement he could, though there is a report that one of the many good stories about the incomprehensibility of *Sordello* began with him. Mason lets us know indeed that none of the family could make much out of that work and did not hesitate to say so. Otherwise Reuben was a very warm supporter with perhaps a special bias toward Browning's dramatic efforts. When Browning's first play, *Strafford*, was put on in 1837 he even bought tickets for members of the family to go and cheer the work on. Later, he took the trouble to send Browning a report on *Colombe's Birthday*, when it was revived during his absence in Italy.[200] When, even later, he wrote, perhaps after a rereading, a favorable opinion of *A Blot in the*

'*Scutcheon,* Browning quite correctly thanked him, "you were always the most indulgent of my critics."[201] Except for *Pauline,* which he had from Browning's father, Reuben was regularly sent copies of his work by his nephew.[202] Like the members of the set, though over an even longer time, Reuben thus gave Browning a fine target to aim at in conceiving of his audience: a person not too quirkily learned or abstruse in his focus but witty, lively, fond of dramatic interplay, and broadly cosmopolitan in taste and mental culture.

"Robert," Elizabeth Barrett Browning wrote in 1848, "though a poet and dramatist by profession, being descended from the blood of all the Puritans and educated by the strictest of dissenters, has a sort of horror about the dreadful fact of owing five shillings five days, which I call quite morbid in its degree and extent, and which is altogether unpoetical according to the traditions of the world."[203] With his various family connections in banking it is perhaps no surprise that Browning should have been prone to keep his personal accounts with a bank clerk's care—even, in his later life, with a touch of avarice. Like his uncles, he could place highest value on affairs of the mind without slighting affairs in the mundane sense. When he gave an account book to his own son in the early 1860s, he was passing on the practical heritage of a family of bankers as if he were a comfortable City man. In it he wrote an "economic precept" rich in the traditions of banking and based on the *Sprichwort* of a famous financier of Queen Anne's time:

'Twas a saying of might with the great Mr Lowndes
Take care of the Pence and not care of the Pounds!
For the Pence may escape you,—light volatile elves:
But the full-bodied Pounds can take care of themselves.[204]

Banker's ways with a penny were only an incidental of Browning's family background. More important, was a sense that he, like his relatives, could deal easily in the terms of the world with the world—the world, that is, of finance and business that was quickly becoming one of the greatest forces, if not the greatest, in Victorian society. Repeatedly we find him, with altogether unpoetical assurance, asserting his confidence in his ability to rise, if he so chose, like any minion of fortune and worm of the hour, to a conventional position of wealth and power. "I have never been at all frightened of the world, nor mistrustful of my power to deal with it, and get my purpose out of it if once I thought it worth while," he wrote Elizabeth Barrett in 1845.[205] In another letter he boasts, "I feel sure that whenever I make up my mind to that, I can be rich enough and to spare—because along with what you have thought *genius* in me, is certainly talent, what the world recognizes as such."[206] Browning might praise his father for being "a perfectly unworldly, good man,—not so much disinterested as without the notion of self-interest" and for not having "a touch of ambition, even a spice of vanity."[207] He himself, even while rejecting banking for a career as a poet, seems in many ways closer to the self-reliant confidence of success of his grandfather or uncles than to the simple unworldliness of his father. Here again, there are the complicated cross relations of three generations of highly talented Robert Brownings. After his father's extreme reaction against worldly success in preference for a life centered on private cultivation and hobbies, Browning would revert to some of the worldly robustness of his grandfather while affirming in a larger way the wider culture and humanity of his father.

Whether Browning really did have, as he boasted to his prosperous, elder friend John Kenyon, "a very particular capacity for being rich, like Chaucer's monk 'to ben an Abbot able,' " is another question and in some ways an irrelevant one.[208] Kenyon, at least, took him at his word and entrusted him with a large legacy in his will, and Browning's business letters to his Uncle Reuben in later years suggest the concern and interest that he applied to his own financial affairs (but also suggest a large element of dependence on Reuben). It is, in any case, one thing to manage an inheritance and another thing to make a way in the world from scratch. From his early years when he lived on his father's generosity, to the years when he shared with his wife her modest income, till later life when he lived in prosperity on Kenyon's bequest, Browning was—fortunately or not—never really forced to put his powers of getting on to a test. But, however great or small Browning's untapped abilities as a financier or worldly administrator may have been, what matters is that he felt himself competent as a man among the men of his age and that, in choosing to devote himself to literature, he considered not that he was unsuited to the more usual pursuits of his time but that he could serve a more significant role as a writer and poet.

To his family connections Browning also owed a certain cosmopolitanism, even internationalism, quite alien to poets like Wordsworth or Tennyson of English country backgrounds. Both the Bank of England and the House of Rothschild were banks heavily concerned in European and international finance and trade. With his father, grandfather, and uncles closely connected to these centers of communication between England and other countries, with one uncle permanently located in the Paris office of Rothschild's, and with both closely in touch with French people and culture, Browning was, from childhood, exposed to interests and concerns that extended beyond London or England to the world at large. Like many middle-class children of the more internationally oriented Europe of the twentieth century, Browning was given special education in modern languages. French and Italian were provided through private tutoring. German was at least begun at The London University in 1828 and taken up fitfully at later times. In the early 1830s Browning even made an attempt at Spanish.[209] Browning became quite a good speaker of at least French and Italian. This stress upon acquisition of foreign languages gave him, as we shall see, the invaluable opportunity to acquire a knowledge of the literary culture of

France, Italy, and even, in part, Germany. But his contact with other countries even went beyond acquaintance with recognized foreign literature. At a time when Paris was as clearly the world center of fashion and culture as London was of finance and trade, Browning followed the cultural and literary life of France with a real and immediate involvement. In a letter to a female friend, Fanny Haworth, we find him recommending *Le Siècle* (for serializing Balzac), a magazine that he read as regularly as any London one: "I receive it from Paris two days old and usually post it off to a friend of mine, as soon as skimmed."[210]

His family associations and connections abroad put him naturally in a position to make friends with persons from other countries. Probably through his Uncle William's literary association in Paris he was put in touch with a French writer and journalist, a M. Desplace, whom Browning, to judge by one of his letters, invited home to dinner.[211] The Rothschild connection probably also procured him an introduction to some "Italian friends," a Countess Carducci and her husband, whom he visited in 1844 at Rome and who returned the visit in London, putting Browning in repayment through a good deal of "weariful sight seeing."[212]

But the most important friendship Browning owed to his family connections abroad is also most typical of the kind of international culture that he shared. This was with a certain French youth four years older than Browning, the Count Amédée de Ripert-Monclar, called simply Monclar. The London Brownings were introduced to him through Uncle William's friendship with Monclar's uncle, the French historian and scholar, the Marquis de Fortia d'Urban, a Paris neighbor of William's with whom he shared an interest in historical research.[213] Although an aristocrat with legitimate claims to a high social position in his native Provence, Monclar had a background very similar to Browning's. Through his uncle he was in close touch with the intellectual and scholarly life of France. His own title derived from the practical financial and legal work of his ancestor Jean Pierre François, first Marquis de Monclar.[214] Like Browning, Monclar seems to have been drawn between the two paths that opened naturally before him: a literary and scholarly career or a practical one in finance and law. Even when Browning first met him he was by avocation a competent lithographer and something of an author; yet he had also held public office in Avignon from 1828 until 1830 when the new government of Louis-Philippe drove him into opposition and even, for a while, into jail. His choice ultimately would be for a practical career, though like Browning's uncles he would not cease to dabble in art and letters and would continue to indulge his literary instincts by publishing works on finance.[215] Particularly at the time when Uncle Reuben astutely introduced Browning to him as a person who could bring him up on political and literary matters in England, the two were as well suited to each other's interests as people from different cultures can be.

Beginning in 1834, Monclar spent a number of summers in England (1834 and 1837 certainly, and possibly others in between). He was there to

Count Amédée de Ripert-Monclar, ca. 1830-1837. Engraving by Joseph Chaix. *Browning's French friend in the 1830s: aristocrat, citizen of the world, writer on finance, lover of the Midi and Italy: "my fine fellow Monclar—one lithograph—his own face of faces."*

Reuben Browning, ca. 1872. Photo. *Browning's uncle—banker, author, amateur of literature and the theater: "the kindest and best friend to me this many a long day."*

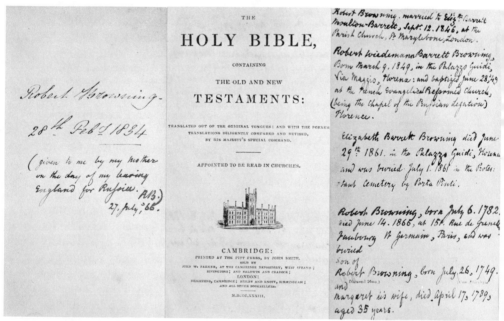

Inscriptions by Robert Browning and His Mother Sarah Anna Browning in the Bible Given Him on His Departure for Russia, February 1834. *Fly with inscription; title page; verso of title with family dates entered by Browning later.*

expand his horizons generally, to improve his English among the natives, and, we are told, to play a modest Scarlet Pimpernelian role as an agent between the French Royalists and the Bourbon refugees of 1830.[216] Monclar's journal of his first "Voyage à Londres, 1834," a careful but none too intimate record of places seen, people met, expenses incurred, at least gives us a record of his ripening friendship with the Browning family.[217] Monclar arrived in London July 20 and settled at 49 Warwick Street, in what he considered the most fashionable area of London. He proceeded to look up connections, including Reuben Browning and Lady Blessington, visit the recommended sights, examine bookshops and printshops, attend an occasional show of Turner watercolors or the theater, wander about the city, and keep a sharp eye out for good looking girls. Robert called once on Monclar, missed him, and left a card. Finally he found him in on August 1. We may be sure that the two, united across nationalities by their similar backgrounds and shared interests, took very quickly to each other. Only to his family and to a very few friends—Domett, his critical supporters W. J. Fox and John Forster, or to Elizabeth Barrett—did Browning choose to disclose his authorship of *Pauline.* Yet Monclar must have been told about it in this first meeting. His journal concludes that Robert is both "aimable" and "homme d'imagination" and expresses a hope to see his poem. Eventually Browning gave him a copy of *Pauline* and even wrote him a long and important letter detailing the history of his artistic development.[218]

A week and a half after the first interview Browning pursued the acquaintance by another call—this time with an invitation to dinner at Camberwell. On August 15 they met by arrangement at the British Museum and Browning led Monclar out to Hanover Cottage. Monclar's journal gives us a rare and genial glimpse of the Brownings at home. Mr. Browning showed the visitor his collection of the works of Junius and amused him with some of his sketches, done "avec une très grande rapidité." Mrs. Browning seemed the soul of goodness. Sarianna called for special attention in the journal for her striking dark hair and eyes and her ladylike accomplishments. Nothing is said of the English cooking, but the evening was clearly a pleasant one. They played music, sang together, drew together: "Elle a été fort agréable." A second and third family evening, September 4 and 14, evoked further complimentary descriptions of the excellent parents, the world of prints and curiosities, and the charming daughter. In sum, he concluded, "Cette famille me plaît extrêmement." Meanwhile Monclar and Robert were becoming close friends. They planned a trip together to the Dulwich Gallery. Robert visited Monclar virtually every other day during the rest of his two-month stay. Monclar calls him "le meilleur jeune homme." Robert in turn seems "extrêmement affectueux." Even when account is taken of the more demonstrative friendships between young men in Victorian times and in French culture, it is clear that Monclar and Browning were becoming quite close acquaintances. The friendship was continued by letter after Monclar returned to Paris September 17. Browning's letters, though not as intimate as those to Domett and always aware of a barrier of language between them, are warm and sometimes quite personal in subject.[219] They are filled with injunctions to Monclar to write and scoldings when he doesn't. At least once, in June-August 1837, the friendship was warmly renewed before both began to drift apart in the 1840s. Monclar's journal of this second visit records more pleasant family evenings, a night together seeing Macready at the Haymarket Theatre, and Browning's sitting to him for his portrait.[220] Browning still speaks very affectionately: "I don't know that I shall leave town for a month," he wrote another friend, "my friend Monclar looks piteous when I talk of such an event. I can't bear to leave him."[221]

Perhaps with the aid of a Berlitz-style *Guide of English and French Conversation for the Use of Travellers and Students*, the two friends managed to enrich personal friendship with substantial communication across cultures.[222] It has been said that their acquaintance even bore direct fruit in Browning's poetic career by immediately influencing his next work in poetry after *Pauline*: that is, that Monclar was the person who suggested the life of the Renaissance physician Paracelsus to him as a subject for a long poem.[223] The suggestion is neither confirmed nor denied by the evidence in Monclar's journals and in Browning's letters to Monclar, though it is clear that Browning did his own research and wrote the work quite apart from Monclar. Perhaps it was as much for his general willingness to share his ideas as for any specific direction that Browning dedicated the work, as promised, and with more than a touch of affection, "To the Comte A. de Ripert-Monclar by His Affectionate Friend." Monclar later took the trouble to do a detailed *analyse du texte*, which he presented to Browning for comment. He must have been at least planning a critical article on the poem.[224] Even when they were losing contact in the 1840s Browning continued to send Monclar copies of his works.[225]

Whatever Monclar's direct effect on Browning's career, his general impact on Browning's developing interests and expanding view of the world was perhaps even more important. In his letters as well as in their personal acquaintance in London we find Browning introducing Monclar to contemporary British culture. In return, while Browning admonished him to keep working at his English, told him of contemporary English literature such as Bulwer's *The Last Days of Pompeii* or the work of the Young Disraeli, and discussed his own work with him, Monclar gave Browning a firsthand report on the literary and intellectual world of Paris. Browning would make Monclar draw pictures of French writers he had seen in Paris such as Hugo or George Sand.[226] His letters to Monclar are full of references to Hugo, Dumas père, or Lamartine. When Browning spoke slightingly of Balzac, Monclar knew enough to correct him and perhaps stimulated Browning to the more serious consideration he would give the Promethean novelist in the next few years.[227]

Association with Monclar also gave Browning some contact with the

French scholarly world of his uncle. Browning evidently helped his friend find a place to publish an English review of a work by the Marquis de Fortia d'Urban,[228] and he seems to have taken a serious interest in other works by Monclar's prolific uncle.[229] Although Browning read Fortia's works—for instance his history of Hannibal crossing the Alps—with interest, they made finally no more permanent impression on him than they did on nineteenth-century historiography. But Browning was at least put in touch with a vigorous foreign world of scholarship and thought. The aged and eminent Fortia, with whom his nephew resided in a villa with a magnificent library in the Rue de Rochefoucauld in Paris, was a member of more than twenty learned societies in France and the rest of Europe.[230] Through him Monclar and Browning both joined the newly formed Institut Historique along with some luminaries such as Thierry and Michelet.[231] If the connection was merely a formal one, it at least gave Browning a feeling of being part of a European intellectual community. In Fortia's work and in his ideas as retailed by his nephew and future biographer, Browning could find something similar to his own father's encyclopedic breadth of learning coupled with more persevering and serious effort. Although a Catholic and moderate royalist, Fortia touched on many of the most important intellectual concerns of the coming age. His persistent work toward accurate historical chronologies led him to at least wonder about the age of the earth, especially as it was illuminated by studies of ancient China and Egypt.[232] Though he took an integrationist stand against the work of Wolf on Homer, he was actively involved in the stirrings of higher textual criticism on the Bible as well as Homer.[233] His efforts, however fragmentary his achievement, suggested a comprehensive approach to history, moving, as his nephew saw it, toward an epic of civilization and the progress of humanity.[234]

The nephew of "one of the patriarchs of French literature"[235] thus turned Browning further toward an awareness of a general European intellectual life. The young count and man of the world was even more influential in introducing Browning to a more immediate, if far more superficial, sophistication. What we know of Monclar—his royalist background, financial acumen, literary avocation, talent as an artist, love of travel, even his courage in opposition to Louis-Philippe and his ultimate fate as a martyr in the siege of Paris—all suggests that he was both a cultivated young aristocrat and a gentleman of the world. Even the report that he, on second thought, tried archly to discourage Browning from writing about Paracelsus because there was no love interest and love, he averred, was a subject about which every young man thought he had something to say, helps fill in this picture.[236] Certainly Monclar's journals show him acutely aware of the attractions of the women he met in London. The portrait of Monclar by Joseph Chaix, which Browning kept in his album, shows similarly a vigorous and energetic person, not insensitive but tuned to the tempo of the active world.[237] Browning seems to have admired, even for a time doted, on Monclar's strong but sympathetic personality. Then, in relating to him, he seems to have been encouraged to develop by emulation a knowing, somewhat detached and modish, if not quite dandiacal pose. His letters to Monclar, even more strained in their attempt at sophistication than his other, usually embarrassed, early correspondence, suggest the direction of Monclar's influence.[238] Browning goes out of his way to add wise comments on the politics of the day, holding up both the Duke of Wellington and his opponent radicals to the cold light of humorous intellectual analysis. Bentham, a writer of whom one would otherwise suppose Browning had never heard, is mentioned more than once with light irony because his big books on legislation had been of special interest to Monclar, as indeed they were to many other non-Englishmen at the time. Browning refers vaguely to happy summer excursions in Walworth and Regent Street, and we can imagine the country rambler turned *boulevardier* and fashionable *flâneur* under his older friend's influence. As with the young Matthew Arnold after him, France and French connections would bring out the worldly sophisticate in Browning. In writing to Monclar Browning tries to speak not as an Englishman to a Frenchman but as one European gentleman to another. He compliments Paris on its hospitality to strangers; he admits that England has its green beauty but expresses his preference for Spain and the South, and for the Romance languages over German.[239] Monclar's son even claimed for Monclar much of the honor of inspiring Browning with his lifelong love of the South and Italy.[240] Coming from the Midi, Monclar had picked up Italian almost as a native tongue and even knew many of the different Italian dialects. He was a connoisseur of Mediterranean culture and his enthusiasm certainly must have communicated itself to his younger and still impressionable friend.

As a final indication of his impact on Browning we have Monclar's own vision of his friend. When he took up a pencil in 1837 he captured Browning in the way he must have most often seen him, in a haughty, almost fierce and rakish pose, closer to the model for a French or Italian aristocrat than for a middle-class English gentleman.[241]

Along with international friendships, travel abroad—formerly the prerogative of aristocracy and rank—was open to the clever son of a London bank clerk as well as to the Parisian aristocrat. In fact, though railway service was only just beginning during Browning's young adult life, and other methods of conveyance—stage or sailing ship—made international travel long and wearying, travel abroad hardly seems to have been considered extraordinary or even particularly unusual in the Browning family. At one point in the long series of visits and letters that constituted his courtship of Elizabeth, Browning confessed that he had been in a "mortal fright—for my uncle came in the morning to intreat me to go to Paris in *the evening* about some urgent business of his." Significantly, it was not the suddenness of this departure for a different country that frightened Browning. It was the fear lest he might be forced to miss his regular day for visiting Elizabeth, and he calmed himself by a glance at the timetables: "I calculated times, and found I could be at Paris to-morrow, and back again, *certainly* by Wednesday—and so not lose you on that day—Oh, the fear I had!"[242]

This particular jump over to Paris and back turned out to be unnecessary. Earlier in life, with less to hold his attention in England, Browning had had extensive opportunities to become acquainted with people and ways of life outside of England. In 1837, and very possibly at other times, there was the visit to Paris with Uncle William and a chance to meet William's French friends as well as to visit the usual sights of the city. Then in 1838, ostensibly traveling under the aegis of a Rothschild's freight shipment to Venice, he made in effect a three-month grand tour of Europe, sailing in April to Trieste and Venice and proceeding from there through Northern Italy, Innsbruck and the Tyrol, to Munich, Frankfort, Cologne, Antwerp and back to England by July.[243] In the fall of 1844 he completed his tour with a circuit of Southern Italy, Naples, Rome, Florence, and Pisa. Both trips, and of course the fifteen years of life abroad with Elizabeth after 1846, contributed to make him feel at ease as a citizen of the world. But, by the time of the trips to Italy, Browning, already twenty-six in 1838, had more serious interests than merely seeing the world. In 1838 he saw his trip as field research for that long poem, *Sordello*, on the life of the Italian troubadour. In 1844 he was deepening his knowledge of a country to which he felt increasingly drawn as both inspiration and theater of some of his finest imaginations.

Although his later experience of Italy had a far deeper and more lasting impact on his character and work, his first trip out of England, a journey made at the end of February 1834 with a Russian embassy to the capital St. Petersburg, had probably a greater immediate effect on the young man. The expedition seems to have been only a very routine one, a mission to negotiate a large Rothschild's loan of 1822. But to a man of twenty-two this was romance enough. Browning, probably as a kind of undersecretary to the Russian Chevalier George de Benkhausen,[244] was thrown suddenly into the company of grown men of international affairs. With his mother's parting gift of a small Bible packed carefully somewhere in his luggage,[245] he found himself speeding by packet and then by a relentless succession, day and night, of stages, to an entirely unknown and still largely primitive country. Browning destroyed the letters he wrote home to his family, but it is not hard to imagine his excitement at the procession of strange scenes, people, and languages that passed as his carriage moved through the Low Lands, across Germany and the plains of Prussia to Lithuania and up along the coast of the Baltic Sea to the Russian capital.[246] Snatches of the experience he remembered and recorded here and there: snowdrops (flowers) seen at Tilsit in Prussia,[247] the endless Russian woods, which he evokes in "A Forest Thought" and more solemnly and majestically in his late poem "Ivàn Ivànovitch" (*Dramatic Idyls*, 1879), the gay peasant life at St. Petersburg. As his father might have, he went about the city on the lookout for scenes worth rendering. A sketch of three Russians lounging outside a building—possibly one of many others—was sent home to his family.[248] Other impressions were hoarded up in memory and even led eventually to some scenes for a play. "It was Russian, and about a fair on the Neva, and booths and droshkies and fish-pies and so forth, with the Palaces in the background."[249]

He was struck by the finery of the Russian court and flattered Elizabeth years later by likening her to "the Queen-diamond they showed me in the crown of the Czar."[250] He had a chance too to observe the surface suavity of diplomatic life. He remembered seeing Sir James Wylie, English physician to the court of Nicholas. The doctor must have made the young man smart with his cool indifference: "He chose to mistake me for an Italian—'M. l'Italien' he said another time, looking up from his cards."[251] We are told, as well, that he met a Russian diplomat by the name of Waring and was impressed enough by his romantic life to use his name for the poem in which he drew the fancy portrait of his own roving and romantic friend, Domett.[252]

Browning's satisfaction with this first introduction to the romance and sophistication of the international world of diplomacy was evidently so great that for a time he seriously considered a career in diplomacy.[253] Although there is no evidence as to how he came to meet Benkhausen, it would seem almost certain that the connection had been through one of his uncles at Rothschild's, probably William.[254] His father was also probably quite sympathetic to the idea of a diplomatic career. Browning applied in 1835 for appointment to another mission, this time to Persia, and this time for the English government.[255] When this application failed, he slowly lost interest in the idea of a diplomatic career, then forgot it altogether as he became increasingly involved as a young poet in the literary life of London. It is an indication of the seriousness of his original intention, however, that the idea was never entirely lost. In 1846 he was thought of as a possible secretary for another mission to St. Petersburg, a mission of humanity led by Moses Montefiore, to plead against a decree injurious to Russian Jews.[256] Deep in his own affairs with Elizabeth, Browning rather coolly turned this offer down. But after his marriage, motivated by his concern for the future of Italy and probably by the feeling that he should have an occupation, he went so far as to ask his influential friend Monckton Milnes to put his name in for the position of secretary to an embassy then contemplated to the Pope. Noting his full command of Italian and adding his frank opinion of his own worth—"many circumstances embolden me to think few others could do so well"—he offered "to work like a horse in my vocation."[257] A mission was never sent and Browning remained with only one profession to the end of his life. Still, even in later life the career of diplomat, combining the adventure of other countries and ways of life with the social position of an authoritative man of the world, held a real appeal. Much later, with equally little practical issue, the idea was reborn in his paternal meddling with his son's choice of career.[258]

Although Browning himself never did enter into the kind of career—in international banking or diplomacy—for which at least part of his family background seemed to have prepared him, the experience that his family connections opened to him in youth and early manhood left a lasting impression on his character and work. This was partly a matter of manners and surface culture. Not only did Browning strike those he met as far from the usual type of "damned literary man," but there was even something in his manner and attitude that seemed foreign or overly sophisticated. To those who knew him in early manhood there was even a hint of dandyism in his appearance. There was Carlyle's early impression from Browning's clothes—the "smart green" riding-costume—that the young man was probably a fellow fit only for "the turf and scamphood." Mrs. Bridell-Fox, daughter of Browning's early literary supporter, W. J. Fox, recalled meeting him in the 1830s: "just a trifle of a dandy, addicted to lemon-coloured kid-gloves and such things: quite the 'glass of fashion and the mould of form.' "[259] In Paris in 1837, as in Russia in 1834, he was taken for a visiting Italian.[260] In later years dandyism faded into a more solidly founded social maturity and even real urbanity as Browning, after years of residence in Italy, came back to London to become the most dined-out and socially available of poets. By then his cosmopolitanism and hint of foreignness might seem a virtue rather than a vice, a redeeming grace on the otherwise respectable poet. Arnould noted that Browning, though he might move "in high, the best, London society . . . has not, and never had, any of the English hard and brusque arrogance about him—on the contrary, was Italian and diplomatic in his courteousness."[261] Nonetheless, the foreign air was still a noticeable aspect of his social personality.

At a deeper level of personality, as well, Browning's early cosmopolitan experience and sense of competence in the great world left a clear impression on him. Henry James remarked after Browning's death that he seemed strangely both the least English and the most English of poets.[262] A warmly patriotic Englishman, a man with a deep respect for the quirky, eccentric character of English life as he knew it in the life of Camberwell or through friends like old Captain Pritchard, a lover of the English countryside, and a man deeply rooted in the evangelical Protestantism of the English nineteenth century, Browning yet came to make continental Europe—Spain, France, Germany, and especially Italy and the Italian character (or characters)—his peculiar poetic province. He may often bring recognizably English or Protestant values into his poems; yet the perspective is finally that of a poetic citizen of the world: a man who has known all classes of men and many different lands and who can make each man speak in his own national or cultural idiom as well as through his own personality. English his work and poetic character may finally be, but it is an Englishness made up of the urbanity and worldly sophistication of his family connections in international affairs as much as of the inner and personal cultivation of his parents' quiet domestic life at Camberwell or New Cross.

At the worst, such cosmopolitanism could make Browning, sometimes like Byron at *his* worst, a mere well-traveled worldling, sometimes like the clerkly side of T. S. Eliot, a poetic parody of a banker. At best, it allowed him to walk with more assurance in that narrow region between unconscious participation in the life of his time and alienation from it where a poet can make art about other men and society and not merely about his own personal experience. Other Victorian poets, with far less sense of personal connection with the active forces of their time—Tennyson, for instance—might attain some of their greatest artistic triumphs in expressing or overcoming their sense of alienation from the age. Although Browning was never to be the opposite, a mere happy child of his time, he had acquired from his earliest experience the habit of looking without as well as within. If he too was sometimes a prey to that sense of the isolated, only too sensitive self, which is at once the precondition and the price of intensified inner awareness, he also had the antidote for it ready to hand. "I *would* travel, in your circumstances," he wrote an unidentified friend suffering in 1874 from serious fits of mental depression, "& see the world, its troubles and sorrows,—also see its resources, refusing none of its various ways of 'ministering to a mind diseased' . . . Don't be above amusement, the relief through change & novelty,—the common way-side diversions from too active a self-consciousness."[263] As a ministry to a diseased mind such a formula may seem both too simple and too common a prescription. Yet, if not the whole answer, it was the answer that would be given again and again by writers who felt the burden of excessive inner preoccupation and morbid sensitivity. To some—Stevenson, Kipling, Hemingway, for instance—the solution was merely adventure or travel, an escape from the force of inner feeling into the romance of real life or real life taken as a romance. To Clough or T. S. Eliot, there were the forbidden delights of play and playfulness, even the joys of a little sordid luxury or elegance. To others like Carlyle, Meredith, Hardy, even Yeats or Joyce, there was the reviving immersion in simple, attainable realities outside the self: the resolve in *Sartor* to make or do something, the movement in *Ulysses* from the overwhelming process of consciousness to the uric smell of burning mutton kidney. Or there was what Browning emphasizes the most here, the attained sense of identity with the human lot everywhere, the hope of Keats's later poetry, the achievement of Dickens or George Eliot at their greatest. Wherever the stress might fall, the essential thing was involvement beyond the self: the awakened mind put to use on the world rather than left to stare vacantly within.

If many of these doors beyond the self were from the beginning opened to Browning by his early life and environment, he had still, both in youth and throughout his life, the greater problem: the problem of maintaining a working balance between inner and outer: the task of reaching a just mean between the extremes of excessive, inward-turned consciousness and superficial, emotionally vacant objectivity; the work of marrying subject to object, the self to the world.

VI
Art

Indeed, in a larger perspective the view of the external and social world that opened out to Browning in his early years—through his observations in Camberwell, through his early exposure to the world of his father's scholarship, through his friends from the suburbs of London, and through the financial and diplomatic connections of his father and uncles—forms a kind of opposing vector to his developing internal sense of self-awareness and self-consciousness. Taken in isolation, not one of Browning's early experiences, whether his excitement in exploring the natural world around Camberwell, or his participation in the domestic circle at home, or his part in the activities of the set, or even his adventure with the mission to St. Petersburg, stands out as unique or unusual. What is striking, however, is the range and breadth of experience to which his home environment and family social position exposed him.

In *Pauline* Browning found within himself "a principle of restlessness" that he inflated into almost a Faustian passion: "Which would be all, have, see, know, taste, feel, all." And in his next long poem, *Paracelsus*, he chose to study a man who would know all things. Yet if Browning's early experience did bring him a good deal of knowledge about men and the external forms of the world, the breadth of that experience was not the result of a disproportionate thirst to try all things and see all lands but a combination of external awareness and internal self-awareness and cultivation. There may indeed be a suggestion of the social experience and worldly knowledge of Browning's favorite Byron in his flirtation with international affairs and diplomacy; there may be a reminder of Wordsworth in his self-consciousness and immersion in the natural world around his suburban home; but taken as a whole his early life seems distinctive precisely because it encompasses so many types of experience, both domestic and social, natural and cosmopolitan, evangelical and sophisticated, internal and external, romantic and classical.

For the young man Browning, such a diversity of experience was to be both a burden and an opportunity. John Stuart Mill, reading Coleridge, Wordsworth, and other romantic writers after a strictly objective and intellectual upbringing, might find two cultures—the urbane, rational, practical culture of much of eighteenth-century England and the subjective, feeling-filled, self-conscious culture of the early nineteenth century—converging in battle within himself. But in Browning's experience both were present almost from the beginning of his life, and he would somehow have to find a reconciliation between them.

"My sympathies are very wide and general," Browning himself admitted to Elizabeth, "always have been—and the natural problem has been the giving unity to their object, concentrating them instead of dispersing."[1] The problem—set for Browning by the open, free, and even permissive nature of the family and suburban society in which he grew up and by the breadth of experiences, both inner and external, which were encompassed in his early years—was one that both critics and sympathizers would observe in Browning all his life. Most often it was put in terms of a division of head and heart. His early friend Eliza Flower, tired of Browning's more assertive ways as he grew older, complained in the late 1830s of his talking of "head and heart as two independent existences" and even wondered if he had a heart. Later, his sympathetic admirer, Edward Dowden, remarked to his friend and future wife, Elizabeth West, that Browning's strength of spirit preserved him from the danger of division in his nature: from the "complex intellect . . . perplexing his heart or moral nature."[2] T. S. Eliot was far more critical. In a famous comment in his essay on "The Metaphysical Poets" he blamed both Tennyson and Browning for failing to unify intellect and feeling: they "are poets and they think; but they do not feel their thought as immediately as the odor of a rose. A thought to Donne was an experience; it modified his sensibility . . . Tennyson and Browning ruminated." This is overstated, but the problem of unifying and focusing his inner and outer experience was certainly a real one for Browning. It was one that was developed by the circumstances of his youth, but it was not one that could finally be resolved within his family and boyhood environment, only through the experiences, actions, and major choices—whether of career, marriage, or settled beliefs—of adult life. In his poetry it would be a problem that would need solving in new terms in every successful work.

If he would have to go beyond his family environment to achieve any satisfactory reconciliation of these different aspects of his experience and personality, he, at least, unlike Mill, was given the opportunity from his earliest years to come to know intimately the forms of achieved order that other men, through their art, had given to their own experiences and perceptions. For appreciation of the arts, whether music, painting and drawing, or literature, was one other particularly prominent characteristic of Browning's early home life and environment. Probably even more than his other childhood experiences, his early and considerable exposure to the arts had a lifelong impact upon his adult personality and, of course, upon his life as a poet. Much as he might change both his artistic tastes and interests in later years, the experiences of early life laid the foundation for the deep and unfailing sense of the reality and significance of art which never left him throughout a long and often discouraging poetic career. Unlike many others who did then, or do in our age, share the sense of division and the need for concentration that he felt, Browning would seek to find some satisfactory unification not only in his own life but also through the special experience of artistic creation.

1 The Artistic Environment

For the Browning family the phrase "appreciation of the arts," with its suggestion of rather passive approval, is too mild. Cultivation of the arts, rather than the more usual concern for family security or social position, provided the center about which most family activities turned. To a large extent security and comfort were sought in this family, unlike that of Robert Browning the grandfather, not as ends in themselves but as preconditions for enjoyment of the arts. As they often have been in more prominent and successful middle-class families, the ambitions and capacities of a rising family were diverted from the pursuit of wealth to the pursuit of culture.

From Browning's earliest years the mere physical presence of works of art in the house must have given him an elemental sense of their reality. Mr. Browning was an addicted collector of prints. While his own taste, as we have seen, was especially for Hogarth and the Dutch school, he was not averse to picking up any picture that caught his fancy, and his prints were thrown together in large portfolios in a haphazard jumble. Browning whimsically complained to Elizabeth: "How some people use their pictures, for instance, is a mystery to me—very revolting all the same: portraits obliged to face each other for ever,—prints put together in portfolios . . my Polidoro's perfect Andromeda along with 'Boors Carousing,' by Ostade,—where I found her,—my own father's doing, or I would say more."[3] Whatever the propriety of that procedure, the portfolios brought a kind of miniature picture gallery into the Browning home where Robert could browse at his leisure. There were music manuscripts as well. At Wellesley College there is preserved a notebook ruled for music in which Browning's father carefully entered compositions or songs that he specially liked. And of course, there was the piano in the parlor, not set up for display but rather, like the modern television, serving as a kind of social center of the home.

Most important, there was—in the place of highest honor among all the thousands of volumes of history, philology, theology, and general reference in his father's collection—a wonderful reading library of the world's literature, classical, foreign, and English. As we have seen, Wanley's *Little World*, the *Biographie Universelle*, and scores of historical tracts and monographs helped open the boy's eyes to the storehouse of wonders in the objective world. But it was not those curious works, which are often overemphasized in accounts of Browning's early reading, but the works of Homer, Virgil, Horace, Shakespeare, or Milton that were most highly valued and most eagerly recommended to Browning by his scholarly father. Nor were the works of literature available to Browning confined to a selection of a few "great books." If, among the special prizes of father and son, there was an impressive and ever-growing collection of early editions of Milton, there was also room for a tremendous variety of lesser writers. Along with the wonders of the great classics, Browning was put in a position to learn to know and admire good minor works such as the Latin poetry of the Renaissance Scotsman, George Buchanan, or the "Fragments" of the early Romantic Henry Kirke White.[4]

Had his parents merely left him to pasture his mind at leisure on the little world of art and literature contained in their home, only given him that permission for which he was in any case so thankful, "to read nearly all sorts of books, in a well-stocked and very miscellaneous library," they would have done a great deal to develop Browning's awareness of the arts.[5] From merely being among books, seeing pictures, or regularly hearing the piano, Browning came to have an easy familiarity with productions that might have appeared forbidding or austere had he first met them through a school assignment. Classics of art, music, or literature became comfortable old friends to the growing boy. A certain Mrs. Cole, visiting the Browning household at New Cross, was dumbfounded to find Browning treating John Bunyan like a familiar old childhood companion: "The conversation fell on 'Pilgrims Progress' & young Mr. Browning fetched from the library a carved head which he called, 'Christian' & stroked affectionately saying he was 'very fond of old Christian.' "[6] Mrs. Cole went away concluding that the family was " 'not orthodox' or at all events was 'very liberal.' "

In his education in art as in most other aspects of his upbringing, Browning's parents seem to have been most concerned with helping him to find his own way, but they were a good deal more than merely liberal or permissive. Both parents communicated their own lively interest in art, music, and literature to their son; and Mr. Browning, especially, was able to place a broad scholarship—and sometimes even a connoisseur's detailed knowledge—at his son's disposal.

Even where, as with the fine arts, the tastes of father and son came to differ radically, Browning leaning toward Italian painters and his father, in Rossetti's exaggerated report, "caring for nothing in the least except Dutch boors," Browning still profited enormously from his father's enthusiasm and knowledge.[7] Reuben Browning recalled that his half-brother was an inexhaustible mine of information, especially about "the lives of the poets and painters, concerning whom he ever had to communicate some interesting anecdote not generally known."[8] Although this recollection may have been colored by hindsight knowledge of Browning's poems, it is obvious that his father's interests and researches, if not always his tastes, were communicated to the poet. A memorandum that he wrote on the life of Adriaen Brouwer, for instance, follows much the same track as Browning's argument in "Fra Lippo Lippi" and may even have given the son some ideas for his own treatment of Lippo as a realist whose spotted personal history is only the excessive expression of his love for the rich texture of life.[9]

Quite above differences in taste was also a common piety toward the fine artistic achievements of the past. In later life, both father and son responded as if with one groan to the destruction of an ancient church in a small French village where they then spent summers, and Browning's father occupied himself making sketches of the old figured ornamental pieces in a last-ditch effort to preserve what he could of something that had once had beauty.[10] No doubt it was during his walks with his father that Browning began to develop those powers of observing art and architecture that he later put to such effective use in Florence.

Probably it was also his father who first took Browning as a child ("far under the age allowed by the regulations") from Camberwell to the nearby Dulwich Picture Gallery, opened in 1814 and throughout Browning's youth the only public exhibition of art in London. In "that Gallery I so love and am so grateful to," as Browning spoke of it to Elizabeth, a gallery which still ranks among the finest small collections in London, Browning found a school of art seemingly created to satisfy his personal needs.[11] Here, probably with the whole museum virtually to himself,[12] he could see representative works of the English, Dutch, Spanish, Italian, and French traditions and a surprisingly large number of works by famous artists, Lorrain, Raphael, Titian, Veronese, Rubens, Watteau, Gainsborough, Reynolds, Murillo, Poussin, and Andrea del Sarto, and even some really outstanding individual paintings: two groups of Spanish peasant boys and a wonderful *Flowergirl* by Murillo, a warmly sympathetic *A Girl at a Window* by Rembrandt, a fine mythological scene, *Rinaldo and Armida* by Poussin. Shunning the usual rapid tour through a blur of pictures, the young Browning came often to study a particular painting or to lose himself in the imaginary world he found: "I have sate before one, some *one* of those pictures I had predetermined to see,—a good hour and then gone away."[13]

From both father and mother young Robert imbibed a lifelong passion for music: "music, my life," as he called it in a gush of enthusiasm in *Pauline*. A family story, likely enough but of uncertain authority, tells of Browning stealing from his bed to hear, with rapt attention and emotion deeply stirred, his mother playing the piano.[14] Evidently she inherited her interest in music from her father and was herself, far from the plain woman she has been called, a cultivated musician and pianist.[15] There probably was much the same close and direct communication of experience and feeling between Browning and his mother in their liking for music as in their appreciation of nature. It was his father, however, with whom he remembered sharing his early delight in the eighteenth-century "Grand March in C Major," supposedly by the Newcastle musician Charles Avison, and "a favorite of my father's." This piece, which became the subject of Browning's later "Parleying with Charles Avison," was carefully copied by his father into the family music book from which father and son played it: "he hummed—or I strummed—its resonancy."[16] Probably with his father, as well, he would have discussed questions about music such as those Avison himself brought up in his *Essay on Musical Expression* (1752), virtually the first extensive treatment of the aesthetics and history of music in English.[17] The Wellesley music book shows that the father was interested in a wide range of composers, from the famous Handel to lesser known greats such as Henry Lawes or Purcell. As with painters, he probably could tell his son a good deal about musicians' lives and careers. His cartoons, as always, reflect his interest. In one sketchbook an aristocrat of musical taste is confronted by the man in the street: "What!—*perfur* Handel to Blackeyed Susan!!! a pretty fellow you are to be a judge a' music."[18]

Art and music were thus important in the parents' lives and naturally became important in the son's. But on no aspect of Browning's development did his parents' enthusiasm and knowledge have a more formative influence than on the growth of his literary imagination. His mother—not often mentioned by biographers in this respect—introduced the very young boy to the world of children's tales. As a grown man Browning complained, not of children's tales, but of patronizing, moralizing, authors who did not really share the imaginative joy of the child. "Fairy stories, the good ones, were written for men & women, and, being true, pleased also children— now, people set about writing for children and miss them and the others too,—with that detestable irreverence and plain mocking all the time at the very wonder they profess to want to excite—All obvious bending down to the lower capacity,—determining not to be the great complete man one is."[19] Very likely Browning in this diatribe was speaking somewhat from his own early experience, especially in view of the evangelical cast of his mother's attitudes. One tale that he recalled in his poem "Rephan," published among the reminiscences of the *Asolando* volume (1889), is precisely what one might expect. The story, "How it Strikes a Stranger," was written by Jane Taylor, more famous as the authoress of "Twinkle, twinkle, little star," who with her sister Ann was enormously popular in the early nineteenth century for her various volumes "for Infant Minds." About the story, which Browning's mother probably read to him among a series published from 1816 to 1824 in *Youth's Magazine*,[20] there hangs something of the oppressive, evangelical moralizing of a Hannah More, and this despite the captivating fantasy of the situation. A man arrives from another star, learns the ways of earthlings, and so on; but in the end we find the point of the whole tale has been to show us this man's surprise when he finds out about death (not known on his star) and discovers that most earthlings go about blithely unprepared for a future life.

Curiously, young Browning was able to throw away the chaff of heavy moralism while going right to the kernel of wonder inherent in the fable. When in old age he recalled Jane Taylor, it was as "noble woman and imaginative writer," and he retold the tale in *Asolando* as a simple fable—despite some traces of his own philosophizing—of a man choosing to leave a perfect star to accept the human vicissitudes of earthly life. In much the same way, despite his mother's good intentions, he seems to have found a good deal of the imaginative vividness of the nonsense play of wit common to the best children's tales. She would read Croxall's *Fables of Aesop* to Robert and his sister, and he, instead of taking benefit from the morals, would be moved to sympathetic agonies by his intense imagination of the events described.[21] He recalled perfectly a bit of another, more naive and purely imaginative children's story, "a legend that delighted my infancy":

> In London town, when reigned King Lud,
> His lords went stomping thro' the mud.[22]

In later life, he was always armed with a good supply of old childhood stories, as when, having a play rejected for performance, he wrote to W. C. Macready, the manager-actor, comparing himself to "the cucumber-dresser in the old story (the doctor, you remember, bids such an one 'slice a platefull—salt it, pepper it, add oil, vinegar etc etc and then . . throw all behind the fire.')"[23] We may wonder if it wasn't this kind of nonsense tale—a kind known to generations of Scottish story-tellers—as much as Sunday school tales, that Browning heard on those times when, we are told, "his mother could only keep him quiet . . . by telling him stories—doubtless Bible stories—while holding him on her knee."[24] Good Bible stories there certainly were, too—stories able not only to capture the moral sense but also to captivate the imagination of the future author of "Saul." In old age Browning congratulated a friend who was writing up some Bible stories: "Most beautiful they are, as you and I have every reason to know—who was taught them, from the beginning of my life almost, by my mother: I hear her voice now repeating the Joseph and his Brethren, David and Goliath, the Contest of Elijah with the Priests of Baal,—all and every available one indeed. There is nothing comparable to them in the whole literature of the world,— nothing I continue to love more."[25] Such a recollection alone should be enough to dispel the view that Browning's mother was merely a straitlaced, dour, and unimaginative Christian.

It was to his father, however, that Browning owed the gift of Fellows' *History of the Holy Bible,* a present he received when seven.[26] And, all told, it was to his father, even more than to his mother, that he owed his early taste and lifelong enthusiasm for literature. What is surprising is the catholicity of Mr. Browning's tastes as a reader. That the bibliophile and philologist, plodding historical researcher and compiler of hundreds of pages of Bible genealogies, should care to help give his son a feeling for the imaginative richness in the biblical stories is unusual enough. That, with all his tedious scholarship, he was himself inspired by the warmest love for works of literature and above all anxious to communicate his enthusiasm to his son is truly astonishing. One might have expected such a devoted antiquary to have been little more than a pedant to his son. He appears instead to have been almost an ideal stimulus to the future poet, willing to share his own interests and enthusiasm without ever forcing them on his son, offering his reading and knowledge as a resource to be drawn upon, not as a burden to be taken up. Browning recalled at his father's death that he used to carry him in his arms when he was little more than a baby and hum him to sleep with translations of the classics set to the homely tune of "In my Cottage near a Wood": "Either Anacreon's Greek, or 'Persicos, odi, puer, apparitus' in a translation, I fancy, of his own:

> Persian pomp, my boy, I scorn
> Why this fading crown compose?
> Seek out on what lonely thorn
> Summer leaves her latest rose."[27]

Although that experience may not have had any significant effect upon Browning's future progress with classical studies, the story suggests the kindness and affection that tempered the formidable cultivation of the father and made of it, from the child's earliest experiences, an easily approachable and very human possession.

An episode known from Browning's sister's report to be not literally true,[28] the story which he delightfully tells in "Development" (1889) of his first introduction to the *Iliad*, does probably provide a very true picture of the way in which Browning was little by little encouraged to appreciate and comprehend works of literature. To understand Homer as a scholar understands him, not as a single man telling a good story but as the collective mythology and world view of an entire culture passed on orally from age to age in a particular dialect of ancient Greek, this, Browning admits in the poem, is no easy task and one sure to deaden the early interests of a child, however curious he may be at first. His father, who had loved the *Iliad* ever since those school days when he had organized mock Troy battles among the boys with battle taunts from Homer, knew this and, Browning tells us in this fable of early home education, when the boy of five asked him innocently about the tale of Troy,

> that instructor sage
> My Father, who knew better than turn straight
> Learning's full flare on weak-eyed ignorance,

wisely refrained from disgorging all he knew on him. Yet with his own easy mastery of the poem he was able to avoid as bad an alternative: to

> leave weak eyes to grow sand-blind,
> Content with darkness and vacuity.

Drawing on household objects familiar to the boy—"our cat—Helen . . . Towzer and Tray,—our dogs, the Atreidai"—he built up the boy's understanding of the new tale on the basis of what was already well known. A few years later, when he felt Robert was ready for it, he found him playing the siege of Troy and offered him "the tale / Properly told," in Pope: thence, with the years, on to Greek and scholarly editions, and finally, with some reluctance, to August Wolf and the higher criticism.

With "no other direction than my parents' taste for whatever was highest and best in literature," as he recalled in later years, Browning thus began a lifetime of incessant imaginative reading.[29] That this novel educational method, if such an application of good sense, knowledge, and kindness can be called a method, proved successful is hardly surprising. Like his father, Browning soon became an enthusiast for literature and reading, so much so that, forgetting the numerous other experiences of his early years at home, in *Pauline* he could remember his "First dawn of life" as "passed alone with wisest ancient books." Nor would his father have been sorry to find his son, after saying that he had only his parents' taste to guide him, adding "but I found out for myself many forgotten fields which proved the richest of pastures." As Browning came increasingly to direct his own reading and studies, his father remained a helpful source of stimulation and encouragement, feeding him with an unending stream of good books—Bunyan, *Robinson Crusoe*, Raleigh's *History of the World*, Milton, Shakespeare, Camoëns, Tasso, his favorite Mandeville, Pliny, Theophrastus and on and on—and no doubt providing interesting commentary as well.[30] Even as a boy, his father found him fit company to discuss Dryden's urbane and difficult "Discourse Concerning the Original and Progress of Satire," which he read to him while they walked together at Nun's Head.[31] With time the father came to be less a kind, informal mentor than an intellectual companion, discussing some point of history with his son or, later, aiding the poet by providing background research for a poem.

In a household so devoted to collections of artistic works, books, prints, even musical manuscripts, it might be expected that Browning would have been encouraged to develop his critical judgment and taste more than his own artistic ability. The fact, of course, is remarkably quite the opposite. Far more than most artists, Browning was given a direct insight into the practice of all the arts before he decided to devote his efforts to one of them. From their father—a person who, Rossetti believed, had "a real genius for drawing" despite his old-fashioned tastes—both Robert and his sister picked up their skill at sketching.[32] One drawing by Sarianna that has survived, a scene in the Pyrenees, though hardly striking, shows a high level of technical competence, and there is also a very fine portrait sketch of her father.[33] Browning himself, having early picked up his father's knack of making quick sketches, would return sporadically to drawing and painting as a pastime in his later life.

In music, Browning's parents even more directly encouraged him to combine appreciation with a practical knowledge of the art. His musical education, consisting of a seemingly endless procession of lessons with various masters, seems more appropriate for a musician or composer than for an interested amateur. Indeed there is reason to believe that both parents and child may have seriously thought of his becoming a musician. During his lifetime a friend reported that Browning had remarked: "I was so fond of music, even as a child that when I was nine years old I should have been very indignant if you had told me that I was going to be anything else than a musician."[34] Earlier he had confided to his friend Monclar that music, more than poetry, had been his chief interest for many years of his life.[35] With a variety of masters, one dimly identified as Mr. Abel and others unnamed, he learned to play piano, cello, violin, and ultimately the organ.[36] Although I know of no mention of Browning's later taking up the violin, there are many testimonies to his competence on piano, organ, or harpsichord. He was at least good enough to win from Mrs. Jameson, when she heard him play the piano in Pisa, some of her none too sparingly dispensed enthusiasm: "Full of science and feeling."[37]

There are no records that Browning charmed anyone, even Elizabeth, with his singing voice, though his valet was impressed by how much opera he could manage in the tub in the early morning.[38] He had singing lessons, however, with four different masters,[39] including Isaac Nathan, the composer who today is still dimly remembered for collaborating with Byron in his *Hebrew Melodies.* Finally, Browning studied musical theory, harmony, and composition with the family's Camberwell neighbor, the composer, organist, and theorist John Relfe. In addition to the skills of playing, Browning emerged from this long program of musical education with the ability to set songs to music and to speak with some authority on musical matters. He even contemplated, probably in imitation of Nathan, who himself wrote musical entertainments, composing an opera to serve as one of the component parts along with *Pauline* in the grandiose scheme of his twentieth year.[40] "I was studying the grammar of music," he later boasted, "when most children are learning the multiplication table, and I know what I am talking about when I speak of music."[41] In fact, he was still far from the competence of a professional musician, and his monologues on music have been criticized, perhaps with some professional jealousy by musicians at a poet presuming to enter their domain, for allowing musicians to employ amateurish musical devices.[42] If he was not entirely up to the standards of professionals and might make himself ridiculous when he insisted that he was an authority on music, he was certainly an exceptionally competent amateur with a thorough grounding in musical theory and history.[43] He was essentially a student not a master, but he had at least learned his lessons well enough to act later as a very decent instructor to his own son. Most important, he had developed an intelligent enthusiasm for music and a taste that was both refined and catholic. Although he chose to write about minor or unknown figures in the history of music who caught his interest for particular reasons, he preferred Bach to any obscure Master Hugues of Saxe-Gotha, Handel to Charles Avison, Beethoven to his onetime competitor, Abt Vogler.[44] Nor did he, in his liking for the more complex classics, overlook fine works such as Gluck's operas, Elizabethan songs, or popular ballads he might hear in the streets at Venice.[45]

With all his musical education, Browning has been frequently criticized for failing to bring any music into the sound of his poetry. In answer he claimed, rather defensively, that he had "given much attention to music *proper*—I believe to the detriment of what people take for 'music' in poetry, when I had to consider that quality. For the first effect of apprehending real musicality was to make me abjure the sing-song which, in my earlier days, was taken for it."[46] Such a statement can't cover over the fact that a great deal of Browning's poetry, especially the more discursive works of his early and late periods, are blunted by a heavy, dull movement that seems to belong more to Browning the man discoursing than to the poet creating. But it should also lead readers of Browning's best works to look more carefully at the rhythmic forms and complex cadences that keep the poetic imitation of speech from becoming mere ordinary speech. Unlike poets who try to make verse imitate song, Browning at his best tried to find a complexity of sound in the normal range of human speech which would be analogous to that in a fine work of music. He may have been quite right in his opinion that his successes depended to a large extent upon his sophisticated feeling for the form of sound in a sister art.

Such rather unusual training, at least for a future poet, helped to deepen Browning's appreciation of both art and music, and it no doubt provided him, whatever his occasional errors, with the technical vocabulary needed to write poems such as "Andrea del Sarto" or "Abt Vogler" in which the other arts are explored from the viewpoint of their creators. Perhaps what was equally or even more valuable was the feeling, which this training gave him, for the life and experiences of artists in other disciplines and for the possibility of art as a way of life. When Domett reminded him in later life of his habit of sketching in youth, Browning's thoughts went naturally from the art to the life of the artist: "He said he remembered it, and that he 'had always envied the life of an artist, i.e. a painter.' "[47] His father was the only painter he knew closely in youth—and only a leisure time painter at that. But in his experiences with his various music teachers he had an especially good opportunity to come to know at firsthand the varieties, vagaries, and possibilities of the artistic temperament.[48] Abel, the pianoforte master, seems to have been, from the one anecdote by which Browning remembered him, a lovely example of the odd, half-melancholy musical character that

Browning captured so well in the scientific speaker of "A Toccata of Galuppi's." "Yes I am in love," Browning recalled his saying, "it destroys my appetite, interferes with my sleep, and considerably breaks in upon my practising."[49]

In the singing master, Isaac Nathan, Browning met a more vigorous and a lighter spirit. A composer of songs and ballad operas, a devoted admirer and friend of Byron, a writer on musical instruction and lighter subjects, onetime tutor to the Princess Charlotte and probably a domestic secret agent for George IV and William II, Nathan opened Browning's eyes to a sophisticated, almost dandified world of opera and song.[50] Tall and handsome with long dark, curly, hair, Nathan was in his element as master of his exclusive Academy of Singing (and comportment) in his Nelson Square house. He made a point of conducting his lessons in an informal (though no doubt elegant) manner and enjoyed making friends with his pupils.[51] To Browning, who came to him probably in his middle or late teens, he even passed on confidences and rumors about Byron's illegitimate child by his half-sister.[52] Although he is remembered for the Hebrew melodies and although Browning recalled that he used "certain traditional Jewish methods" in voice training, he was far closer to the cosmopolitan world of European music than to his own cultural traditions.[53] Personally he was irascible, sentimental, or improvident by turns, but also lively and often charming—so charming that he even persuaded one of his aristocratic pupils to leave her family and marry into relative poverty with him. If not ultimately a great composer, he was a brilliant musical character who had a high ideal of music and a great reverence for genius. He was, as he wished to be, an unusual combination of intelligence and passionate feeling. With an interest in musical history and aesthetics and an equal love for poetry, he was not only a good teacher of a skill but someone who could stimulate Browning's interest in the nature of art and the idea of the artist.

Finally, perhaps as a welcome balance to Nathan, there was Browning's most serious master, the composer and musical theorist, John Relfe. "Great John Relfe, Master of mine, learned, redoubtable," Browning calls him in the "Parleying with Charles Avison" (1887). Although his reputation has kept less well than that of Nathan, he was a master of a more complex art and to Browning, who knew him when he was already in his fifties, a more impressive and serious figure. Son of a distinguished organist at Greenwich Hospital, musician in ordinary to George III, composer of songs, cantatas, sonatas, and hymns, a serious and learned writer on *Principles of Harmony* and other subjects in musical theory, he no doubt opened to his student the higher and grander realms of musical experience.[54] It was with him especially that Browning studied composition and musical theory and he recalled him as "my instructor in counterpoint . . . a thoroughly learned proficient."[55] He also remembered, on two occasions, a certain tension that developed between his own intuitive, enthusiastic approach to assigned problems and the master's more methodical and sober method: "How did you get this?' he would say, and I used to answer, 'Oh, I don't know exactly how,—but it's right, isn't it?' I don't mind saying that they always *were* right, but my methods vexed his soul terribly."[56] If Browning had a chance to play the clever schoolboy, the experience with Relfe also opened his eyes to the importance of craft and intellectual control in the highest reaches of an art. It suggested the way in which seriousness can be a precondition to the most exalted form of artistic enthusiasm. Beyond the technical facts of his art, Relfe, like Browning's own Abt Vogler in the monologue of that name (1864), felt the mystery of music's effect on the human mind: "Secret springs . . . too metaphysical in their nature, and lofty in their origin, for the philosopher's eye to explore."[57] Indeed, there was a real connection between Vogler and Relfe, for the work of the once famed master of the lost high art of extemporization, Abbé Georg Vogler, had provided Relfe with part of the basis for his revised system of thorough bass.[58] From Relfe, Browning probably first heard of Vogler, and when he set out to portray the eighteenth-century musician with his lofty enthusiasm and his sense of a higher order of reality coming to him through the harmonies of his organ keyboard, Browning probably drew heavily upon his recollection of his own organ master.

Childhood lessons might thus give Browning some intuitive understanding of the relation between an artist's personality or life and his work, as well as some grasp of the principles of the art. Of course, they did not make him a competent artist. Likewise, a family in which literary efforts were a normal pastime did not make Browning into a poet, but this environment probably did help to prepare him, in understanding and perhaps somewhat in the basic skills of rhyming and verse, for the more serious and far more difficult attempts of his later career. At least in the development of his own early habit of versifying, the example set by his family was obviously important. His mother was an accomplished storyteller. His father, likewise, had a knack for mixing fiction and historical lore into everyday situations until reality was viewed through the ordering artifice of story. In what was probably a not untypical incident he could thus mystify a small boy whom he came upon fishing in one of the canal-ditches near Camberwell: "He bade a little urchin we found fishing with a stick and a string for sticklebacks in a ditch—'to mind that he brought any sturgeon he might catch to the king'—he having a claim on such a prize, by courtesy if not right."[59]

His efforts in verse had much of the same quality. His father, Browning said in later life, was an "adept" at verse though "of an earlier bygone school."[60] Evidently he recognized the authority not only of the classics such as his favorite Horace but also the great neoclassics, Dryden and Pope. As with his drawings, however, his verse most often paid its homage to the more playful and vigorous traditions of the previous century than to its more elevated classics. Generally, his compositions were ephemeral attempts at imposing an order on experience, very like his similar efforts in impromptu sketches. His grandson recalled Mr. Browning's "extraordinary facility for writing verses'' and also the brief life of these creations—"generally assigned to the waste paper basket.''[61] The verses, which he "was in the habit . . . of dashing off without a moment's hesitation,'' were mostly epigrams, whether on political or social events of the day or on the eternal verities of life.[62] His emphasis—as in the following impromptu reflection on an old beauty—was usually on prominent rhyme and sprightly comic turns.

> Now if Old Homer tells the truth
> Each goddess has Eternal youth.
> This a young goddess that we know
> Was 20—40 years ago.[63]

His facility at rhyming, which Browning held to be greater than his own, was generally available for any good use. He helped teach Browning his Latin declensions by joining the forms to grotesque rhymes; years later he taught his grandson and others the principles of anatomy with the aid of verses from an "Anatomical Parish":

> And in vestry affairs that the clerk Gastroenemius
> In all parish matters so very abstemious.[64]

Other literary exercises were a bit more serious, though not much so. An epitaph on a poet picks up the strength of eighteenth-century satirical verse:

> Here lies—after living in troublesome times—
> Of glory—war—fire & combustion—
> G——T——, the Poet, composer of Rhymes
> And Dealer, by wholesale, in fustian.[65]

He was even capable of his own real fustian, as an anagram poem, lambasting a "Bob Ho——y a Clerk at the Bank" in the finest, playful cockney, reveals. It begins

> A was an Ass, call him Bob if you will
> B Bilk'd the waiter when paying his bill
> C was the Coachee and he was bilk'd too
> D was (in classical language) a Do,[66]

and continues on through the alphabet until poor Bob has landed his drunken, offensive self in jail. His more serious works that have survived are far less impressive than these jeux d'esprit. A versification of three stanzas from Psalm 124 is pious but dull and simple.[67] A meditation on the Crimean War beginning "Think on the weather—all around / The Snow lies deep upon the ground,'' is cosy and similarly pious, but quite second-rate.[68] Probably he was at his best when he was able to combine his wit and intellectual play-fulness with his modest and kind disposition, as in the "Epitaph on a Dog" which has some of the warm humor of a similar one by Robert Frost:

Alas! poor Dash's days are up: he
Is now what you and I must be:
I knew him when he was a puppy,
That's more than you can say of me.[69]

With such an example before him, it is no mystery why Browning took instinctively to verse making, as he did to drawing or music. The general at-mosphere of encouragement for the arts and for artistic expression was probably more important in the family life than any specific training the son may have obtained from his ever producing father. Certainly Browning learned his father's skills at impromptu verse, but, as we shall see when we look at his early poetic development in detail, he quickly moved toward models closer to his own time and temperament. In a broader way, how-ever, the family's artistic life, and especially the practice of his father, did provide an approach to art that would prove of permanent value. This was less any specific skill or taste than a way of thinking about art and the mak-ing of art. The great danger to a poet in the age in which Browning was growing up was that, with the success of the romantic revolution, sincerity and directness of expression, the triumphant forces of reform against the hollow uses of the past, might themselves become mere fetishes and open the way to a disregard for the necessary craft and sense of style inherent in all art. Although Browning, like virtually every other poet of his age, would respond very strongly to the attractive new attitudes and new poetic voices of the romantic poets, he had, from the example of his father, a founda-mental sense of the formal necessities of art. If his father probably failed to produce anything of lasting value just because he was unable to find a per-sonal role and aim to go along with his technical competence, there was no doubt of his mastery of the formal side of the arts he tried.

Indeed, the father set a model not only for the craft necessary in art —the deliberate mastery of a particular style of expression which his car-toons and epigrams reveal so immediately—but also for a self-conscious awareness of different forms and their possible relation to each other. His attitude toward different styles was really the equivalent of his universal ap-proach to history. Each style that he found in the great record of the history of art was noted and carefully catalogued in his mind along with other sorts of information. Inasmuch as he had little deep personal involvement in his art or in that of others, he was able to enjoy works from diverse periods with an easy catholicity of taste. To live with him was thus to have a con-stant reminder of the variety and diversity of possible artistic form. His col-lections of prints were great mélanges of different painters and periods rep-resenting a miscellaneous history of style. The family music book[70] is a most extraordinarily eclectic musical scrapbook with entries ranging from serious works by Handel, Purcell, or the religious music of a Mr. Clifton to operatic airs, "Rule Brittania," Renaissance love lyrics, and the "Highland Laddie." It is a splendid little collection that suggests that family playing and singing ranged easily, and without excessive fear of incongruity, over a wide variety of Western types of music.

In the father's art itself, there was the continual playing with styles, the habit that made him such a natural parodist and satirist. His poems mixed Homeric goddesses and real old women, cockney language and white-gloved analytical detachment, or anatomy and parish business. His drawings played even more obviously with contrasting styles. Not only did his cartoons generally depend upon the mixture of high language and low persons, or sometimes low persons dressed up in high costume but speaking low language, but he even liked deliberately to parody various styles as an art in its own right. One notebook contains a number of serious parody sketches, including one of Holbein, one from an "old painting," one Dutch grouping, and even a study of the style of a South Sea idol.[71] Another has a good imitation Rembrandt teasingly entitled "a real Rembrandt—quite brown with age" and an elaborate parody, "The Poacher" pasted beside a print of Roubiliac's "Bishop Hough's Monument in Westminster Cathedral" to invite comparison.[72] Styles, like historical facts, were mere grist to his unusual mind and emerged, in his representation, more clearly, if less complexly, defined than in the original. However much Browning might lean toward a simpler, "sincere" personal art, or a simple copying of one form in his early poetic development, it would be hard for him, with his father's example before him, to forget the possibilities inherent in an art that is formally conscious of itself. Like it or not, he could not escape the cosmopolitanism that was a part of his artistic heritage from his father. As he expanded his own awareness of different artists and different forms of art, he would only grow further into this heritage and put himself at a further remove from the simple sincerity of the poet who ignores the richness of achieved form available to him from his predecessors.

2 The Significance of Art

It is clear that Browning's early exposure to the arts gave him a rich opportunity to come to know a variety of works of art and to understand something of the creative activity of artist, musician, and poet. Beyond these evident facts of his early life, speculation as to the impact of this experience with art upon the boy's developing tastes and artistic preferences is both more interesting and less certain.

What indications there are as to the young Browning's response to the experience of art, though mere hints at best, do at least suggest a fairly consistent tendency in his preferences and enthusiasms. And despite the large and obvious differences between the various forms, there is an overriding similarity in the way in which he speaks, especially in *Pauline*, of his experiences with art, music, and literature.

Robert Browning Sr. as Parodist

Left: A Real Rembrandt—Quite Brown with Age. Pen and ink by Robert Browning Sr.

Center: Bas-Relief on Bishop Hough's Monument in Worcester Cathedral. Engraving by Heath of Roubiliac's sculpture.

Bottom: The Poacher—a Parody on Bishop Hough's Monument. By Robert Browning Sr.

Above: Dulwich College, ca. 1840. Engraving by Lacey.
Dulwich: village, school, picture gallery: "A green half-hour's walk over the fields."

Right: Two Spanish Peasant Boys. Painting by Murillo.
One of Browning's favorites at the Dulwich Picture Gallery. "I have sate before one, some one of those pictures I had predetermined to see,—a good hour and then gone away."

Isaac Nathan. Painting. *Browning's singing master: composer, essayist, friend of Byron.*

Grand March Attributed to Charles Avison. Copy by Robert Browning Sr. in the family Book of Music. *"A favorite of my father's; he hummed—or I strummed —its resonancy." "Somehow coldness gathered warmth."*

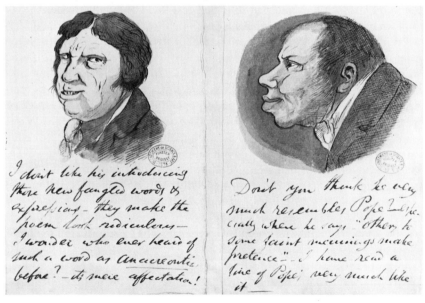

Literary Discussion at the Local. Cartoon by Robert Browning Sr. Left: *"I don't like his introducing those new fangled words & expressions—they make the poem look ridiculous—I wonder who ever heard of such a word as* Anacreontic *before?—it's mere affectation!"* Right: *"Don't you think he very much resembles Pope?—especially when he says 'Others to some faint meanings make pretence'—I have read a line of Pope's very much like it—."*

His preferences are perhaps most clear in the fine arts where very quickly he veered away from his father's beloved Dutch realists to the Italian and Spanish schools. We may form an idea of his early taste from the group of works at Dulwich which he especially recalled in praising that childhood haunt to Elizabeth: "Those two Guidos [Guido Reni's *St. John the Baptist* and *St. Sebastian*], the wonderful Rembrandt of Jacob's vision [*Jacob's Dream*, now ascribed to Aert de Gelder], such a Watteau [either the *Fête Champêtre* or the *Bal Champêtre*],[73] the triumphant three Murillo pictures [i.e., Murillo's *Spanish Flowergirl, Two Spanish Peasant Boys, Two Peasant Boys and a Negro Boy*], a Giorgione music-lesson group [now no longer ascribed to Giorgione], all the Poussins with the 'Armida' and 'Jupiter's nursing' [*Rinaldo and Armida* and *The Nurture of Jupiter* and a number of others]."[74] Only the most general qualities unite this potpourri of quite wonderful paintings from different schools and periods. Yet they do suggest a consistent tendency that would sharply distinguish Browning's taste from that of his father. In all the paintings, there is not only a scene, usually an outdoor one with an extensive view, but a central person or persons, creating an interplay between landscape and human form or character. In all there is, if not a story, at least a striking situation or pose, as in the captivating Murillo *Two Peasants Boys and a Negro Boy,* where the artist catches the three boys—two sitting and the third with a water jug on his back leaning down to them—in a moment both ephemeral and seemingly eternal.[75] Perhaps what most relates the works is just this larger tension or struggle between life, vibrancy, and movement and countering, controlling patterns of order, arrangement, and harmony imposed by the artist. In the *St. John the Baptist* of Guido Reni, for example, St. John—the predominating and large figure—preaches with one arm extended to the side of the canvas, and the poised grace of his half-sitting, half-standing body forms a center of order in a wilderness scene that, with a ring of trees and unsettled sky, appears to swirl uneasily about him. Similarly, among the many fine Poussins at Dulwich, Browning's choice fell not on the calm, reposed *A Roman Road* but on two works in which characters are posed in brightly opposing colors as on a stage in a moment of strong activity. It is only through the larger, geometrical patterns of the total composition that the movement is finally kept in balance.[76] Or again, the *Jacob's Dream*, which he took to be Rembrandt's, interested him just because it seemed to be a composition made up of very rapidly painted strokes.[77]

Another favorite work of the young Browning and one that continued to exert an influence on him throughout his later years, was the *Andromeda* of Polidoro da Caravaggio (or Caldara, ca. 1500-1543). Originally one scene in a fresco series for a Roman villa, Polidoro's design for the maiden perilously situated between the monster's ravages and possible rescue by the hero Perseus had been stylized and made more boldly dramatic in a striking eighteenth-century engraving by Volpato in the Piranesi series.[78] Almost certainly this was the print that Browning rescued from among his father's boors and placed over his desk at Camberwell, then later transferred to his

New Cross room.[79] For this, we can have an even better indication of what he found striking, for he evoked the picture in *Pauline* as, no doubt, he looked up at it from his desk in writing. Later in life Browning would see a special significance in the story of Perseus rescuing Andromeda from the monster as a symbol of his own less mythic rescue of Elizabeth Barrett from her supposed monster-father. But his initial response to the design in *Pauline* is more immediately to the situation and the peculiar tension between destructive forces and a redeeming artistic order:

> Andromeda!
> And she is with me—years roll, I shall change,
> But change can touch her not—so beautiful
> With her dark eyes, earnest and still, and hair
> Lifted and spread by the salt-sweeping breeze;
> And one red-beam, all the storm leaves in heaven,
> Resting upon her eyes and face and hair,
> As she awaits the snake on the wet beach,
> By the dark rock, and the white wave just breaking
> At her feet; quite naked and alone,—a thing
> You doubt not, nor fear for, secure that God
> Will come in thunder from the stars to save her.

Changeless in the pose in which the artist has captured her, she is yet within a threatening, emotionally, even sexually charged landscape where movement and contrasts of dark and light wage an endless contest against the larger controlling vision of the artist.

Browning's early taste in music is far less apparent than that in art, for even the one work that he did remember liking particularly, that "Grand March" he and his father attributed to Avison, he later, in the "Parleying," admitted was something of an odd choice. Probably far greater composers, such as Bach and Handel and especially Beethoven, whom he has Pauline place along with Shakespeare and Raphael in her pantheon of creative geniuses in the strange note in French in *Pauline,* were more constant passions even in youth. Whatever work he enjoyed, the boy certainly found music an emotional stimulation as well as the technical art he learned from his music masters. When, again in *Pauline,* he attempted to transpose his early impressions of listening to music into verse, the result, though in a less tortured vein than the description of the *Andromeda*, was somewhat similar. Music, he declared, "is earnest of a heaven, / Seeing we know emotions strange by it, / Not else to be revealed." Further, he thought of music not only as an expression of the emotions but as an organizing force that brought them into a strangely harmonized dance, a dance that yet led the listener into new and unexplored realms of experience. Music is like a voice,

> A low voice calling Fancy, as a friend,
> To the green woods in the gay summer time.

And she fills all the way with dancing shapes,
Which have made painters pale; and they go on
While stars look at them, and winds call to them,
As they leave life's path for the twilight world,
Where the dead gather.

The vagueness, the tantalizingly evocative imagery, the mixture of abstraction and sensuality all suggest Browning's poetic immaturity and the particular influence of Shelley at the time he wrote these lines. Yet the underlying attitude toward music ran deeper than the style of expression and had hardly changed more than fifty years later when, in the "Parleying with Charles Avison," he spoke in quite different language of music as a never-to-be-finished attempt to puzzle out the relationship between feeling and intellectual knowledge:

To match and mate
Feeling with knowledge, make as manifest
Soul's work as Mind's work, turbulence as rest
. . . . .
Give momentary feeling permanence.

He would thus return again and again to the problems of the aesthetics of music because music seemed to reveal, in its ultimate and simplest form, the problem of all the arts, that of the relation between form and feeling, between a work of art as we look at it objectively and the work as we receive it when it has full effect on us. Music, most precise, even scientific of the arts in form, was also most immediate in its impact, seeming—as Browning would say in different ways from *Pauline* to "Abt Vogler" to the "Parleying with Charles Avison" at the end of his career—to speak directly to the soul and to speak, as if in a Platonic language, of harmonies from some finer sphere. The general problem of the relationship between external and internal, the outer object and the internal subjective experience, was here most radically clear. Three notes combined—as he has Abt Vogler exclaim —achieve the essential aesthetic miracle: to the internal sense of the listener they produce not merely an objective fourth note but a star, an experience of transcendent beauty.

As with other ideas that Browning would work out fully in his poetry, his concern with the effect of music grew in prepared ground. Browning's instructor Nathan, for instance, had a lively nontechnical interest in the psychology of music. His textbook on music spends a great deal of time discussing the history and aesthetics of music and stresses again and again the age-old notion that music works directly on the passions or inner soul. Although we don't know whether Browning read the work or was merely exposed generally to Nathan's attitudes through instruction, one major example he gives for the power of music to tune the soul is especially suggestive.

"The temporary derangement of Saul gave way," he observed, "to the harp of David." In that way David proved himself a true musician: "Soul itself was taken for the instrument to be touched and played on by the contrivance of harmony, and he only who could tune, temper, and modulate, this exquisite piece of spiritual mechanism, was acknowledged as a true musician, and real master of the science."[80] Similarly, in Avison's *An Essay on Musical Expression* he would have found the view that music directly strikes the passions reduced almost to a science. Particular forms, sharp or flat keys, slow or lively movements, especially the "Variety of Intervals, from a Semitone to a Tenth . . . do all tend to give that Variety of Expression which elevates the Soul to Joy or Courage, melts it into Tenderness or Pity, fixes it in a rational Serenity, or raises it to the Raptures of Devotion."[81] Browning would draw on such ideas for detail in his poems, as in the equation between specific notes and emotional states evoked in "A Toccata of Galuppi's" (1855), but the overall idea was nothing new and had indeed been the theme, as Avison himself notes, of Dryden's "Alexander's Feast." Such works, and certainly his contacts with musicians, were most valuable in helping Browning find a way of expressing the strong effect of music on him in revealing sudden moments of personal order and harmony. Merely through hearing or playing a work of music, his own problems of a felt division between inner intensity of feeling and growing external mastery and sophistication seemed to be resolved, at least while the music lasted. But the difficulty, as Pauline points out in her note in French in *Pauline,* would still arise when he tried in serious composition of his own to find a resolution himself. Browning allows Pauline to express his own doubts as to whether he will ever achieve either the more important concentration of conception or even the formal concentration of ideas in execution of a Shakespeare, a Raphael, or a Beethoven.

Possibly because music—at least when performed—seemed most easily and immediately to satisfy his craving for unification, Browning put more of his emotional energy, in the years before *Pauline,* into it than into writing. To his friend Monclar he confessed that he turned most often to the other arts, to drawing and especially to music rather than to poetry, when "real and strong feeling called for utterance." Even in 1837 it seemed easier to express feelings "in harmonic combinations or melodic amplifications rather than in language."[82]

Of course, reading is another form of creative activity, if less obviously active than playing an instrument or singing. And in reading the imaginative triumphs of others, if not in his own early poetic efforts, Browning was able to satisfy much the same desires for coherence and unity. Not that his early reading in literature suggests any simple pattern of preference or taste. Homer, biblical tales, old fables and stories, Bunyan, the poetry of Francis Quarles, these and a host of other books which he read in childhood, have in common at most only a strong appeal to the young imagination. Despite particular enthusiasms, especially for the two poets, Byron and Shelley, his appetite for books, like that of his father, grew more and more omnivorous as he matured. But here again, Browning's retrospects in *Pauline* upon his early reading do at least indicate the particular way in which he responded to his early reading and, as with art and music, give us some idea of the place of this experience in his life.

Speaking in *Pauline* of those "wisest ancient books," the Ovidean fables and the story of the *Iliad,* which were his earliest recollections, he noted especially the stimulation that they provided for his own imaginative faculties:

> All halo-girt with fancies of my own,
> And I myself went with the tale—a god,
> Wandering after beauty—or a giant,
> Standing vast in the sunset—an old hunter,
> Talking with gods—or a high-crested chief,
> Sailing with troops of friends to Tenedos.[83]

Reading became an occasion, in fact, for creation of his own very intense vision:

> I tell you, nought has ever been so clear
> As the place, the time, the fashion of those lives:
> . . . . .
> never morn broke clear as those
> On the dim clustered isles in the blue sea:
> The deep groves, and white temples, and wet caves.

Reading in the Greeks—"for which I have always had a passion"[84]—was, like his interest in music, not merely a pastime or an enjoyment but an emotional commitment and a form of creative activity in itself.

The "old lore" most often referred to in *Pauline* is that embodied in the Greek drama that Browning probably read in translation as a boy and then came to again in his teens when he studied Greek. For each play to which he alludes, the *Ajax* and the *Antigone* of Sophocles, the *Agamemnon* and the *Choephori* of Aeschylus,[85] Browning presents an encapsulated picture founded upon a particular incident. The result, though based on passages from the dramas, is virtually Browning's own dramatic scene, far more drawn out into metaphorical oppositions and with a weaker philosophic and ritualistic foundation than the Greek originals. Orestes in the *Choephori* is thus recalled in the vignette:

> the boy,
> With his white breast and brow and clustering curls
> Streaked with his mother's blood, and striving hard
> To tell his story ere his reason goes.

Even when he does speak of fate in Greek terms, as with the *Agamemnon,* the picture becomes at once more emotionally charged and more symbolically compact than in the Greek original, itself the work of the most highly colored and metaphorical of the Greek tragedians:

> the king
> Treading the purple calmly to his death,
> —While round him, like the clouds of eve, all dusk,
> The giant shades of fate, silently flitting,
> Pile the dim outline of the coming doom.

This is not to say that Browning ignored the works that he read; only that in his reading, as in his appreciation of pictures or music, he showed a tendency to respond neither to calm, reflective, purely intellectual art nor to purely emotional, unordered works, but to look for a union of artistic order and vivid emotional content. In light of the diversity of experience, both inner and emotional and external and objective, to which Browning's home environment exposed him, this kind of interest in art seems hardly surprising. With the "problem," as he described it, of giving unity to "very wide and general" sympathies he quite naturally responded most fully to artistic creations that imposed a unifying order on a strongly felt substance. What is surprising is that, even in *Pauline,* Browning seems to have been aware of this process. In a poem that, in its elaborate disguise, in its confused, almost chaotic structure, especially in its disturbing succession of emotional tones —ranging from ecstatic to deeply contrite—is almost an epitome of the young Browning's unfocused interests and feelings, the recollections of art serve as organizing and tempering moments. For instance, before he turned to the *Andromeda* above him Browning had fallen into one of those fits of self-accusation and despair only too common in the poem:

> I begin to know what thing hate is—
> To sicken, and to quiver, and grow white,
> And I myself have furnished its first prey.
> All my sad weaknesses, this wavering will,
> This selfishness, this still decaying frame.

And his recollection of the familiar work of art functioned as a sudden release and expression, in better controlled form, of these disturbed and self-destructive feelings:

> But I must never grieve while I can pass
> Far from such thoughts—as now—Andromeda!

In the passage in which he stripped his mind bare in order to dissect his various powers, he was even more explicit. After speaking of his intense self-consciousness and his restless desire to experience all things, he acknowledged one other essential power without which he would have been made helpless by the very strength of the others:

> of my powers, one springs up to save
> From utter death a soul with such desires
> Confined to clay—which is the only one
> Which marks me—an imagination which
> Has been an angel to me.

When we look back on Browning's youth across the history of his later career as a poet it seems obvious that he did have a very special power of imagination. Yet if we put aside such hindsight knowledge for a moment and consider Browning simply as a young man beginning to find his own interests and to think of choosing one way of life or another, it is equally obvious that such a special power would be brought forth or not brought forth, called out in one form or in another, by the particular circumstances of his early experiences. In Browning's case the opportunities he had to use his imaginative powers in art, music, and literature gave him the experience denied to many talented persons of other backgrounds or circumstances, those mute inglorious Miltons of all ages and places. And, unlike many a talented person exposed to a similar cultivation who remains in a larger way indifferent to art, Browning felt, from his other experiences and from the kind of personality that they helped to create, a need to turn to the study of art and the practice of his imagination as a way of organizing and understanding life. His experience led him to seek organization and coherence through imagination and art. In return, as we shall see, his imagination would slowly learn, as he grew as an artist, to focus back on life in the process of fulfilling itself.

3 Perishable Idols

In the melodramatic, strained speech that pervades *Pauline* Browning lamented, among the other curses of art, this worst of realizations:

> And then know that this curse will come on us,
> To see our idols perish—we may wither,
> Nor marvel—we are clay; but our low fate
> Should not extend [to] them, whom trustingly
> We sent before into Time's yawning gulf,
> To face what e'er may lurk in darkness there—
> To see the painter's glory pass, and feel
> Sweet music move us not as once.

Involving much of himself in the works of art he studied, he felt, in plainer words, an equally strong disappointment when he could no longer respond to them. This realization is another result of his early exposure to art and one that helped determine the direction of his later life and affected his decision to be a poet.

What, if any, specific works the twenty-year-old Browning had in mind when he wrote this passage is not made explicit. Those two most serious "idols," Byron—from whom Browning probably even took the term[86]— and Shelley, were as we shall see, very much in his mind as he wrote *Pauline*. But he was not ready to say absolutely that either had entirely perished to him. His relations with two other artists, however, illuminate most clearly the process he tries to formulate in *Pauline* precisely because, though they had their importance for him, they did not affect his whole personality so deeply and complexly as his greater idols. Both artists, the English composer and Newcastle organist Charles Avison (1709-1770) and the Dutch artist, Gérard de Lairesse (1640-1711), are discussed by Browning himself in his later recollections in the *Parleyings* (1887). His experience of disillusionment with their works—with a book by Lairesse read in a translation entitled *The Art of Painting* and with Avison's "Grand March"—suggests the general way in which Browning developed through his enthusiasms for the work of others.[87] From idealization, he would, as he came to comprehend their achievement, swing round to inevitable disillusion. As he thus proceeded from work to work of the past, he was learning to grow from dependence on the past to a sense of the need for his own independent work in the present.

Lairesse's work, written when blindness made the painter turn from painting to discussing paintings, was a leisurely manual of art, incorporating his opinions on technique, painters, and the proper subjects for art (five-hundred pages of this in the English translation).[88] When he looked over the book in 1874, Browning, remembering his early enthusiasm, was moved to write on the flyleaf: "I read this book more often and with greater delight, when I was a child, than any other; and still remember the main of it most gratefully for the good I seem to have got by the prints, and wondrous text."[89] For a while, at least, the young boy, delighting especially in the descriptive "walk" he took with Lairesse to learn what was desirable in landscape painting, found in the work a satisfying school for his imagination. Here was, he must have felt, the ordered, coherent expression of his own still incoherent early passion for nature.

In fact, Lairesse's view of the proper treatment of nature in art hardly seems compatible with what we know of Browning's own intense delight in wild landscape. Lairesse was a strong champion of the ancients over the moderns; his tastes in landscape were quite rigidly neoclassical with a decided preference for the beautiful over the natural. He thought the proper subjects for art were found exclusively in classical story and expected his landscapes to have a goodly sprinkling of classical deities and creatures. Perhaps moved for a time by the very unclassical abundance of this huge and generously illustrated neoclassical handbook, Browning became an enthusiast for both the view of art and the author. In the "Parleying with Gerard de Lairesse" he recalled

> the man I loved
> Because of that prodigious book he wrote
> On Artistry's Ideal.

But sooner or later, perhaps with Browning's developing consciousness of his own quite different interest in nature, what had seemed a satisfying imaginative experience became so no longer. "Bearded experience bears not to be duped / Like boyish fancy," he wrote in the "Parleying," but the disillusionment probably preceded the literal growth of a beard, possibly setting in not long after his "youth's piety" led him to study the deity-filled paintings at Dulwich then ascribed to Lairesse.[90] Certainly by the time he came to write *Pauline* the scales had fallen from his eyes and in his brisk erratic tour through the woods and fields, he offered, as he did much later in the "Parleying," a "walk" (or hop, skip, and a jump) of a very different, much more energetic and realistic sort. What for a while had seemed a vital exercise of the imagination had become, with his own growth, a one-sided, limited work: the work, as he explains in the "Parleying," of a mind bent on excluding much of the force of real experience in order to create its own ideal beauty. Ironically, it was the strange chapter in which Lairesse set out to describe a truly horrible landscape as a lesson to his students in what to avoid as positively "unpainterlike" that finally most influenced Browning. As DeVane showed, Browning drew his own most poetically fruitful landscape, the impoverished wasteland of "Childe Roland to the Dark Tower Came," in large part from conscious or unconscious reminiscences of Lairesse's lesson.[91]

Another recorded disillusionment, among, no doubt, many such experiences with early favorite works of art that were grieved down in silence, was the "Grand March" attributed to Avison that he had enjoyed with his father. In fact a rather unspirited work, it had managed for a while to catch his boyish imagination as it did again in an odd moment of recollection when he wrote the "Parleying." "Somehow coldness gathered warmth," and raised the boy in a moment of enthusiasm "twixt earth and air." Then he must have found himself brought down heavily to earth and left "to rub eyes disentranced," just as he was again in the "Parleying with Charles Avison" when for a moment he recollected his early experience. What for a time had seemed, as Browning formulated it in the "Parleying," to bring together all parts of his being, soul and mind, feeling and knowledge, in one coherent powerful order became a dead and unsatisfying creation, "The figured worthies of a waxwork show."

In the "Parleying" Browning went on to propose a theory of musical history based on a continuous progress of changing taste. Music was the closest expression of the imaginative state of a particular age, but it was also the most evanescent.[92] But this somewhat questionable general theory of progress in the arts was a less important product of Browning's disillusionment than the intuitive understanding that such experiences with art gave him, early in life, not only of the significance of the art of the past but also of its insufficiency. Not that Browning's early exposure to the arts led him finally to a contempt for the works of the past. Even in the "Parleying" he hails the works of Homer and Michelangelo as unchanging and immortal, and perhaps there have been few poets who cultivated so diligently the odd volumes or out-of-the-way paintings as well as the great works of the past. But unlike his father, who seemed to browse forever in the storehouse of man's past achievements, he found—as one after another idol perished for him—that he was left with an unsatisfied desire to recover the unity of form and emotion that had seemed for a while permanent.

Deep and early experience with the arts thus served in the long run to suggest to the young Browning a means of reconciling his finely developed inner self-consciousness with his widely dispersed external interests and experience, while at the same time tantalizing him with its inadequacy. Perhaps it helped, as well, to at least point the way toward a more satisfactory resolution of the complexities of his personality by his own endeavors at art.

His experience directed him, at any rate, away from his childhood environment, away from simply accepting the ideals provided for him by the tastes and interests of his parents and toward the harder quest for his own models and ideals. His early, independent, and fruitfully unsuccessful attempts to find suitable models for the development of his own interests in writing poetry are the subject of the second part of this study. They show, even in the poor forms of youthful precocity and the confused assertions of young manhood, the emergence of an individual temperament and poetic voice from the fertile soil of his childhood circumstances and family life. His inheritance from family and past was, indeed, an exceptionally rich and full one. Learning the right use of it, as he began to develop his own way in life and his own way as an artist, would be his own responsibility and the problem of his future.

Part Two
The Development
of a Poetic Nature:
First Steps

Preceding pages: Perseus and Andromeda. Engraving by Giovanni Volpato, 1772, of the fresco by Polidoro da Caravaggio.   *Browning's favorite print, hung over the desk where he worked.*

Andromeda!
And she is with me—years roll, I shall change,
But change can touch her not.   *(Pauline)*

VII
Precocious Beginnings

Browning's early environment is a book in which much can be read about the forces active in forming his character and the possibilities open to him as he grew. Yet a child is not a passive vessel to be filled by his parents, or even a blank slate to be written upon by his early circumstances. To know a child's environment is not necessarily to know what kind of person he will develop into. Even in early childhood, he is forced to confront difficult or really irreconcilable alternatives and to make decisions whose importance he may only come to understand much later. By placing ourselves in another person's situation, we may recreate something of the experience he had. But it is only by the decisions that he takes, or fails to take, by those possibilities that he makes realities, that individual character is created. Embracing or disputing the expectations and attitudes of the world around him, a child gives a direction to his personality. He becomes a part of life through the interaction of his self-consciousness with the world.

The prominent aspects of Browning's home life and environment suggest a good deal about his developing personality precisely because Browning, for the most part, seems to have had little quarrel with them. Rather than choosing between piety and knowledge of the world, between cosmopolitanism and domestic cultivation, between love of nature and love of art, Browning characteristically developed sympathies sufficiently "wide and general" to embrace them all. As a mature artist he would have to struggle in greater earnest with the seeming incompatibilities of these early influences. For the time being, they simply grew into the being of the developing boy. Again, some concerns that would later loom large in his life did trouble his adolescence but without really leading to any decisive issue. Browning's religious life, for instance, fluctuated widely in youth. A "passionately religious" child in nursery years; a bored, restless youth at Mr. Clayton's services; a practicing vegetarian and sometime atheist in his teens; a guilt ridden, even morbid enthusiast at twenty writing his confessions in *Pauline*: he could be all these things, and yet only over the succeeding twenty-five years and more would he begin to resolve these conflicting reactions and formulate his personal religious beliefs.

Likewise, there are stories enough of Browning's passing, passionate admiration for various young ladies. Sharp, as always a good raconteur and a bad authority, avers that there was a married woman fifteen years Browning's elder to whom he vowed his soul at age ten or slightly thereafter.[1] As we shall see, he certainly had a very warm admiration for Eliza Flower not long afterward and a close friendship with her sister Sarah. Then there was a mysterious "handsome girl" with whom he fell in love when she stayed at the Camberwell house on a visit.[2] Or there is the persistent rumor in the Browning family that Robert was in love with his half-aunt Jemima, sister of Reuben and William Shergold, only a year older than her nephew, and "as beautiful as the day."[3] With the poetess Fanny Haworth, the "English eyebright" of *Sordello*, there was certainly, as Browning confessed to Elizabeth, some kind of light literary fever in the 1830s. But so many swallow-flights of passion don't announce the spring of more serious involvement. It would not be until the rather late relation with Elizabeth that he would begin to face the deeper commitment of intimacy.

These, and many other strands of his future life can be identified in his early years but remain vague and indefinite. A context may be set in his youth, but it is only with greater maturity and experience that a direction to his growth clearly emerges. We are halted, as always, in our attempts to see specific patterns of development by the arbitrary limits placed on our knowledge of Browning's early life. We know that the child is father to the man, that somewhere in the chrysalis the more complex organization of the future is forming. But the stages in this development are often left all blank, with only beginning and maturity to attest that there have indeed been stages in between.

For two strands of his development, his early tentative steps toward his future career as a poet and the growth of his mind in reaction to his education, similar lacunae are inevitably present. Here, however, the gaps are not quite so absolute. It is impossible to give a month by month or even year by year account of either, though such a detailed account would seem far more important to an understanding of Browning and his poetry than the list of endless days of visiting and dining out that we can chronicle to our heart's content in his later years. Still, with all the holes that must be left unplugged and all the important questions that can only be given probable answers, overall patterns in his development do emerge. In the years that lead up to his first confused, but not inconsiderable published work *Pauline,* we can already see important steps taken toward his mature conception of himself as a poet and toward his mature ideas about man and society. If there is still much more growth that must come after *Pauline* before he can begin his real work, there is at least a beginning and—more important—there is a direction, a chosen way on which he may concentrate his future efforts as a man and artist. By *Pauline*, he has found, or at least is finding, his vocation. The path to this point, vague as it must often be, deserves as careful scrutiny as possible.

1 An Itch for Rhyming

In a family where all forms of art were part of the daily life, where the mother enjoyed reading poetry and the father wrote verse extemporaneously, whether for the purpose of counting his blessings from the Lord or lambasting a fellow employee at the Bank, it was no sign of particular genius in Browning that he began to make his own verses almost as soon as he could talk. In the family context verse was not a special art reserved for special experiences and emotions but merely an alternative form of expression along with talking, music, or drawing. To Elizabeth, Browning recalled producing "verses at six years old, and drawings still earlier."[4] But he had been making rhymes before this and admitted another time that he couldn't "remember the time when I did not make verses and think verse-making the finest thing in the world."[5]

With his father's example before him, he began most naturally in his comic, epigrammatic style. His first recorded outbreak shows him already a master of occasional verse, though the couplet is a foot short of the neoclassic ideal. It was inspired by some nasty medicine:

Good people all who wish to see
A boy take physic, look at me.[6]

Although this was perhaps a work of unconscious felicity, there is no doubt that Browning picked up from his father an elemental command of the craft of verse at a very early age. In following his father's bent for impromptu verse, as he did his habit of extemporaneous sketches, he early obtained a facility with odd meters and rhymes and probably learned directly from him the grotesque rhyming that they both liked to use in humorous verse. Such an unforced and easy beginning at verse would ultimately have a great deal to do with Browning's mature ability to make use of a greater variety of verse and voice than any poet in his century. It also probably gave him the bias toward poetic garrulity against which he would have to fight, and not always successfully, throughout his poetic career. When poetry in the best sense wasn't forthcoming, he could, like his father, keep churning out verse and worse.

Writing verse after his father's fashion was little more than an acquirement, a skill a gentleman would learn along with sketching or piano playing. Browning was obviously precocious. To the poet's scalawag acquaintance, Thomas Powell, Browning's father boasted he once had had nearly a hundred specimens of his verse, most of it probably dating from his childhood.[7] They were, the elder Browning bragged on somewhat dubious grounds, written extemporaneously and without any alterations. The one example he gave was probably not untypical, an effusion "On Bonaparte." "Remarkably beautiful," the proud father noted, "and had I not seen it in his own handwriting I never would have believed it to have been the production of a child." Browning, who made sure that none of these works survived to let his readers form their own judgment,[8] had a far more critical attitude. "You see," he told Domett, "when I was not even a boy, I had fancy in plenty and no kind of judgment—so I said, and wrote, and professed away, and was the poorest of creatures."[9] We need not applaud the loss of verses that could hardly lack interest. Yet they would probably tell us next to nothing about Browning himself, about his developing mind or personality. Evidently what was striking was simply his precocious talent in spinning rhetoric and rhyme out effortlessly. Powell was probably thinking of the juvenile works he had seen through Browning's father when he wrote in an 1846 review, ostensibly with reference to *Pauline* and to *Paracelsus*: "One remarkable peculiarity . . . is the finish of his style. In the mechanical he was perfect from the first."[10]

If Browning tried to suppress *Pauline* in part because it revealed too much about him, he almost certainly destroyed this earliest work, and even his teenage efforts, because they revealed too little. They were, and were almost bound to be, works of poetic parroting, strings of phrases, rhymes, and attitudes borrowed wholesale and stuck together with little conscious aim. Rhyming was done merely because he felt an almost innate "itch" for it.[11] Probably sound and the most obvious effects of rhythm mattered far more than sense or expression. In *Pauline* Browning in fact spoke of his earliest, almost instinctive poetic effusions as a strange kind of utterance not yet matured to the point of meaning: music waiting "on a lyrist for some thought, / Yet singing to herself until it came." His sister recalled (so Sharp asserts) that he would go round and round the dining room table spanning out his meters on the mahogany of the top.[12] In the 1840s Browning similarly recalled to Domett, "In my youth (*i.e.* childhood) I wrote *only* musically—and after stopped all that."[13] Probably the complexity of most adult poetry, which combines music, feeling, and thinking, was simply beyond his capacities. Although he wrote a great deal of verse, he gave himself more fully as he explained to Monclar, to art and especially to music.

What seems important in this one facet of many in an active and intelligent boy is not the accomplishment or lack of it, but the early hints of some more individual and personal direction. For mere precocity can be the deadliest of dead ends. Without the development of some personal relation to an art, a talent merely blossoms early, shrivels, and dies. In the event, Browning did not develop any distinctive personal voice even in his teenage writing and he was led by the inner logic of his development into a long period in his later teens when he was a reader rather than a writer of poetry. However, there was a seed of growth even in his earliest writing, an instinct for personal mastery that led him away from his father's rather timeless and impersonal displays of wit and talent and into a dialogue with the poetry and poets of his age. Rather than resting content with merely parroting his father's somewhat old-fashioned style and wit, he sought, almost from the beginning, to pick up the coming styles of verse and the attitudes embodied in them.

Sharp reports that Browning did honor his father's ideals sufficiently to begin translations of Horace's odes sometime before his teens and to strike up an Horatian ode in English in his amorous campaign for the heart of the married woman he supposedly loved at age ten.[14] Whatever grain of truth may be in these reports, there is no doubt that his father's favorite Horace, the poet about whom he even planned an historical novel, would ultimately have a large influence on the subtlety and formal complexity of Browning's best short poems. But it was not his father's ideal that first caught his attention, nor did the Latin poet's perfection of form command his boyhood emotions. Born, as he claimed to Elizabeth, "supremely passionate" and certainly encouraged in direct expression of feeling by his family's emotional warmth and artistic involvement, he was, like many of his generation, ready to respond to any apparently sincere expression of feeling.[15]

There had been one man who had had the artistry to succeed supremely well in gratifying this kind of taste in readers of the late eighteenth and early nineteenth centuries. He was the Scot James Macpherson who had come forward to deliver to the world the poems of the ancient Gaelic bard or scop, Ossian. The grown Browning would come to the conclusion, along with the preponderant critical opinion, that the self-styled translator was far more nearly the father than the midwife to the poems he presented to the world.[16] As a very little boy, though, he must have heard about or read a credulous account of the poems of Ossian that stirred deeply his sense of wonder and drew heavily on his childhood reservoir of feeling. At the most he saw only a few scraps of Macpherson's poetry, quoted in another work. But, following much the same process of looking in his heart and writing as Macpherson himself, he began to compose his own poems of Ossian. The result, which was hidden under the cushions in the couch for safekeeping, seems to have been a somewhat more vigorous variation on the heavy pathos of Macpherson's Ossian. Whereas one of Macpherson's heroes usually overcame his opponent by decorously slipping a blade in his side and then proceeded to the main business of tears and mourning, Browning at about five years old was more direct. In the one scrap he quoted to Elizabeth, he indicated murder by an ominous four stars (****) and had his hero exclaim boldly "And now my soul is satisfied."[17]

Although the Scots rhetorician Hugh Blair had, without a twinge of conscience, compared Macpherson's Ossian to his forefunners in the epic, Homer and Virgil, Ossian's was a grand style easy to pick up and mimic even from a few scraps and not hard to surpass in its vague melancholy and loosely evocative landscapes. Long before the boy bought himself a copy of the whole of Macpherson's Ossian and found with it the damaging argument of Malcolm Laing that Macpherson seemed more often to be translating lines from the standard classics than from some Scots original,[18] he must have given up this mimicry of what was mostly a forgery. The style and emotions were too easily caught even by a boy. When Browning refers to them in later life—for instance in his report to Domett that the publisher Moxon smiled "grimly with a super-*Ossianic* joy of grief" over a failure he had himself predicted[19]—they are understood for what they are, merely a set of attitudes.

2 Giants of Old

Ossian stands at the gateway to the new romantic literary age into which Browning was born. The vagueness and suggestiveness of a translation of a distant poetry from a misty time allowed Macpherson's admirers, like the little boy Browning, to feed into their reading whatever emotions and sentiments were not being gratified by the more critical and intellectual classics, Dryden, Pope, or Thomson. His appetite whetted by the mere promise of Ossian (a promise no modern reader can any longer find), Browning apparently felt his way intuitively toward similar ways of fulfilling vague, emotional longings through literature. In *Pauline* he speaks of making "rude verses" in his early boyhood on "those old times and scenes, where all / That's beautiful had birth for me." There the scenes, rather than of Macpherson's Scotland, were probably classical Mediterranean ones, seen through a diaphanous gauze of romance.

From the vague sentiments and sad lands of Ossian and from his own visionary dreams of clustered isles, deep groves, white temples, and wet caves, Browning soon moved on, however, to the far more substantial realities of feeling and expression in the poetry of the English Romantics. Ossian had been truly a precocious interest. Browning probably began to read some of the Romantics only toward the beginning of adolescence, in that period he speaks of in *Pauline* when he turned from his earlier writing to gaze "on the works of mighty bards." Although there is no evidence that makes explicit how much of Wordsworth or Coleridge he knew in boyhood, it seems very likely that he read their poetry carefully and extensively and that, as with Ossian, he made some attempt to assimilate and master their very new forms of expression. From one of the two surviving poems of Browning's youth, "The Dance of Death," which he modeled on Coleridge's "Fire, Famine, and Slaughter," it is certain that he did, to some extent, confront Coleridge's poetry.[20]

Wordsworth, however, he probably read and admired even more fully. That Browning was deeply grounded in the work of the greatest of the first generation of English Romantics is obscured by his own famous pronouncement on him. In "The Lost Leader" he immortalized the later Romantics' reaction against Wordsworth's political and social apostasy into Toryism and toadying. His letters to Elizabeth are similarly full of jokes and sneers at the aged laureate's unnatural appearance at court in a bag wig. Browning caps his feelings with the notorious statement that he could not find the energy to cross the room "if at the other end of it all Wordsworth, Coleridge & Southey were condensed into the little china bottle yonder."[21] What his slurs on Wordsworth conceal is that Browning, like Shelley, earned his right to criticize Wordsworth's latest stance by his appreciation for his earlier achievement. To the president of the Wordsworth Society, which he joined in old age, he set the record straight: "I keep fresh as ever the admiration for Wordsworth which filled me on becoming acquainted with his poetry in my boyhood."[22] That his statement was not a hollow testimony is made clear in subsequent letters where he endorses as old favorites early works that even a Wordsworthian may pass over in rereading, such as "The Reverie of Poor Susan" or "Goody Blake and Harry Gill."[23] His repeated preference for Wordsworth's "first sprightly runnings" exceeds even the conventional view that the early poetry is best and suggests that Browning retained a personal and lifelong fondness for what he read as a boy.[24] He read *The Excursion,* evidently knew something of the later sonnets and poems, and eventually saw *The Prelude* when it was published, [25] but the early ballads and poems like "Resolution and Independence" or "We Are Seven" had the lasting impact of things that have been early personal possessions.[26]

Inspiration from reading Wordsworth and Coleridge may have had something to do with a more serious outpouring of verse at about age twelve. We simply don't know because nothing from this period has survived. From what information there is, however, it appears that a more recent, major voice among the Romantics had begun to have a primary, though probably not exclusive, influence on the boy's idea of what poetry could be. This was, of course, Lord Byron, whose European name and fame had penetrated to Camberwell while his equally great contemporaries, Keats and Shelley, remained unknown. In May 1824, when Browning was just turning twelve, the news of Byron's death at Missolonghi was bursting over England. Browning may have heard of him before then as the great scandal and great poet he was. If he hadn't been looking at Byron before 1824, he certainly turned his attention then to the man whose death made him overnight a hero. Byron became his chief poet and evidently his personal hero as well.[27] To Elizabeth he confessed that he had, despite periods of estrangement, by and large retained his "first feeling for Byron"; and this feeling took decidedly the form of teenage worship: "the interest in the places he had visited, in relics of him: I would at any time have gone to Finchley to see a curl of his hair or one of his gloves."[28] It was probably this sudden attention to Byron and the natural identification that a boy makes with his hero that stirred Browning sometime after his twelfth birthday to take up poetry somewhat more seriously himself. This is probably the period Browning speaks of in *Pauline* as a return to verse writing on new terms. Now, he was beginning to make a deliberate effort to match his predecessors by imitation:

And I began afresh; I rather sought
To rival what I wondered at, than form
Creations of my own; so much was light
Lent back by others, yet much was my own.

For a brief time he put on the robes of his later vocation. He became for a year or two a marvelous "boy poet" with grown-up poetic ambitions. He was, as he reminded W. J. Fox in 1833, "at that time a sayer of verse and a doer of it," a role he wouldn't take up fully again until he was twenty.[29]

The result was not merely some occasional poetic play but "a book of verses" consisting, as Browning sneered at it later, of "a batch of performances of all sorts and sizes."[30] At the time he was serious enough about this work, and vain enough of his young talents, to give the whole the fancy title, "Incondita" with its ambiguous suggestion both of self-deprecation—crude confusions—and also of superior unconcern—mere trifles. The volume was shown to friends and Browning is reported to have been at one point quite anxious to have it published until, as we shall see, he was kindly dissuaded by W. J. Fox.

If Byron was the chief inspiration of "Incondita," as all indications suggest he was, it is not hard to imagine what general kind of verse Browning was writing. No one has successfully captured Byron's vigor, breadth, and exceptional capacity for mixing varieties of tone and attitude. But his more obvious attitudes and tricks of style were only too easy to imitate or parody.[31] The master parodist, Browning Sr. found it easy enough to mimic Byron lamenting the death of a dog.[32] By contrast, his more earnest son evidently followed the amorous and egotistical Byron of *Childe Harold's Pilgrimage,* the childish side of the "childishest childe" that he went out of his way to ridicule in his maturity in *Fifine at the Fair* (1872).[33] To Elizabeth he admitted his dislike for Byron's "trenchant opinions" and disclaimed any identification in his lovemaking with the stereotyped Byronic effects: "attitudinizing à la Byron, and giving you to understand unutterable somethings, longing for Lethe and all that."[34] Yet in these later attempts to dissociate himself from Byron he seems to protest somewhat too much, as if he had found himself at one time only too easily able to take up Byron's attitudes and still had to ward off temptation. In *The Inn Album* (1875) the "Elder Man" mocks the "Younger Man's" Byronism—"had loved, and vainly loved: / Whence blight and blackness." Yet satire is coupled with candid recollections of his own similar boyhood folly—a touch which Browning probably drew from his own experience: "just for all the world / As Byron used to teach us boys." Even as late as *Pauline* Browning would hardly be free from the attractions of Byronic posing. In the "Incondita," love agonies and great-souled broodings were probably welcomed wholesale. Sharp reported that Browning even told him one of the works was explicitly based on Byron (rather, one must fear, as The Return of Dracula is based on its original): a work called "Death of Harold."[35]

It is easy to censure the obvious kind of dishonesty in this species of poetry, poetry that picks up someone else's easiest points and becomes an even slicker version of the original, completely up-to-date and almost immediately out-of-date. Such quickly became Browning's own view of the "Incondita" and the prime reason why no verses were left for posterity to shake a finger at. Browning, indeed, not only anticipated his critics' sneers but even supplied the moral and meaning of this experience for the biographer. This is in the so-called "Essay on Chatterton," a review article Browning wrote in 1842. There, in his attempt to rescue the great romantic ideal of Chatterton as a wondrous boy-genius from the undeniable evidence that he had been guilty of presenting his own work as the poetry of the medieval monk Rowley, Browning was led to draw some generalizations about the boyhood work of poets in general. The case that he makes to excuse Chatterton for his boyhood dishonesty is put in a more general framework, which fits what we know of Browning's own early work and seems almost certainly drawn from his own experience.

His argument, which is weakened in Chatterton's case by the assumption that Chatterton was both a genius and a sincere and kind person, is that the young poet will always begin to find an outlet for his creative powers by mastering current models rather than by initial displays of originality: "Genius almost invariably begins to develop itself by imitation."[36] Chatterton has merely allowed himself to pass over the fine line that divides the necessary work of imitation—the natural way to begin finding his own expression—from outright imposture and forgery. The beginning artist must be a thief. Paradoxically, it is only when he acknowledges his theft by ascribing his work to the real source from which it came that he is deemed guilty. Chatterton's excuse, as Browning forges it for him, is his youth. He was led into a fatal falsehood in a way that Browning can understand as only too natural for a young poet. He was, Browning emphasizes (using an example that suggests he was thinking of his own early work), no mature imposer like Macpherson "producing deliberately his fabrications to the world and challenging its attention to them."[37]

The whole line of defense is especially interesting because it fits Browning's early situation far better than Chatterton's. Whereas the marvelous boy chose to frame his forgeries in an idiosyncratic, medievalized Renaissance style that, if generally imitative, was also quite personal and, in some ways, quite original, Browning's own imitations, from the honest forgeries of the dishonest Macpherson to the later mimicry of the Romantics in the "Incondita," follow his models explicitly. Young genius's object is simply "to compete with, or prove superior to, the world's already recognized idols, at their own performances and by their own methods."[38] Only after mastering the current models does the poet begin to develop faith in his own powers and to find an outlet for his powers through an expression which embodies his own personal outlook and beliefs: "No longer taking the performance or method of another for granted, it supersedes these by processes of its own."[39]

From such an explanation of childhood work one can easily understand Browning's total disregard for his own juvenilia. Even when not passed off as forgeries, they are in this analysis no better than such. This criticism seems rather harsh. Yet the two examples of early work that were somehow spared Browning's rage, "The Dance of Death" and "The First-Born of Egypt," do on the whole confirm this estimate. The judgment is all the more convincing because these two works, preserved in the transcription of Sarah Flower, were probably among the latest of his childhood efforts, works written at fourteen after the entire "Incondita" had been put behind him.[40] Although "The Dance of Death" was clearly suggested by Coleridge's similar "Fire, Famine, and Slaughter: A War Eclogue" (1798), neither of Browning's poems is literally an imitation. Both are essentially his own independent creations and both reveal very considerable technical abilities at verse making and quite a mature vocabulary and command of language. "The First-Born of Egypt" seems generally as close to Byron as "The Dance of Death" is to Coleridge. But it has no specific antecedents and is quite an interesting attempt to bring alive a biblical story.

Although in no sense slavish copies of any models, the poems have, however, a hollowness, a lack of central purpose or inspiration. They are essentially pastiches of description and sentiment without a controlling intention. Browning works his own variations on romantic images and feelings, but altogether the poems amount to little more than five-finger exercises. This lack is particularly apparent in "The Dance of Death." Coleridge's verses, certainly not among his finest work, were themselves a parody of another work, the witches scene in *Macbeth*. He made his weirds the forces of destruction in war and used them to frame a searing criticism of William Pitt, which, as Browning noticed to Elizabeth, he went to elaborate embarrassed efforts to cool off in a later prose note.[41] For all Coleridge's later efforts to claim it was merely a jeu d'esprit, his work has a controlling intention as biting, political protest and a unifying dramatic and rhetorical aim behind the play with grotesque images. By contrast, though one critic sees some promise of the later dramatic monologue in Browning's four ghastly speakers, Pestilence, Ague, Madness, and Consumption, his poem is essentially a rather meaningless piece of horror. Each speaker is allowed to have his inhuman gloat over the havoc he wrecks among mankind. The more full and fanciful the language, the more absurdly awful the effect. Splendid formal powers are hooked to a mere schoolboy fascination with the instruments of torture, and since the ills who celebrate their successes are remediless, the more effective the irony grows, the more ridiculous the poem becomes in its inhuman perspective. Consumption claims the prize, and well may have it for the Ovidian richness with which he contrasts his ugly power with his beautiful victims:

Tell me not of her balmy breath,
Its tide shall be shut in the fold of death;
Tell me not of her honied lip,

The reptile's fangs shall its fragrance sip.
Then will I say triumphantly
Bow to the deadliest—bow to me!

"The First-Born of Egypt," which describes at first hand the vengeance of the passover, or rather the moment of realization after the slaughter, is altogether more impressive. Each person, whether hardened in sin or a poor, loving, blind father, finds his hopes blighted by the catastrophe, and the poem is unified by the stress on the varying capacities of different persons to feel fully an identical loss. Yet, though the poem has the organizing force of the romantic and sentimental assumption of shared capacities for feeling between author and reader, there remains an overall impression that the poet is playing with ideas and feelings beyond his personal experience. Byron would have built up our feeling over this rather unpalatable show of superior striking force to read a lesson against the Old Testament God of wrath and curse the curser. Browning's willingness to turn verse on this subject may suggest he was already beginning to think freely about the literal truth of the Bible. But unless an attempt at irony colossally misfires at the end, we are left with an obvious conflict between the personal feeling the description arouses and the conclusion—that all acknowledged "In silence the dread majesty—the might / Of Israel's God, whose red hand had avenged / His servants' cause so fearfully." Again Browning seems to have no central direction or attitude, only a series of received feelings and descriptions upon which he improvises his own versions to suit his subject.

Much the same lack of fundamental organization can be demonstrated on the local level of word choice, images, and historical and literary allusions in both the poems, but boyhood works of such an obviously immature nature need not be arraigned in full critical court. Rather, the impression remains, for all their limitations, of extraordinarily precocious powers and of a surprisingly rich range of literary and historical reference. Even in his very early efforts, there is displayed the abundance and richness of powers that Coleridge found to be the mark of exceeding promise in his discussion of Shakespeare's early work.

Although he possibly wrote some poems after these two, they appear to be not only his only surviving juvenilia but his latest. Both in *Pauline* and, more explicitly, in the letter to Monclar about his poetic development, Browning implies that after the imitative inspiration of the "Incondita" period he turned away from writing poetry. Real feeling, he told Monclar, then began to find easier expression in music. Never, he emphasized, did he cease to hold "a poet's calling in pre-eminent reverence."[42] However, with growing talents but no adult experience and no direction emerging for his poetic efforts, he must have felt himself at least at a temporary dead end as a poet. He had precociously tried to assume an adult role but had not gotten beyond the limits imposed by his youth. He was still a boy-poet, a boy playing at the role of a man without the means to go beyond the imitation essential

to all such play. In the Chatterton essay Browning even implied that this
activity had little more ultimate significance than play. It was a mere flexing
of the poetic muscles before the dawn of serious development. In his "faith
in the world" which comes from the naive "short-sightedness of infancy"
the boy merely picks up and copies whatever fashionable idols are before
him.[43] The process, as Browning presents it, is essentially directionless and
the particular idols chosen irrelevant.

In fact, this was certainly not true of Chatterton, whose one contribution to English poetry was his first imitative style, nor, though Browning
may not have wished to admit his debt to his predecessors, was it true of
him. If his juvenile poetry writing did not lead him to the main thing, the
development of a personal aim and direction as a poet, it was far from irrelevant to his development. From studying and imitating romantic poets such
as Coleridge, Wordsworth, and Byron, Browning was picking up at a very
early age the new ways of thinking about the poet and the new ways of writing developed in their generation. His early imitations inoculated him for
life against the ordinary Victorian disease of echoing and reechoing the
cadences and attitudes of those three poets. (Shelley would be a harder
problem for him, as we shall see.) However, even in his mature work when
he moved away from an excessively personal voice and concern in poetry—
as well as in his earlier long works with obvious ties to romanticism, *Pauline, Paracelsus,* and *Sordello*—Browning would stand firmly on the general
base laid down by the great Romantics. With them, he would accept the
premise central to modern poetry: that the poet must develop in his own life
and work his own conception of his role rather than accept a ready-made
model provided by society or criticism. Such a tradition demands that a
poet neither become permanently a disciple nor seek disciples.[44] We should
not look for nor will we find many specific formal devices or themes passed
on from the Romantics to Browning. Rather, to make his own way in his
mature poetry, he would choose to borrow styles or ideas eclectically from
writers such as Donne, Ronsard, Samuel Butler, or even Balzac, who
weren't so immediately his predecessors. In a general way the language of
his poetry would be the language of the Romantics. With his own peculiarities added, whether through the dramatic diversity of his best monologues
or through the rather harsh Browningese of some of his later work, he
would essentially adopt the use of a speaking voice for poetry, a language
apparently emanating from an individual personality rather than merely
following a traditional form. From the entire generation of romantic poets,
through probably especially from Wordsworth (and from Wordsworth's
practice, not his theory), he acquired a sense of the strength of an unrhetori-
cal language for poetry that approached ordinary language in diction,
phrasing, and cadence, without actually becoming merely everyday speech.
His speakers in the dramatic monologues express their own personalities,
not their poet's, and they often use language or metrical forms appropriate
to their historical time and place. Yet in his best works Browning mines a

lode of poetry opened up first by the Romantics. At base, the monologues are a dramatic application of the essential romantic genre, the first-person utterance shaped in form around the character and personal concerns of the speaker: organic form used with dramatic distance. In the short view his poetry would move in an anti-romantic direction; in the longer vision, his work with the dramatic monologue seems an inevitable child of the romantic revolution in poetic form.[45]

Browning's debt to Wordsworth or Coleridge was only of this important but most general sort. They were among "the giants of old," as he spoke of the Romantics in 1868, "the great extinct race" on whose shoulders he and virtually all poets since have stood in their basic forms and concerns.[46] However, their subjects and specific interests were different enough from Browning's to keep him from ever feeling their achievement as a burden or obstacle to his own. He developed along his own lines, even in his way of looking at nature. And he appreciated their parallel but finally different forms of perception and expression without ever feeling greatly in their debt. Similarly, Browning admired the work of Burns and Scott, whom he probably, though not certainly, also knew in his youth, as well as other more minor romantic writers, without ever finding their example particularly powerful or compelling in his mature work. Like Wordsworth or Coleridge, Burns may have encouraged Browning generally toward a speaking, colloquial voice in poetry. Scott's success in the historical novel was not so much a specific model for Browning as a general influence working through both Scott and his followers to turn Browning's attention toward the use of past epochs in literature.[47]

His most serious boyhood idol, Byron, was rather a different matter. Browning would quickly turn against the posing and posturing of Byron's weaker side, though not before he had done some imitations in parts of *Pauline.* But, as he confessed to Elizabeth, he continued, despite ups and downs, to retain his admiration for Byron. Even when he was publicly attacking the side of Byron that pretended to care only for oceans, not for man, he swore, "I never said nor wrote a word against or about Byron's poetry or power in my life."[48] For all the obvious differences between the self-magnifying Regency Lord and the Victorian author of "so many utterances of so many imaginary persons, not mine," Byron's influence on Browning was probably as great as that of any modern poet except Shelley. And, though Shelley would have, as we shall see, a far stronger emotional impact on Browning and a greater effect upon his life, Byron was in many respects a far more kindred spirit.

This is a truth that does not appeal to the legion who come to Browning through the attraction of Elizabeth Barrett and his love relation with her and who sentimentalize his vision and his earlier life only to posit an unreal disjunction between his private self and his later public role in London society. Browning, like Byron, was in fact both a man of the world and a sensitive private temperament throughout his entire life. If anything, his family situation and connections and his father's wide learning gave him, as we have seen, the instincts of a cosmopolite at a far earlier age than Byron himself. His later experience in young manhood in London society and abroad only increased the breadth of his social experience. Even his friends in the set swore by Byron as their kind of poet.[49] Far from being merely a fashionable model that he latched onto in his early poetry, Byron appealed to Browning for very fundamental and important reasons. In him he found the same combination of breadth of interest and experience with depth of feeling and self-consciousness that his early experience was giving him. In Byron there was both sophistication and feeling, geographical and historical breadth along with ever more complex inner awareness. There was the same sympathetic reaching out for more and more experience and the same problem of giving unity to his impulses, of concentrating instead of dispersing them. In historical terms there was the same need to link the eighteenth and nineteenth centuries, to combine the width of social vision of the Enlightenment with the depth of perception of the romantic revolution.

The full impact of his idolization of Byron, which amounted to far more than its first fruit in the boyhood imitations, is suggested by a passage in *Pauline*. He is almost certainly thinking especially of Byron when he speaks of his first serious reading in the "mighty bards":

> the first joy at finding my own thoughts
> Recorded, and my powers exemplified,
> And feeling their aspirings were my own.
> And then I first explored passion and mind.[50]

Byron, certainly—if other bards as well—seemed to embody Browning's own personal feelings and difficulties. In imitating him he began to find a vocabulary for understanding his needs, a vocabulary that persisted even in the phrase "passion and mind" in *Pauline*. Had Browning been able to accept not only Byron's perception of the problem of a diversified intellectual and emotional sensibility, the problem of heart and head as Browning formulates it in his own works of the 1830s, but also Byron's attitude toward it, he might have gone on to be merely a minor nineteenth-century follower of Byron. But if he recognized in Byron the closest approach to his own situation, he was not willing even in boyhood fully to accept Byron's way of resolving the complexity he felt. Browning would graduate from Byron to Voltaire and leave a personal legend of being something of a scoffer in adolescence. He retained a capacity for trenchant, sometimes brutal, satirical thrusts throughout his life. He was not willing, however, to follow Byron into a poetry that primarily celebrated and glorified his personal complexity. And he was not willing to reduce the complexity he found within himself and the world to Byron's ironic contrast between his greatness of feeling and the incapacity of the world to satisfy it.

Such a reaction against Byron's egotistical but glorious attempt to integrate his vision of self and the world seems implicit even in the abandonment of the presumedly Byronic "Incondita." Posing and self-aggrandizement were to be put down, not celebrated. By the time of "The First-Born of Egypt" he was simply unwilling to take the next Byronic step and assert, as Childe Harold certainly would have, had he been present, that the wide vision of God's workings, epitomized by the vengeful slaughter of these innocents, is a matter for irony. He admits that our capacity to feel and to be hurt by experience is undeniable, the more so when we look on the broadest view of human life. However, the future author of both *Pippa Passes* and *The Ring and the Book* can't bring himself to scoff even at this worst of God's faces. There is a confused fear and wonder, an immature, uncertain response, but also an unwillingness to separate himself from human life and set up a mill of irony on the site of a bleeding and complaining heart.

The unwillingness to follow Byron was virtually a moral one, epitomized by, but not limited to, his later explicit criticism of Byron's posturing and egotism. At some time in his teens his reaction was solidified by the knowledge, communicated to him by his music tutor Nathan, that Byron's Byronism wasn't all pose.[51] The story of Byron's child by his half-sister remained a reality in his view of Byron throughout his life. By itself it didn't turn Browning away from Byron or qualify his respect for Byron's powers, but it probably was an added factor in his rejection of the Byronic magnification of self. Even in the period when he was questioning his religion he found it hard to ignore the biblical logic of knowing men by their fruits.

Unwilling to follow Byron's bold course, Browning was thus brought to a dead end in his poetic growth after the "Incondita" not only by his immaturity but by a specific problem that he was unable to resolve. How could he manage to express the breadth of mind and feeling that he found in Byron without following Byron's own path as a poet? Although his mind and sensitivity would continue to grow throughout his teens, he would see no way in poetry to bring them together. Not until age twenty, when he wrote *Pauline,* would he even make the attempt. In the interim, while the boy-poet grew into a man, Browning's interest in poetry and art would not cease. Nor would he cease to develop his understanding of possible forms of art or roles for the artist. But perhaps in reaction to Byron and to the superficial breadth of his own early poetry, his development for the next six or eight years would be in a rather different direction. In the interests encouraged by his friendship with the Flower sisters and in his passion for Shelley's poetry and for Shelley the poet, he would enrich the idealistic and inward-turned side of his nature almost at the expense of the breadth he had learned from Byron. The immediate result would be in the short run far more disbalancing than his early experience with writing imitative poetry. He would be encouraged in the natural idealism of adolescence almost to deny a part of his character and experience; and the experience with Shelley and Shelley's poetry would pose problems of poetic identity that he would be long in resolving. It was almost a matter of hopping from pan to fire. Yet out of this troubled and confusing experience would come the beginnings of a sense of his own identity as a poet and the start of a vocation. Ironically, his first task would then be to find a way, though not Byron's way, to work back toward the breadth that he had achieved so easily and glibly as a boy-poet but that came much harder to the more earnest young man.

Sarah Flower Adams. Portrait by Margaret Gillies.
Poetess and actress.

VIII
A Sentimental Education:
The Flowers

Few writers maintain a high estimation or even much affection for their boyhood work. But Browning's understanding of the failure of his work, its imitative and, to him, deeply alien nature, led him to early and particularly determined efforts to destroy every structure in this land of false imagination and plow its fields under with salt of oblivion. His own copy of "Incondita," carefully stitched by his mother (if we can believe William Sharp) in hopes of publication, was quickly destroyed. Copies of other poems were preserved by his parents only by concealing them from their son's Saturnian fury.[1]

The decision to turn against his firstborn was accelerated, if not precipitated, by his earliest, and surprisingly trauma-free, experience with a critic. Seeking to help him find a publisher, Browning's mother is said to have turned to her friend, Eliza Flower, who knew about publishing through her father's work and friends. Eliza, in turn, showed Browning's poems to her family friend, the Unitarian minister, writer, and crusader, W. J. Fox.[2] Fox read the verses with interest and had one interview with the boy. His courtesy and kindness attained a rare success. He managed to persuade Browning of his truly high opinion of his promise and talents: "which verses he praised not a little; which praise comforted me not a little." At the same time he got across his blunt opinion: such premature publication would be a mistake. Having "prophesied great things of the future," he advised the boy "to consign the present work to the fire."[3] Fox in 1824, in an article for the first issue of the new *Westminster Review,* had attempted to curb the excesses of Byron fever that were infecting England by criticizing the new spirit of affectation and levity in literature. With unwonted thunder he demanded whether "every stripling who can indite a pretty verse, or fabricate a readable paper for a magazine, is to find nothing in heaven or earth,

Eliza Flower. Engraving by E. Bridell-Fox.
Musician and composer.

in life, mind, or morals, important enough to make him serious, or interesting enough to demand emotion?"[4] Tactfully in conversation, or perhaps through Eliza,[5] he may have communicated his similar reactions to *this* stripling's imitation of Byron: specifically that it contained too great a splendor of language and too little original thought.[6] The criticism, explained directly to Browning years later, is remarkably close to his own analysis of the problems of juvenile writing. It would have been easier to swallow from Fox because Fox was genuinely impressed by his talents. About two years later Sarah forwarded to Fox the two slightly later poems (which have thus survived) with the obvious expectation that he would be pleased to see new work from the person he would remember as "the boy" Browning.[7]

The odd, single meeting with Fox was a thread that would lead unexpectedly to important events in Browning's life in the 1830s, when their acquaintance was renewed with the publication of *Pauline*. Fox was to be Browning's "literary father," even his "Chiron in a small way," above all a sympathetic friend in the London literary world who would generously extend both his kindly enthusiasm and practical assistance.[8] The more important immediate effect of this first appeal to Fox, however, was not Browning's relation with him—he only saw Fox that once—but his renewed contact with some old friends, Eliza Flower and her sister Sarah. With both sisters, Eliza, nine, and Sarah, seven years his elder, Browning had long been acquainted, possibly as early as age six or eight.[9] Their acquaintance, turned into friendship by the relation begun with "Incondita," lasted until at least 1827 when Sarah wrote her famous letter to Fox describing her crisis of faith in the authenticity of the Bible after discussions with Browning. Following a lapse of some years, the friendship would be renewed in 1833, then no longer as an informal comradeship between a boy and two young women but as a more formal adult acquaintance. Although it is difficult to be certain exactly how well Browning knew them in their earlier relation, and it is clear that he saw them frequently in the 1830s, it seems probable that the sisters exerted the greatest influence on Browning in his early adolescence, especially in the period after "Incondita." Later, they were merely two among many literary and artistic acquaintances. In his youth their very unique qualities—for they were both exceptional persons—would have had their full impact. Coming under their influence at a time when his dissatisfaction with the "Incondita" left him with no clear opinions or beliefs about art, except a conviction that he must find something more meaningful than mere, simple imitation, he was naturally drawn strongly toward them as models of artistic activity.

Both sisters were, in quite different ways, creative artists in the widest sense. Indeed, one explanation that has been offered for Browning's early acquaintance with them is that Eliza may have been asked by Browning's mother to give him music lessons.[10] Such a supposition would at least help explain the odd acquaintance of a young boy with a girl nine years his elder. Eliza and her sister lived north of London at Dalston near Hackney with their widower father Benjamin Flower, the printer, nonconformist lay preacher, idealist political radical, onetime supporter of the French Revolution and onetime political prisoner. Through a mutual friend, a Miss Sturtevant, probably ultimately through the family minister George Clayton, who was first cousin to the girls, Browning's mother came to know Eliza as a friend and sister lover of music, and may well have asked her to give Browning lessons.[11] Eliza was certainly well qualified to be a music teacher.[12] She had been intensely and single-mindedly devoted to music since earliest childhood when she had amazed a village organist by her ability to compose songs.[13] In her thinly masked portrait of her as the sensible sister in her novel, *Five Years of Youth or Sense and Sentiment* (1831), her acquaintance Harriet Martineau described her as a natural musical genius, a judgment that was shared by everyone who knew her:

> She had that natural taste for music—the ear and soul for it—without which no teaching is of any avail. She sang much and often, not because she had any particular aim at being very accomplished, but because she loved it; or, as she said, because she could not help it . . . Everything suggested music to her. Every piece of poetry which she understood and liked, formed itself into melody in her mind, without an effort; when a gleam of sunshine burst out, she gave voice to it; and long before she had heard any cathedral service, the chanting of the Psalms was familiar to her by anticipation.[14]

Much in her family circumstances contributed to nourish this talent into serious musical endeavor rather than into the mere musical accomplishment of a young lady of her time. Her mother, an Eliza Gould, had been unladylike enough herself to progress from school teaching to marriage with a political prisoner whom she had visited in jail to express her sympathy with the cause of freedom of the press. At her death, when Eliza was only five, Eliza and her younger sister were given an upbringing both "original and erratic" by their father who gave them the intellectual training, if not the broad experience of the world, of educated young men of the time.[15] Because of the unusual circumstances of her childhood and education, and also, to some degree, in spite of them, for the father was evidently somewhat domineering in a kind way,[16] Eliza developed into a self-directed and serious musician. In 1831 she even appeared to Martineau, who was herself fighting for an independent woman's voice in the male world of achievement outside of the home, as almost a model of the new woman who would be able to avoid not only the trammels of conventionality but also the self-imposed shackles of sentimentality. A few years later, Harriet found herself less pleased with Eliza's strange relationship with W. J. Fox in which, apparently without sexual intimacy, she supplanted Fox's wife and took over as the mother of his children, his devoted housekeeper, and his amanuensis and helpmate in his various social and moral crusades. This affair, or lack of it, has ever since rivaled the notorious formal approach to a *ménage à trois* of her friend Harriet Taylor with Mr. Taylor and Mr. Mill in its ability to provoke hot gossip long after the principals, whether condemned as fleshly or dismissed as Platonic, have turned to dust.

Interesting as it is, her domestic arrangment should not obscure her real accomplishment and the greater promise which remained unfulfilled at her death from tuberculosis in 1846. All those who knew her personally rather than condemned from a distance saw her not as an appendage to her more widely famed companion but as a person of considerable independent vocation, even as an artistic genius. She was a fine performer.[17] She was a composer who published a book of musical settings to themes from Scott's Waverley novels, song sequences in Fox's *Monthly Repository,* and occasional ballads, most notably the once-famous, "Now Pray We for our Country."[18] After the initial scandal of her life with Fox, she became highly respected among the congregation of Fox's independent Unitarian South Place Chapel at Finsbury, where she was choirmaster. She adapted music from classical composers for their advanced, nondoctrinal hymn book and found her life's work in composing original music for other hymns.[19] The form now seems unfortunately a tomb in which her talents will lie buried till the resurrection of high musical seriousness in Protestant hymn singing; in her age, the *Westminster Review* could distinguish her both as the greatest composer of her sex and as the finest religious composer of her time.[20]

Close acquaintances not only admired her professional abilities but held her almost in awe as a person of high intellect and sound judgment. To Browning's later friend, the self-important John Forster, she would become one authority to whom he would bow both on matters of literary judgment and for adjudication of disputes between himself and Browning.[21] Other friends of Fox paid their homage to her, for instance Leigh Hunt or the actor Macready.[22] John Stuart Mill perhaps rendered the highest tribute to her capacities when, in the passage in his *Autobiography* in which he extolled Harriet Taylor with rhetoric rarely applied to humankind, he placed Eliza next to the throne (or pedestal) as a "person of genius, or of capacities of feeling or intellect kindred with her own."[23] If these weren't qualities enough for one woman, Eliza, with dark eyes, long dark hair in streaming ringlets and a "fragile sylph-like figure" was exceptionally attractive in a romantic, airy way.[24]

Sarah, who was generally called Sally or Sallie as Eliza was always Lizzie, was to Harriet Martineau a less glowing example of the coming woman. To Eliza's "Sense" she was cast to play "Sentiment," a girl who through miseducation and a natural weakness of will squanders high native gifts and succeeds neither in the traditional role of women nor in finding a new vocation for herself. Other writers speak of her "too exquisite temperament,"[25] and she does seem to have been too much a prey to her own emotions and subject to hysterical breakdowns. Yet in retrospect we may be more impressed by her versatility and talents and by how much she did manage to do before she became, after 1837, progressively more invalid, growing deaf and dumb and slowly dying from tuberculosis. She shared her sister's love for music and, more than Eliza, took a strong interest in the visual arts, even writing articles on art and society. Her main bent, however, was toward writing itself and the drama. She was remembered by friends for her fine readings from Shakespeare. Before the breakdown in her health, she had even begun commercial acting at Richmond and Bath and received some critical notice.[26] The high-water mark in her literary career would be reached in 1840, of course, with the lyrics for the hymn "Nearer, My God, to Thee" which, like all exceedingly popular works of art, can be too easily underrated. It is a poem of real power. The long dramatic poem *Vivia Perpetua*, a work rather similar in type to Browning's own *Paracelsus* and probably written not too long after, has some quite splendid individual passages which at least suggest her promise as a poetess. In intellectual range and lyrical boldness she was certainly the superior of many of the better-known fashionable bluestocking versifiers of the day.[27] For Fox's *Monthly Repository* she could also write competent, if somewhat overly flowery, prose articles and stories, which embody some of the progressive social concerns of Fox's circle.[28]

Sarah was, like Eliza, very attractive in a similarly romantic, if not so aloof, way. She married the intellectual steamroller William Bridges Adams in 1834, a man who wrote fiery articles for radical causes, including woman's liberation, under the name of Junius Redivivus and then, his patrimony exhausted, went on to become a captain of industry and an authority on railroad carriages and hardware. It was perhaps an ill match for a woman who was called sweet-tempered by all who spoke of her, though there is no evidence that Adams's acrimony as a writer was carried into the domestic sphere. Like Fox with Eliza, he certainly did not discourage Sarah from developing her talents.

When Browning knew them in his boyhood, of course, most of the Flowers' work was in the future and both girls were just emerging into full possession of their artistic abilities and personal attractions. Although the specifics of his relationship with the sisters are as vague as every aspect of Browning's early years and more boldly overwrought with undocumented rumors and traditions, it would probably be hard to overstate the general impact of these remarkable women on the boy. It does seem at least clear that Browning came to know them both fairly well. If both appeared in Browning's preteen years rather vaguely as family friends or, in the case of Eliza, possibly also as a music mistress, with the "Incondita" they entered solidly into his life. While Eliza was performing the practical service of putting Browning in contact with Fox, she did him the even greater kindness of herself making a sympathetic and careful reading of his poems. Taking due account of his age, she was very enthusiastic about them. She copied them out, and showed them to her sister who apparently caught from her (as she often did) the spark of enthusiasm.

Henceforth he was their "boy poet," a prodigy whom they may have associated romantically with mingled images of wondrous boy Chattertons and untutored geniuses of nature such as the milkmaid or plowboy poets of the eighteenth century. The evidence strongly suggests that he in return directed some of his first stirrings of adolescent feeling away from poeticizing and toward the sisters, especially Eliza. At least for a while his attention, as he explained to a friend years later in his long and embarrassed campaign to recover and destroy all evidence of this period, was engrossed with writing "verses and letters" to Eliza instead of playing "cricket and trapball."[29] We may wonder, as always, at Browning's excessive fear of having his early, very natural foolishnesses made public (without going out of our way to expose our own); but he was probably quite correct in calling these lost items "purely nonsensical." Possibly they were outrageously and gloriously so: precocity may have prevailed here as elsewhere.

Beyond the obvious fact of Browning's early adolescent idealization of Eliza and the concomitant infatuation, there is, however, little here to tickle the tooth of scandal. Although he almost certainly did write amorous poems of some kind to her at this time, the unendingly repeated assertion that she is the Pauline of his first published poem, written seven or eight years later, is baffling. Even if we trust the single authority for this supposition, Browning's friend and biographer Mrs. Orr, who says that, despite Browning's denials, if anyone inspired *Pauline* it was Eliza, we may, probably should, remain thoroughly skeptical.[30] For if we read the poem at all, it is just the premise itself that seems most unlikely. Pauline gives her name to the title, suggests that the speaker write a poem, and holds tight to him while he probes his psyche and memory at length. Otherwise, she hardly seems to exist. She is obviously not the real cause of the poem, nor felt as the inspiration, nor much material to its subject, which is the inner life of the author himself. Such as she is—and at best this is a very pallid literary ghost, even if Browning's undirected sexual feeling is not—Pauline is distinguished by her habit of writing in French, her origin in a distant land such as Chateaubriand might have imagined, and her sweet native songs. Eliza, of course, fits none of these qualifications, though she no doubt was "a key to music's mystery" like Pauline. She also was clearly entirely out of touch with Browning not only when *Pauline* was written, but even at the time when she is said to have first become the speaker's beloved. At most, Eliza may be said to lurk somewhere vaguely behind the shadowy figure of the poem in the idea of a woman half motherly and half sexually attractive who kindly indulges the speaker in his growing pains of guilt and irresolution. Only in this very limited sense—that Browning was recalling and utterly transforming his earlier feeling for her—can the tradition that Eliza was Pauline be correct. Zealots, of course, may apply the technique of earnest unlockers of Shakespeare's sonnets and find a verbal key in a tribute to her, "dear as a winter *flower*" (italics mine). But the least subtle skeptic will find other women in Browning's life—Sarah, his sister or mother, or a brief unnamed passion of his late teens—for whom an equally strong, and equally irrelevant case could be made.[31]

The serious influence that Eliza and her sister exercised on Browning was, of course, not that of early lovers but of very talented and cultivated young women friends who could communicate ideas and passion for music, literature, and art. At most, the puppy sexual attraction that Browning naturally must have felt for two such open and romantic older young women probably only helped, through the beneficent effects of necessary sublimation, to make their world of interests and enthusiasms more attractive than they might otherwise have been to someone his age. His very serious interest in music (which every parent who tries knows no lessons alone can buy) no doubt caught fire at the living flame of Eliza's musical devotion. Whether or not she ever served as his tutor, she must have given him the far more important education of direct contact with her musical thinking and enthusiasms. Very long after whatever love he may have felt for her had died away, his truly Platonic passion for her musical abilities was as strong as ever: "I never had another feeling," he wrote a year before her death, "than entire admiration for your music—entire admiration—I put it apart from all other English music I know, and fully believe it is *the* music we all waited for."[32] Even long after her death he spoke of her as "a composer of real genius."[33]

For Sarah's work he had evidently somewhat less enthusiasm. Although he observed St. Perpetua's day in one letter in tribute to her play, he later objected to a comparison Fox made between her and Elizabeth Barrett and criticized some of her popular verses (these quite rightly) as doggerel.[34] Her sweeter, less self-secure ways naturally bred less esteem. At the same time, they allowed greater ease and familiarity, though probably not the kind of familiarity Betty Miller speculates upon.[35] On a subject of tremendous concern to both of them, the authenticity of the Bible as the essential, perfectly trustworthy word of God, Browning had at least that one long talk with Sarah, if at the expense of provoking one of her crises of confidence and driving her in turn to seek an older counselor in Fox.[36] Her easy enthusiasm and readiness to be persuaded made her a very warm admirer of Browning's poems, especially because she was quick to romanticize him as a boy genius. The letter sending to Fox "The First-Born of Egypt" and "The Dance of Death," which Browning must have shared with her or Eliza, calls the poems "gems" and (apropos of mines) wishes "they were *mine* with all my soul—and I'm sure it would be worth all *my* soul if they were." Elsewhere in the letter she confidently speaks of the work as "that Genius's poetry."[37] Such lack of concern for critical judgment, though it suggests that there must have been many others called genius by her who are not now remembered, was not necessarily a bad influence on such a young talent. If Browning seems not to have written much more until *Pauline*, he still had been encouraged by Sarah to think highly of his abilities. Such praise even for boyhood efforts may have made him the more ready to try his talents seriously when he later turned back to poetry.

Her passion for poetry and literary achievement was not only highly complementary (and complimentary) to Browning's own passion but probably also played some part in creating his own enthusiasm. She was fond of giving dramatic readings from Shakespeare, and we may at least suspect that it was from her, as much as from his father and Uncle Reuben or his acting at school, that Browning first learned to daydream about Shakespeare's characters. Her renditions of Madge Wildfire or the Cid, done up with costume and dramatic action, were, like Charles Mathews's monopolylogues, primitive dramatic monologues in the general tradition out of which Browning would develop his mature art.[38] It is also very likely that Sarah and Eliza were both important to Browning in making him aware of contemporary literary figures and ideas. From the perspective of the Browning family, the Flowers were directly connected with the literary and intellectual world which they themselves admired but existed outside of: hence the appeal to them over the "Incondita" poems. In the 1830s they would provide through Fox most of Browning's immediate contacts with that world. Even in their earlier acquaintance they may have given Browning the sense that there were such worlds for boys to grow up to conquer.

"To me their friendship, a love as of two elder sisters . . . was indeed a liberal education," gushed a young man who knew them in a similar relationship at a later date.[39] For Browning, likewise, the acquaintance may be called an education, even to some degree that opening of the mind and encouragement to independent thinking which is a liberal education. On the whole, however, the distinctive training they offered might better be called, without irony, a sentimental education. To know them was to share, even more than specific skills or information, a special outlook on life and art, and a particular culture, which their unusual background and abilities had allowed them to develop and which few observers failed to notice. The same young man comes closer to defining their ambience when, in a further fit of praise, he says: "With their love and feeling for music and pictorial art, and their high poet-thought, they were such women in their purity, intelligence, and high-souled enthusiasm, as Shelley might have sung as fitted to redeem a world by their very presence."[40] Probably long before they knew of Shelley, they were indeed establishing their own special post-Jupiterian better world on the twin bases of high spiritual enthusiasm and the religion of art.

In this religion Eliza, with her whole-souled devotion to music and to all high causes, was a saint. Sarah, less able to exist unintermittingly in her sister's realms of lofty inspiration and emotion, was the high priestess, praising Eliza and exhorting herself toward a state of perfect feeling and assurance, which she only rarely attained. The litany was in essence, purity, nobility, and enthusiasm, repeated over and over again, one meaning in varying words.

Although both ultimately were to have more than their share of human trouble, anguish, and pain, they aspired to attain, even in this world, the exalted state of soul traditionally said to be reached only beyond death. Both were working toward, and under Fox's tutelage would arrive at a

Christianity entirely purged of what Fox called the "sour milk of Calvinism." Salvation could be universal and the seeds of salvation could be found by each individual within himself, ready to be nurtured into full spiritual growth. Without being too clear about the formal theology, the girls were, as Martineau perceptively observed, attempting to go back to Eden's garden. In her novel, they are pointedly pictured as engrossed in reading the passages about the garden in *Paradise Lost*. Years later, Eliza would give her second collection of religious music the title "Heaven upon Earth." (The final volume, "Life in Death," seems almost supererogatory.)

Their optimistic and love-centered religious outlook, combined with their relatively sheltered lives in country town and suburban village, enabled them to adopt a peculiarly innocent and untroubled form of romanticism, what might be, to an antiromantic such as Irving Babbitt, the ultimate abomination because of its ultimate faith in human nature. To conceive of their perspective we must imagine a Wordsworth never disillusioned in his first faith in the French Revolution, a Coleridge married to his truelove in opium-free bliss, a Byron seeing nothing around him to raise his sense of irony, or, above all, a Shelley whose early heresies were welcomed by Oxford and Sir Timothy as the earnest firstfruits of an aspiring soul and a proof of his noble spirituality. With their faith in the goodness of feeling, they were able to obliterate all distinction between religious aspiration and artistic inspiration. In Sarah's *Vivia Perpetua* (1841) Christian belief is a noble inspiration that carries the soul beyond earth:

> Hast not felt thy soul
> To swell and press against this limiting earth?
> Hast never thirsted for a perfect truth.

Such feeling then necessarily leads to art:

> Think, with what joy, what loving adoration,
> Would burst the song of praise from forth our souls.[41]

Indeed, Christ himself is no more nor less than "the immortal Poet of Humanity" who wakes other souls to their potential for artistic feeling:

> His life a poem, that will yet create
> Myriads of poems, deathless souls of men,
> Regenerate by his divine example![42]

As a corollary, when her religion seemed threatened, as it was after the discussion over the authenticity of the Bible, Sarah was likely to feel a parallel crisis in aesthetics: Handel's "Messiah" then "dwindled to a mere musical enjoyment."[43] Sarah's own writing was a matter of sincerity to feeling and overflow of emotion without any of the scruples over form or personal preparedness felt by the great Romantics: "The spontaneous expression of some strong impulse or feeling at the moment . . . she wrote when she felt that the spirit moved her."[44] Nor was she bothered much by the greater Romantics' periodic states of inner deadness and dejection. When excited by anything, she admitted with perfect candor, she was subject to "feeling like a runaway horse."[45] Although her best poetry grew out of a hard-earned sense of the difficulty of truly attaining spiritual elevation, she more often celebrated, in an ultrasimple romantic form, the direct path from beauty or nature to religious feeling.[46]

With a similar intuitive leaning toward an uncomplicated romanticism which celebrates the validity of immediate feeling, Eliza's first work, the music for Scott's Waverley novels, magnified the human passions embodied in popular traditions. She was presented to Scott as a "young enthusiast" by a friend and wrote him herself of her high feeling for "Scotch scenery and the sound of Scotch song" which "could not help glowing under the influence of *her poetry*."[47] The motto for the attractive volume, from *The Lady of the Lake*, identified enthusiasm with art: "If one heart throbs higher at its sway / The wizard note has not been touch'd in vain."

From secular to sacred enthusiasm was an easy step, or possibly no step at all. Eliza and Fox ultimately selected passages for their hymn book by preference from nonreligious poets, including Byron, Coleridge, Shelley, and even Browning himself.[48] All high attainments of humanity were by definition religion as well as art. In admiring Eliza's musical art, Sarah was probably not overstating Eliza's own view of what she was doing when she repeatedly spoke of her music as a holy thing. A composition is referred to as "a lovely heaven-born seraph-child."[49] A performance of an adaption from Mendelssohn is "inspired, simple, fervent, musical expression. Lizzie the while," she observes, "with heart, soul, voice, finger, frame, seeming all but borne upward by the strain, as on wings to heaven." She assures her correspondent, "you would have *religioned* in it, and her enjoyment of it."[50] Sarah's most hyperbolic, but also rather attractive, tribute to her sister, the poem "A Summer Recollection" (1836) even speaks of her as "a saint divine" and boldly asserts, "On Earth there is no purer, brighter Heaven."[51]

From our distant perspective, which clarifies the larger scene even while it makes it impossible to see the full complexity of life and detail, it seems obvious that the two sisters were both a very rare source of enrichment to Browning's early life and also a rather strange, even exotic model for creative activity. If through their help he came quickly to realize the limits of the imitative "Incondita" and was put in wider touch with what was going on in contemporary literary and artistic life, he was also encouraged toward a new bias. Here, unlike the earlier imitations, the bias was not merely toward a past style and a pose but toward an entire, rather one-sided view of art and the aim of the artist. Remarkable and talented as they were, Browning's friends must seem to us oddly lopsided in their art and opinions. While they devoted all their attention to illuminating brilliantly the top room of the tower of art with every candle of spiritual emotion they could light up, they left all the other rooms of art almost totally dark. Intent on attaining and expressing their own most exalted states of soul, their general feelings of spirituality and purity, they neglected the usual concerns and subjects of art: the complexity of man, society, and the world in its unspiritualized and unregenerate state. For them art was not so much about life as a mission in life. Their ultimate aim in art, like the hopes of the religious to establish Christ's kingdom on earth, was, as Sarah put it, to render "the whole world . . . one vast spectacle of moral, intellectual and physical beauty." In that dim future "universal love shall have wrought out universal beauty."[52]

We need not cynically disparage the obvious good intentions behind such a view of art or presume that there must be some neurotic motive for the sisters' focus on love, beauty, and spirituality. But, like John Stuart Mill, when he liberated himself from the very different, though equally single-minded focus of the early Utilitarian reformers, we may wonder whether such a brave new world, thus perfected and simplified by art, could really make us happy. Mill himself, with the highest appreciation for the value of their kind of cultivation and ability, could also see, sympathetically but justly, what was lacking in the Flowers' kind of art. He described Harriet Taylor, Eliza's friend and fellow enthusiast, as one general kind of personality, the "received type of feminine genius." Bright and noble to the outer world, on the inside she is "a woman of deep and strong feeling, of penetrating and intuitive intelligence, and of an eminently meditative and poetic nature."[53] Good as all this is, the problem with this attractive role (which Mill felt Harriet later overcame) is that there is not enough relation between this inner sensitivity and the world. Genius is turned excessively inward until it may seem wasted in mere celebration of sensitivity. Power unexercised in the world becomes pent up until the force of character needed to achieve specific goals is lost.

Women like the Flowers might be especially susceptible to such imbalance, but the difficulty was a more general one into which talented women, still largely isolated and overprotected by society, were only more likely to fall. With his own somewhat isolated upbringing, his general sensitivity and self-awareness, Browning himself—or at least one part of his character— was especially attracted by the sisters and their world. Seeming to open up new experiences, in reality they gave encouragement to romantic tendencies already present in his life. It would be too much to say that Browning was in any sense a disciple of that "very remarkable person," Eliza, or her sister.[54] But it is undeniable that, at least for a time, they drew his attention and encouraged him toward a similar ideal of an exalted, spiritual, and enthusiastic kind of art.

Beyond this general recognition of their importance to him, it is impossible, for mere want of information, to chronicle their specific influence. Outside of the lost verses to Eliza and the two poems of age fourteen that have survived, Browning apparently was not writing poetry in his early teens; certainly none has been preserved. We may suspect that it was largely because of Eliza's influence that in this period he focused more of his attention on music than poetry, and on music understood as Eliza understood it —as the medium of emotion and feeling par excellence. Yet we have no music by Browning from the time and no way to measure her influence here. *Pauline*, written after the break in their acquaintance, obviously shows a general compatibility with both sisters' ideas of art and artistic sensitivity, however little can be said about Eliza's personal part in it. However, there is a more obvious lyrical influence working in *Pauline*. And, if any relation between Browning and the Flowers can be extrapolated from the speaker of that poem's relation to the imaginary Pauline, it is surely dissonance, not harmony, that is expressed. The character Pauline represents an attractive, but rather naive artistic simplicity that Browning must contrast to his own more unsettled and complex state: a state that remains what it must be despite all regrets, guilty feelings, and promises to be again what he has been. Like Schiller's naive poet Pauline is to sing her "native songs, gay as a desert bird / Who crieth as he flies for perfect joy"; she is—in the passage that seems most applicable to Eliza—"a key to music's mystery when mind fails," an example of art at its most intuitive and most purely emotional.

When, with the publication of *Pauline*, he began to see the sisters again, Browning was already clearly beyond the reach of their direct influence. Although Sarah considered him "unexceptionally poetical" (except for his nose, which was a problem), he was no longer the boy-poet who had come to them earlier.[55] His intellectuality, his growing cosmopolitanism and ambitiousness, his consciousness of powers seeking mastery and understanding through art, all made him far less attractive to the Flowers. If they accepted him as a bright part of their society, they also—especially Eliza—became increasingly critical of his divergence from their ideal of life and art. In a copy of *Pauline* that purports to be Sarah's, some pencil marginalia—presumably also hers—make this attitude very clear. Purely lyrical passages are marked with evident enthusiasm and applause for Browning's abilities, but the very unlyrical complexity of the character that he attempts to analyze in the poem is deplored with equal feeling. His statement that his selfishness is "satiated not" is seconded in the margin: "true!" His craving after knowledge is stigmatized "*vanity*." Talk of his content with a simple life is censured: "True to [?] the perfected soul but not of yours RB, alas." Worst of all, the Byronic allusion to "deeds for which remorse were vain" is confirmed: "*true!* poor lad."[56]

The import of these markings, which are either by Sarah or outright forgeries, is clearly echoed by other comments by the sisters. Eliza wondered if this new Browning even had a heart and complained that he had "twisted the old-young shoot" of her affection for him "off by the neck."[57] In Browning's first longer successful work, *Pippa Passes,* she saw only an "exquisite subject" ruined by "the egoism of the man." In fact, the subject is riddled with temptations to sentimentality and jejune spiritual optimism that are only controlled by Browning's artistic mastery: the puppetry, or overall vision of the workings of many lives in a small town that Eliza found so offensive: "as if God worked by puppets as well as Robert Browning."[58] Ironically, Eliza has been said to be the model Browning had before him for the central character when he wrote *Pippa*.[59] There is even less apparent reason for this than for the coupling of her and Pauline, for the uneducated silk worker of Asolo seems, to say the least, not much like the highly cultivated, English musician. However, in celebrating the power of song and innocent goodness, Browning may have been abstracting at least some of Eliza's most distinctive qualities. She seemed to Browning, at any rate, to fit the overall mood of the piece, and he even suggested seriously that she compose accompaniments for the lyrics.[60]

Although there can be no obvious equation between the innocence of Pippa and that of Eliza, the different views of *Pippa* are perhaps symbolic of the change in the earlier relation between Browning and both Sarah and Eliza. While Browning continued to value their special qualities, the lyrical sincerity and simple assertion of what seemed most obviously good, he came to see it as one part of the more complex human scene, no less good but limited by its very innocence to seeing only certain aspects of reality. He began to practice a more complex art not by turning cynically against their simpler, lyrical ideal, but by incorporating it into his overall vision of the different possibilities in life and art. Eliza by contrast, found his vision less poetic, in her sense, for trying to be comprehensive rather than merely personal. Here again, as with the far simpler attempt at imitation in the "Incondita," Browning was learning that someone else's aims in art, someone else's style and values, could not simply be appropriated wholesale. His own different and more complex circumstances and needs made it impossible for him to be satisfied with the kind of art and artistic vision that would suffice for Eliza or Sarah. Their kind of radical subjectivity might satisfy one side of his nature, but it did so only by famishing his other more social and intellectually ambitious qualities. Contact with these remarkable women helped him develop in one direction but eventually drove him on, unsatisfied, to seek a more complex idea of art and a more complex style of expression.

IX
Sun-Treader: First Flight

Much the same process was to take place with an influence which followed the "Incondita" and the association with the Flowers in time and which, if anything did, seized Browning and forced him into a half alien, half sympathetic mold. This was, of course, the influence of Shelley's poetry and the conception of Shelley the man that Browning induced from his work: that influence which, to judge from many accounts of Browning, was the single inner event of his first twenty years and the only begetter of his mind and poetry. On the contrary, far from merely molding an unformed and shapeless young man after his image, Shelley, like the Flowers, was able to have such a strong influence on Browning because he appealed so forcibly to one side of his character and experience. Almost magnetically, he drew out, then focused and concentrated Browning's emotional sensitivity and the idealistic tendencies of his family and family religion. Here, however, the influence, though no less eccentric than the Flowers', was that of major genius and compelling creative power. Browning's understanding of Shelley would intensify and complicate itself with his attempts to free himself from the limitations of his early conceptions of him. The process of finding his own way, a way that would give artistic expression to his own complexity rather than parrot the stranger and possibly greater complexity of Shelley would not come merely from a few years of personal growth but from years of effort in the 1820s and 1830s. In some sense, it would even require a lifetime of effort to comprehend the special power of his predecessor and to integrate him into his own wider vision of life.

1 Shelley Discovered: "A Spell to Me Alone"

How Browning came to know the work of the poet who had died at twenty-nine in the Gulf of Spezia in 1822 is still something of a mystery, though that it should be a mystery is itself somewhat strange. Unlike his friend Byron, Shelley had attained some notoriety but no accompanying fame as a poet during his lifetime. Save among a very narrow circle of friends and admirers, he was virtually unread. Except for *The Cenci*, which was printed first in Italy and then again in England, none of his works had even gone into second editions during his lifetime. His reputation might have expanded after his death, but it was, rather, contracted by his father's insistence that nothing of his be published or reprinted. Mary Shelley, in hope of support from her father-in-law, agreed to suppress the splendid volume of *Posthumous Poems* in 1824 and to do nothing to keep Shelley's name before the public. Unsold copies of previous works were sent to the office of Leigh Hunt's brother and nephew, John and Henry Hunt, where they were evidently available on demand to those who already knew of Shelley but were neither advertised nor distributed.

Shelley was thus not only virtually unknown but almost unavailable in the 1820s. The one exception, his early doctrinaire *Queen Mab*, which was repeatedly issued in pirated editions intended for a particular market of tin-eared freethinkers, was hardly likely, as Shelley himself had realized, to help the poet's serious reputation. An old story, probably originating with William Sharp's biography, claimed that Browning first stumbled over this bad work of a good poet, advertised in a bookstall, as "Mr. Shelley's Atheistical Poem: very scarce."[1] Sharp had a talent for imaginative elaboration, but he did know Browning and may be recalling something of what was told him.

It is possible Browning did at some time obtain *Queen Mab* in this way, but he himself left a clear record in a different work about his "first specimen of Shelley's poetry." This specimen was, in fact, the only other place where he was likely to have met with Shelley: one of a few unauthorized editions published by William Benbow of High-Holborn in 1826 and 1827, perhaps with some collusion on the part of Shelley's well-wishers.[2] The one Browning had was a collection mostly of lyrics taken from the *Posthumous Poems* entitled *Miscellaneous Poems,* by Percy Bysshe Shelley (1826). It was a cheap little volume, no more than three inches wide and four inches long, with unimpressive brown covers. In a note he added on the back of the front cover in 1878 Browning explained that it was a gift of his cousin, James Silverthorne; he probably received it some time in late 1826 or 1827.[3] How Silverthorne happened to give him this work is a further mystery. A strange comment made by Fox about six years later in a descriptive piece suggests that the first interest in Shelley might even have begun, fittingly enough, with a hint from Eliza. "L[izzie]," he says, lost a poem of Shelley's on a picnic last autumn and where it was lost "this spring some one found a delicate, exotic-looking plant, growing wild on the very spot, with 'Pauline' hanging from its slender stalk."[4] The incident had some real basis. Eliza had managed to lose Browning's own copy of *Rosalind and Helen*, which he had loaned to Fox in 1833 after *Pauline* was published.[5] But the implication seems to be that this is a fanciful way of recalling an earlier discussion of Shelley's poetry, when Browning himself was a younger, impressionable sensitive plant.

However he and his cousin happened first to take an interest in Shelley, Browning's enthusiasm was strongly whetted by the poems in the Benbow volume. He naturally wanted more; but he was stymied by Sir Timothy's efforts to kill his dead son's reputation, a more reprehensible activity than his more understandable hostility to Shelley's actions when he was alive. With Browning, who would come to play a small part himself in elevating Shelley to fame as a major English poet, the strategy rather backfired. The mystery surrounding this unnatural procedure with the work of a poet but recently dead only served to stimulate his interest. The first hint of martyrdom, as always, worked to push distant spectators into roles of partisans and converts. Ultimately, Browning wrote to the *Literary Gazette*—a miscellany of prose, poetry, reviews, and literary notices—to ask where he could find Shelley's works. What is probably the answer, printed in the regular section in which the editor replied "To Correspondents," appeared on November 24, 1827: "K. may [,] we presume, get the information he seeks at any publisher's; at Messrs Hunt and Clarke he is sure of it."[6] By such a cloak and dagger procedure Browning, or rather his mother who bought him the books, was finally led to the offices of the Hunts, by then evolved into Hunt and Clarke, York Street, Covent Garden.[7] There they indeed got the "goods," goods which today could only be had by stealing from the most precious collections of rare book libraries. Aside from *The Cenci*, which he probably bought in the English second edition, he was able to obtain first editions of all Shelley's major publications except the *Alastor* volume of 1816 (the poem itself he had in *Posthumous Poems*), the suppressed satire *Oedipus Tyrannus; or Swellfoot the Tyrant*, and possibly *Hellas*.[8] Very likely, though there is no positive evidence of this, he also picked up one of the pirated *Queen Mab* editions either from Hunt and Clarke or from a different bookseller at about this time.[9] From Hunt and Clarke he did obtain at least two other treasures, Keats's *Endymion* and the great *Lamia* volume of 1820.[10]

Eventually Keats would be virtually as important a poet to Browning as Shelley and in some ways a closer fellow spirit. Even his first reading gave him a lifelong interest in Keats. But his focus was now to be primarily on Shelley and on the splendor of works like *Prometheus Unbound, Adonais, The Cenci, Epipsychidion*, or the famous shorter poems and lyrics of the *Posthumous Poems*. Between this reading and the writing of *Pauline* was to be the time, if any, when, in the words of Browning's friend Arnould, "Shelley was his God."[11]

In attempting to assess what in fact this means, what effect Shelley did have on Browning, the harm of Sharp's otherwise pleasant little anecdote, as with most biographical myths, is less the single distortion of fact than the waves of implication that have become attached to it.[12] What still needs to be emphasized against the earlier impression, is how comprehensive a range of Shelley's work Browning was able to read and respond to almost immediately. Far from having to surmise Shelley's mature complexity and greatness from the half-success, half-silliness of *Queen Mab*, Browning first saw a volume that contained, with the notable omissions of "The Cloud" and the "Ode to the West Wind," virtually all of Shelley's finest short poems. Then within a short time, he acquired almost all the poems and dramatic poetry Shelley had published. Only the great "Defence of Poetry," which was not to be published until 1840, would remain an important blank spot in his awareness of Shelley's multiplex literary abilities. Although he came under the influence of Shelley's ideas and ideologies—from the simplicity of vegetarianism to the complexity of millennial political ideals—at the deepest level he had to absorb the impact not just of a few troubling ideas but of Shelley's total, strange and perplexing genius. This influence, this covering angel, as Harold Bloom might call him, from the shadow of whose wings Browning would devote a huge amount of his creative labors to set himself free, was to be not one aspect of Shelley, or one distorted side of him, but his full complex power.

The effect of one writer upon another writer who comes under the power of his genius is bound to be a confused mixture of inspiration and benefit on the one hand and misdirection and harmful distraction from more natural tendencies on the other. In the case of Shelley, who perhaps more than any modern poet, has exercised a special and profoundly strong influence on many of his successors—Hardy and Yeats, along with Browning, are only the most obvious examples—the impact is almost certain to be peculiarly powerful. To this assertion both admirers and detesters of Shelley are likely readily to agree, but the grounds of agreement are not likely to be the same. To the admirer of Shelley, the strength of the influence is a measure of Shelley's own strength as a poet and the successor's problem is the problem of all disciples of true master-spirits: that to break away from the master on one's own is to become necessarily something less than the model. To others, the influence of Shelley is particularly strong because peculiarly bad: it holds out the great temptation of all simplicities that attempt to appear as greatness. What probably should be recognized here, and most often is not, is that Shelley was both a magnificent and a terrible example, at once the glory and the negation of humanity, a poet who will never be soberly enshrined in the prophet's corner where his admirers might wish to place him nor ever safely locked away from harm as those who dislike or fear him may wish. He will have his impact, and that often a total one, on those who feel his unique force. He will never, save on some improbable second Shelley, pass on his power to his beneficiaries without also loading them with impossible visions and unattainable poetic aims that they will have to come to terms with or fail trying.

Having said so much of the complexity of Shelley, it is particularly humbling, as a way to understand Browning's own early reactions to Shelley, to try to define more exactly in what this complexity consists. For there is the certainty that such an attempt with a poet like Shelley can only lead to iteration of simplicities. But at that price, it is perhaps still worth recalling the ways in which Shelley's unsteady and fitful brilliance can be seen somewhat steadily and somewhat wholly. In part, and as a beginning, we must recognize in him the heir to both the Enlightenment and the French Revolution, asserting his belief in the need for total political and social revolution and regeneration in a time, in the teens of the nineteenth century, of particularly great repression and reaction. His chosen role was thus to embody what he considered the highest aspirations of his society while expressing most vigorously his sense of alienation from what society actually was and from the traditional religious and social institutions on which it rested. Such radical commitment and radical alienation left his work strangely divided. He could be at one time the poet who envisioned in rosy symbolic terms the new social order of heart's desire. At other times, or even in other parts of the same poem, he could be the most bitterly insightful realist, even a scientific analyst, about the abusive state of things as they are.

For all the sincerity of his social concern, Shelley's profound alienation was both result and cause of a deeper focus on his isolated self, an even more radical development of romantic tendencies toward individualism than his political and social attitudes were of Enlightenment criticisms of the social order. While Wordsworth or Keats might attempt to relate their moments of intense personal insight to their normal selves and normal experience, Shelley could dwell through entire poems, and evidently through much of his life, in the realm of purely subjective lyrical or symbolic imagination. Intensely self-conscious but without conscious critical embarrassment, he seemed able at times to substitute the world of his own feelings and imagination for external reality entirely.

Although as social radical and as radical realist, Shelley can be defined, even placed within some kind of tradition of ideas, as lyricist and visionary his position is and probably must remain uncertain, ambiguous, even mysterious. Here is both his obvious power and his greatest limitation. Some of Shelley's most skeptical critics have wanted to dismiss this side of him entirely by claiming that his poems are essentially defective as works of art, that they act only as imprecise vessels to receive predisposed vague sentiments on the part of the reader, that they represent, in effect, a rarified form of sentimentality. This may be true, as with the bad work of other poets, of Shelley at his worst. But it is not a sufficient dismissal for the splendid though strange works of Shelley's lyrical or symbolic imagination. The best of these exist as full creations and must have their independent effect on the reader who is not himself a prefilled vessel, predisposed to dismiss Shelley however he finds him.

The grain of truth in the accusation of imprecision and vagueness is, however, that far more than most poetry, this work of Shelley's will leave readers who have had the experience of the poetry thoroughly divided about the meaning of the experience. As with any puzzling, mysterious, and moving performance, interpretations of the same experience may vary from charges of charlatanism up the gamut to proclamations of a religious miracle. While Shelley has not escaped the charge of fraud, his work has more often been explained away, even by those who admit its power, as an aberration, especially as a psychological deviation. Few poets (indeed few politicians, either) can escape the charge that neurosis or psychosis is at the base of their unusual power. In Shelley's case it *is* hard to deny that his poems grow out of experience often open only to those, like him, who are cut off from the ordinary relations of society and the ordinary repressions of everyday consciousness. Although we may prove, as commentators have, that Shelley is hardly ever lacking in intellectual force and virtually never writes without trailing a considerable baggage of classical and scientific knowledge, we will have to acknowledge that he deliberately chooses to write in the areas of abnormal or partially unconscious human experience rather than in those of daylight consciousness. The stuff or fabric of his particular vision is, in the largest sense, not merely a social vision but an exploration of the inner self and emotions, conscious and unconscious, in their fullest complexity. Shelley, of course, intends to harrow the unconscious to bring out only what is good there, working against the tyranny of repression inside himself as much as in his society. But the noble enterprise is a dangerous one that threatens to destroy not only unnecessary repression but normal conscious order and that may end up running on the knife-edge of insanity. The cloth of an abstract vision drawn from within threatens at every moment to be rent through by the working of the powerful emotional chemicals from which it is made. Constructive vision then yields to the destructive force of madness. Celebrating in his best poetry the unlimited power of love, Shelley celebrates an ambiguous force, a pulsing essence of the unconscious which may work for good or turn terribly to ill depending on how it is used.

To those who fear this force it seems half mad to play with it at all. Literature for them becomes somehow less itself for trying to go beneath the surfaces of things. For others, this is the noble task of the hero of the unconscious who reveals our deeper selves to us even at the risk of madness or absurdity. He is a visionary philosopher who speaks in the special language of symbolic poetry of aspects of man not open to analytical discourse. With a different view of the unconscious, a seemingly slight variation that really opens into essential philosophical dichotomies, the inward-turned imagination reveals not merely the ultimate parameters of the personality but special kinds of truth that are only found in this way. In this view, Shelley's uniqueness is not merely a personal aberration but an approach to a more universal truth than men usually may obtain. Depending on what this truth is taken to be, Shelley's role itself seems to vary. To the Jungian, Shelley is discovering, in his personal inspiration, innate forms and symbols behind all conscious thinking. To the Platonist, he is a seer expressing in symbolic forms the certain and unchanging realities beneath or above the fluctuating appearances of things. Or, despite his early militant atheism and lifelong agnosticism, he is seen as in essence a part of his reader's own religion or mysticism, a poet whose utmost exploration of his own powers has led him to the sources of divinity planted in his deepest being. If he is not Christ himself, he has at least found the Christ within, or so the Christian rationalist for Shelley would have it.

Whichever view of Shelley one leans toward (and it is possible to incline toward more than one at a time) what is important in assessing Shelley's influence on the young Browning, who read him intensely, fully, and evidently repeatedly, some time after his fourteenth year, is not so much how Shelley's strange power is to be explained but the fact of its power and strangeness. To feel the strength of his poetry was to be challenged both into new states of awareness and into new conceptions of the possible roles of the artist. And the challenge was no less strong for coming in a form so open to a variety of interpretations about its ultimate significance. Indeed, Browning can be said to have spent a good deal of his critical energy in his teens and twenties, and even intermittently throughout his life, in repeated efforts to deal with the complexity of Shelley: understanding one facet of his genius or coming to terms with one perspective on his strange power only to find new challenges opening before him.

Browning's later views of Shelley, when he had arrived at some clearer conception of his own life and work, are still complex but at least fairly definitely formulated. In the early 1850s when he wrote the poem "Memorabilia" and the so-called "Essay on Shelley," for what turned out to be spurious letters of Shelley, he obviously still had the very highest opinion of Shelley's personality as well as his work. To hear a chance word by someone who knew the poet—as Browning does in "Memorabilia"—was still to feel that a myth was suddenly thrust into his everyday world. But in the "Essay" he also put Shelley's special genius decidedly in perspective. It was identified specifically as only one kind—though a great kind—of poetic power. Browning called it subjective, and contrasted it to a kind he obviously valued at least equally and leaned toward far more in his own work: the objective poetic genius he identified with Shakespeare. Later, as more of the facts of Shelley's life became available to him, Browning became even openly critical of him.[13] In his relation with his first wife he seemed to Browning, as to many persons since, "half crazy and wholly inexcusable."[14] The poet came to appear a "poor silly boy," and even the poetry seemed at times also a diminished thing, though Browning never entirely lost his ability to catch fire over Shelley's dramatic poetry and his fine lyrical descriptions.[15]

At age fourteen or fifteen, however, Browning had neither the real knowledge of Shelley's life nor enough experience of his own life and poetry to see the poet plain and the poetry in perspective. Shelley's obvious power, brought home with added force by the mysterious, conspiratorial manner in which his works had to be obtained and by the legend planted in his poetry and taking root around his strange death and stranger life, seized the teen-age boy and threw him for a time into the heart of Shelley's mystery.

2 A Poetic Conversion

The total impact of Shelley on Browning was all the greater because Browning read him at a time when he was open to more than one aspect of his genius. From what Browning would later stigmatize as his "foolish markings and still more foolish scribblings" in the Benbow *Miscellaneous Poems*, we can still obtain a fairly good idea of "the impression made on a boy by this first specimen of Shelley's poetry." Despite Browning's indus-trious efforts to smear across, blot over, scratch through, or cut out effu-sions of his earlier self, his overall enthusiasm and at least some of his spe-cific interests are obvious in Pottle's careful report of marginal markings and the few comments left untouched.[16] What is most clear is that Browning first responded to Shelley in the way that seems somehow right and just: not as a thinker, nor as a strange personality, nor as a moral or religious force, but simply as a master of language and simple expression. With a few nota-ble exceptions, what he had in the Benbow volume was a concentrated col-lection of Shelley's finest, and often most personal, lyric pieces, the shorter works that Mary Shelley copied out of the various manuscripts left unpub-lished at Shelley's death for the *Posthumous Poems*.

To be sure, there were also more complicated works such as the frag-ments of "Prince Athanase," "Mont Blanc," or the unsuccessful but inter-esting dramatic start, "Charles the First," and we have no right to conclude from lack of markings in some parts of the book that Browning was not in-terested in these. But the positive evidence all suggests that he was heavily attracted by the simpler, but subtly impressive lyrical ability of Shelley. Except for the ubiquitous "To a Skylark," his favorites seem to have been poems that don't stand out in Shelley's total work but that are extremely fine lyrics. Largely free from the peculiarities of Shelley's genius at its great-est and strangest, they are perfect little poems of description or lyrical feel-ing. Some are really love lyrics like the charmed and romantic "Lines to an Indian Air" (now, through Browning's own report of a manuscript he saw in Italy, titled "The Indian Serenade"), which seems to have been his favor-ite poem in the volume and which he would still call "a divine little poem" in the 1850s.[17] Another favorite, "To Mary," beginning "O Mary dear, that you were here," reveals Shelley in a rather rare mood of simple, per-sonal feeling that demands no more abstract or complicated expression. Others were equally uncomplicated but effective poems of description like "Dirge for the Year" on the age-old theme of seasonal death and rebirth, "To Night," the most heavily marked poem—probably because of its strik-ing beauty as a lyrical invocation and evocation of a state of mind—or "On the Medusa of Leonardo da Vinci" with the more gothic attraction of terror and beauty mixed in a descriptive word-picture.

Shelley's power to create myth, even at the simplest level of giving form to lyrical emotions, similarly caught Browning's attention in his first reading. The poem "Arethusa," for instance, returns to the origins of myth in its account of Alpheus chasing the river Arethusa down to the sea and presents this in the heightened opposing symbols of romantic myth-making. A poem not marked but very much imprinted on Browning's mind, "The Two Spirits," gave him another first impression of Shelley's striking power in wrapping opposing images into spontaneous symbols and mythic tales. One spirit chooses the earthly path below; the other resolves, in a kind of purely symbolic language, to soar aloft:

I'll sail on the flood of the tempest dark,
With the calm within and the light around
   Which makes night day:
And thou, when the gloom is deep and stark,
Look from thy dull earth, slumber-bound,
My moon-like flight thou then mayst mark
   On high, far away.[18]

Two poems that come closer to Shelley's habitual concerns with his role as a poet and with the role of the poet in society, "Stanzas Written in Dejection, near Naples" and the "Hymn of Apollo," deserved Browning's attention—though not, perhaps, quite the "splendid" he wrote above the "Hymn." They are simpler and more conventional treatments of these subjects than Shelley makes at his highest level of inspiration, for instance in *Adonais* or the "Ode to the West Wind."

As he revisited the Benbow poems at age sixty-six, Browning scribbled on the inside cover a last sigh in the form of the opening from Shelley's famous "A Lament," which he must also have first read in this same volume: "O world, O Life, O Time!"[19] No doubt he intended some irony. With time he, like the Shelley of the poem, felt the loss of his early idealized vision, only his early idealization was of the poet himself and his lament was over the lamenter. But the primary feeling is, I think, personal; he glances back at a state of youthful enthusiasm that can never be recaptured in the soberer reading of age. In the rather ratty little volume he had found poetry that spoke in highly emotional, musical, sometimes even incantatory language about subjects that appealed simply and directly to him. Even more than in his friendship with the Flowers, he had found here a vehicle for the expression of his own highly developed inner consciousness and feelings, his love of nature, art, and music. Without cynicism we can add that Shelley, young poet himself, was a natural lightning rod for Browning—as he has been for thousands of other young readers—who attracted the free flowing sexual energy of adolescence, much as the more tangible but perhaps less apprehensible attractions of Eliza had a few years before. Before he became something at once more complex and more troubling to Browning, Shelley must have appeared on a more immediate and human level as a kind of ideal companion, someone who seemed both to echo and perfect his own secret aspirations and feelings. A brief allusion in Browning's *Trifler* article to one of the lesser Benbow poems that caught his attention is indicative of this first experience of Shelley. In reading "Love's Philosophy," Browning had crossed out part of the subtitle calling it an imitation from the French and correctly substituted "Anacreon ode."[20] In the *Trifler* he pays a tribute to Shelley by linking him through this poem to the great Greek lyric poet from Teos. Just as Anacreon, considering how all things in nature take up moisture, "did set himself seriously to drink," so in "Love's Philosophy," "from an accurate consideration of the osculatory propensities of mountain, wind, and flower, the sweet poet of our days did determine sedulously to kiss."[21] "Sweet poet of our days" may call up Keats, or Leigh Hunt, or even "Anacreontic" Moore more readily than Shelley for most readers of the Romantics. But to Browning, Shelley appeared first with a very human face. It was only as he proceeded from his initial feeling for Shelley's lyric and expressive abilities that he began to see in Shelley something more than a sympathetic, sweet companion.

Even this partial, first reading of Shelley probably had a serious effect upon Browning. There is no evidence that he began to strike out his own verses in response. Browning seems in fact not to have been writing any poetry between the verses associated wtih the Flowers and the composition of *Pauline* at twenty, a period of as long as six years. Music and reading in Greek literature, not writing poetry, were then the primary forms for his creative emotions.[22] Still, Shelley's lyrics had found a responsive chord in Browning's feelings, and the effect was at least to show the future poet that English poetry, as well as music, could embody his emotions and concerns.

Had this been all the impact Shelley had on Browning, it would have been a great deal. It was, rather, merely the beginning. Browning's own description in *Pauline* of reading Shelley is founded on the age-old rhetorical idea that poets work by delighting to instruct. The only difference is that Browning views the entire experience as a far more emotional and personal event. Shelley's message, his larger vision for mankind, came, Browning recalled, "Clothed in all passion's melodies, which first / Caught me . . ." The result was what we have seen: after reading Benbow he was set "as to a sweet task, / To gather every breathing of his songs." Finally, as he read through most of Shelley's poems he began to see, worked everywhere into the fabric of the poetry, something more than the superficial sweet melodies of passion:

> woven with them there were words which seemed
> A key to a new world; the muttering
> Of angels, of some thing unguessed by man.
> How my heart beat, as I went on . . .

The process seems ultimately closer to that of conversion than rhetorical persuasion. Convictions and feelings unformed within him—"Much there! I felt my own mind had conceived, / But there living and burning"—became organized into a full and central commitment. The development seems a natural one in view of Browning's reading. From the fairly simple, if sometimes nearly perfect, lyrics of the Benbow volume he proceeded to the more complex, if also less uniformly successful, major psychological and philosophical poems and poetic dramas. There are no clear indications of the order of his reading or any full ranking of his particular enthusiasms. Throughout his life Browning could quote widely and appropriately, either from memory or from quick reference to the text, from a great range of Shelley's poems. Enthusiasm led him to examine fully not only the minute, lesser figures embroidered on the larger tapestry of Shelley's imagination but even the tattered or snarled sections that others usually pass by. Like most readers he responded easily to the splendid flights of fancy and imagery in "The Sensitive Plant" or "The Witch of Atlas." "The whole poem abounds," he still raved over "The Witch" in his old age, "in passages of extraordinary beauty."[23] He probably enjoyed the more abstract "Julian and Maddalo" almost equally.[24] Nor did the sentimental haze around *Rosalind and Helen* keep him from penetrating its strangely subversive and probing analysis of political and social standards. Nor was he even deterred, as strong readers have been, from getting at the symbolic heart of the tale of Laon and Cythna in *The Revolt of Islam* by its dull romance plot or its philosophical encrustations. In his volume there are pencil marks throughout from careful reading and even rereading.[25] The symbols of the poem, or at least the impressive, idiosyncratic emblem of the eagle and serpent, stayed with him all his life, to reappear, painted boldly by his son at Browning's own suggestion, on the ceiling of the room where he died in 1889.[26]

Browning certainly read *Adonais*, one of the two master works in which Shelley's aspirations to a language elevated beyond language and to a passion purified of all objects are most nearly fulfilled. The other, *Epipsychidion*, he also must have read, though he does not refer specifically to it.[27] If his ability to recite "The Cloud" in its entirety from memory is any indication, he virtually immersed himself in many of the great lyrics and shorter poems.[28] When he needed an example of Shelley at his best to contrast with his juvenile gothic novel *St. Irvyne*, Browning reached, however, for "a chorus in the 'Prometheus Unbound' or a scene from the 'Cenci.' "[29] Apparently the great epic drama was for Browning, as for most readers, a central work from his first acquaintance. We know from a comment to Elizabeth that he planned, probably sometime in the early 1830s or even earlier, to pay it the high compliment of imitation by a parallel restoration of the *Prometheus Firebearer*.[30] *The Cenci*, despite splendid writing and its interest as a dramatic experiment, seems an odder first choice. Initially he may have warmed to the noble character of Beatrice, but the play as a whole presents the other side of Shelley, not the angel muttering about heaven but the man dismayed at the hell of human life. It seems likely that his respect for it grew with time until, in the "footnote" to it, the little poem "Cenciaja" (1876), Browning would call it a "superb Achievement." He also read that truly superb, if not fully achieved, work of Shelley's darker vision of reality, "The Triumph of Life." Indeed, he read it carefully enough to remember even a footnote perfectly, though there again appreciation may have developed with his own maturity.[31]

Certainly, when Browning explains further in *Pauline* that "the whole / Of his conceptions" slowly dawned on him as he kept reading in Shelley's poetry, he is not speaking about Shelley's tremendous sense of alienation from society and pessimism over things as they are, that realistic side of Shelley which is present all along but comes out so forcefully in his last great work. Rather, he began to find in Shelley ideas and opinions about what might be. Shelley began to appear as instructor as well as master poet. Presumably under his tutelage, he swore off eating his fellow creatures. In even more direct discipleship, he studied the social and political ideas of the master and with perhaps more sanguine hopes than Shelley himself, he began planning for a total reformation of government and society. The influence of Shelley was thus in part intellectual, providing a political philosophy and a point of view. Here the conversion was intense but relatively short lived. By the time he wrote *Pauline,* he had not only become disillusioned with Shelley's political ideas but was even able to put this entire part of his intellectual development in a cogent and coherent autobiographical perspective.

The full story of this affair with Shelley's opinions properly belongs with the larger one of Browning's education and early intellectual history, where we shall return to it. In the development of Browning's artistic sensibility, however, it was the reformer himself, far more than his opinions and philosophy, that mattered. By the "whole of his conceptions" Browning intended Shelley's social and political opinions, but, as even the most casual reader of Shelley knows, the whole of his conceptions includes a very special and prominent conception of himself. At the worst, and especially to those in any case out of sympathy with Shelley, this may seem mere personal egotism writ large in his work. Bleeding in metaphor right before us on the page, falling upon the thorns of life in the thick of black and white, he seems, even when we know the traditional ritual he is invoking, to make impossible demands on our ability to take him as seriously as he takes himself. Yet in his best poems, or in the best parts of his best poems where the strain of self-pity is not so intrusive, he not only makes such demands but succeeds in obtaining our agreement. As with some of the greatest poets, he makes his elevated conception of his own role central to the poetic statement. In lyrics or in long poems such as *Adonais* or *Epipsychidion,* where the poet speaks directly, we imbibe his vision as a part of his projected role: in *Adonais* that of a poet speaking of poetry; in *Epipsychidion* an idealized lover speaking of the forces of eros on a metaphysical level. In other poems

Shelley gives us something only apparently different, a character as the central focus: Prometheus, Prince Athanase, or the poet of *Alastor*. Although Shelley may seem to suggest some criticisms of the character in the poems, he is finally not interested in creating characters separate from himself. Rather, as in most romantic dramatic works, the character is an idealized and projected version of the poet himself, a medium by which he can either criticize and understand aspects of his own psychology or embody his own aspirations at the highest level of idealization. Thus, if there is a warning in *Alastor* (as well as a celebration of the special experience of the poet), in *Prometheus Unbound* there is an extraordinary elevation of self into a mythic role as poet of the cosmos and redeemer of the world.

No one, of course, identifies Shelley literally with his characters or even with his assumed roles as prophet and poet. However, while some readers grant his seemingly extravagant role as a license necessary for the poet and focus on what he has to communicate in this role, others, no doubt with encouragement from Shelley's own example, focus as much on the person who takes on these roles. These readers—and they certainly included Browning—reason, in effect, that if Shelley is not literally either his characters or the poetic roles he assumes, he nonetheless must possess their special qualities in order to feel his parts as totally as he does. From there it is an easy step to recreate Shelley in the image of his poetry. Focus turns from the poetry and its obvious display of extraordinary powers of imagination to the poet as an embodiment of his own imagined idealisms.

It is easy to stand back and point out the obvious flaw in this way of reading and in this way of thinking about a poet's projected selves. However, to the poet who makes his inner experience the essential subject of his poetry, who attempts through imagination to ignite the spark of divinity he feels within, confusion between self and poetic role or character is almost a temporary necessity. If he wishes, as Shelley did, to find only what is good within and offer this as an ideal for mankind, he must to some extent block out the rest of his ordinary self and pretend for a time that he is indeed only what his idealisms assert. By the same token, the confusion between the real Shelley and his idealized projections is almost inevitable for a while in a person who is himself capable of poetic creation. If the poem makes a strong impact it will lead the poet-reader to identify with the poet himself and thus to take on his own confusion between reality and role.

Some such process seems to have taken place as Browning read Shelley. On top of his admiration for the poetry there sprouted an even more deeply felt enthusiasm for the man. If familiarity can breed contempt, it is also true that ignorance may foster love. Browning claimed that even in 1852 when he wrote the "Essay on Shelley" he had only the works to go by, "having no knowledge of his life."[32] But his ignorance when he first read him was of course far more profound. In *Pauline*, he stresses that he first knew Shelley as an unknown poet who seemed almost a private possession. Not only were his works hard to find but there was almost no information about his life save for the facts about the melodrama of his death. Unless he had some anecdotes from his cousin or from a person like the music instructor Nathan, he would have had little more than Mary Shelley's brief preface to the *Posthumous Poems* by way of biographical information. And this was an encomium rather than a memoir. Shelley is there briefly portrayed virtually as he idealized himself, "the wise, the brave, the gentle," who has been basely attacked for "his fearless enthusiasm in the cause which he considered the most sacred upon earth, the improvement of the moral and physical state of mankind."[33] He is a "bright vision" marvelously occupied in his quiet life of study, love of nature, and good will for man. His death is presented with emotion laden, though not insincere, purple description.

When Browning learned, later in life, more of the complex truth about Shelley the man, he blamed his mistaken impression specifically on his trust in "the testimony of untruthful friends."[34] Browning eventually met virtually all of Shelley's friends and surviving well-wishers, but it isn't hard to guess the person he was especially thinking of. Mary Shelley expressed her regret in her preface that Leigh Hunt had not been able to provide a full biographical notice. In the event, he did just this, though four years later and for his own *Lord Byron and Some of his Contemporaries*. He certainly justified Mary's faith in his liberal treatment of his old friend. Because it elevated Shelley at the expense of the more famous poet of the title, the book caused a great literary stir when it appeared in 1828. Browning's references to it in later life suggest that he probably saw or bought it at the time.[35] The side of Shelley's life that would cause Browning many years later to reevaluate Shelley entirely—his treatment of his first wife, the suicide Harriet—is essentially glossed over by Hunt. Browning felt he was misled by Shelley's friends on three specific matters, and all three are indeed misleadingly treated in Hunt: first, that Harriet was essentially an uneducable person incompatible and impossibly mated with a person of Shelley's genius; second, that they parted by mutual consent; and third, that Shelley had lost custody of his children after Harriet's death merely because of prejudice against his lack of religion.[36] Browning was ultimately to learn that Harriet had been improving herself by studying the odes of Horace and playing Mozart, that Shelley had deserted her, and that Lord Eldon had made clear that desertion, not agnosticism, was the reason for the decision against giving Shelley custody of the children.[37] Hunt's whitewash, for such it amounts to, ultimately did his friend more disservice than kindness. Encouraging an unreal idealization of Shelley the man, it ultimately led people like Browning, in reaction, to devalue the poetry as well as the very human— indeed, as Browning came to suspect, sometimes half-insane—poet.

When he first read Hunt, Browning was no doubt more swayed by his praise of Shelley than by the omission of criticism. For Hunt's raw impressions of his friend have here been filtered and purified through his literary imagination into a saint's life. Shelley is not only pure white, a kind friend, lover of mankind, sage student of nature and literature, but even pure angel. Since Matthew Arnold, the association between Shelley and angels seems, of course, natural; but Hunt is rather in earnest: Shelley looked like "John the Baptist or the angel whom Milton describes as holding a reed 'tipt with fire.' "[38] He is not only a selfless reformer working for the good of mankind, but, by a strange though not really illogical process of reversal, Shelley the atheist and agnostic is turned in Hunt's account into a model of true religious feeling. "Mr. Shelley's disposition may be truly said to have been any thing but irreligious," Hunt asserts, and finds occasion to contrast his active and sincere goodness to the hypocrisy of the formally religious.

What he read in Hunt about the man Shelley would thus have confirmed and consolidated Browning's unreal idealization of him. Hunt's lifelong penchant for idolizing literary persons by the machinery and attitudes of religious superstition seems to have even awakened in the young Browning, as it did in the young Keats, a kind of secular reverence. Browning recalled that he went so far as to draw up some rough sketches of an incident described by Hunt. Like a pietistic rendering of a saint's good deeds it was presumably an account of one of Shelley's noble actions.[39] It was to be called, "Percy Bysshe Shelley—Cor Cordium," with the incident quoted in full as a saint's actions might be cited beneath a picture. Later, when Browning got to know Hunt, he would be among the favored few who would be given a real icon, a copy of the bust of Shelley by Marianne Hunt, Leigh's wife, which Browning set on the way up the stairs at New Cross.[40]

Without excessive cynicism over such literary enthusiasm, we may suspect that with Browning, as with Hunt, a large amount of emotion originally connected with religion was being transferred to this secular saint and martyr. Sharp's anecdote about *Queen Mab* has led to an easy identification of Browning's late adolescent skepticism with the influence of Shelley. If Shelley no doubt encouraged Browning in his reaction against the regime of Dissenter orthodoxy at Clayton's church and against mindless faith in what he had been told, his influence also cut in the opposite direction. Religious emotion, which he had deprived of an object by reading skeptics such as Voltaire, found a new channel in Shelley. Shelley himself conceived of his role as closer to that of a latter-day prophet with a new dispensation than to that of a destroyer of religion itself. The mature Shelley was careful to distinguish between the false conception of God, which he railed against, and the higher good, which—with Plato or the historical Jesus—he humbly served. Hunt's implication, which really underlies his entire defense of Shelley, that there may be more true religion in the so-called infidel Shelley than in canting and spiritually dead orthodox Christians, even suggests a way back into the fold by a different door.

Indeed, it is just the path Browning seems to have followed between the unsettled period when he first began to read Shelley and the time when he composed the tentative assertions of *Pauline*. Although it would be quite wrong to assert that *Pauline* represents a secure assertion of faith against earlier doubt, there is at least a spasmodic thrust toward a vague profession of faith.[41] In the process Shelley and Christ, far from being antithetical powers, are joined together among the forces of light by Mrs. Browning's idealistic son. In *Pauline*, Browning frequently expresses a sense of guilt or pained regret over the period of skepticism when he denied even God's existence and fell, he believes, into contorted and debased spiritual states. But Shelley has no association with those rather embarrassing recriminations. Browning's "Hell-dress"—what we would call his normal anxiety about a growing independence of judgment in religious matters and the state of confusion that naturally accompanies it—is certainly not the mantle Shelley wears. Like a figure of divine energy in Blake's drawings, Shelley is for Browning a "Sun-treader," one whose spiritual energies are associated with the active power in the single source of all light. More than merely a religious influence, he sees Shelley as a source of immediate spiritual strength.

During his spiritual doubts one central truth seemed clear and unchanging: Shelley's purity. With this certainty he could at least set a limit to the corrosive workings of his skepticism and "wandering thought": "that one so pure as thou / Could never die." In short, and he is here in fact addressing Shelley's spirit, Shelley's greatness seemed a guarantee that man, or at least such a man, was, in more than a metaphorical sense, immortal. Although the poem then goes on to recount the loss of his secular faith in Shelley as redeemer and reformer of this world, there is no repudiation of Shelley's spiritual power. In the final address to him, following the profession of faith to Christ himself, Browning mixes God, moral absolutes, and Shelley into one vague whole on the side of light: "Sun-treader, I believe in God and truth / And love." He addresses Shelley himself as a kind of trustee to his newfound and still precarious pact with God and goodness. Like one who has just escaped physical death and seeks the assurance of his friends, Browning explains, he himself has just escaped from spiritual death and he "would lean" on Shelley and depend on him when he fears that he may again succumb to gloom or spiritual paralysis. For Browning, the Christ-like Shelley seems naturally to serve as intermediary with Christ, just as Christ does with God. Faith in Shelley has opened the way for Browning's religious feelings to find their way back to their origin.

3 Ambiguities: Pauline

All this, it hardly need be said, is a great deal to load onto any mere man and poet, however great his abilities. Browning's ultimate reaction against Shelley seems predictable and the whole process perhaps a little unfair to Shelley, much as his own exalted view of his role may have encouraged it. More important to Browning's own development, he was obviously creating an impossibly high ideal for himself of what a poet should be. He was not merely hero-worshiping a human genius but elevating genius to divinity. Although the problem of coping with his own impossible vision of Shelley was to remain with him for many years, it was a difficulty that was bound to make itself felt almost immediately. Browning's first serious interest in becoming a poet himself was called forth by Shelley's influence, and naturally it was called forth in Shelley's image. The idealization was as natural a part of the process. As a boy he had had, as he explained to his friend Monclar in the letter of 1837, a sense that poets were grand things, but the "Incondita," as we have seen, seemed to him a puppet-like affair because he had not developed any sense of himself as a poet. While he displayed cleverness, his feeling had no direct means of becoming involved in his work; he wrote not from the concerns of his whole being but from a polished corner of his personality. What was missing Browning called the sense of a "poetic nature."[42] Today it might be called a sense of identity as a poet, the coming together of a personality around a vocation and a chosen role. Hence, as he also explained, the strange period when music, more than verse, commanded his greatest emotional commitment. In his extended reading of Shelley, Browning not only experienced a resurgence of interest in poetry but found, unreal as it may have been, a model for a poetic nature. In effect, he apprenticed himself out psychologically to his own conception of Shelley and, over a period of about five years, began to try to make himself into a poet on the same mold.

In this process *Pauline* is both the first fruit and the greatest tribute of the student to his chosen master. It even seems likely that one of the major motivations for this first poem after adolescence was in fact a desire to celebrate and proclaim his allegiance to the master. In the mature "Essay on Shelley" he hints that he had even imagined at one time that he might serve as the instrument to spread Shelley's reputation: "The signal service it was the dream of my boyhood to render to his fame and memory." If so, he had waited too long and was finally pushed to tardy activity by the march of events. In *Pauline* Browning refers topically to Shelley's emergence as a recognized major poet and contrasts this new fame to the obscurity in which Shelley had existed when he first loved him. The passage about "His award" —"the award of fame to him, the late acknowledgement of Shelley's genius," as Browning glossed it in the copy of *Pauline* returned to him with John Stuart Mill's comments—may refer to the slow spread of knowledge about Shelley from remarks in works such as Hunt's, or Moore's life of Byron.[43] However, Browning was probably thinking more specifically of something he had been reading in the influential magazine *The Athenaeum*. This was a series of articles entitled "Memoir of Shelley," and written by Shelley's cousin and friend from school days, Captain Thomas Medwin. The articles were featured for weeks and included a number of unpublished items by Shelley, among them the poem "Similes," which Browning read then, "to remember it all my life."[44] It was followed by a series, lasting for months, of selected unpublished prose and poetic pieces. All told, the series was a very high public affirmation of Shelley's importance, and would have appeared as such to Browning when he read it. Browning was struck by the story Medwin tells of Shelley's strange dream a few nights before his death in which he met his double as a cloaked figure who finally revealed his identical face to him and demanded, Shelley to Shelley, "siete satisfatto?"[45] He would have found in Medwin a great deal more of this side of Shelley than in Hunt, much more about Shelley's interest in dreams and unconscious experience, a fuller sense of his physical and even social weaknesses, and an explicit treatment of Shelley's occasional approaches to insanity.[46] The account thus gave him a more complicated view of Shelley's genius and especially of the strangeness at the heart of it. Still, it did nothing to contradict the roseate picture in Hunt. Shelley's possible insanity is romanticized as an essential part of his imaginative genius, and the sullied areas in his relation with Harriet are whitewashed by the same omissions Hunt had made. Medwin stresses Shelley's movement away from early atheism; he asserts that his poetry will promote "that greatest and best of truths, the immortality of the soul." He sums up Shelley's personal virtues by an Italian's observation that he was "veramente un angelo."[47]

The "Memoir" appeared in July and August of 1832.[48] Browning was evidently already writing *Pauline* at the date given at the end of the poem, October 22, 1832,[49] and it is thus not unreasonable to suppose that Medwin's public acknowledgment of Shelley had led him to begin his own even more personal tribute to the poet, soon afterward.[50] Whatever the inspiration, however, it is clear that *Pauline* celebrates Shelley not merely with reverence but with the even greater tribute of imitation. Commencing seriously as a poet, he begins by trying to appropriate the master's role and powers. Although by 1832 he had already questioned and largely rejected Shelley's social role as a vehicle of regenerating revolution, he still aspired to put on Shelley's mantle as a poet of moral and religious inspiration. Perhaps because he knew he was not going to have to make good on his claims at the end of his poem, it was in the last forty lines that he dared to state this role most explicitly. The poem itself, he can there assert, is a proof that he has, for all his self-doubts, been "visited" by higher powers through his imagination. The language is vague, but it is clear that he has in mind something like Shelley's own intuitions of intellectual beauty. "Beauty rose" on him: that is, he has acted as a receiver for something beyond him and normal human experience. In the future he hopes "beauteous shapes will come to me again, / And unknown secrets will be trusted me." The conception of the artist implied here, as Robert Preyer has pointed out, has affinities with the tradition of occultism in which the artist is a necromancer in touch with spiritual secrets.[51] Browning alludes obviously to this tradition in *Pauline* by the prefatory Latin quotation from the letter to the reader of Cornelius Agrippa's *De Occulta Philosophia*, a work he read in a worm-eaten anthology of treatises on magic, formerly the property of Sir Kenelm Digby, in his father's library.[52] It has affinities as well with the modern revision of this conception of the artist in the symbolist tradition in which the poet, through the images he finds, is similarly, if more vaguely, in touch with something beyond ordinary existence. Above all, this conception of the poet is the same as his view of Shelley's own role, a combination of religious and imaginative powers. He rises to the ultimate assertion of this role at the end of the passage: "I shall be priest and lover as of old." In the final revision in 1888 he further enlarged it to "priest and prophet," though the change is, like most revisions in *Pauline*, a clarification, not a rewriting from maturity.

By whatever it is called, the poet's function—as in most (though not all) of Shelley—is to look within his own mind and his own special experience for the subject of his poetry. Again like Shelley, he only carries the focus of all English romantic poetry on the poet's personal and imaginative experience to an extreme. The poet is not merely analyzing his inner consciousness by reporting the images thrown up from his unconscious, but he is functioning as a Prometheus or Isaiah of the soul, a bringer of new knowledge of man's eternal situation to his mundane ordinary self. In a splendid image for this process—and one probably borrowed from Shelley[53]—he proposes to his friend Pauline that they

> go together, like twin gods
> Of the infernal world, with scented lamp
> Over the dead, to call and to awake,
> Over the unshaped images which lie
> Within my mind's cave.

Thus conceived, this Aeneas-like visit to the inner lower world of images seems almost an heroic enterprise. In practice it is the far easier task of writing a certain kind of vague, image-filled, pleasant, and not always very meaningful poetry. *Pauline* is spasmodically sprinkled with such poetry, and it is in these sections that Browning appears, despite some fine passages, most derivative of Shelley. Although a poet may speak of capturing a world beyond this world, he is in fact stuck with manipulating the poor images of this world in the hope that they will somehow catch fire. Browning's are all the less likely to do so for being warmed over from Shelley. Although his specific echoes of Shelley need not be detailed here, particularly since they have been studied thoroughly a number of times,[54] it is worth noting that his appropriation of images from Shelley arises not so much from specific borrowings as from the natural overflow of a mind filled to brimming with the peculiar imagery and symbolism of Shelley's poetry. *Pauline* abounds with images of fiends, witches and snakes (both, as in Shelley, eccentrically positive), caves, and chained spirits. There are the same vaguely connotative words—dim orb, dominion, radiant, presence, and so on—by which Shelley attains his mind-stunning, hypnotic effects. Above all, he presents images in loosely connected, soft and feminine lines in which the sense of logical connection is suppressed and the concretion of image on image makes an almost abstract pattern of words.

In this, Shelley's very special métier, the young Browning is, however, a far cry from the master. Whatever he might have developed into in time had he continued this kind of verse, in *Pauline* he is able to match Shelley's brilliance only in a chance image or phrase, not in the kind of extended passage so common in Shelley where image added to image creates new myth. Although it has interesting scenes and complex psychological fancies, as a whole the poem fails to fulfill the intentions of poetic priesthood. It does not really attempt to present an entire ethical, social, or religious vision as Shelley's best poems do. It may be a fine tribute to Shelley. As an imitation it is essentially a failure. It tells us of Browning's personal identification with Shelley but does not achieve success in bringing to fruit this grafting of self onto another.

With his lifelong distaste for self-revelation, Browning had many personal reasons for disliking *Pauline* and for attempting, as long as he could, to suppress it altogether. In this failure of intentions, he had also very valid formal reasons for his antipathy to the work. Quite correctly, he told Elizabeth that it was, in contrast to the mere limited achievement of his earliest unpublished work, quite simply a failure "ambiguous, feverish," without overall unity. The feverishness may be attributed to the obvious cross-buffeting of inexperience and high excitement. The ambiguity—used not in our modern sense of deliberate multiplicity of response but as an indication of real confusion—is most apparent in the central uncertainty over his relation to Shelley. Desiring to be a poet such as he conceived Shelley to be, he nonetheless found himself taking a rather different, overall perspective on the role of the poet and on the relation between the poet's special imaginative experience and his larger existence as a person.

The difference in perspective is registered most obviously in the overall form of the poem. It is clearly not modeled on any of Shelley's finest works. As a poem that primarily discusses rather than enacts the poet's function, *Pauline* is closest to Shelley's own somewhat agonized exploration of the poet's role in *Alastor* and the fragments of "Prince Athanase," both, it should be noted, works of his early maturity and themselves somewhat closer to the romantic poem of self-exploration than to Shelley's most famous works. Browning probably read the brief "Prince Athanase" in the Benbow volume, and he had *Alastor* in his copy of *Posthumous Poems*. Most commentators have been ready to consider these essentially as models for the plan and scope of *Pauline*.

Although the overall similarities between works about the poet's role are obvious, a comparison only serves to point up fundamental differences even here between Browning and Shelley. As Harold Bloom has observed, despite the often-noted disparity between Shelley's Preface to *Alastor* and the poem itself, *Alastor* has a single concern: the personal price that must be paid, in alienation and finally in death, for the attainment of ultimate vision.[55] Here and in "Athanase" where the poet-figure is prematurely grayed by his single-minded preoccupation with personal vision, Shelley explores, in the most radical terms, the consequence of Romantic self-consciousness. Insisting on no less than total commitment by the prophetic poet to his internal vision, he is equally honest about the necessary loss in individual personality and even, partially, in humanity. The exposition, for all its apparent complexity, is really splendidly logical and simple. Resolving to be more than human in his ethical perspective, Shelley can put away, while still realizing the cost, all complexity of usual personal growth and development over time. Whereas earlier Romantics such as Coleridge and Wordsworth were concerned with mediation between the self and the imaginative vision, Shelley prepares the way for vision by immolation of the self: he then rises from the ashes of self to the great triumphs of visionary power of his finest work.

Much as he aspires to Shelley's priestly and visionary vocation, Browning's own perspective on the role of the poet comes, by contrast, far closer to that of less radical romantic predecessors, whether Coleridge, Wordsworth, or Byron himself. *Pauline* is, in fact, a very different kind of poem about the poet's self. Far from being an abstract and lyrical quest romance, it is a somewhat realistic and autobiographical history of the self. If, as Browning liked to assert, the voice we hear in the poem is that of the "Poet of the batch" from a longer unfinished series of productions with different speakers, he is a poet who speaks in an ordinary world in which his lyrical moments are only part of the total circumstances of his life. We have not the abstract poet-figure pursuing his abstract epipsyche to his ruin but a young would-be poet trying to place his poetic experience in relation to his own ongoing life. The genre in which this very mixed bag is to be packaged, if we must package it, is not one defined by Shelley but the larger one present in all European romanticism and made explicit in Browning's subtitle: the confession.[56] Inasmuch as it is very much a poem about the author's religious life as well as his imaginative life, it seems, if anything, a return from the often more abstract romantic treatment (and Shelley's particularly abstract treatment) to the origins of the confessional genre in religion itself. Following the ideal of Browning's own liberalized Calvinist church, the poem works through self-examination, self-reproach, and a full baring of conscience to a confession and profession of faith.[57] As a spritual confession it may be incomplete and somewhat unconvincing, but it clearly borrows this religious form for poetic purposes.

With less clear evidence we may suspect that the archetypal romantic confession, that of Jean Jacques Rousseau, was also in Browning's mind as a model along with Shelley's poems. Browning's passion may have been for Shelley, but he knew Rousseau familiarly and his poem seems to possess more of the fever of life and self-analysis that Shelley himself found in Rousseau than the sense of ultimate certainty of Shelley.[58] In addition, a partial association with Rousseau might be one reason for the French tone, Pauline's French language and the Swiss scenery of her native land. But from Rousseau the genre of course branched out endlessly into every corner, English and continental, of the wide domain of romanticism that stretched out behind a young Victorian poet. From Goethe's *Werther* to Wordsworth's figure of the Solitary in *The Excursion*, from Chateaubriand's romances to Byron's *Childe Harold*, Browning had no end of prototypes for his own attempt to portray and understand his role as a poet in relation to his own life and growth.

The unconscious vacillation toward and away from Shelley in the form of the poem causes a major aesthetic problem that is evident in the mixture of lyrical, conversational, narrative, and even epistolary (if Pauline's note may be considered a piece of letter writing) stances. But, beneath the formal confusion is an even more important confusion of attitude and poetic identity in relation to Shelley. The impression of ambiguity is complicated especially because Browning seems aware of his attraction and repulsion but uncertain how he feels about his own uncertainty. On the one hand, the poem is suffused with guilt, and much of this guilt seems to attach to his past failure to reach both the personal purity and the prophetic stance that he believes Shelley embodied. The guilt over Shelley is not, as Betty Miller suggested, the opposite of his guilt over lapses from religion. Rather, he is troubled by a similar feeling of failure in both areas—failure to live up to the high ideals that he had insisted on professing. The guilt is similar, too, to the mixed emotion he may be obliquely expressing about Eliza Flower in the address to Pauline. He hopes to be better but is fully aware that he has not existed on her level of purity since childhood.

Set against the guilt and the regrets and the promises to be better in the future, there is, however, an answering sense of vitality and even satisfaction with his more complex if less exalted personality, that intricate web of sensibility and fundamental good sense that we have been watching develop in this study. The guilt might continue, even persist into the 1850s, but, equally, the vigor of a different talent, sprouting away both from his ideal conception of Shelley and from Shelley's poetry, can be traced as early as *Pauline*. Although the weak confessional form of the poem was an experiment that Browning would never try again, some particular facets of *Pauline* already suggest the emergence of his later orientation as a poet.

Even in the least convincing element of the poem, the prop figure of Pauline, which he drags on to motivate a speech that obviously needs no external motivation and to reassure a growing spirit that has no lack of assurance, there is a wide swerving away from the Shelleyan model. This is no search in Shelley's manner for the ideal companion soul or epipsyche. When he read the poem in 1833, John Stuart Mill recognized immediately how unreal a figure Pauline was, and in the comment written in his copy he expressed the sly wish that this lover could meet "a *real* Pauline." But lack of reality does not guarantee any high degree of ideality. For all her fine native French, love of music, perfect features, and free-spirited approach to her unlegitimated relation to the speaker, Pauline is not a Platonic ideal of woman but, as Mill's comment implies, the work of a young man's rather realistic, self-indulging imagination. She is far more daydream than vision or poetic fantasy. As such, her particular unreality is composed of the very real, if not very realistic, emotional and sexual needs of a young man. In part, she serves the impulse, which Betty Miller oddly took for the whole of Browning's emotional needs, to return to a comforting and reassuring motherly figure as an antidote to the necessary poisons of confusion and insecurity present in all growth and change. This is the weakest side of Pauline, and she does seem at times to be created after the narrower side of Sarah Anna's religion, reproving roving thoughts and social deviance as Coleridge's unfortunate wife, the pensive Sara, had in his own early explorative poem, "The Eolian Harp." Far more than poor Sara Fricker, however, the imagined Pauline is not only cuddling but cuddlesome, rather explicitly presented as an object of physical desire in this pre-Victorian work. Although the rest of the poem hardly matches the enticements of the opening invitation to Pauline to embrace, she certainly comes closer throughout to being an imagined real object of desire than any visionary projection of soul's desire.

The vitality of a mind excited by experience of ordinary reality intrudes even more blatantly and far more attractively in another part of the poem where Browning is talking about something he really has experienced fully. This is the passage, already discussed in relation to Browning's early experience in nature,[59] in which he revels in an imaginary rush through the countryside with poor Pauline evidently hanging like a modern motorcycle bride from his coattails. Although this is obviously written in a romantic and even pre-romantic descriptive tradition, Browning emphasizes the vitality of the actual scene rather than his own feelings or responses to it. His own emotion is a general, inner sympathy with the external world rather than an experience of something more than nature through nature. Shelley was, of course, a habitual student of nature and a person capable of very close observation. But nature was for him primarily a book of symbols that could tell him, or that could be made to reveal, deeper truths behind nature. If we set a passage from Shelley—for instance the invitation to Emilia at the end of the *Epipsychidion* to fly with him to an island—against Browning's description, the contrast between the two is immediately apparent. Shelley's imaginary flight, which may have indeed inspired Browning's, opens the way for his projected soul-longings to escape into a scene of nature reworked to fit the millennial aspirations of the heart. It is no longer, as it is in Browning, outer reality perceived with intense feeling but a new interior landscape painted with the colors of pure imagination.

Browning's need to present his experience in the complexity with which it came to him is even more evident when he turns from describing imaginary persons or real landscapes and focuses upon himself, especially his mind and emotions. This section, expecially the long central passage in which he claims to strip his mind bare to its essentials, is easily the most interesting part of the poem and the part which displays most original concerns and capacity of mind. He does not found a school of psychology or even propose a fully coherent theory of mind and emotion. But he does show a new thrust of interest that can be properly said to represent an important development not only away from Shelley's special, radical view of the imagination but even away from the habitual concerns of most of his romantic predecessors. Their emphasis had been in large part upon the psychology of the imagination, upon understanding and expressing that power capable of forming unity from disparate realities or able to project a larger vision of life from the mixed stuff of reality. Whether their assertions were relatively modest, as with Wordsworth, or radical, as with Shelley, their preoccupation was with man's faculties as poet and creator: they looked less on man in his complex and varied capacities as a social and ethical being than on his special abilities as individual perceiver and creator. Although Keats might aspire to an art that went beyond the artist's concern with his own powers and reached out to touch and befriend ordinary men, Wordsworth might try to press himself into the alien mode of sage and ethical philosopher, or Byron might actually transcend his self-involvement in the social satire of his latest work, virtually all the major writers of the generation before Browning in practice found the center of their creative life in exploring their own special artistic sensibilities, however egotistical or however broadly sympathetic they might be.

Browning is, of course, far from being free from his own egotistical concern with his special abilities and artistic potentialities in the self-analysis of *Pauline*. What is new is the insistence upon understanding his special power of imagination in the context of a broad analysis of self. The quality of his interest is analogous to that in the early poems of Tennyson of almost the same time. He explores the power of romantic imagination as a strong, indeed often overwhelmingly strong force within the self, but he continually relates it to the more ordinary needs and problems of the artist as a human being. In Tennyson's early poems on art we are made to see not merely the imaginative, creative center of the artist but its relation, good or bad, to the whole ongoing (or isolated and slowly dying) life of the personality. Similarly, in Browning's analysis he tries to place his experience with art in relation to the total needs and capacities of his personality. Imagination is explicitly presented as a power working within a larger plane of conscious existence. This full existence he in turn analyzes somewhat murkily into three faculties: first, explicit self-consciousness, second what he calls "self-supremacy," but what we might call the will or ego, the capacity for taking hold of the world in which the self finds itself and bending it to use, and finally, that restless centrifugal force that leads him to seek out ever more broad experience: "Which would be all, have, see, know, taste, feel, all." These together make the "myself." However, the analysis presumably applies to the essential conscious self—though often conscious to a lesser degree—of all people.

Within this framework, he then explains the peculiarity that leads him to artistic expression as a specially strong imagination, encouraging him, as we have seen, to seek in art a reconciliation of his disparate experience.

Rather than isolate imagination he treats it in the context of other powers or passions that seem particularly strong. He thus finds in himself a basic religious yearning. Later we are told of a passion for knowledge and of a balancing or competing passion for love. If imagination is made central, it is not placed at the center itself. Browning seems to be groping toward a psychology of art in which, without denying the huge power of the imagination as the Romantics had discovered it, he can reintegrate it with the other aspects of mind and personality, which it can serve as an illuminating and unifying force. Ultimately, imagination, as Browning uses it in his mature art, may even find its function in portraying the complexity of man rather than in seeking to demonstrate its powers in a vacuum or striving primarily to analyze its own nature and the nature of art.

In applying his own imagination in *Pauline* to an act of self-examination, Browning carries his interesting but still somewhat overly formal analysis of faculties of the mind to a further realization. This is the truth enunciated somewhat mystically and theatrically in the epigram that Browning took out of context from Marot's "Huictain":

> Plus ne suis ce que j'ai été,
> Et ne le sçaurois jamais être.[60]

No doubt he selected the epigram to call attention to the streak of Byronic posturing over a sense of guilt that runs through the weaker side of *Pauline*: that sense of unutterable deeds ("for which remorse were vain") that have wrought unutterable changes (which never do get uttered). But it also captures the essential theme of Browning's autobiographical reflections, the sense of the growth and change of personality over time. In part, he denies such change explicitly. The essential qualities of his personality, really the strengths of the various aspects of his consciousness and will, seem to him present before all circumstance. And though much of this study has been devoted to showing the influences in an environment that encouraged and shaped his developing tendencies, there was no doubt a predetermined, even biological reality that preceded all experience and that determined the relative force with which he would seek out experiences or, when found, fully incorporate them in his personality. Yet most of Browning's history, as he proceeds with his almost Freudian intention of "calling / The dark past up—to quell it regally," is then a history of change and development.

We shall look at that history in detail in considering Browning's education since it is essentially a history of education and of his growth through reaction to the norms of his society, to its critics, and to his own decisions about his education. What needs to be emphasized here is the obvious conflict between this view of the self developing and changing over time—especially the mind developing in its capacities by expanding its knowledge of external reality—and the static idea of truth embodied in the outlook of his first ideal. Shelley might elaborate and expand his vision, even, as some of

his students have emphasized, change some of the essential terms of his philosophy. He dealt, however, not in development but in ultimates. Change,
as in his own master Plato, is the enemy of the One. Life, in his most mature
vision, is not a process of struggle through adversity toward an emergent
truth but a slow triumph of the forces that wear men down from the vision
of good and perfection to the multiplied dust of nothingness. Not in life but
in death, or in the higher death to life of a mind focused on the images of
eternity, is truth to be sought. Staining life must be renounced or tran-
scended to reach the white radiance of eternal certainty. Although Shelley in
his life could work in small ways for the reform he sought, in his conceptions the past, whether of society or self, must not be dealt with, built upon,
and mastered; it must be swept away in a sudden movement from present to
millennium. And, in Browning's view of him, Shelley himself had no need
of any personal growth.

Over this issue of growth the underlying conflict with Shelley comes most
fully to a head. Although Browning intends to portray his experience as a
sad falling off from his best self, he cannot help presenting it as a vital, and
on the whole positive, movement through youth to an ever fuller sense of
who he is and where he is going. The price of development has been guilt
over change; yet as guilt finds expression and is confessed, the moral seems
to be that the development has been worth the price. From confession and
despair he even moves to the opposite extremes of spastic triumph in his
imaginative powers and too easy professions of renewed faith in Pauline,
God, Shelley, and his own priestly aims.

W. S. Swisher and Robert Preyer have suggested that some of the passages in *Pauline* that are most imitative of Shelley in symbolic or mythic
manner may even have essentially a psychological and descriptive function.[61] The strange dream sequences that Browning recounts might be read
as personal, dream analyses of guilt rather than as Shelleyan mythic creations woven from the stuff of the unconscious. The difference is as great as
the issue between Freud and Jung, and Browning himself seems here—as in
other parts of *Pauline*—simply unsure of whether he is functioning as self-
analyst or prophet. In the first role he appears far more able than Shelley to
admit the ambivalence in the work of the imagination when it seeks light by
brooding over the images within the unconscious mind as they are revealed
in dream or introspection. Light exists with dark, good instincts with bad,
images of creation and growth with those of guilt and death. Shelley, of
course, sees a huge fabric of both good and evil; but he tends to project those
outside of himself. Browning's more contorted visions of "dreams in which
/ I seemed the fate from which I fled"—dreams in which he is a fiend who
has defiled a white swan by holding it to him or a witch who seduces and
drags down a young god to her level—suggest that he finds the Shelleyan
task of opening up the unconscious self a much more dubious enterprise:
one yielding not only splendid visions but also the pain of old anxieties released and new fears discovered.[62] The confession may have provided a nec-

essary and useful step to self-understanding, but it is the work of analysis, not Shelley's work of liberation. Having followed his master into the world of dreams and lyrical meditation as a priestly vocation, he seems instinctively and almost despite himself to react against this unbaring of the unconscious self as the dangerous and magical process his preface from Agrippa claims it is. "NAM ET EGO VOBIS ILLA NON PROBO, SED NARRO." He is not necessarily approving all he has found, merely telling it as he found it.

His reaction away from Shelley's penetrating and strangely lucid and untroubled enterprise of seeking poetic inspiration within himself has been looked upon as a deliberate and narrowing flight from the deeper self: a Victorian act of pure will and self-repression.[63] However, the poem suggests rather the healthy development of the ego from self-examination to resolution based on self-knowledge. Browning has found that he has "nursed up energies" that "will prey" on him and that he is capable of self-destructive, uncontrolled feelings of hate. Above all he has discovered that he is continually beset by feelings of guilt over (what we would call) a rather natural "hunger for / All pleasure, howsoe'er minute" and over his inability fully to live up to his own excessive idealism. His best instinct is not to deny these realities of the self but to give them vent and room. If he sometimes feels the attraction of narcissistic withdrawal—"my soul's idol seemed to whisper me / To dwell with him and his unhonoured name"—his instinct is primarily not to yearn after Shelley as Shelley had after Adonais, but to turn his imagination more fully on reality. Imagination and feeling are not repressed but allowed to expand in confronting the outer world or the substantial reality of dramatic scenes. Hence the release of energy in describing realistic nature or in recreating the scene of the *Andromeda* print or the old stories from Homer and the Greek tragedians.

4 Pauline: *Alternatives*

The movement toward a greater sense of reality and a fuller psychological realism is thus a swerve away from Browning's professed model and ideal and generally a turn away from the central preoccupation of romanticism with the powers of imagination. At moments, however, it seems to bring him not forward but back toward the stance of another admirer of Shelley who yet insisted upon going his own way, Browning's first idol, Byron. For of all the English Romantics, Byron most fully balanced the quest for the unworldly experience of the imagination with an equal thirst to apprehend fully his own character and the real world in which he lived. Like Byron, Browning pays homage to the moments of transcendence that he can share with Shelley, but he focuses on dramatizing his own character and on understanding the relation between his self-conscious sense of inner power and his experience in the gross but unavoidable realities of human existence. As he thus reacted from Shelley, Browning almost naturally fell back into something like Byron's complex presentation of self, now understood more fully than in boyhood. Very likely his close knowledge of Byron, especially

220 / The Development of a Poetic Nature

of the parallel confessional work *Childe Harold's Pilgrimage,* even suggested some of the forms in which to present his revelation, as well as the
more obvious posturing of guilt that appears throughout *Pauline.* His position is in many ways very similar to that of the older Byron in cantos three
and four of *Childe Harold.* Like Byron, if with somewhat less theatricality,
he attempts to take stock of his present self in relation to his past and his
theme, again like Byron's, is the realization, "I am not now / That which I
have been."[64] With Byron, too, he has come to realize that the powers of
imagination may be destructive rather than liberating to the artist. His sense
that inner energies can prey on him if they find no proper outlet may even
echo Byron's own realization in the poem Browning knew so well: "Yet
must I think less wildly:—I *have* thought / Too long and darkly, till my
brain became, / In its own eddy boiling and o'erwrought."[65]

Although he thus seems to arc back from his identification with Shelley
to his old ideal, not only in the occasional Byronic posturing but even in his
more serious presentation of himself, this new Byronism was at most a way
station, not a final stop. Even in *Pauline* he is not content merely to present
his problems and to point out, as Byron had with increasing fineness and
wit in his latest work, the ironic disparities between the imagination's limitless aspirations and the limits of self and reality. The quest through imagination for an ideal state beyond the ordinary self, which Shelley had inspired, had led him to the point where he could understand rather than
merely mimic Byron's attempt to integrate reality and imagination. But this
understanding did not fundmentally alter his earlier revulsion from Byron's
egotism and isolating irony—a revulsion all the more strong because Byron's
wit had apparently been so easily available to him during his adolescence.
Throughout *Pauline* he as vehemently rejects (and censures in his earlier self)
the self-sufficiency and bitterness of Byron's habitual stance as he strongly
accepts the need for Byron's directness and sense of reality. In embracing
Shelley he had rejected the cynicism he felt in Byron for what seemed a finer
faith. Although this had proved impossible as a total creed, he was still unwilling to turn back wholly to Byron. With his entire generation, he never
lost his admiration for Byron's strength and abilities, but he continued to
seek some more positive alternative.

What that alternative would ultimately be is clear enough in the late
poem "At the Mermaid" (1876), where Browning anachronistically has
Shakespeare criticize "your Pilgrim," Childe Harold, for his jaundiced and
egotistical complaints over life. Even in *Pauline*, Browning seemed to feel at
least intuitively that Shakespeare, not Byron, was for him the real alternative to Shelley. In *Childe Harold* Byron moved in successive cantos away
from the original pretext that Harold was a dramatic character and toward
the direct expression of his personality and opinions that we find in the last
two cantos and, most maturely developed, in *Don Juan.* By contrast, Browning moved in *Pauline* in just the opposite direction. If he fell into something very close to a Byronic stance in his swerve away from the alien aims
of Shelley, it was finally Shakespeare's very different dramatic example that

he held before himself as he finished *Pauline*. Both Shelley and Byron may be more present in the poem itself than Shakespeare; but it was decisively toward the greater dramatic poet and away from both early models that the experience of *Pauline* began to lead him.

Browning almost certainly knew a good deal of Shakespeare by the time he wrote *Pauline*.[66] He had acted at school; he had heard about plays and the theater from his father, from his Uncle Reuben, and no doubt from Sarah Flower and others; he had seen Richardson at Camberwell Fairs; he had already gone, very likely with his cousin James Silverthorne, to the regular theater as early as 1830, when he saw *Hamlet,* and probably earlier.[67] However, the stronger influence of Shelley had cast into shadow the different possibilities that Shakespeare could open to his growing personality and nascent sense of identity as a poet. What evidence we have suggests indeed that it was only at the time when he was struggling in *Pauline* to understand the problems of following Shelley that he began to see clearly the alternative that Shakespeare offered. The result is a curious and yet rather splendidly insightful afterthought, a notation left on *Pauline* as if for his own benefit and his eyes alone. This is the little, odd dating at the end, "Richmond, *October* 22, 1832." It follows three lines that end the poem with a direct address to the reader:

> All in whom this wakes pleasant thoughts of me,
> Know my last state is happy—free from doubt,
> Or touch of fear. Love me and wish me well!

"This transition from speaking to Pauline to writing a letter to the public with *place & date,* is quite horrible," John Stuart Mill complained in the margin of his copy. The flourish, a kind of dramatic bow before the audience such as sometimes completes a play, *is* strange, part of the general formal problems of the poem. Browning's explanation is revealing and to the point, however: "Kean was acting there: I saw him in Richard III that night, and conceived the childish scheme already mentioned: there is an allusion to Kean, page 47. I don't know whether I had not made up my mind to *act*, as well as to make verses, music, and God knows what,—que de châteaux en Espagne!"[68] The final lines—a bit of overt acting—as well as the dating from Richmond, are, in effect, a sudden jump out of the confessional form and into the drama and a sudden and final swerve away from the lyrical and personal model he had been celebrating.

Browning continued the swerve when he attempted, evidently first about October 30, 1833 after he received back the Mill copy, to provide for himself a history of the composition of *Pauline*.[69] If Mill's criticism of the morbid self-consciousness he found in the poem did not, as has been argued, alone turn Browning against this early work, it at least forced him to reconsider the poem and his attitude toward it.[70] His explanation of the genesis of the poem in what he calls a "childish scheme," was written at the opening of the copy Mill had read. He is already quick to belittle his own work, and he does so by casting it as one part of a larger "foolish plan" to produce a series of works seemingly written (or composed, since one is an opera) by different persons. Although the forms are those of major works, poem, novel, opera, or speech, the implication is that his intention was from the beginning largely dramatic: as in his Uncle Reuben's favorite monopoly-logues of Charles Mathews, he would "assume and realize I know not how many different characters." Browning claimed elsewhere that he had proceeded so far with this plan as to have finished a second piece, "Pauline, Part 2," which he decided to destroy, as well as some other uncompleted work.[71]

This explanation distances Browning a long way from this work. If it were accepted fully it would mean that *Pauline* should be viewed not as an intimate, confessional work by Browning about his internal development but as a detached look at one kind of personality, as essentially a dramatic monologue. Only a very few readers have been ready to accept this view of the poem.[72] It seems rather blatantly an attempt on Browning's part to wish his first work away as it is and replace it with what he might have wished it to be after the fact. What seems actually to have happened is that Kean's acting in Shakespeare began to suggest to him a different kind of art as he was in the midst of writing *Pauline*. Sarianna, who was his only confidante while the work was in progress, recalled quite explicitly that it was while he was finishing the poem, not—as he implies—while he was conceiving it, that he was seeing Kean. In her remembrance, he composed the end of the poem in his head on one of several trips he made to Richmond around October 1832.[73] Although he may have been meditating a larger scheme before *Pauline*, he only began to fit *Pauline* into it (if even then) as his interests turned away from a personal or lyrical ideal in the process of writing. In his comment in the Mill copy the confusion in his intention is still acknowledged. After explaining the work as part of a dramatic series, he admits, "the present abortion was the first work of the *Poet* of the batch, who would have been more legitimately *myself* [Browning's italics] than most of the others; but I surrounded him with all manner of (to my then notion) poetical accessories, and had planned quite a delightful life for him." In other words, *Pauline is* what it appears, a personal confession with obviously fictional details, the chief accessory being Pauline herself and the delightful life planned for him being the trip in the woods and the stay abroad in her native land envisioned at the end. Where Browning wanted to go—as a poet that is—if not where he had been in this poem, is obvious. In the few cases where he revealed the work to friends he insisted upon adding a digest of his explanation as a kind of official addition to the work: "the history of it," he explained to Elizabeth when she wanted to see it, "what is necessary you should know before you see it.[74] Only, the candid admission that this work had essentially himself as the imagined speaker was quietly dropped. In the copy he gave to the man who planned to revive *Pauline* after forty-four years of interment, he wrote merely, "Mr. V. A. (see page second) was Poet of the party and predestined to cut no inconsiderable figure."[75] His public statement, when he finally felt obliged to reissue the poem in 1868, explicitly claimed *Pauline* as his first work of "poetry always dramatic in principle, and so many utterances of so many imaginary persons, not mine." It is an early attempt at a "dramatis persona" and only fails from want of "craftsmanship and right handling."

What was the attraction of Shakespeare and especially of Edmund Kean in *Richard III* to the poet writing *Pauline*? The answer, I believe, is that Kean in Shakespeare provided an especially attractive bridge for Browning from his role as an imitator of Shelley to the kind of dramatic realism that was more natural to his character and background and that was emerging, despite himself, everywhere in this Shelleyan poem. The response seems to have been as much to Kean the man as to Shakespeare. In building his permanent fame as a Shakespearian actor, Kean had always used a personal interpretation that threw the main character into bold relief as a central consciousness in the play. He was a prime creator of the nineteenth-century method of acting Shakespeare by stressing vivid portrayal of individual characters rather than the dramatic interplay of characters, plot, and poetry. To admire his acting was to feel the particular consciousness of one individual character even more distinctly than Shakespeare had intended and to feel simultaneously the greatness of Kean's own character as it mixed with his part. When Browning saw Kean at the small, Georgian, King's Theatre on the Green at Richmond, there was a further reason why his attention would have been called to the actor as man as well as the actor as part. Kean was wasted and sick and would be dead in slightly more than half a year. He had taken over management at Richmond so that he might live in the adjoining house and save all his energy for acting. He was carrying on more through spirit and will (and ample potions of hot brandy in his exhaustion between scenes) than anything else. On the whole he had in fact declined greatly from his days of glory in 1814 when he had exploded on the London theatrical world with his interpretations of Shylock and Richard III. Yet he was still capable of extraordinary moments when he seemed to open up the depths of consciousness in one of his characters.[76]

What Browning thus saw was human will triumphing through its own ongoing life and decay (and the scandal of his private life that Browning either hadn't heard about or kindly overlooked). It is this endurance of spirit that he remarks in his tribute to Kean in *Pauline*. He imagines himself in Kean's position, "gifted with a wondrous soul" but "in the wane of life." Then, as in Kean's aged acting:

> there shall come
> A time requiring youth's best energies;
> And strait I fling age, sorrow, sickness off,
> And I rise triumphing over my decay.

The tribute was all the more sincerely felt because Browning had had an opportunity at some point even to meet and shake hands with the frail, little

Reminiscent Bust of Shelley. Sculpture by Marianne Hunt.
One copy of the bust was set on the way up the stairs in the Brownings' home at New Cross. "Shelley's 'white ideal all statue-blind' is—perfect,—how can I coin words?"

Edmund Kean as Richard III. Engraving of the painting by T. J. Hall. *"I shall warm as I get on, and finally wish 'Richmond at the bottom of the seas,' &c. in the best style imaginable."*

The King's Theater, Richmond. Engraving.   *Kean's theater and last home.*
"Kean was acting there: I saw him in Richard III that night, and conceived the child-
ish scheme already mentioned . . . I don't know whether I had not made up my mind
to act, *as well as to make verses, music, and God knows what,—que de châteaux en*
Espagne!"

man with the grand head and ever-passionate involvement in his acting.[77] Kean struggling to redeem the shadow of his former magnitude thus offered an alternative role with which Browning could identify and served as a release for many of the most healthy instincts working in *Pauline*. Kean was a model not of prophetic unworldliness but of the soul put to drag road metal through the efforts of real life and yet managing to find its greatest nobility in the process.

What was attractive to Browning about *Richard III* itself, a play that would remain a favorite even though he knew and appreciated Shakespeare's greatest mature works, seems at first more mysterious. That he identified with Kean in the leading role of Richard is clear enough even three years later when, in a letter to Fox about *Paracelsus*, he unconsciously slips into the role himself. Mill, he tells Fox, must not be "an idle spectator of my first appearance on any stage (having previously only dabbled in private theatricals [i.e., *Pauline*]) and bawl 'Hats off!' 'Down in front!' &c., as soon as I get to the proscenium; and he may depend that tho' my 'Now is the winter of our discontent' be rather awkward, yet there shall be occasional outbursts of good stuff—that I shall warm as I get on, and finally wish 'Richmond at the bottom of the seas,' &c. in the best style imaginable."[78] The line was Kean's showstopper. As he said "In the deep bosom of the ocean—buried" he paused before buried and slowly unfolded his arms. "In a style of deliberate triumph uttering his words with inward majesty, [Kean] pointed his finger downwards, as if he saw the very ocean beneath him from some promontory, and beheld it closed over the past."[79] Browning's bit of fustian bravado in taking on the part is extremely suggestive, connecting by association Mill's criticisms, Kean and *Richard III, Pauline,* and his efforts to go beyond that work to a more public style in *Paracelsus*. Above all, it seems to imply that Kean in the part of Richard helped open an emotional synapse that could release and order energies pent up by Browning's attempt to mold himself on his conception of Shelley and the Shelleyan poetic role.

Now Richard is, of course, a villain and, compared to later hero-villains such as Macbeth or even Edmund, a rather obvious and direct one. We don't have to suppose that Browning in any sense denied this to understand what he saw in the character. In a way somewhat similar to Blake's and Shelley's useful misreading of Satan in *Paradise Lost,* he could make a personal and creative use of this bad overreacher. In the leading part Kean called his attention not to the condemnation heaped on Richard by all those around him but to the central fire of Richard's admirable energy and subtle intelligence. "By Jove, he is a soul!" Byron had exclaimed over the part years before: "Life—nature—truth, without exaggeration or diminution."[80] The energy Shakespeare gave Richard, enhanced and made credible by Kean's genius, was in fact not primarily the energy of villainy—the play indeed begins slowly and weakly with Richard's evil machinations—but the amoral energy of the individual will and ego carrying on in the face of hopeless circumstances. Kean as Richard was able to persuade his audience to detach themselves from the failure of his logic and the blatant injustice of his cause and he was finally able to win from them admiration in the last two acts for the relentless force of will that brings Richard to his furious and un-silenced end. Above all, Richard's force—the force of splendid conscious-ness and penetrating mind—cuts through the oppression of bad conscience and the impotence of guilt. The audience could perceive how abominable his guilty actions were; but they were even more directly involved in the vi-tality of his speech and thought.

There is no need to suppose that Browning had any remotely similar reasons for guilt to understand how he could respond so strongly to Rich-ard's ability to make the best possible case for himself in every situation. His own anxieties—to use the term as Harold Bloom has so productively and relentlessly applied it—were as much over his relation to Shelley and the role of the poet he offered as over any more usual guilt about religion or morals. For his own pressing needs as a growing personality, Richard could be, for all his evil, a liberating force. Attacked wholesale by conscience, Richard fights back for his bad self. His philosophy, abominable in moral-ity and statecraft, is a word of health to the consciousness plagued by the re-proaches of idealisms that it cannot in any case maintain against its full per-sonality. "What is done," he advises, "cannot be now amended." So at the end of *Pauline*, Browning resolves to turn his back on what has troubled his conscience: "No more of the past—I'll look within no more." Richard argues, "Plead what I will be, not what I have been—/ Not my deserts, but what I will deserve," and Browning assures Pauline, "You'll find me better —know me more than when / You loved me as I was."

If anything, the example of Kean, Richard, and Richard's author was thus influential as a way out of the big professions, concomitant despair, and endless labyrinth of confessional vacillation in *Pauline*. Here was an ac-tor who grew in the struggles of life and a character who showed the way to decisive speech and action under a far greater and far less tolerable burden of bad conscience and guilt. Above all, here was a writer who found a place in his work for more than just a part of his own emotions and personality. Here was the entire drama of conflicting emotions, intellect, and will that Browning himself had been experiencing and that, against his own lyric in-tentions, he had been trying to express in *Pauline*. But in Shakespeare, per-sonal confusion and emotional muddle were projected and ordered into ob-jective, dramatic form.

It is one thing to recognize Shakespeare as a supreme example of strong feeling and emotion brought into dramatic order and to learn fully our own partial sentiments and unexpressed attitudes by hearing them brought to full objective existence in his characters. It is quite another matter to achieve what he has achieved. Browning was destined to spend at least six years of his early career in an unsuccessful effort to make himself into a dramatic poet in the full sense. In the end he would never attain in his plays, nor even in his best dramatic monologues, Shakespeare's vigor and directness and

Shakespeare's capacity for projecting living and independent characters out of his own imagination and experience. In the process of writing *Pauline*, however, he was at least enabled to see beyond Shakespeare's classic greatness into the personal uses of his kind of art and the type of artistic sensibility he must have possessed. Very possibly the strange and oddly self-conscious and apologetic note that he added under Pauline's own signature was a tardy recognition of how far this work was from the kind of art he admired in Shakespeare. As we have noted, along with Beethoven and Raphael, Shakespeare is cited as an alternative ideal that Pauline finds far superior to the practice of her rhapsodist. She sees in Shakespeare a concentration of ideas and a larger artistic order, based first on a unified conception and then on an orderly execution. She doubts that either one is possible for this poor poet and wonders whether the whole shouldn't be burned—"mais que faire?"

Toward the end, Pauline is made to function as critic as well as supportive lover. By way of apology for this first work he reminds her that she had pronounced that "a perfect bard was one / Who shadowed out the stages of all life" and that this work was merely the first stage, done according to orders. The implication is again that *Pauline* is already seen as a tentative for a poet, not an example of his mature work: that in the future he will move from the vagueness of an adolescent poem about adolescence to works that treat, as Shakespeare does, the full complexity of human life. Ultimately in the 1888 revision, "shadowed" would become the even more objective and Shakespearian "chronicled," but the direction is already clear in the early reading. By the end of his career Browning may have felt he had some just claim to turn the shadows of unaccomplished poetry into the reality of chronicled achievement.

Despite Browning's ecstatic professions, at the end of the poem, of his priestly role, there is thus a rather clear direction developing out of the failure of *Pauline*. With Shakespeare as a lodestar, Browning was headed—before he received any additional shoves from unfavorable reviews or frank comments from Mill—toward a less personal and on the whole less lyrical and more dramatic and objective art. Far from undergoing the alienation from his true self that this process has sometimes been called, he was really moving in the direction of fuller self-realization through art. Although he would almost never again try to express directly his own life and feelings, he would find in a more objective and a more realistic art a fuller vehicle for the complexity of a personality which suffocated in the narrow lyric and personal concerns of *Pauline*. Not that he really would be able at this early a point in his life and career to carry out his resolve to "look within no more." In his two succeeding major works, *Paracelsus* and *Sordello*, he would continue to be essentially preoccupied with the overwhelming problem of *Pauline*: What kind of poetic role should he adopt and what kind of poetry should he write? As such, they are still far closer, if not to Shelley, at least to Byron's similar attempts to objectify his own personality and problems in dramatic or narrative form than to anything of Shakespeare's. However, unlike Byron, he would there be seeking the solution not by endless probing within but by attempts, not always very successful and often too labored, to place his own problems in a larger, external, and universal context. He would try to talk not about himself and his specific problems but about the general conditions of poets and poetry in at least a partially realistic and historical context.

5 The Shelleyan Heritage

The poem in honor of Shelley is thus also a poem, from the view of Browning's own development, of farewell to him. Henceforth Browning would drop almost entirely the attempt to imitate Shelley's lyrical or mythic form and style. By the time he published *Paracelsus* in 1835, he could even take it as a singular insult and annoyance to find the *Athenaeum* review of August second dismissing his second work as only an imitation of Shelley.[81] If there were still some borrowings or unconscious echoes, the tone of the whole was realistic and dramatic; in intention it was far from Shelley or even the aims of *Pauline*.[82] There is, of course, an overall similarity between *Paracelsus* and most of Shelley's work in the focus on the poet-figure and his quest, a focus that is continued in *Sordello* as well. But, if anything, Browning uses the quest as a way of criticizing rather than imitating Shelley. The study of the too ambitious spiritual quester gave him a chance to isolate and evaluate some aspects of Shelley's own unflagging quest without having to criticize him directly.[83]

Even within *Pauline,* side by side with the extravagant praise there were also indications that Browning already realized consciously that he must cut himself loose from his first master if he would develop his own way as a poet. Apparently he found that he could express his need to grow away from the shadow of an influence more easily in abstract terms. He specificially applies his general perception that there are idols in the arts who must perish to us as we grow to self-reliance even to favorite poets:

> witness this belief
> In poets, tho' sad change has come there too
> No more I leave myself to follow them:
> Unconsciously I measure me by them.
> Let me forget it.

He means, much as he would rather not acknowledge it, that he is beginning to find his own sense of identity as a poet, that he not only measures himself by them but also them by himself. As this identity grows, he begins to perceive Shelley as a distinct and different person from himself. As he celebrates Shelley's glory and new fame he simultaneously mourns his loss as a poetic double, as a part of his own growing personality. He realizes he cannot be Shelley:

For never more shall I walk calm with thee;
Thy sweet imaginings are as an air,
A melody, some wond'rous singer sings,
Which, though it haunt men oft in the still eve,
They dream not to essay; yet it no less,
But more is honored.

His method of exorcising a past influence is thus the same as that he used with his friends the Flowers: he praises highly and then begins to go his own way.

Shelley, however, was not so easily to be declared dead and buried honorably somewhere in the back of the mind. Browning happily moved away from the priestly poetic role he still held up for himself in *Pauline,* but he was not willing to challenge directly the ideal of an almost religious function for the poet as revealer of ultimate and spiritual truth. He was likewise not able to see Shelley himself as merely another of his childhood idols to be thrown off with maturing judgment. Through Shelley, he had had an experience both extraordinary and strange, and his own need to proceed in a different direction in no way canceled out what he had felt through Shelley's imaginative and mythic genius and his abstract moral fervor. The experience had touched him like a religious conversion, and though he might turn his attention to more ordinary life, he would carry it somewhere in his mind along with his more specific religious ideas as a kind of ultimate: not for him, perhaps not for this world at all, but no less real as an experience of a spiritual state penetrating beyond this world.

How much Browning felt, at some level, that he was betraying the highest aims of the poet in not reviving and continuing the role he saw and even exaggerated in Shelley will perhaps always be a matter of speculation or dispute. It is quite certain that he bore no enduring feeling, such as Betty Miller tries to suggest, of betraying the ideas and radical politics of Shelley. These he had rejected quite consciously and deliberately before *Pauline.* Similarly, he felt little of the guilt that a backsliding freethinker might feel in returning to religious belief. Shelley's religious skepticism had never been a primary influence on Browning, though Sharp's little anecdote about *Queen Mab* has misled most commentators into thinking it was. He was quick to dissent from a passage on skepticism in ''The Sensitive Plant,'' when he quoted it to Monclar, with the comment that here the master is wrong.[84] On minor matters such as vegetarianism he was even more outspoken against the master's position. Carlyle was pleased in 1842 with Browning's ability to run logical circles around the American transcendentalist fellow traveler Bronson Alcott for his solemn vegetarian creed.[85]

Browning would remain, however, rather acutely conscious of Shelley as the embodiment of one poetic road not followed. Certainly he often felt Shelley looking over his shoulder as he wrote during the first twenty or even thirty years of his career. As late as 1862 he could still complain, with obvious application to his early worship of Shelley, of a precocity that "binds its author to many a crude, wrong & untrue profession of faith which seriously hampers him after & long after."[86]

Although *Paracelsus* (1835) as a whole represents both a departure from Shelley and even a criticism of his ideas, the long scene at the end of Part II between Paracelsus and the poet Aprile seems deliberately contrived to apologize for most—or all—poets' inability to live up to the Shelleyan ideal. Aprile is not a study of Shelley but of a poet whose too eager desire to love and celebrate every aspect of this world leaves him, at his death, unfinished in his task and far from attaining the ultimate aims of poetry. The song "Lost, lost," almost an explicit imitation of the style of the lyrics in *Prometheus Unbound* and represented as being sung by all the spirits of past poets, bemoans yet another poet who has failed in the ultimate priestly aims. The nature of that failure is made explicit in the considerable additions to the song made for the collected edition of 1849. He has failed in the highest Shelleyan aims: he has not spoken "God's message" and he has left "The world, he was to loosen, bound." However, he works through his guilt at his failure to attain these highest aims in the course of the scene. Aprile's final insight at the moment of death is that only "God is the PERFECT POET" and hence, as the explicitly Christian additions of 1849 make clear,[87] that man is only the part, and should not feel a burden of guilt because he is not God, the whole; man finds through his partial achievement his larger dependence on God and God's support. Aprile apparently is crowned, despite himself, by his sainted peers as he speaks his last words. To be less than divine on earth may be not failure but humanity.

Still, Shelley returns to haunt *Sordello* (1840), there specifically as a pure spirit who must be placated, or even exorcised, in an opening apostrophe before Browning may go his own different way:

> thou, spirit, come not near
> Now—nor this time desert thy cloudy place
> To scare me, thus employed, with that pure face![88]

He is too pure a spirit with too pure an art—and not merely for the gross impurities of *Sordello* but for most of Browning's mature art. Others might simply ignore Shelley's special art and special kind of purity and go their own way unbothered. Browning, like the small but important minority of readers who continue to admire Shelley's poetry, could not. To dismiss Shelley he had to apologize. He continued to dream of an art and artistic role far from his natural bent and his real achievement. To Elizabeth he confessed a secret longing to look directly in his heart once again and write what he called "R. B. a poem."[89] Shelley seems always near when he thus speaks, as he often does to Elizabeth, of a deeper inner self only rarely expressed. Unlike Shelley, who looks from his tower up to infinitude, Browning sees himself as a consciousness imprisoned within the self as in a lighthouse, "wherein the light is ever revolving in a dark gallery, bright and alive, and only after a weary interval leaps out, for a moment, from the one narrow chink, and then goes on with the blind wall between it and you." There is always the longing, at once liberating and destructive, to "knock the whole clumsy top off my tower." Then, from that romantic wish there is inevitably the sensible return to his own full self and the paramount problem of finding not full expression but any expression at all: "Of course, every writing body says the same, so I gain nothing by the avowal."[90]

Finally, there is again and again the recognition that had begun in *Pauline*: that strange and wonderful as Shelley's poetry was and his character appeared, his view was not the entire view of life open to the artist. Shelley's place was secure in his pantheon yet he could agree entirely with Elizabeth's description of his limitations in "A Vision of Poets" (1844): "Shelley's 'white ideal all statue-blind' is—perfect,—how can I coin words?"[91] The "Essay on Shelley," prefixed to the spurious *Letters* of Shelley in 1852, contains some of Browning's highest tribute to Shelley's unique genius. However, the drift of the whole argument is to solidify his very tentative swerve away from Shelley in *Pauline*. Now the alternative, Shakespeare, is unmistakable. Shelley is given all due honor, but not as the essence of genius, only as a superb example of one kind of genius. Browning may aspire to unite both his objective and subjective poet, but he acknowledges the purely subjective role and then, in effect, puts it on the shelf. The way is cleared for the tremendous and very un-Shelleyan achievement of *Men and Women*. If, as has been eloquently but not entirely convincingly argued, "Childe Roland to the Dark Tower Came" is a poem that reflects his sense of guilt over his abandonment of Shelley and the romantic quest Shelley represents,[92] it is clear that he has mastered the guilt sufficiently to prevent any block in the magnificent achievement of this poem (really a deliberate parody of a Shelleyan quest) or the others of *Men and Women*. Browning finds his place as a poet, not as a prophet. He is content by and large to define his role as that of the poet in "How It Strikes a Contemporary." There the poet is an ordinary man—if not simply a man among men—whose eye is primarily on this world not the next. "For," as the "Essay on Shelley" insists, "it is with this world, as starting point and basis alike, that we shall always have to concern ourselves: the world is not to be learned and thrown aside, but reverted to and relearned." The poet thus is not a seer or priest who reports on God to his less insightful brethren. Rather he is content to file his modest but illuminating reports on the ways of this world to an eternal audience. After 1855, particularly when he became disillusioned with Shelley the man as he came to know more about his real life, it was Shakespeare, not Shelley, with whom Browning would identify, as in "House" or "At the Mermaid," on the rare occasions when he used a poet as an image for himself.

In the long process of disengagement from the start Shelley had given him as a poet, Browning not only learned to live with his own inability to follow the ultimate priestly or prophetic role. He also quietly reshaped his original, disturbingly powerful vision of Shelley as a sun-treader of irresistible personal and poetic force into a more manageable and tolerable form. The process, a logical and necessary one for coping with an outgrown but unforgettable force in his life, might even be dignified by Harold Bloom's conception of a saving or creative misprision. In Browning's case this is hardly a matter of misreading the poet he knew so well. It is rather a process of creative emphasis on what he finds useful to him in Shelley and a concurrent de-emphasis of what is disturbing or impossible. In the two important ways in which Browning comes to reevaluate Shelley as poet, he is, if anything, done more than justice. We might even say that Shelley is subjected to the age-old treatment for those of unwanted but undeniable power: he is kicked upstairs.

First, Browning came to overvalue the one side of Shelley that could be some kind of model to him as he worked away from his major influence. This is the side he identifies in the "Essay on Shelley" by citing "successful instances of objectivity": "Julian and Maddalo," the "Ode to Naples," and the work he rated so highly, the drama *The Cenci*. He even flirts there with the idea that Shelley's more famous work was only a kind of apprentice effort for future objective poems of this kind. Although finally he piously rejects this heretical notion, he clearly found it useful to think of his own dramatic and more objective works as still following the master's lead even as he went his own way. In 1879 Browning would even testify in court that Shelley was "A great dramatist—almost as great as Shakespeare."[93] Poets are not subject to charges of perjury on their critical opinions even when offered in court, but Browning is obviously rating this side of Shelley more by a personal than a critical standard. *The Cenci* has some moments of magnificent poetry and an overall power of acute contrast between white and black, pure and horribly evil characters. But it is also terribly flawed in its dualistic and even paranoid vision of reality, really a subjective symbolic projection offered as objective drama. It is, as well, weakly derivative in dramatic form for all the greatness of some poetic passages. However much Browning may have been dazzled by Shelley's creation of Beatrice Cenci, the splendid soul who is at last driven by outrage to kill her father, he could not have learned much from Shelley's Godwinian idea of tragedy as the study of character flawed by confrontation with things as they are. His focus as he developed would be rather on the opposite, on the possibilities of growth in character through experience in reality and on the internal failures, through self-deception and casuistry, by which a character fails to grow. At most he shared with this side of Shelley only an overall dramatic focus, an emphasis on minutely delineating states of thought and feeling rather than on presenting overt dramatic action. In the undeniable power of Shelley's creation, however, Browning did find an authorization for his own course. In dramatic work he could follow Shelley without feeling the burden of his past achievement; rather quickly, he could redefine the focus of dramatic poetry to suit his needs without ever having to acknowledge fully his independence.

Second, Browning eventually also kicked upstairs Shelley's major poetry in his efforts to come to permanent terms with his early enthusiasm. The process is, indeed, endemic to those who have loved Shelley, as it is to those who have come under Blake's influence. By Shelley's friends Browning had been given, virtually from the start, a view of Shelley that tended to downgrade his human struggles and embalm him safely away as a sweet-smelling saint. With time Browning himself further elevated Shelley from a poetic role to an almost symbolic ethical or religious role. Shelley becomes incorporate with his own absolute symbols, becomes, as Keats does to Shelley in the *Adonais*, not so much a real poet as an idea.

In the "Essay on Shelley" Browning doesn't so much extend as confirm and ratify the process by his mature judgment. He insists upon typing Shelley as one kind of poet, the subjective. He then defines the role Shelley successfully filled in terms so exalted that it is clear no mere human poet like himself can follow him. As earlier, Shelley's character is painted in colors of impossible nobility and humanity and he is explicitly rationalized to fit the Christian faith. Had he lived, Browning is certain, he would have become a Christian. This assertion is necessary, not to placate the ghost of Sarah Anna's orthodoxy by willfully distorting Shelley, but because Browning still views Shelley's poetry, in serious and sober prose, as a form of revelation, or the nearest human approach to it. "He digs where he stands"—into his own soul as the "nearest reflex of that absolute Mind." Thus working up "that mighty ladder . . . through himself to the absolute Divine mind," Shelley reaches his proper poetic end, a vision beyond this world to eternity and divinity: "Not what man sees, but what God sees—the *Ideas* of Plato, seeds of creation lying burningly on the Divine Hand." With his deliberate modesty, Browning in this way fulfills, as he explains at the end of the essay, his boyhood aspiration to pay some humble tribute to Shelley.

Thus elevated, Shelley the poet, rather than being a role model who interferes with Browning's more natural growth, has a new importance. He is virtually a part of his theology, a human link to the divine world that lies, in Browning's essentially Protestant outlook, beyond a worthy life in this world. If he has breathed easily in the world of spirit where other poets dare not even venture, his poetry, like the most visionary parts of the Bible, can give the earthbound poet his best knowledge of the highest reaches of human imagination and the highest level of language. Nor is this idea of Shelley as visionary poet much likely to be affected by any biographical news about the limitations of the boy and young man Shelley. Indeed, if we can trust the report of his trustworthy valet, even in later life Browning treated Shelley's poetry and Plato's *Republic* as personal bibles.[94] These were the works he consulted most regularly, perhaps along with the Bible. Although he moved steadily toward the role of the objective poet both in his dramatic experiments and in his mature dramatic monologues, the last thing Browning wanted was to portray man as incapable of those moments of religious or eternal insight that he found more habitually in Shelley. "However cloud-involved and undefined may glimmer the topmost step" of the Platonic ladder of perception, there was no doubt in his mind as to the existence of the ladder itself or of where it led.

As creatures from that place, Shelley the poet and Shelley's poetry thus became both symbol and usable metaphor for man's highest nature. Shelley's poetry is, again in the language of the Essay, "a sublime fragmentary essay towards a presentment of the correspondency of the universe to Deity, of the natural to the spiritual, and of the actual to the ideal." As such, his work offers to the more objective poet a mine of ideas and metaphors for keeping man's spiritual hopes continually present in poems that are themselves focused on his present condition. Both through the obvious borrowing of images of light, star, radiance, and so on,[95] and through more complex reworkings of Shelleyan effects, Browning would use what he had learned from his first poetic master to make his own poetry something more than mere realism. With hints of a greater reality and higher insight worked everywhere into his characters, Browning's poetry is not merely an objective report on man's physical and mental condition, but a vision of a creature with spiritual aspirations progressing through this world to an ultimate destiny beyond the world. In large part through Shelley's permanent influence on him, Browning became a poet of reality touched by the higher Reality Shelley seemed to reveal. His work is about real men troubled by their own fitful visions of something beyond their normal experience. In such a way, an influence which might merely have overshadowed and destroyed Browning's own different propensities would be converted into a beneficial part of his distinctive vision of life. Without following him in his own desperate and splendid mission, Browning would be able to build upon some of the best insights of his romantic predecessor as he performed his own different task of renewing poetry's age-old (and in Browning's sense objective) role of achieving the fullest possible view of man and his society. If some of Shelley's vision and intensity is lost as it is thus moralized, his essential insights into the heights of man's imagination are not. In his best poems Browning fits them into an accordingly complex and open-ended view of man's total nature and possible sublimity.

At the time he published *Pauline* this ultimate integration of the insights he had gained from Shelley into his mature poetic work was, of course, a thing of the distant future. At the time, he was left with quite a desperate situation. His identification with Shelley had focused most of his energies on assuming the role of poet. His initial and decisive swerve away from Shelley in that poem then left him with virtually nowhere to go. In his first work he was in effect both honoring and bidding farewell not only to Shelley but to the larger tradition of romanticism that he might naturally have followed. Although his profession of faith in *Pauline* might seem to sound for an instant the note of a new age, the note of Victorian spiritual affirmation as it is found in the sunnier (and often more superficial) works of the successors to the Romantics, he really had no obvious new path before him by which he could go beyond the past. Far from having settled his mature role as a poet, he was to begin almost a decade of restless and often futile groping for a new role to replace his lost ideal. *Pauline* might initiate the break with the past and the beginning of a movement toward a new, more realistic poetry focused on the subject of man's complex nature and experience. But it achieved no solutions to both problems that he would have to face successfully in making himself into a different kind of poet: finding a specific subject matter for his poetry and giving it a suitable poetic form.

Both those tasks were made enormously more difficult for him by his turn away from Shelley and from the role of the subjective poet. Whereas the subjective poet may merely dig where he stands and shape his ore—lead or gold as it may be—after one form that seems almost naturally generated by his personal subject matter, the more objective poet, who wishes to see man steadily and whole, can hardly rely upon his personal experience alone. He must know man in his various forms and conditions; he must know his opinions and states of mind; he must know the variety of the world and the very different societies in which men may live; he must have a command of various kinds of language and expression in order to represent the variety of personalities and moods that he studies. The poet who digs where he stands may make his whole work from the intensity of his perception or recreation of one simple personal experience. The success of the objective poet will depend not only on his native abilities but upon the breadth and depth of his education.

In Browning's case his family and home environment had given him an exceptionally broad introduction to life from the start. The influence of the Flowers and especially of Shelley had moved him decisively toward personal involvement in art and toward a view of himself as creative artist. And he had been brought quickly to an early crossroads in his development. However, while his sense of himself as a poet had been growing, a process probably even more important to his ultimate role had been taking place. This was the slow emergence of his own personal convictions as a result of his formal and informal education, convictions that would bolster with serious practical resolution his very tentative hopes of becoming a poet. In the process of making decisions about future goals that arose in his education, he came slowly to determine his personal relation to his society, rejecting more usual ways of life and careers for the special vocation of a thinker and poet. At the same time, in slowly learning to direct his own education, he came to general convictions about the nature of knowledge and about the kind of understanding that he as a poet would wish to have and express. Browning's education, not merely the loading on of a particular intellectual and literary baggage but the development of a personal focus on knowledge and a personal orientation to it, is thus as central to his ultimate development as a poet as his early experience with art and tentative artistic roles. In the long run it set the context of his mature efforts at poetry, and it led him to the decisions about his life and personal values that would take him beyond the ''private theatricals'' of *Pauline* to a final commitment to the incredibly difficult occupation of the serious poet. The development of Browning's mind in this full sense is the subject of the final part of this study.

Part Three
Education

Preceding pages: The University of London, 1829. Engraving by Thomas Higham. *The new main building of The London University, now University College London.*

X
Schooling and Society

Browning's early poetic development and the influence of Shelley on it have been repeatedly noticed in studies of him and his work. His education, by contrast, has been acknowledged, if at all, only superficially. Whether he even had any schooling and formal training seems sometimes to be a matter of question.

With the opportunities available to Browning in his father's collections of books and art and, even more, in his father's wide scholarship and greater curiosity, a very large part of his education obviously had nothing to do with schools and formal study. Long before reading and writing were officially taught to him at school, the experience of literature and books had been made an essential part of his life at home. Later, much of his education was literally home education, with supervision by his father and special tutors. And even when Browning began to shape and direct his own education, his standards differed from those of his family primarily in the degree of his commitment and the seriousness of his aims. Browning's own statement years later about his home reading—"I had no other direction than my parents' taste for whatever was highest and best in literature"[1]—has even been taken as an epitome of his entire education. G. K. Chesterton, for instance, actually paying tribute to Browning's learning, remarks, "If we test the matter by the test of actual schools and universities, Browning will appear to be almost the least educated man in English literary history."[2] Others have routinely applauded the open-spiritedness of an education of random reading; or, with Santayana's horror before possible intellectual barbarism, they have deplored, with unconscious anachronism, Browning's failure to receive the benefit of a rigorous public school.[3]

Important as his home and parents were to his education, attractive or unattractive as the picture of an untroubled childhood of browsing in a family library may be, for Browning, as for everyone, getting an education was a far more complicated and difficult process than mere random absorption of art and literature in his home. In fact, all real education, home education as well as formal instruction in schools, is essentially public not private. To the extent that it is education, it not only stimulates emotions and imagination but puts a child, well or worse, in contact with the inherited knowledge of the past, both as specific information and as ways of thinking or conceptualizing. In doing so, all but the most idiosyncratic courses of instruction necessarily embody the general assumptions of the society in which the child grows up about what knowledge and which ways of thinking are of importance. Even in home education, a child is brought in contact not only with the values and interests of his parents but, to a greater or lesser degree, with the standards and disciplines of the larger outside society. As John Milton and John Dewey would both agree, education has as its ideal and ultimate aim, to prepare the child to enter his society and to perform "justly, skillfully, and magnanimously" the offices, "both public and private" of citizenship. As such it provides, in whatever form, the first opportunity for the child to define his place in society and to develop his own values in relation to those of his society. In the long process of education that extended from a dame's school for virtual infants to the strenuous independent reading and study of his early adulthood, Browning absorbed a great deal of knowledge and information that formed his later personality and interests as a poet. Yet probably more important, his education, particularly his formal education at school and for one year at The London University, provoked Browning to make increasingly more deliberate and permanent decisions about his real interests and values. And in making these decisions, he not only shaped his future character but began, if only by tentative steps, to express that character for the first time.

1 Educational Alternatives

Where there is general agreement about the content and structure of education for persons of a particular class, a child is likely, after all griping and protests during the process, to accept the body of knowledge and the ways of thinking taught to him as natural and inevitable and to expect much the same for his own children. Or, rarely, he may, in disagreeing with the values implicit in his education, take a clear position against the views of his society. Browning's parents, however, and, as he grew up, Browning himself, faced a far more complicated situation. For the early nineteenth century was a time when education at every level was touched by uncertainty and controversy. Much of this began in a new concern, felt by men as different as rational, radical reformers and Evangelical leaders in the Church of England, with the miserable or nonexistent education of the working classes. In Parliament Henry Brougham was initiating the long fight that would lead, after endless delays and partial actions, to the beginning of a compulsory system of education in 1870.

Thus began a long-range social revolution, a lumbering start toward more democratic educational institutions. Along with this larger social change, a more immediate, if quieter crisis was developing in the education of the middle and wealthier classes—a crisis not so much in the social distribution of education as in the content and form of instruction. The Brownings and other families like them found themselves living in a time of increasing uncertainty about the proper end and best methods of education. Although there had always been differences between individual schools, or even between different masters of a particular school, on the whole the traditional schools for quality education, the public schools and the endowed grammar schools, had in the past embodied a reasonably coherent educational approach. Dr. Johnson had tersely, but not unfairly, epitomized their business in his definition of a grammar school: a place "in which the learned languages are grammatically taught." Mathematics might take an important secondary position in some of these schools, and frills such as modern languages be offered at others for an additional fee. But the essential curriculum was study of Latin and Greek. Although nineteenth and twentieth-century opponents of the classical tradition would probably have recognized many of their own ideals in the original intentions of the Renaissance humanists for a broad training of the mind through the classical languages and ancient learning, by the eighteenth century both theory and practice in traditional schools had settled into a more narrow, less universal system. Vicesimus Knox, for example, headmaster of Tunbridge School in the late eighteenth century and author of a widely used school text, thus justified the traditional study of the classics primarily on formal and moral grounds. "Classical discipline," he asserted, makes for the "enlargement, refinement and embellishment of the mind"; at the same time, the hard application to grammar and memorization strengthens the character. The instructor, usually a divine, should keep a wary eye out for the appearance of the old Adam and use the rod, if necessary, to put down "the vicious propensities of human nature."[4] Intense focus on a limited number of selected authors and passages and on the niceties of language and translation, as well as the writing of Latin verse, was thought to give a tone to the mind and provide a common core of culture for the educated classes. Strenuous drill formed the moral powers and could later, it was believed, be turned to account in any discipline of life.

By the time of Browning's birth, these arguments, though endorsed by Oxford and Cambridge and legally bolstered by a court decision prohibiting a change in the curriculum of endowed schools,[5] were becoming increasingly less persuasive to many teachers and parents. Not only had the emphasis on moral discipline and formal training sapped the original educational value of the classics as a body of great literature and ideas and as a theater for the study of history, but with the growth of modern knowledge and arts it became increasingly less possible to defend the classics as the only languages of learning and literature. Two hundred years before, Bacon had criticized the teaching of "words not things," and his phrase became the by-word for critics from Locke to Jeremy Bentham who argued for a curriculum of practical and scientific knowledge to replace unappetizing and unprofitable "dry husks of ancient learning."[6] Locke had marveled: "When I consider what ado is made about a little Latin and Greek, how many years are spent in it, and what a noise and business it makes to no purpose, I can hardly forbear thinking that the parents of children still live in fear of the Schoolmaster's Rod."[7] Practical men of the middle classes, anxious to buy their sons the training that would let them make their way in the world, were not slow to pick up such hints and to look for alternatives to the traditional schools. Oblivious to the danger that practical knowledge and scientific study could degenerate into a new kind of pedantic rote learning with hard facts replacing hard grammar, practical parents and utilitarian reformers alike called for a new modern scientific and mathematical curriculum to replace the old.

Other critics placed greater stress on teaching the attainments of a gentleman of the world. They would replace or at least enrich the classical curriculum with modern languages, especially French, and with drawing, fencing, and music. Most important, during the first thirty years of the nineteenth century, critics of the classical training stressed the need for a more historical and intellectual approach to classical culture and a broader study of English history and literature. Samuel Butler, grandfather of the novelist and headmaster of Shrewsbury years before Thomas Arnold began to revise the teaching of classics in the public schools on historical lines, could admit that public schools seemed often, in their concern with philology, to "neglect the sense for the sound."[8] By the 1820s, with a clearer sense of what was lacking in the classical curriculum, Macaulay and other critics of the educational status quo in the *Edinburgh Review* mounted a scathing attack on the philological approach to classical studies. Above all, they saw a lack of historical perspective: "attention is distracted from the really important lessons of history and philosophy to grammatical and metrical trifling"; grammar is taught by memorization of "needless rules and technical divisions are multiplied without mercy"; the "triteness of the subjects" for Latin themes reinforce the essential mindlessness of the process.[9]

During the late eighteenth and early nineteenth centuries, attacks on the traditional classical curriculum were swelled by a new humanitarian and romantic sentiment that found the discipline of the classical schools and the attitude toward children's moral and emotional growth, which they represented, both cruel and damaging. Even many of those who approved of the intellectual rigor of the classical training could suspect the Christian qualities of a famous flogger like Dr. Keate of Eton who was reputed to have told his young charges: "Blessed are the pure in heart. If you are not pure in heart I'll flog you."[10] To thoughtful parents, the great public schools especially, with their combination of frequent birchings, established bullying of younger boys, and loose or nonexistent social supervision, could seem very negative schools for character. One writer blamed Eton, with pious exaggeration, for giving a boy "a confirmed taste for gluttony and drunkenness, an aptitude for brutal sports and a passion for female society of the most degrading kind."[11] Another writer, a self-styled member of Cambridge, in an anonymous history of his own education written as a tract, could seriously portray his education at a private classical school and later at a public school as a shocking descent from the civilization of his family life.[12]

Dr. Johnson's justification of flogging—"children being not reasonable can be governed only by fear"—was, though merely tossed off in conversation, very much to the point. Educational reformers, especially after Rousseau, were increasingly persuaded that, if their needs and limitations were respected, children were naturally reasonable; and they were inclined to stress the value of adjusting education to the natural process of growth of the child rather than bending or breaking him through an imposed system and discipline. Reformers such as Richard and Maria Edgeworth complained of the stultifying effects on individual talent of a system that drills boys as if they were in the army: "perhaps, in the whole regiment not one shall ever distinguish himself from the ranks."[13] Whatever are a boy's abilities, the anonymous Cantabrigian complained again, "his inclinations, his taste, his turn of mind, they must take one direction wherein he must acquit himself successfully, or be punished by his master and degraded in the eyes of his school-fellows."[14] In the same vein critics called for healthier school environments, more imaginative means of presentation, and a concerted effort to develop a model social community in the school. Carlyle's cry in *Sartor Resartus,* from his own experience with the old schooling, for an education that would reach beyond the mechanics of the humanities to touch the student's human soul with the life of the past, gives voice to the slowly stirring discontent of two or three generations. "Innumerable dead Vocables (no dead Language for they themselves knew no Language) they crammed into us, and called it fostering the growth of mind. How can an inanimate mechanical Gerund-grinder, the like of whom will, in a subsequent century, be manufactured at Nürnberg out of wood and leather, foster the growth of anything; much more of Mind, which grows, not like a vegetable (by having its roots littered with etymological compost), but like a Spirit, by mysterious contact of Spirit, thought kindling itself at the fire of living thought."[15]

2 *The Very Respectable Establishment Opposite Rye-lane*

Far more than today, education was considered in the early nineteenth century to be essentially the responsibility of the child's parents. In the Browning family, as in many intelligent middle-class families of the day, this was not merely a matter of financial responsibility but also an intellectual, even moral, responsibility. According to cousin Cyrus Mason's account, there was a tradition of independent thinking on education in the family that went back to Reuben Browning, the great-uncle to the poet.[16] In the tutoring and encouragement that Reuben had given Browning's father, even rather against the wishes of Browning's grandfather, he had made the general educational questions of the day a matter of immediate concern in the family, especially to Browning's father whose difference from his own father, even his oddness, was in large measure a result of his own education.

When he set out to provide an education for his own son, Browning's father was confronted, in the general failure of confidence in the established schools, with a bewildering variety of opinions about the best kind of education. And he was faced with almost as many alternative ways of providing him instruction. Anyone with a house and some credentials could, in the eighteenth and nineteenth centuries, set up what was essentially a small business as a schoolmaster. Any reader of Dickens can easily believe that many masters were bores, charlatans, or brutes. But the prevalent dissatisfaction with the older schools also encouraged a number of well-educated and talented men to establish independent schools of real merit. Many originated as academies for Dissenters who found the connection between the established schools and the state religion unpalatable. Others catered to the growing middle-class need for practical, scientific, or professional instruction. There were numerous innovative schools offering a wider range of subjects and inculcating cooperative, progressive social attitudes. There were also a large number of private or collegiate schools offering much the same classical instruction as the established schools but in a smaller, home-like environment, with less bullying, closer supervision, and often special tutors for additional subjects at fixed rates.[17] Perhaps just because of the uncertainty about the best kinds of school, home tutoring—either by a special tutor who lived in (sometimes even a prominent man of learning in an aristocratic household), by a local master who took on students, or even by an educated father—was not at all considered, as it is today, eccentric or antisocial. It was a common and often preferred alternative to the public schools for wealthy and aristocratic families.[18]

In the context of these widely differing educational possibilities in a time of general disagreement about the best form of education for the middle and upper classes, the program chosen for Browning appears neither particularly unusual nor especially undisciplined and informal. In fact, the school finally settled on, the Peckham School near the Brownings' Camberwell home, "chosen for him as the best in the neighborhood,"[19] was far closer to the conservative classical standard than many schools available elsewhere to sons of the middle classes. It was, indeed, a step backward from the kind of progressive, mixed curriculum the elder Browning had enjoyed at the Rev. A. Bell's school at Cheshunt, where French and "every other Branch of useful Literature" were all regular parts of the offering along with the classics. There, too, the classics must have been more than merely a set of grammatical rules to be memorized for the boys to be inspired to spend play time acting out the Trojan War.[20] At Camberwell, nothing really comparable was available. Both the older local endowed schools, Alleyn's College at Dulwich and Jephson's Free Grammar School, had fallen on evil days: the famous old college was not merely out of touch with modern needs but corrupt and decadent. Jephson's was under local attack for failing to expand the curriculum beyond Latin and Greek.[21] Other schools were church or charitable ventures aiming at providing a minimal education to at least some of the local people.   AGE 5

Browning was first sent, probably at about age five, to a local dame's school. Crabbe's definition of that kind of establishment—"Where a deaf, poor, patient widow sits / And awes some thirty infants as she knits"— would no doubt apply, but some reading and writing were taught as well. Browning's experience there, though he surely had little conscious part in it, was nonetheless indicative of his later experience. A hubbub was raised about the mistress because, it was alleged, she favored Master Browning while neglecting the other students. No doubt, the bright, already well-informed young boy was spoiled by his teacher. But the result was that Browning was thus set apart from the other boys and asked, finally, to leave. If the event made any lasting impression, it must have been to bolster any feelings of self-regard that had already been built up at home; and the experience may have suggested to the young boy, in a vague way, that his education would inevitably follow a different path from the other boys'.

However this may be, after a year or two of elementary studies at home, Browning was sent, probably about age seven, to the lower school at Peckham run by two spinsters, the Misses Ready, sisters to the master. The school was a weekly boarding school with weekends at home. Even with the promise of weekly release, Browning's first response was the unmitigated woe of homesickness. An anecdote records that he found a face carved in an old cistern and projected his sense of loss of identity onto the dead object, ritually repeating "In memory of unhappy Browning."[22] It is not hard to guess what psychoanalytical interpretation could make of the incident, but what is certain is that nothing that afterward happened at the Misses Ready fundamentally altered Browning's naive sense that the process of going to school was one of alienation from his truer self.

A "petty" or preparatory school in the classical system had two aims. First, it "taught the three R's , the counties of England, the dates of the English monarchs, and the Latin declensions."[23] Second, it took upon itself the duty of stirring principles of piety and Christian morality into its unjelled charges. No doubt Browning did complete his rudimentary education—he speaks in a note in the Mill copy of *Pauline* with familiar contempt of " 'Brown, Smith, Jones & Robinson' (as the spelling books have it)"—and begin the long road to Latin grammar. Nor was there mistreatment or exces-sive discipline. If there were punishments they were, at any rate, not the essential foundation of the learning that they often were in the public school system. But with weekend reminders of what imaginative reading might be like, the boy was more sensitive than his fellow sufferers to the dullness of the traditional procedure. "Children's wits are weak, active, and lively, whereas grammar notions are abstractive, dull, and lifeless; boys find no sap nor sweetness in them," Charles Hoole lamented in 1660.[24] With essentially the same curriculum in 1820, the Misses Ready faced the same problem.

The attempt to form moral and religious character "by an incessant iteration of moral saws" was, on its own terms, an even more failing enterprise.[25] Elizabeth Barrett later spoke of Browning as "educated by the strictest of dissenters"; but the Peckham school was, if anything, a fairly typical Church of England private school and was sometimes referred to, probably beginning at a later date, as the Peckham Collegiate School.[26] The religious fare was not so much denominational as traditional and pietistic. Quarles's emblem poems, standard reading in petty schools since the seventeenth century, were supplemented by heavy doses of Dr. Watts's *Divine Songs Attempted in Easy Language for the Use of Children* and his *Psalms.* Browning, who had read Quarles at home, liked this reading; he appreciated Watts's greatness as a hymn writer. But the future scrutinizer of the motives of bishops, daily afflicted by a superior pompous morality along with morning hair brushing, learned to go beneath the ostensible morality to evaluate the spirit it represented. Browning was soon forcing his mother to see the unconscious and comic brutality that motivated the good sisters' moral indoctrination. He would imitate their furious hair combing and their equally ferocious condemnation of fellow humans to perdition:

> Lord, 'tis a pleasant thing to stand
> In gardens planted by Thy hand.
> . . . . .
> Fools never raise their thoughts so high.
> Like *brutes* they live, like BRUTES they die.[27]

When exactly Browning came to understand what was involved in this teaching is unclear. Clearly, though, the whole experience of learning to evaluate this procedure of rote inculcation was as important an event in Browning's education as any at the Misses Ready. Browning frequently quoted Watts in later life, sometimes seriously, sometimes in fun, but always with the self-conscious awareness of an educated mind that understands the uses and misuses of pious sentiments.[28]

The Reverend Thomas Martin Ready, who like his father, the Reverend Martin Ready, was master of the Peckham School, taught, like his sisters under him, a very traditional classical curriculum. Ready eventually took a degree from Cambridge and left school teaching altogether for a comfortable vicarage.[29] Nevertheless, the Brownings' opinion that Ready's school was the best to be had in the Camberwell area seems to have been true. To a local historian it was, "the very respectable establishment opposite Rye-lane." In contrast to the famous but moribund Dulwich College, it could brag of university scholars and eminent graduates: "Many youths educated at this school have become eminent in after life and a few have taken a high degree as wranglers at the Universities."[30] Well-to-do, educated families like the Dometts and their cousins, the Curlings, sent their children there.[31] One of the graduates, William Channell, a school friend of Browning's who shared Browning's low opinion of his school, later became a prominent judge.[32] Indeed, the appeal of the school was probably as much social as educational. As a collegiate or classical school, it offered an aura of gentility to its middle-class patrons. An advertisement for a rather similar school conducted by a clergyman at Leicester suggests the tone: an "old-established seminary . . . young gentlemen are expeditiously instructed in every branch of classical, polite and useful literature, as may best suit their future destination, whether the Church, Army, Navy, Commerce, or the more retired scenes of private life."[33] The fee for Ready's as for other schools of the kind, was probably rather stiff, possibly twenty to thirty guineas, a very considerable sum.[34]

In principle, a family-like environment was created with the master as paterfamilias of his home business. There was a chapel built next to the schoolhouse by Ready's father, probably for daily observance while the schoolboys fidgeted.[35] There was also a recreation area with a walled playground and a greenhouse. Browning spoke to Alfred Domett in young manhood "of the disgust with which he always thought of the place" and recited verses (the "three years" is misremembered) he had gone to the bother to compose in order to exorcise it:

> Within these walls and near that house of glass,
> Did I, three (?) years of hapless childhood pass—
> D____d undiluted misery it was! [in a suddenly deepened tone].[36]

The verses were none too good, and looked at objectively, things at the school were not that bad. There was the inevitable rite for the younger students, being "bullied by the big boys."[37] Still, there were also things to be learned from bigger boys, such as sailor terms from Edward Domett, Alfred's brother, or schoolboy talk: Browning responded to a searching query of John Stuart Mill's in the margin of *Pauline* with, " 'that's tellings,' as schoolboys say." There was the fun of being the center of attention in matches of wit against older boys.[38] And there was even recognition for his varied artistic talents. His pen and ink caricatures were remembered years later; he directed and acted in school productions of plays such as Nicholas Rowe's *Royal Convert* (1707) and even had some of his own boyhood dramatic works put on.[39] In more just moments, Sarianna reported, Browning "always acknowledged the boys were most liberally and kindly treated."[40]

It is worth acknowledging as well, as neither Browning nor his biographers have, how much, even at times inadvertently, was given to Browning in the old classical system. After obtaining the rudiments of grammar in the lower school, Browning probably passed into Ready's classes at about age ten and remained there till age fourteen.[41] Browning's father later spoke of six years of "unwearied application to the Greek, Latin, & French languages." French came later, but Browning evidently studied both Latin and Greek with Ready.[42] Latin would have followed a fairly standard syllabus, the Latin New Testament, Latin selections, Ovid, Caesar, Terence, Virgil, Horace, Cicero, and exercises in writing Latin verse.[43] He probably began Greek in the first year at the upper school or later. Even more than with Latin the focus would have been on grammar and memorization of rules. Yet, before leaving Ready's, Browning would have done some reading in the Greek Testament and Greek poets such as Lucian; and he would even have had a taste of his favorite Homer in the original. In both languages daily work focused intensively on short passages for translation and grammatical analysis. In a boarding school such as Ready's, there might be three or four lessons per day, broken only by meals, exercise, or chapel.[44]

Such constant attention to language and to the meaning of words, as apologists for the classics never lost a chance to point out, couldn't help but strengthen the student's vocabulary and give him a sensitivity to the nuances of language, which is often not developed in more extensive reading in foreign languages or English. In addition, the amount of time spent working over selections from major authors couldn't fail to give a gifted child like Browning some glimpse, if only darkly through the hack work of schoolboy translation, of their real dignity and literary value. "They taught me nothing there," Browning told Domett; yet he must have had, like other gifted boys put through the classical education, enough training to see what was of value in classical literatures and to encourage him, in his own way and by his own choice, to continue the study of the classics after he left Peckham. Lest, for his educated scorn for the limitations of his education, Browning be mistaken for uneducated, it is important to understand that his education at Ready's was, by the standards of the day, quite solid and very conservative. At Ready's he was given the foundation in classics which was, till the end of the century, the necessary intellectual baggage of the educated man.

The truth was, that though he did what was necessary to keep up with assigned work and though he made a reputation for his cleverness and talents, Browning was increasingly in revolt against the conservative educational standards of his day. At home his father and his books were always present to remind him of a wider world of knowledge, and a more liberal approach, than the endless progression of grammatical exercises at Ready's. Indeed, though the foundations of Greek were probably laid at Ready's, it may very well be, as the fanciful account of his introduction to Homer in the poem "Development" suggests, that the main inspiration for his progress in Greek came from his father's own unquenched enthusiasm. Then again, although he had no desire to put one impulse from a vernal wood above the imaginative literature he was reading at home, like Wordsworth or Rousseau before him he no doubt found his daily, drawn-out lessons had less impact upon him than his intense experience of external reality around Camberwell and Dulwich. Finally, there was always the immediate contrast between the culture and liveliness of his own family and the conventional and dull minister and his prim sisters.

The young admirer and imitator of Byron might have been happy to rise immaculately above his school and master in serene contempt. But for Browning, as indeed for the young Byron, direct outspoken rebellion was not so easy. Browning later admitted that he had conceived a certain contempt for the other schoolboys and for the master himself. In a refinement of this spirit seven years after he left Ready's, he scribbled on the inner page of a letter a biting, condescending epigram on one of Ready's sermons at Kennington. "Impromptu on hearing a sermon by the Rev. T. R.—pronounced 'heavy'—

'A *heavy* sermon!—sure the error's great,
For not a word Tom uttered had its weight.' "[45]

A similar lampoon appeared in the *Trifler* and, though unsigned, is almost certainly another venting of Browning's contempt for his old master:

"I wander from the point!" cried Tom—
It was an idle fear—
How could he ever wander from
What he was never near![46]

Confronting in Ready, however, the first representative of the society outside his family with an important role in his life, the schoolboy, for all his scorn, was pulled as well by a desire to please and conform. The verses which he remembered from his school days speak very differently of Ready:

We boys are privates in our Regiment's ranks—
'Tis to our Captain that we all owe thanks![47]

Browning, "always neat in his dress," easily won the master's affection with such orthodox sentiments and became, at least for a time, his privileged pet.[48] In return, Browning was evidently given a certain license to indulge his penchant for clever mischief, even working his pranks against the master himself. At the breakings-up, ceremonies that began holidays, when parents were invited, the pattern was the same. Browning never had a prize, though typically schools of this sort went out of their way to please as many parents as possible. Yet it was Browning who would direct the school plays and Browning, too, who came forward in the immaculate dress of a white-gloved young dandy to deliver his own rhymed address with heavy oratorical gestures.[49] Nor was the adolescent Browning as immune as he may have told himself to the authority traditionally given to the master by society. More than twenty years later Browning recalled in detail a classmate translating Virgil "after this mode, 'Sic fatur—so said Aeneas,—lachrymans—*a-crying*' . . our pedagogue turned on him furiously—'D'ye think Aeneas made such a noise—as *you* shall, presently?'"[50] Dull Tom had a side Browning knew enough to beware, and there is no record that he ever let himself run seriously afoul of him.

What we can laugh at as the unfortunate conjunction of a clever, unusually gifted boy with a conventional, conservative schoolmaster and future minister had for Browning, even when he wrote *Pauline* six years later, overtones of a nearly traumatic collision. In the result, rather than spearing Ready with a thrust of his wit, he was himself left a casualty with an intense sense of alienation from his former self. His various stratagems to gain attention and respect only served to deepen the sense of shame and the feeling that he had somehow lost touch with his former self.

> I lost myself,
> And were it not that I so loathe that time,
> I could recall how first I learned to turn
> My mind against itself; and the effects
> In deeds for which remorse was vain.

Even when allowance is made for the strained and self-indulgent introspection of *Pauline*, the statement is very strong. It suggests that Browning's school experiences, if primarily in a negative way, had a decided impact upon his developing character.

The cause, rather loosely given in *Pauline*, for this period of anxiety and alienation from himself is restraint—"long restraint chained down / My soul till it was changed." Restraint, of course, suggests the conditions of regimental school life that led Browning to adopt, as he had never needed to at home, methods of "cunning, envy, falsehood." More than this, though he may have chafed under the none-too-rigorous discipline at Ready's, it was far more the intellectual restraint—forcing his mind to run in narrower, more formalistic channels than it had before—which seemed to be killing his earlier self. In *Pauline*, he opposes restraint to the unrestrained joy and self-development of his early reading before school years. Whatever skills in language he learned at Peckham, the classical education seemed, as it did to other rebels from the system,[51] not only to narrow his education to formal points of grammar and language but almost to kill his interest in the humanities altogether.

With many boys the response to such miseducation was automatic: leave pedants and books behind as soon as possible and take up some more exciting occupation. For Browning the reaction was far more complicated and interesting. What he had previously taken up from his family without conscious purpose or understanding, the pleasures of imagination and wide reading, he now elected more deliberately. Without rejecting the knowledge Ready taught, he rejected the spirit in which it was presented and the narrow uses—class exercises and periodic class prizes—to which it was reduced. Leaving Peckham at the earliest normal age, fourteen—the age when other boys might leave for special professions and trades—Browning, a different boy with new skills, a wider knowledge of his own character, and some ideas on what passed for knowledge in the world, turned as he explained in *Pauline* to the "old delights" of reading and "The still life I led apart from all," in order to renew contact with his earlier self. His parents certainly concurred, probably even encouraged him, in this decision. However, it is probably not incorrect to see in this decision the first conscious entry of the young Browning himself into the quiet conflict that his father had waged against the narrow construction put upon the significance of letters and humane knowledge by most of his society. In rejecting, not merely intellectually, but with his full being, the limited views of the development of the mind represented, for society, by dull and conservative men like Ready, Browning was committing himself, more deeply than he understood at the time, to his father's personal battle for a wider vision of knowledge and the humanities.

3 Interlude: Home Tutoring and Millennial Hopes

From fourteen to sixteen Browning's education, thanks to his father's generosity, was essentially that of the son of an aristocrat of his age. Middle-class home, middle-class milieu notwithstanding, he was given attainments and a freedom to develop his imagination and personality that would have made him, even if he had had no further education, a gentleman by the standards of his time. Harrow, the public school favored by many great families among the Whigs, then established the standard for the broad cultivation of a gentleman by providing, in addition to the classics, lessons by special masters in French, Italian, drawing, fencing, broadsword, dancing, and music.[52] And there were not a few less prominent schools that appropriated these subjects to add polish to the education of the well-to-do middle classes. "All defects," Vicesimus Knox had complained of the academies and private schools, "are supplied in the money-making world, by the superior excellence of dancing, French, drawing, fencing and music masters, all of them far-fetched and richly remunerated."[53] Knox's crotchets could do nothing to change the situation. For the intelligent middle-class parent, such attainments were a worthwhile purchase: a voucher that his son would pass as a cultivated person in society. Mr. Browning's willingness to pay for tutors no doubt flowed from a more sincere belief in the intrinsic value of the subjects. However, this period of home education, while restoring to Browning his old freedom to develop after his own fashion, hardly cut him off, as is often suggested, from the learning of other boys of his day. Far more than Ready's training, home tutoring put Browning in a position throughout his life to enter easily into the society of cultivated men of all classes.

The solid grounds of Browning's musical education, under various tutors, were laid during this interlude.[54] He was trained in the genteel, if useless art of fencing and the more modern one of boxing.[55] There was opportunity to develop his own furious style of horsemanship on Uncle Reuben's horse—the mad careening that so annoyed his more pedestrian cousin.[56] There was time, too, for drawing, gardening, dancing, and other such pleasant subjects that were being incorporated into the self-styled progressive schools of his day. On the surface, at least, the man being formed from the boy was not a bookish recluse but, with all its good and bad, the nineteenth-century version of the complete English gentleman.

The business of this unbusiness-like period of his education, however, was not merely the surface attainments of the gentleman of his time. The broadening knowledge of a foreign language and literature, the first addition made by reformers to the classical curriculum, was the primary goal set by Browning and his father for this time. The centrifugal forces of the French Revolution had whirled to England a supply of educated French gentlemen without profession or trade and there was no difficulty finding near Camberwell a man offering his French accent in exchange for English guineas. The man found was named Auguste Loradoux, lived at nearby Walworth, styled himself *Professeur de Langues,* but was "my old French Master" to Browning.[57] That he had some claim to professional status other than the self-assumed title is suggested by his troubling to publish, along with a Charles LeRoy of Camberwell, a text of *Gil Blas* expurgated "à l'usage des écoles." Still, this impression is undercut by Browning's claim that he himself did most of the work—"I '*did*' for my old French Master, and he published."[58] He knew the classics and gave Browning translations from Greek to French poetry as exercises, but then he had the quantities wrong. Browning, who found him a decent person, protected him from knowledge of his ignorance, obligingly, if somewhat patronizingly scanning "Aristogeiton" with "votre nom" by dropping the *e.*[59] If Loradoux was no candidate for the Académie Française, he was at any rate able enough as a teacher to give Browning a lifetime foundation in speaking French and to start him on a critical appreciation of French literature. After the deadness of Latin by rote, the slow growth of the power to think and express himself in a living language, learned from a native speaker, must have been exhilarating in itself. The young man, who could still in 1832, for no apparent reason except his love for French (and perhaps an association between his confessions and those of Rousseau), have his imaginary lover speak in academic French in a footnote, was for a time probably infatuated with the sound and flow of French. Years later he still slipped, possibly with affectation but, if so, certainly with unconscious affectation, into a French phrase—"Tomorrow morning I leave for the country—not, I fear, to see Leicester—mais ça viendra avec le bon temps"[60]—or a French locution in English—"There,

you have a list of my doings actual [present] and intended.''[61] More productively, from speaking French and from practice in writing French verses—at
one time ''as easily as English''[62]—the future poet was expanding his awareness of possibilities of expression and sentiment not often explored in English. In time, in poems such as "Count Gismond" (1842) or the French
"Claret" of "Nationality in Drinks" (1845), Browning's feeling for the
even flow and graceful elevation of French would enable him to bring into
English some of the elusive essence of a foreign mentality.

Most important, two years of constant daily work at French gave
Browning a solid taste of a foreign philosophical and literary tradition.
Even at fourteen, in the "Dance of Death" fragment, Browning had preten-
tiously attached two verses—in translation and rather insipid as well—from
Madame de Staël as an indication of his cosmopolitan reading. There is no
evidence that Loradoux was any more inspiring as a teacher than Ready,
but at least he could count on his student's interest in the subject. Nor
would introductory reading like the satirical, picaresque adventures of *Gil
Blas de Santillane* be likely, in the way of thirty lines from Caesar or Cicero
for parsing each night, to dampen his student's enthusiasm at the outset.
What other works Browning read for his lessons isn't known: certainly
enough of the courtly poetry of the Renaissance to find an aptly Byronic
headquote in Clément Marot for *Pauline;* probably also a good deal of his
more innovative contemporary Ronsard, who is given a chance in "The
Glove" (1845) to make some cutting remarks about Marot's translations of
the *Psaumes de David.* Almost certainly, he also read Molière, whose doctors he speaks of with familiarity in his letters,[63] and the great tragedians.
Well along in his studies he was very possibly introduced to the pleasures of
Rabelaisian humor and philosophy. In any case he captured the spirit of this
relaxed period of growth and education in Rabelais' name in the later poem,
"Sibrandus Schafnaburgensis" (1845) where crabbed pedantry is tossed
aside for the refined pleasures of an attic *fête champetre:*

> a loaf,
> half a cheese, and a bottle of Chablis
> . . . . .
> Over a jolly chapter of Rabelais.[64]

Then and later, Browning read a good deal of French literature. Elizabeth
Barrett might complain of his lack of interest in her idol, George Sand, but
couldn't deny his breadth of reading in the classical masters and in French
plays and vaudevilles.[65] More important than any specific reading, Browning's wide exposure to French literary traditions fostered from an early age
a literary cosmopolitanism that encouraged innovation and independent
thinking. Keep in mind, he wrote a fellow writer in the 1860s who was working at careful analysis of character, "the immeasurable superiority (to my
mind) of French models than English: oh, I know what the clever English

find it useful to say!—and I say,—Bosh!''[66] Such things are not, of course, always ordered better in France, and Browning himself was also sometimes prone to turn subtle French analysis of character into mere English turgidity. However, for a writer, who might, like many talented persons in the nineteenth century, have found the greatness of the English literary tradition a constricting and paralysing standard of excellence, awareness of the different kind of excellence achieved in the French tradition—that the house of literature, indeed, has many mansions—was an important kind of mental freedom.

French and French literature were Browning's primary occupation during this interlude at home. Both Latin and Greek were kept up, however, by regular reading. It was these subjects that Browning would elect to pursue on an advanced level when he entered The London University. Most important, though still with the encouragement and guidance of his father, Browning was beginning to exercise the freedom of adult scholarship: self-directed general reading aimed at a fuller understanding of man and his world. This process, undertaken simply by wide pasturing in his father's library, has seemed a haphazard procedure to later writers accustomed to lists of great books or standard curricula in general education as the means to such general knowledge. However, what Browning may have lost in this time from lack of system was in good part made up for by the genuineness of his motivation. Whether reading well-known works or out-of-the-way oddities his father had picked up, Browning read not to know the "right" books or to fulfill a school requirement but to find out from each work what understanding of life it offered. "Great books" were read not as an end in themselves, as merely so much educational baggage to be loaded in, but as a means to wider knowledge of humanity.

There was, in any event, very little in the way of systematic approaches to general knowledge to be found in Browning's day and it was almost inevitable that he would spend a good deal of time in undirected exploration until he began to find his own way. Most of the sciences by which the twentieth-century student tries to organize his understanding of man and society were in their infancy or barely existent in the early nineteenth century. Psychology in England, despite the fundamental criticisms Coleridge was making of it, still followed the arid path laid down by Locke and his eighteenth-century disciple and systematizer, David Hartley. It attempted to explain not behavior or creative thinking but merely the processes of reasoning by a mechanical model. Anthropology and comparative studies of different societies hardly existed as disciplines. What information was available had to be sought in undependable random sources such as accounts of voyagers and colonists. Bentham and his Utilitarian followers were calling attention to the need for a systematic analysis of the institutions of society and their relation to individual humans, yet they themselves tended to reduce men in society to crude and mechanistic models. There was really no descriptive sociology that attempted to explain the complexity of present social organization.

Economics (political economy) alone, primarily because considerations of value had been almost entirely laid aside, might seem, from the work of Adam Smith, Malthus, and Ricardo, to be becoming an organized discipline of knowledge. Most of all, though there were many writers of memoirs and histories, and some outstanding individual historians from classical times to Gibbon, there was not the consolidating enterprise of history that there has been in the later nineteenth and the twentieth centuries. Obtaining any coherent and dependable view of the past was a work of individual exploration and scholarship, not a matter of consulting the current authorities. Early nineteenth-century thinkers as diverse as John Stuart Mill and Thomas Carlyle could even question whether previous historians had brought any idea of a different past to life. Carlyle saw only mountains of dry-as-dust annals and unimaginative accounts; Mill questioned whether, before Coleridge, thinkers had possessed any sense of a separate past time in which man and his society might be fundamentally different from the present.[67]

With no clearly organized modern body of knowledge the student had really only two options: he could acquiesce in the view, long outdated but still endorsed by his society's educational system, that general knowledge was simply a matter of classical learning, or he could set out on his own to read his way to wisdom. For the enterprising reader there are, of course, many possible ventures toward wisdom and no sure roads to success. If the account in *Pauline* can be taken literally, Browning had turned first, even before he left Ready's, to eclectic reading in poetry as a source of general understanding of man through the ages: seeking, in the boisterous phrasing of *Pauline,* "to know what mind had yet achieved." His first mighty bard was, as we have seen, the Byron whose worldliness and breadth of experience attracted him at the time of the "Incondita" and continued to exert a less intensive influence throughout his youth. In the hero of Missolonghi Browning had, of course, found a boy's political ideal, as well as a poetic model. Byron's emotional, somewhat superficial but certainly sincere and fearless championship of the cause of liberty—especially the spread of liberty abroad at the time of general reaction and repression after Waterloo—probably set for life Browning's similar allegiance to the grand old cause of European liberalism. He certainly prepared the way for Browning's deeper and temporarily more important, conversion to Shelley's political views.

Shelley's greatest impact upon Browning was, as we have seen, as a personal and literary model, as a poet only recently dead who seemed for a time to embody Browning's own aspirations and views of his role as a poet. It was certainly his growing passion for Shelley's poetry and for the man as he conceived him that led him to begin to look seriously at his ideas—not the ideas that drew him to look at the poetry. Browning even attempted, when he read *Pauline* over in 1867 for reissuing, to suggest that his entire interest in Shelley had been essentially a personal or poetic one: "And my choice fell / Not so much on a system as a man."[68] If he did come to Shelley's ideas through Shelley the man and poet, there is also no doubt that for a considerable time Shelley then came to affect Browning as much through the content of his works, his ideas and explicit doctrines, as through his personality and poetic genius.

What precisely in the Shelley he knew so well—from the ridiculous of his early philosophizing in *Queen Mab* (the village atheist, as Chesterton called Hardy, blaspheming over the village idiot) to the sublimity of his uncompleted "The Triumph of Life"—most influenced his thinking is hard to say. As we have seen, Browning probably did read Shelley's *Queen Mab*, though not as his first acquaintance with him, and he may have come under the influence of the skeptical religious thinking of this work. But if so, there is little evidence of it in all that he says of Shelley. And Browning found no difficulty, as he passed out of his general phase of early religious doubts, in carrying Shelley with him back toward a more religious, if not explicitly orthodox, viewpoint. If anything, Shelley's free speculation on religion probably tended to open Browning's mind to the possibility of varieties of religious viewpoints and feelings rather than to convert him to a rigid, rational skepticism.

It is true that Browning did undergo a decided conversion under Shelley's influence into that different credo, in which the lion foreswears the lamb altogether, vegetarianism. Presumably under the tutelage of the long note to *Queen Mab* that amounted to a small treatise and was in fact later published as such, Browning resolved to live (and claimed he did so for two years and more) on bread and potatoes.[69] The sincerity of such a conversion, especially in a time before year-round fruits and vegetables—not to mention protein substitutes—were conceived of, can hardly be doubted. But neither atheism nor vegetarianism were central to Browning's response to Shelley's ideas. In the self-proclaimed admirer of both Plato and Bacon, Browning found, more than specific ideas and beliefs, an overarching and contagious faith in the power of the human mind. Shelley's words, it should be recalled, seemed to Browning a new language, an act of entirely different mental conception:

A key to a new world, the muttering
Of angels of some thing unguessed by man.

And it was not merely specific doctrines but, "the whole of his conceptions" that eventually dawned on him as he read.

What the whole of his conceptions—this Shelleyan revelation—seems to have been was a way of talking about possibilities rather than realities. In Shelley the secular saint, "believing" in mankind and "devoting all / His soul's strength" to their good, Browning saw not a specific system of thought but a general commitment to saving mankind. Man would be saved not by faith in an afterworld but by the poet's new conceptions, his "hopes and longings" for a regenerated, renewed secular order. Had he known

Blake at this time, Browning might have felt much the same enthusiasm for his general conceptions as he did for Shelley's. Both writers were part of the larger movement of European thought from other-worldly religious ideals to a secular idealism, a conception—parallel to the millenarian strain in Christianity—of a new apocalypse for man now and on earth. Such ideas were, of course, not limited to poets and poetry. Converted, as he explains in *Pauline,* by the grandeur of Shelley's hopes, Browning, like the prose prophet Thomas Paine, made "liberty" his intellectual and moral absolute: "I was vowed to Liberty." As most often, the term liberty was used vaguely precisely because it was meant to carry such a range of values. Not specific political freedoms alone but a large and open-ended promise of a renewed life and society, liberty was essentially the freedom of mind that made such a vision possible. Like Shelley, Browning began himself to conceive of a better possible world set up against the real one:

Men were to be as gods and earth as heaven,
And I—ah, what a life was mine to be!

Such ideal aspirations for man, rather than a specific program for improvements and reform, were typical of extreme romantic social thought. Crane Brinton remarked concerning Shelley, "his central principle is simply revolution by miracle, the conquest of the promised land by a mere sounding of the trumpets of desire."[70] To Shelley this would not have seemed a criticism. The miracle he sought was the regeneration of man, and his method was the contagion of his own idealism, expressed in his poetry. "The great instrument of moral good is the imagination," he proclaimed in "A Defence of Poetry" (1821, published 1840), because it elevates each individual directly to a higher understanding and more elevated feeling. As an ideal, the drama of ancient Athens appeared in his view to be a theater for the entire society that acted upon men like a religion: "The Athenians employed language, action, music, painting, the dance, and religious institutions to produce a common effect in the representation of the highest idealisms of passion and of power." To fulfill this conception, Shelley wrote the *Prometheus Unbound,* embodying consummately in Prometheus the most splendid of abstract idealisms and demonstrating, somewhat less successfully, the miracle of regeneration that results from these virtues. With the same outlook, Browning's idealism led him to dream, at least, perhaps shortly after his first enthusiasm for Shelley's vision or possibly some years later, about writing a companion work to restore "the Prometheus πυϱϕόϱος [firebearer] as Shelley did the Λυόμενος."[71] He planned, as he recounted to Elizabeth, to show in the same abstract form of myth how Prometheus first achieved "the salvation of man" and how his ideal action would bring in and of itself a revolution. Prometheus would be led off at the end to be bound, but the mere might of Jove would stand under a new, unceasing threat of apocalyptic revolution: "Might in his old throne again, yet with a new element of mistrust, and conscious shame, and fear, that writes significantly enough above all the glory and rejoicing that all is not as it was, nor will ever be.''

Certainly Browning's reading and intellectual life during this period of home education was not confined solely to poetic and philosophical speculation and rosy visions of an ideal world wiping out the solid and not so unpleasant realities of late Regency Camberwell. He continued that diverse incidental reading among the curious knowledge and wide assortment of literature and history in his father's library that had begun when he learned how to read. Yet all that is known of these two years suggests that the greatest influence upon Browning's mental development came from works, like Shelley's, of intellectual and imaginative exploration. Quite naturally he was first attracted by the most open advocates of intellectual liberty and the free use of the mind, by those writers of the eighteenth-century Enlightenment and the romantic idealism of the early nineteenth century who had, like him, liberated themselves from the narrow, Christian classicism of the Thomas Readys of the time. Along with Shelley, we are told, he was reading the complete works of Voltaire, a more acid and specific critic of the old ways, if a less volatile prophet than Shelley for the coming new order of things.[72] From other Enlightenment thinkers, probably Diderot and Rousseau especially, as well as from earlier speculative minds such as the Renaissance occult philosopher and physician Cornelius Agrippa, Browning must have found other hints of a possible new order of things as he continued the survey of ''passion and mind'' that he recalls in *Pauline*.[73]

Samuel Johnson, with some correctness, might have seen in such a program of reading an invitation to useless curiosity and a capitulation to the dangerous prevalence of the imagination, but for a growing and curious mind of Browning's time a period of immersion in the currents of European radical speculation and secular idealism was both inevitable and necessary. All of the major English romantic writers from the Pantisocratic Coleridge to even the lukewarm radical disciple of Leigh Hunt, John Keats, had had to come to some terms with the stirrings of new thought, at the same time critical and corrosive, enthusiastic and idealist, that found their greatest expression in the French Revolution. Even Browning's older contemporary, Carlyle, the splendid castigator of abstract speculation, had himself been trained on the radical speculation of the Scottish Enlightenment. While Browning was reading Voltaire and Shelley, the young Alfred Tennyson, age fourteen, another early enthusiast for Shelley and Byron, was putting the scientific speculative skepticism of the eighteenth century into the eloquent arguments of the Devil in *The Devil and the Lady*. For more than two centuries the European mind had been setting itself free from the literal Christian vision of a world created in 4004 B.C. and ordered by hierarchies of political and religious authority established by God in perpetuity. The process, sporadic at first, had burst into full and open speculation toward a new vision of the universe and society with the writers of the French Enlightenment, and it flared up again, after the French Revolution burned out, in the writings of poets like Byron and Shelley and in the more directed and practical radicalism of the liberal reformers and the Utilitarians. Although thinkers as different as Locke and Shelley, Voltaire and Rousseau, looked hopefully toward a new knowledge, a modern vision of man and society to replace the older orthodox vision, their greatest legacy to the nineteenth century was a critical and destructive one. A student of the early nineteenth century who set out, as Browning did, to explore the "mind" of his time would find that studying modern knowledge of man and society led him primarily not to a new vision of man but to the complementary extremes of skepticism and speculation. In addition, to the young Browning modern knowledge was bound to seem especially tentative, even somewhat insubstantial, because reading and the direction of his interests did not lead him, as we shall see, into the most fully articulated modern disciplines: mathematics, physics, astronomy, geology, or economics.

The effect on Browning of this period of free reading in skeptical and romantic writers was, however, less that of religious crisis and depression than of intellectual exhilaration and giddiness: "I dreamed not of restraint but gazed / On all things: schemes and systems went and came." The speaker of *Pauline* looks back on this time as splendid but also unbalancing. Absolute freedom sent his mind into a whirl of systems and open possibilities, and his only steady belief was in the fitful star and tossing bark of Shelley's genius. The little that is recorded of the impression Browning made on others during this period also suggests abrupt and uneven mental independence. It was during this time of free reading that Browning was moved, as we have seen, to share his doubts on the genuineness of the Scriptures with Sarah Flower, only to lead the would-be spiritual adviser into a maze of perplexity of her own. As his reading and thinking continued, Browning's puzzlement probably did begin to turn into assertiveness and paradox-posing, as Mrs. Orr reports in very decided terms: "He set the judgments of those about him at defiance, and gratuitously proclaimed himself everything that he was, and some things that he was not . . . it distressed his mother."[74]

Parents who would be dismayed if their children did not think for themselves can still be less than content with the rough adolescent path to independence. Even Browning as a much older person—himself a father of a difficult son—could condemn his early self as a puppy worth little.[75] More fairly, we can understand the petulance of a clever boy brought up at one remove from the realities of London life and confronted, in his first exercise of freedom, with authoritative challenges to traditional ways of thought and with emotional calls for the immediate regeneration of society. Scorn for all that seemed arbitrary and outdated, impatience at the ridiculous delay in the making of the new secular Jerusalem, would seem to justify minor breaches in the present social order and some unleashing of the old Adam at home.

Fortunately, the Brownings took their stand far to the left of Tory politicians, reactionary divines, and other presumptive supporters of the ancien régime. Browning's freethinking might distress his mother, yet both parents' traditions and ways of life had encouraged him to work out his own independent view of things. If the first consequences of his independence distressed them, it was they who had encouraged his free study at home. Nor was there any suggestion that some other procedure should be followed or that the devils of open inquiry should be forcefully driven out of him.

XI
The London University

That a new procedure was ultimately devised was Browning's decision alone. Whatever uneasiness his independence of mind caused at home, the thrust of his idealism was directed not toward his sympathetic parents but outward toward his society. He was going through a period of conflicting feelings and attitudes, but his instinct was a healthy one: to test his new ideas and idealism by engaging with the world. The note of engagement, of commitment to ideas not as abstractions but as approaches to life, sounds throughout the discussion of this period in *Pauline*. He "threw" himself, he recalls, to meet "What then seemed my bright fate." His vows to the abstraction, liberty, were to bring immediate and concrete change. The hopes for a regenerated future were to live in the present as heaven on earth. New conceptions would necessarily bring a new life: "My whole soul rose to meet it."

What possible activities if any, Browning considered appropriate to throw himself into in order to effect the immediate realization of his ideals, isn't known. There is no indication that he followed his master, Shelley, in throwing pamphlets out of the window in the hope of turning passing pedestrians into proselytes. Nor did he strike any more general blow for freedom that might have brought him into conflict with the law. Even Shelley had advocated not direct action but passive resistance and faith in the miraculous revolutionary power of the liberated mind. Imbued with a similar faith, Browning, not surprisingly, threw himself not into direct action but into further education.

From our perspective, a perspective founded on that very recent idea that we think of as age-old, the idea of the liberal arts education, it is not hard to propound what kind of further education Browning should have sought. After the extremes of meaningless discipline and free reading in speculative works, the future poet needed the firmer and wider grasp of human life and society that contact with a variety of literary works and study of history and the history of thought could bring. He needed training in subjects like philosophy and comparative religion: training not in mere linguistic skills, but in the careful use of language in complex questions of philosophy and ethics. Above all, he needed close personal contact with some of the other talented people of his time who were equally devoted to the idea of development of mind but had also taken some of the hard steps along the way to mental cultivation: contact with men who could show him that to criticize the present and to imagine a rosier future were, though essential, only the simpler, first steps in education; that further education would require a much harder discipline, the wide reading and careful reflection needed to explore the infinitely complex nature of man and society as they are at present and to understand the infinitely subtle ways in which the present is simultaneously formed from the past and divided from it. It is easier, indeed, to outline some such program of education for Browning than to suggest where, in 1828, he might have found it. Oxford and Cambridge, still closed to those outside the Church of England by various tests, offered a core curriculum of classics, theology, and—at Cambridge—mathematics: in effect a continuation of the more conservative classical grammar school subjects. Although the social life was liberal, even indulgent, to the rights of young gentlemen to get to know the world, liberty of the mind was not encouraged. Doubtless the enthusiast for Shelley, like the young Oxford author of *The Necessity of Atheism,* would have found there not guidance for broadening and deepening his intellectual inquiry but the machinery of ostracism and expulsion. High costs (Oxford and Cambridge generally required the very large sum of two hundred pounds or more per year) and religious tests made these universities, in any event, out of the question for Browning. Unless a student was willing to adventure to the then remote Scottish universities or the even more remote German ones, there was no other alternative to private tutoring or home education.

1 *Fair Girl That Comes a Withered Hag*

The announcement that there was suddenly an additional alternative, a new university in London itself, must have first struck Browning as a confirmation of his hopes for the dawning of a new world. The creation of a new university, after centuries of hegemony by the upper-class and Church of England institutions, was another sign of the quiet stirrings of evolutionary change that were thawing England in the years after Napoleon's defeat. The new university, located in the metropolis, was set up quite deliberately as a challenge to the religious, social, and educational order established in Oxford and Cambridge. It was called The London University (later University College in the larger University of London) and was created by an ad hoc alliance among various groups that were excluded, socially or intellectually, from the old universities. Catholics, Dissenters, Jews, and free thinkers joined to create a nonsectarian university: a phenomenon inconceivable to many traditional educators who, with Thomas Arnold, a man far from the religiously ultraconservative, thought of the new creation not as a university at all but as "that godless institution in Gower Street." Some supporters saw the university, as well, as an instrument for educating and training a new ruling class, the middle and professional classes of London— "the glory of England"[1] as James Mill called them in arguing for the university—and a class that was coming, in any case, to play an increasingly important role in England's political and intellectual life. Location in London and a nonresidential system put university education within the reach of comfortable, commercial families like the Brownings. Money, not social position, opened the way to the new university, which was formed like a venture company with places open to those who, like Browning's father, took shares of one hundred pounds. At that price it was not quite the "humbug joint stock subscription school for Cockney boys" John Bull dubbed it, but it was certainly a step toward opening higher education to the middle classes.[2] Most important to Browning, the university seemed created with just that faith in the importance of mind to which he himself had been converted. In fact, a poet, Thomas Campbell, had first suggested the idea of the university. Innovative educational thinkers as diverse as the theoretician Jeremy Bentham, Henry Brougham, the persistent practical reformer, and the young Macaulay gave their support to the venture. They and many others must, like Browning, have been able to envision in the new institution some solid realization of their own vaguest hopes.

Behind most thinking on the new university was a conception, ultimately stemming from the ideas of Francis Bacon, and still traceable today in the theory of the multiversity, of the university as a compendium of all knowledge possessed by the society. Where Oxford and Cambridge provided instruction almost exclusively in a few subjects deemed essential to the development of a gentleman's mind, the founders of The London University, seeing potential use to society in all knowledge, sought as wide a curriculum as was practically feasible. On the German or Scottish model, and both served as examples for the new university, authorities would offer a smorgasbord of lectures on their various specialties, what Coleridge called, when he saw it in practice, a lecture-bazaar.[3] Stress was put, as in the teaching of Bentham in his *Chrestomathia* (1815), on "useful learning," on knowledge as the means to social improvement and regeneration. Professional, medical, and legal subjects as well as training in physical sciences were offered along with arts subjects.

It is not hard to see how such plans would excite the young enthusiast for Shelley, especially when they were still unfixed and floating before the university, being erected in the north of London in 1827 and 1828, had yet taken settled form. Through Sarah or Eliza Flower, Browning may have first learned of the venture from W. J. Fox, who had acted as a leader of the dissenter supporters of the university.[4] However he became interested,

Hon.ᵈ Sir

As a parent anxious for the welfare of
an only Son and desiring to avail myself of
the favourable opportunity that now offers of
placing him in the London University, I find
myself at a loss to know in what manner I should
best proceed, & therefore trespass upon you in hopes you will put
me in a way most likely to attain the object I
have in view. —

I have an only Son — now in his Sixteenth
Year, — & have brought him up in strict conformity
with every requisite mentioned in page 23 of the
Prospectus; and can add, moreover (with the
most grateful feelings of a Parent) this Test of
his Moral character — that I never knew him
from his earliest infancy, guilty of the
slightest deviation from Truth. —

His abilities will undergo a scrutiny

Letter of Robert Browning Sr. to Thomas Coatts [Coates] Esqre, April 22, 1828.
Application to enroll his son at The London University.

before judges, better qualified than I am; but I can answer for his unwearied application, for the last 6 years, to the Greek, Latin & French languages; — And he so earnestly desires I would interest myself in procuring his admittance, that I should feel myself wanting as a Parent, were I to neglect any step to procure what he deems so essential to his future happiness.—

Under these circumstances, I should be greatly indebted to you, Sir, if you could inform me, how I may become a shareholder, & what steps will be requisite for the attainment of my object; especially, whether it would be proper to make a personal application to Mr Horner? and the communication will greatly oblige,

Your obedient Humble Servt

Robt Browning Junr

Hanover Cottage
Southampton Street Camberwell. April 22d. 1828

Browning's decision to attend the university, indicative of his unsettled mood, seems to have been both sudden and enthusiastic. On April 22, 1828, only five months before the first classes were to begin, Browning's father wrote to the Secretary, Mr. Coates, enrolling his son and, in the process, making it perfectly clear that his son was nervously at his side hurrying him along.[5] After noting that Browning, "only Son" that he was, should qualify both by "his unwearied application, for the last 6 years, to the Greek, Latin & French languages," and by his "Moral character"—"I never knew him from his earliest infancy, guilty of the slightest deviation from Truth"—he explained that he was writing because his son "so earnestly desires I would interest myself in procuring his admittance, that I should feel myself wanting, as a Parent, were I to neglect any step to procure what he deems so essential to his future happiness." The tone, indicating an affectionate parent's dutiful submission to his son's wishes—a rarer event in that time than in our own—makes it clear that this educational decision was essentially Browning's own. Naturally the expenses, the one-hundred pound share to be credited toward tuition of about twenty-one pounds a year, were borne by the kindly passive party, in total a burden equal to about one-third of one year's income. The other party, active and enthusiastic, was registered on June 30 as number sixteen in his class, "Robert Browning: age 16: Hanover Cottage, Southampton Street, Camberwell," and began lectures with the first class at the university in late October.[6]

Sixteen was not young for attending the university; admission was open even to students two years younger. Yet sixteen *is* young, and it is natural for a boy Browning's age to have overly high hopes for his first flight on his own. The reaction, when reality turns out not to be what was hoped for, can be both traumatic and very educational. Browning's enthusiasm for The London University did not, indeed, survive the reality. The entire experience, however, brought him to decisions that would partly shape the course of his future life.

In the schematic mental history that he outlined in *Pauline,* disillusionment follows almost immediately upon the most exalted hopes and high enthusiasm for the future. He had expected a "fair girl" but had found in reality not the creature of his dreams but "a withered hag." Browning associates this disillusioning transformation directly with his entry at London, with his first lonely reaction to urban life. This initial disappointment was real enough. In order to attend early classes Browning had taken lodgings near the Bloomsbury site of the university, presumably at a student rooming house, in or near Bedford Square.[7] It is not hard to imagine the effect of drab loneliness, lodgings, and the colorless Bloomsbury section of London on the sixteen-year-old. The university building itself, reputedly admired by Browning's father as "a chaste and truly classic specimen of Grecian architecture,"[8] may have given Browning an early intimation of the dehumanization that ideals can undergo in becoming realities. To the novelist William De Morgan, a son of a professor and a student at London after the building was complete and the institution fully established, London still seemed to offer no visible humanizing symbol of university life, "nothing in the places of study, in their antecedents and surroundings, to catch and hold the imagination . . . the banquet of learning before me ungarnished and colourless."[9] Browning, pent, like Coleridge at Christ's Hospital, in "the great city," began to dream of "woods and fields" (*Pauline*) and, no doubt, of the lost society and affection of home life. Greek and Latin classes had been changed from 8:30 to 9:30 for the convenience of students coming from homes "in the villages around London."[10] Browning decided after a week in lodgings to save money, improve his board and meals, and commute from home. The decision was not, as it has been portrayed, one to retreat or pull out from the university or from the life of his fellow students. London had no collegiate life and was designed as a commuter school to keep costs down. Outside of classes, there were few, if any, opportunities for student social life with the exception of a formal debating society. Most of his fellow students were, like him, day students from nearby suburbs.[11] Browning felt intuitively the disparity between high hopes and a reality different only in being drabber, more confining, and less comfortable than the one he had known. However, it was only in the course of the year that he became altogether disillusioned about his hopes for education at London.

If he was unhappy with the student life and surroundings, he could still find, like the majority of students everywhere who must pursue knowledge outside the endowed cloisters of the privileged few, a new world of the mind through university subjects. The speaker of *Pauline* remembers not just early loneliness but also the solitary joy of reading and meditation: "yet I was full of joy—who lived / With Plato—and who had the key to life." For a variety of reasons, however, The London University did not engage itself intellectually with the self-motivated student of Plato. After all the trumpetings of educational revolution, the university seemed almost ironically unable to accommodate a student who took its claims seriously. This was less, or not at all true in medicine or the physical sciences where London took an immediate, national lead in many disciplines. The trouble in other fields, especially in the humanities or social sciences, was that the organizers were not yet able to produce what they proclaimed. The young Macaulay had hailed the new university as an alternative to the standard core curriculum of Latin, Greek, and mathematics. Instead, subjects like history, English, or philosophy would, without the long years of language work and philology, offer a modern training for the mind and develop sound ideas.[12] In practice, however, the university took only very limited steps toward the modern liberal arts curriculum.

There was even a touch of irony in Macaulay's high hopes for the university because history and an historical approach to other disciplines was above all the key that was lacking to open these disciplines. Neither of the two historians who were—whatever their limitations as scientific researchers—to play the greatest part in awakening Browning's generation to the importance of historical process, Macaulay himself and Thomas Carlyle, appeared in the chair of history, a chair still unfilled when Browning arrived. Carlyle, still virtually unknown, had thought of applying for a professorship but had been discouraged. The chair of philosophy was also vacant in the opening year. Where the positions were not actually unfilled they often seem, by our present standards, only half filled. English was offered as a course subject: a real innovation. Yet in practice the emphasis was placed not so much on study of literature and the historical and intellectual context of literature but on memorizing etymological, grammatical, and philological information. If Browning went to the first lecture of the main course, he would have heard the young professor, the Rev. Thomas Dale, offer his discipline as an expedient to ambitious young men for "preparing their weapons and polishing their armour" for the "arena of public or professional life."[13] And the lover of Shelley might have been less than sympathetic to the Anglican divine's righteous and rhetorical rage against writers who used their genius for "the excitement of unholy passions, the palliation of guilty indulgences, the ridicule of virtue, or the disparagement of religion."[14] Surely the educator might begin by drawing meaningful distinctions between such different qualities! Dale also offered a series of lectures, beginning later in the year and evidently intended as an extra to the regular curriculum, on English literature. Even these began with three hours of history of the language, and the coverage, by different genres, was probably both superficial and abstract.[15]

Lacking any very positive direction for innovation in the humanities and history commensurate with its lead in the sciences, London fell back on the rather conventional standards of the day for liberal arts. The university statement followed Cambridge University in defining "the essential parts of a liberal education" as classics and mathematics; other studies, such as modern languages, were "ornamental accomplishments."[16] Browning, enrolled for a regular program of study in Greek and Latin, was not only receiving what he might have received at Cambridge or Oxford, he was also receiving it from Cambridge men, and not merely from Cambridge men but from Trinity College men. In the same year Alfred Tennyson entered Trinity itself and, along with his friends, was soon convinced that the established program of liberal education was a mere husk of learning, the special province of "hard-nosed angular little gentlemen" who liked the discipline and competition for its own sake. At Cambridge the famous Apostles club was formed expressly to get away from the formal liberal arts to a fuller liberal cultivation of the mind: "It existed to remedy a fault of our education. Its business was to make men study and think on all matters except mathematics and classics professionally considered . . . To my education given in that society I feel that I owe every power I possess . . . from the Apostles I, at least, learned to think as a *free man*."[17]

While his contemporaries were turning away from classical philology at Cambridge, Browning, a student looking for something new at a self-proclaimed innovative university, found himself receiving, in effect, a course in extension from Trinity. Both of his two professors in the classics were young Trinity men who had had the interest and physical stamina to spend some years at Jefferson's new University of Virginia. Both were then called back to join England's own new venture. Nonetheless, T. H. Key was probably not far from the Trinity angular, philological norm and rather likely to dispirit the already disgruntled student of Ready's. A mathematician, later author of a *Latin Grammar* (1846), contributor to the Philological Society, and Headmaster of a university prep school, he left a later student, Walter Bagehot, moaning, "My head is now full enough of queer etymologies, and examples of all manner of changes of all manner of letters . . . There is no connected system as yet to help the memory."[18] Faced with a blitz of derivations and disconnected word-lore, Browning must quickly have wondered what advantage his long trip each day into London was over reading Latin literature at home. The class met for almost ten hours a week. Browning, probably qualified for the Livy and Cicero of the upper class, must have done a good deal of reading in Latin and strengthened his already adequate command of the language. Nor was Key, whatever his limitations as a great light, known as a bad thinker. It seems unlikely, however, that Browning gained very much from the lessons that he wouldn't have had in some other way. The single exception is very likely the word enclitic, used for a semi-dependent grammatical form, which Key was self-consciously proud of introducing into school grammar.[19] His pupil uses the word too in "A Grammarian's Funeral" (1855) and ascribes the grammatical discovery to his heroic grammarian. The definition is revealing: "Dead from the waist down."

His Greek classes under Jefferson's "boy professor," George Long, were probably somewhat different.[20] Twenty-eight, but a veteran of teaching Edgar Allan Poe and other Americans, Long was already writing on Greek authors and editing texts; later he became an authority on Latin law, editor of the *Penny Cyclopaedia,* and translator of Marcus Aurelius and Epictetus. He was a scholar and thinker of real ability. With him Browning had also ten hours of classes a week, probably the higher class on Aeschylus and Herodotus or the middle class on Aeschylus and Xenophon.[21] Long offered two things that would have been of value to Browning. One was close and well-informed study of Aeschylus, a writer, if we can believe *Pauline,* already close to his heart from early reading. In the 1870s Browning took upon himself the role of defender of the later Euripides against the ancient gibes of Aristophanes and the lesser barbs of modern scholars. But it was Sophocles and especially Aeschylus that he mentioned in *Pauline,* and he would have been glad to study the *Prometheus Bound* further. When Browning discussed the play seventeen years later in the letters with Elizabeth he spoke of it with affection among "books I loved once."[22] In the same correspondence, his knowledge and command of the scholarship on Aeschylus—the various editions, plays known only from fragments, Aeschylus' life and outlook on life, even the *Scholia* (a copy of which he sent to Elizabeth)—is thorough and impressive.[23] The only thing he didn't tell Elizabeth, who must have been duly impressed by his scholarship, was that he had learned it from a professional scholar well versed in English and German historical research.[24] His work with Long gave him, if not the equipment of the professional scholar, at least the background of a well-informed inspired amateur and the tools to study Greek literature on his own. Although he would turn away increasingly from Greek attitudes and classical ideas of form in his mature years, it would not be from lack of understanding of the originals.

The other benefit Browning derived from contact with Long was some approach to history through the context Long provided for literary study. Here Long was in the vanguard of Victorian classical study. His concern with understanding classical civilization as a living culture, not merely a dead grammar, would eventually earn him Matthew Arnold's highest tribute: comparision with Dr. Arnold himself.[25] At Long's introductory lecture, the stress on cultural and historical context was a prominent feature. Facing squarely the utilitarian educational standard implicit in the new university, he asked how studying Greek could be called "useful knowledge." In large part, he answered, Greek is useful because it can give us an understanding of the manners of other times, of the origins of political institutions, and generally a sense of man's existence in an historical process.[26] To make sure that this was the effect of his Greek course he provided readings in Herodotus and, as he explained in the opening discourse, used his lectures to add historical and cultural background. In theory, at least, it was a course on Greek literature and civilization: a course that would make the student conscious of the interrelation of society, individual men, and art in history.

How much Browning received from this emphasis is uncertain. When he speaks with casual assurance in a letter to Elizabeth of Prometheus' bitter complaints over a punishment he had yet deliberately chosen, it is hard not to believe that Browning had learned not just Greek vocabulary and syntax but also a sense of a way of life. "That was the old Greek way—they never let an antagonistic passion neutralise the other which was to influence the man to his praise or blame. A Greek hero fears exceedingly and battles it out—cries out when he is wounded and fights on, does not say his love or hate makes him see no danger or feel no pain—Aeschylus from first word to last . . . insists on the unmitigated reality of the punishment."[27] Perhaps, and this is after all the best that can be said of any teacher, Long opened some new vistas and prepared the way for Browning to go further on his own in later years.

Whatever his ultimate influence, Long's immediate impact was not entirely positive. In practice, his pedagogy came far closer to the old daily parsing than he wished to suggest in his first lecture in a school stressing innovation and payment by the number of students that professors attracted. Although he was an innovator in turning away from antiquated grammar school practices such as teaching Greek through Latin, he continued to adhere to the traditional view of the classics as, above all, "an intellectual exercise," a "mental discipline," the verbal equivalent to mathematics. Not long into the year he honestly issued a "Supplement" to his original statement, explaining that historical study would have in practice to be put off until the basics of language were mastered. After this experience, in his later writing on pedagogy, he expressed only a very qualified approval of an historical approach.[28] His historical light, in any event, was aimed primarily down the relatively narrow roads of legal and institutional history. Over the year, Long may have fitted increasingly into Browning's general idea of a fair maid turning into something less attractive on closer knowledge. As a man and teacher Long was sarcastic and distant. One student remembered especially his "caustic irony, accurate and almost ostentatiously dry learning and profoundly stoical temper."[29] Whatever intellectual awareness he nurtured, he was not likely to inspire increased enthusiasm in the young poet.

At a deeper level Browning may have sensed that, along with the good he could receive from a man of Long's abilities, there were also dangers to which he was especially susceptible. Throughout his life, it was in the field of study that he pursued under Long—Greek drama especially—that Browning made the greatest claim to full scholarly knowledge. And it was on those subjects, where he considered himself a learned as well as inspired amateur, that he came closest to pedantry and a pedant's quarrelsomeness. Replete with something more than a little bit of knowledge, he threw himself in later years into a number of unseemly controversies in which the poet yielded to the poet-pedant. He came forward as the defender of Euripides, the least popular of the three great tragedians, and devoted two long poems (*Balaustion's Adventure* and *Aristophanes' Apology*) to the venture. He raised a stir of scholarly dust over his crotchet, direct transcription of Greek names into English rather than the traditional latinizations (Herakles for Hercules). Like others before him, he nearly brought the whole classical, scholarly world down on him by arguing for the supremacy of the moderns over the classical greats. His translation of the *Agamemnon* (1877) is perhaps the high point of his serious scholarship and the nadir of his poetic career. It is so careful and literal a translation as to be almost unreadable. It is the kind of work good students do; and it has found and been recommended for only one use, as a trot for other students. It has been explained as a backhanded hit at the classicists of his day, but if so, it only shows how dangerous it was for his poetry when he took them too seriously. It is probably more simply explained as the triumph of his literal, scholarly instincts over those of the poet. Of course, scholarship and learning need not turn into pedantry and willingness to place detail over spirit; but they have often tended to these extremes, and Browning had few examples of humane scholarship placed before him in his formal education. The future world authority on Roman law threatened to bring out the narrower side of Browning's interest in knowledge just because he was a man, unlike Ready or Key, of undoubted power and progressive thought. In ultimately *not* following Long, Browning not only gave the world a poet but also spared her a heavy-handed if thorough and committed scholar.

What benefit the poet derived from the closer study of Greek drama and Greek life can be seen in the splendidly evocative and yet controlled fragment, "Artemis Prologuizes" (1842). When he was not bound to literal translation, the freer form of imitation—here of the *Hippolytus* of Euripides—brought out all Browning's intuitive understanding of the spirit of the ancient drama. Noting the fact that Browning composed the poem while in bed with a fever, Douglas Bush suggests that "it needed illness to make Browning a classicist." It took, perhaps, a forced stay away from notes and scholarship to focus his attention on the essentials of the literature itself. In any event, it was not in scholarship, but in the creative application of scholarship to poetry that Browning would succeed as a student.

In electing Latin and Greek, Browning was following explicitly the program of liberal education set out by the university. He also enrolled for a subject officially "considered more in the light of ornamental accomplishment," beginning German. The choice belies the description. Inasmuch as he was already proficient in three languages, the decision to start another language, and a hard one associated with the most recent movements in thought and scholarship at that, was an objective indication of the intellectual ambitions that he speaks of in *Pauline*. Here, at least, London did offer something new in the humanities. Interest in Germany and in the new intellectual movements afoot there was still relatively new, although thinkers like Coleridge, De Quincey, and Carlyle had called attention to the romantic philosophical movement, and occasional professors, like Long, had incorporated German scholarship into their work. The German university was one of the primary models for The London University and, as the coming language of scholarship, German was necessarily given a place in the curriculum.

When in *Paracelsus* (1835) Browning set out to portray a restless mind on a quest for universal knowledge, he chose two German universities, Würzburg and Swiss German Basel, as setting and context. For him, as for Carlyle in *Sartor Resartus,* the German university was associated with an almost overreaching thirst for a universal science and a knowledge of all things. The same association and the same quest led Browning to the German language, and his immediate impression must have been that his hopes would be fully realized. His professor, Ludwig von Mühlenfels, was beyond question authentic, a German scholar from Heidelberg recently escaped from a Prussian political prison where ("an old story") his liberal activism had landed him. He did no lasting writing or scholarship, publishing only texts and lectures for English students and writing on political questions. However, there was no question about his universal curiosity and his capacity for theoretical thought. Friend of Felix Mendelssohn, in touch with the most recent German thought and scholarship, including the new critical approach to mythology and religion, *he* was no doubt the right experience even if his course was not. On October 30, 1828, Browning would have heard him, in his opening lecture, speak in praise of the German language and culture in an accent he felt obliged to apologize for, and in a rhapsodic vein strange, if somewhat wonderful, to English ears. His observations, too, commonplaces of German romanticism, were still rather unusual ones in England. He spoke of the relation between language and national character, of the association of different dialects with different folk characteristics, and of the importance of popular speech in general as the truest expression of national character, "morals and customs" and "the inexhaustible humour of the people."[30] His subject would have been of interest to the young poet naturally alert to other countries and peoples from his family's connections abroad. In fact, Browning would later make the complexities of national character and the greater complexity of finding appropriate language for national characters the subject of some of his finest short poems. The professor's corollary idea, that nations develop like humans from undifferentiated childhood to modern, complex, and differentiated characters —an idea of organic evolution in history long in the air in Germany but still new in England—would have been of equal interest. When von Mühlenfels went on, with a kind of visionary enthusiasm, to speak of German literature —"The immeasurable empire of ideas and perceptions . . . The boundless world of imagination and reflection is the scene of its brightest triumphs"[31] —the enthusiast for Shelley and Plato could hardly have withheld his approval. Still less could he dissent from the German patriot's warm and lofty, if fittingly vague peroration on the glories and responsibilities of liberty.

Another printed lecture, dated 1829, which may or may not have been the same as any Browning might have heard in the previous year, is intriguing because it outlines two of the ideas that would be central to Browning's own thinking. Attempting to survey the cultural development of man from earliest times to the present, von Mühlenfels gives a progressive and modernist view of history very similar to that which Browning would express in his works from *Paracelsus* on. In his view, history is a slow working toward the ultimate spiritual perfection of man, a process that is being fulfilled simultaneously by the spiritual endeavors of individuals and by the organic growth of the race.[32] This is, of course, the overall vision of human progress that Browning would dramatize in his study of the aspirations of Paracelsus, a master spirit who aimed to lead the way in the more sluggish development of the race as a whole. In his schematic view of history, von Mühlenfels likewise seems to foreshadow Browning's own views as they are expressed in the major monologues on classical limitations and Christian aspirations: "Karshish," "Cleon," and "A Death in the Desert." Man has progressed, in the German professor's view, from the passionate childhood of early biblical times, to the formalistic, action-centered, and self-suffi-cient boyhood of the race in the classical period, then finally to the more complex aspirations of the Christian age, especially in its further develop-ment after the Protestant Reformation. Like the mature Browning, he ad-mires the virtues of the classics but sees them as only a step toward the higher spiritual aims of the moderns.

Even more interesting is his transformation of this historical outline into aesthetic categories, a translation Browning repeatedly makes in his historical monologues and presents directly in the "Essay on Shelley." Von Mühlenfels' terms are also those the mature Browning uses: objective and subjective. Classical art he defines as epic and objective, centering in direct portrayal of "the life of man as it appears in action" and finding immediate and complete expression in its form. Early religious poetry is the contrary, lyrical and subjective, aiming—much as Browning will have his lyrical singer David do—to express the inexpressible, spiritual states too exalted to find any objective form that can fully embody them. Finally, von Mühlen-fels posits a modern, dramatic poetry that is at once external and internal, objective and subjective. Better than Browning himself in his own attempt to use the vocabulary of objectivity and subjectivity in the "Essay on Shel-ley" (1852), von Mühlenfels is able to define modern art as a mixture of both qualities: an art, indeed, much like Browning's own mature work, in which objective form is given to the complex subjective reality of the indi-vidual personality and consciousness. "It is the individual character, the personality of man, which is sketched, both in the subjective and objective . . . the union of personality and universality."[33]

Whether Browning was in fact exposed to these leading ideas of von Mühlenfels' and, if so, whether they had a direct influence on him remains unclear. They were certainly not original or unique ideas but only more elaborate commonplaces of romantic critical thought, and could have come to him by any number of paths. Yet they would be central concerns of Browning's poetry, and some seeds of later growth may very well have been planted by this first exposure to the elaborate critical discourse of German romanticism. Certainly von Mühlenfels must have seemed, at least initially, to be about to open up something new, if not the wholly new world Brow-ning had hoped for.

If his experience at London taught Browning one thing, however, it was the difficult lesson all must learn: the tiring disparity between the feast that our imaginations can prepare for us in anticipation and the nourish-ment that we find before us when we really arrive at our imagined goal. Higher hopes made it an especially hard lesson for Browning who, in his plans to sit directly at the feast of German scholarship and imagination, was hardly prepared for the barbarities of learning German. Such, at any rate, is the best conjecture the few facts that survive allow. When Browning despaired of German grammar and etymologies—von Mühlenfels promised to put off the lectures on culture and literature until the language was mastered—is uncertain. There is no evidence that he left these classes before his others, though that is possible.[34] The later history of Browning's flirtation with the German language would suggest that he had made more than an acquaintance with it in his formal studies but not quite reached a reading or speaking knowledge. He knew the language well enough to use, rarely, German words in letters,[35] and to keep coming back for sporadic affairs with it the rest of his life. In 1834 he seemed ready to give up and admit he wouldn't know German.[36] Then in 1842 he was trying to blow life into the old flame. "Do you prosecute German-study?" he asked Domett, "I read pretty well now."[37] Less optimistically he reported the next year, "How do you get on with German? I read tolerably—and find the best help is Schlegel and Tieck's translation of Shakespeare";[38] even more modestly and realistically in 1878: last year "revived my acquaintance with German."[39] If none of these encounters really struck out fire, they showed, at least, that Browning was able to use his early experience with German to maintain some direct contact with German writers and thinking. His intellectual journeys and real travels on the continent would both tend to take him south not north. But he had enough feel for German culture and ways of thinking that he could return, in a number of fine poems after *Paracelsus,* to German settings and characters—not only in the spoofs of German spiritual pride in "Johannes Agricola," German military brassiness in "Nationality in Drinks," or the burgher temperament in "The Pied Piper of Hamelin," but also in the more sympathetic and subtle treatment of the higher reaches of Gothic character in "Master Hugues of Saxe-Gotha" or "Abt Vogler."

Whatever new sights into varieties of culture and human nature were ultimately opened through von Mühlenfels' German lessons, the image of a German professor that was left in Browning's mind was indicative of his reaction to the new German-model university in general. In *Paracelsus* the ordinary class of professors, the Tritheims who, unlike Paracelsus, are content to promulgate indifferently the good and bad of the present system of learning, are held up for scorn as "pedants" teaching "idle arts" to "plodders." "A Professorship / At Basil! [*sic*]" Paracelsus scoffs at his own title. In the half-comic, half-visionary *Christmas-Eve and Easter-Day* (1850), Browning takes his readers on a whirlwind trip to a lecture room in the modern German university world at Göttingen; but the portrait of the professor there, if more realistic and complex, is no less negative. Perhaps much like the liberal von Mühlenfels, the German professor is an exalted, high-minded intellectual, a "studious / Martyr to mild enthusiasm" with "a wan pale look, well nigh celestial,— / Those blue eyes had survived so much!"[40] At the same time, his quest for abstract purity is a life-consuming, physically and intellectually consumptive enterprise. He has trodden underfoot "all the fleshly and the bestial" and has lost in the process all vitality. "Sallow, virgin-minded," he is plagued by hoarseness, racked by fits of coughing and spitting. His discourse, an intellectual and metaphysical rationalization of Christ, is both rhetorically exalted and spiritually meaningless. His critical function, subjecting everything to the power of his mind, is like that of a scientist pumping air out of a bell jar: as he achieves a greater and greater purity he is approaching an absolute nothingness:

> the Critic leaves no air to poison;
> Pumps out by a ruthless ingenuity
> Atom by atom, and leaves you—vacuity.

As the year went on, Browning was coming more and more to see his education at London as just this kind of pumping process, not opening a better world but merely drawing away his vague enthusiasm for universal knowledge. The process was, indeed, twofold. On the one hand, both the teachers at London and the curriculum in the nonscientific fields were certainly ill suited to engage the concerns and interests of the young poet. Browning, on the other hand, was being put through an experimental test of the enormous educational goals he had so easily declared. While he was becoming disabused of his hopes in the university, he was also learning to criticize his own aspirations and to adjust them to more realistic aims.

2 A Practical University

Realism and realistic aims were, of course, faiths upon which the university was founded. Explicitly dedicated to Baconian and Benthamite ideals of useful knowledge, the university saw its function as both to further knowledge and to train the competent professional classes of the future. In the university, the utilitarian forerunners of modern theorists of a social meritocracy placed particular stress on what an official statement called "the useful intercourse of theory with active life."[41] Pronouncements by the university and by virtually all the lecturers encouraged students to think of their education realistically as an instrument to social success and advancement. Traditional subjects were justified, as in Long's opening lecture, on grounds of their utility for men planning legal or other public careers. More than many twentieth-century service or multiversities, London mixed together professional and liberal arts education. Law (part of the General Department) and medicine (in a separate department) were alternatives to the liberal arts education and together enrolled the majority of students. Medicine, especially, was the most cohesive and immediately successful of the programs, ensuring, indeed, the success of the university as a whole in its first years.[42] The professional slant of the university naturally encouraged a spirit of realistic competition for success as the first step in a professional career. But the spirit of getting on was also an intrinsic and firmly instituted part of the university educational system. Even the poet Campbell, the idealist among the founders, had defined the university in a hardheaded way as a place for "effectively and multifariously teaching, examining, exercising, and rewarding with honours in the liberal arts and sciences, the youth of our middling rich people."[43] Even more explicitly,

Bentham founded education upon the competitive, self-regarding virtues, euphemistically labeled, "the comparative proficiency principle" and the "place capturing principle."

In practice, the university encouraged competition by yearly prizes given at the end of the term. At the same time, students were discouraged from pursuits that did not advance their future careers, such as work on a student newspaper.[44] The one activity that was established among the liberal arts students would have been sanctioned by university theorists and university officials alike. This was a Literary and Philosophical Society that met for weekly debates in the mathematical lecture room. The debates—"eloquent weekly outpourings of these young aspirants for fame," one participant recalled—suggest something of the character of Browning's fellow students. Talented and ambitious young men—some, like the younger brothers of John Stuart Mill or T. B. Macaulay, from quite illustrious families, others, like the young John Forster, later lawyer, critic, and friend of Browning and Dickens, obscure men of talent from the provinces—sought at London the foundation of public and legal careers. If they were not all as anxious to excel in their academic work as university officials might have wished, they were generally highly motivated by a realistic desire to make friends and to win reputations for ability at the university. Some others, like the Reithmüller who brought a bottle of asafetida into a lecture room, were given to an even more realistic pursuit of the greatest immediate happiness and liberty —to "oysters, fog (smoking) and grog," or to "long, long rambles through the crowded streets of London."[45]

From both forms of student realism, the variety officially encouraged and the age-old form of student life that flourished in any case, Browning found himself separated by temperament and interests. If he was coming to realize that the regeneration of the world was not as philosophical a matter as it might seem from reading Shelley, he was not much attracted by the prospect, offered by the economists and utilitarian social thinkers of the day, of seeking the slow evolution of the Platonic good by the unrelenting pursuit of conventional success and his own self-interest. Even if learning could not immediately transform reality, it was still learning and knowledge —not the personal and practical uses to which they could be put—that he wished to obtain at the university. Nor was he likely to find in the less highly driven students much sympathy for Shelley or Shelley's ideas, however much he and they might agree about the pleasures of rambles through London. Altogether, Browning must have felt most strongly the differences between himself and the other students. In the seat of practical learning he was conspicuous, more conspicuous than Arnold's scholar gypsy would have been had he turned up at Oxford, for his romantic style and appearance: "a bright handsome youth," as a classmate recalled, "with long black hair falling over his shoulders."[46] His independence and self-motivation might win the respect of fellow students.[47] Yet he sensed a deep difference between himself and them. Other students—much as he has Paracelsus speak of them—seemed by his standards to be almost all motivated by false or insincere ends. "Each has his end to serve, and his best way / Of serving it." Outside of these there were only a very few, "A scantling—a poor dozen at the best," who were truly motivated, who "really come to learn for learning's sake; / Worthy to look for sympathy and service."[48]

As he looked back from a distance of six years it was easy thus to separate himself from other students as the saving remnant from the unelect. At the time, the presence of other students with strong, different motivations and competitive spirits probably posed, as it has for other poets who have found themselves in institutions devoted to the mind but not to producing poets or artists, a considerable challenge to Browning's security and sense of self.

In this light, it is difficult, as Betty Miller has pointed out, not to see a dim reflection of Browning's own career at London in the account of Paracelsus' erratic education at Würzburg. The experience there is not one of simply rejecting the false aims of other students. Rather, Paracelsus speaks of being drawn by the spirit of competition into striving for what others do: "plunging" into the competition, "Not pausing to make sure the prize in view / Would satiate my cravings when obtain'd— / But as they strove I strove." Worse, he realizes the superiority of his own aims only by finding out his unsuitability for attaining the goals sought by others. While "the meanest plodder" makes his deliberate way to the specific goal he seeks, Paracelsus, aspiring to more but not clear what that more should be, finds himself left behind, "a slow and strangling failure." Paracelsus' agonized and rather rationalized account suggests that Browning knew at first hand the painful process by which an individual learns to separate out his own goals from those set before him by his society and by his peers. Indeed, he may have actually felt the sting of failure when he sat down at the detailed and rather literal exams in his classics courses in March.[49] Certainly he took no prizes. The impression in *Paracelsus* is of a struggle to maintain and redefine a personal identity against the clearer identities and aims of others. He evidently went through a period when dissatisfaction with himself—"I loathed myself"—joined with confusion and indecision: "I was restless, nothing satisfied, / Distrustful, most perplex'd." Yet beneath his hurt pride and pridefulness he felt himself establishing his own identity and aims by contrast to those of the other students: "A mighty power was brooding, taking shape / Within me." Finally he came to understand the difference between his educational aims and the utilitarian ones of his fellows. If he wanted to succeed as the other students, he would only have to put the immediate uses of learning above the learning itself:

Know, not for knowing's sake
. . . . .
Know, for the gain it gets, the praise it brings,
The wonder it inspires, the love it breeds.

All this is put in the inflated, self-justifying speech of Paracelsus, and it suggests that Browning had difficulty talking about this experience dispassionately and objectively. In *Pippa Passes* (1841) another student, the art student Jules, studying in Italy, is portrayed with greater objectivity at the same moment of self-consciousness. His awakening is a far more bitter one. Only when he realizes that he has been gulled and made a fool of by the other students, does he really begin to formulate clearly his own aims and to understand his differences from the others. Paracelsus' superficial, rather defensive scorn for the other students is replaced by an acknowledgment, probably closer to Browning's own experience, of the sway that their values have had over him. Their voices have broken in upon his inner confidence, destroying his faith in his original aims: "Oh," he exclaims, "to hear / God's voice plain as I heard it first, before / They broke in with that laughter! I heard them / Henceforth, not God!"[50] Unpleasant as it is, the contact with others is, however, a necessary step in Jules's development as an artist. Shunning their ways and values, he sets out to find a path as an artist more suited to his own personality and ability. The experience is a necessary form of destruction, drawing a clearer sense of identity out of the conflict of different personalities and values. Symbolically, Jules breaks up his old works at the end to begin his new career afresh.

It would be misleading to elaborate too closely the possible similarities between Browning at London and his fictional students. Both Paracelsus and Jules draw out and project a relationship to other students that would have been only implicit in Browning's own reactions to his fellow students and that was, in any case, only one aspect of his response to London. However, his total experience, both with the education offered and with the orientation of the university and his fellow students, led him to much the same place as his characters. Like them, he decided finally to leave university and fellow students alike and strike out on his own. On May 4, 1829, after close to an entire academic year, Browning's father wrote to the Warden Leonard Horner: "I am very sorry to communicate my son's determination to withdraw from the London University, (an event as painful as it was unexpected)."[51] Both the late date and the suddenness of the decision indicate that Browning, far from merely slipping away from the university without really trying it, had come to a decisive resolution after a considerable trial.[52]

3 Some Practical Decisions

Whoever made the ultimate decision for Browning's earlier withdrawal from Ready's school, there is no doubt that this decision was one made entirely by Browning himself. After seeking out London on his own, he continued to direct the course of his education by withdrawing when he found the work and atmosphere unattractive and unprofitable. It was essentially an educational decision, but in determining the nature of his education he was taking an important, hardly reversible, step in defining his own identity and his relation to his society. This is true, of course, of all people. However, because Browning was finding that he had to decide his own way in every aspect of his education rather than merely fit into an accepted form offered ready-made by his society, his education reflects with especial clarity his growth as an individual.

His decision to withdraw from the university even had the effect of bringing to a head some specific practical questions that had sooner or later to be faced. First of all, Browning could hardly hope to ignore the immediate financial implications of his withdrawal. If the privilege of exercising the freedom to direct his own education was his, the practical burden of this freedom was laid, as it often is in the independent decisions of a young student, squarely upon his father. Since the fees were deducted from the original one-hundred pound subscription, the father of "an only son" was left with three years of prepaid tuition on his hands. Presumably the tuition could have been transferred to another student but there is no evidence that this was done.[53] It was a large sum for the family to lose. Moreover, though they may have only vaguely guessed the ultimate implications of their son's decision, the elder Brownings were in fact taking on the full support of a student, age seventeen, who would remain essentially still a student in their house for the next seventeen years. Browning was still young and he was already living at home at the time he gave up London. It was a natural arrangement in an affectionate family and at a time when middle-class boys often remained in their homes until they were sufficiently prosperous to set up their own households. However, as time went on and there seemed no prospect of their studious son ever supporting himself, both Browning and his parents must have sensed the real extent of the commitment. Browning's sudden entry and equally sudden withdrawal from the university are indicative of the confused aims and adolescent uncertainty of that period of his life. But he was never deliberately careless of or indifferent to his family. He never considered it necessary to the development of himself and his art to alienate friends or family or to exploit them to attain his own goals. As time went on, he would become increasingly more conscious of the extent of his debt to his family and of the impossibility of ever repaying it. The effect would be to make him also increasingly aware of the seriousness of the task of self-education that he had taken on in leaving London.

The situation was, for all the goodwill in his family, bound to be a difficult one. It left him open in his own mind, and still leaves him open, to the moralist's charge of using his parents and of failing to make his own way in life. Worst of all, it probably did exert a subtle break upon the development of his independence as a thinker and as a poet. Even a grown child cannot live merely as a gentleman boarder in his own family, and Browning's gratefulness to his parents naturally led him to continue the affectionate and close relationships of earlier years. It is perhaps as silly for us to be shocked by the idea of a grown man continuing the habit of kissing his mother good night—which Browning indeed did until his marriage—as it was for Victorians to applaud such a sign of filial affection.[54] But the mere closeness of family affections, even, as in Browning's case, where a reasonable person will find little evidence of overt incestuous desires or oedipal fixation, will tend to discourage a person from looking outside the family for friendship. And it may make it more difficult, as it probably did for Browning, for a young adult to develop fully an independent style of life.

The situation *was* difficult, and Browning, as well as his parents, would pay a price for his decision to take up for an indefinite time the life of a student at home. Yet it is difficult to imagine any other alternative open to him. In reality, his decision to leave The London University was the first substantial practical step toward his ultimate choice of a full-time career (if it can be called a career) as a poet. In leaving London he was putting behind him the variety of careers most naturally open and suitable in his society to a person of his abilities and background. London was just the place to give a son of the London middle class an opportunity to rise into the highest positions open to mere talent in Victorian England.

Browning's family had hopes, evidently, that he would follow the most obvious of these paths, The London University's highroad into the legal profession.[55] Although, as we have seen, the exotic and rather unrealistic idea of a career in the most gentlemanly of nineteenth-century professions, diplomacy, could tempt Browning now and then throughout his early years, the very real and practical prospect of a legal career was a bitter notion to him, bitter because it was indeed such a real possibility and such a reasonable choice. Even in the 1840s a well-wisher such as the aged lawyer and essayist Basil Montagu could still suggest that Browning was just the type of young man who needed a good profession like the law, and he even offered to train him gratis.[56] Browning was grateful, *and annoyed,* and confided to Elizabeth that he would rather spend his days grooming horses—"rather do it all day long than succeed Mr. Fitzroy Kelly in the Solicitor-Generalship."[57] Kelly was indeed a case in point, and a sore one at that, because he had risen through the Bank of England along a path that would have been easily open to Browning himself had he been a lawyer.[58] At other times he could admit the attractions of the genteel life of the London lawyer, "the sweets which time and prescription, and sociality, and classicality of a sort, and *lucri odor,* help to wring out of London Law-Life!"[59] Despite close friendships with lawyers, his opinion of a legal career remained acid, even rather snobbishly so. "I have always had a supreme contempt for the profession, and the lawyers in my poems get the benefit thereof," he wrote a year before his death, probably thinking of his satirical treatment of the two lawyers in *The Ring and the Book.*[60]

In 1829 what he had seen of the law was primarily his fellow students at London and the atmosphere of clever young men ambitious to trade their intelligence and knowledge for status and power. However valuable a contribution many of his classmates might make to Victorian society and government, from Browning's point of view he was no doubt right in decisively rejecting the law for himself. For anyone interested in literature or the disinterested use of the mind, the law in nineteenth-century England was a temptingly attractive halfway house. Lawyers such as the part-time play-wright T. N. Talfourd, the essayist Montagu, the poet B. W. Procter, or the critic John Forster, to name only a few not unknown friends of Browning in the late 1830s and 1840s, constituted virtually the literary intelligentsia in early Victorian England. As such their contribution was not in itself nega-tive or negligible. They provided much of the fuel to keep a lively and grow-ing industry of literary periodicals going; they provided reviews of books and plays above the level of mere hack writing; they maintained a contact between literature and the practical world. They even included men of real talent like Forster, Procter, or A. W. Kinglake, the author of *Eothen,* a brilliant work of travel literature, who, Browning suggested, seemed embar-rassed as a lawyer by his unexpected success as a writer.[61] Important writers such as Thackeray or Macaulay might begin as lawyers and turn more di-rectly to letters. But though the cultivated lawyers and other professionals did much to maintain the general intellectual life of Victorian England, they established too often merely a high level of mediocrity. In a review of Wordsworth, written before she knew Browning, Elizabeth Barrett rather acutely noted why: " 'Art' it was said long ago, 'requires the whole man' and 'Nobody,' it was said later, 'can be a poet who is anything else'; but the present idea of Art requires the segment of a man, and everybody who is anything at all is a poet in a parenthesis.'' She added that the refusal of the "Tennysons and Brownings" to be anything but poets was both necessary and promising.[62] Essentially the problem was the same one Browning had felt intuitively at The London University. When the uses of knowledge were elevated over knowledge or literature themselves, writing and the arts in general became only serious amusements, exercises of the mind, the attain-ments of an intelligent gentleman—all these, but not serious ends in them-selves, not endeavors into which to throw one's very best efforts. The tal-ented boy who pursued his Greek and Latin diligently in order to prepare himself for the linguistic and oratorical contests of his future career might become an accomplished student of the classics; he might in later life be-come a gracious reviewer and Sunday scholar or even a regular contributor to polite annuals of poetry; he might be indeed a cultivated and accom-plished person: but he was not likely to develop any genius he might have for the highest works of literature.

In choosing the disinterested education of a thinker or poet rather than the cultivation of a practical man in a practical age, Browning was thus es-sentially already beginning to live the life of the poet with its full-time com-mitment to study and work. Whether financial support for such a career comes (as it did in Browning's case) from the family or from patrons or impersonal government and private foundations, it is never given, except by blind fortune and good luck, to a would-be artist without some test of his seriousness, without some hurdle that must be cleared. Browning's parents probably had little objection to his studying at home, but they were reluctant to accept the implication that he was preparing for no profession. Although he says little about any opposition from his parents to his plans, the terms in which he does speak of his choice of a way of life suggest that the placid family life was more than once disturbed by debate over his future. Acknowledging to Elizabeth that he had enjoyed what was most important to him, "this careless 'sweet habitude of living'—this absolute independence of mine, which, if I had it not, my heart would starve and die for," he admitted that he had had to fight "so many good battles to preserve" this freedom.[63]

It is hard to imagine that the battles of will between an independent-minded son and indulgent, loving parents were earthshaking or long inconclusive. But the issue was important. Browning's father, if no lawyer, was a banker who carried leisure-time art, literature, and self-cultivation to their perfection as a way of life. In refusing to follow suit, Browning was making a decisive break with his family, even while he was moving in a direction that their entire way of life implicitly encouraged. Most of all, he was, in a quiet way, fighting a round of the artist's good fight with society. His father's youthful revolt had ended strangely in an uneasy truce with conventional middle-class ideas. Like Wemmick, the modest clerk in Dickens' *Great Expectations* who returns home each night to his miniature suburban castle in Walworth to indulge all the fantasy and imagination he had suppressed during the day, he made a life of outward conformity and the fullest, private imaginative liberty. Like many sons of onetime rebels, Browning was intuitively breaking his father's uneasy truce and returning to carry the unresolved issue with society to a fuller conclusion.

In truth, what he faced in his family's objections to his decision was less their values than the values of work and self-reliance of middle-class English society. In the succeeding years he would have to assert and reassert his decision to go his own way, even at the price of scandal for going his own way at his family's expense. His direction would have to be asserted more against the numerous Basil Montagus of his world, who wished him well but wished him occupied at some practical employment eight or ten hours a day, than against his own family. "At a word," he offered to Elizabeth in talking about their future plans, "I will do all that ought to be done, —that every one used to say could be done, and let 'all my powers find sweet employ' as Dr. Watts sings, in getting whatever is to be got."[64] "Everyone," bolstered with the authority of pious religion, was a hard, if intangible, force to stand up against. And they were always tangibly present among relations like the Masons who looked on the progress of their spoiled prodigy cousin with an unpleasant mixture of grudging admiration and puritanical envy. Everyone needed to be reminded, always does need to be reminded (*we* even need to be reminded when with Betty Miller we begin to envy and condemn his freedom) that, as Elizabeth replied, for a person of real artistic abilities "an exchange of higher work for lower work . . & of the special work" he is "called to, for that which is work for anybody," is not only a betrayal of his talents but a loss to everyone, to society itself.[65] The burden of the proof that he did have a special calling fell—and must fall—on the artist. For Browning, the consciousness that everybody was watching him skeptically to see if he really was the genius his way of life seemed to assert was to be a goad toward serious endeavor as an artist and at times toward a destructive drive that prevented his natural growth and forced him into premature and overly ambitious efforts.

His decision as to what kind of education to give himself thus made Browning confront seriously, for the first time, the intertwined question of what kind of career he would pursue. In this, as in the decision to remain living at home as a student, the full impact of his decision was not felt at once. Rather it would grow upon Browning over the years until an early and none too clear decision would come, through the repeated reaffirmations of more mature experience, to have the finality of a personal fate. The process of Browning's education had at least brought him by 1829, three years before he actually began writing, to take the first decisive steps in the making of his life's work.

Letter of Robert Browning Sr. to Leonard Horner Esqr., May 4, 1829. *Announcing his son's decision to withdraw from The London University.*

XII
Rededication:
Toward Humanity
and the Human Past

In the spring of 1829 his immediate occupation was not, however, the work of a poet. Whether he realized it consciously or not, his business was to be the making of a poet. And this was as much, or more, a matter of developing his mind and views as it was the process of attaining a sense of identity as a poet. At the same time that he was trying to come to personal terms with the view of the poet's role that he had found in Shelley, he was undergoing an even more important development in his views of man and society, moving toward a new vision of knowledge that would set the direction of his education and mature work.

He had first to take stock of where his sudden and dislocating period at London had brought him and decide where he should go from there. He had chosen The London University as the mecca to his hopes for knowledge that would be a regenerating wind to sweep away the evils and weaknesses of present life and society and bring on a sudden golden age. Where had his experience brought these hopes? He had found not the realization of his ideals but the center of what was already a strong movement and would be the strongest force for change in the nineteenth century: the movement for practical and scientific application of knowledge to the general improvement of mankind. From the spirit of that enterprise, superficially so like his own convictions, he recoiled with an intuitive sense that it was not for him. With an equally strong intuition, he must have realized that the university's failure to offer anything in the humanities that could inspire him, as the professional and scientific offerings inspired the more practically oriented students, indicated a weak side to the entire enterprise of the Utilitarians and practical men. Although they might begin with the same goal of a regenerated humanity, their rush to bring practical, easily apprehensible aims to speedy fruition led them to a new distortion of humanity, an imbalance that would feast man's practical side but famish the more complex levels of his humanity. This perception of the dangers of too direct and practical an onslaught on human perfection was one that linked Browning, despite himself, with the more conservative (in 1829) romantic writers, Wordsworth, Coleridge, and Southey, who all had had deep reservations about the new enterprise and the new education. But the perception was more than the political attitude of one persuasion. Even the radical Shelley had warned in the "Defence of Poetry" (not then known to Browning because not published until 1840) against the dangers of utilitarian views usurping all other ways of conceiving of man and society. "Their [the Utilitarians'] exertions are of the highest value, so long as they confine their administration of the concerns of the inferior powers of our nature within the limits due to the superior ones." But "an unmitigated exercise of the calculating faculty" on every level of man's life will bring not regeneration but worse degradation.

Browning reacted at London not from a version of his own ideals, but from a debased, practical alternative to them. To a more roundly and solidly persuaded utopian, the experience need not have affected his own beliefs. But for Browning, tenuously inspired with an untried enthusiasm caught from a heterogeneous literary and philosophical tradition, this first disappointment provoked a development that would undoubtedly have come sooner or later. Sometime during the year, perhaps at the same time that he decided to give up the university, his poorly built erection of millennial hopes fell with a dull inner thud. With a natural emotional logic, though without any real logical necessity, the disappointing failure of his first venture suggested to Browning that the entire scheme was merely unreal, visionary only in this weak sense, not prophetic of the great day to come. Carlyle describes a similar process of disillusion in his reaction to the University of Edinburgh, one of the progressive universities that London had emulated. Under the guise of Teufelsdröckh in the spiritual autobiography, *Sartor Resartus,* he criticized the self-proclaimed rational and practical university for giving its students finally a sense of intense unreality, pumping, like Browning's Göttingen professor, the life out of reality, and leaving only vacant systems instead of life: "We boasted ourselves a Rational University: in the highest degree hostile to Mysticism; thus was the young vacant mind furnished with much talk about Progress of the Species, Dark Ages, Prejudice, and the like; so that all were quickly enough blown out into a state of windy argumentativeness; whereby the better sort had soon to end in sick, impotent Scepticism; the worser sort explode (*crepiren*) in finished Self-conceit, and to all spiritual intents become dead."

From the windy argumentativeness of a humanly barren education, Browning naturally first rebounded, even during the year at London, toward the most substantial realities, those of everyday life in the world outside the university. Exploring the objective world on his own was in any case, if we follow Browning's own short spiritual biography in *Pauline,* a part of his original plans:

> to look on real life
> Which was all new to me; my theories
> Were firm, so I left them, to look upon
> Men and their cares, and hopes, and fears, and joys.

However, his first deliberate and self-conscious observation of the fantastically broad, even bewilderingly diversified, scene of life that London offered a wide-eyed young student only served to finish the blow that his disillusionment with The London University had struck at his great plan. Grasping for solid realities to balance the vacuity of his education, he began to see that his own schemes, if more attractive than the utilitarian enterprise, were equally vacuous:

> And suddenly without heart-wreck I awoke
> As from a dream: I said, 'twas beautiful
> Yet but a dream, and so adieu to it.

Pauline thus presents schematically a psychological moment of disillusionment that must in fact have developed slowly and over time. Browning's early structure for dealing with the world—really, we might say, an attempt of an inexperienced person to substitute a simpler world for the one he had not yet faced—was totally crumbling:

> First went my hopes of perfecting mankind,
> And faith in them—then freedom in itself
> And virtue in itself—and then my motives ends
> And powers and loves, and human love went last.

As in the case of the "better sort" in Carlyle's analysis, the disillusionment took the form of a kind of general skepticism, a lapse of all ideals in the cessation of his greater idealism.

What is most surprising in this crash is that Browning could characterize it, writing only three years later in *Pauline*, as a fortunate fall. The moment of disillusionment is presented even as a kind of revelation, as a negative epiphany through which he attained important awareness. If he felt a new burden of guilt—"as some temple seemed / My soul, where nought is changed, and incense rolls / Around the altar—only God is gone"—he also felt that an impossible weight of idealism had been lifted off his shoulders. The spirit was virtually exhilaration:

> I had oft been sad,
> Mistrusting my resolves: but now I cast
> Hope joyously away—I laughed and said,
> "No more of this"—I must not think.

Disillusionment even seems to have brought new powers. No longer bound by his own moral vision, he became aware of faculties for responding to the mixed stuff of present reality that had been atrophying within. In a different way from the Utilitarians, he also had been oversimplifying human nature, and his own nature, to bolster his theories. Now he felt disillusionment "no decay" because it helped him discover the possibilities of his own nature: "new powers / Rose as old feelings left—wit, mockery, / And happiness." The experience was an elemental but essential one: that of sensing fully and immediately his own natural vitality, of feeling, "buoyant and rejoicing," the powers of "youth or health" that continued through all dream shipwreck. His hopes for man's immediate regeneration, his plans to play some vague, messianic role, might evaporate under the piercing beams of experience, but beneath all there was a solider sense of self that did not vanish.

His immediate reaction to London was thus to move from abstract ideas and abstract ideals to a vital, if basic, realism. It was at this time that he probably first began to reflect upon his own psychology, especially on that fundamental quality of being, the sense of "intensest life, / Of a most clear idea of consciousness / Of self," upon which he founded his self-analysis in *Pauline.* Free from the discipline of London, "defying all opinion," he could continue to feast, as well, on the salutary realities of simple, external observation. By renewing contact with those immediate realities, he could settle a mind dizzied by his own speculative vacillations and by the dry abstractions of London. There were the old haunts around Camberwell and Dulwich to find again, and the greater world of the entire London area, barely scratched on the surface so far, to explore more fully. There were long rambles, perhaps with his cousin James Silverthorne, in the woods and country, excursions to Dulwich or to suburban towns in other parts of London, shops and sights in London itself, endless business along the Thames and the docks out to the east, fairs, and plays, and even the opera: a gypsy life with gypsy freedom, sometimes even the chance to meet with some real Gypsies and listen to their stories. Restless, set free from the unifying force of his idealism, he would try out everything and look into all walks of life and ways of being: "I grow mad / Well-nigh, to know not one abode but holds / Some pleasure—for my soul could grasp them all."

The aspiration for unlimited experience was a permanent element of Browning's personality, but it was especially intense at this time. Through the old sea-captain and family friend, Pritchard, Browning was admitted to the lectures at Guy's Hospital, presumably the famous ones in midwifery, of Dr. Blundell, Pritchard's cousin and later a sometime member of the set.[1] Browning's father had hopes that he might catch a passion for medicine. But, what was unappealing as a discipline and possible profession at The London University, was of great interest to the amateur inquirer just because he could focus clearly on the general mystery of life revealed in medical science without being lost in the abstractions of the discipline.

Skepticism, freedom, and outdoors exploration might have led, in a different person, to the life of an adventurer, whether the stylized one of Shelley's friend, Trelawny, or the career in deadly earnest of the grown Rimbaud. With Browning, though high hopes for education and knowledge had taken a severe setback in the disillusionment at London, skepticism did not develop into any real cynicism. If anything, as he explains in *Pauline*, his emotions still instinctively leaned toward the Shelleyan hope that he might be the instrument for a social renewal, that "the words / He utters in his solitude shall move / Men like a swift wind." In reverie at night he would return to that dream, only to have to dismiss it again before the harsher illumination of reality: "morn / Came, and the mockery again laughed out." On introspection, he found that he had not really discarded his earlier ideals but merely tempered them in the cold water of reality. He maintained his faith in liberty, if not in its immediate triumph; he still felt the same sympathy for others, if also a new awareness of "the woes I saw and could not stay."

Despite some doubt of Shelley, some sense that his special luster had been partly the effect of a glorious haze of unreality, Browning, as we have seen, did not at all turn his back on his poetry; nor did he scorn Shelley's social and political idealism just because he could no longer completely share it. If unlivable, ideals like Shelley's still appeared splendid. What began to emerge, however, was more a Keatsian than a Shelleyan attitude toward knowledge and the uses of knowledge. In *Pauline* he recalled a thought of this time, "that it were well / To leave all shadowy hopes, and weave such lays / As would encircle me with praise and love." Knowledge might be a friend to man in his present state, not just an instrument for transcending that state at some future time. Simultaneously, he began dimly to realize what had been missing in his education at London and why it had seemed so tasteless to him. Knowledge might not only serve man in his present state: it might also be knowledge of man in his present state, a knowledge turned to human realities rather than to abstractions.

This realization came to Browning, or at least is habitually expressed by him, as it is by Tennyson, as a problem of the proper limitations of knowledge or of the proper moral uses of knowledge. Central to both *Pauline* and *Paracelsus* is the discovery, first made at this time but ratified repeatedly in the following years, that the pure aspiration for knowledge can become destructive. Not that the "craving after knowledge" is in itself a bad thing. The speaker of *Pauline* even sees it as some indication of the soul's aspiration toward a higher sphere of existence, almost as a proof of immortality. The danger is that it will then outstrip and unbalance our moral sense, our capacity for love, which might also be infinite but must in the real world find a limited real object. Knowledge unrestrained thus threatens to sever our means of contact with life and other people. In this way it can be perilously wild, a "sleepless harpy" that would prey on our normal human nurture. In terms remarkably similar to those with which Tennyson speaks of uncontrolled wild knowledge in *In Memoriam,* CXIV, Browning explains his reasons for chaining down his aspiration for infinite knowledge.

> I considered whether I should yield
> All hopes and fears, to live alone with it,
> Finding a recompence in its wild eyes;
> And when I found that I should perish so,
> I bade its wild eyes close from me for ever.

This attitude is not, as it has been characterized, a form of compromise or betrayal of the mind to social or religious orthodoxy or to the moral authority (as it is presumed) of his mother.[2] As an idea it is not even a departure from Shelley, who, like Blake, could symbolize ultimate evil as the uncontrolled power of abstract reason, Urizen for Blake, Jupiter in Shelley's *Prometheus Unbound.* Browning had tended, in his first enthusiasm for the radical critique of things as they are made by writers as different as Shelley and Voltaire, to respond to the overall similarities between the opinions of thinkers of the Enlightenment and their romantic successors. He was now focusing on their differences. Like all the English Romantics he had sensed the danger of thinking that elevated one aspect of human nature at the expense of all others. Like them he was coming to stress the importance of feeling and love as the humane and human forces that could balance the tendency of the mind, when left to itself, to move into abstraction.

However simple the formulation sounds—love to be balanced against knowledge—it was a truism that Browning meditated upon and took home to heart with time. In *Paracelsus*, he made the opposition the central and stated theme of his hero's education. Paracelsus, like the young Browning, aspires to a Promethean knowledge of all things. What he must learn, what is even rather inartistically shoved before our attention as The Theme of the poem, is that he will never have any success in his quest for knowledge unless he begins, like the opposite personality, the poet Aprile, to aspire to love as well. What he must learn in fact, is the nature of man. The realization of the importance of love, and of man's emotions in general, comes, at last, as a new understanding of man's proper humanity:

> Love, hope, fear, faith—these make humanity;
> And these I have lost!

The insight is in a sense trivial; yet no part of Browning's formal education in the humanities so far had kept clearly in focus the mixed nature of the object of study: human nature, both mind and feeling.

Less obvious and more interesting is the understanding to which Browning leads his student-protagonist at the conclusion. A failure in his own attempts to integrate his aspirations to love and knowledge, Paracelsus attains, before his death, to a Pisgah-sight of the promised land of a better-tempered knowledge. He has not succeeded in joining love and knowledge, he finds, because he has focused his study on the wrong subjects. Like Browning himself, his gaze has been only upon the future possibilities of man: seeing no reason why man should not immediately be "all-sufficient," he has looked only forward:

> I would have had one day, one moment's space,
> Change man's condition, push each slumbering claim
> To mastery o'er the elemental world
> At once to full maturity: then roll
> Oblivion o'er its work, and hide from man
> What night had usher'd morn.

Now he realizes what Burke had reprimanded the sympathizers of the French Revolution for not acknowledging and what Wordsworth and Coleridge learned in their own disillusionment with the Revolution: that the future must develop out of the past, that if we are to understand man's future we must comprehend his past. Looking only for the millennium to come, Paracelsus, like Enlightenment thinkers from the heights of Voltaire to the nadir of Henry Ford in our own century, placed no value upon knowledge of the past for itself:

> I saw no use in the past: only a scene
> Of degradation, ugliness, and tears;
> The record of disgraces best forgotten;
> A sullen page in human chronicles
> To be erased.

Understanding man's mixed emotional character, Paracelsus now leaves a different legacy to those who follow him. Past and present are not irrelevant absurdities to be swept away by a better future. They are a story of man's long and painful process of emergence into light and joy. Each stage in the journey is valuable in itself. We prepare for our own better future, and actually achieve it, by realizing sympathetically the evolution of mind and love in the past. "Not so," Paracelsus apostrophizes the future student of man,

> wilt thou reject the Past,
> Big with deep warnings of the proper tenure
> By which thou hast the earth: for thee the Present
> Shall have distinct and trembling beauty, seen
> Beside its shadow—whence, in strong relief,
> Its features shall stand out: nor yet on thee
> Shall burst the Future, as successive zones
> Of several wonder open on some spirit
> Flying secure and glad from heaven to heaven;
> But hope, and fear, and love, shall keep thee man!

The physician's last lecture was not a new one in the nineteenth century. It even sounds as if it had been drawn wholesale out of some corner of Wordsworth's *The Excursion*. The importance of this revelation was that it came at the beginning, not the end of Browning's imaginative life, and that he resolved in his education, as later in his best poetry, to put it strenuously into practice. When Paracelsus speaks finally of what this study of the past might be, his turgid exposition catches a bright flame of sincerity, even eloquence. After his long and disappointing vague search for the future, the past, as an object of knowledge, has the imaginative attraction of a complex but definite real thing. In the better student love will find its object, along with knowledge, in contemplation of the complex and mixed fates of previous men. With the sympathy of love their struggles, even their failures, will reveal man's nobility, if also his limitations:

> To trace love's faint beginnings in mankind—
> To know even hate is but a mask of love's;
> To see a good in evil, and a hope
> In ill-success. To sympathize—be proud
> Of their half-reasons, faint aspirings, struggles
> Dimly for truth—their poorest fallacies,
> And prejudice, and fears, and cares, and doubts;
> All with a touch of nobleness.

XIII
A Poet's Education: Tradition as Found

Just as he first turned instinctively from the university to the external objective world, Browning thus turned, as he began to take up his education again, to the tangible subject of man's past. Browning's education to this point had followed the erratic course of a person seeking, beyond his immediate subjects of study, the proper values to direct his future education. More than this, in a time when there was exceptional disagreement about the aims of education, he was finding out for himself, in settling the direction of his studies, many of the values by which he would shape his life and future work. However, his new focus on humanity as it is, and upon the human past, was to be far from merely another stage in his education. It set the direction, in fact, of a continuous process of study and education that would last the rest of his life. His way once chosen, his development would be toward wider knowledge and deeper understanding. It was a broad way, a very wide focus: as much a way of looking at life and at man's nature as an educational direction. But it was a way so firmly chosen that when, more than thirty years later, he had to plan his own son's education, he fell back instinctively on what he himself had come to. The accepted education in society, "Greek, Latin, & gentility," was then still essentially what it was in Browning's boyhood. His choice was again to go his own way, seeking a broad training in the humanities rather than a more narrowly focused discipline. He insisted upon "generally enlarging the knowledge" by "various studies," and he sought an education of the full being, not merely development of mental powers and abstract reasoning: "He should advance generally, not at the expense of any faculty mental, moral or physical."[1]

The education of the father was not necessarily right for the son, especially when the special virtue of the son was not, as it turned out, self-motivation and originality. But for Browning, the direction of his own education after London was probably exceptionally beneficial, especially because it was settled early enough in his life—at age seventeen—to be decisive in the development of his mind. And, while his interests were coming closer to those of his own father, Browning was unlikely to limit the use of his studies to the father's antiquarian and dilettante pastimes. Even Browning's outward stance, the role he assumed as he settled into a life of independent study, was far removed from his father's convivial, armchair scholarship and artistry. Whereas his father fetched books for citation over the dinner table or lightly turned off satirical sketches in company, Browning took on the habits of a serious and professional student. From the glimpses that letters give us of his life at Camberwell and later at New Cross, he seems to have assumed, as far as the realities of comfortable suburban existence allowed, the stance that he, like Yeats after him, found in an attractive form in Shelley: that of the Prince Athanase, the young scholar seeking truth in solitary study and meditation. The realities were, at Camberwell, a small smoky room, "a horrible smoky room" in fact, and small enough at times to remind him of Lear's "walled prison."[2] At New Cross, with three floors, there was a bit more space for the poet-scholar in residence. Browning's study, "the little writing room of mine," was on the top floor, evidently adjoining a larger room where his father's books were kept.[3]

The "walled prison" to which Lear dreams of going with Cordelia is a narrow place, but is to be the home of imagination and renewed understanding. In his small room, working at his lift-top desk, leaning back to finish a book ("read, read, read"), or getting up to pace to the window and stare out on the surrounding green, Browning sought by regular study and contemplation to call up a balanced view of man and man's past. Whether in his reading or in his own writing, the working imagination could bring a living world into the small, empty room. "I really had you *here*," he wrote the actor Macready about one of his plays, "in this little room of mine, while I wrote bravely away."[4] As symbols of meditation, of the mental activity that can call life out of things past, there were even two skulls set up before him, "each on its bracket by the window."[5] At New Cross the effect was completed by the lingering presence of a tradition that the study, "this old room where I sit all day," where "few brooms trouble walls and ceiling," was once the clandestine chapel of a Catholic family.[6] Dressed by preference in a workaday blue shirt,[7] with no company except at times a crafty spider, "so 'spirited and sly,' " watching him as he worked out of a tooth in the skull, Browning made his mind and world by solitary labor and concentration.

1 Curious Knowledge

Long, dutifully detailed lists of books read are surely among the bald spots of biography. Inasmuch as Browning's study at home began a process of regular reading and education that lasted the rest of his life, any catalogue of his reading would also be interminable. Confronting seriously the challenge of his father's six thousand books, Browning had exceptional opportunities for varied and extensive reading. Free public libraries did not exist at the time; fashionable circulating libraries offered primarily novels and recent literature. But Browning had, in his father's library, something close to the depth of classical literature in many languages and historical works and documents of a small college library.[8]

Of course, the mere presence of books does not ensure a reasonable education, and, as many commentators have suggested, the range of reading available at home tempted Browning to some extent into the obscure corners of literature, those "forgotten fields" in which he acknowledged finding rich pasturage. The pedantic streak that Greek studies brought out at London could even find new expression in the pedantry of the self-educating: the pride in mere acquisition of unusual facts and out-of-the-way bits of information. The first task Browning imposed upon himself as he began his own education was a strange project: "reading and digesting the whole of Johnson's Dictionary."[9] Whatever benefit he may have derived incidentally from the incisive personality he could find lurking behind even the most innocent definitions, the venture as a whole was probably a singularly dubious one. For most of us with memories of shifting sand, it would be merely time wasted. Browning's exceptional memory—"I who . . . can forget nothing (but names, and the date of the battle of Waterloo)"—made it a more perilous task.[10] From this exercise some of Browning's tendency to long words and obscurity as well as his best successes in finding the right word for a character may possibly stem.

His extensive browsing in other reference works and in odd collections of stories and anecdotes was also, to an extent, an indulgence of his penchant for mere information, a continuation of the encyclopedic curiosity he had acquired from his father in childhood. He seems to have read through works like the standard, *Biographie Universelle* (1822) or Pilkington's *Dictionary of Painters* (1805) as well as Collier's *Great Historical Dictionary* simply for amusement.[11] He sought similar diversion in old books of jest and anecdote such as his childhood acquaintance, the seventeenth-century *Wonders of the Little World* of Nathaniel Wanley, to which he evidently often returned, or the Latin collection of humorous tales *Jocoseria* of Otto Melander. If Browning did delight in the recherché information he drew out of such works, even at times delighted in surprising people with the appearance of deep scholarship that such information could give, he was far from confusing it with a real education. In the footnote of *Paracelsus* in which it is mentioned he sees the *Jocoseria* for what it is: "such rubbish." And the *Biographie* is quoted critically as merely a handy work of reference. Like modern readers of detective stories or second-grade historical novels, he could take his amusement in odd corners of knowledge without giving his whole mind to them.

Browning's fascination with what one critic has called "esoteric tidbits of information" was not intended as an alternative to a more methodical study of the humanities.[12] But it was not entirely a frivolous interest either. In his undirected reading before London, he had met his age's lack of any systematic body of material for a general education outside of the classics by taking up one intellectual faith. Now, disillusioned with systems, he could find, in the detailed and out-of-the-way curiosities of man's past, vestiges of the complexity of human nature that all systems tended to overlook. What seems a weird or gothic interest was in reality a means for developing a cosmopolitan, even rather classical outlook. Nothing human was to be strange to his interest; and in the most forgotten backwaters of recorded history and anecdote he might hope to find the most revealing indications of man's nature or the possibilities of his mind and imagination. The odd series of works that he recalled in old age in the *Parleyings with Certain People of Importance in their Day* (1887) is by no means the record of Browning's main reading interests in youth or young manhood for which it is sometimes taken;[13] still, it suggests the way in which Browning could find food for thought in the lives and work of obscure, even mediocre persons. If Christopher Smart and Bernard de Mandeville interested Browning as men of genuine, if minor, genius, he recalled the eighteenth-century Whig politician, George Bubb Dodington, whose *Diary* he probably read at some time in early life, only to show what reflections of value might be gleaned from even such a booby's life. The aged Browning, probably not unlike the younger Browning, saw in Dodington a man—as he was—of some ability and intellect, a man also of some importance in politics and the literary life of his time but in the end held up to his generation and posterity as an egregious coxcomb and fool. What interested Browning was not these curious details about a nearly forgotten person, but the inner facts he could deduce about Dodington's philosophy of life from his strange conduct and the strangely straightforward, even naive revelations of his *Diary*. In politics only for personal benefit, but making the greatest show of patriotic intention, he amazed Browning not because his motives were bad but because he was such a direct, simpleminded, naive, kind of hypocrite. Dodington's failure provided instructive insight into more complex characters. If politic success were merely a matter of saying one thing and doing another, every petty person of some talent would prosper. True greatness of this kind—and Browning in 1887 thought of a great politician whom he had admired but had not respected, Disraeli—would have to come from more subtle, more connived stratagems than such as a Dodington employed.

Out-of-the-way places in history could thus give Browning the start to insight into the nature of politics in general. Other odd corners of knowledge provided, in very different ways, insight into the complexities of the human mind. Browsing through the work of the obscure Renaissance physician, Giovanni Battista della Porta, Browning discovered, as he reported to Elizabeth, an evocative example of the natural tendency of the mind to think in metaphors. "He avers that any musical instrument made out of wood possessed of medicinal properties retains, being put to use, such virtues undiminished,—and that, for instance, a sick man to whom you should pipe on a pipe of elder-tree would so receive all the advantage derivable from a decoction of its berries.''[14] From such reading, endless observations and anecdotes, of course, could be drawn. What is important, however, is that Browning was not indiscriminately studying everything that he happened upon as if all works were of equal literary or historical importance. Instead he looked for the glint of universal significance that might, even in the most inert materials, show man to him in a new or fuller light.

From rare works in his father's collection and various compendia of biographies and biographical anecdotes, Browning kept unconsciously storing up, as he had been since childhood, images of humanity that he would often draw upon for incidents or entire poems years later. As we have seen, stories or persons he had first met in works such as Wanley, or images he found in the descriptions of art books such as Lairesse's *The Art of Painting* would surface as the conscious or unconscious inspiration of later poems. And that process continued in his occasional reading all his life. "An old peculiarity in my mental digestion," Browning observed after explaining that he had written a poem in 1883 from an incident he had ingested forty years before, "a long and obscure process. There comes up unexpectedly some subject for poetry, which has been dormant, and apparently dead, for perhaps dozens of years.''[15] Although the process of gestation was not always a guarantee that the lead of obscure sources would be turned into the gold of general human insight, he had no intention to baffle his readers by the extremes of his scholarship. Nor did he, with the innocent arrogance of the self-educated, assume that everyone would share his odd bits of knowledge. In a letter that should have been required reading for all the industrious source hunters who have grunted and squabbled over the (mostly) unpalatable mulch that nourished Browning's poetic crop, he admonished a good friend to forget about sources and the real incidents and look at the story in the poem itself: "If you would—when you please to give them your attention—to confine it to the poems and nothing else, no extraneous matter at all." It is not the raw fact, which can come from anywhere, but what is seen in it or made from it that is important. "You imagine that with more learning you would 'understand' more about my poetry—and as if you would somewhere find it already written—only waiting to be translated into English and my verses: whereas I should consider such an use of learning to be absolutely contemptible: for poetry, if it is to deserve the name, ought to create—or re-animate something—not merely reproduce *raw* fact taken from somebody else's book.''[16]

2 A European Culture

Reading in obscure and forgotten sources was an important part of Browning's education, one that he had begun in early childhood but that he sought more deliberately when he turned to his own education for his career as poet. It gave him, in his works as well as his conversation, a command, as

Elizabeth noticed, of "curious knowledge as well as general."[17] However, Browning did not suddenly abandon the high road to general knowledge for the dirt byways of random reading. Rather, his reading suggests a new and conscious effort to appropriate a usable past to his personal needs, to find in the various traditions of his culture those writers and thinkers who could most help to suggest directions for his own developing views and modes of expression.

Most apparently, he kept up his command of the old languages of learning and continued to expand his general reading in them. Through his early school work, his study at London, and his reading in the 1830s, he had at least the education in the classics of a modern undergraduate concentrator. If the ways of teaching the classics to which he had been subjected had left him less than enthusiastic, he had not lost his immediate pleasure in the best works of the past. Nor did doubts about the way in which the classics were taught ever lead him to doubt, as one might expect he would have, the place of the classics "in anything like an 'Education' which deserves the name."[18] First among the "old delights" that return in *Pauline* "like birds again," when Browning turns to a life of private study, is what he had been studying less happily at London: Greek drama. The favorite passages that he had freely translated from Sophocles' *Ajax* and Aeschylus' *Agamemnon* and *Choephori* were annotated in the margins by Browning with the original Greek in the copy John Stuart Mill looked at, as if to show that the enthusiastic reader of earlier days had also become a competent scholar.[19] From chance references in his early letters and from echoes in his poems, it is clear that Browning came to know many other Greek plays, among them Aeschylus' *Eumenides* and *Clytemnestra,* Sophocles' *Oedipus at Colonus,* Euripides' *Hippolytus, Iphigenia at Aulis, Iphigenia in Tauris,* the *Bacchae,* and *The Trojan Women.*[20] His first enthusiasm for Aeschylus was undimmed in *Sordello* where the murky, metaphysical dramatist is made to stand (we might say sit) along with Sidney as an imaginary audience to the far murkier modern epic, in order to pay a complicated tribute to Walter Savage Landor. The undated fragment, called "Aeschylus' Apology," possibly from the 1840s, is a far more splendid—and also more critical—tribute to Aeschylus' intellectual and imaginative power. Even in its unfinished form the monologue magnificently evokes the gloomy fateful vision of Aeschylus, as he broods over his life minutes before his own absurd fate is to be completed. While Aeschylus thus continued to be for him, as he had been for many Romantics, an example of terrific imaginative power, his own reading was probably leading him increasingly to understand and respect the latest and least appreciated of the Greek dramatists, the tragedian Euripides whom Browning in later life defended vigorously in *Aristophanes' Apology.* That later defense did little for Browning's poetry. In Euripides himself, however, he may have found something of a personal model. As he turned increasingly against the classical spirit and toward a consciously modern literature, Browning was a good enough classicist to find classical precedent for his attitude. Euripides could have shown him a writer, even in classical times, moving away from the accepted and recognized forms, consciously introducing modern language, ideas, and even a degree of psychological realism.

Greek drama was one area of the classics in which his reading and interest continued to grow. Another was the great lyric and epic poets. His enthusiasm especially for Homer and Virgil, for Anacreon, Ovid, and Horace, is patent in his early works. Not only, as we have seen, was translation and imitation of Horace connected with some of his boyhood efforts at poetry,[21] but his early published works, especially *Pauline, Paracelsus,* and *Sordello,* are littered, almost in the Elizabethan manner, with reminiscences and allusions to the classical past. Side by side with his direct description of nature in *Pauline,* are the lovely, if heavily literary reminiscences of classical mythology from Ovid, Homer, and Virgil. The Ovidian style and the direct allusion to mythology disappeared quickly as Browning developed his own form of poetry. But if he refused to adopt classical models, or after the single splendid tour de force of "Artemis," to imitate classical forms directly, he showed his continued saturation in the great poets in more indirect ways throughout his work.

In poems such as "Karshish" and "Cleon" (1855) as well as more direct statements such as the "Parleying with Gerard de Lairesse," Browning would separate himself from the tendency of his century to return to an idealized classical or neoclassical world. But if the classical past was not for him the model that it often seemed to a contemporary such as Matthew Arnold, it was nonetheless a storehouse of perceptions about man and of poetic ideas. Browning would return to it in his poems again and again not to dwell permanently but to draw upon it for expressions and ideas—there are almost one hundred borrowings or echoes of Homer, Horace, Ovid, and Virgil, in *The Ring and the Book* alone—or to allude to familiar apothegms or maxims. Above all, the best classics were a common cultural heritage that he could assume he shared with both his characters and his readers—a common experience through which the present could be better understood. Even poems on the most modern of subjects might ask the reader, through the hint of a classical quotation or a general parallel to the situation in a classical work, to see the universality in the apparently modern. The source in Horace's *Odes* (III.iii.1-8) for the idea and title of the poem "Instans Tyrannus" (1855) lets us see the hollow boasting of this tyrant as just another incident in the endless struggle between the unjust in power and the just men who stand up against them. Similarly "Love Among the Ruins" (1855), representing an incident in modern love, updates the pastoral vision of country innocence and love opposed to urban corruption and power only to show that it is one universal way of looking at human experience in all ages.

The classical world was indeed a theater, not the only one but a particularly complex and interesting one, in which human nature and the human imagination could be seen on display. We know that Browning continued not only to read deeper into the best writers but also to extend his knowledge into lesser and even obscure writers. There were gifts of an Epictetus from his learned Uncle Reuben, and works like the *Characters* of the late Greek philosopher Theophrastus or a venerable 1505 edition of the *Letters* of Pliny the Younger from his father, gifts from scholarly gentlemen to a scholarly young man.[22] Before 1846, letters and poems allude not only to standard authors such as Hesiod, Pindar, Herodotus, Thucydides, Lucian, Terence, Lucretius, Cicero, Livy, and Juvenal, but to a host of little known writers such as the Greek poets Alciphron and Colluthus mentioned in *Pippa Passes*. In his letters during the 1830s, as those to W. J. Fox—"my Chiron in a small way"[23]—he sometimes even makes a display, verging on pretentiousness, of his classical learning. Or he castigates his opponent roundly in Greek as truly a trifler in the discourse on debt.[24] The poet who ruined one monologue of his major work by insisting upon the realism of an Italian lawyer writing his brief as well as his bad jokes in Latin, was competent enough in that language to converse freely in it with a French priest on his honeymoon—discussing, the astonished Elizabeth reported, "at three in the morning whether Newman and Pusey are likely 'lapsare in erroribus.' "[25] And he would keep up both Latin and Greek and keep extending his reading all his life.[26]

Keeping up his French was not even in question. He continued to be in touch with his tutor and probably saw a good deal of him during the work on the *Gil Blas* textbook. Then his family connections in France and his friendship during the 1830s with Ripert-Monclar gave him frequent opportunity to improve his speech and writing. While he probably kept working at standard authors, with French as with the classics he was developing his own preferences and critical opinions. In his letters to Monclar he repeatedly comments with enthusiasm on contemporary French authors, Hugo, Balzac, Lamartine, Sue, or even the minor dramatist Drouineau.[27] Among the famous writers whose likenesses Monclar drew for him during a visit in England were Dumas père and George Sand, and he evidently read widely in modern French romances in the early 1830s.[28] Between that time and his correspondence with the avid reader of French novels, Elizabeth Barrett, Browning developed a salutary critical distance from what was merely sensational in contemporary French literature. Reading George Sand's novel *Consuelo* in 1845 to please Elizabeth, he found it merely "what in conventional language with the customary silliness is styled a *woman's*-book," that is, pretending to a boldness that it didn't really achieve: "timid in all the points where one wants, and has a right to expect, some *fruit* of all the pretence and George Sand*ism*."[29] Dumas, too, he came to see as primarily a writer of sensational incident. "Are there 'new effects?' " he asks Elizabeth of *Monte Cristo*.[30] Along with opinions as to what "seems all false, all writing," grew also a sense of what was, to his mind, first-rate and useful in modern French literature. He spoke of Musset and Lamennais with respect.[31] Victor Hugo, however, then not the weighty patriot and author of the weightier *Légende des siècles,* but a rising star, only ten years older than

Browning himself, author of a riot-provoking play, of passionate lyrics of love, and of a novel, *Notre-Dame de Paris,* of a striking epic scope, was a real discovery and one made at least as early as 1833.[32] "*There* is a head 'for remembering!' " he assured Elizabeth when he sent her a portrait, probably another one of those Monclar had drawn.[33] A copy of *Notre-Dame* was sent to Domett in New Zealand with the injunction, you "shall read," and a promise of more Hugo to come.[34] By the 1850s enthusiasm had become mere solid regard—Browning, Elizabeth reported, had vowed never to sit in the same room with Frances Trollope, "author of certain books directed against liberal institutions and Victor Hugo's poetry"—but such institutional respect never faded into mere indifference. Like Tennyson and Browning, like, indeed many writers of the nineteenth century, Hugo published too much, and he may now seem simply too much of an institution, too classically romantic to be read with pleasure. Who is the greatest French poet? André Gide asked, and answered, "Victor Hugo, alas." But to the young Browning the enthusiastic, courageous young French genius, speaking out his faith in liberty directly and fully against old Europe, must have seemed only a somewhat less fine but more imitable Shelley. Especially in *Notre-Dame* he could find, as if Hugo had been following just his own line of mental development, not only broad hopes for the future but also a new depth of concern with the detail of man's life in historical process and with the possible emotional significance of present human existence, even under the most wretched circumstances. Perhaps, as well, the serious melodrama of plays like *Hernani* or *Lucrèce Borgia* even provided something of a model for Browning's own theatrical ventures in the late 1830s and 1840s.

Even greater than for Hugo, far greater than for the great English novelist of the past generation, Scott, or for Dickens in his own generation, was Browning's admiration for Balzac. To Monclar Browning had remarked glibly of a "convulsive" school led by Sue and Balzac. When Monclar stuck on the observation and defended Balzac, Browning was driven in embarrassment to read him in earnest.[35] Then the discovery of Balzac's enormous series of novels, *La Comédie humaine,* appearing for the first time throughout the 1830s, turned Browning against all French romance-writers whatsoever: "I bade the completest adieu to the latter on my first introduction to Balzac."[36] Like all readers (like Balzac himself who cried out from his death bed for the doctor of his stories) he was overwhelmed by Balzac's ability to call up a total, seemingly real world. The interweaving of the same characters from book to book—"that very ingenious way of his" —seemed to him to keep the stream of life moving in the midst of art: "They keep alive, moving—is it not ingenious?"[37] He would "devour" the tales as they came out in feuilletons in the daily *Siècle,* two days late from Paris, and was so taken by the fictional reality that he begged a friend to visit the scene of *Béatrix* when near Bordeaux.[38] In 1866, still a warm admirer of Balzac, he went himself to Le Croisic—"glorified to me long ago by the Beatrix [*sic*] of Balzac."[39] In another part of the French Atlantic sea-coast was the town of St. Aubin where he would find his own inspiration in the realities of provincial life for his most Balzacian of works, the *Red Cotton Night-Cap Country* (1873). But more than his subjects and realism, Balzac's "faculty,"[40] his larger, almost visionary concern for the entire scope of human life and his vigorous language, bringing poetic strength and freedom of expression to the portrayal of reality, was immensely important as a general influence on the man who would move poetry in the direction of the novel, just as Balzac had moved the novel in the direction of modern poetry. Here, as with Hugo, was another model for the development of his own mind away from abstract subjects and into the complexity of life itself.

While reading further into the classics and French literature, Browning was also going through the mental discipline of acquiring a reading and speaking command of yet another language, Italian. Although the German had not gone as well or as far as he might have wished, he pursued Italian seriously and regularly. His enthusiasm for this new study probably even acted to dampen his interest in the harder Northern language, though it is unclear whether Browning took up Italian while he was at London, or, as seems more likely, after he left.[41] The appeal of Italian for Browning is obvious. Far more than German, it was the language he associated with the later English Romantics, his favorites, Byron, Keats, and Shelley. German might be the language of the most advanced scholarship and science of his age; but Italian was the language for those, like Browning after The London University, who sought not abstract systems but direct contact with the richness of man's experience.

As it happened, the instrument for learning Italian was near at hand: another "professor" of languages, an Angelo Cerutti who lived elsewhere but had his largest clientele among the culturally aspiring middle-class residents of Camberwell.[42] He had been giving lessons at a Goodson school where he recorded Browning's sister, *"damigella per nome Browning,"* as among his pupils as early as the summer of 1828.[43] Through her Browning must have caught the idea of taking lessons, as later Browning's French tutor, Loradoux, and his singing master, Mr. Abel, probably did from him.[44] Browning perhaps began in the fall of 1829, and both he and his sister were still working with Cerutti in early 1830 when he published an edition of Bartoli's *De' simboli trasportati al morale* as a text for reading practice.[45] Cerutti returned to Italy for two years in 1830 and 1831, but lessons were probably continued thereafter until his longer absence after 1836.[46]

We know far more about this Italian in England Cerutti than we have any apparent right to. He took unwonted pride in his work as grammarian, publishing not only an Italian grammar and bowdlerized editions of Italian authors for his English students, but even a treatise on Italian grammar for Italians. He styled his great work *Grammatica filosofica* and himself not only grammarian but philosopher. Finally he published a long querulous two volume autobiography with "moral and philosophical digressions."

His life as a whole has some of the mixture of ignobility and heroism of that of the scholar-hero in Browning's "A Grammarian's Funeral." Such as it was, his position as a grammarian (*"la cima di quel monte"* he dignifies it in the *Vita*) was attained in spite of a constant and losing battle with fortune, lack of students, English fogs, family sickness and deaths, envious fellow grammarians, and, above all, lack of funds and hovering debtors. But even the tired man who included in the title of his autobiography the indication that he was, as if unexpectedly, *still* living (*"lui vivente"*) and who digressed most often to complain of his present poverty, looked back with gusto upon the time in his life when he was tutoring at Camberwell.

When Browning knew him the man was young, self-educated, and imaginative in temperament. He was also frankly romantic, paying court with only partial success to a series of English girls and students, including the attractive young pupil who shared lessons with Browning's sister Sari-anna.[47] When Browning, sixteen years later, was paying his own court to Elizabeth he told her playfully that he sought a proof of their love by a bookish version of "forget-me-not": reaching up for any book in his library and reading his fortune from whatever page chance might offer. The book turned out to be Cerutti's grammar and, for all his dread of turning up a page of conditional tenses or single numbers, Browning found the hopeful and highly romantic message, "If we love in the other world as we do in this, I shall love thee to eternity," in a section of "Promiscuous Exercises."[48] The choice of such a passage was less of a special omen of good fortune than Browning wished to believe. Cerutti's method emphasized reading from classical authors as well as memorizing grammatical rules. Under the romantic grammarian, "amorous strains and sublime conceptions"[49] from Dante and Petrarch, the twin fountainheads of western poetry of love, were part of the study of Italian from the beginning.

Both Cerutti's method and his personality put Browning in contact with a very different kind of formal knowledge from that he had found at London. In the preface to the grammar Browning used, Cerutti even directed a few snide and superior snipes at the new rational university at London. "Students who breathe the scientific air of an University," he observed, would have no need of his method, for they would look on learning a language as merely a matter of applying abstract rules.[50] His point, delivered in this backhand way, was that language is a subtle art to be learned only by adjusting to the ways of thinking and expression natural to another language. In learning Italian from Cerutti, Browning was thus encouraged especially to acquire a sense of the complex differences in attitudes and forms that give identity to different cultures. The interest in Italian culture and Italian character thus begun, would lead Browning—with additional encouragement from his friend Ripert-Monclar—a long way: both to visit and finally to settle in Italy, and to make Italy and Italian thought and society the context, often even the subject itself, of many of his best works.

After the beginning work on language, Cerutti emphasized reading in the best Italian literature. Although his tastes were somewhat narrowed upon the classical works (he digresses, for instance, to criticize Alfieri) he was genuinely interested in Italian literature. He complained, indeed, about the lack of serious literary students among his English pupils, and must have been glad of the opportunity to read with Browning.[51] He himself had picked up his learning by wide reading in famous authors and boasted in his autobiography that this kind of education was far superior to the outmoded methodical studies of the universities.[52] Claiming a vague affinity to Rousseau in his contempt for formal studies, extolling the importance of extracurricular experience with love and the theater in a balanced education, Cerutti was not only a sympathetic spirit for a university dropout to work with; he was also some kind of living proof that independent reading could make an educated mind.

The work Cerutti edited for first reading was the *De' simboli trasportati al morale* of Daniello Bartoli (1608-1685), a late humanist and educator, historian of the Jesuits, author of both devotional works and treatises on subjects such as ice and sound. The *Simboli* had undergone a revival in the nineteenth century because of the interest Leopardi and others took in Bartoli's rich and polished prose. Even so, Browning read him primarily as a convenient model of prose style. He took the *Simboli* with him in his voyages to Italy to refresh his Italian, "yawning over" it and turning with relief to write "Home-Thoughts, from the Sea" and "How They Brought the Good News from Ghent to Aix" (1845) in the flyleaf.[53] His impression of Bartoli, in a letter discussing one of the symbols or short tales that he moralizes, is that he is a "very clever man" who says foolish things "in choice Tuscan."[54] Although he chose Bartoli as his subject in one of the *Parleyings,* even there Browning showed little respect for him and used him primarily as a stalking horse. Browning looked upon his work as he did other curiosities, useful for the insights it gave into the lore of history and scholarship, but not for that reason to be confused with the works of literature of value in themselves.[55]

Italian could open up this and other sources of story and detailed anecdote. When Browning came to read up on the background for *Sordello* or even for some of his more successful later poems on Italian subjects, his curiosity sometimes led him into too much local history and detailed lore and threatened to drown his readers in curious anecdotes. However, the work Cerutti assigned his advanced pupils was not eccentric but central to Italian and European culture alike. *At* the center, of course, was Dante. Like all serious students of Italian Browning under Cerutti worked methodically through Dante.[56] The experience left him not merely a competent student of Italian but a lifelong lover of Dante. He would return to him not only for specific information in writing *Sordello* but also merely for the pleasure of rereading.[57] With Cerutti Browning probably also read Petrarch, a usual study for advanced students. If so, he had from earliest exercises to most advanced study an exposure to the sources of the poetry of idealized love in the singers of Beatrice and Laura. Although we have no authority to conclude that this alone shaped Browning's own love poetry in this tradition, since he had a close or closer contact with the Petrarchan tradition in the English Renaissance poets, certainly this reading expanded and quickened his appreciation of this special realm of experience and language. Sentimental romanticizers of the Brownings call forth cynical disparagement of this side of Browning. Yet if his love poems sometimes fail, more often through excessive cleverness than excessive sentiment, he also achieved, in poems as diverse as the troubadour "Rudel to the Lady of Tripoli" (1842), the personal "By the Fire-Side" (1855), or the Platonic love language of Caponsacchi and Pompilia in *The Ring and the Book,* as fine a restatement of the Petrarchan tradition as any modern writer.

Standard, advanced reading also included Tasso, Ariosto, and Boccaccio's *Decameron,* for which Cerutti had a special student text but which still must have had its unexpurgable vitality and interest.[58] Most important, Cerutti was able to show Browning enough of the richness and variety of Italian literature, even while he was putting him through the necessary drudgery of grammar and vocabulary, to whet his appetite for continued reading on his own. Tasso, interesting to Browning through both Byron and Shelley, Luigi Pulci, the burlesquer of epic and stylistic model for Byron's *Don Juan,* Machiavelli, and Alfieri's plays are all mentioned in Browning's correspondence. Browning was sufficiently expert on Tasso even to be asked to review a biography for Forster's *Foreign Quarterly Review.*[59] Although Browning tended to share his tutor's low estimation of modern Italian writers—Alfieri "writes you some fifteen tragedies as colourless as salad grown under a garden glass with matting over it"[60]—Cerutti had converted him to the Italian classics.

Independent reading during the thirties in Greek, Latin, French, and Italian thus gave Browning an unusually broad background in the major classical and romance literatures. On top of all this, there was his considerable exposure to German. There was a foray into learning Spanish, evidently successful enough to let him read Calderón, no doubt on an inspiration from Shelley who had been reading him avidly right to his death.[61] Finally, he showed a warm appreciation for writers such as the Portuguese Camoëns, or even more exotic Arabic writers whom he knew only in translation.

Even by 1833, Browning appears, in one briefly illuminating account we have of him, as an exceptionally proficient linguist and student of foreign literature for his age. A Katie Bromley (later Mrs. George Hering) was a close friend of Eliza Flower and recorded her impression of the young man whom she met with the Flowers at the home of W. J. Fox. She was deeply annoyed at his self-conscious manners and the poorly disguised young conceit that was evidently fanned by the attention he was given at Fox's. But she was duly impressed when he quoted effortlessly from an Italian poem that happened to be mentioned and then as effortlessly translated the poem into fluent and lovely English with a shrug of his shoulders.[62] At other times, though with the same "distressingly" self-conscious disparagement of his own efforts, he translated "splendid scenes" from Victor Hugo's "Lucretia [Lucrèce] Borgia."[63] As a mature matron Katie was less critical, but she still recalled these occasions years later: "To meet this plain-looking boy, to listen to his silvery voice, to marvel at his easy translations from many tongues, became to us a recurring intellectual treat."[64] Browning at twenty-one seems to have been received virtually as a special expert on continental literature. The diary, which breaks off the next year, provides an extraordinary glimpse of Browning's early sophistication in languages and literature, if also a reminder that he was very young and, with his clumsy attempts to disguise his awareness of his talents, far from the mature social graces that would please a young lady.

Of his education, as well as his talents, it leaves little doubt. Having started to study languages as a part of the general cosmopolitan situation of his family, he was rapidly acquiring the intellectual equivalent of worldly cosmopolitanism in a broad knowledge of European literature and culture. Like the diplomat or international banker that he might have been had he followed only one side of his nature, he was becoming not merely an educated English gentleman but an educated European.

3 The Legacy of Protestant Culture

Along with this European cultivation Browning was sending his intellectual roots further into his own literature and into the Protestant culture that Matthew Arnold identified as a native, Bible-nurtured Hebraic tradition. If his culture was far from the narrowly Hebraic fundamentalist and chauvinistic Protestantism that his enemies and too familiar friends have found in him, it was also a long way from the internationalism and deliberate deracination of the expatriate modern writers of the 1920s. Ezra Pound might rightly see in Browning's scholarly *Sordello* something of his own voyage out of historical continuity in search of more universal literary traditions; but he was only seeing one side of his mentor.

The period of Browning's most deliberate education, in the late 1820s and 1830s, was also the time of his greatest religious uncertainty. Browning professed no creed, public or personal. *Pauline* and *Paracelsus* stressed heavily the problem of faith and of the nature of man's religious aspirations, but neither presented a coherent answer to the kind of ultimate questions the young man had first dumped in the lap of his friend Sarah Flower. There is no evidence, however, that Browning ever turned away from religious concerns for an unconcerned skepticism; and while he remained in doubt about his own beliefs, he was, like other Victorian doubters, continuing to explore and absorb the fervidly felt, and often splendidly expressed, heritage of Protestant English Christianity and the English Bible. Browning had read and studied the Bible itself so carefully even in childhood that its events, so far removed in time and place, seemed to him, as to generations of English Protestants, a natural part of his immediate experience of life. Although Browning was aware of the difficulties his poetry might seem to present because of his out-of-the-way reading, he seems to modern readers, even seemed to many readers in a Bible-reading age, cruelly indifferent to their problems with biblical references. Even the pious and far more religiously preoccupied Elizabeth found she had to notify Browning that he was overrating his readers' Bible scholarship. The umbrella title of his most important early series of publications, *Bells and Pomegranates*, she pointed out, having herself only dimly recognized it from Exodus (28.33-34), could leave even his best and most friendly readers confused and completely mystify those who were not equipped to play Oedipus to his sphinx.[65]

Such familiarity with the Bible was, of course, the result of upbringing in a creed that stressed the word of the Bible, both Old and New Testament, and it was strengthened by his mother's imaginative storytelling from the Bible.[66] But Browning's knowledge of the Bible went beyond mere conventional absorption and enjoyment of the stories in childhood. For one thing, his religious tradition, Bible-studying rather than fundamentalist, encouraged full and scholarly consideration of the text rather than literalism. The Bible was for him a work of literature and a work of history as well as a work of religious doctrine. In the 1860s, especially in the poems of *Dramatis Personae,* Browning would attempt to establish his own personal position against the conclusions drawn from the new historical and textual interpretation of the Bible by continental writers such as Strauss and Renan; but he was never, like the fundamentalist, opposed to the process of critical discussion and scholarly investigation of the Bible. His own study of the Bible was less a matter of textual and historical investigation than a broad and undoctrinaire appreciation of its moral and religious insights. Without settling on the Unitarian theology of his *literary* mentor in the 1830s, W. J. Fox, Browning probably shared with him the view that the Bible could be a source of ethical wisdom quite apart from theological doctrines. Browning was even closer to the approach of the Camberwell preacher whom he seems to have preferred to the family minister after his period of open religious doubts in the late 1820s and early 1830s, Canon Henry Melvill. Melvill, who was also a favorite of John Ruskin, was an Anglican trained at Cambridge and formerly a tutor at St. Peter's College.[67] In 1830 he took in hand the Camden Chapel in Camberwell, a schismatic offshoot of the parish church which had attempted an Evangelical middle way between Establishment and Dissent since its foundation in 1795.[68] Melvill, who was styled locally "Melvill of the Golden Mouth" in tribute to his "powerful and affecting eloquence," quickly became the most popular preacher in the area, drawing hearers, in the tradition of the Chapel, from a variety of different churches, Establishment and Dissenting, and eventually making it necessary to enlarge the Chapel.[69]

Sarianna recalled going herself to Melvill's sermons as early as his first year in the ministry and the family probably acquired copies of his published sermons as early as 1833.[70] It is not clear when Browning began attending; certainly by the early 1840s he went regularly and probably had been going since the early or middle 1830s.[71] What attracted him in Melvill was probably not just the "deep rich voice trembling with earnestness" which Sarianna remembered all her life.[72] The family minister, Clayton, was of course himself unsurpassed for earnestness. Rather, it was what impressed Ruskin, the combination of earnestness with learning and literary eloquence.[73] Sermons were worked over, as one hearer observed, as if they were to be heard by the entire nation.[74] The result was discourses that are still readable and that reflect a fine intelligence, wide learning, and a refined control of language all placed at the service of his persistent but not overbearing concern with the essential aim of his mission: to persuade his hearers of the need for Christ's mediation in their salvation.

This emphasis, which is a commonplace in Browning's later comments on religion in his poems, was obviously an age-old Christian belief when Melvill recited it, and there can be no grounds for attributing Browning's later beliefs specifically to Melvill's influence. Perhaps Browning was more particularly struck by Melvill's fondness for arguing against natural religion by positing a sensitive spirit from pre-Christian times who can approach in his speculations the views of Christianity but who is stymied when he faces the problem of personal mortality: the argument that Browning would dramatize most explicitly in the monologue "Cleon."[75] Melvill's importance to Browning as he began to work out his own opinions and religious focus was probably even more as an example of serious religious discourse than as a source of ideas. Like Browning himself as he became disillusioned with his early faith in the speedy regeneration of the world through man's mind, Melvill based his religious thinking upon a direct attack on the self-sufficiency of the intellect. Again like Browning, he did not end up opposed to the progressive intellect of the time but merely insisted upon the necessity for balance, a balance that he formulated explicitly in terms of matching knowledge with spiritual progress so that "knowledge of God" might lead in the "vanguard of the host of information."[76] In his sermons he attempted himself to lead the way by calling his suburban parishioners to acknowledge the intellectual value of their moral and religious heritage: "We fear, for example, that the intellectual benefits of Scriptural knowledge are well-nigh entirely overlooked; and that, in the efforts to raise the standard of mind, there is little or no recognition of the mighty principle that the Bible outweighs ten thousand Encyclopedias."[77] From a man with Melvill's broad learning and sophistication, this injunction, fortified by the example of his fine and balanced commentaries in his sermons on passages from the Bible, probably helped encourage and shape Browning's serious return to the Bible and religious literature as a young adult student.[78] Although he had not been raised in any strict sense in a sectarian Dissenter environment, he was moving in his respect for Melvill as in his reading toward an ever more central appreciation of the inheritance of his Protestant tradition.

The Reverend Henry Melvill at Camden Chapel (Episcopal), Camberwell.

Above: North East View of Camden Chapel, 1825. Water color by G. Yates.

Left: The Reverend Henry Melvill, ca. 1832. Engraving by J. J. Williams. *"Melvill of the Golden Mouth," eloquent, learned, earnest, literary: whose sermons Browning and his sister attended in the 1830s and 1840s.*

Below: West End of Camden Chapel, 1825. Water color by G. Yates.

Ruskin, who admired Melvill greatly, though he came in time to see the intellectual limitations in his orthodoxy, felt the preacher's strongest point was his literary quality. Not only were his sermons models of Ciceronian polish but his careful exegesis of individual passages was for Ruskin a life-long example for sound, close textual analysis, something very close in its breadth of focus to literary discussion and critical appreciation.[79] Browning must have appreciated Melvill's unsurpassed ability to open up a biblical text to its full meaning. But even more than a learned and cultured divine such as Melvill, Browning came to focus his mature interest in the Bible on its literary and humane value. In the stories and wisdom of the special culture recorded in the Bible he sought not only religious insight and a chance to exercise his talents at explication but universal understanding of man's experience. His letters show him again and again falling back upon a comparison between his own experience and a story or saying from the Bible. Keats or Tennyson suffering from adverse reviews recalled to Browning Hezekiah going softly all his years "in the bitterness" of his soul.[80] Elizabeth was warned from Matthew not to neglect her own poetry: "Do not be punctual in paying tithes of thyme, mint, anise and cummin, and leaving unpaid the real weighty dues of the Law."[81]

Such casual allusions in letters suggest how available the Bible was to Browning and how easily he could draw more extensively on it for the language of a poem such as "Saul," in which the spirit of the biblical world becomes the substance of the poem. Even poems not specifically on biblical subjects might often be saturated with echoes, conscious or unconscious, from the Bible. In *The Ring and the Book* alone, there are over five hundred quotations or adaptions from virtually every part of the Bible.[82] Above all, the Bible, known as well as Browning knew it, represented an endless resource for moral or religious ideas and language. Browning is not piously afraid even to set scripture against scripture, to give hypocrites and villains, as well as earnest thinkers, a chance to draw their arguments from Bible quotation. Like a confident Jesuit, he felt that truth could not fail to emerge out of the debate, at least to the serious reader. With generations of English writers, he could find in the Bible a source not only for richness of thought and experience but, especially in the King James Version, for splendid language and power of expression. Browning's echoes from the Bible are as often imprecise adaptations or evocations of biblical language as direct quotation. It was not a matter of filling out his poems with reference to the Bible. The Bible was so much a part of his personal culture that he did not so much allude to it as use it naturally as an integral part in his habitual way of expressing thoughts and feelings. As such, like Browning's thorough grounding in the classics, it gave a richness and extension to his language that the modern writer who lacks this resource will have difficulty matching.

Eventually his interest in the Bible led him, sometime after 1835, to take up Hebrew. At the time he didn't maintain his command—"I could read what I only guess at now,—thro' my idle opening the hand and letting the caught bird go.'' But the start was good enough to let him return to Hebrew more seriously in the 1870s and 1880s.[83] Even in his first bout with the language, he learned enough to find an apposite quotation in Hebrew for a kind word about him on a scrap of letter from Walter Savage Landor: "a good report maketh the bones fat."[84] He at least went far enough to gain a feel for the unique power of a language totally different from European languages. Alfred Domett recalled talking with Browning when he was just beginning Genesis and how enthusiastic he was about the verbal force of the original: "the fine effect . . . of 'God said, let there be Light—and then was Light'; how the two parts of the verb in the Hebrew, each a single word, sounded—the last like the immediate echo and repercussion as it were, of the first, like two claps of the hand, one quick upon the other."[85]

While he deepened his perception of the central work of the entwined Hebraic and Christian traditions by studying Hebrew, Browning also widened his understanding of the traditions of Judaism and Protestantism. If he was not the fire-breathing anti-Papist he has sometimes been taken for, he had, both by upbringing and temperament, a natural distrust for institutional and authoritarian Catholic tradition.[86] But he was far from a fundamentalist disregard for religious tradition itself. His curiosity about the Old Testament and the commentators on it as well as his sympathy for Judaism as the root of Protestant Christianity led him naturally from the old testament to rabbinical writings both in the biblical period and after. Like his father, who seemed to one friend to know "even Talmudic personages personally,"[87] he studied the religion by understanding the perceptions and philosophy of individuals in the tradition. In poems good, preachy, or bad, Browning would later use rabbinical figures, real or composite, like Ben Karshook, Ben Ezra, and Jochanan Hakkadosh, almost as stalking-horses for his own religious opinions. Whatever the success of their monologues as poems, they indicate the connection Browning was able to make quite naturally between his own situation as a thinker on religious questions and the position of religious thinkers in the Judaic tradition. For both, the essential tradition was that of individual men seeking the just or religious life. The tradition existed not so much in institutional continuity as in the similar religious problems faced by individuals in every generation.

With a similar concern Browning studied other Christian and non-Christian writers and thinkers not to assimilate a specific faith or tradition but to deepen his understanding of individual religious experience. In some sense his interest was even, like that of William James at the end of the century, in the varieties of religious experience. In some of the poems and plays written in the 1830s the subject was explicitly that of religious oddity or aberration. The play *The Return of the Druses* (written late 1830s and published in 1843) is a study of religious imposture in the context of the belief of the Eastern cult, the Druses. Although the story was almost entirely Browning's own, he had evidently first become interested in such an exotic subject by reading about the Lebanese sect's belief in successive incarnations in Collier's *Dictionary* and the *Biographie universelle* and also in *A Dictionary of All Religions* (London, 1704), a primitive work of comparative religion since attributed to Daniel Defoe.[88] Although both the *Biographie* and Defoe's hack work were superficial, they opened the way for closer reading about the sect, and they opened Browning's imagination to the very different possible manifestations of religious feeling. Possibly it was the discussion of antinomianism in Defoe's *Dictionary* that led Browning in a similar way to Johannes Agricola, the sixteenth-century sectarian who asserted the independent validity of faith without works.[89] The result of this interest, the remarkable early poem "Johannes Agricola in Meditation," is a brilliant, if somewhat loaded—even caricatured—pathology of distorted religious emotion. Although the subject of the poem is ostensibly Agricola's antinomianism, Browning's approach is to understand the doctrine as the religious state of mind of an individual, that is, to understand the doctrine by understanding the kind of mentality to which it would appeal. Agricola, supremely confident of his own election and serenely contemptuous of the merely just who, he knows, will burn in Hell, is an example of the mad mind in which alone, in Browning's opinion, such a belief could take root. A similar approach is implicit in the later "The Bishop Orders his Tomb at St. Praxed's Church" (1845) where the corruption and insecurity of the Renaissance Church is understood through the psychology of a corrupt prelate. Implicitly, the orientation was toward a human norm for religious belief. If Browning did not go as far as Freud would in understanding all religion as a product of abnormal psychology, he insisted on seeing religious belief not as abstract doctrine but as an integral and essential part of a human's personality.

Even while his own convictions remained imprecise, studying the varieties of religious life—even those for which he could find no inner sympathy —was at least a way of finding which traditions he would reject. At the same time, Browning's reading was leading him to develop a sense of a tradition of religious experience with which he could identify. The tradition was English and Protestant, but again it was not a tradition of specific doctrine but of a general religious outlook. It was a tradition expressed in the great works of general literature on religion rather than in the sectarian tracts of his childhood evangelical training. Browning's reading in English Protestant writers was in fact only one part, if a prominent part, of a deliberate study during the 1830s of English literature as a whole. For to acquire a thorough knowledge of the literature of his own country was to become aware of a general religious tradition that permeated it.

Even in his childhood reading he had picked up unconsciously a feeling for this religious literary heritage. Quarles, Bunyan, even the hymns and songs of Watts, which he sometimes ridiculed, had had a considerable part in the foundation of Browning's education and personality. If Watts mainly suggested an ideal of sweet, even saccharine harmony in social life and religion,[90] Quarles's *Emblems*—"my childhood's pet book"[91]—touched a higher level of pious verse, both finer in the complexity of its apparently simple art and more profound in its vision of man's religious life. Reading in his father's large eighteenth-century edition with the original illustrations to the poems, the boy had found religious ideas presented in a direct, immediately apprehensible form. In one poem from the *Emblems* the aspiring Soul was illustrated as "a squat little woman-figure with a loose gown, hair in a coil, and bare feet," and the world through which it must pick its way to holiness as a "terrestrial ball" redeemed from abstraction by the absurd prominence given to the town of Finchley: "the evident capital of the universe," Browning recalled, "and Babylon's despair for size,—occupying as it does a tract quite equal to all Europe's due share on the hemisphere."[92] As in the greater religious poets of the early seventeenth century, the juxtaposition of man's general spiritual aim and his particular circumstances comes home with force: Finchley, the place where one starts out, the correlative to every man's local beginnings, makes a distant religious idea—the religious quest of man's life—into a personal reality in even a child's imagination.

In a different way the same was true, of course, of that other favorite childhood book, Bunyan's *Pilgrim's Progress*. Although purveyor of low Protestant doctrines in contrast to the high Anglican, even borrowed Catholic ideas of Quarles, Bunyan brought to Browning, as to generations of English children of all creeds, a tangible and emotionally compelling representation of the idea of the personal religious life. Browning read Bunyan so well and so often in childhood and later that he could brag in 1882 that he had written his own late poem, "Ned Bratts," from the story of Old Tod in Bunyan's *Life and Death of Mr. Badman* without ever needing to look up the text. There, a scoundrel and his wife repeat the tale of their conversion by the word of God as it came through Bunyan's mouth. But it was as much the form of this message as Bunyan's religious teaching that affected Browning. Religious conversion and the turning of the soul to fight the devil in the world could be seen through Bunyan's eyes not as a distant and lifeless ritual but as a reality as solid as the lives of tinkers and sordid publicans like Old Tod and his sluttish wife. Such stories, as well as the very real and walking abstractions of *Pilgrim's Progress* must have indicated to Browning from very early in his life that important religious questions could be found in the spiritual lives of ordinary people and that they could find expression in their language. Browning's father did much the same thing when he translated the journey of *Pilgrim's Progress* into his own simple visual language in the beautiful illustrated map leading through town and country to the celestial city.[93]

During the period of self-education in the 1830s neither Bunyan—still in 1879, "the object of my utmost admiration and reverence"[94]—nor Quarles was given up. Browning's interests took him, however, in the direction of more sophisticated expressions of English Protestant opinion. He read widely in the religious poems of Quarles's more cerebral contemporaries: Donne, probably Vaughan, even the Catholic Crashaw. Most certainly he knew George Herbert's *The Temple* intimately enough to find or perhaps recall from memory an appropriate quotation from it for a friend's book.[95] The quotation, a passage on spiritual aspiration from "The Church Porch" displayed a theme that was central to Browning's own individualistic outlook even at a time when he was far from professing a particular creed. However, unlike many of his own readers, Browning was not reading Herbert for the message. To admire *The Temple* at all in an age when there was no fashionable bias toward Metaphysical poets was to appreciate both Herbert's ability to see the simplest matters from a complex and intellectually challenging religious viewpoint and his quiet but almost absolute control of a simple, pure English.

Inasmuch as he liked the second greatest English religious poet not because he thought he ought to but because he did, Browning felt no artificial inhibition from responding to the different power of the greatest. There is no evidence that he had read Milton in his childhood. Throughout the 1830s, however, he seems to have made a gradual study of practically all of Milton's works. This was partly a result of his interest in the English Civil War generated during work on the play, *Strafford* (1837). But an edition of *Paradise Regained* and *Samson Agonistes* with his name was inscribed 1832, and probably he read these after *Paradise Lost*. Gifts from his father of the *Poems* and the essay *On Education, Eikonoklastes, The History of Britain*, as well as a 1669 copy of *Paradise Lost* attest to his continuing and broadening study of Milton.[96] As he came to know Milton's life and works with increasing depth, Browning found in his strong and clear voice an authoritative example of a poet and of a religious thinker. From the master keeper of literary relics, Leigh Hunt, Browning eventually inherited a prize possession, the lock of Milton's hair admired by Keats in Hunt's panoply, "a real authenticated lock of *Milton's Hair*." But a more authentic tribute to Milton's authority occurred spontaneously as Browning read and defensively tried to answer the marginal criticisms John Stuart Mill had written in his copy of *Pauline*.[97] Mill stigmatized as vulgar the use of "so" at the opening of sentences to mean accordingly. Browning responded by an appeal to the classical master and displayed a number of similar usages in *Paradise Lost*.

More important, Milton suggested to Browning an ideal of religious and poetic fortitude to which he could recur in his own struggles as a poet. Milton had damned individual, military heroism in his creation of Satan in *Paradise Lost*, but Browning could find in him a different, internal and spiritual heroism: the heroism of the poet himself in *Paradise Lost*, daring to venture into the highest religious questions, or that of Christ in *Paradise Regained*, exercising an heroic fortitude of intellect. Most attractive to Browning would be *Samson Agonistes*, where the central figure is an individual human endeavoring to follow the will of God against the entire world around him. A passage Browning picked out for his friend R. H. Horne in 1843 suggests the kind of inner heroism of the spirit that attracted Browning in Milton. Samson tells the Philistine warrior to bind on all his finery and "all thy gorgeous arms," but he himself will fight in the simplicity of his inner conviction: "I only with an oaken staff will meet thee."[98] Of course, as a poet who insisted upon writing about religious belief in the nineteenth century, Browning had to be far more concerned with asserting the possibility of any religious faith at all than with justifying the ways of God to men. But if Milton's heroic construction of a total vision of the universe from his religious beliefs was not a possible model for poetry in the nineteenth century, his example was at least an encouragement to Browning, as it was to Blake, in his own different struggles. For more than thirty years, he would find a general public essentially hostile to his work and indifferent to his concerns, but he had at least the recollection of a greater poet who had continued, undismayed, to express his views and publish his work despite the far more severe and active hostility of his age.

At his highest Milton is, of course, not merely the poet of spiritual fortitude but a seer whose religious vision, reaching beyond physical realities, looks into a pure, white light of higher reality. If his attempts to translate this vision into seeming realities often give a ludicrous overtone to the descriptions in heaven in *Paradise Lost,* his attempts to capture directly, or at least speak of, the sublimity of God as light are, as in the invocation to light in Book III of *Paradise Lost,* splendid, as close to what we think of as sublime as anything in English poetry. If Browning was necessarily alienated by his upbringing from the Catholic traditions of mystic transcendence through sensuous material objects of contemplation, he had in Milton a model of poetry that could express the highest religious aspirations by reaching through description up toward the inexpressible. The effect—the communication of the incommunicable—was at the least a psychological reality. Somehow Milton had found a way of making real to his reader a world incomprehensible in the terms of the world he knew from experience.

In another work of an English writer, "A Song to David" of Christopher Smart (1722-1771), Browning found, in a very different style, a similar attempt through language at a religious vision beyond all expression. Browning read that one great poem, written after the poet had suffered a mental breakdown and while he was in debtor's prison, around 1828 and was so impressed by its lyrical splendor, especially at the time when he was under the full influence of Shelley, that he memorized the whole.[99] In the late "Parleying with Christopher Smart," Browning recalled finding the poem among the other competent but unexciting works of the translator of Horace and versifier of the Psalms through the metaphor of a man who explores a large, well-furnished but conventional house. In one room, and in one room only, he finds sudden, wholly dazzling splendor. Browning thought of Smart's poem as standing alone, amid the more commonplace reality of most eighteenth-century poetry, near the level of the exalted vision of Milton or the lyric intensity of a great romantic poet such as Keats (or, no doubt, though in 1887 he doesn't speak of him, Shelley). His poem, a lyric naming of the glories of the creation, does—in its intent, if not in its language—recall the Milton who had recreated man's unfallen perfection in *Paradise Lost.* Accepting the tradition that Smart scratched the "Song" with a key on the wainscot of his cell during a period of madness, Browning speculated that in the heightened consciousness of his manic insanity Smart saw through the ordinary reality of everyday life to the unfallen glory of God's world hidden beneath our ordinary perceptions. Like Adam in the garden, this once he was able to name the "real vision" of things with "right language." As—in the manner of the Psalms and in the manner Browning would borrow in his "Saul"—he catalogued the chain of glories of the world from the simplest things to the most exalted, Smart seemed to Browning to be penetrating directly through the world to a spiritual reality:

> pierced the screen
> 'Twixt thing and word, lit language straight from soul,—
> . . . . .
> Fire suffused through and through, one blaze of truth.

What Smart revealed to Browning was a kind of religious mysticism or ecstasy compatible with the Protestant separation between nature and spiritual reality. Working at first only with the materials of nature perceived with proper feeling, Smart rose to an abstract but highly sensuous and compelling symbolic creation, at once concrete and visionary. For Browning, Smart's great achievement in the poem was an indication that the way to religious vision could be by a transcending leap of faith from the world into eternity rather than, as in Catholic mystic tradition, by a sensual and emotional use of mediating symbols. For Smart, God's immanence was evident in nature, and more directly within man himself, if he but had eyes to see Him. Like Milton or Bunyan, Smart was thus an indication that the traditions of his own poetry, English and Protestant, did not preclude the expression of the highest religious vision. That the latest writer could preserve and transmit this tradition only in the enthusiasm of what ordinary men had to consider a manic folly was a reminder to Browning that the more direct belief of the Renaissance was not available to him. Even thus transmuted, a living tradition was at least made available to Browning, one from which he could develop his own tentative assertions in David's rapture in "Saul" or in the more genial flight of transcendent enthusiasm of an Abt Vogler.

Above all, to know a tradition was to have a context for understanding the kind of experience on which it was founded. Such probing into this Protestant tradition in the process of self-education was giving him the sophistication and depth to comprehend the problems he faced as a poet, especially his problems in coming to terms with Shelley's influence. For this was also broadly a tradition in which Shelley's lyrical vision, and especially Shelley as Browning saw him, could easily be placed: the tradition of Protestant seers, of poets who could see directly and subjectively into Divinity through themselves. In 1887, perhaps as a token of his later distrust for Shelley, he placed Smart between Milton and Keats, not Milton and his own first idol. Yet clearly he had seen the subjective poet par excellence much as he saw Smart; far more than Keats, Shelley fits as the modern extension of this celestial railway. But the effect of seeing Shelley in an entire tradition would be not to increase Browning's emotional dependence on him. Rather it prepared the way for Browning to understand more dispassionately Shelley's special genius. By wide reading he was thus slowly developing a context for his more immediate concerns as a poet and a critical perspective on his current preoccupations.

4 Starry Paladins: Renaissance Ideals

In his self-directed reading during the 1830s, Browning was not only finding roots in the specifically religious works of his own country. He was, even more, making contact with the enormously rich tradition of English literature as a whole. Even biographers who have denigrated Browning's formal knowledge have admitted that his familiarity with English literature indicated some kind of deliberate, "more constant study."[100] What needs to be added is that in a time when English literature barely existed as a school subject and, where it existed at all, was likely to be mainly a matter of grammar and philology, a good general knowledge could be acquired only through a deliberate course of self-education. The concentrated study of English literature which now, as a college major in English with lectures and a preselected and traditional syllabus so often provides the bulk of the formal education of the young writer, had, in Browning's day, to be attained through the industry of the writer himself or not at all. Browning's curiosity had been nurtured by his father, of course, even before he began his independent reading after The London University. Dryden's "Preface" to the *Satires,* the work Browning recalled his father reciting to him at Nun's Head, was probably not the only piece of English literature read aloud to him during the childhood walks; and in his boyhood Browning had delved into works such as Horace Walpole's letters, as well as the more obviously attractive writings of Shakespeare, Pope, or Defoe.[101]

What he added to this initial sampling of English literature in his late teens and early twenties was a slowly growing sense of tradition, a sense of a national literature growing and changing over time. In his general reaction against his earlier, abstract, and future-oriented thinking he slowly developed a view of literature not only as a set of timeless works of imagination but also as a cultural growth that develops as an ever expanding tradition that nourishes its future upon its past. His new concern for the reality of the past fostered in him an embryonic historical sense, or rather, that simultaneous awareness of the pastness of the past and of its presence in the mind of the student in which T. S. Eliot, in "Tradition and the Individual Talent," sees the origin of the idea of tradition.

Merely to conceive of the idea of literary tradition is not, of course, to possess a literature as one's own tradition. Tradition, as Eliot also insists, "cannot be inherited, and if you want it you must obtain it by great labour." Browning's father could begin to form his son's taste; Browning's experiences at London and after could direct him toward an understanding of literary tradition as a concept; but his way thereafter had to be an individual one, leading, through his particular choice of reading and his special interests, to a personal participation in a literary tradition and to an independent perspective on the past. Still, if Browning had necessarily, as Eliot asserts all men must, to recreate the past from the viewpoint of his own present, he had also—unlike people of two or three generations earlier—the advantage of inheriting some overall historical framework of understanding from previous students. The benefit was, above all, in having a wide range of important authors from virtually every period of English literature already identified and placed in some historical relationship.[102] If the critical discourse of the preceding generations had sometimes run only to excessive abuse or unreasoned enthusiasm, the students of the late eighteenth century, such as Thomas Warton, as well as their romantic successors, had at least insisted that the study of English literature had to be an historical one: that the focus could not be merely upon the modern literature currently in fashion and its immediate predecessors.

Above all, they had called attention to the span of riches in English literature, not only the classics like Chaucer, Spenser, Shakespeare, and Milton but the large number of other fine writers of the past who had been virtually forgotten. By focusing on the value of the works of the distant past, they had helped to suggest that the cultural values and literary modes of former times, far from being merely artifacts of barbarous ages that had since been surpassed, were major factors in the development of past excellence and were worthy of sympathetic study. In his own study of English literature Browning clearly drew upon this historical background. He even came in time to take it for granted. When in 1845 he happened upon an early work of the American James Russell Lowell, *Conversations on Some of the Old Poets,* he was astounded by Lowell's naiveté in proclaiming his "discovery" of old poems "(out of a roll of dropping papers with yellow ink tracings, so old!)" that had been recognized as classics of English for a generation. "Here, with us, whoever *wanted* Chaucer, or Chapman, or Ford, got him long ago—what else have Lamb, & Coleridge, & Hazlitt & Hunt and so on to the end of their generations . . what else been doing this many a year? What one passage of all these, cited with the very air of a Columbus, but has been known to all who know anything of poetry this many, many a year?"[103]

Even as early as the 1820s, Browning was familiar with some of the writing of the romantic critics, and Hunt, at least, would become a personal acquaintance during the 1830s.[104] It is unclear how deeply he read in any of them. He would not have been inclined to substitute the authority of recent critics for that of the recent professors at The London University and he no doubt shied away from looking upon Hazlitt's lectures or Lamb's essays as textbooks. Rather, they were, like Keats's sonnet on Chapman's Homer, testimonies to the new enthusiasm for the English literature of the past. They provided the sense of excitement, of possible discovery, that sent Browning to look at the works for himself and develop his own critical evaluations. In Hazlitt's *Lectures on the English Poets* (1818) he would have found the declaration that poetry, unlike science, rises to its highest level in the earlier stages of a civilization, and that in England, "the four greatest names in English poetry, are almost the four first we come to—Chaucer, Spenser, Shakspeare, and Milton." Whether he read this, or whether he read Lamb or Hazlitt's work calling attention to the value of the virtually forgotten dramatists of Shakespeare's time, or whether he had even picked up an enthusiasm from Keats's poetry, Browning's attention was turned decidedly toward the earlier writers.

Chaucer, a poet to whom the mature Browning would often be compared for realism and psychological astuteness as well as for his general vigor—that quality that Hazlitt called gusto—was read fully. Browning was able to quote from memory both from the *Canterbury Tales* and *Troilus and Criseyde*.[105] But, except for Chaucer, his focus was not on the very earliest English literature. Although he could have found in the scholarship of his day a guide to other Middle English literature and to Anglo-Saxon, he seems only to have attained a nodding familiarity with Chaucer's contemporaries and predecessors, and no Anglo-Saxon at all. He refers only vaguely to the mystery plays of the Middle English drama and to the English ballad tradition.[106] Later he would parody old forms, as in "The Heretic's Tragedy" (1855), subtitled "A Middle-Age Interlude," or pick up some of the cadence and force of Anglo-Saxon in a poem with a very un-Anglo-Saxon sentiment—"Prospice." But along with Hazlitt, Hunt, and Lamb, his interest was primarily in the Elizabethan and seventeenth-century writers. What has sometimes been called the Elizabethan revival of the early nineteenth century was primarily a revival of interest in the Elizabethan and Jacobean dramatists, the first recognition of a neglected heritage that has not been forgotten since. Although Browning would, in his own work in the theater in the late 1830s, increasingly turn away from their model, he read Shakespeare's great, if lesser, contemporaries carefully and probably quite extensively. He refers familiarly to Ben Jonson, Middleton, James Shirley, and Webster in his early works and letters.[107] In Marlowe he took sufficient interest to make serious plans for writing a play on the mystery of his death —called off, perhaps fortunately, only when he found it had just been done by another Elizabethan enthusiast, R. H. Horne.[108]

Then, as now, reading the other dramatists of the English Renaissance was both an end in itself and a road back to Shakespeare. If respect for the Elizabethan and Jacobean drama in general was just budding in the early nineteenth century, love of Shakespeare had bloomed into full worship, and the young Browning joined wholeheartedly in this exaltation. Shakespeare was become less writer than god—"the greatest man that ever put on and put off mortality" to even his finest critic, Coleridge. Browning could see, even poke fun at the growing idolatry of his age: Shakespeare as the measure of all things was becoming not a specific writer but an abstraction of virtue. If Shakespeare unlocked his heart with the key of the *Sonnets,* the cantankerous speaker of "House" in the late *Pacchiarotto* volume explains in exasperation, why then . . . well . . . well . . . the less *Shakespeare* he. Yet Browning was no less a Shakespeare-idolater, and in the same volume he actually succumbed to the universal temptation to justify his own opinion through the bard. In "At the Mermaid" Shakespeare is brought back to life to have a last say, in Browningesque fustian, against Byronic posturing and sentimental, mawkish poetry of self-revelation. His influence was, indeed, fundamental and inevitable. He is "in our very bones and blood, our very selves." The idea of a tercentenary celebration struck Browning in 1864 as absurd: "The very recognition of Shakespeare's merits by the Committee reminds me of nothing so apt as an illustration, as the decree of the Directoire that men might acknowledge God."[109] The comparison was, indeed, serious. If, as Aprile says in *Paracelsus* in his final insight, "God is the PERFECT POET, / Who in his person acts his own creations," then Shakespeare, the poet who most fully captured the vitality and complexity of creation, is like him in aim if not in power. Browning directly asserts this view, which parallels Coleridge's idea that Shakespeare's imagination is the secondary power closest to God's own primary creative force, in "The Names (To Shakespeare)" (1884). There Shakespeare's creation is "man's most of might . . . one remove / Though dread—this finite from that [God's] infinite." As much as he had the Bible, Browning piously revered and studied the works of this lower God.

Browning, of course, had begun to experience Shakespeare's dramatic genius as part of a living stage tradition as early as 1830.[110] His subsequent enthusiasm for the two greatest Shakespearian actors of his day, Kean and Macready, and then his own attempts to write verse plays would keep Shakespeare in the theater very much before him for many years. Browning studied Shakespeare, however, not only on the stage of his day but as a literary master. As we have seen in looking at *Pauline,* Shakespeare quickly assumed a fundamental place in Browning's poetic development as a different kind of literary idol from Shelley. And this master, like that other, was gleaned endlessly for literary ideas and expressions. His early letters show Browning again and again drawing from the wealth of Shakespeare in his memory just the quotation or allusion he needed to make a point. He refers familiarly to at least fifteen of the plays, as well as the sonnets, and probably had studied most of the other plays as well. He alludes repeatedly to *Lear, Macbeth, Othello, Hamlet,* and *The Tempest,* and he must have studied each more than once or twice. He even took the trouble to look into a facsimile reprint of the first quarto of 1603 of *Hamlet* and his father gave him a 1612 quarto of *Richard III*.[111]

It is as difficult to assess the immediate impact of Shakespeare's many successes upon Browning as it would be to deny his ultimate importance. Eventually, in the "Essay on Shelley" Browning came, as we have seen, to acknowledge him directly as the epitome and ideal of one kind of poetry, the master of the objective poetry toward which he himself had clearly been moving. His later "Caliban upon Setebos" (1864) is an even greater tribute to a master, a variation on a theme which takes Shakespeare's great play as a central possession of literary culture, an imaginary world that has become a reality like the historical past. The impression is that Browning kept studying and restudying at least his favorite plays and growing in his understanding of Shakespeare's genius and variety as he himself grew as a poet. In the meantime, his careful reading in Shakespeare, as also his reading in the greatest plays of Shakespeare's contemporaries, gave him, not only in *Pauline* but in later work as well, an implicit ideal against which his own early, very un-Shakespearian work could be sized up.

At the most conscious level, Shakespeare seemed, in Bishop Blougram's terms, sheer "power and consciousness and self-delight," an example of freedom and unhampered creative development that Browning could hold before himself in his own efforts to grow. Defending his unusual choice of the exotic Druses as a subject for a play, he thus naturally appealed in 1840 to the actor-manager Macready, who was then playing in *As You Like It,* by the precedent of Shakespeare: "I intend to be with you in a day or two under the greenwood at Arden—but, ask me whence the 'banished Duke' comes, why they banish him and how,—and you confound me . . . Surely such matters are the *donnés*."[112] At a deeper level Shakespeare's incredible ability to make different characters live in their own distinctive speech and language and yet to give each, villain or villein, his own special kind of eloquence—creating everywhere real speech that is also golden speech—was a pervasive influence on Browning. In his dramatic poems of the 1840s even more than in his plays of the 1830s, Browning used Shakespeare's mastery of dramatic character through distinctive language, his ability to give metaphor, allusion, and argument to speech without losing a sense of individual character, as a standard to which he could aspire if not always reach. The result, as Robert Langbaum has pointed out, was something quite different from Shakespeare: characters divorced from the context of society and worldview in which they were bedded and evaluated in Shakespeare's plays; works that are sometimes Shakespearian but never Shakespeare.[113] But if Browning, with his entire century, tended to read Shakespeare with too little sense of the unity of the plays, too much as brilliant creations of character and splendid language in the manner of Kean's Richard, Browning as a poet was using his education in Shakespeare to create tradition in just the way Eliot would say he must. From his interaction with the great dramatic speech of the English Renaissance he was fitted to bring into English nondramatic poetry the vigor of dramatic speech and dramatic character. A living tradition is not the imitation of the past but a new growth from the vigor of sound roots.

Unlike some of the Romantics who were interested in Elizabethan drama, Browning's study of Renaissance English literature was focused as much on nondramatic poetry as on the stage. His "loving, life-long familiarity with the Elizabethan school" allowed him to maintain contact with the greatest body of poetry as well as the greatest drama of his country.[114] As in all his reading in poetry, he made what he read a permanent possession, memorizing poems he particularly liked until he could astound acquaintances in his maturity by his repertoire. "[He] knows by heart, I should think, all the verse that has ever been written," a Mr. Smalley exclaimed. "You will hear him, when he is in the mood, pour out quotations without number of verses by poets without name or fame."[115]

Not that he focused upon minor poets to the exclusion of major ones. When his contemporaries spoke of sixteenth- and seventeenth-century nondramatic poetry it was most often to focus, as critics had in the eighteenth century, on Spenser and Milton. With them, Browning certainly read and knew *The Faerie Queene* as well as Milton.[116] It is true, however, that Spenser had nowhere near the importance for him that Milton had. He might sympathize with Spenser's overall assertion of a philosophy of moral aspiration. In a larger view, Spenser was a part of the Protestant tradition of individual responsibility and of the religious life lived and proven in the world that Browning also found in Milton or Bunyan. But Spenser's fantastically imaginative work with its varied but highly elaborate language and poetic forms and its splendidly fanciful settings and episodes was for Browning more a monument to be once admired than a living tradition with which he—in the way Keats had—could make significant contact.

The writers with whom he could identify were both more masculine in their expression and more willing to expose directly the personal conflicts as well as the ideals of their age. Sir Philip Sidney appealed to Browning, as he did to his own age, even more as a personal figure than as a writer. It is thus Sidney whom Browning calls up, along with living friends and other unidentified great writers of the past, to stand as an audience to his otherwise unread epic *Sordello*. The choice of Sidney may appear merely another unexplained obscurity to readers of the poem. For Browning it must have seemed quite logical to think of the great example of an Elizabethan man and writer as an ideal and sympathetic audience for his own account of the conflict between the aspiring man and the aspiring poet in his hero, the troubadour Sordello. Sidney, "the starry paladin" of "silver speech," was not merely an aristocrat to be contrasted to the popular audience for whom Browning had to write in his plays—those ordinary seekers of amusement whom he refers to in a letter to Domett, borrowing hypothetical names from Sidney's *Defence of Poesie,* as the Stokeses and the Nokeses of the world.[117] He was also a master with whom Browning could partially identify and in whom he could see, honestly admitted and eloquently displayed, the struggle between the desire to realize an ideal as man and writer and the limitations of the natural man. If the terms of Browning's own struggles would not be exactly the same as Sidney's—not, for instance, in his life simply between Reason and Desire, or in his writing, between making a golden, ideal world and writing history—still the sense of debate and of honest inner combat allowed Browning to feel a continuity between his own concerns and Sidney's.

With another poet, John Donne, the identification was even more immediate. Donne had never been as completely forgotten as his twentieth-century revivers liked to imply. He was republished in the eighteenth century in a sympathetic edition, which included Walton's eulogistic "Life of Dr. John Donne" and which was given to Browning by his onetime friend Thomas Powell in 1842. He subsequently was included in a number of anthologies or series of English poets that Browning might have seen.[118] Browning could also have found critical generalizations mixed with rather high praise of Donne's learning and ingenuity in the discussion of the Metaphysical poets in Johnson's "Life of Cowley," and he would have been able to sample very generous selections from many of Donne's best poems there as well. Among his immediate predecessors, Coleridge, Lamb, De Quincey, Landor, and Hazlitt had noticed Donne, only Hazlitt unfavorably. Donne was, however, still sufficiently obscure in the early nineteenth century that Browning could consider him, if not a personal discovery, at least a kind of personal possession. Elizabeth wrote about him to Browning as "your Dr. Donne" and again "your Donne."[119] Later Alexander Grosart would dedicate his edition of Donne (1872) to Browning as Donne's modern literary patron in the age before Eliot.

Browning's acquaintance with Donne began long before Powell, probably knowing of his interest in him, gave him the edition. Even before he went to The London University he had set to music the "Song" ("Goe, and catche a falling starre") from the *Songs and Sonnets*.[120] It would seem likely that he already knew the other departures from the Elizabethan love lyrics in that volume. Browning evidently was reading Donne right up through the 1840s, but again the 1830s would seem to be a time of especially concentrated study. He quoted Donne familiarly in the *Trifler* article of 1835.[121] He even remembered a delirious period during a sickness in 1834 when he imagined that he had to "go through a complete version of the Psalms by Donne, Psalm by Psalm!"[122] Fortunately Donne never did a version of the Psalms, though he had praised Sidney's. That this should be the form of Browning's nightmares suggests how deliberately he was reading in even minor works of the Renaissance at the time. Browning came to know—and in these cases came to know with pleasure—a very wide selection of Donne's poetry. He shows an acquaintance not only with well known poems such as "A Valediction: forbidding Mourning" from the *Songs and Sonnets* but also with the "Epithalamion" and with poems from the *Elegies,* the *Verse*

Letters, and the *Epicedes and Obsequies.*[123] In *The Two Poets of Croisic* (1878), Browning still recalled Donne's notoriously obscure work, the bitter unfinished satire *The Progresse of the Soule* (written 1601), apparently a life-long favorite of his. He worked a quotation from it into his own poem.[124]

What Browning found in the "reverend and magisterial" Donne was not very different from what his more militant advocates in the early twentieth century claimed to discover. Less than T. S. Eliot did he hope to recapture through Donne the religious vision and intellectual climate of Donne's age. The certitude that a relation between heaven and earth could be found, the conviction that the world could be understood in the terms of religion if the exploration were pushed deeply enough, these assurances that underlie even the most agonized spiritual and poetic struggles of Donne, were acknowledged but not assimilated by Browning. The unified picture of the world of nature and religion that permitted Donne in a poem like "A Valediction: forbidding Mourning" to unite love and death, religious, spiritual union and sexual consummation by the single, certain metaphor of a compass was not one that could be revived by a nineteenth-century poet, however much he might wish to. When Browning, very likely following Donne or other poets of his school, would attempt a similarly elaborate image, as in the ring metaphor of *The Ring and the Book* or the prismatic image of "Numpholeptos" (1876), the result was not necessarily inferior to Donne, but it was something different. Instead of bringing his explorations to a static, unifying conclusion, a long conceit would lead Browning ever more deeply into the complexities and uncertainties of his own ultimate vision of reality.

If Browning found it impossible to become a disciple of Donne in an age profoundly different from Donne's, he was able in a different way to establish poetic commerce with his overlooked predecessor. Here again the creation of his own personal sense of tradition began in his education. Reading Donne early in life side by side with the romantic literature of his day, Browning was able to gain an intuitive feel for a very different kind of poetry and a very different motivation for writing poetry. If he was obliged, nonetheless, as Eliot charged, to find ways to ruminate over the intellectual fodder of his age because he could not believe in Donne's unifying solutions, he could at least expand his own sensibility to include much of what was very different in Donne's tradition. Browning found in Donne in a prominent, accentuated form many of the special qualities of Renaissance verse and drama in general that had been largely lost from later English literature. That Donne in his century was himself a rebel in his personal reuse and adaption of the traditions of his age probably served only to make his particular qualities even more attractive to Browning. Donne carried to an extreme the tendency of all English Renaissance writers to welcome logic, argument, and the use of reason as well as feeling into a poem. Even more than Shakespeare, he suggested to Browning a kind of poetry very different from the highly metaphorical and emotive poetry of the great Romantics or more sentimental survivors such as Thomas Moore. In Donne argument was not a foreign, discursive element imposed upon the more "poetic" qualities of the poem. It was a distinct and important pleasure in itself, a very real part of the art. Not only argument but deliberate mis-argument or over-argument—the casuistry for which both Donne and Browning have been blamed—was not a flaw but a kind of extended figure of speech, one other aspect of a poem in which the poet could please by his extravagant skill. Browning, whose interest in the knotty *Progresse of the Soule* is revealing, found in Donne that argument provided the backbone of most of his poems. Like Donne, he would later organize most of his own poems around argument.

Browning also found that Donne, like any good advocate, asserted the freedom to build his argument out of the materials and language that seemed most fitting to his purpose. He had, as his modern apologists have told us a thousand times, no preordained poetic diction or rhythms (though he always sounds a great deal like his favorite poet) and he had no preconceptions about the content and subject of poetry (though at base he always wrote about the great subjects of his age, love and religion). Browning discovered in him a rough, colloquial language that had the force of spoken English. He must have noticed, as he also did in the drama of the Renaissance, high and serious matters juxtaposed to ordinary or "low" subjects and events and have felt that the effect was not so much the mockery and irony that he was unable to accept in Byron but a fuller sense of the deeper relations between things. He saw that Donne could even take delight in the deliberate awkwardness of erudite words or the universal Elizabethan custom of punning carried to a new extreme. He found continual experiments with meter and rhythm and everywhere the form adapted to the needs of the statement rather than imposed by convention: form enwrapping "the thought as Donne says 'an amber-drop enwraps a bee.' "[125] Above all Browning certainly saw that, in his attempts to draw out and fully express his meaning, Donne felt free to develop complicated conceits, complex intellectual metaphors that made demands upon the reader's mind as well as his emotions and imagination.

That Browning would follow Donne in most of these qualities is no proof that Donne's influence was decisive in his own development. Certainly Browning's mature poetry shared qualities with Donne's, but it was not fundamentally the same kind of poetry. Joseph Duncan is no doubt correct, however, in asserting that Browning's enthusiasm for Donne at least served to reinforce his own tendency toward an informal, colloquial language and an argumentative, intellectual content in his poetry. In an even more general way Donne, like the very different Milton, helped as well to secure Browning's determination to shape his own education. Both reminded him of an earlier ideal of the poet not only as a man of special sentiment and perceptivity but also as a man of extraordinary knowledge and wisdom. In his lifetime progress as a poet from lover of woman to lover of

God, Donne always insisted upon the dignity of his incessant labors as a scholar. He was not embarrassed as a poet by his extensive and often curious knowledge and reading. He wrote not only as a learned scholar with endless information but, in some sense, also as an intellectual poet, a poet who insisted upon bringing his special learning to bear upon the most general questions of life. He offered his lovers not merely passion but a self-conscious understanding of their relation to literary convention and to traditional wisdom about the universe. As a poet of religious experience, he spoke both as every religious man and as the learned Dean of St. Paul's.

The idea of a poet as scholar and intellectual was of course, one that Browning had already discovered and emulated in the most self-consciously learned of the romantic poets, Shelley. To find it in Donne, Milton, and other poets of the Renaissance was to be assured that this was not merely a peculiarity of Shelley to be classed finally on a level with his vegetarianism. It was a promise that the poet need not take his stance as a man of only private feeling impotent in his sensitivity against the masculine force of hard-headed scholars and thinkers. At the price of hard labor and independent thinking, he could, like the poets of the Renaissance, speak out on the large, general questions of his age, and he could write not only from awareness of his own experience but the historical experience of mankind.

It would be tedious to catalogue Browning's other reading in writers of the Renaissance and perhaps misleading as well, since a writer who is mentioned only once or twice in Browning's poems or correspondence may not have been as important to him as others who happen not to be mentioned at all. From Bacon's imposing *Novum Organum* to the biting satire of Bishop Hall, to the pleasant, minor poetry of George Wither, he seems to have at least looked thoroughly into the variety of earlier English literature. The accessibility of the earlier literature as a whole was, in any case, more important than the influence of all but a few writers. Exploring a realm opened up to him by the scholarship of the previous generations, Browning was one of the earliest writers to benefit (and perhaps to suffer in some ways, too) from what Kenneth Clark, speaking of the similar development in the visual arts, has called the museum view of art. With the scholarly recovery of the distant and often forgotten past, the artist was able to form himself not merely by imitating the ideas and styles of his immediate predecessors but by absorbing eclectically attractive qualities from works of quite different periods. The past was, of course, always more accessible to writers than to artists, but the renewed interest in the literature of the English Renaissance and the special circumstances of Browning's self-education made it especially possible for him to achieve intercourse with earlier writers and to create his own sense of tradition in the process of his education. In this way tradition could be for him simultaneously a rooting of his vaguer, adolescent aspirations in the reality of the past and an act of personal freedom— finding those aspects of the past that could be made to grow anew and flourish in the different circumstances of the present. For Browning as a poet it meant especially that he would be able to draw easily and intuitively upon a wider range of styles and sensibilities than would be available to a writer with a lesser experience in literature of other times.

5 Excellent and Indispensable Eighteenth Century

Browning followed, even outdid, most of his romantic predecessors in looking back beyond the literature of the past century to the greater glories of the Renaissance imagination. But he was less intolerant and scornful than some of the Romantics of the body of literature written since the Restoration, which, until the romantic reaction, had been considered the modern literature of a more advanced and civilized age. His father's rather conservative taste had led him naturally to introduce Browning first to the accepted classics of his own youth, no doubt Pope, Johnson, and Swift as well as Dryden and Defoe. Browning naturally read, if without any special enthusiasm, standard prose such as the correspondence of Horace Walpole or the *Letters* of Chesterfield to his son.[126] He was in the same casual way familiar with the major playwrights of the Restoration and eighteenth century. He speaks familiarly of Nat Lee's *Caesar Borgia* and of Colley Cibber's adaption of *Richard III* and acted Nicholas Rowe's *The Royal Convert* at school.[127]

Without expecting to find any new revelation or surprise, Browning continued his reading in Restoration and eighteenth-century literature during the 1830s. The importance to him of this nearer tradition was less in specific personal discoveries and influences than in the philosophy or overall perspective on life it offered. In the absence of fully developed formal disciplines in psychology, political theory, economics, or sociology, the persistent curiosity of eighteenth-century writers and philosophers about the nature of man and society encouraged an intelligent and reasonable outlook on immediate human and social reality. Although Browning had been influenced for a while by the more abstract, radically critical conceptions of Voltaire or Shelley, his reading in English writers of the eighteenth century gave him fundamentally a commonsense approach to man's ordinary nature and to social reality.

It was especially the prose writers rather than the poets of the period on whom Browning appears to have concentrated. In the 1830s his father fed his slightly wayward son solid works like Locke's *Essay on the Human Understanding* or Bolingbroke's *Letters on the Spirit of Patriotism*.[128] Even when Browning read the poetry it was, to judge from the few references he makes in his early years, the least poetical of all poets of the age of prose, the scurrilous satirist and burlesquer, Samuel Butler, whom he picked up.[129] If Browning's deepest sympathies and respect went out to the moral independence and religious vision of the greatest poet of the Puritans, another part of him could join with Butler's practical and social perspective on the absurdities of the Presbyterian knight-errant Hudibras and his argumentative Independent squire Ralpho. Where Milton aspired to describe a total moral and religious universe unknown to ordinary experience, Butler was content to establish a reasonable point of view upon the common reality before him. Similarly, where the wit of a Renaissance poet like Donne was a subtle instrument that devised complex paradoxical unities, Butler's wit was a bludgeon to beat the absurdities out of his opponents and demonstrate brutally the contrast between high talk and low reality. In Butler, as in Donne, Browning could find food for his own delight in casuistry, but Butler's object in spinning long discourses and theological arguments for his characters was to ridicule, not to persuade and astound. As in Browning's monologue "Johannes Agricola in Meditation," where we join the author in enjoying the full ingenuous absurdity of the speaker, the protagonists in *Hudibras* were given leisure (modern readers would say, too much leisure) to string themselves up by their own pedantry and illogicality. In Butler there was always the implied test of abstract argument against concrete, ordinary reality. At the end of a long harangue by Hudibras that brings the first canto to a climax, Butler drops us and his mock hero back heavily to earth: the foolishly resounding speech receives answer in kind in a "blast of Wind" from the leader's horse. Butler prefers even a sordid reality to the gaseous nullity of words without reality.

It is not clear exactly when Browning read *Hudibras,* though he knew it by 1835. In his general reaction against Shelleyan, millennial thinking and against the abstractions of The London University, Butler's skeptical, realistic vision would have probably seemed a more than usually attractive alternative. As he worked back toward a sense of the real world left behind in his speculations, he may even in the early 1830s have taken a passing interest in the practical observations of another arrant realist, that Mr. Worldly-Wiseman of letters, Lord Chesterfield, whom he certainly read. In his limited outlook onto the world of society and government, he at least, like a lesser Machiavelli, told his son and his readers not what men should be but what they were. Browning was turning away from the kinds of public ambitions that Chesterfield had for his son. In order to understand the realities of society he was, however, not above inquiring into the ways of the world and informing himself about the common politic arts.

He found an even clearer alternative to his earlier way of thinking in the 1714 work of the Anglicized Dutchman, Bernard de Mandeville, *The Fable of the Bees,* which was given to him by his father on February 1, 1833, shortly after he had completed *Pauline.*[130] Whether or not his father intended it as a contribution to Browning's resolve, in the poem, to turn back to real life from his millennial ideals, it was certainly an ideal choice. Mandeville, a physician with a sharp, rather annoying independence of mind, had ventured to write a poem, "The Grumbling Hive," giving his waspish views on society under the transparent allegory of a beehive. To push and to amplify this rather pedestrian piece of doggerel he then proceeded to surround it in successive editions with an ever growing mass of brilliant and paradoxical prose explication that was really a series of essays on the nature

of man and society. Browning's love for wit was stimulated by the brightness and boldness of the paradoxes and ironic thrusts in a work purporting,
as its subtitle proclaimed, to establish the shocking maxim, *Private Vices,
Publick Benefits.* Without much concern for philosophical consistency or
overall logic, Mandeville, in his various prefaces, introductions, inquiries,
remarks, and dialogues, delighted in a series of ad hoc arguments establishing in different ways his central and in fact quite ambiguous paradox. More
than even Donne or Butler, Mandeville was, for Browning, the model ar-
guer, the great example of a maker of cases and virtuoso special pleader.
Long before Browning tried out, as Professor Smalley has shown, the
method of advocacy logic in the so-called "Essay on Chatterton," he found
the art of deliberate case-making finely and consciously developed in Mandeville.[131] In a letter of March 1833 thanking W. J. Fox for helping him with
a notice of *Pauline,* he even speaks of a " 'case' which leaves my fine fellow
Mandeville at a dead lock," that is, Fox's unprecedentedly selfless kindness.[132] Two years later, in that short-lived periodical *The Trifler,* published
by Browning's friends in the set, he was himself trying the same kind of
paradoxical prose case-making, as he took for his subject the Mandevillean
(and Keynesian) premise that debt is better than liquidity and proceeded to
use Mandeville's favorite device of confusing abstract and specific meanings of a word, in this case, moral debt and cash debt. He even acknowledges "the subtle Mandeville" in the essay as a forerunner in the casuistic
subject at hand and appeals to him as an authority on the problem of moral
debt.[133]

What especially would recommend Mandeville as a model of a "fine
fellow" to the young, independent scholar was the provoking boldness of
his examples, annoying enough in his own day to drive Augustan society to
minor repressive action, and perhaps even more stinging in pre-Victorian
times. Not only did he treat Church and other public institutions with a
cold and inquiring intellectual curiosity, but he even subjected those more
established informal institutions, manners, female chastity, and decency, to
unembarrassed and penetrating scrutiny. That a chaste female would blush
at indecent observations made in her presence that she would hear whitely
and willingly if she were hidden in the next room was the kind of disturbing
truth that Mandeville kept uncovering in his cases. Mandeville's society was
shocked at such lucidity of perception; but the young Browning had found a
kindred spirit, now not an idealist and millenarian who looked beyond society and the present condition of man, but a realist who could see through
and into them. Probably at this time Browning scribbled an entirely sympathetic allusion to the *Bacchae* of Euripides on the title page of his *Fable:*
"The fool will consider the words of a wise man absurd."[134]

Mandeville's doctrine, that personal qualities generally and perhaps
rightly condemned by moralists in the individual—prodigality for instance
—were nonetheless essential to the general well-being of society, seemed to
the aged Browning when he wrote the *Parleyings* to chime with one of his

own favorite ideas: that moral evil must be accepted as a condition to the attainment of moral good. However, it was not the possibility of drawing this different, if analogous moral argument from Mandeville's social and economic views which attracted Browning in 1833.[135] The letter to Fox mentioning Mandeville in fact emphasized the essential quality of Mandeville's work, its realistic, even skeptical view of mankind. Mandeville might be at a deadlock before Fox's act of kindness, but before the run of mankind his skepticism seemed all too justified. Mandeville did not convert Browning to a merely pessimistic view of human nature, but, in the particular circumstances of Browning's own intellectual growth, his skepticism provided a healthy antidote to Browning's feeling of disillusionment with ideal hopes for human nature. Beneath the irony and *épate* of Mandeville's wit Browning could sense a positive spirit of "bright humour and sound practical sense" whose real aim was not to disparage man but to cut through unrealistically elevating or denigrating views of man to a just appraisal of his nature.[136] If he missed the possible heights that Smart or Milton attained or the subtle complexities possible to Donne, he at least saw average man steadily and whole. To Browning he was, as he dignifies the physician in the *Parleyings,* a "sage," a man who surveyed the human scene with "homely wisdom, healthy wit." Like that of the twentieth-century sage Freud, Mandeville's wisdom was primarily a result of his clear focus on men's motivations rather than on their rationalizations for what they do, or really, on the contrast between the two. As a physician, Mandeville had himself written on insanity and the abnormal passions that disturb mankind. His more general view in the *Fable* stressed that man's passions, his bodily needs and his unending quest for self-esteem, could neither be slighted by society nor ignored by moralists and students of mankind. Society for Mandeville was indeed, as it essentially was for Freud, a large instrument for flattering or sublimating man's basic passions into generally productive forms; but it could not exist without the motivation from those passions.

The effect of this doctrine on a thorough student could be, as it was for Browning, a guarded optimism. If man was no better a creature than, underneath, most of us always suspected, he was at least no worse. His worst qualities were on the whole necessary ones. Evils over which moralists or puritan zealots grew hysterical might be turned by proper understanding to the general good; despite all its imperfections, the world could seem reasonable, if not ideal. Rather than teaching a general misanthropy, Mandeville actually inculcated a tolerant and social attitude. His preferred companion for conversation, as he describes him in the *Fable,* is a man educated in much the way Browning was being educated: Latin, Greek, modern languages, some science and history, but also training in music and art, dancing, fencing, and riding, and experience from travel. The educated gentleman, Mandeville insists, should not be overstrict in denying himself normal pleasures. Above all, he should not stop his education after school; he should be a person who "still improves himself and sees the world till he is thirty" at least. Here was confirmation of the path Browning had chosen for himself, scholarship and study of man that led to further development of himself and an ever broadening awareness of his fellow men and society.

Mandeville, of course, was just one of many influences on Browning's thinking as the young man followed his own direction in his continuing education. In Adam Smith, or in his ideas received at second hand, he may have found similar and perhaps too optimistic views of the larger order that lies behind the apparent confusion of society. In the course of his reading Browning probably found much of the same focus on man as the proper study of mankind in Pope, or more complexly in Swift or Samuel Johnson. Browning shows an early familiarity with *Gulliver's Travels* by an allusion to the "Voyage to Lilliput" in the *Trifler* article of 1835.[137] Although there are few specific allusions to either Pope or Johnson, the impression remains that they were quite well known to Browning, as they almost certainly were to his father.[138] But the particular influence of Mandeville, coming at the time when Browning was anxious to turn from abstractions to look on "real life," is indicative of what he found generally in the practical focus of the eighteenth century on man and society. Here again, Browning was acquiring a tradition, this time more a tradition of ideas and attitudes than one of expression and sensibility, without necessarily confining himself within the original limits of the tradition. The ideas of Mandeville and thinkers like him would be of enormous use to Browning in some of his finest poems, not only in studies of the pathology of the passions such as "Porphyria's Lover" (1836) but also in more subtle characterizations of motivation. The envious brother of the "Soliloquy of the Spanish Cloister" (1842) is an admirable application of Mandeville's insight into the predominance of the passion of envy and a finely ironic analysis, à la Mandeville, of the process of rationalization by which men attempt to whitewash their lower motives. The famous "Caliban upon Setebos" seems an ideal illustration of Mandeville's theory that primitive man's thinking is a projection outward of inner states of emotion, especially fear.[139] Yet while relying on ideas like Mandeville's for insight into his characters, Browning never allowed himself to accept Mandeville's rather low expectations of what man could be. If an opponent of Mandeville's such as Shaftesbury might be wrong in holding up a too lofty ideal for most men, he might be rightly describing the possible attainments of some men. The power of the one great poem of Mandeville's unreasonable contemporary, Smart, or the higher reaches of man's spirit manifest in the works of earlier literature or in the romantic overthrowers of the eighteenth century, reminded Browning of the things that were not conceived of in Mandeville's philosophy. If he would not inscribe himself as a disciple of Mandeville and other similar reasonable men of the eighteenth century, Browning could certainly be their diligent student. And, like Matthew Arnold, he would continue to find the century and its tradition of thought an indispensable background to his own thinking.

There were, of course, many other specific works that Browning found of special interest in his course of reading. He continued to broaden the solid base that his family circumstances had given him in musical history and the history of the fine arts. He also continued to read the modern authors, the Romantics whom he had begun to know in boyhood and adolescence, a reading that expanded in the 1830s into a full awareness of contemporary literature. But even this look at merely some of the past authors with whom he seems to have found a particular affinity, either because of their style and outlook or because of their opinions and ideas, suggests the quality of Browning's education after The London University. The extent of his accomplishment in languages and the breadth of his reading in the literature, general history, and philosophy of his own and other Western traditions are obvious and impressive. Equally, his deeper response to certain writers or traditions shows him continually working in his acquisition of knowledge to turn the usable past into a personal possession. Writers and their works existed for him in a historical past context that was valuable and interesting in itself. But they also transmitted attitudes or forms of expression that might come alive again in a different context for the modern reader. Education was, in this sense, a form of parleying or grappling with the past in order to seize its value in the present. As he gained a fuller appreciation of man's past, Browning was also making himself, expanding his ideas and his range of expression, finding and shaping the traditions in which he worked.

XIV
A Poet's Education:
Limits and Promise

Although Browning's reading seemed, in the 1830s especially, to follow a deliberate course of education, filling in gaps in general knowledge and developing his mind, the process was, of course, an unending one. He would continue all his life to expand and deepen his awareness of man's past, and he would continue to make from his particular interests bridges by which he could connect the past to the present and participate in traditions he had renewed for himself. What such an open and expanding process of education did not and could not lead to was the increasing coherence and unified way of thinking of a mind devoted to one discipline of thought, whether science, medicine, law, or a particular field of scholarship. Each of those disciplines accepts a particular tradition, a specific way of thinking and reacting to new information, and builds within its framework. Even a thinker like Browning's contemporary, John Stuart Mill, who spent much of his life expanding the limits of his own Utilitarian heritage, did so by attempting to translate concerns left out of his tradition by his predecessors into the language of his tradition, in the process enriching the language but not abandoning it. By contrast, Browning was forced to live with the incoherence and shifting viewpoints of the generalist. Despite the professional manner in which he set about his education, the process was finally bound to seem somewhat unprofessional and erratic. At best, he was making a series of amateur raids, no matter how orderly, upon the infinite body of general literature and knowledge, and his understanding would never attain more order and precision than the ordinary common language in which it would have to be expressed. At most he could hope to integrate as much of his learning as possible into his own personality and his own personal vision of the world. To a thinker or philosopher who accepts a specific intellectual framework for integrating all experience, a generalist such as Browning must always appear, as he would in retrospect to the philosopher George Santayana, a barbarian of knowledge—a bear, even a deliberate and self-possessed bear, foraging aimlessly for honey in a great forest. Yet, if Browning's kind of education led on only to more education, not to a settled system of thought or to a set of definite theories, it was perhaps the necessary education for a modern writer who would take human life as a whole and not some small corner of our existence as his subject.

A necessary liability, however, is not an excuse. Having said so much about the strengths of Browning's education, it is worth asking how well Browning was able to guard against the dangers of imbalance and dilettante superficiality consequent to any such general education? The answer is that Browning's education was both thorough and, following the limitations of such an enterprise, exceptionally full and comprehensive in the areas on which it focused. Although he was not trained as a critic or literary historian, he received and went on to give himself a very thorough fundamental understanding of Western man's literary history and generally of the history of his creative spirit. At the same time, his focus upon literature in the widest sense—as creative achievement, philosophy, and a part of cultural and social history—made his literary study a training in the humanities as a whole rather than merely in belles lettres. The weaknesses in Browning's education were not those of superficiality or dilettante failure of concentration in what he did study. Rather they occurred in the important areas of knowledge that he did not sufficiently survey or comprehend even in a general way. These were especially the sciences and, though only initially, history.

1 Science: The Failure to Connect

The problem of the sciences was not Browning's alone. It was a problem that seems to have been built into the kind of education that was emerging from dissatisfaction with the classical system and that was probably intrinsic to the new sciences that were just arriving. In Browning's time a few self-styled progressive middle-class schools placed their emphasis solely upon scientific training and scientific thinking, rather than upon an expanded program of modern languages and literature. But the effect of such premature attempts to extend the viewpoint and disciplines of the emerging physical sciences to the entire program of education was, as Browning seems to have sensed at London, a foreshortening and truncating of man's understanding of his own nature and of the nature of his society. Wholesale application of the science of some parts of nature to the different nature of man could only lead to the pedantic pseudoscience of hard facts that Dickens found so easy to satirize in *Hard Times*. The undecided question as to the place of science in ordinary education (not a debate on the significance of science itself, which has become increasingly obvious and uncontested) has raised continuing controversy, from the disagreements between Thomas Huxley and Matthew Arnold later in the nineteenth century to their echo in

C. P. Snow and F. R. Leavis in the twentieth. Granting with the critics of scientific education that science cannot simply be made the center of ordinary education, the practical question still is, as it was in Browning's own education, how the nonscientist can attain scientific knowledge and scientific thinking sufficient to deal with the reality of science in modern life without actually undergoing the training of a scientist.

Browning's solution, like that of most nonscientists, was a mediocre one: to learn about science, to learn how to talk about it, without actually learning to follow the process of thought in particular sciences. There is no indication that Ready provided any kind of scientific training at his school. Nor is there reason to believe that the young university student who was repelled by his preprofessional fellow students ever joined the future scientists at their lectures. This is not to say that he was indifferent or hostile to the idea of studying the physical world in itself. Medical lectures at Guy's Hospital were a great attraction as long as there was no question of his becoming a doctor himself. The enthusiast for nature, especially for nature not as a general conception but as a world full of strange and interesting creatures, had a deep curiosity about zoology and biology. Similarly, the young enthusiast for Shelley, admirer of Bacon, and believer in the regeneration of the world would never really loose his first faith in the progress of mind triumphing over nature. If much of *Paracelsus* was devoted to showing the need for a human as well as theoretical focus in the pursuit of knowledge, it was still a work whose hero is an early precursor of medical science. Paracelsus himself is made into far more—and perhaps also something less —than an early scientist; but the entire work presumes that we should join with him in contemning the medical ignorance of his age and that we should think of our own times as, by contrast, scientifically enlightened.

The limits of Browning's education in science are most obvious, however, in his inability to provide meaningful bridges between his general faith in the progressive development of science and his enthusiasm for specific facts or practices, that is, in his failure to understand scientific thinking. In *Paracelsus* he talks about the progress of the scientific mind but gives us no specific idea of what, if anything (except for the dubious benefit of laudanum), Paracelsus himself contributed to the emergence of modern medical thinking. It is the general theory of knowledge and life that Browning gives him, not his scientific hypotheses, that are to be taken seriously. Similarly, Browning was aware of the great enterprise of chemistry in France since the work of Lavoisier, but when he alluded to it in a letter to Elizabeth, he singled out not the theoretical advance but only what struck the wonder of the nonscientific mind, the technical accuracy of the methods: "the fine French Chemical Analysts bring themselves to appreciate matter in its refined stages by *millionths*."[1] This is as much a philistine view of science as admiration for the length of a poem or the number of rhymes it contains is of art.

The physician and earnest member of the Browning Society, Edward Berdoe, has alone claimed for Browning the status of a scientific poet and asserted that "in him . . . the poetic and scientific methods . . . are truly combined."[2] Bernard Shaw, who assumed the role of devil's advocate before the society, was closer to the truth when he pointed out that "though he had hitherto regarded himself as an arrant sciolist in scientific matters, he had picked up in the course of his general reading all the knowledge . . . which Dr. Berdoe had praised Browning so highly for possessing."[3] Browning had the interest in science of the dilettante general reader, but his education did not give him the tools and curiosity to penetrate the surface of scientific advances and meditate upon the deeper implications of nineteenth-century science for man's vision of himself.

The limitations of this part of his education are nowhere more clear than in his odd relation to the most significant scientific advance of the century, the expanding vision of geology and biology that led finally to Darwin's *On the Origin of Species* in 1859.[4] Tennyson sensed the beginnings of this new view of man's origin and explored its deeper implications even before Darwin's theory was fully developed. Other writers ignored the issue entirely. Browning's position was anomalous. One of the earliest enthusiastic prophets of evolution, he remained until the end of his life ignorant of the essentials of Darwin's theoretical revolution. Berdoe, defining "the scientific habit of mind" as a purely empirical interest in detail, exclaims of Browning: "What a scientist he would have made!" And he certainly shared Darwin's enthusiasm for prying into the remotest details of natural life. One diligent student has even found that Browning, if ornithological competence is any test, exceeded even Tennyson in prowess as a naturalist, boasting seventy-two distinct species of birds in his poetry to Tennyson's paltry sixty.[5] More than most poets and even long after *Pauline,* he delighted in accurate description of nature, as if he naturally had some of Darwin's own passion for empirical accuracy.

The enthusiasm that he felt for the details of external nature led him, in the culminating, deathbed speech of Paracelsus, to give his hero a visionary statement of evolutionary faith. In this vision of past and future, creation proceeds to ever higher aims spurred on by the infusing love of the Creator for the joy and vitality of his universe. The implication of the passage is that man is a higher development of the animals, fulfilling in his consciousness their lesser qualities. At the same time, as in the far more tortured and thoughtful meditations of Tennyson on evolutionary development in *In Memoriam,* the entire process is understood in the light of an ethical and religious faith that evolution is truly progress. From the power of "young volcanos" and "savage creatures" seeking "Their loves in wood and plain" up to the Hallam-like ideal man of the future, God is present as an incessant force in the evolution, perhaps even performing a continuous act of creation over time: an idea Browning would later play with in the drama *Luria* (1846).

Browning could have found or heard about the idea of a meaningful, directed evolution in the scientific theory of the French biologist Lamarck (1744-1829), who suggested that animals' changes in response to their environment were inherited by their offspring in an endless process of refinement and improvement. He might have found a similarly optimistic and teleological idea of evolution more rhetorically expounded in Goethe's poems on the metamorphoses of plants and animals (1790 and 1806) or in the forsaken garden of literary biology of Darwin's grandfather, Erasmus Darwin (1731-1802), author of *The Botanic Garden* and the prose *Zoonomia, or the Laws of Organic Life.*[6] But the passage in *Paracelsus* seems more a sudden inspiration on Browning's part, perhaps a sudden realization for himself of a general idea that was very much in the air, than a versification of a scientific theory. Between the facts—the vivid perception of the variety and vitality of natural phenomena—and the general metaphysical master idea of evolution there is nothing but the sudden spark of faith. There is, indeed, no science at all. Nor, though there are indications in the passage that Browning was aware of current geological ideas of cataclysmic change, is there any sense of science as an ongoing enterprise building on specific previous work. Browning's favorite textbooks in biology are the Roman compilations of curious and often highly dubious animal lore of Pliny the Elder and Aelian, fine sources for poetic fancies but hardly suitable for Berdoe's "scientific poet."[7]

After the publication of Darwin's theory of natural selection Browning was to develop gradually from an early prophet of evolution to a fairly direct opponent of the theory insomuch as it threatened to provoke a total reassessment of traditional views of man and religion.[8] Although his sympathy with science thus became increasingly more strained, his position was still not one of hostility to science itself. He argued merely that scientific theories dealing with natural phenomena give us no evidence, one way or the other, about the original creation of the universe or about the spiritual destiny of man. But his assertion that he was never against Darwin—"all that seems *proved* in Darwin's scheme was a conception familiar to me from the beginning"—only against Darwin's "philosophy," hardly confronts the primary ethical problem that Darwin's theory posed to his contemporaries.[9] What Darwin had uncovered was not the idea of evolution as a philosophical conception but the brutal mechanism, survival of the fittest, by which organic nature was ordered. Unlike the younger poets of the later nineteenth century, such as Thomas Hardy, Browning was unable to respond to the ultimate challenge of natural selection to his breed of Mandevillean optimism because he seems never to have really comprehended Darwin's central conception. In the 1880s he still speaks of changes brought about by "desire and will in the creature" as if Darwin had merely provided new evidence for Lamarck's older theory of the inheritance of acquired characteristics.[10] Small wonder that he felt he had anticipated Darwin since he turned Darwin into only a more thorough fact collector and less competent metaphysician than the poet: "Whatever his merits as an investigator," he is reported to have said of Darwin, "his philosophy is of little or no importance."[11]

Browning's on-again, off-again affair with evolution is symptomatic of the limitations that his education, like that of most nonscientists since, imposed on him. To Berdoe's flattery he responded modestly and honestly: "You so generously estimate my attempts to make use of the few materials of a scientific nature I have had any opportunity of collecting: would they were of more importance:—but my gratitude to whoever takes the will for the deed is all the greater."[12] Because of the failure of his education to match his will to acknowledge and evaluate science, Browning's lifetime response as a poet to one of the primary forces of his age was little more than he thus claimed. He collected materials, observations on the refraction of light in a prism, images of geological change, details of the apparatus of a chemical laboratory, fragments from the language of mesmerism or archaeology, and, as poets have done in every age, he put them to his own use: made them serve his aims of communication. To say that Browning was a scientific poet because of this activity is merely to say that he was and is a modern poet, that he appropriated the common language and popular ideas of his day. In this sense we have had many scientific poets. In fact, as scientific ideas and practices become increasingly a part of common life, we have nothing but scientific poets. However, if Browning was one of the earlier poets to insist upon expressing not merely a poetic sensibility but the full range of speaking and thinking of his age, he was not equipped to be a poet like his peer Tennyson who spoke authoritatively to the problems raised by the advance of scientific theory and the vision of man and the universe that it was developing.

In his younger years, when a science like biology was still primarily a heterogeneous mixture of classification and muddled metaphysics and theology, the lack of scientific training was less of a liability. Browning could respond to the general problem of matching intellectual advance with emotional and spiritual advance without any very clear vision of what the intellectual advance actually was. In his later years, however, the weakness of his education would become an increasingly severe limitation in his poetry, especially since he would insist upon dealing with man's condition in the most general terms. His pronouncements on matters such as evolution or the condition of faith would take on a note of hollow assurance from his failure to comprehend fully what really were the grounds for the doubts and concern of the younger generation that was growing up in the Darwinian world. By not sufficiently understanding the ways in which scientific advance and discoveries had themselves led to a qualification of the earlier nineteenth-century optimism about the advance of mind and knowledge, Browning would be increasingly cut off from the intellectual life of the later nineteenth century. Even worse, he would be cut off from one kind of self-knowledge, unable to understand the reasons for the disparity between his consciously professed faith in progress and the increasingly gloomy vision projected into many of his later works. Because his ideas of the progress of science and mind stemmed largely from the general philosophical faith of the Enlightenment rather than from any real understanding of science, they were not much subject to growth with experience. It was again Tennyson, not Browning, who was capable of the public reexamination of his earlier faith in progress in the splendidly self-conscious "Locksley Hall Sixty Years After."

Along with this weakness in the physical sciences, Browning's education was scanty in most other areas of conceptual or scientific thinking. Just as he had little theoretical comprehension of the physical sciences, he seems to have had, from the paucity of references to them, little distinct understanding of the near-sciences of human and social behavior that were beginning in the nineteenth century. He was close to practical economics and banking through the family profession, but he showed no interest in the new theoretical approach to political economy of Malthus and Ricardo. From references in letters to Monclar we know that he at least knew Bentham's work.[13] Yet he clearly took little interest in those first attempts to create a science of laws and society and perhaps saw Bentham himself in much the same light as his father saw phrenologists. Nor is there any indication that he took much interest in the practical schemes for a utopian society proposed by Robert Owen and Charles Fourier, or in the well-organized Saint-Simonian brotherhood that had so interested John Stuart Mill and Carlyle during the 1830s. "Fourier's scheme" is mentioned in *Christmas-Eve and Easter-Day* (1850) only to be labeled as a "mere" theory to be toyed with in thought. Here again, as in his reaction to The London University, Browning seemed instinctively to shy away from disciplines that threatened to reduce the complexity of life to simplified and often dehumanizing schematic representations. But once again, as with the sciences, his failure to explore the theoretical conceptions of social thinkers would leave him, even where his intuitive sympathies might be on the side of the angels, increasingly unable to confront, in depth and on its own grounds, one important community of the developing thought of his age.

Readers of the more muddled arguments of some of Browning's longer and less successful monologues complain, as well, of his lack of formal training in mathematics and logic.[14] The logic of this, however, is itself suspect. Given Browning's love of casuistry and mis-argument, more formal training in logic might only have added fuel to the fire of his deviousness. Certainly, though Browning had enough mathematics to keep his scrupulous financial accounts, he had as little higher mathematics as most gentlemen of his day, indeed probably even less. The loss for him, as it still is for most nonscientists today, was in not having the basic tool for theoretical and conceptual thinking. Without mathematical training, he would be discouraged from looking into any specialized discipline, from physics to economics, which used mathematical analogues. Although most disciplines were still far from the wholesale use of mathematical language of twentieth-century science, the lack of mathematics still tended to cut Browning off from an entire way of thinking, even—as it began to appear with the publication of *Alice in Wonderland*—a new way of talking about life in literature.

Beneath Browning's general agreement with the earlier Victorian faith in the advance of mind one may even suspect a hostility or, at least, indifference to scientific enterprise. To the extent that he could see the quest for knowledge, as he does in *Paracelsus,* as a part of the larger human desire for self-knowledge and a fuller life for all, it commanded his enthusiasm. But he had already turned away from the more arid, practical scientific spirit—increasingly specialized and divorced from other aspects of life—as he found it at The London University. As we have seen, the message of *Paracelsus* was as much the danger of knowledge by itself as faith in evolutionary advance. Perhaps his uneasiness about science was even reflected in his unwillingness after *Paracelsus* to write about scientists. We have in the monologues artists, lawyers, musicians, poets, priests, grammarians, indeed virtually all the professions except scientists. Karshish the physician, "picker-up of learning's crumbs," is a student of all things, far from a modern scientific researcher and sympathetic because of his general interest in philosophy and religion. When the speaker of "A Toccata of Galuppi's" (1855) confesses to an interest in modern science—"physics, something of geology, / Mathematics"—we can't help observing his gloomy distance from life, his wistful yearning for the light gaiety and splendor of the dead Venice that Galuppi's old music brings to his mind as he plays it. And we can hardly miss the contrast between his emotional response to the past—"Dear dead women, with such hair, too"—and his hollow "triumph o'er a secret wrung from nature's close reserve" in the scientific present. Unless it could keep its attention focused on the general aspects of man and nature—a condition harder and harder for modern science to meet—science almost seemed to Browning another form of pedantry, a contrived escape from life. What he didn't appreciate adequately was the extent to which the pedantry, the specialization of the scientist, could ultimately work enormous changes in man's world and his view of himself.

2 History: Prelude

If Browning was thus in his education moving away from serious intellectual engagement with one major thread of modern thought, he was as clearly moving toward involvement with another, history. However, his journey to a sophisticated view of history was to be a slow one over many years. His turn in his reading away from visionary systems and projections of his imagination into the future and toward the reality of man's past achievements had been essentially a turn toward historical knowledge. His education after London seems almost a saturation of his mind in the past. His reading in the *Biographie Universelle,* in miscellanies of anecdotes, or in out-of-the-way narratives and firsthand accounts brought him into direct contact with the crude but essential stuff of history, the myriad grains of sand of individual lives, each with its own vitality and its own special sense of being alive, that make up history. If history is, from one view, the essence of innumerable biographies, Browning was beginning to get some sense of history through his casual reading merely by developing a feeling for the variety and complexity of past lives and ways of living. Moreover, through deeper focus on important individuals, especially writers and artists, and through wide and varied reading in original works from one period of history such as the English Renaissance, he was attaining an intuitive feel for the social, cultural, and intellectual differences between his own time and past periods.

While he was building up in all his reading an increasingly solid sense of the past, Browning was also, from the evidence we have, taking up the family penchant for amateur history. Indeed, with the example of Uncle William's work on the *History of the Huguenots* and his father's ceaseless, if less fruitbearing, research, it is hard to imagine how he would not have also developed some sense of himself as an amateur historian. As early as *Paracelsus* he pretended to the role of factual historian as well as fictionalizing poet. While the poet mixed imaginary and factual events to develop his personal ideas through the character of Paracelsus, the research student appeared pompously at the end to establish the historical credibility of the story.[15] "The liberties I have taken with my subject are very trifling," he proclaimed at the beginning of the notes, "and the reader may slip the foregoing scenes between the leaves of any memoir of Paracelsus he pleases, by way of commentary." The gesture and tone are those of Uncle William justifying his *contes* as true history. Although the subsequent fourteen pages of notes demonstrated that Browning had indeed done a good deal of reading in historical accounts of Paracelsus, they hardly served to turn his would-be poetic gold into the weightier stuff of history, and they did reveal that Browning's approach was strictly amateur. Like anyone who wades into the great ocean of history without much training or much forethought about historical problems, Browning merely got up this one subject—reading everything about Paracelsus that he could get his hands on—without obtaining any fuller perspective upon Paracelsus' age or his larger historical position.

Such pedantry—another example, in fact, of the tendency to overcaution and scholarly defensiveness that he showed in his forays into Greek subjects—has contributed to the impression that Browning had only a meager, desultory education. It appears to be, again, the pedantry of the self-educated or partly educated who cannot get a perspective on the woods because they have not yet learned what to look for in scanning individual trees. But though such educational limitations continued all his life to qualify Browning's forays into Greek philology or his few ventures into the sciences, he was, in his serious historical education, merely making a poor beginning when he wrote *Paracelsus*. In effect, he was forced to commence at the level of his most influential teacher. With no direct exposure to history either in school or at The London University, he naturally began with his father's way of viewing history. This, it should be clear, was essentially the perspective not of the historian but of the amateur antiquary, of a man who had spent his life ferreting out bits of information eclectically from the endless mass of documents and sources. Indeed, Browning's father had even less overall method than the usual antiquary, for in his enthusiasm he took all of history as his special province. If his encyclopedic range of curiosity was instrumental in interesting Browning as a boy in many areas of history and in imparting his enthusiasm to him, the father's example also threatened to lead him, as a grown man, into a bog of aimless scholarship and undirected curiosity. Not untypical was the father's interest in every detail and every opinion relating to the controversy over the Junius *Letters*. The long-smoldering question of the authorship of these scandal-provoking letters, which the spilling of much ink had not at all served to put out, was indeed just the kind of issue that could capture the antiquarian imagination of Browning's father permanently.[16] Browning was early introduced to the mystery of this curiosity of eighteenth-century history, probably even in the 1820s.[17] But he was not destined, like his father, to remain in the chamber of historical maiden-thought forever, and he would ultimately come to see the larger irrelevance of such historical buffmanship. By the time of the correspondence with Elizabeth, the question had clearly come to seem merely one of his father's crotchets. One day Browning had to write a hurried apology to her for not responding to an earlier letter she had sent, inside yet another book on the Junius question. After expressing all regrets, he then frankly admitted that it might have been a long time before he had found the letter in the volume: "My own Ba is entreated to observe, that when she sends me reviews about herself, and songs by herself; and a make-weight book about 'Junius' happens to be sent also . . I do not ordinarily plunge into the Junius-discussion at once—perhaps from having made up my mind that the Author is Miss Campbell!"[18] Though for all Browning cared the author might as well have been the Miss Campbell whom a foolish rumor had it he was about to marry, fortunately the elder Browning still cared. It was he, poking into the book with the "lucky inspiration of curiosity," and not Browning, who had found the letter!

Browning's later experience would lead him similarly to develop beyond the limitations of his father's conceptual views of history. He might read with interest a book like Sir Walter Raleigh's *History of the World* (which his father gave to him),[19] that outdated if fascinating work of universal history beginning with a retelling of the Bible. But he would increasingly break away from the kind of literal-minded research and curiosity without perspective that led his father, in the nineteenth century, to devote much of his time to the Nomenclator, his elaborate genealogy of biblical families. When Browning later turned back to biblical events in his poetry, as in "Saul" (1845; 1855) or "A Death in the Desert" (1864), it would be to reimagine and revive the milieu and spirit of the time, not to display his scholarship in minutiae of biblical history.

The process was one of slow maturation of interest in the past, not of any sudden insight that took him beyond his father's attitude toward history. Indeed, Browning's finest work in bringing alive in his poetry the rich texture of the mind and culture of a past time seems a natural outgrowth of his father's simpler but exceptionally strong historical curiosity. One of his father's cartoon series speaks admiringly of Scott's novels, especially *The Heart of Midlothian,*[20] and it may well be that the father could point out to his son in another writer what he himself could not fully achieve: a vivid reconstruction of a past era. Scott's revolutionary use of the novel as a vehicle for reviving the complexity of past life in the mind of the present certainly came to represent a natural model for the development of historical thinking in the Browning family. No doubt swayed by admiration for both Scott's genius and his extraordinary success, Uncle William, as we have seen, followed his rather dry historical study of the Huguenots with more lively imitations of Scott's historical novels.[21] His long flirtation with the literary uses of history also led him to make an unsuccessful bid for popularity in a series of shorter historical tales published in his *Leisure Hours.*[22] Unlike his nephew, he wrote no historical dramas. But he was sufficiently interested in the subject to write a critical essay "On the Earl of Essex as Dramatised by Various Authors."[23] With such a vital concern with history before him, it was thus only natural that Browning too should gradually move away from mere antiquarian research to develop in his plays and poetry a living vision of the past parallel to Scott's (and his own favorite Hugo's) achievement in the novel.[24] William's perplexities in his enthusiasm for history in literature also suggest, however, the kinds of problems his nephew would have to face. Like Bulwer-Lytton and others who followed in the wake of Scott's success without Scott's central idea of the imaginative creation of a total past culture and way of life, William seemed finally unsure what it was he wanted to imitate in Scott. His essay "Hints for Novel Writers" takes an antiquary's pedantic pleasure in scoffing at Scott's glaring historical errors—as if literal accuracy were the measure of Scott's ability to bring another age to life. Yet he can't deny Scott's greatness: "The charms he has thrown around our legendary history, have awakened a feeling of inquiry, which has led to rich discoveries in our annals."[25] He feels the importance of Scott, but he can't quite see what it is. And so in his own attempts, as in those of a better writer such as Lytton, he tends to reduce the literature of history to accurate factual detail and fanciful romance plots. What gets lost is just what his nephew would have to learn to recover: the ability to bring alive through history an entire different world as a theater for the study of human nature.

Browning's full development as a poet of history could not, however, emerge merely from his first attempts at self-education. Rather, he would learn to incorporate an historical perspective in his works through confronting again and again in efforts such as *Strafford* (1837), *Sordello* (1840), *The Return of the Druses* (1843), or the early dramatic monologues set in the past the problem of historical context. Ultimately he would go further in history than he would in science because he would keep forcing himself to deal with historical problems directly in his works. Perhaps even more important, he would have the good fortune in the late 1830s and 1840s to complicate his understanding of history by coming to know personally and even, to some extent, by working with two practicing historians: one a very competent researcher and biographer, John Forster, and the other, one of the two greatest historians of his age, Thomas Carlyle.

With history, Browning's education was thus less a preparation before his literary career than a result of his first ten years of work. The story of the growth of his understanding of history and of his ability to recreate a convincing historical past in his poetry consequently belongs with that of his early literary career. As he developed, he would never actually become a historian himself, or even take the attitude toward accuracy in retrieving the past of a professional historian. But he would come to use the perspectives and conceptions of historical thinking as a fundamental, perhaps even the fundamental organizing principle in many of his best poems.[26]

3 *Education: Conclusions*

There were, of course, many other lesser areas of knowledge on which Browning's self-education in the 1830s merely or hardly touched. But the easy snobbery of the institutionally certified against the self-educated should already have enough to feed upon, and what should be emphasized is rather the strength of Browning's training in comparison to that of the usual well-educated person of his day, and perhaps even of our own. Even with his weakness in the entire area of science and conceptual and mathematical disciplines, Browning's education appears remarkably well balanced in comparison to that of many of his contemporaries. In very different ways, it was an education as remarkable and as comprehensive as that famous one that James Mill forced upon his pliable son in his own reaction against the usual education of the day. As with Mill, a new kind of education was really added onto the old rather than merely substituted for it. Browning had as good an education in the classics as university graduates of his time. This was important not only because of its value in itself but because it allowed him to go his own way in the rest of his education without having to spend his life continually justifying the choice he had made. Inasmuch as knowledge of the classics would continue to be the special badge of the educated man for another hundred years, Browning had, at least, not cut himself off from one of the essential qualities of the mind of his time. Even if his own leaning would take him increasingly away from classical standards and models, he would be able to speak on questions of taste and style, as he could not on scientific questions, with the authority of a person who has fully comprehended the alternatives. At base, he had the security of knowing that, with or without a university education and however else he might direct his studies, he had attained the acknowledged credentials for an educated person of his day.

To this usual gentleman's education Browning had added a broad background in European language and literature, wide general reading, and both an extensive and deep knowledge of his own cultural, religious, and literary traditions. His election to the recently formed Institut Historique de Paris (now the Société des Études Historiques) in 1835 as a corresponding member has been seen as merely a courtesy bestowed on him by his highly connected friend Ripert-Monclar, who was himself a member. But if it was no great honor it was at least some indication of Browning's satisfaction with the progress he was making in his self-education. For the section of the large body that he chose to join he was in fact already quite well qualified. This was the third division, Histoire des Langues et des Littératures.[27] Although there is no evidence that he ever took an active part in the work of the Institut, Browning must have felt that his membership, along with French writers such as Lamartine, the critic and scholar J.-J. Ampère, and Eugène Sue, was a strong incentive to further study.[28] He had no reason to blush before the association of his name with theirs, for his knowledge of literary history was already outstanding for his age and not contemptuous by the standards of present doctoral study in comparative literature. More than many modern students he also had an interest in literature in the widest sense, including philosophy and the cultural and social context of literature, as well as in more strictly aesthetic concerns. If his understanding of historical thinking was still somewhat naive, he was at least beginning to work toward a larger sense of the whole life of a period of the past, a life refracted equally in its literature and in the various aspects of its history.

The danger of Browning's kind of education and of his independent course of reading was that it might have made his mind into a useless curiosity shop of odd information. Worse, it might have produced a true pedant, an earnest Mr. Casaubon of letters pretending to seek the key to life by running away from its complexity into an obscure corner of learning. Or, in reaction to his father's dilettante antiquarianism, he might have developed, as indeed he seemed to whenever he took on an academic subject directly, into a truly scholarly and dry-as-dust antiquary. What kept the poet from becoming an epicure of knowledge like his father or merely a thorough grammarian, philologist, or antiquary was a less easily definable, but very important, quality of his education: essentially the relation it bore to other aspects of his life. Although much of his education was the result of lonely self-discipline, it never became an enterprise that had to sever him and alienate him from other men. At times Browning could feel the isolation necessary to a life of long and intensive reading—"the fact is I live by myself," he complained to a friend in a moment of discouragement[29]—but he was far less cut off in his education than he might seem to be. For one thing, his education, no matter how serious, was never a matter of training his mind and filling his memory at the expense of his other faculties. Like many middle- and upper-class Englishmen, Browning and his father accepted and blended together Greek ideas of the harmony of body and mind and English ideas of gentlemanly moderation. Consequently, as we have seen, Browning's intellectual education was combined with training in fencing and boxing, and a good deal of walking, riding, and outdoor exercise. Body was not bruised to pleasure soul; and yet, contrary to the bully public school methods for mass-producing sound minds in sound bodies in the later nineteenth century, in Browning's education soul also was not sacrificed for the good of body. If Browning was being made into a scholar and a gentleman, he was also being given a chance to develop into both a practical and a sensitive person. While he was working at learning six languages and getting lots of physical exercise, he was also developing into a sensitive amateur musician and artist and beginning to acquire the feeling for previous works of music and painting that would lead him to the subjects of many of his best poems.

In another realm he was learning the practical arts of gardening and agriculture and looking with a curious and open eye upon the hundreds of special skills and trades practiced around London and its suburbs. He was picking up the vocabulary of the workaday world of "hods of mortar & heaps of lime, and trembling tubs of size, and those thin broad whitewashing brushes I always had a desire to take up and bespatter with," and getting the feel, if only in imagination, of being part of it.[30] If, even in his plan to look on real life, he could not have firsthand experience of every occupation and way of life, he at least continued to have abundant curiosity and an inquiring eye. Reading and actual experience blended to give him a very wide range of practical knowledge, and practical knowledge, whether of arts or agriculture, kept his reading from leading him away from life and encouraged him to connect past and present, abstract and concrete. It was this spread of knowledge, his ability to relate different areas of learning and practice, that especially impressed Browning's contemporaries. Elizabeth, no doubt a prejudiced witness, testified, "I must tell you, quite startling & humiliating, to observe how you combine such large tracts of experience of outer & inner life, of books & men, of the world & the arts of it; curious knowledge as well as general knowledge . . & deep thinking as well as wide acquisition."[31] But she found a less partial witness, the historian Kinglake, who remarked on the breadth and interconnection of Browning's knowledge after spending a few days with him in a house with a large library. He came away, she reported, " 'quite astounded by the versatility of your learning'—& that, to complete the circle, you discoursed as scientifically on the training of greyhounds & breeding of ducks as if you had never done anything else all your life."[32]

Most important, for all the independence of his education, Browning had frequent opportunity throughout his early years to try his mind against other educated minds and to learn to bring the knowledge he gained in his reading to bear in conversation. Much as he might develop away from him in the course of his education, Browning's father was an ever present and interested listener with whom learning could turn into discussion and living culture. His mother was less well read but would have been interested in talking about poetry and music as well as questions of religion or ethics. His sister shared both his tutor and his enthusiasm for Italian, and, more generally, lived almost too much in the circle of her brother's interests. And beyond the immediate family was the society of his two scholarly uncles, Reuben and William, each with somewhat different intellectual and literary interests. There had been schoolfellows at Ready's with whom to share talk about classes and studies and there was the company of his music-loving cousin James Silverthorne. His various tutors in music and languages, most of them not a great deal older than himself, were also companions with whom he could try out ideas and pick up new ways of viewing what he had been reading.

Above all, his friends in the early 1830s, the Frenchman Ripert-Monclar and the members of the set, provided an equivalent to the kind of intellectual companionship many people find most important in university education. With Monclar Browning could share and develop his interests in history and in French literature. In the debating and conversation society of the colloquials he had an opportunity something like Tennyson's in the more famous Cambridge Conversazione Society to try his wits against a wide variety of educated minds, to present his thoughts and reading to people of different backgrounds and interests, and, in the process, to learn to separate what was merely a peculiar interest of his own from those subjects of general interest to all men. As from all interaction of good minds, the result was a developing sense of standards of excellence in thought and expression and an ability to distinguish between what was more and what less important. If the Apostles had to create an institution apart from the university of their time to serve such a function, Browning had much of what was truly important in a university education without being at a university. Of course, success in communication, whether in writing or in conversation, is not merely a matter of education or early experience. Browning especially would have a long fight ahead of him before he could find adequate ways to communicate his reading and experience. Much labor at writing and a great deal of experience in society would be required before Arnould could exclaim in 1843: "Browning's conversation is as remarkably good as his books, though so different: in conversation anecdotical, vigorous, showing great thought and reading, but in his language most simple, energetic, and accurate."[33] Such acclaim is given not to an education but to the greater effort of putting an education to use. In the set, however, Browning at least had the opportunity to lay the foundation and to begin to learn how to bring his knowledge forward to other men and adjust his ideas to their criticisms.

If Browning's education was on the whole only a preparation for the harder education to come, the education of experience as a writer, it was at least a remarkably broad and effective preparation for a person who would take general knowledge as his special concern. At the same time, the preparation was itself very much of a beginning, probably an even more important beginning to his lifetime career than the more apparent start with the publication of *Pauline*. Large early poetic aspirations, plans for great works, secret publication of an early volume of intimate verse: these are experiences that have begun many a legal or business career. They imply nothing beyond the work in hand and require not a long-range commitment but merely current enthusiasm and the willingness to hazard a relative's money with the vanity press. But in the course of his education Browning had come to make a much more definite commitment to a career in literature. With each stage of his education, and particularly in the decisions made at The London University and afterward, Browning had taken more and more control of his own education, in effect had come to direct the development of his own mind. When he resolved to leave London and thereafter to pursue a general education on his own, he was taking a greater degree of personal responsibility for his future than he had in any other action in his life. At the same time, in taking this one responsibility he was placing himself in a position where he would be obliged to continue on the course he had set. He would have to redeem the promise of his self-education through his future career. Like Paracelsus, whom he portrayed as bearing the burden of justifying the independent educational course he had chosen for himself, he would feel himself placed under the necessity of bringing some truth or some achievement back from his voyage of independent exploration.

By itself such a burden of responsibility was not necessarily a healthy or productive development. Although the choice of independence was the first important action of maturity, it might have also left him, like many another self-willed and independent person, futilely grasping at some kind, any kind, of success, that might seem to justify his headstrong act. Indeed, Paracelsus' life, as Browning tells it, is made up of just this kind of urge to premature success or attainment, and his redemption is only that he is finally capable of discarding such false achievements in his greater aspiration to more substantial attainment and values. As with Paracelsus, Browning's early commitment in his education to some greater achievement than that of the usual careers would lead him into a dark and enormous wood of perplexed motive and unresolved ambition. It would take him more than ten years of effort as a poet to emerge into some satisfying accomplishment.

If the independence of his education thus only served to impose a burden of even greater independence—perhaps the greatest problem he was to face in his entire life—it also had set him at least a few steps along the path by which he would ultimately find a meaningful field for the exercise of his talents. For in the broadest view his education can be seen as the early and dimly understood struggle to broaden the vision of the humanities of his day. His first reaction against the moribund and narrowed classical and religious humanistic traditions of his time in favor of the broader vision of philosophers like Voltaire and poet-prophets like Shelley was a recapitulation in his own terms of the earlier revolts of the Enlightenment and romantic writers against the limited vision of man of the past. Then, in his further reaction against the unreality and the overly simplified and future-oriented vision of both the utilitarian utopianism behind The London University and the secular millennialism of Shelley, he turned almost instinctively toward the reality of man's past and present complexity. He turned, indeed, to that focus on man's historical condition that would be the great field and occupation of nineteenth-century humanism. In turning back to the reality of man's past achievement and the web of his historical development he was at least beginning to make his way toward a new and revived conception of the humanities: an ideal of knowledge as understanding of man's nature in all its complexity, both that of historical circumstance and individual aspiration.

The groundwork for this vision was being laid in his education, and in some sense we can say that Browning had already chosen his career in the early 1830s along with his education. He was to be in the broadest sense a man of letters, and in some vague sense he saw himself as a humanist, a person who would bring new knowledge of man to his fellows. But the road through to this uncharted ambition was in no way clear and, more than many writers, he would have to undergo an especially long period of indecision before he really found his way. The road to the humanism he wished to attain would indeed take him, as had his education, through many half-successes and false starts until he saw his mature direction. At the end of the tunnel, perhaps already dimly visible to him in the early 1830s but not yet attainable, was the unity of his mature work, the dramatic monologues of the 1840s and the even greater work of *Men and Women* and *The Ring and the Book* beyond.

Into that promised land this study may look but does not pretend to enter. What we have seen is rather something of the complexity and mystery of the development of creative genius, no less a mystery for being seen in some of its detail and complexity. For what is most striking in Browning's youth is just the amount of mental and emotional living and complexity that is packed into a few short years, as if the real mark of genius were no more than the capacity, in the fullest sense, to make the most of the moments as they fly past. In his home life and early environment he had undeniably great opportunities for growth and diversity. But it was the privilege of his special capacities to take hold of these as they passed rather than stare at them in blank unchanging inapprehension.

As we have seen, great opportunities for growth were also the seeds of great problems in finding direction and coherence in his mind and personality. But here again, what is striking is the thrust to grasp and meet realities rather than to flee from them. Although no final sense of identity as a poet was possible for him in his boyhood years, he seems to have sought, almost as soon as he could perceive something of his own nature, to find a means by which he could construct a satisfying unity of personality. Neither early verses, nor his flirtation with Byronism, nor his longer and premature emulation of Eliza Flower or Shelley, could wholly satisfy his instinct for relation and fullness of understanding. Still, in each of his premature efforts toward his ultimate role as an artist there was a movement, even though sometimes a dialectical movement, toward the complex poetic role that would ultimately suffice.

The growth that we have traced last, that slow evolution of a sense of the past and of the traditions of his culture that was the main part of Browning's education, is again most remarkable for its comprehensiveness and fullness. The complexity is not merely a matter of much study and reading. Many men have learned more and better. What is impressive is rather the way in which, in virtually every area, he used his education to deepen previous interests and experience, to confront the diversity of early experience rather than to escape from it. He never threw off entirely the subjective and religious tendencies of his youth but turned them to the study of the romantic tradition and the great religious writers of the English heritage with the result that he broadened and deepened them into maturity. The social and superficial cosmopolitanism of his family situation became the deeper cultivation of the student of the entire tradition of European culture. His interest in the curious works of his father's library and mind developed into a growing sense of the complexity and richness of man's history and man's nature. Nothing important seems to have been discarded or cut out; but all was transmuted from the confusion of boyhood impression and enthusiasm into the worthier coin of adult comprehension within the framework of tradition and a broad sympathy for human nature and its manifestations, from its merest quirks to its highest intentions.

Slowly he was building up an understanding of man in which the first great thrust toward creativity in his imitation of Shelley could be broadened and educated. Without losing the original need to express himself—to find the artistic "vent," as he observes in the "Essay on Chatterton," "for impulses that can find vent in no other channel"[34]—the impulses themselves were being broadened and universalized until their release would ultimately open the way not merely for an expression of one boy's condition but the condition of man in general. The need would still be for concentrating, rather than dispersing, the complexity of his understanding and feeling. But the moments of concentration, when they came, would be not idiosyncratic personal statements, nor mere copying of the form and viewpoint of others, but unique wholes, new ways of perceiving and understanding man and his works, a further step in the ever more complex development of our culture upon its earlier self and of man's ever re-forming vision of himself through the eyes of his artists.

Appendixes

Appendix A Ancestry and Contemporary Relatives of Robert Browning

I. The Woodyates Brownings

1. Robert Browning, great-great-great-grandfather? (1666?-?).

The earliest ancestor for which a specific lineage has been asserted, this Robert Browning is known only by an entry, probably by Uncle William Shergold Browning, in a book in which he recorded the Woodyates Brownings. He is identified only as "Robert Browning b. W. Hon about 1666."[1] Presumably he migrated to the hamlet of East Woodyates, Dorsetshire, for the same record has his son Robert born there. His other son would be Thomas, the first family holder of Woodyates Inn. There are no Woodyates parish records before 1704. This is obviously a vague and possibly faulty family record, but it should probably be distinguished from the earlier famous or exalted antecedents asserted only by family legend.[2]

2. Robert Browning, great-great-grandfather (1695?-Nov. 1746).

Son of the above; W. S. Browning's entry indicates he was born at Woodyates in 1695, though there is no separate record of this. There are records of him at Woodyates from the register of births, marriages, and deaths at the Pentridge parish church after 1719[3] and in other local records. He married Elizabeth Pethebridge (?-1759) sometime before 1719.[4] Her origin is not known. They had at least four children (see Chart 1) including the twin eldest sons, Robert Jr., who died at 25 leaving one son himself, and Thomas, great-grandfather of the poet. Family tradition suggests another daughter, Christiana, who married a Seymour,[5] though this might have been inaccurate or mistaken.

Furnivall claimed this Robert was head butler at one time to a Sir John Bankes of Corfe Castle, but no John Bankes of this time has been found.[6] If he was not a head butler, there is no evidence that he was of more elevated class. Other records from Woodyates suggest he was a substantial citizen in the small hamlet but certainly not part of the gentry. A head butler's position might indeed have been beyond his reach. He was churchwarden twice, in 1725 and 1731, and an Overseer of the Poor seven times.[7] He also served twice on the jury of the out-hundred court at nearby Cranborne.[8] Robert's property was rated to the poor at the modest amount of seven and one-half pence, but he was sufficiently prosperous for his widow to be in a position to leave a legacy of one hundred pounds (then a large sum of money) to her grandson Thomas

Pethebridge Browning (son of the twin Robert who died young) out of an unspecified larger estate. When he was buried on Nov. 25, 1746, Robert was merely called Robert Browning, not Mr. Browning; but clearly he was in a comfortable and respectable position, and whatever his occupation, could probably look back on a relative rise to prosperity through his lifetime. Like many of those who rose within the traditional parish structure to a place of some independence, he and his family, as indicated by his wife's one known book, by the names given to his children, and by the tone of his wife's will, combined hard work and shrewd, worldly activity with puritanical biblical culture. Elizabeth probably died in 1759, the year her will was proved.

3. Thomas Browning, great-grandfather (Sept. 30, 1721-Sept. 5, 1794).[9]

Son of the above; he married Jane Morris from nearby Cranborne (1729-July 16, 1773) before 1749. Nothing is known about her background. They had seven children (three died young) of whom the eldest was Robert Browning, grandfather of the poet, and the next oldest was Reuben Browning, who also migrated to London (see below). Another son, William Browning, was placed well in the navy as midshipman. The family tombstone in the Woodyates Pentridge Churchyard, entries on which begin for Brownings of this generation, records his early death by drowning in Antigua.[10]

Cyrus Mason and Vincent Baddeley, both descendants of the Woodyates Brownings, were loath to trace the family back to the middle-class profession of innkeeper. In fact, it is hard to imagine how else in the rough upland Dorsetshire chalk country—sometimes described by Thomas Hardy—they could have had any independent position, since they were clearly not local gentry. Woodyates Inn was a property holding, belonging to the family of the Earls of Shaftesbury and used as the name for a part of the hamlet of East Woodyates. Under the name of Woodyates Inn, the property was leased in 1733 to Thomas Browning, presumably the brother of Robert Browning, great-great-grandfather of the poet. It was leased again in 1760 to his nephew Thomas Browning, great-grandfather, along with some additional pasture land and, in 1779, it was re-assigned by Thomas to William Shergeld (or Shergold), the husband of his daughter Christian Rose.[11] As the Reverend Anthony Lane has shown, there is mention of an inn at Woodyates Inn as early as 1685; by 1750, when the London to Exeter route came across the downs, it was an important landmark and so recorded in the standard history of Dorset first compiled in this period. Local tradition even has it that George III stopped there.[12]

Such a proprietorship, really a considerable and complicated private business, gave Thomas a prominent position in his hamlet, second only to the local gentry in the area. Like his father, he was given, apparently not always entirely at his own desire, responsible local positions: churchwarden close to a dozen times, overseer of the poor five times.[13] As innkeeper, he was evidently ready to get his hand into any profitable enterprise, including transportation and hospital space for midwifery.[14] One surviving letter to his son, the grandfather of the poet, after he had sold the inn shows him busy transmitting drafts for money, sending flitches of bacon and other goods to London, and complaining about the threshers of his wheat. He is literate and a newspaper reader up on the news.[15] Most indicative of his substantial position are his ambitions for his sons, Browning's grandfather Robert and William, who were both placed in national, as opposed to local, positions from which both might—and the one who survived did—rise to something like national importance. He himself owned fine furniture from Chippendale;[16] his burial on September 10, 1794, was recorded with the distinction of Mr. before his name.

4. Reuben Browning, great-uncle (Sept. 1756-Jan. 29, 1827).

Cyrus Mason makes important claims for this Reuben as a source of the more literary cultivation of Browning's father and through him, of the poet himself. Cyrus's account of the family, which is vague or wrong in many particulars about the early period (Cyrus himself was born 1828 or 1829) is also the only source for his view of this Reuben. However, as the step-grandson of Reuben (see Chart 3) he has a special claim to authority for family tradition here. Probably he exaggerates Reuben's importance but can be trusted for the general view of his personality. Almost certainly Reuben did not come to London until after 1785, the date Mason wrongly gives for the arrival of Robert Browning, grandfather of the poet, in London.[17] He settled in Camberwell and is possibly an unidentified Browning who lived very near the poet's parents' residences in Southampton Street.[18] Mason implies, but is not certain, that he was a schoolteacher of some sort (p. 54). His primary occupation, however, was, like his brother, who probably found him the job, at the Bank. He was appointed April 29, 1790, pensioned May 6, 1819.[19] He married a Widow Mason who had a son John. Widow Mason was attracted to what Mason calls Methodism, though it may have been a Dissenter church, even Congregationalism. By 1829 her son was baptizing *his* son at the York Street Church that the poet's family also attended. This may have been the Widow Mason's church all along and hence the original place of contact between Brownings of Woodyates and Wiedemanns of Dundee. Eventually Reuben, like his nephew after him, followed his wife away from the traditional parish affiliation of the family in the Church of England (pp. 62-64).[20] What is most important is that Reuben opposed his brother's more worldly influence on his children in both his families by his quiet emphasis on literary culture and full self-development. Mason is quite clear that Browning's father sought in this Reuben both the love and culture he found lacking at home and that he imparted a similar cultural interest to his son. We may suspect as well that hostility between the two brothers, of which Mason speaks, may have placed Browning's father as a child in the intolerable position of being a shuttlecock between them.

Mason cites two books from Reuben's library, neither very revealing: W. Webster, *Arithemetick in Epitome* (1729), a schoolbook inherited from his father and uncle, and a Salmon's *Geography*, evidently with a poetic inscription (?) to a William Longman, whom Mason tries without evidence to connect to the publisher.

5. Robert Browning, grandfather (July 26, 1749-Dec. 11, 1833).

The oldest son of Thomas and given, as with at least seven generations of Brownings (the twins Thomas and Robert alone muddle the succession) the name of Robert, he was born to succeed and did. He was baptized September 12, 1749 in the Church of England in which he remained until his death. Through the influence of his father's landlord, the fourth earl of Shaftesbury, evidently by way of the M.P. for Salisbury who was a director, he received an appointment to clerk in the Bank on August 24, 1769, shortly after his twentieth birthday. On April 29, 1784 he was promoted to First Clerk (later called Principal Clerk) of the Bank-Stock Division, duly listed on the masthead in the *Royal Kalendar* for 1785 and thereafter until his retirement on October 31, 1821. His salary was £ 561 at its highest and his pension was a very generous £ 421 a year.[21] Bank stock was a speculative commodity at the time and his position gave him connections with private bankers, especially Nathan Rothschild, by which he was able to place his sons William and Reuben. His position as Lieutenant in the Honourable Artillery Company was a common part of Bank service. His social position was obviously comfortable and secure. Documents preserved at Baylor describe him in 1771 as "Robert Browning of the Bank of England Gentleman" and in 1784 as "Robert Browning of the Bank of England & in the City of London Esquire."[22]

He married Margaret Tittle, grandmother of the poet (see below) on October 13, 1778. They settled in Battersea where Browning's father was born in 1782. There was another child, Margaret Morris Browning, born in 1783 (see below). In 1784, they moved to Camberwell where a third child, William, born the same year, died in infancy.[23] Before Margaret Tittle died in 1789, the picture by the significant painter, Wright of Derby, left a record of the social status of the young family as well as a testimony to Margaret's handsome good looks.

In 1794, Robert remarried the well-connected Jane Smith of Chelsea and settled there, evidently at No. 7, Great Cheyne Row, where at least his eldest son from this marriage, William Shergold Browning, was born.[24] He had nine children from this second marriage, the last when he was sixty-five. Mason speaks of a long residence at Peckham, though this may be misremembered for Chelsea. Sometime about 1820, he moved his family to a grander house at Islington in the North on or across from Colebrook Row, a substantial place as Cyrus Mason remembered it, with a large garden going down to the New River.[25]

Robert lived well but probably did not die rich. He provided for his widow and helped in various ways to set his children up for themselves. His will, written August 21, 1819, with Codicils of January 14 and June 8, 1829 and October 28, 1833, gives his unmarried daughters two hundred pounds and a share in the entire estate after the death of their mother; probably by then there was not a great deal to be distributed. He was loyal to those who were loyal to him, but Browning's father and his sister Margaret Morris were given only the customary ten pounds for a mourning ring on the pretext that they had already inherited money from their mother's relatives. Jane Eliza, who, to her father's displeasure, married Reuben's stepson John Mason, was excluded from the eventual division of the property by being given a smaller specified sum; Thomas, who evidently shared the father's hot temper, was given only fifty pounds on the death of his mother.[26]

Books known to have belonged to this Robert Browning are:

Brookes, Thomas. *Precious Remedies Against Satan's Devices.*[27] London, 1656. (Note by Robert Browning, 1811, and another by the poet, 1873 [see also note 11 above]: Bertram Dobell Catalog. *Browning Memorials.* London, 1913, item 57.)

Gerrans, R., trans. *Travels of Rabbi Benjamin, Son of Jonah of Tudela.* London, 1784. (Note by the poet, indicating his grandfather's name among the subscribers: *RBJW*, p. 39, RB to Julia Wedgwood, Aug. 19, 1864.)

Martyn, William. *The Historie, and Lives, of Twentie Kings of England.* London, 1615. (Autographs from 1790 to 1863, five generations of Brownings: Thomas to Robert Wiedeman Browning: book at Baylor.)

Quarles, Francis. *Emblems, Divine and Moral: Together with Hieroglyphics of the Life of Man,* 2 vols. London, 1777. (Stamp of "Rob. Browning" and authentication by the poet: Bernard Quaritch Catalog No. 326. *Rare and Valuable Books, Including Books of R. B. Browning, Most of Which Have Interesting Inscriptions.* London, June, 1913, item 104.)

Smith, Samuel. *Joseph and his Mistresse, the Faithfulnesse of the One and the Unfaithfulnesse of the Other, Laid Downe in Five Sermons.* London, 1619. (With stamp of "Rob. Browning" and authentication by the poet in 1873: Sotheby, item 1103.)

_____. *Noah's Dove, or, Tydings of Peace to the Godly.* London, 1619. (With note by the poet identifying book as his grandfather's: Henry Sotheran Catalog 737. *Old Engravings and MSS, Books, and Relics of R. and E. B. Browning.* London, 1913, item 235.)

Spurstowe, William. *The Spiritual Chymist; or, Six Decads of Divine Meditations on Several Subjects.* London, 1666. (Autograph of Robert Browning, 1783 and 1793: Mason. "Kinsfolk," p. 54; Spurstowe was one of the Smectymnuus whom Milton defended: another indication of the puritan tendencies of the grandfather.)

Tugenious. *Scots Poems Wrote by Tugenious before 1600.* Edinburgh, 1761. (With stamp of "Rob. Browning": Mason. "Kinsfolk," p. 44; not identified.)

The Young Gentlemen and Ladies' Monitor. N.d. (Autograph, 1783, by Robert Browning: Mason. "Kinsfolk," pp. 42-43; not identified.)

II. The Tittles of Jamaica and St. Kitts

1. Edward Tittle, great-great-grandfather (?-buried June 27, 1742).

Jeanette Marks's years of digging in colonial records tell us much about the West Indian background of Browning's paternal grandmother, though there are major lacunae, and her judgment is not always unquestionable.[28] Edward Tittle probably began as a bright apprentice in Port Royal, Jamaica, in the late seventeenth century, very likely as an indentured worker over from England. He remained cordwainer or shoemaker all his life, but became the major leather goods supplier in both Port Royal and the growing new town of Kingston. He married Lucy Molison (1679-Nov. 11, 1744; sometimes Lucia Mollison) who helped him expand his holdings into land, city property, cook houses, and even a tavern. "Slowly, methodically, and energetically multiplying their possessions,"[29] the Tittles rose in the expanding colony in one generation to a position among the well-to-do middle-class gentlemen and not far below the more aristocratic Barrett family of Jamaica from which Elizabeth would emerge. Their daughters were married to men described as gentlemen and they themselves were given velvet palls, a mark of distinction, at their burials.

Edward Tittle had four children who bore his last name (see Chart 2). Because she accepted Furnivall's groundless assertion that Browning's grandmother was a mulatto, Marks was anxious to trace an interracial origin and argues that Tittle's son John was not by his wife. This is possible, since even one of their own children, Mary, is known to have been born out of wedlock, but the issue remains unclear. Certainly there is no evidence to recommend Furnivall's contention to those not already persuaded of its truth.[30] What is clear is that the Tittles were rising, even more quickly than the Brownings of Woodyates, to a position where they looked beyond immediate needs and their immediate lives to the larger world.

2. The Reverend John Tittle, great-grandfather? (?-Nov. 1758).

Marks assumes that this son of Edward Tittle, possibly not the son of Lucy Molison, was the father of Margaret, paternal grandmother of the poet. The only grounds for the supposition, other than the unlikely correlation with Furnivall's claim of mulatto blood (see above), are that his wife was also named Margaret and that he settled at St. Kitts. By 1748, when he made his will, he had had no issue, after fifteen to seventeen years of marriage, though Margaret (born 1754), her brother, and her sister, may have come in a flood of late blessings before John's death. John's brother, Edward Tittle, the other possible great-grandfather, did settle in St. Kitts in 1763 after his brother's death.[31] At that time the two families must have virtually merged around the St. Kitts interest; consequently the question of paternity is relatively unimportant.

Marks pushes a view of John Tittle as frustrated and self-defeating; this is based largely upon his correspondence with his superior in the Church, Edmund Gibson, Bishop of London, in which he frequently bewails his difficulties as a prelude to asking the Bishop for his influence in London in his affairs.[32] Like many persons in his age and especially in the islands, he was endlessly involved in lawsuits and disputes and always afraid that his enemies would hurt his "interest" (his euphemism for his non-priestly concerns) unless he kept pressure on his friends. But the larger picture shows, rather, a very successful secular career, if perhaps at the expense of his higher vocation. He managed to attain three livings in the rich plantation island of St. Kitts; he married a daughter of a St. Kitts surgeon, George Strachan, of sufficient means to make it worth his trouble to go to law to obtain a fair share of his estate when he died; with a silent partner in London with whom he was forever at war or law, he took on a major plantation for which his managing fees alone were   150 a year, a comfortable enough sum in itself. Beyond the Bishop of London he also had a friend back in England in the Earl of Warwick, with whom he had an appointment as chaplain. His "interest" was such that, like the Barretts, he was often in London to look after his affairs directly.

His will of 1748, with gifts of £500 and £400 to brother and sisters and with mention of additional slaves he held on Jamaica, suggests the Lord had smiled upon his ministry greatly, nor, though Marks cites a mortgage of over £1000 for a piece of land on his removal to Jamaica just before his death, is there any indication that he failed later.[33] Certainly his brother, who was prosperous in Jamaica, considered the St. Kitts interest important enough to warrant his relocating the family there after his brother's death. This priest was thus, like his father, the founder of a line. The Tittles would still be at St. Kitts, and still major planters, when Browning's father was sent out by his father to claim his mother's part. Whatever his worldliness, John no doubt also represented a considerable step upward in the education of the family; legal and financial records probably give us even a biased view of his concern for lucre. The one record of the rest of his life, his parish book entries, struck Marks as showing both great care in his duty and some cleverness.[34] But he was not bothered, as his presumed grandson, the poet's father, would be, by the slave system upon which it all rested, nor was he excessively troubled by the isolation and tedium of plantation life.

3. Margaret Tittle, grandmother (1754-April 17, 1789).

No information about the Tittle family in St. Kitts after Edward's settlement there in 1763 is known except through Browning family tradition and a few Browning items relating to the Tittles. From a copy of her Camberwell tombstone made by her son,[35] we know Margaret was born in St. Kitts thirty-five years before her death in Camberwell in 1789. That she had at least one brother and one sister is indicated by the reference in the will of Robert Browning, grandfather, to an "Uncle Tittle and Aunt Mill."[36] Uncle Tittle is probably the uncle from St. Kitts who was killed by his slaves and whose cufflinks were passed on first to Robert Browning, grandfather, and then to the poet.[37] Aunt Mill must have been Sarah Mill, whose name appears on a friendship coin with Robert Browning, grandfather.[38] As the Tittles were no doubt as much in need of London friends in this generation as in the one before, they were probably anxious to maintain good relations with their relative in the Bank of England.

Other than this and the facts of her marriage to Robert Browning, grandfather of the poet (see above), nothing is known of her except what can be divined from her attractive portrait by Wright of Derby,[39] and this is largely her obviously handsome dark-haired appearance, her aristocratic bearing, and the culture that moved her to pose with Thomson's *Seasons*. Presumably she had a solid claim to a part of the St. Kitts plantations and was an attractive match for the ambitious grandfather. In her right, her single surviving son, the poet's father, would have had good claims and better prospects on St. Kitts; he probably did receive from Uncle Tittle and Aunt Mill enough to make his own household a bit more comfortable and to make it not impossible for him to send his own son to university or to underwrite most of his early publications.[40]

III. The Wiedemanns of Dundee

1. William Wiedemann, great-grandfather (?-buried Aug. 16, 1777).

In most accounts this William, grandfather of the poet's mother, has been simply conflated with his son, also William, into a hybrid mariner from Hamburg. William the elder was not a mariner but a sugar refiner. He was probably an immigrant to Dundee, Scotland, but very likely came not from Hamburg, but from Holland. Dutchmen, at least, were most common in the Dundee Sugar House, built in the Sea-Gait (or Gate), Dundee, in 1751, where they provided the necessary skilled labor.[41] Like all the rest of Browning's ancestors, this one evidently prospered through native wit and hard work. By 1769, he was able to purchase a large separate house with a good-sized garden on Sea-Gait Street near the refinery.[42]

William's wife's name is not known. She outlived her husband and was evidently left well-off. The first Dundee Directory, published in 1782, lists her as one of the Merchant Company,[43] which suggests her husband may have developed from sugar work to more general activities as a merchant. It is possible William and his wife had more than the one child, Browning's grandfather, who is recorded as "eldest lawful son and heir."[44] William was buried in the Howff in 1777;[45] his wife presumably died sometime before their son sold the family house in 1787.

2. William Wiedemann, grandfather.

No exact dates are known for the father of Browning's mother. Millar was wrong in conjecturing that he was born about 1766.[46] A better guess might be about 1745-1750, in which case he may have been born in his father's native country, presumably Holland. This William Wiedemann was called a "mariner," which presumably meant a shipping merchant who kept his own vessel.[47] He was probably relatively prosperous, though nothing is known of him after 1787.

He married Sarah Revell, probably a Scotswoman, as all biographies have claimed. The birth and baptism of Browning's mother is recorded in a Dundee Register of baptisms in the Church of Scotland as June 13 and 16, 1772;[48] they had at least one other daughter, Christiana (see below under Silverthornes). On May 7, 1787, William asserted his possession of his father's house by taking sasine and then sold it June 21 for £251 to a partner of the Sugar House Company. Inasmuch as both daughters appear next in London, it is likely that he emigrated there after the sale. Probably his wife as well as mother was dead by then, though this is unsure. There were Revells in Camberwell as early as 1780 and in 1813 both a William and an Elizabeth Revell lived near the Brownings on Southampton Street—possibly relations of the maternal grandmother.[49] William Wiedemann was dead by 1811 when Robert Browning, grandfather, waited on an uncle (perhaps a Revell) rather than the father of Browning's mother to warn him against his son. Browning's maternal grandparents were Christian and probably, like her, rather pious (though Christiana was a common name). The grandfather's drawings suggest he had some leaning to art or draftsmanship.[50] The Scots background as it was given to Browning's mother was a more important and immediate influence on the poet than the great-grandfather's European culture, though the love of music probably came through him.

IV. Contemporary Relatives[51]

1. Family of Robert Browning, grandfather, and Margaret Tittle

Margaret Morris Browning, aunt (Oct. 2, 1783-1858). A shadowy figure, Browning's paternal aunt was never married and seems to have had no means of support beyond her inheritance from her mother or the Tittle family.[52] The only record of her appearance is the romanticized account of Cyrus Mason who quite wrongly has her and her mother descended from French aristocratic refugees. Under this delusion her dark hair is recalled along with "foreign mysterious movements and profoundly expressive dark eyes."[53] She was evidently reclusive and seen mostly at family funerals. Mason speaks of a tradition that this "eccentric Aunt Margaret was detected mysteriously crooning prophecies over her Nephew, behind a door at the house at Camberwell."[54] There is no collateral evidence for such egregious eccentricity and no evidence that she had much part in any way in her nephew's development. This is probably more Mason moonshine. Alienated from her father by his second marriage and, like her brother, under the influence of her Uncle Reuben, she probably was, as Mason generally implies, a mixture of shyness, strangeness, and independent dignity.

William Browning, uncle (Dec. 2, 1784-Dec. 12, 1784).[55]

2. Family of Robert Browning, grandfather, and Jane Smith

Jane Smith Browning, step-grandmother (April 29, 1771-July 4, 1848). Daughter of James Smith of Bremhill, Wilts (1735-1799) and Jane Young of Glasgow (1740-1814), Jane Smith was born and lived at Chelsea. She was vaguely related to some Seymours of Somerset and was second cousin to Lord Macartney,[56] Ambassador to China: a likely match for the ambitious grandfather of the poet who himself thought of a marriage of convenience after Elizabeth's death. From Mason's account of her in old age she was apparently, widow's cap notwithstanding, a very handsome woman: "her face really attractive, her abundant hair smoothed over her temples under her widow's cap, its broad white strings falling gracefully over the body of her black silk dress . . . what a serene, beautiful picture of age she represented."[57] Even in old age, however, she was evidently a pretty kitten with claws. Her spiteful jealousy, which banished Margaret Tittle's portrait and kept Browning's father from going to university,[58] was still active when she moved to New Cross probably sometime around 1841 and settled at Albert Terrace on the Old Kent Road not far from the Hatcham house of her stepson. Sitting in state at her window she had nasty comments to make about whatever displeased her, especially "stuck-up" Sarianna, Browning's sister, and that "home-made poet" who had eloped with Elizabeth. She was dead, however, before she had the opportunity Mason's imaginative memory gives her, of seeing her stepson waving at her and the widow von Muller next door. The tale must have been made up on the basis of the brief reference in the *Times* report to the poet's father waving at the widow as he came home. This may lead us to doubt Mason's other best anecdote, that of the poet's appearance before her, just before he eloped, to exclaim that the Book of Common Prayer made a monstrous mistake in forbidding a man to marry his grandmother and to give her one reverent and impressive kiss.[59] In fact, Browning probably saw less of her than of his uncles and aunts because of the difficult relations between his father and grandfather. The one record of any literary exchange, again testified to only by Mason's esemplastic memory, suggests that there was little intellectual sympathy between them. She asked him to write so "ordinary folk" could understand him; and under this baiting he haughtily replied that he did not write for this generation—possibly meaning as much her kind as her age.[60] Tensions across the larger family, which the poet avoided by the distantness that Mason so deplores, no doubt often began with Jane Smith. It should be noted that she was only a year older than her stepdaughter-in-law, Browning's mother, an additional cause for family difficulties.

William Shergold Browning, half-uncle (Feb. 3, 1797-Feb. 1874). The eldest son of the second family of Robert Browning, grandfather, William was born in Chelsea, and apparently with less chafing at the bit than his older half-brother, he eventually entered the Bank of England, probably sometime before 1820. When his position was eliminated, his father placed him in the Paris office of Rothschild's through his acquaintance with Nathan Rothschild, presumably in 1824, the year he went to Paris. He was there until at least 1846.[61] In Paris he lived at rue Laffitte, No. 15; later he was at 3 Camden Place, Greenwich.[62] He married Louisa Mansir, sister of the Mansir who married his sister Mary. They had ten children (see Chart 4) all of whom were probably somewhat known to the poet from his visit in Paris with them.[63] Browning entertained his daughter Louisa Jane on her honeymoon and, late in life, established a friendly relation with William's grandson, a talented lawyer and writer on Australian law, Robert Jardine Browning. Members of William's family, like all the contemporaries of the poet, usually combined business or professional careers with an interest in arts or scholarship. Because of his Paris position and acquaintances, his family was especially well traveled.[64]

William's publications were:

A Flemish Legend. (No copy found; this title is listed among his publications in *Hoel Morvan;* hence issued before 1844.)

The History of the Huguenots during the Sixteenth Century. 2 vols. London, William Pickering, 1829. (This work has a complicated bibliographical history: dissatisfied with Pickering, William evidently republished with Whittaker and Co., London, 1829. Pickering reissued the original edition at least twice, in 1839 and 1845, but also issued a third volume in 1839, which carried the account from 1598 to the present. Then, in 1840, Whittaker and Co. reissued this revised edition and followed with second, third, and fourth editions in 1842, 1842, and [184?]. The new edition was issued by Lea and Blanchard in America, Philadelphia, 1845. There was also a translation into German of the first edition by Karl Herzog, Leipzig, 1830-1831. The history was favorably reviewed in the *Gentleman's Magazine,* 99 [Oct. 1829], 347.)

Hoel Morvan; or the Court and Camp of Henry V. 3 vols. London, T. C. Newby, 1844.

Leisure Hours. London, Whittaker and Co., 1841. (Reissued by Galignani, Paris, 1841; subscribers to the original issue included Reuben and Sarianna Browning, Mrs. Mansir, and Mrs. Silverthorne.)

The Provost of Paris, a Tale of the Court of Charles VI. Paris, G. G. Bennis, 1833.

William also wrote for the *Gentleman's Magazine* and other periodicals. *Leisure Hours* reprints some reviews and articles.

Christiana Browning, half-aunt (March 1, 1799-Feb. 7, 1825).

Jane Eliza Browning, half-aunt (Sept. 15, 1800-1880). According to the account of her son Cyrus, Jane Eliza, like Browning's father, came under the influence of her Uncle Reuben from Woodyates. She married John Mason, stepson of this Reuben, whom she met at her uncle's house. Cyrus implies that this marriage and the "Methodist" influence of Reuben and his wife, the widow Mason, was not to the taste of her father. Possibly "Methodism" had always been Congregationalism. Certainly by 1829, when they baptized a daughter there, the Masons were affiliated with the same church as the poet's family.[65] Her father gave her a dowry of one hundred pounds but restricted her in his will to one hundred more at the death of her mother.[66] The Masons seem to have resided around the early 1820s in Camberwell, then went north to Islington to be near the old head of the family, then eventually followed Jane Smith Browning back south to New Cross.[67] They had nine children who, like the rest of the family, pursued a variety of professional or artistic careers. Cyrus speaks with great respect of his father's culture and his love for poetry.

One has the impression from Mason's account, however, that they were somewhat in the position of poor relations and, following the family wherever its center seemed to be, were rather envious onlookers of the more prominent members of the family: the old patriarch Robert, the poet's father, Reuben, or William. In the few glimpses Mason gives us of them, they seem always grudgingly focusing their attention on the young poet, half envying him, half wishing he and his family would pay them more attention. Overcoming their puritanical scruples about the "propriety" of the theater, they went as "family" to the production of *A Blot in the 'Scutcheon* (1843) but, when things went poorly, were afraid to support their relative (and probably somewhat gratified at his failure). They seem to have taken most interest in the failure of *Sordello,* which became a standing family joke.[68] When Browning eloped with a famous and not penniless poetess the last straw to break envy's back had been placed and they resolved to think and speak of him no more.

Cyrus Mason, cousin (1828 or 1829-Aug. 8, 1915). More than fifty years later, this Mason had his famous kinsman still very much in mind and found a minor niche for himself with posterity through his manuscript account of "The Poet Robert Browning and his Kinsfolk," which no student of the poet can completely ignore and no student should completely trust. Like most of the family, Cyrus had had aspirations toward art, had even gone to Paris to paint, but he then ended up as a secure government employee—albeit a lithographic draftsman—in Melbourne, Australia. Mason, who is said to have looked much like the poet, evidently continued to dream of higher uses for his abilities, to draw, and to scribble endlessly.[69] After a visit back to the old country, his attention turned to family pride and his long-standing jealousy of his older cousin, by then buried in the Abbey. The result is the manuscript used cautiously throughout this study as one of the few firsthand accounts of the poet's family life. Because of Mason's peculiar slant it is, however, far less helpful and far less trustworthy than it ought to be. Much of it is taken up with misty attempts to establish the aristocratic background of a family whose middle-class origin is heavily underlined by everything of a factual nature he recounts and is, indeed, epitomized by the prosperous Australian looking back for a pedigree. Then his argument turns entirely on his assertion, an uninteresting one in any event to a post-Victorian age, that the poet was consistently ungrateful to, and strangely neglectful of, kinsfolk. The charge tells us much about the Mason family's combination of envy for the poet's abilities and success and their thwarted desire to find in him a patriarch to replace the old Robert Browning. It also tells us something about the kind of nearby influences from which the poet had to free himself, even at the cost of some resentment, in order to go his own way in life. But it makes Mason's descriptions both one-sided and rather biased. In addition, Mason, about seventeen years younger than the poet, relies only on vague family traditions for much of what he says about the family background and the education of the poet. Finally, he clearly read most of the published material about Browning (with growing indignation that rosy references to the Browning clan didn't fill each page) and accounts which seem like memories, and may have seemed so to him, are often repetitions of published details. His best stories for the period he knew are rendered suspicious by his ability to manufacture a tale about Jane Smith Browning and the widow von Muller that is impossible because of the former's death in 1848 even before the poet's mother died.

As to Browning's relation with kinsfolk, Mason seems only right in his general view that Browning chose not to center his life upon the extended and extensive Browning family. To those who were generous and sympathetic to him, his father, mother, sister, and his Uncles Reuben and William, Browning returned friendship and generosity, though he would acknowledge that he remained in their debt all his life and had rather let them spoil him. The sole exception might be his Aunt Silverthorne, who evidently did feel he had unnecessarily neglected her family in the 1850s (see below). Mason can only cite one instance of his mother's kindness to the poet, some rocking to whispered poetry when he was an infant,[70] and there is much opposing evidence of the Masons' spite. Kind Uncle Reuben is even ridiculed as something of a fool to help the poet. Apparently there were fights between the Masons and Reuben's family in later years.[71] It should be noted that there is evidence of kindly relations between the poet and some of his other aunts (see below, Louisa and Mary).

Reuben Browning, half-uncle (April 11, 1803-Sept. 6, 1879). The poet's kindly favorite uncle was for a long time a happy bachelor, taking his morning swim in the New River near the family house at Islington, indulging his penchant for the theater, able to afford the horse that the poet exercised for him and able to offer generous gifts and help to his talented nephew.[72] Sometime shortly after the poet married and a good time after his fortieth birthday, he too took a wife, Margaret Lewis, a Welsh woman from Penhelig, Aberdovey, and became a family man whose home was a rendezvous for Brownings from around the world.[73] After living near the Brownings at Albert Terrace in the 1840s, he settled his family at 9 Victoria Road, Old Charlton (near London) and later at "Penhelig," Morland Road, Addiscombe (near Croydon).[74] He and his wife had eight children (see Chart 4) who remained on friendly terms with the poet and were, indeed, given a contingent benefit in his will; there is no evidence of any Masonic annoyance with the poet from this part of the family.[75] They were a cultivated family who combined, as usual with the Brownings of the poet's generation, art and professional careers; music was an especial interest and one daughter, Christiana, was a composer. Three surviving photos from his middle age show Reuben as round faced and affable.[76]

Like William, Reuben was placed through his father's influence at Rothschild's where he distinguished himself without extinguishing his literary and scholarly interests. He joined the office at St. Swithin's Lane in the City where he remained until his death sixty years later.[77] His publications were:

Compulsory Immediate Convertibility of the Bank Note a Failure. N.p., 1868. (A pamphlet of 8 pp.)

The Currency Considered with a View to the Effectual Prevention of Panics. London, 1867. (An *Addenda* of 15 pp. was published, London, 1868; and there followed a revision: *Reflections on the Currency, with a View to the Effectual Prevention of Panics.* London, 1869.)

A Few Observations on the New Stamp Act, 17 & 18 Victoria, c. 83. London, Coventry & Co., 1854.

The Finances of Great Britain Considered. Comprising an Examination of the Property and Income Tax, and the Succession Duty of 1853, pts. 1, 2. London, 1859. (No more were published.)

Letters on Financial Subjects. The Greater Portion of which Appeared in the "Daily Telegraph." London, 1866. (Published under the pseudonym, Brutus Britannicus.)

He also addressed the Liverpool Financial Reform Association, Nov. 1859. There are a series of technical letters to W. E. Gladstone on the use of annuities to raise government funds: May 31, June 2, 14, 14, 1856, BL, Add. MS. 44,586, fols. 187-206. His "Fictional Account of the Last Judgment," the story of the bank clerk, Cher, is at Baylor.

Mary Browning, half-aunt (March 21, 1805-Aug. 1864). Mary married Robert Mansir, brother to William Shergold Browning's wife, in June 1831, and had one son by him. He was dead by August 1834 when Ripert-Monclar reported meeting a widow. She remarried to a Dr. G. Mason of Lincoln (apparently no relation to the other Masons). Nothing is known of her relation with her nephew the poet; but, contrary to Cyrus Mason's assertions, he bothered to see this relative after his return to London in the 1860s and at her death spoke warmly in a letter to her sisters of "her old fullness of life" and his hopes for reunion after death.[78]

Louisa Browning, half-aunt (1807-Sept. 6, 1887). Louisa was a spinster and kept school with her sister Sarah at Dartmouth Row in the town of Blackheath southeast of London. Her father notes in a codicil to his will that he gave her two hundred pounds to set up the school. Apparently Jemima was also involved in the school until her marriage.[79] Louisa and Sarah, at least, lived at the school and later at 1. Maitland Park Crescent, Haverstock Hill, N.W., London. Letters testify to a cordial relation between her and the poet.[80]

Thomas Browning, half-uncle (April 15, 1809-1878). Thomas was the scapegrace of the family, a man, according to Mason, who knew him in Australia, with his father's pride and hot temper but without his solidity.[81] He was handsome and extravagant and was early involved in a conflict of will with his father. After three years at the Bank he was finally shipped out (apparently at Reuben's expense) to Tasmania in 1829.[82] He became a shipping clerk there, later moved to Melbourne, Australia, where he died. His father left him only fifty pounds and nothing at all if he tried to borrow on it. There is no evidence of relation between him and the poet, though he is a reminder that there were strong tempers in the family.

Jemima Smith Browning, half-aunt (July 5, 1811-Nov. 26, 1880). In her nephew's view she was the beauty of the family, "beautiful," indeed, "as the day." She takes on additional interest from a persistent rumor in the Browning family that the poet's admiration even mounted at one time to love. He is said to have kissed the stone steps of the chancel where she stood before going into the vestry when she was married.[83] One can imagine fanciful admiration being mistaken by the family for passion, though it is possible Browning did feel something more than mere admiration for this attractive aunt only one year older than he. Her marriage in 1845, just when Browning began to develop his own serious interest in a woman, *is* interesting and tempts speculation into Browning's emotional development that facts can't establish.

She apparently was involved in Louisa's school in Blackheath (see above) until her marriage to a William James Hixon in 1845. They had four children.

Sarah Browning, half-aunt (Sept. 9, 1814-Nov. 1902). This Sarah, even confused with her niece Sarianna of the same age at her death, kept school and lived with her sister Louisa (see above). Like Louisa, she seems to have had at least cordial relations with her nephew the poet. Cyrus Mason visited her shortly before her death when he made his trip back to England; he gives a very romanticized description of her as an example of the family's physical and genteel perfections from clear complexion and robust temperament down to filbert nails.[84] Between the lines one sees a rather prim old maid, much offended, like Mason himself, at stories that the Browning family might have had ancestry other than blue British.

3. *Silverthorne Family*

Christiana Matilda Wiedemann, aunt (?-late 1850s?). No record of the birth of the sister of Browning's mother has been found, though probably she was somewhat younger than Sarah Anna. She probably came south from Scotland with her sister and settled with her at their unidentified uncle's house in Camberwell or Peckham. Before 1804 she married a William Oliver Silverthorne (1773-June 16, 1844) a brewer in Camberwell who worked the family Brewhouse on Peckham Road near the junction with the Browning's Southampton Street.[85] They had four sons, William, James, John, and George (see below). A letter of Browning's of 1844 refers to William Oliver Silverthorne's death after a "frightful visitation."[86] There were warm relations between their household in Camden Row near the brewery and the Browning family. On Sunday both families went to the York Street Church. The poet spoke affectionately of "dearest aunt"; she cared enough for him to put up a rather sizable thirty pounds for the publication of *Pauline,* which his parents didn't know about,[87] though there is no evidence that he had other debts to her.

After the death of her son James in 1852, the family business was sold and eventually she went with John and his family to the continent. She died at Marconnelle, Pas de Calais, probably in the late 1850s. Her grandson recalled bitterness over Browning's failure to pay attention to her in this late period,[88] bitterness which may have begun with the poet's failure to attend James's funeral (see below). The contingent benefit given in his will to the children of his cousins is proof that Browning never ceased to acknowledge debt to his aunt and a close relation with all the Silverthornes. But this may be one case where Browning did neglect kinsfolk who had helped him—if only through inadvertance and preoccupation with his own relation to Elizabeth, not ill-will or aloofness.

James Silverthorne, cousin (Feb. 12, 1809-May 19, 1852). James or Jim, eldest surviving son of Christiana, was not the closest to the poet's age [89] but common enthusiasms made him a best friend throughout their youth. Like his brothers, he was a good musician and had, as well, ambitions to become an artist, or at least took serious interest in art. His associations with Browning,[90] over Shelley, Beethoven, and the theater, suggest he was both intelligent and cultivated. After his father's death in 1844, he took over the family brewery, apparently with disastrous consequences.[91] He married Jane Street Hayman and had one child, Edward Christian Silverthorne, who ultimately worked for Rothschild's, probably through some aid from the Browning family. James died in May, 1852. A letter of RB's about a year and a half later indicates that his wife planned to remarry and that his death had led to his mother's breaking up the home where she had remained with her son and his family. [92]

There were certainly cordial relations between James and Browning during the former's lifetime[93] and the poem "May and Death" is one of the few intimate tributes Browning left of anyone. But Sarianna felt her brother had been wrong in neglecting to come over from Paris to James's funeral[94] and this perhaps contributed to later misunderstanding with the Silverthornes (see above).

William Wiedemann Silverthorne (Feb. 13, 1804-died young?), John Silverthorne (March 7, 1811-1862), and George Silverthorne (April 26, 1813-?), cousins. Both John and George were of ages to be friends of the poet, though they were not as close friends as James. Except that they, too, were musical and were called wild youths, little is known about either. They both must have married and have had children by 1864 when Browning left a contingent benefit to the children of the three cousins in his will. John had at least one son living in 1903. Certainly he and his family, and possibly George, as well, went with their mother to France.[95] William Wiedemann almost certainly died before he could have known the poet.

Genealogical Charts

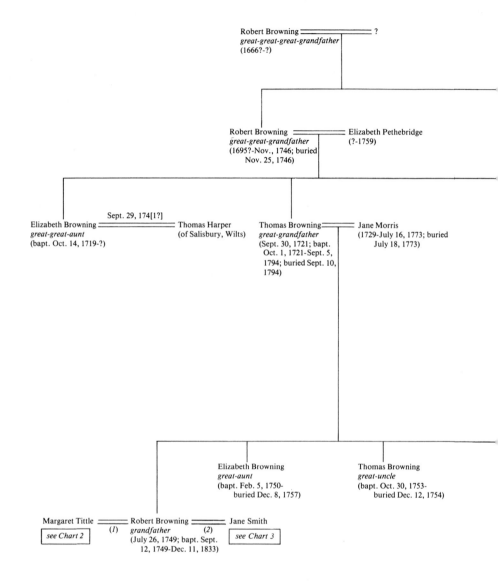

Robert Browning ══════════ ?
great-great-great-grandfather
(1666?-?)

Robert Browning ══════════ Elizabeth Pethebridge
great-great-grandfather   (?-1759)
(1695?-Nov., 1746; buried
Nov. 25, 1746)

Sept. 29, 174[1?]

Elizabeth Browning ══════════ Thomas Harper   Thomas Browning══════════ Jane Morris
great-great-aunt   (of Salisbury, Wilts)   *great-grandfather*   (1729-July 16, 1773; buried
(bapt. Oct. 14, 1719-?)   (Sept. 30, 1721; bapt.   July 18, 1773)
                                                      Oct. 1, 1721-Sept. 5,
                                                      1794; buried Sept. 10,
                                                      1794)

Elizabeth Browning   Thomas Browning
great-aunt   *great-uncle*
(bapt. Feb. 5, 1750-   (bapt. Oct. 30, 1753-
    buried Dec. 8, 1757)   buried Dec. 12, 1754)

Margaret Tittle ══════════ Robert Browning ══════════ Jane Smith
see Chart 2   (1) *grandfather*   (2)   see Chart 3
                   (July 26, 1749; bapt. Sept.
                   12, 1749-Dec. 11, 1833)

[a]Most variations from Furnivall's genealogy, "Ancestors," p. 45, are explained in the text of Appendix A. Information on the family of Thomas Pethebridge Browning and on the Mason family (*Chart 3*) is from Mason, "Kinsfolk," Appendix 3.

368

Chart 1 Woodyates Brownings[a]

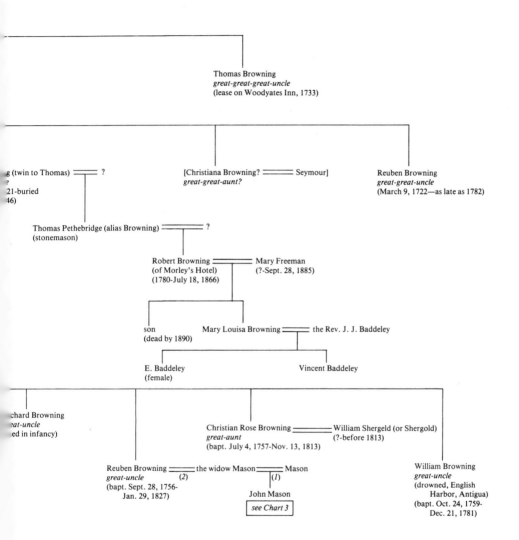

Thomas Browning
great-great-great-uncle
(lease on Woodyates Inn, 1733)

g (twin to Thomas) ══ ?
21-buried
46)

[Christiana Browning? ══ Seymour]
great-great-aunt?

Reuben Browning
great-great-uncle
(March 9, 1722—as late as 1782)

Thomas Pethebridge (alias Browning) ══ ?
(stonemason)

Robert Browning ══ Mary Freeman
(of Morley's Hotel)   (?-Sept. 28, 1885)
(1780-July 18, 1866)

son
(dead by 1890)

Mary Louisa Browning ══ the Rev. J. J. Baddeley

E. Baddeley
(female)

Vincent Baddeley

chard Browning
at-uncle
ed in infancy)

Christian Rose Browning ══ William Shergeld (or Shergold)
great-aunt   (?-before 1813)
(bapt. July 4, 1757-Nov. 13, 1813)

Reuben Browning ══ the widow Mason ══ Mason
great-uncle   (2)   (1)
(bapt. Sept. 28, 1756-
Jan. 29, 1827)

John Mason
| see Chart 3 |

William Browning
great-uncle
(drowned, English
Harbor, Antigua)
(bapt. Oct. 24, 1759-
Dec. 21, 1781)

369

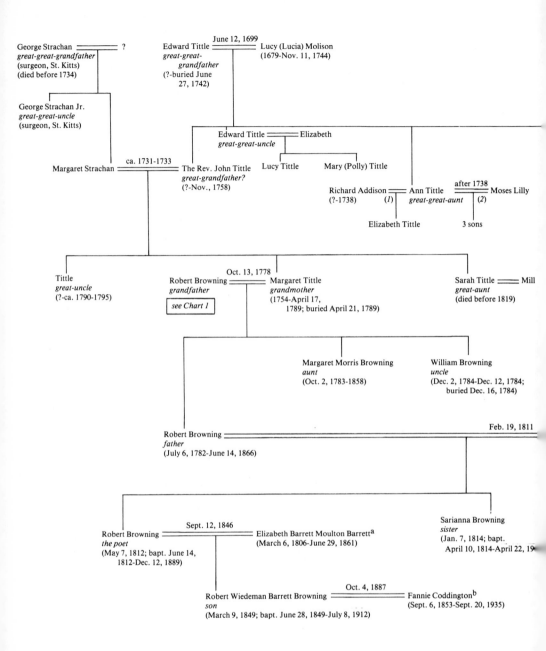

George Strachan ══════ ?
great-great-grandfather
(surgeon, St. Kitts)
(died before 1734)

George Strachan Jr.
great-great-uncle
(surgeon, St. Kitts)

June 12, 1699
Edward Tittle ══════ Lucy (Lucia) Molison
great-great-grandfather
(?-buried June 27, 1742)
(1679-Nov. 11, 1744)

Edward Tittle ══════ Elizabeth
great-great-uncle

Lucy Tittle   Mary (Polly) Tittle

Richard Addison ══════ Ann Tittle ══════ Moses Lilly
(?-1738)   *(1)*   *great-great-aunt* after 1738 *(2)*

Elizabeth Tittle   3 sons

ca. 1731-1733
Margaret Strachan ══════ The Rev. John Tittle
great-grandfather?
(?-Nov., 1758)

Tittle
great-uncle
(?-ca. 1790-1795)

Oct. 13, 1778
Robert Browning ══════ Margaret Tittle
grandfather
[see Chart 1]
grandmother
(1754-April 17, 1789; buried April 21, 1789)

Sarah Tittle ══════ Mill
great-aunt
(died before 1819)

Margaret Morris Browning
aunt
(Oct. 2, 1783-1858)

William Browning
uncle
(Dec. 2, 1784-Dec. 12, 1784; buried Dec. 16, 1784)

Feb. 19, 1811
Robert Browning
father
(July 6, 1782-June 14, 1866)

Sept. 12, 1846
Robert Browning ══════ Elizabeth Barrett Moulton Barrett[a]
the poet
(May 7, 1812; bapt. June 14, 1812-Dec. 12, 1889)
(March 6, 1806-June 29, 1861)

Sarianna Browning
sister
(Jan. 7, 1814; bapt. April 10, 1814-April 22, 19_)

Oct. 4, 1887
Robert Wiedeman Barrett Browning ══════ Fannie Coddington[b]
son
(March 9, 1849; bapt. June 28, 1849-July 8, 1912)
(Sept. 6, 1853-Sept. 20, 1935)

[a]For the Barrett family see the extract from the College of Arms, Jeannette Marks, *The Family of the Barrett* (New York, Macmillan, 1938), p. 536 f.

[b]For the Coddington family see Maizie Ward, *The Tragi-Comedy of Pen Browning (1849-1912)* (New York, Sheed and Ward and the Browning Institute, 1972), p. 114*n*.

**Chart 2 Tittles of Jamaica and St. Kitts;
Wiedemanns of Dundee; Silverthornes; and the
Immediate Family of the Poet, Robert Browning**

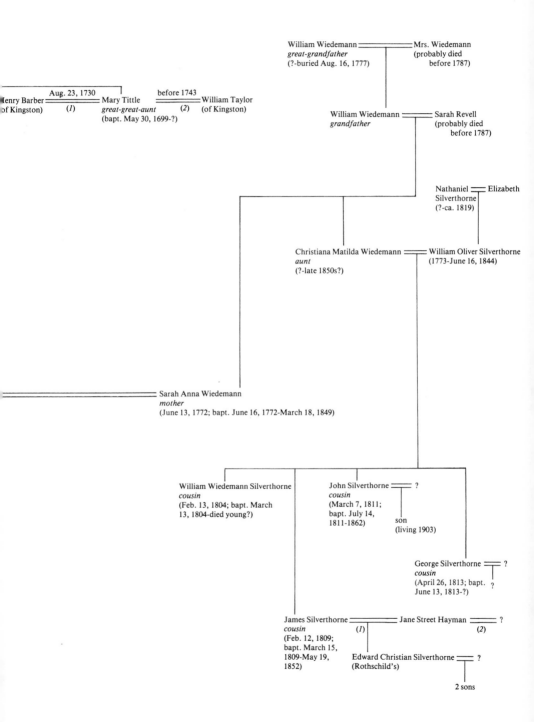

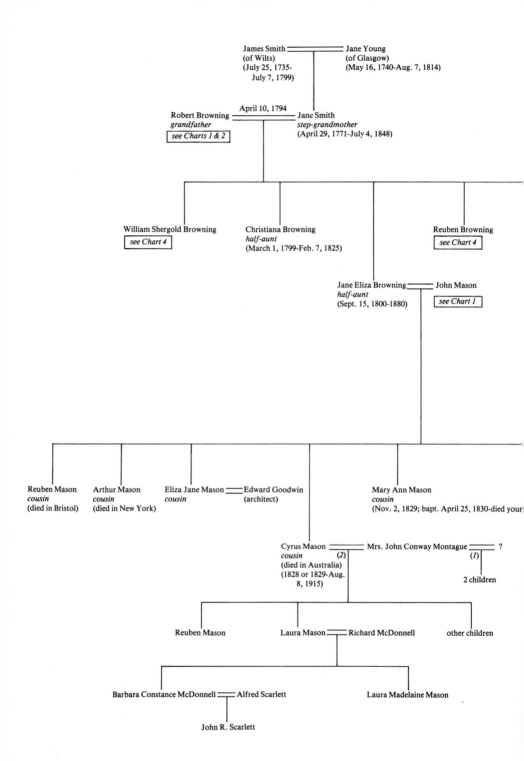

James Smith
(of Wilts)
(July 25, 1735-
July 7, 1799)

Jane Young
(of Glasgow)
(May 16, 1740-Aug. 7, 1814)

April 10, 1794

Robert Browning
grandfather
see Charts 1 & 2

Jane Smith
step-grandmother
(April 29, 1771-July 4, 1848)

William Shergold Browning
see Chart 4

Christiana Browning
half-aunt
(March 1, 1799-Feb. 7, 1825)

Reuben Browning
see Chart 4

Jane Eliza Browning
half-aunt
(Sept. 15, 1800-1880)

John Mason
see Chart 1

Reuben Mason
cousin
(died in Bristol)

Arthur Mason
cousin
(died in New York)

Eliza Jane Mason
cousin

Edward Goodwin
(architect)

Mary Ann Mason
cousin
(Nov. 2, 1829; bapt. April 25, 1830-died your

Cyrus Mason
cousin   (2)
(died in Australia)
(1828 or 1829-Aug.
8, 1915)

Mrs. John Conway Montague
(1)

?

2 children

Reuben Mason

Laura Mason

Richard McDonnell

other children

Barbara Constance McDonnell

Alfred Scarlett

Laura Madelaine Mason

John R. Scarlett

Chart 3 Family of Robert Browning,
Grandfather, and Jane Smith

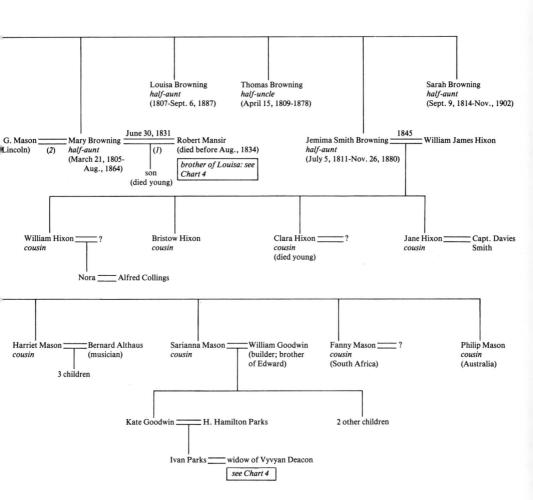

Louisa Browning
half-aunt
(1807-Sept. 6, 1887)

Thomas Browning
half-uncle
(April 15, 1809-1878)

Sarah Browning
half-aunt
(Sept. 9, 1814-Nov., 1902)

G. Mason === Mary Browning
(Lincoln)   (2)   *half-aunt*
                    (March 21, 1805-
                    Aug., 1864)

June 30, 1831
=== Robert Mansir
(1)   (died before Aug., 1834)

brother of Louisa: see
Chart 4

son
(died young)

Jemima Smith Browning === William James Hixon
half-aunt   1845
(July 5, 1811-Nov. 26, 1880)

William Hixon === ?
cousin

Bristow Hixon
cousin

Clara Hixon === ?
cousin
(died young)

Jane Hixon === Capt. Davies
cousin   Smith

Nora === Alfred Collings

Harriet Mason === Bernard Althaus
cousin   (musician)

3 children

Sarianna Mason === William Goodwin
cousin   (builder; brother
                            of Edward)

Fanny Mason === ?
cousin
(South Africa)

Philip Mason
cousin
(Australia)

Kate Goodwin === H. Hamilton Parks

2 other children

Ivan Parks === widow of Vyvyan Deacon

see Chart 4

373

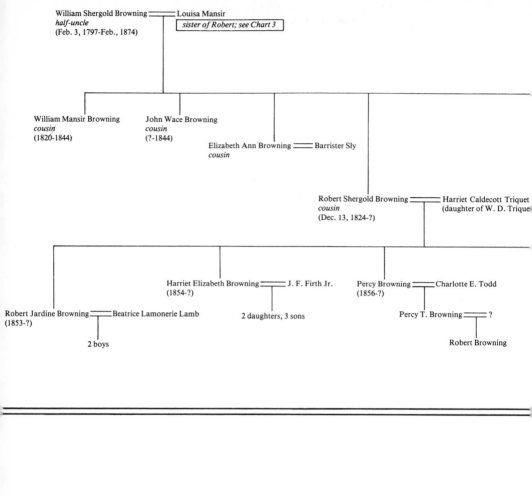

William Shergold Browning ══ Louisa Mansir
half-uncle
(Feb. 3, 1797-Feb., 1874)

┌─── sister of Robert; see Chart 3 ───┐

William Mansir Browning
cousin
(1820-1844)

John Wace Browning
cousin
(?-1844)

Elizabeth Ann Browning ══ Barrister Sly
cousin

Robert Shergold Browning ══ Harriet Caldecott Triquet
cousin (daughter of W. D. Trique
(Dec. 13, 1824-?)

Robert Jardine Browning ══ Beatrice Lamonerie Lamb
(1853-?)

2 boys

Harriet Elizabeth Browning ══ J. F. Firth Jr.
(1854-?)

2 daughters, 3 sons

Percy Browning ══ Charlotte E. Todd
(1856-?)

Percy T. Browning ══ ?

Robert Browning

Christiana Browning
cousin
(composer)

Robert Reuben Browning
cousin
(?-1887)

Michael Browning
cousin
(Rothschild's)
(1850-July 7, 1893)

William Browning
cousin
(ca. 1855-Sept., 1889)

Thomas Henry Browning ══ ?
cousin
(?-May, 1893)

Thomas Browning
(South Africa)

Captain Robert Seymour Brownin

? ══ Michael Browning ══ ?

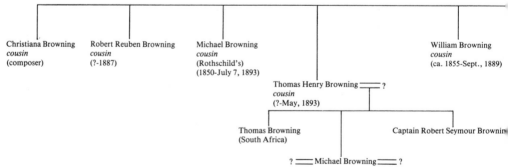

[a]Information from Elaine Baly, "Talking of the Brownings—Robert's Relations," *Browning Society Notes,* 3 (Dec., 1973), 8-11, as well as from Furnivall, "Ancestors." Baly omits two of William's sons, who died young.

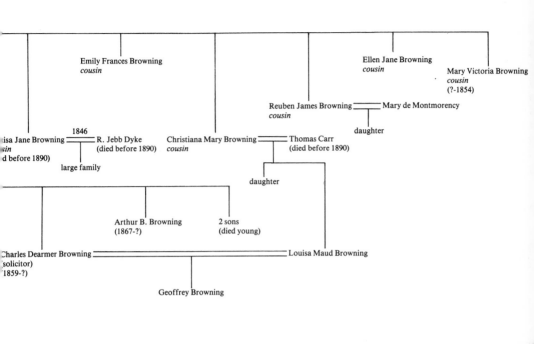

Emily Frances Browning
cousin

Ellen Jane Browning
cousin

Mary Victoria Browning
cousin
(?-1854)

Reuben James Browning ══════ Mary de Montmorency
cousin

daughter

1846

isa Jane Browning ══════ R. Jebb Dyke
sin   (died before 1890)
d before 1890)

Christiana Mary Browning ══════ Thomas Carr
cousin   (died before 1890)

large family

daughter

Arthur B. Browning
(1867-?)

2 sons
(died young)

Charles Dearmer Browning ══════════════════════ Louisa Maud Browning
solicitor)
1859-?)

Geoffrey Browning

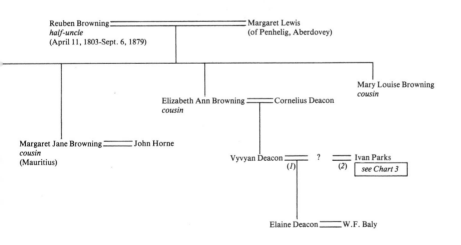

Reuben Browning ══════════════════ Margaret Lewis
half-uncle   (of Penhelig, Aberdovey)
(April 11, 1803-Sept. 6, 1879)

Mary Louise Browning
cousin

Elizabeth Ann Browning ══════ Cornelius Deacon
cousin

Margaret Jane Browning ══════ John Horne
cousin
(Mauritius)

Vyvyan Deacon ══════ ? ══════ Ivan Parks
                          (1)   (2)   see Chart 3

Elaine Deacon ══════ W.F. Baly

375

Appendix B Checklist of Sketchbooks, Notebooks, and Manuscripts of Robert Browning Sr.

I. In Public and Private Collections (by location)

Bank of England, Archives Section

1. "Bevan Scrapbook of Cartoons," ca. 1832, many on the Reform Bill, Acces. No. 4826, classification No. 741.5, presented by R. A. Bevan.
2. "Scrapbook of Cartoons," some ca. 1832, Acces. No. B 707/2, classification No. 741.5, formerly the property of Mrs. M. M. Stephens and presented by the Governor of the Bank, 1953.

Armstrong Browning Library, Baylor University

3. "Adriaen Brouwer," notes on his life and work, not cataloged.
4. "The Christian Virtues," brief note, dated Paris, Oct. 10, 1858.
5. "Military Engineering Sketches," vol. I of Drawings, Carson, No. 29, Herring, I., A.[96] Same as Dobell Catalog (see below), item 74.
6. "Nomenclator," 94 pp. and "Speed," 19 pp., genealogies of the Old Testament, dating after 1841, Carson, No. 28, Herring, I., I.
7. "The Old Schoolfellow," Carson, No. 30, Herring, I., C; repro. Herring, pp. 30-71.
8. "One hundred and Forty-Four Caricatures," Original Contributions, ca. 1830-1835, Carson, No. 31, Herring, I., G.
9. "Pencil and Ink Drawings of Scenes," vol. II of Drawings, Carson, No. 32, Herring, I., B.
10. "Sketch Book," scrapbook formerly the property of R. Wilkins Rees, cartoons, epigrams, sketches of the family, not cataloged, Herring, I., H.
11. "Small Sketch Book," Percy Cosier Collection, cartoons and parodies, not cataloged, Herring, I., F.
12. "Thirteen Sketches of *Bells and Pomegranates,*" inserted in RB, *Dramatic Lyrics* (1842) and *Dramatic Romances and Lyrics* (1845), Carson, No. 33, Herring, I., E. Cf. G. S. Layard. "Browning as Illustrator," *The Sketch,* 25 (Feb. 22, 1899), 200; rpt. *The Critic,* 34 (April 1899), 301.
13. "Twenty-Five Drawings," sketches and cartoons, Carson, No. 27, Herring, I., D.

Boston Public Library

14. "Thomas Ingall Sketchbook," cartoons by RB Sr. and RB. Partly pub., "Sketches by Robert Browning and his Father," *More Books: Bulletin of the Boston Public Library,* 1 (Sept.-Nov., 1926), 260-266.

British Museum

15. "Sludge, the Medium" Ashley MS. 2588, Herring, IV., A.
16. "The Medium," Ashley MS. 5720, ca. 1860, Herring, IV., B.

Fitzwilliam Museum, Cambridge University

17. "Letters to RB and Sarianna Browning," 14 letters, 5 to Sarianna, 9 to RB, [1849]-1866, and a plan of the Road Murder, Herring, III., A.
18. "Junius," essay of 6 pp., Herring, III., B.

Humanities Research Center, University of Texas

19. "Copy-book," Browning Collection, genealogies of popes and kings, Herring II., C (part 2).
20. "Notebook with Index," with signature of R. H. Griffith, notes on historical reading, dating as late as 1860, Herring, II., B. Same as Dobell Catalog (see below), item 70.
21. "Scrapbook," cartoons including "Ghost Story," dating as early as 1818, Herring, II., A. Cf. "A Curious Relic of the Browning Family," *The Bookman* (London), 10 (April 1896), 11-13; rpt. *The Bookman* (N.Y.), 3 (May 1896), 229-231.
22. "Scrapbook," Browning Collection, maps of *Pilgrim's Progress,* cartoons, poems, Sarianna Browning's portrait of RB Sr., Herring, II., C (part 1). Cf. Alice Corkran. "Chapters from the Story of my Girlhood," *Girl's Realm,* Nov., 1904, pp. 280-283, 285.

Robert Browning Fellowship Hall, Walworth

23. "The Nomenclator," 196 pp. (in a box), genealogies of the Old Testament, as submitted to a publisher with a note by RB, also "Preface" to this by RB and EBB in EBB's hand. Items 210 and 211 in the *Browning Bulletin* of the Robert Browning Settlement [London, 1928].
24. "The Nomenclator" (2 vols., brown covers): No. 1, 96 pp. inscribed to Anthony Snellgrove, Nov. 1856; No. 2, 66 pp. inscribed to Anthony Snellgrove. Items 136 and 137 of the *Bulletin.* I did not find item 133, a "Speed" presented at the same time to Snellgrove.

University College London, D.M.S. Watson Library

25. "Correspondence," Correspondence Nos. 655, 1252, 2 letters concerning RB's application to and withdrawal from The London University; pub., H. Hale Bellot. "Browning as an Undergraduate: Entry and Withdrawal," *Times,* Dec. 17, 1926, p. 15.

Victoria and Albert Museum

26. "Caricature Drawings," Forster Collection 48.D.1, Herring, VI.

Wellesley College Library [97]

27. "Book of Music," copies of songs and lyrics, Herring, V., B.
28. "Waltham Drawings," Marks Collection, cartoons and sketches done for the Waltham family, Peckham, 1826, Herring, V., D.
29. "The Widow of the Wood," novelistic account, sent in letters to Mrs. von Muller, April 3, 1851 and probably other dates, Herring, V., A.

Yale University, Beinecke Library

30. "Fifty Pen, Pencil, and Watercolor Sketches."

Private Collection

31. "Cartoons of Colleagues at the Bank," Mrs. Dorothy Gwyther, London.

II. Recorded, Location Now Unknown (by publication) [98]

Bertram Dobell Catalog. *Browning Memorials.* London, 1913

32. "About Fifty Humorous or Grotesque Drawings," item 69 (probably same as No. 30 above).

33. "Book Containing Genealogical Memoranda Relating to Leading Personages of the Old Testament," item 72.

34. "Drawings," chiefly in pencil, some architectural, item 66.

35. "Four Coloured Drawings, Copied From, or Imitative of, the Works of the Dutch Artists," item 68.

36. "Genealogies of the Old Testament," 395 pp., item 584.

37. "Grotesque Figure Drawings," some colored, item 65.

38. "An Index to the Persons Mentioned in the Works of Horace," item 585.

39. "Memoirs of the Roman Poet Horace," 1830, unfinished novel of 104 pp., item 230.

40. "MS Book Containing Memoranda on English and Scottish History," item 71.

41. "Nomenclator," over 100 pp., item 73 (possibly same as No. 6 above).

42. "Notebook," notes on Caesar Borgia and Italian history, dated Nov. 10, 1810, Mr. Hawkins's, 17 Manor Place, Walworth, item 283.

43. "Sketch Book," including cartoons of *Pilgrim's Progress,* item 67.

44. "Sketch Book," rough pencil views of scenery and notes, as late as 1848, item 401.

Ifan Kyrle Fletcher Catalog, No. 29, 1941, p. 6.

45. "Six Original Sketches of Humorous Characters," dancing master and others, Herring, VII.

Kitton, F. G. "Robert Browning the Elder, as a Caricaturist," *Art Journal*, 3 (Feb. 1896), 55-58.

46. "Sketchbook," with Introductory Notes by Reuben Browning and a note by Robert Wiedeman Browning.

Nicoll, W. R. "Robert Browning's Father," *Bookman* (London), 42 (May 1912), 63-73.

47. "Hamelin," complete poem on subject of the Pied Piper (wording slightly different from the 60-line fragment quoted in Griffin and Minchin, p. 21).

Sotheby & Co. Catalog. *The Browning Collections.* London, 1913.

48. "The Nomenclator," ca. 350 pp. (2 MSS, probably 2 parts), item 129 (includes "Preface"; possibly same as Nos. 23 and 24 above).

Stead, F. H. "Browning's Father: Caricaturist, Verse-Writer and Humanitarian," *Putnam's Magazine,* 7 (April 1910), 853-860.

49. "Sketches," belonging to Anthony Snellgrove.

Appendix C Contributions of Robert Browning
to *The Trifler*

In the Houghton Library, Harvard University, there are two issues of *The Trifler,* the amateur magazine edited on purely casual principles by Browning's friends in the set. The copies, Numbers one and two, January and February, 1835, are inscribed by an unidentified editor, probably one of the Dowsons, "To Robt Browning Jr Esq with the Editors [*sic*] regards." [99] It is likely that these are the only copies extant, and also that these two numbers were all, or close to all, that were ever published. Below are given the texts in full of the prose essay, certainly Browning's, and the "Epigram," which should probably be ascribed to him. The essay that his "Strictures" answers is printed first for comparison. I have not altered punctuation or spelling.

I. Essay on Debt, Signed C., the Article
Which Provoked Browning's "Strictures"

"Let it be your first care not to be in any man's debt."
Johnson.

The state of existence familiarly known as being *over head and ears in debt,* is not by any means *exclusive;*—on the contrary, it seems open to men of every rank and character, is *enjoyed* by communities as well as individuals, and in its most enlarged form takes the name of *national.* Debt indeed is a kind of social disease, wide-spreading in its ravages, but of no specific type; it springs from an endless variety of causes, and is marked by symptoms the most dissimilar. In the incipient stages it imperceptibly undermines the constitution, but it soon festers into a gnawing ulcer, or "gangrenes to black mortification." It may be hidden from other eyes for a time, but it is a cancer "rankling in the riven breast," which often grows incurable from concealment. It is at once a consumption of the stamina of the body, and a paralysis of the powers of the mind. The patient becomes emaciated, but the approved practice is to treat his disorder like a plethora; an abstemious regimen is prescribed, which, by subduing the quickened pulse and calming the fevered brain of dissolute excess, may reinvigorate the shattered frame of an impaired fortune.

The malady is contagious, and the benevolent often endanger themselves by their kindness to its victims. Honor and worth are not proof against it, and genius too frequently pines and sinks under its attacks; but the most malignant case is that of the spendthrift, in which the disease quickly runs to its crisis. Its course may be traced in the scion of an ancient house who upholds the dignity of his family by making over to the Jews the acres that are his only in expectancy, in exchange for the means of supporting a reckless extravagance; or in the upstart who establishes himself as a man of *ton,* by squandering the hoards he has lately inherited in the hells of St. James's or at Newmarket. He gets involved in debt, and is haunted by duns; writ follows writ, and he is hunted by bailiffs, till at length he is forced altogether off the stage, or at least has to change the scene;—his choice lies between King's Bench or the Fleet and "beyond Dover," unless indeed in a lucky hour St. Stephen's open its doors. In the end he becomes a "man on town," a *roué* and a *blackleg;* or if he has been taught wisdom, it is too late, and it is better to be a fool than go to his school to learn it.

Poverty and debt are nearly allied, but their influences are not alike baneful. The poor man may look his fellows boldly in the face, and "with virtue conquer extremities;" the man in debt feels lessened in his own eyes, and prefers living by his wits rather than his industry. Poverty may stimulate to exertion; debt cramps the energies of the soul and saps the independence of character. The gay may affect to view the evil lightly, but the wise man will agree with the moralist, and "not accustom himself to consider debt merely as an inconvenience, knowing that he may find it a calamity."

C.

II. Browning's Answer to the Essay on Debt

SOME STRICTURES ON A LATE ARTICLE IN THE "TRIFLER," IN A LETTER TO THE AUTHOR THEREOF.

"Naturally at a new author I doubt, and stick, and do not say quickly, Good: I censure much and tax."[100] I am ordinarily of Donne's mind; but in the instance of a certain lucubration in the number of last month, I confess, I doubt nothing and stick not to say as much,—deliberately, Bad! As for the censuring and taxing, take the present as an earnest; and I will wager (having gained somewhat by the ousting of Sir Charles)[101] that already the writer of the same,—instinctively apprehensive,—doth babble of "the common courtesy *due* to a stranger;" for 'tis of a truth the ungracious dissertation on debt and debtors, that I take on me to reprehend: at least, friend, I will owe *thee* nothing—I exult inordinately at the opportunity for rating thee roundly, which thine own flimsy reasoning hath furnished. I will neither re-read thine exercitation, nor more curiously consider my notions of its scope and tendency, nor charitably impute some better and less obvious motive to thee than is apparent in thy shallow performance—for this, and more, I fairly *owe* thee, and from all this dost thou voluntarily exclude thyself. I make no account, accordingly, of thy sophistries severally and in detail, but record generally that thou, ω μάταιε,[102] didst "stand up in the sun to shame creation," by an attempt to loosen and destroy the very tenure by which thy race doth exist and possess it.

For to be man is to be a debtor:—hinting but slightly at the grand and primeval debt implied in the idea of a creation, as matter too hard for ears like thine, (for saith not Luther, What hath a cow to do with nutmegs?)[103] I must, nevertheless, remind thee that all moralists have concurred in considering this our mortal sojourn as indeed an uninterrupted state of debt, and the world our dwelling-place as represented by nothing so aptly as by an inn, wherein those who lodge most commodiously have in perspective a proportionate score to reduce, and those who fare least delicately, but an insignificant shot to discharge—or, as the tuneful Quarles well phraseth it—

> "He's most in DEBT who lingers out the day,
> Who dies betimes has less and less to pay."[104]

So far, therefore, from these sagacious ethics holding that

"Debt cramps the energies of the soul," &c. [105]

as thou pratest, 'tis plain that they have willed on the very outset to inculcate this truth on the mind of every man,—no barren and inconsequential dogma, but an effectual, ever-influencing and productive rule of life,—that he is born a debtor, lives a debtor—aye, friend, and when thou diest, will not some judicious bystander,—no recreant as thou to the bonds of nature, but a good borrower and true,—remark, as did his grandsire before him on like occasions, that thou hast "paid the *debt* of nature." Ha! I have thee "beyond the rules," as one (a bailiff) may say!

Then, do but see, how, acknowledging, as thou needs must, this great original debt, on surveying more narrowly thy condition, thou wilt find that innumerable other debts, unperceived before, have thee fast, couldest thou even evade this primary obligation—as Gulliver only set free by a mighty wrench his head, to discover that the rest of his body was wholly subdued by minute lets and manacles. [106] Thy connexion with society, or political debt—is it not of such remote and hoar antiquity, that the impassioned Jean Jacques hath expended his best wit in the endeavour to ascertain the "origin of the social contract?" [107] Thy more immediate relation to the same, or moral debt—hath not the subtle Mandeville specially addressed himself to the task of accounting in some measure for the multiplicity of thine owings under that head, and establishing the "original of moral virtue?" [108] —And, miserable, couldst thou slip eel-like, nay, Wellesley-like, [109] from even these—could'st thou by searching find out some conjuncture wherein, to thy thinking, nothing did oblige thee—some untrodden path wherein thou wert seemingly free to follow thine own bent,—wouldst thou not say, in default of all other claims on thee, "I owe it to *myself* to do thus and thus?" Beset as thou art on every side by these evidences of thy debts "ut numero carrentes arenæ," [110] — the ledgers (as it were) wherein they are registered opened wide before thee, with here a sophist urgent on their venerable standing, there a moralist voluble on their magnitude,—over thy shoulder a poet rendering more formidable the sum total in flourishes of red-ink,—under thy nose a spruce humanist jotting down an unexpected demand on any the most trifling appropriation thou mayst meditate;—in the teeth of all this, I ask, wilt thou still designate *debt,*—nothing reserving, nothing qualifying,—as a disease, an ulcer, and what not? or wilt thou not rather, convinced that these things are so, closely surveying the conditions of human existence, the way which flesh cannot but go, the restrictions to which flesh cannot but submit, and impressed with this doctrine so universally, so unremittingly,—wilt thou not rather submit with docile alacrity to the manifest necessity which hedges thee round and hems thee in, and, conforming thyself to a debtor's estate, make it thine only business to contrive how best cooperating with the design of thy being, thou mayst *owe* more and more—as from an attentive observation of the bibulous properties of sea, earth, sun, and moon, the drouthy Teian did set himself seriously to drink [111] —as from an accurate consideration of the osculatory propensities of mountain, wind, and flower, the sweet poet of our days did determine sedulously to kiss? [112] I put it to thee, friend, and with no ill-will, trust me, but rather in pity;—can it be that thou hast really lived hitherto ignorant of this important dogma? That, far from endeavouring to follow out in right earnest its minutest bearings, in their genuine spirit, thou hast, mistaken man, deemed thy solitary thwartings and withstandings of its operation nothing less than virtues, and hast plumed thyself thereon proportionably? Is it even so? Well may Professor Füglistaller thus versify:—

"Agamus ergo, meditemur
  Imbellis vis quid valeat;
Homuncionem despicemur,
  Qui, quæ intendit, nesciat." [113]

I cannot withstand the itch of proselytizing, and scruple not to promise myself that the arguments I shall adduce will work their due effect in thee; but these I reserve for a separate communication, partly by reason of their magnitude, embracing as they do all the advantages which shall accrue from thy adoption of this principle in thy every-day practice, and partly because the wind bloweth sweetly from the Park, and the two strangers in dingy apparel and bright neckchains,[114] who have so fancied the singing of the goldfinch in my window as to listen thereto beneath during the last two hours, have at last disappeared, and a sally is no longer inexpedient.

Z

III. *"Epigram," Probably Another Comment by Browning on his Schoolmaster, Thomas Ready*

EPIGRAM.

"I wander from the point!" cried Tom—
It was an idle fear—
How could he ever wander from
What he was never near!

There is no external evidence that the "Epigram" is by Browning; but comparison with Browning's known epigram on Ready of 1833 with its similar subject, scorn, and familiar "Tom," makes the attribution extremely likely:

Impromptu on hearing a sermon by the Rev. T[homas].
R[eady]. pronounced 'heavy'—
"A *heavy* sermon!—sure the error's great,
For not a word Tom uttered *had its weight*."[115]

Browning's other epigrams on his school and schoolmaster are quoted in chapter x.

Appendix D Sarah Flower Adams' Marginalia in Her Copy of *Pauline*

The copy of *Pauline* (1833) in the Widener Collection, Harvard, can be tentatively identified either as that possessed by Sarah Flower Adams or as a deliberate forgery on both external and internal evidence. External evidence consists of a manuscript note in an unidentified hand on the inside front cover, "This copy was given to Sarah Flower Adams the author of Nearer my God to Thee and the original Pauline by Robert Browning," and an unidentified sales catalog clipping inserted in the copy, "This Copy was given by the author to Sarah Flower Adams, author of 'Nearer My God to Thee,' who, at least in part, inspired the poem. From the library of Walter B. Slater." Presumably both assertions derive from the same unidentified source. Their vague claim, however, is substantiated by the character of the pencil annotations, a number of which clearly appear to be contemporary with the work and written by someone who knew the author. The tone is also compatible with all that is known of Sarah's character, a mixture of enthusiasm for egregiously poetic passages and disapprobation of RB's self-involvement. A comparison of the handwriting with that in the facsimile of the manuscript of "Nearer, My God, to Thee,"[116] although somewhat inconclusive due to the small number of samples and differences in date, suggests that Sarah's authorship of the marginalia is not improbable. In light of this evidence it seems correct to assume that the copy is either Sarah's with her marginalia or a deliberate forgery purporting to be hers. Inasmuch as Slater was a regular purchaser from the forger T. J. Wise, the second possibility should not be discounted,[117] though as a major collector Slater would be a likely buyer for a legitimate find as well.

The marginalia are in very light, sometimes illegible, pencil. They consist of exclamations and brief observations and a number of marginal lines marking passages of special interest. They are apparently all from the same hand. Page references below are to the original edition of *Pauline;* the line numbers are those used in the Ohio edition of *The Complete Works of Robert Browning,* vol. I (1969).

Reference		Marginalia
p. 11	I have felt this in dreams—in dreams in which / I seemed the fate from which I fled; (ll. 96-97)	[lines marked]
p. 12	entire page (ll. 106-122)	[lines marked] [one to two illeg. words followed by] all

Reference		**Marginalia**
p. 16	entire page (ll. 171-186)	[lines marked] what poetry [or] very pretty [? almost illeg.]
p. 17	Its course in vain, for it does ever spread / Like a sea's arm as it goes rolling on, / Being the pulse of some great country—so / Wert thou to me—and art thou to the world. (ll. 187-190)	[lines marked]
p. 19	I was thine in shame, / And now when all thy proud renown is out, / I am a watcher, whose eyes have grown dim / With looking for some star (ll. 225-228)	pretty!
p. 25	They came to me in my first dawn of life . . . Sailing with troops of friends to Tenedos;—(ll. 318-325)	[lines marked; last line also marked by an *X*]
p. 26	On the dim clustered isles in the blue sea: / The deep groves, and white temples, and wet caves— / And nothing ever will surprise me now— / Who stood beside the naked Swift-footed, / Who bound my forehead with Proserpine's hair. (ll. 331-335)	[lines marked]
p. 27	In deeds for which remorse were vain, as for / The wanderings of delirious dream; yet thence / Came cunning, envy, falsehood (ll. 349-351)	*true!* poor lad.
p. 28	For music, (which is earnest of a heaven, . . . Where the dead gather (ll. 365-374)	[lines marked]
p. 29	I had done nothing, so I sought to know / What mind had yet achieved. No fear was mine . . . To rival what I wondered at (ll. 338-391)	[lines marked; first two underlined; rest marked in margin; last also marked with *X*]
p. 39	Decays. Nought makes me trust in love so really, (l. 554)	[line marked]
p. 40	As the delight of the contented lowness / With which I gaze on souls I'd keep for ever / In beauty —I'd be sad to equal them; / I'd feed their fame e'en from my heart's best blood, / Withering unseen, that they might flourish still. (ll. 555-559)	true to [?] the perfected soul but not of yours RB, alas. [and two lines drawn under entire comment]
p. 42	My selfishness is satiated not, / It wears me like a flame; (ll. 601-602)	true!
p. 44	This restlessness of passion meets in me / A craving after knowledge: (ll. 620-621)	*vanity* [and "passion" underlined]

Reference		Marginalia
p. 46	passage on Andromeda (ll. 655-667)	ah so alive [? illeg.]
p. 53	Still, as but let by sufferance; the trees bend / O'er it as wild men watch a sleeping girl, (ll. 772-773)	[lines marked]
pp.55-57	footnote (after l. 811)	[Pauline's note is lightly but entirely crossed out]
p. 64	I am very weak, / But what I would express is,—Leave me not, (ll. 924-925)	pretty—[lines marked and underlined through "is,"]
pp. 64-65	I hope in myself—and hope, and pant, and love— / You'll find me better—know me more than when / You loved me as I was. (ll. 933-935)	[lines marked]
p. 66	Most stinted and deformed—like the mute dwarfs / Which wait upon a naked Indian queen. (ll. 956-957)	[lines marked]
pp. 67-68	Feeling God loves us, and that all that errs, / Is a strange dream which death will dissipate; (ll. 978-979)	[lines marked]
p. 70	And I shall see all clearer and love better . . . I shall be priest and lover, as of old. (ll. 1012-1019)	[lines marked]

Notes

Abbreviations

BAF	*Browning to his American Friends: Letters Between the Brownings, the Storys, and James Russell Lowell, 1841-1890,* ed. Gertrude R. Hudson (New York, Barnes and Noble, 1965).
Baylor	The Armstrong Browning Library, Baylor University.
BL	The British Library at the British Museum.
Broughton	Leslie N. Broughton, Clark S. Northup, and Robert Pearsall, *Robert Browning: A Bibliography, 1830-1950* (Ithaca, Cornell University Press, 1953).
DeVane, *Handbook*	W. C. DeVane, *A Browning Handbook,* rev. ed. (New York, Appleton-Century-Crofts, 1955).
DI	*Dearest Isa: Robert Browning's Letters to Isabella Blagden,* ed. Edward C. McAleer (Austin, University of Texas Press, 1951).
Domett's *Diary*	*The Diary of Alfred Domett: 1872-1885,* ed. E. A. Horsman (London, Oxford University Press, 1953).
Furnivall, "Ancestors"	F. J. Furnivall, "Robert Browning's Ancestors," *Papers of the Browning Society* (London, 1889-1891), III, 26-45.
Griffin, "Domett"	W. H. Griffin, "Robert Browning and Alfred Domett," *Contemporary Review,* 87 (Jan. 1905), 95-115.
Griffin, "Early Friends"	W. H. Griffin, "Early Friends of Robert Browning," *Contemporary Review,* 87 (March 1905), 427-446.
Griffin and Minchin	W. H. Griffin and H. C. Minchin, *The Life of Robert Browning,* rev. ed. (London, Methuen, 1938).
Irvine and Honan	Park Honan and William Irvine, *The Book, the Ring, and the Poet: A Biography of Robert Browning* (New York, McGraw-Hill, 1974).

LEBB	*The Letters of Elizabeth Barrett Browning,* ed. F. G. Kenyon, 2 vols. (London, 1897).
LL	*Learned Lady; Letters from Robert Browning to Mrs. Thomas FitzGerald, 1876-1889,* ed. Edward C. McAleer (Cambridge, Mass., Harvard University Press, 1966).
LRB	*Letters of Robert Browning,* ed. Thurman L. Hood (New Haven, Yale University Press, 1933).
Mason, "Kinsfolk"	Cyrus Mason, "The Poet Robert Browning and his Kinsfolk by his Cousin," ed. Willard C. Turner, unpub. M.A. Diss., Baylor University, 1971 (the MS is at Baylor).
Miller	Betty Miller, *Robert Browning: A Portrait* (New York, Scribners, 1953).
NL	*New Letters of Robert Browning,* ed. W. C. DeVane and K. L. Knickerbocker (New Haven, Yale University Press, 1950).
Orr	Mrs. Sutherland Orr, *Life and Letters of Robert Browning,* rev. F. G. Kenyon (London, Smith, Elder, 1908).
RBAD	*Robert Browning and Alfred Domett,* ed. F. G. Kenyon (London, Smith, Elder, 1906).
RBEBK	*The Letters of Robert Browning and Elizabeth Barrett Barrett 1845-1846,* ed. Elvan Kintner, 2 vols. (Cambridge, Mass., Harvard University Press, 1969).
RBJW	*Robert Browning and Julia Wedgwood: A Broken Friendship as Revealed by their Letters,* ed. Richard Curle (New York, Frederick A. Stokes, 1937).
Sharp, *Life*	William Sharp, *Life of Robert Browning* (London, 1890).
Sotheby	Sotheby & Co. Catalog, *The Browning Collections. Catalogue of Oil Paintings, Drawings and Prints; Autograph Letters and Manuscripts . . . Which Will Be Sold by Auction, by Messrs. Sotheby, Wilkinson, and Hodge, London, May 1, 2, 5-8* (London, 1913).

Note: Because Browning's correspondence is scattered in dozens of published editions and articles or still available only in manuscript, full dates for letters cited are given in normalized form in the notes. Brackets around a date indicate that it is conjectural. Where the editor of a letter has already made a conjectural dating, this has been followed, but doubts or corrections have been added. As an aid to future identification of published letters, *the page reference given is to the page on which a letter begins.* RB and EBB stand for Robert Browning and Elizabeth Barrett (married or unmarried), RB Sr. for the father of the poet.

Quotations from Browning's poems are from first editions through *Christmas-Eve and Easter-Day* (1850) unless otherwise indicated. For works published later than this, citations are from the Macmillan text, *The Complete Poetical Works of Robert Browning,* ed. Augustine Birrell (New York, 1915).

Notes

Chapter I   *Introduction: Seeing Young Browning Plain*

1. The birth and baptism were recorded by George Clayton, the family minister, in the Register of Baptisms, Locks Fields Walworth, p. 12v, Census Office, the Public Record Office, London (this is the original called in from the church in 1837).

2. Orr, p. 32, RB Sr. to Thomas Powell, March 11, 1843; "Browning's Letters," *The Critic,* 8 (Jan. 2, 1886), 11.

3. *DI,* p. 145, RB to Isa Blagden, Jan. 19, 1863.

4. E. V. Lucas, "Robert Browning: a Castigation," *Methuen's Annual* (London, Methuen, 1914), p. 47.

5. Sarianna Browning told Browning's biographer, Hall Griffin, that the circumstances of "Development" were real, but the central incident, the Troy game, was fanciful: Robert Wiedeman Browning to Hall Griffin, Nov. 11, 1902, Hall Griffin Papers, BL, Add. MS. 45,563, fols. 186-194.

6. "More legitimately *myself* than most of the others" (other early works he contemplated): RB, Marginal MS note, *Pauline* (1833), Mill copy, p. 4, Victoria and Albert Museum, Forster Collection.

7. W. C. DeVane, *Browning's Parleyings, the Autobiography of a Mind* (New Haven, Yale University Press, 1927). DeVane's work is an admirable study of the sources and ideas in this poem and offers a number of insights into Browning's thought even in his early life. But it should not be misused, as Griffin and Minchin's revised biography has used it (pp. 6, 9-10, 15-16, 19), as a substitute for biographical study of Browning's early reading and the influences on his developing mind.

8. Orr, chap. iii, is the only record for most of these. Mrs. Sutherland Orr was RB's closest woman friend in later life; she was also "authorized" to write RB's life by Sarianna Browning who gave her help and read her manuscript: Sarianna Browning to Michael Field, [ca. July, 1890], BL, Add. Ms. 45,856, fols. 46-46b; Hall Griffin Papers, BL, Add. MS. 45,563, fols. 61-63b. Nonetheless, both Sarianna and Robert Wiedeman Browning frequently expressed dissatisfaction with parts of her work.

9. *RBEBK,* I, 334 (letter 181), RB to EBB, [Dec. 21, 1845]; F. H. Stead, "Browning's Father," *Putnam's Magazine,* 7 (April 1910), 860, Sarianna Browning to A. G. Snellgrove, April 3, 1890.

10. This general portrait of the early Browning is confirmed not only by Sarianna (ibid.) and RB's later recollections (*RBJW,* p. 84, RB to Julia Wedgwood, Oct. 17, 1864) but also by persons who knew Browning in youth: the Rev. Edward White who knew RB from church: see "Mr. Browning's Religious History," *British Weekly,* Dec. 20, 1889, p. 117; also White's open letter to Herbert Stead, June 5, 1895, MS, Newington District Library. The letter has him with pale complexion, "black flowing hair," and omits the inaccurate black eyes of the article; see also W. S., otherwise unidentified, who knew him at The London University: "Correspondence," *Times,* Dec. 14, 1899, p. 9. There are also the slightly later recollections of Emma Young: Griffin, "Early Friends," p. 440; and Domett's *Diary,* p. 178.

11. Sotheby, item 172, RB to Anne Egerton-Smith, [ca. Oct.-Nov. 1876].

12. RB Sr., "Pencil sketch of Robert Browning," "Thomas Ingall Sketchbook," MS, Boston Public Library, fol. 49 (picture 163): this may date as late as the 1830s; RB Sr., drawing identified as "supposed early portrait of R Browning," "Sketch Book," MS, Baylor (No. 10, Appendix B): certainly of a young man with wavy curls, but not necessarily RB. Grace E. Wilson, *Robert Browning's Portraits, Photographs, and Other Likenesses and their Makers* (Waco, Texas, Baylor University, 1943), p. 24, reproduces a portrait of a boy, age 12, by E. Bridell-Fox, by vague tradition a copy of an early sketch of RB by RB Sr. The present location is not known. It may be another portrait by E. Bridell-Fox of Robert Wiedeman Browning?

13. Described, Wilson, *Robert Browning's Portraits,* pp. 29-33. Wilson reports the Beard original in the Rischgitz Collection at the National Portrait Gallery, London, but this is only a copy of the engraving and is located at the Radio Times Hulton Picture Library. I conclude the Beard sketch is lost. The Armytage engraving was made for R. H. Horne's *A New Spirit of the Age* (London, 1844). James Charles Armytage (1820-1897) was a well-known English engraver. I have not been able to identify Beard. Evidently in 1854 another engraving was made from the Beard sketch, probably from the Armytage engraving, by John Sartain (1808-1897) for the *Eclectic Magazine,* 31 (April 1854), p. 433 f. (not from a Lawrence original as Broughton, entry C126, implies). The engraving is signed "Yours very truly, Robert Browning." On the complicated history of the Ripert-Monclar portrait(s) see n. 241, chap. v. Even more puzzling is the silver-copper daguerreotype reproduced by Wilson, p. 27, attributed to the Royal Polytechnic Institute, and dated by Wilson as 1835 (at Baylor). Inasmuch as the daguerreotype process was invented in 1839 and not available commercially until about 1840 in London, this cannot be a photograph from 1835. The portrait appears to be of RB and of about the same date as the Beard drawing. Possibly the daguerreotype is a photograph of a drawing of 1835; the portrait looks more like a drawing than a photograph. It seems to be a photo (reversed) of the head in the Armytage engraving but with a different, simpler drawing of RB's body in less formal garb. Possibly this is a photo of the lost Beard original from which the engraving was made; the fancier dress could be the engraver's addition. Cf. Sotheby, item 1235, which confuses the photo with the Armytage engraving.

14. Visa of RB, St. Petersburg, March 31, 1834, MS, Baylor; kindly trans. for me by Mr. Scott Ward.

15. Catherine (Katie) Bromley, quoted in A. M. W. Stirling, *The Merry Wives of Battersea and Gossip of Three Centuries* (London, Robert Hale, 1956), p. 122 (source not identified); E. Bridell-Fox, "Robert Browning," *Argosy,* 59 (Feb. 1890), 764.

16. M. D. Conway, "Robert Browning," *New York Evening Post,* Dec. 17, 1889 (copy at Baylor); and also Conway's *Autobiography, Memories and Experiences* (Boston, Houghton Mifflin, 1904), II, 22; *William Allingham, A Diary,* ed. Helen Allingham and D. Radford (London, Macmillan, 1907), p. 240. Both recollections are from a first meeting April 12, 1836 at Leigh Hunt's. Carlyle's recollection to Conway is also of a later visit to Hatcham.

17. *NL,* p. 262, RB to Madame Bessie Rayner Belloc, March 18, 1881. This was on the occasion of RB's first visit to Carlyle's house, ca. May 1840.

18. Joseph Slater, *The Correspondence of Emerson and Carlyle* (New York, Columbia University Press, 1964), p. 329, Carlyle to Emerson, Aug. 29, 1842; Carlyle to John Sterling, July 28, 1842.

Chapter II   Camberwell and New Cross

1. An old pamphlet describing the church (n.d.), BL, Map Room, MS. XL.39.A. The old church was enlarged in 1825. The present church was built on the site of the old one after a fire in 1841. Standard works on Camberwell's history and antiquities are Douglas Allport, *Collections Illustrative of the Geology, History, Antiquities, and Associations, of Camberwell, and the Neighbourhood* (Camberwell, 1841); William H. Blanch, *Ye Parish of Camerwell* (London, 1875); Philip M. Johnston, *Old Camberwell: Its History and Antiquities* (Camberwell, priv. prnt., 1919), mostly on church relics; H. J. Dyos, *Victorian Suburb: A Study of the Growth of Camberwell* (Leicester, Leicester University Press, 1961), uses Camberwell as a model for a classic study of the expansion of Victorian London; John Summerson, *Georgian London* (London, Pleiades Books, 1945), pp. 255-271, discusses the early development of London's suburbs. Extensive collections of local history are located in the Newington District Library, Walworth and the Minet Library, Stockwell.

2. Engraving from a painting by H. Prosser, "North View of St. Giles Church, Camberwell" (Engelmann, Graf, Coindet & Co., n.d.), Newington District Library.

3. At least two nineteenth-century views of this old inn are available: "The Rosemary Branch in 1800," Newington District Library, reproduced Blanch, *Parish*, p. 370: a painting by H. Prosser, "Rosemary Branch," BL, Add. MS. 25,112, fol. 15. The quotation is from Blanch, *Parish*, p. 368.

4. "Camberwell Mill" (1825), Newington District Library; another print (1816) shows a windwill at Dulwich Common.

5. "A New and Accurate Survey and Map of the County of Surrey Oct. 28, 1763," BL, Map Room, Maps XL.8.6.

6. "View of London from Camberwell" Newington District Library. There is also an earlier "View of Camberwell from the Grove" (n.d.). The quotation is from an article on Grove Hill in *The Mirror of Literature, Amusement, and Instruction,* Feb. 26, 1825, clipping at Newington District Library.

7. "Knight's Hill Farm" (n.d.), Newington District Library.

8. Reputedly he lived in the attractive mansion known as the "Old House on the Green" at Camberwell Green. Newington District Library has two eighteenth-century views of the house.

9. A print (probably around 1800) of an Italianate house in a park, entitled "Villa of John Rolls Esq. New Cross Kent Road," BL, Map Room, Maps, 25.C.26, fol. 26.

10. T. B. Macaulay, *The History of England from the Accession of James II* (Boston, 1849), I, 274.

11. "A New Map of London and its Environs" (1823), BL, Map Room, Maps 3479 (36). Summerson, *Georgian London,* pp. 255-271, describes four stages of early suburban development generally, though not necessarily, succeeding each other: expansion within the old villages; construction of new villas; new development along roads in terraces, semidetached, or detached houses; estate development between main roads.

12. J. Arnould to A. Domett, Apr. 18, 1874, Hall Griffin Papers, BL, Add. MS. 45,560, fol. 69.

13. By G. Yates, Add. MS. 25,112, fol. 14.

14. G. Yates, water color of "Camberwell Charity Schools" (1825), BL, Add. MS. 25,112, fol. 10; another by Yates, BL, Add. MS. 25,112, fol. 12.

15. "Plan of Grove Hill Camberwell Surrey belonging to J. C. Lettsom M.D. 1792," Newington District Library.

16. Allport, *Collections of Camberwell*, p. 102.

17. Charles Dickens, *Pickwick Papers,* chap. lvii.

18. Pigot and Co., *London & Provincial New Commercial Directory* (London, 1823), p. 10 (description of Camberwell).

19. Letter of Feb. 26, 1845, Hall Griffin Papers, BL, Add. MS. 45,560, fol. 44.

20. *RBEBK,* I, 103 (letter 48), RB to EBB, [June 24, 1845].

21. Orr, p. 25.

22. Blanch, *Parish,* pp. 186-187. Most of what was celebrated as progress was in fact merely huge growth, from about 11,000 at RB's birth to about 39,000 as early as 1840 when the Brownings removed to less settled New Cross: Ibid., p. 75.

23. Arnold, *Friendship's Garland* (1871).

24. Robert Wiedeman Browning to Hall Griffin, Nov. 11, 1902, Hall Griffin Papers, BL, Add. MS. 45,563, fols. 186-194.

Chapter III   Family

1. Furnivall, "Ancestors," p. 31, asserted the African origin. The family story that RB Sr. was told at St. Kitts to sit in the segregated part of the church is, as Orr early noted, inexplicable. He was blue-eyed and very English in appearance and complexion. Possibly this was a response to his liberalism, not his coloration, or perhaps he wandered, like the proverbial Englishman, in the noonday sun. Furnivall had the story from Robert Shergold Browning (son of Uncle William), letter of March 5, 1890, MS, Huntington, FU 159; however, he gives a mistaken age for the residence at St. Kitts and the story seems to have been unknown to RB Sr.'s immediate family. A "Memo" MS, Robert Browning Fellowship Hall, Walworth, by Anthony Snellgrove (the younger), RB Sr.'s fellow employee at the Bank, specifically confirms that RB Sr. was light, not dark in complexion and notes that Furnivall had his information from another employee (Bevan) who never saw RB Sr. Mason, "Kinsfolk," p. 48, gives another family legend about the Tittle background, equally unfounded: Margaret Tittle was of French descent —aristocratic refugees, of course! Furnivall, "Ancestors," demonstrated the lack of evidence for attribution of Jewish origin. The discussions of these questions have been logically unsound and morally vacuous.

2. Oscar Browning, *Memories of Sixty Years at Eton, Cambridge, and Elsewhere* (London, John Lane, 1910), p. 6. RB told Moncure D. Conway that the family descended originally from a DeBruni: *Autobiography, Memories and Experiences* (Boston, Houghton, Mifflin, 1904), II, 23. The Brownings also claimed unproven kinship with the extinct gentry family of Brownings of the manors of Melbury Sampford and Melbury Osmond: Furnivall, "Ancestors," p. 35. Mason, "Kinsfolk," pp. 19-32, asserts—but does not demonstrate—the same connection. His muddled method, looking for recurring first names, shows the woolgathering of family pride at its fuzziest.

3. O. Browning, *Memories,* p. 6. A book given to RB (Sr.?) in 1847 by M. Galtons Fall, Elizabeth Charlotte, *Derry, a Tale of the Revolution* (London, 1843), at Baylor, confirms family interest in this presumptive forebear. Christiana Browning (daughter of RB's Uncle Reuben) to F. J. Furnivall, [ca. 1890], MS, Huntington, FU 72, asserts the connection also. One possible connection between Londonderry and Woodyates is suggested by the fact that Thomas Earl of Londonderry held manors at Woodyates and Gussich St. Andrews in the eighteenth century: John Hutchins, *The History and Antiquities of the County of Dorset* (London, 1774), II, 221.

4. The arms were taken from a family, Bruning, of Wilts and Derby without authorization from the College of Arms: "gules two bands wavy or and argent": Furnivall, "Ancestors," p. 36; O. Browning, *Memories,* p. 6. Maggs Bros., *Catalog,* No. 338 (London, 1915), item 150, is a framed coat of arms of the poet. The motto was used on stationery and the arms at the Palazzo Rezzonico in his old age.

5. Sotheby & Co., *Catalogue of the Papers of Lt.-Col. Harry Peyton Moulton-Barrett* (London, May 1937), lot 6, EBB to Arabel Barrett, Feb. [1847].

6. Appendix A summarizes information available about Browning's known ancestors and the relatives, outside of his immediate family, contemporary with his early life. Information given in the text below about his paternal and maternal forebears is substantiated in the Appendix. For the Woodyates Brownings see Appendix A, section I.

7. The Tittle family background is summarized, Appendix A, section II.

8. J. A. Giuseppi, "Families of Long Service at the Bank of England," *Genealogists' Magazine,* 10 (Sept. 1949), 403.

9. Mason, "Kinsfolk," pp. 53, 60.

10. Ibid., p. 78.

11. A list of books known to have been his is given in Appendix A, section I.

12. Orr, p. 4.

13. *LRB,* p. 289, RB to Edmund Gosse, Feb. 23, 1888.

14. RB Sr. was born July 6, 1782 at Battersea, London. He died June 14, 1866 at Paris, 151, rue de Grenelle, and was buried in the grounds at rue de la Chaise: Sarianna Browning to J. M. Campbell, May 24, 1892, MS, Humanities Research Center, Univ. of Texas. He left no will.

15. From his "Uncle Tittle and Aunt Mill," as Browning's grandfather noted in his will, 1819: given in full, Furnivall, "Ancestors," pp. 39-40. Their identity is discussed in Appendix A, section II. Tittle was almost certainly dead before he went to St. Kitts. It is not clear whether RB Sr. received money from both or just from Tittle; there is no date for Sarah Mill's death. On the amount of the legacy, probably small but not negligible, see also Appendix A, section II.

16. *RBEBK,* II, 1003 (letter 523), RB to EBB, [Aug. 26, 1846]. From Bank records it appears that the other capacity was as an apprentice to William Manning, a West India merchant and director of the Bank: Giuseppi, "Families of Long Service," pp. 404-405. Manning was in the firm of Porcher & Co. He had married into a Ryan family of St. Kitts and was director at the Bank from 1790 on (governor 1812-1814). He was the father of the cardinal.

17. Ibid.

18. Mason, "Kinsfolk," p. 45, recalled that RB Sr. told him of trading a pineapple for writing paper in St. Kitts. Mason makes a silly effort to argue that only the cultural isolation, not the system of slavery, was responsible for his return. That slavery made a large impact on RB Sr. is evidenced by his frequent drawings of slaves as servants in his cartoons, mostly sympathetic.

19. Advertisement for a school "At Cheshunt in Hertfordshire," MS, BL, Department of Prints and Drawings. The Rev. A. Bell was clergyman at the Dissenting Chapel in Cheshunt Street, Cheshunt (now rebuilt as Cheshunt United Reform Church). The exact location of the school, described as a "healthy situation," is not known. (Information kindly provided by Mr. Jack Edwards, Librarian, Public Library, Cheshunt.) Kenyon was also at a Dr. Sawyer's Fort Bristol School, Bristol, and the Charterhouse, London, and Mrs. Andrew Crosse, "John Kenyon and his Friends," *Temple Bar,* 88 (April 1890), 478, identifies the Fort Bristol School as the one RB Sr. attended with him (as does the *DNB,* s.v. Kenyon). However, Orr, p. 97, mentions a "Rev. Mr. Bell at Cheshunt," probably from family information; and this is confirmed by RB's own reference to Cheshunt: William Knight, *Retrospects* (New York, Charles Scribner's, 1904), p. 87, RB to William Knight, Jan. 10, 1884. The association with Kenyon was probably early; Kenyon speaks of RB Sr. as an "early schoolfellow" (John Kenyon to Anna Jameson, Feb. 13, 1846, MS, Wellesley), and Kenyon's poem (see note below) suggests the schoolboy battles were out of Pope's Homer, not the Greek.

20. John Kenyon, *A Rhymed Plea for Tolerance* (London, 1839), p. 22: passage marked by RB Sr., presentation copy, Wellesley.

21. Mason is not generally trustworthy on earlier family history. Appendix A, section I, discusses this Reuben and the grounds for accepting some of Mason's testimony concerning him.

22. See the discussion of Jane Eliza Browning, Appendix A, section IV.

23. *RBEBK,* II, 1003 (letter 523), RB to EBB, [Aug. 26, 1846].

24. Orr, p. 5.

25. *RBEBK,* II, 1003 (letter 523), RB to EBB, [Aug. 26, 1846].

26. Giuseppi, "Families of Long Service," p. 404; nominated by Manning. RB Sr.'s direct association with Manning explains how he could obtain a position at a time when his

father would not have been in a mood to help him. Furnivall, "Ancestors," pp. 30-31, notes that the examination consisted of polite questions about his trip to St. Kitts. The employment, like the small private income, would have been a source of aggravation to his father.

27. A Notebook of his is dated "Nov. 10, 1810: Residence at Mr. Hawkins, 17 Manor Place, Walworth": Bertram Dobell Catalog, *Browning Memorials* (London, 1913), item 283.

28. As Griffin and Minchin, pp. 4-5, noticed, RB's claim in the letter of [Aug. 26, 1846] that the grandfather hated RB Sr. until a "few years" before he died, seems to conflict with the tone of his will of 1819. Probably there were at least formal relations between the two families in the 1820s.

29. Mason, "Kinsfolk," pp. 80-81: Mason states that the poet's family had moved there first and were thus joined by the others. Elaine Baly, "Talking of the Brownings—Robert's Relations," *Browning Society Notes,* 3 (Dec. 1973), 5, has the widow moving to Albert Terrace first. Mason's memory must have precedence over family tradition here, though he may be wrong.

30. An article on Grove Hill in *The Mirror of Literature, Amusement, and Instruction,* Feb. 26, 1825, clipping at Newington District Library.

31. A cartoon by RB Sr., "Scrapbook of Cartoons," formerly property of Mrs. Stephens, Bank of England, Archives Section, fol. 57, has a young man told that he will never do at the Bank: "they drink nothing but Small beer—& are obliged to put on a clean shirt every other Sunday." Another in the "Bevan Scrapbook," also at the Bank, fol. 47, jokes about reform sweeping away sinecures at the Bank for relatives.

32. Correspondence concerning RB Sr.'s application for a ticket to the British Museum Reading Room, William Smee to Sir Henry Ellis, Nov. 8, 1847, BL, Add. MS. 48,340, fols. 91-92b. Furnivall, "Ancestors," p. 31, quotes a friend on RB Sr.'s popularity at the Bank.

33. He started in the Accountants Office; in 1811 he was appointed to the Dividend Room of the Consols Office from which he never changed until his retirement: Giuseppi, "Families of Long Service," pp. 404-405. Orr, p. 13, notes that he refused an offer to found a branch office in Liverpool in later years. Richard Garnett reported to Hall Griffin that a man who knew RB Sr. at the Bank felt he was not a very efficient clerk: Hall Griffin Papers, BL, Add. MS. 45,564, fols. 112-113b. His one activity at the Bank of any note was deplorable: he was innocent subscribing witness to the power of attorney of a Henry Fauntleroy, who was later found to be a forger and hanged: George Borrow, *Celebrated Trials, and Remarkable Cases of Criminal Jurisprudence from the Earliest Records to the Year 1825* (London, 1825), VI, 563.

34. Sarianna Browning to Anthony Snellgrove, June 22, [1866], MS, Private Collection of Mrs. Dorothy Gwyther, Whetstone, London.

35. Robert Wiedeman Browning to Hall Griffin, Nov. 11, 1902, Hall Griffin Papers, BL, Add. MS. 45,563, fols. 186-194.

36. Orr, p. 15: a letter of Dec. 26, 1870, recalling Browning's father in later years in Paris.

37. Robert Wiedeman Browning to Hall Griffin, Dec. 8, 1904, Hall Griffin Papers, BL, Add. MS. 45,564, fols. 123b-124.

38. Mrs. Kate Lemann to Hall Griffin, Oct. 31, 1901, Hall Griffin Papers, BL, Add. MS. 45,564, fols. 81-84. The "Waltham Drawings," MS, Wellesley, provide a warm record of his sociable use of art with another family, that of a C. Waltham, Esq., of Peckham.

39. Mason, "Kinsfolk," p. 93.

40. RB Sr.'s appearance was described, F. H. Stead, "Browning's Father," *Putnam's Magazine,* 7 (April 1910), 856, Sarianna Browning to Anthony Snellgrove, April 3, 1890. The only picture of him as a younger man is a portrait "Miniature," artist unknown, at Wellesley. It shows a decent looking person in the garb of the Regency period. There is a later picture of him, p. 858, by Josephine Meyer, from a photograph. See also the portrait sketch by Sarianna Browning, "Scrapbook," MS, Humanities Research Center, Univ. of Texas (No. 20, Appendix B). There is another photograph of him in the "Caricature Drawings," MS, Victoria and Albert, Forster Collection 48.D.1 and also in the Browning Photograph Album, Balliol Col-

lege (repro. Irvine and Honan, p. 300 f.). There is a supposed self-portrait, "Sketch Book," MS, Baylor (No. 10, Appendix B).

41. The social position of the Bank of England clerk is discussed in R. H. Mottram, "Town Life," *Early Victorian England: 1830-1865,* ed. G. M. Young (London, Oxford University Press, 1934), I, 177-179. Mottram concludes that the clerk at the Bank represented the "highest type of executive the City could produce," outranking all other clerks and standing only just below the administrative and professional classes. As with the parallel work in the East India House, a position was part specialized occupation, part sinecure. Hours were 9:00-3:30; many clerks had second employments or small businesses; until the 1830s there were over forty holidays; there were possibilities for overtime pay and supplies of free paper (some of RB Sr.'s MSS are on discarded ledger paper). Pensions were certain.

42. The birth and baptism three days later were recorded in the parish register. See the summary of information on the Wiedemann background, Appendix A, section III.

43. Orr, p. 18, citing RB as source. Sotheby, item 301, lists some of his drawings, with signatures of Christiana and Sarah Anna.

44. *LRB,* p. 23, RB to Sarianna Browning, July 2, 1849. The name Wiedemann may have been Anglicized even earlier; see the record of RB's mother's birth, Appendix A, section III. RB's son sometimes wrote Wiedemann.

45. Hence the point of RB's grandfather waiting on him: *RBEBK,* II, 1003 (letter 523), [Aug. 26, 1846]. If so, the father was probably dead by 1811. There were Revells (grandmother's maiden name) near the Brownings in Camberwell: see Appendix A, section III, part 2. Silverthorne is sometimes wrongly identified as John Silverthorne: See Appendix A, section IV, part 3.

46. RB Sr., Sketch of "Sarah Anna Browning," "Waltham Drawings," MS, Wellesley, fol. 30. There is a supposed sketch of her by RB Sr., "Sketch Book," MS, Baylor (No. 10, Appendix B). The identification, as with the sketches supposed of RB and himself, is conjectural.

47. The early relation with von Muller is made clear in both the accounts of the breach of promise case of July 1, 1852: von Muller v. Browning: "Law Report," *Times,* July 2, 1852, p. 6; "Court of Queen's Bench," *Morning Chronicle,* July 2, 1852, p. 7 (copy at Boston Athenaeum). Muller is sometimes spelled with an umlaut.

48. Mason, "Kinsfolk," p. 67.

49. He was labeled a dotard even by his own lawyer: see reports in the *Times* and *Morning Chronicle,* cited above. Damages were 800 pounds, which RB Sr., with the support of his superiors at the Bank, refused to pay. A letter, RB to Reuben Browning, Dec. 31, 1858, MS, Wellesley, suggests that a small settlement could have been made—although it was not—to allow RB Sr. to return home. Mason is probably right in charging RB with some of the blame for the case since he acted in a precipitant manner that prejudiced the case against RB Sr. Yet he was persuaded that RB Sr. was in the hands of blackguards and certainly they were ready to profiteer when they could.

50. Mason, "Kinsfolk," pp. 94-95.

51. Orr, p. 14.

52. Henriette Corkran, *Celebrities and I* (London, Hutchinson, 1902), p. 14, claims he "would have dressed most shabbily and have been extremely untidy" without Sarianna.

53. Mason, "Kinsfolk," p. 93.

54. Ibid., p. 84.

55. *LRB,* p. 284, RB to Robert Wiedeman Browning, Jan. 25, 1888.

56. F. H. Stead, "Browning's Father," *Putnam's Magazine,* 7 (April 1910), 857. Browning called the disease *"tic-douloureux"*: D. S. Curtis, "Robert Browning," diary entry for Nov. 12, 14, 1855, MS, Baylor. Tic douloureux is trigeminal neuralgia, an intensely painful inflammation of the masticatory nerve in the face. Sarianna suffered from a similar complaint, and Orr is probably right in seeing Browning's own headaches in the 1840s as a similar illness. Certainly Browning identifies the two frequently in letters to Elizabeth. Mrs. Browning died not from this but from an illness leading to heart failure: then called "apoplexy" (Domett's *Diary,* p. 212) or "ossification of the heart" (*LEBB,* I, 399, EBB to M. R. Mitford, April 30,

1849). She died March 18, 1849, age 76: recorded, *Gentleman's Magazine,* 31 (May 1849), 557; also entry 78 in the continued Register of York Street Chapel: The Robert Browning Settlement, *The Browning Bulletin* [London, 1928], item 10. She was buried at Nunhead Cemetery.

57. *RBEBK,* I, 403 (letter 207), RB to EBB, [Jan. 19, 1846]; *LEBB,* I, 369, EBB to Sarianna Browning, [ca. June 1848].

58. Entries for RB Sr. in the Camberwell rate books, Newington District Library, locate the family: 1) 1813-ca. April 25, 1816 on Southampton St. (now Way) near Dowlas St. (earliest entries call this area merely Back Settlement); the rate paid was substantial for the area, though many paid more; 2) ca. April 25, 1816-ca. Nov. 4, 1824 on Southampton St., next to the Common (i.e., the Cottage Green, a block north of the former residence); the entry for April 25, 1816 has the Brownings at both addresses; 3) ca. Nov. 4, 1824-1840 on Southampton St., described as "House"; the entry for Nov. 9, 1826 is Wells St., possibly a temporary residence or a clerk's error. The rating of Feb. 6, 1839 gives the residence one vote, a gross rental of 33, and a rateable value of 30: voting under the Reform Act was the prerogative of the substantial middle class; many Camberwell houses had no votes. In the rating of Nov. 4, 1824, last of several that year, Browning was crossed out and Captain Lamb written in. The move to New Cross was about Dec. 1840. The third Southampton St. house, called Hanover Cottage, was probably one of the three separate cottages labeled "Hanover Cots." on the north side of Southampton St. just west of Grove Place (present Coleman Road) about three blocks south of the Cottage Green in J. Dewhirst, "Map of the Parish of St. Giles, Camberwell" (London, W. Wheeler, June 1, 1842), Newington District Library. The cottages have large gardens backing onto lanes and fields. The name was used by the family: it appears on a calling card of RB's of 1834, Private Collection, and in RB Sr.'s correspondence over RB's entry to The London University.

59. This and other information about the Camberwell residences is largely derived from Robert Wiedeman Browning to Hall Griffin (with Sarianna's answers to Griffin's queries), Nov. 11, 1902, Hall Griffin Papers, BL, Add. MS. 45,563, fols. 186-194; also, Sarianna Browning to Jeanie Morison Campbell, July 14, 1899, MS, Humanities Research Center, Univ. of Texas.

60. The details from "Development," *Asolando* (1889), are authenticated by Sarianna in the letter of Nov. 11, 1902, cited above.

61. *LRB,* p. 5, RB to Laman Blanchard, [April 1841]. Even Sarianna confessed she had no idea what was meant by a goose pie: letter of Nov. 11, 1902, cited above. The residence is probably the property numbered 36, "Mansion, Garden, & Orchard" in a "Plan of an Estate Belonging to the Worshipful Company of Haberdashers . . . at New Cross in the Parish of Saint Paul Deptford Surrey" (London, John Lane and Co., 1854), The Manor House, Lewisham Library. This is south of the Old Kent Road (or Kent Road, now New Cross Road) and just west of the railroad cutting. In the St. Paul's Rate Books for 1841 Robt. Browning is written in as a new occupier of a "House Garden & Premises" (assessment No. 7 for 44 pounds). The assessment is repeated in 1842. According to Sarianna the landlord next door was a Mr. Halcombe. He (as Holcombe) is listed next to RB Sr. for a large assessment on land and property in 1841 and 1842. He probably occupied property 37 on the Plan of 1854 which included a pond. Both 37 and 36 are among his many holdings on the Plan. There are buildings on the Plan called "stables and yard" further south along the railroad cutting from the house probably occupied by the Brownings (property 67, also held by Holcombe). These are likely to have been the Brownings' stable. There is a view of the site of the Brownings' house in a print by E. Duncan, "View of the London and Croydon Railway From the Deep Cutting Made Through the Hill at New Cross Looking Toward the Greenwich Railway" (London, Day & Haghe, June 1, 1838), The Manor House, Lewisham Library. There are two large houses, one long two story one furthest from the tracks, one three story one, and a third, lower building nearest to the tracks. Mrs. Joan Read, Administrative Assistant at The Manor House, Lewisham Library, identifies the smaller building as the Brownings'. However, this building is too small to fit the descriptions of the Brownings' house and is on the site of the stables in the Plan. It probably is the stables. The three story house should be that of the Brownings from both location

and size (though it does not look like a goose pie). The rural nature of the area is clear in the print: even the railroad was partially shielded from view by the depth of the cutting. I am indebted to Mrs. Read for this information about the Hatcham location and for letting me read her, "The Manor of Hatcham: Aspects of its Development 1600-1900," Diss. Univ. of London, 1973. Albert Terrace, the residence of Jane Browning's family, was probably the same as Hatcham Terrace, a row on the north side of the Old Kent Road, slightly closer to London than the Brownings' lane.

62. *RBEBK,* II, 627 (letter 316), RB to EBB, [April 16, 1846]. See also the letter to Campbell of July 14, 1899, cited above.

63. *RBEBK,* II, 1003 (letter 523), RB to EBB, [Aug. 26, 1846].

64. Miller, p. 20.

65. Macaulay, in his *History of England,* I, 334, remarks, speaking of progress, "It may well be, in the twentieth century, that the peasant of Dorsetshire may think himself miserably paid with fifteen shillings a week; that the carpenter at Greenwich may receive ten shillings a day." See also W. J. Bate's useful discussion of the value of money, 1800-1820, in his appendix to *John Keats* (Cambridge, Mass., Harvard University Press, 1965), pp. 711-712. RB Sr.'s salary was reported by Furnivall, "Ancestors," p. 30, as £ 275 when he retired. However, the notation on his letter requesting a pension for reasons of health indicates his real salary was £305 including £30 of emoluments. The retirement pension granted at two-thirds salary Jan. 20, 1853 was two-thirds of this figure. See William Whitla, "Letters of Robert Browning and his Sister to the Snellgroves," *Browning Society Notes,* 4 (July 1974), 13, RB Sr. to the governor of the Bank of England, Jan. 14, 1853. The salary was reported as about £ 320 in the "Law Report" of the von Muller judgment, *Times,* July 2, 1852, p. 6. He is there spoken of as living as a man of 500 or 600 pounds would, "in a quiet gentlemanly way." Miller assumes, in speaking of the family being poor, that RB Sr.'s legacy from Uncle Tittle and Aunt Mill was very little. But the Tittles were much more prosperous than she implies (see Appendix A, section II); his sister with a similar legacy apparently had enough to live on (see Appendix A, section IV, Margaret Morris Browning); the implication in RB's grandfather's will as well as in his conduct in demanding reimbursement from his son for his education was that the sum was at least appreciable. It is probably reasonable to assume that the Brownings had some useful extra income from this source.

66. Mason, "Kinsfolk," pp. 95, 128.

67. H. C. Minchin, "A Letter from Hanover Cottage," *The Bookman,* 86 (April 1934), 6, RB to E. F. Haworth, [ca. Aug. 1, 1837].

68. *RBEBK,* I, 16 (letter 7), RB to EBB, Feb. 11, 1845.

69. The family clock, Sotheby, item 1303, is now at Baylor. The teapot is Sotheby, item 1333.

70. H. C. Minchin, "A Letter from Hanover Cottage," 6, RB to E. F. Haworth [ca. Aug. 1, 1837]. Minchin, probably correctly, takes "M." to be RB's mother.

71. Mason, "Kinsfolk," p. 84.

72. *RBAD,* p. 126, RB to A. Domett, July 13, 1846.

73. Donald Smalley, "Joseph Arnould and Robert Browning: New Letters (1842-50) and a Verse Epistle," *PMLA,* 80 (March 1965), p. 95, J. Arnould to RB, Dec. 6, 1848.

74. Their mutual friends included Arnould, Chris Dowson, Domett, John Forster, E.F. Haworth, John Kenyon, and Capt. Pritchard. Pritchard left her a legacy of one thousand pounds and MSS, books, and papers (Desborough, Young & Desborough to Sarianna Browning, Oct. 19, 1859, MS, Baylor).

Sarianna (Jan. 7, 1814-April 22, 1903) was baptized at the York Street Congregational Church, April 10, 1814 (birth and baptism entered as Sarahanna by George Clayton in the Register of Baptisms, Locks Fields Walworth, p. 17, now in the Census Office of the Public Record Office, London); educated at Miss Goodson's School, Bower Place, Camberwell; lived with her family; with RB Sr. in Paris, 1852-1866; with her brother until 1889; with her nephew, primarily in Asolo and Florence, until her death; buried at the Protestant Cemetery outside the Porta Romana, Florence. See: "Miss Browning," *Athenaeum.* No. 3940 (May 2, 1903), pp.

564-565; S. G. Pomeroy, *Little-Known Sisters of Well-Known Men* (Boston, Dana Estes & Co., 1912), pp. 143-179: dutiful but comprehensive. There are important MS collections of her correspondence at Balliol College Library, Oxford (to Robert Wiedeman Browning and Fannie C. Browning and from B. Jowett to her); at Baylor (to Anne Egerton Smith and to William Allingham; also letters to her from J. M. Campbell and Joseph Milsand); at the BL (to Michael Field, Add. MS. 44,856; some fragments are also pub., *Works and Days from the Journal of Michael Field,* ed. T. and D. C. Sturge Moore [London, John Murray, 1933], pp. 218-222); at the Humanities Research Center, Univ. of Texas (to J. M. Campbell); at Huntington (to H. F. Martin and F. J. Furnivall); and in the private collection of Mrs. Dorothy Gwyther, London (to Anthony Snellgrove, the younger, pub. by Whitla, "Letters of Robert Browning and his Sister to the Snellgroves," pp. 13-24; one other letter is at Morgan, and another at the Fitzwilliam Museum, Cambridge). There are photographs of Sarianna in the Browning Photograph Album, Balliol College (repro. Miller, p. 192 f., and Irvine and Honan, p. 300 f.), at the Humanities Research Center, Univ. of Texas, at Scripps College, and probably elsewhere. A portrait is reproduced in Henry Sotheran Catalog No. 737, *Old Engravings and MSS, Books, and Relics of R. and E. B. Browning* (London, 1913), item 405. There is a caricature by RB of her, "Thomas Ingall Sketchbook," MS, Boston Public Library, fol. 68; see also Bertram Dobell Catalog, *Browning Memorials* (London, 1913), item 75, and front., a sketch of Sarianna attributed to RB but probably by RB Sr. (see Sarianna to J. M. Campbell, April 16, 1892, MS, Humanities Research Center, Univ. of Texas, where she speaks of finding a picture of her at 12 by RB Sr.).

75. *LRB,* p. 179, RB to H. Buxton Forman, July 2, 1877.

76. Robert Wiedeman Browning to Hall Griffin, Nov. 11, 1902, Hall Griffin Papers, BL, Add. MS. 45,563, fols. 186-194.

77. Mason, "Kinsfolk," p. 104.

78. Henriette Corkran, *Celebrities,* p. 15.

79. Angelo Cerutti, *Vita* (Florence, 1846), I, 332.

80. Henriette Corkran, *Celebrities,* pp. 10, 15. M. D. Conway, *Autobiography, Memories and Experiences* (Boston, Houghton, Mifflin, 1904), II, 24.

81. *LEBB,* II, 122, EBB to M. R. Mitford, July 15, 1853.

82. Her copy of Tolstoy's *Katia* (Paris, 1886) is at Baylor; her other French editions are given in Sotheby, items 1163, 1164.

83. J. Arnould to A. Domett, July 28, 1844, Hall Griffin Papers, BL, Add. MS. 45,560, fol. 36.

84. Alice Corkran, "Chapters from the Story of my Girlhood," *Girl's Realm,* Nov. 1904, p. 284.

85. Ibid., p. 286. The friend was, of course, Anne Egerton Smith.

86. Jeanie Morison [Campbell], "Robert Browning and Elizabeth Barrett Browning," *Chamber's Cyclopaedia of English Literature* (Philadelphia, J. P. Lippincott, 1904), III, 556; Henriette Corkran, *Celebrities,* p. 17.

87. [W. H. Grove], "Browning as I Knew Him, by his Valet," *Sunday Express,* Dec. 4, 1927, p. 466: "Wobert, why don't you mawwy one of these ladies who is so fond of you." Baly, "Talking of the Brownings," p. 11, asserts from family tradition that the poet and his Uncle Reuben had a milder similar speech problem. I know no confirmation of this from their contemporaries.

88. D. S. Curtis, "Robert Browning," diary entry for Nov. 12 & 14, 1885, MS, Baylor.

89. "Voyage à Londres, 1834," MS, Private Collection.

90. Sarianna Browning to Michael Field, Feb. 27, [1897], BL, Add. MS. 45,856, fol. 114.

91. Silverthorne (1st name illeg., but identified as son of John) to Hall Griffin, Jan. 22, 1903, Hall Griffin Papers, BL, Add. MS. 45,563, fols. 204-206, recalled sacrifices for his education, possibly the money spent for The London University. It is not clear how this would have been Sarianna's own sacrifice.

92. *LL,* p. 24.

93. Domett's *Diary,* p. 213.

94. RB Sr. to RB, June 15, 1849, MS, Fitzwilliam Museum, Cambridge University.

95. C. G. Duffy, *Conversations and Correspondence with Carlyle* (New York, 1892), p. 58.

96. *RBEBK,* I, 25 (letter 9), RB to EBB, [Feb. 26, 1845].

97. *RBEBK,* I, 32 (letter 11), RB to EBB, March 1, [1845].

98. Orr, p. 32, RB Sr. to Thomas Powell, March 11, 1843.

99. *LRB,* p. 172, RB to Norman MacColl, June 13, 1876.

100. "Michael Field" recorded seeing the proof sheets: *Works and Days,* p. 207.

101. *The Diaries of William Charles Macready 1833-1851,* ed. William Toynbee (New York, G. P. Putnam's Sons, 1912), I, 392 (entry for May 1, 1837).

102. Kate Lemann to Hall Griffin, Jan. 29, 1905, Hall Griffin Papers, BL, Add. MS. 45,564, fols. 169-170b.

103. Alfred Domett to RB, Aug. 20, 1846, Alexander Turnbull Library, Wellington, New Zealand. Cf. also the comment in Domett's *Diary,* p. 213 about RB Sr. speaking of his son "as *beyond* him."

104. *RBEBK,* I, 398 (letter 205), RB to EBB, [Jan. 18, 1846]. These were probably the "Thirteen Sketches of *Bells and Pomegranates,*" MS, Baylor, or similar sketches.

105. RB Sr. to Sir Henry Ellis of the British Museum, Oct. 18, 1847, BL, Add. MS. 48,340, fols. 91-92b.

106. On the rather strained relations between the family of the poet and the Masons, see the discussions of Jane Eliza Browning (Mason) and Cyrus Mason in Appendix A, section IV, part 2. With many of his relatives in the second Browning family and among his cousins, the Silverthornes, on his mother's side, the poet had, by contrast, a close and agreeable relationship that reinforced the open-minded and intellectual orientation of his immediate family. See the discussions of the Silverthornes in chap. v, section 3, and of Reuben and William Shergold Browning in chap. v, section 4.

107. *RBEBK,* I, 398 (letter 205), RB to EBB, [Jan. 18, 1846].

108. *RBEBK,* II, 775 (letter 402), RB to EBB, [June 12, 1846].

109. This implication, that RB was "pushed" or "trained" by his parents according to a "system" runs through Mason, "Kinsfolk" (see esp. pp. 12-13). Mason gives no evidence for this and there is nothing in the character of RB's parents, esp. the father, or in the records of family life to substantiate it. The "system" was freedom and encouragement for the growth of RB's mind. Mason's motive for his view, jealousy over a cousin's ability, is obvious. The "system" of Great-Uncle Reuben, as Mason himself describes it, was nothing more than freedom and wide reading in liberal subjects.

110. Not entirely, however: see the account of Thomas Browning's conflict with his father, Appendix A, section IV, part 2.

111. Both men are discussed in chap. v, section 4.

112. Mason, "Kinsfolk," p. 88.

113. RB, "Notes in Correction," MS, Baylor, The history of the links is discussed in Appendix A, n. 37.

114. Hiram Corson, "Robert Browning." *New York Evening Post,* Dec. 17, 1889 (clipping at Baylor).

Chapter IV   Self-Consciousness

1. *Pauline* (1833), Mill copy, Victoria and Albert Museum, Forster Collection.

2. *RBEBK,* I, 74 (letter 31), RB to EBB, [May 24, 1845].

3. *RBEBK,* I, 16 (letter 7), RB to EBB, [Feb. 11, 1845].

4. "Self-consciousness" in the sense of being aware of one's own identity was used as early as Locke's *Essay Concerning Human Understanding* (1690) but the sense of distinct inner

perception, of a faculty akin to outer perception of the world but focused on inner consciousness, becomes common only in the nineteenth century, as does the modern common sense of morbid pre-occupation with oneself. RB uses the compound himself in a letter to Ripert-Monclar, March 2, 1835, MS, Private Collection, and again in *Sordello,* Book II. He uses "consciousness" in the sense of intense inner awareness twice in *Paracelsus* and six times in that most self-conscious of works, *Sordello.* Geoffrey Hartman, *Wordsworth's Poetry, 1787-1814* (New Haven, Yale University Press, 1967), pp. 343-344, discusses the origin of the compound and suggests that Coleridge uses it in the romantic sense (*Biographia Literaria,* chap. xii, thesis 6) as a German import.

5. Another observer, who knew RB personally, a Catherine (Katie) Bromley, remarked in her diary of 1833 on his social self-consciousness: "Robert talks immensely, and how self-conscious: To me, distressingly so": quoted A. M. W. Stirling, *The Merry Wives of Battersea and Gossip of Three Centuries* (London, Robert Hale, 1956), p. 121, from a MS diary reported at Old Battersea House. I have not been able to locate the Diary. There were MSS at Old Battersea House, Battersea, but the house has changed hands and many of the possessions have been sold.

6. RB's early exposure to the romantic poets is discussed in chap. vii, below.

7. On RB's reading of Smart see chap. xiii, section 3, and n. 99, below.

8. *RBEBK,* I, 398 (letter 205), RB to EBB, [Jan. 18, 1846].

9. This view has been most strongly put forward by Miller, pp. 6-15. It has been rather uncritically repeated (by Irvine) in Irvine and Honan, chap. i. Irvine generally relies on previous secondary works for this part of his study and did not have the benefit of Maisie Ward's helpful criticisms of Miller.

10. Orr, p. 18.

11. Domett's *Diary,* p. 212.

12. *LEBB,* I, 321, EBB to Sarianna Browning, [ca. Feb., 1847].

13. *LEBB,* I, 396, EBB to Sarianna Browning, [April 1, 1849]; Orr, p. 154, EBB to M. R. Mitford, April 30, [1849]; also letters to Mrs. Jameson of April 30, Aug. 11, and Oct. 1, 1849, MS, Wellesley. A lock of hair from Mrs. Browning, inscribed with RB's initials, the date Sept. 14, 1836, and a notation by Sarianna that he kept this with him throughout his life testifies to his lifelong filial piety, conventionally expressed (now at Wellesley).

14. *RBEBK,* I, 142 (letter 72), RB to EBB, [Aug. 3, 1845]; *RBEBK,* II, 1010 (letter 526), RB to EBB, [Aug. 27, 1846]; also W. R. Benét, ed., *From Robert & Elizabeth Browning* (London, John Murray, 1936), p. 21, EBB to Arabel and Henrietta Barrett, Oct. 2, 1846. Cousin Cyrus Mason's repeated assertion that this was not the case has no apparent foundation.

15. Jeanie Morison, "Robert Browning and Elizabeth Barrett Browning," *Chamber's Cyclopaedia of English Literature* (Philadelphia, J. P. Lippincott, 1904), III, 551: "those who know best say that his mother's was, out of sight, the strongest influence on his life." J. M. Campbell was a friend of Sarianna and apparently thus cites an opinion traditional in the Browning family.

16. Domett's *Diary,* p. 212.

17. See n. 46, chap. iii.

18. "Voyage à Londres, 1834," MS, Private Collection.

19. Edward Dowden, *The Life of Robert Browning* (London, Dent, 1904), p. 5; Donald Smalley, "Joseph Arnould and Robert Browning: New Letters (1842-50) and a Verse Epistle," *PMLA,* 80 (March 1965), 99, J. Arnould to RB, March 23, 1849.

20. Orr, p. 18.

21. *LEBB,* I, 402, EBB to Sarianna Browning, May 21, 1849; *LEBB,* I, 396, EBB to Sarianna Browning, April 1, 1849.

22. Orr, p. 18. Miller casts Mrs. Browning as in every way the domineering and dominating authority in her family.

23. *RBEBK,* II, 1025 (letter 532), RB to EBB, [Aug. 31, 1846].

24. The story is told by W. J. Stillman, *The Autobiography of a Journalist* (Boston,

Houghton Mifflin, 1901), I, 278-279. Stillman, a sometime journalist, traveler, and artist, knew Sarianna in Paris in the late 1850s and heard the family story from her. Whether the details are to be relied upon or not, the general import of the story can, I think, be trusted.

25. Alice Corkran, "Chapters from the Story of my Girlhood," *Girl's Realm,* Nov. 1904, pp. 285-286.

26. Mason, "Kinsfolk," p. 92.

27. *RBEBK,* I, 463 (letter 233), RB to EBB, [Feb. 15, 1846].

28. EBB to Fanny Dowglas, Sept. 6, [1847], MS, Huntington, HM 4900.

29. In the original draft of "Dejection" as a letter to Sara Hutchinson, *Collected Letters of Samuel Taylor Coleridge,* ed. E. L. Griggs (Oxford, Clarendon Press, 1956), II, 438.

30. *The Complete Poetical Works of Robert Browning,* ed. Augustine Birrell (New York, Macmillan, 1915), pp. 1331-1332. The Dows were William Alexander and A. Dow, to whom the poem was inscribed from their "Sincere Friend." They lived at 13 Nelson Sq., Southwark. RB's "Address Book," MS, Yale, also has "9 King's Bench Walk Temple," Dow's law address. Dow (?-1848) was a Special Pleader to the Temple, a friend of Forster and admirer and sometime legal consultant to the actor Macready. DeVane, *Handbook,* p. 556 asserts without evidence that Dow's father, James Dow, M.D., lived in Camberwell and Dow appears in Macready's diaries as living there in 1833: *The Diaries of William Charles Macready 1833-1851,* ed. William Toynbee (New York, G. P. Putnam's Sons, 1912), I, 41. Contrary to DeVane's implication, RB seems not to have met Dow until after 1835 when he moved in the same set as Forster and Macready; very likely Macready's entry for Feb. 1, 1836 records their first meeting: I, 272. The inference of early acquaintance is based on the poem, incorrectly published as "Lines to the Memory of his Parents," which Browning wrote for the tomb of Dow's father in St. Mary's Church, Barnsley, Yorkshire. See E. G. Bayford, "Poem by Browning," *Notes and Queries,* 193 (June 12, 1948), 248-249, for a transcript of the full poem from the tombstone. The elder Dow died in 1832 but the tomb was erected later by Dow and his sister Margaret. RB joked on March 20, 1837 about how Dow had been twisting his arm to fill out the poem to include his mother and a brother and sister who had died young, clearly implying that the poem had been written only very recently: *Diaries of Macready,* I, 380.

31. Orr, p. 154, EBB to M. R. Mitford, April 30, [1849].

32. *RBEBK,* I, 142 (letter 72), RB to EBB, [Aug. 3, 1845].

33. See the discussion of Melvill below, chap. xiii, section 3.

34. Browning's mother appears as No. 78 in the first list of church members in 1806. Very possibly she had been a member before this. Browning's father was No. 425 in 1820 though he attended earlier. Relevant church documents are listed in the Robert Browning Settlement's *The Browning Bulletin* [London, 1928].

35. G. K. Chesterton, *Robert Browning* (New York, Macmillan, 1903), p. 12.

36. *RBEBK,* I, 509 (letter 255), RB to EBB, [March 3, 1846], speaks of Clayton's father, John Clayton (1754-1843), also a minister, as an "Evangelical." I deliberately use the term evangelical with a lowercase *e* to distinguish the general religious movement, in which Clayton even as an Independent is included, from the more specific Evangelical Movement within the Church of England.

37. Thomas W. Aveling, *Memorials of the Clayton Family with Unpublished Correspondence* (London, 1867), pp. 13-44, recounts John's early career, primarily quoting an unfinished memoir by George Clayton. John Clayton (1754-1843) was a student at the Countess of Huntingdon's Trevecca College (later Cheshunt); after his conversion he became minister of the prosperous Congregational Church in Little Eastcheap, London. He remained friends with many Anglican divines. In a sermon, *The Principle of Union Among the Disciples of Christ, Explained and Enforced* (London, 1831), copy BL, George Clayton encouraged his congregation not to isolate themselves from Anglican or Methodist brothers in Christ.

38. Edward White, a member of the congregation, reported in the *British Weekly,* Dec. 20, 1889, p. 117. George Clayton (1783-1862) joined the Locks Fields congregation in April, 1804 at age twenty. Clayton's brothers, John (1780-1865) and William (1784-1838) were also

Congregational evangelical ministers. There are published sermons and books of devotion by the Claytons in the BL and elsewhere as well as the records of an unfortunate pamphlet controversy waged by the father against theatergoing.

39. Frederick Rogers, *The Early Environment of Robert Browning* (London, priv. prnt., 1904), p. 15 (a copy of this rare pamphlet is at Baylor; another at Newington District Library).

40. Ibid., p. 12.

41. Pigot and Co., *London & Provincial New Commercial Directory* (London, 1823), p. 79. The church held 2000. It was completed in 1790, though the first minister was appointed in 1793. Clayton followed Philip Mills and Edmund Denham as the third pastor: John Waddington, *Surrey Congregational History* (London, 1866), pp. 322-330. The church survives as a shell and facade on present Browning Street (now used as a theater set factory). Edward White's open letter to Herbert Stead, June 5, 1895, MS, Newington District Library, reports the social status of the church. Prominent church members included Joseph Cottle, brother of Amos and friend of Charles Lamb.

42. Rogers, *Early Environment,* p. 13. The rate books, Newington District Library, show Clayton lived genteely in Camberwell in a house with stable and garden. At other times he lived out in the country.

43. Aveling, *Clayton Family,* p. 219. Clayton was educated at Reading with a Dr. Valpy and at Hoxton College.

44. Ibid., pp. 453-458. See also the fuller but less objective account of her in Joseph Sartain, *The Life of Mrs. George Clayton* (London, 1844), detailing her rise from theatrical world to evangelical sainthood. Mrs. Clayton, née Whennell (1779-1842) was succeeded by Mary Giles, whom Clayton married in 1845. Church works included a Benevolent Society, a Sunday School, a Vestry Library, and a Missionary Society: the Victorian evangelical spirit militant: see *A Pastoral Letter from the Rev. George Clayton to his Flock* (London, 1837).

45. Bertram Dobell Catalog, *Browning Memorials* (London, 1913), item 119. W. R. Nicoll, "Robert Browning's Father," *Bookman* (London), 42 (May 1912), 64-65, prints some of these religious poems copied by RB Sr. for widow von Muller. From Dobell's description he is probably wrong in taking these as versifications by RB Sr. of Clayton's sermons. The samples given, weak Miltonic lines on biblical themes, would do little credit to either RB Sr. or Clayton.

46. Edward White to Herbert Stead, open letter cited above.

47. Aveling, Clayton Family, p. 224. Portraits confirm this description. Besides the front. in Aveling, *Clayton Family,* there is one by G. Baugnet (J. Hogarth, n.d.) and a print, "Revd. George Clayton" (Williams and Son, Sept. 1, 1843), at Newington District Library.

48. Edward White to Herbert Stead, open letter cited above. The hair was dark brown, not actually black.

49. Rogers, *Early Environment,* p. 8, notes that Sarah Anna kept a missionary box for the London Missionary Society and later subscribed a fixed amount each year until 1847. Sarianna's contributions are often mentioned in her correspondence to Anthony Snellgrove, MS, Private Collection of Mrs. Dorothy Gwyther, Whetstone, London. The Clayton Jubilee Memorial Schools were founded in his honor.

50. *LRB,* p. 23, RB to Sarianna Browning, July 2, 1849.

51. The Bible given to Browning on Feb. 28, 1834, Sotheby, item 369, is now at Wellesley (cf. Sotheby, item 369); there is a Latin *Novum Jesu-Christi Testamentum* (Limoges, 1812) at Baylor inscribed to RB by his mother. The Concordance is Sotheby, item 600. Her "Commonplace Book," Dobell Catalog, *Browning Memorials,* item 460, consisting mostly of biblical texts, suggests the same interest. It dates from before her marriage.

52. George Clayton not only used the term *evangelical* for his family's religious mission but also described his father's development as an explicit part of the Evangelical movement. Even after his technical break with the Countess of Huntingdon in joining the Congregational Church, John remained on friendly terms with her; he was also closely connected with the work of the Clapham Sect through friendship with John Thornton, a close associate of Wilberforce: Aveling, *Clayton Family,* pp. 4, 90-91.

53. Copy now at Baylor.

54. *The New England Mind: The Seventeenth Century,* rev. ed. (Boston, Beacon Press, 1961), p. 389. That this was still the theology at York Street is indicated by a "Solemn Covenant with Almighty God, Made through His Beloved Son Jesus Christ, and by the Aid of His Holy Spirit" left by Clayton's wife: Aveling, *Clayton Family,* p. 458; also Sartain, *Life of Mrs. Clayton,* pp. 32-35.

55. Coles, *Practical Discourse,* p. 186.

56. Her copy is at Baylor: a gift to her before her marriage from an otherwise unidentified Mrs. Burton.

57. *Spiritual Gleanings,* p. 95.

58. Ibid., pp. 93-94.

59. Ibid., p. 161.

60. RB to W. C. Macready, Sept. 6, [1841], MS, Scripps College.

61. Coles, *Practical Discourse,* p. 102.

62. *Spiritual Gleanings,* p. 102.

63. Copy at Baylor.

64. *Advice,* p. 91.

65. Ibid., p. 96.

66. Ibid.

67. Aveling, *Clayton Family,* pp. 249, 266, quoting an unpublished "Diary." The present location of the "Diary" is unknown. None of Aveling's frequent quotations from the "Diary" refers to the Brownings. Aveling provides a number of indications that some members of the Clayton family were driven by the atmosphere of too self-conscious religion into morbidity; a daughter went insane; a sister spent her life generally in depression about her spiritual state.

68. Orr, p. 25.

69. Edward White, reported in the *British Weekly,* Dec. 20, 1889, p. 117. Griffin and Minchin, p. 50, report that White also recalled an open rebuke from Clayton to Browning for inattention. This is not in the *British Weekly* article they cite or in White's later open letter. Possibly it was an elaboration in one of the articles that reprinted White's comments.

70. M. D. Conway, *Autobiography, Memories and Experiences* (Boston, Houghton Mifflin, 1904), II, 26, Sarah Flower to W. J. Fox, Nov. 23, 1827. RB's relation with the Flowers is discussed in chap. viii, below. E. Bridell-Fox, in her "Memoir" to Sarah's *Vivia Perpetua* (priv. prnt., 1893), speaks of RB "anxiously discussing religious doubts and difficulties" with Sarah. The tone, coming from her personal knowledge of Sarah, is the correct one for the incident.

71. [William Grove], "Browning as I Knew Him. By His Valet," *Sunday Express,* Dec. 4, 1927, p. 466 (copy at Baylor).

72. George Eliot, *Scenes from Clerical Life,* chap. x.

73. E.g., Miller, p. 11: "The ideals of Shelley and those of Sarah Anna Browning could not continue to exist under the same roof."

74. Sotheby, item 596: now at Baylor.

75. Sharp, *Life,* p. 22.

76. *NL,* p. 341, RB to unidentified correspondent, March 9, 1887.

77. RB to Charles Dickens, [Oct. ? 1841], MS, Huntington HM 18459.

78. Alice Corkran, "Chapters," p. 285.

79. W. J. Stillman, *Autobiography,* I, 278.

80. Orr, p. 27.

81. Sarianna Browning to J. M. Campbell, Feb. 8, 1893, MS, Humanities Research Center, Univ. of Texas.

82. Alice Corkran, "Chapters," p. 285.

83. *RBEBK,* I, 355 (letter 189), RB to EBB, [Jan. 4, 1846].

84. "Scrapbook" (No. 21, Appendix B), MS, Humanities Research Center, Univ. of Texas; Sarianna speaks of the cat in a letter to Jeanie Morison Campbell, [Sept. 25, 1899], MS, Humanities Research Center, Univ. of Texas.

85. Orr, pp. 26-27.

86. Orr, p. 74. Sarianna did recall a favorite toad: Robert Wiedeman Browning to Hall Griffin, Nov. 11, 1902, Hall Griffin Papers, BL, Add. MS. 45,563, fols. 186-194.

87. *RBEBK,* I, 351 (letter 187), RB to EBB, Dec. 31, 1845.

88. William H. Blanch, *Ye Parish of Camerwell* (London, 1875), p. 7.

89. Sotheby, item 798.

90. E.g., "Thomas Ingall Sketchbook," MS, Boston Public Library, fols. 42v., 56.

91. Sarianna Browning to J. M. Campbell, July 14, 1899, MS, Humanities Research Center, Univ. of Texas.

92. *RBEBK,* I, 509 (letter 255), RB to EBB, [March 3, 1846].

93. Print of "A Cottage Near Dulwich," formerly at Dulwich Library (copy now in the Newington District Library).

94. A print, "View of the Gipsy House in Norwood, Surrey 1803," suggests the kind of primitive encampment RB might have seen, BL Map Room, K.41.13.1. The Gypsies moved from Norwood to Dulwich Wood sometime between then and 1812: Griffin and Minchin, p. 55.

95. Mrs. Sutherland Orr, *A Handbook to the Works of Robert Browning* (London, 1886), p. 55.

96. Sharp, *Life,* p. 105. Sharp virtually implies that Browning composed *Strafford* and *Paracelsus* in the Dulwich Wood by night: p. 62.

97. The eighteenth-century historian and poet Maurice: quoted Blanch, *Parish,* p. 282.

98. John Scott, author of *Amwell.* Quoted, Douglas Allport, *Collections Illustrative of the Geology, History, Antiquities, and Associations, of Camberwell, and the Neighbourhood* (Camberwell, 1841), p. 94.

99. Again the source is the somewhat dubious one of Sharp, *Life,* p. 62.

100. Jack Herring, "The Baylor Browning Letters: Plans for a New Edition," *Browning Newsletter,* No. 1 (Oct. 1968), p. 14, RB to Alfred Domett, Dec. 19, 1841.

101. RB to F. O. Ward, Friday Morning [ca. Feb. 7, 1845], MS, Baylor.

102. *RBEBK,* II, 627 (letter 316), RB to EBB, [April 16, 1846].

103. *RBEBK,* I, 353 (letter 188), EBB to RB, Jan. 1, 1845.

104. *RBEBK,* I, 438 (letter 223), RB to EBB, [Feb. 6, 1846].

105. Sharp, *Life,* p. 96: reported from a conversation with RB.

106. W. C. DeVane, "Sordello's Story Retold," *Studies in Philology,* 27 (Jan. 1930), 15-16.

107. Hartman, *Wordsworth's Poetry:* see especially the Introduction to Notes, pp. 343-344. Hartman notes that Wordsworth speaks often of "consciousness" but does not create the compound "self-consciousness." My summary of both Wordsworth's ideas and Hartman's are bold and bad observations on an exceptionally subtle process. I see no reason to assume that RB's own development was through Wordsworth, though he knew him at an early age. Rather, and only in gross outline, there is a parallel development of sensibility through certain similarities in experience.

108. *RBEBK,* I, 499 (letter 250), RB to EBB, [Feb. 27, 1846].

109. *DI,* p. 171, RB to I. Blagden, Aug. 19, 1863.

110. *LRB,* p. 159, RB to Anne Egerton Smith, [Aug. ?] 16, 1873.

111. *RBEBK,* I, 355 (letter 189), RB to EBB, [Jan. 4, 1846].

112. Stopford A. Brooke's broad discussion of RB as a poet of nature in his *The Poetry of Robert Browning* (London, Thomas Y. Crowell, 1902), pp. 57-114, is still the fullest treatment of the subject.

113. Conway, *Autobiography,* II, 31.

114. Alfred Domett to RB, Jan. 30, 1846, MS, Wellesley.

Chapter V   Objectivity

1. G.K. Chesterton, *Robert Browning* (New York, Macmillan, 1903), p. 11.

2. Griffin and Minchin, p. 12. Henriette Corkran, *Celebrities and I* (London, Hutchinson, 1902), p. 13, mentions Ostade and Teniers. A letter, RB to Mr. Courtney, March 30, 1876,

MS, Baylor, lists RB Sr.'s prints, including Brouwer, Teniers (probably the Elder), and Dou, as well as Rembrandt, Van Dyck, and some minor painters. There is an interesting MS, "Adriaen Brouwer," by RB Sr. at Baylor—evidently a memorandum from earlier reading— showing interest in his life and work.

3. Alice Corkran, "Chapters from the Story of my Girlhood," *Girl's Realm,* Nov. 1904, p. 284.

4. There are fine studies of figures, not cartoons, e.g., in "Caricature Drawings," MS, Victoria and Albert Museum, Forster Collection, 48.D.1, fols. 87-98; "Pencil and Ink Drawings of Scenes" and "Twenty-Five Drawings," MSS, Baylor (Nos. 9 and 13, Appendix B); and "Fifty Pen, Pencil, and Watercolor Sketches," MS, Beinecke, Yale. Many of the cartoons verge on more serious attempts at genre sketches.

5. Frederick Locker-Lampson spoke of RB Sr.'s "great love and admiration for Hogarth," Orr, p. 15, Frederick Locker-Lampson to RB, Dec. 26, 1870.

6. The "Scrapbook of Cartoons," formerly property of Mrs. Stephens, Bank of England, Archives Section, contains a series of 140 studies of customers who have come to the Bank for "The Unclaimed Dividend."

7. F. G. Kitton, "Robert Browning, the Elder, as a Caricaturist," *Art Journal,* 3 (Feb. 1896), p. 57.

8. "Caricature Drawings," MS, Victoria and Albert Museum, Forster Collection, 48.D.1, fols. 17-36.

9. "Scrapbook," MS, Humanities Research Center, Univ. of Texas (No. 21, Appendix B).

10. "Thomas Ingall Sketchbook," MS, Boston Public Library, fol. 22. One of his books, much marked, was Charles Bell's *Essays on the Anatomy of Expression in Painting* (London, 1806): Bertram Dobell Catalog, *Browning Memorials* (London, 1913), item 41. Sir Charles Bell (1774-1842) was a standard author of anatomical textbooks. There are other similar sketches in the "Thomas Ingall Sketchbook" and still others are noted in F. H. Stead, "Browning's Father," *Putnam's Magazine,* 7 (April 1910), 857.

11. "Fifty Pen, Pencil, and Watercolor Sketches, " MS, Beinecke, Yale. The sketch, identified only as after one by Cross, is from John Cross's *An Attempt to Establish Physiognomy upon Scientific Principles* (Glasgow, 1871). Cross was a medical doctor and a serious authority on anatomy. But his physiognomy is more interesting for its evolutionary approach to comparative anatomy than for its often silly and sometimes racist assertions about the relations between physical and moral characteristics. It is, however, a mine of metaphors for the artist or poet seeking physical correlatives for invisible moral qualities.

12. *The Characters of Theophrastus,* trans. Francis Howell (London, 1826). The copy was sold, Sotheby, item 1160, and is now at Baylor.

13. Ibid., p. xiv.

14. Alice Corkran, "Chapters," p. 281. Henriette Corkran also told him how as a girl she heard "stories of mysterious murders" from him, Henriette Corkran to Hall Griffin, Nov. 15, [1904], Hall Griffin Papers, BL, Add. MS. 45,564, fols. 96-96b.

15. Furnivall, "Ancestors," pp. 31-32. Professor Richard D. Altick kindly located the place of the execution, Horsemonger Lane Gaol, not in a direct route from New Cross to the City. Another time when he was late for a train in Paris, he excused himself excitedly: "Just bought this for five sous, *The Manning Murderers,* with a picture of the kitchen where the body was buried!" (Henriette Corkran, *Celebrities,* p. 12).

16. Henriette Corkran, *Celebrities,* pp. 12-13. RB Sr. to RB, [n.d.], MS, Fitzwilliam Museum, Cambridge University, contains a discussion and separate plan of the Constance Kent case at Road, with a psychological analysis of the 16 year old girl. A book at Baylor, William Wills, *An Essay on the Rationale of Circumstantial Evidence* (London, 1838), is inscribed to him by the author (not the later playwright). It is filled with curious analyses of difficult murder cases resolved by strenuous ratiocination. RB Sr. took a similar interest in cases of contested titles, e.g., the Berkeley Peerage Case, on which there is another book at Baylor.

17. Sotheby, item 173.

18. *LRB,* p. 6, RB to E. F. Haworth, [ca. Dec. 30, 1841].

19. The *Novum Jesu-Christi Testamentum* (Limoges, 1812), at Baylor, given to RB by his mother has grotesque faces on the cover, presumably by RB, also in the manner of RB Sr.

20. Domett's *Diary*, p. 145: Robert Curling, Domett's cousin.

21. There are a large number of these in the "Thomas Ingall Sketchbook."

22. Alice Corkran, "Mr. Browning," in "Scrapbook of Clippings," Boston Public Library, R.9.119.1.

23. D. S. Curtis, "Robert Browning," diary entry for Oct. 15, 1883, MS, Baylor. Browning spoke of the elephant that his father took him to see as a boy. RB could have seen lions at the Camberwell Fair, as well: RB Sr., Stephens "Scrapbook of Cartoons," fol. 80.

24. "Thomas Ingall Sketchbook," fol. 7.

25. "MS Collections for History of Camberwell Made by R. Symmes," BL, Add. MS. 6167, fol. 71.

26. Douglas Allport, *Collections Illustrative of the Geology, History, Antiquities, and Associations, of Camberwell, and the Neighbourhood* (Camberwell, 1841), p. 86; William H. Blanch, *Ye Parish of Camerwell* (London, 1875), p. 313.

27. *Observer*, Aug. 19, 1832: quoted in Blanch, *Parish*, p. 313. Protests had begun as early as 1823.

28. In the Newington District Library collection. There is also a scrapbook of prints and clippings on the Fair, "Camberwell and Peckham Fair," SC. 791.6 CAM.

29. *DNB*, s.v. Richardson, John.

30. "Caricature Drawings," MS, Victoria and Albert Museum, Forster Collection, 48.D.1., fols. 62-71, 81-86.

31. *DI*, p. 355, RB to I. Blagden, Jan. 23, 1871.

32. Jim Kimball, "A Ruskin Letter to Mrs. Browning," *Browning Newsletter*, No. 8 (Spring 1972), p. 47; corrected, David J. DeLaura, "Ruskin to Browning: A Letter Reread," *Studies in Browning and his Circle*, 1 (Spring 1973), 33-34, Ruskin to EBB, [Oct. 18, 1856].

33. Grace Prestwich, *Life and Letters of Sir Joseph Prestwich* (Edinburgh, 1899), p. 17.

34. *LRB*, p. 217, RB to F. J. Furnivall, Apr. 15, 1883.

35. In the Newington District Library Collection.

36. "Thomas Ingall Sketchbook," fols. 33, 37.

37. Ibid., fol. 38.

38. Ibid., fol. 77. Ingall considered the area, later Wyndham Road, as very rough. It is similarly described in Blanch, *Parish*, p. 341, as an area where hawkers, costermongers, chimney sweepers, and donkeys abounded.

39. "Thomas Ingall Sketchbook," fol. 15: also explained by Ingall.

40. *RBEBK*, I, 509 (letter 255), RB to EBB, [March 3, 1846].

41. *RBAD*, p. 50, RB to A. Domett, March 5, 1843.

42. The comparison is interestingly made by Jack Herring, *Browning's Old Schoolfellow* (Pittsburg, Beta Phi Mu, 1972), pp. 19-21.

43. BL, Ashley MS. 2588; cf. Browning's poem "Mr. Sludge, 'The Medium' " (1864). W. R. Nicoll, "Robert Browning's Father," *The Bookman* (London), 42, No. 248 (May 1912), 63-73, publishes the full text of RB Sr.'s Hamelin poem. A part from a different MS of only 60 lines and with somewhat different wording, dated March 2, 1843, is given in Griffin and Minchin, p. 21. A note by the father to Thomas Powell explains that he began it not knowing his son had written on the subject. Cf. the report in *Books and Letters Collected by William Harris Arnold* (Jamaica, N.Y., 1901), item 40, that RB told T. J. Wise that the father wrote his poem first. RB Sr.'s written note, of course, carries authority. RB Sr.'s poem is closer to doggerel than RB's and spiced with bankers' jokes.

44. "Thirteen Sketches," inserted in *Bells and Pomegranates*, III, VII (1842, 1845), MS, Baylor. Probably these are some of those referred to by Elizabeth, *RBEBK*, I, 415, 506 (letters 212, 252), EBB to RB, Jan. 24-25, 1846, [March 1, 1846].

45. Sotheby, item 342.

46. A spoof by James White (London, 1796). The copy is now in the Victoria and Albert Museum, Forster Collection.

47. Books of his listed in Sotheby and the resale catalogs or at Baylor.

48. Sotheby, item 583, RB's note.

49. *LL,* p. 87, RB to Mrs. FitzGerald, Sept. 4, 1880.

50. *LL,* p. 192, RB to Mrs. FitzGerald, Dec. 4, 1886.

51. Henriette Corkran, *Celebrities,* p. 14.

52. *NL,* p. 343, RB to an unidentified correspondent, April 23, 1887; the "Memoirs" are listed, Dobell Catalog, *Browning Memorials,* item 230.

53. *LRB,* p. 105, RB to Baron Seymour Kirkup, Feb. 19, 1867.

54. His interest in the Junius question is discussed in chap. xiv, below.

55. Robert Wiedeman Browning to Hall Griffin, March 12, 1904, BL, Add. MS. 45,563, fols. 231-233b.

56. *LRB,* p. 97, RB to Robert Wiedeman Browning, [June 15, 1866].

57. "Military Engineering Sketches," MS, Baylor.

58. Dobell Catalog, *Browning Memorials,* item 230.

59. The work survives in a number of forms, ranging from about 110 pages to 395 pages, sometimes consisting of a full "Nomenclator" and an abbreviated "Speed," probably based on the earlier work of Speed. See Nos. 6, 23-24, 33, 36, 41, 48, Appendix B. One of the Browning Settlement copies (No. 29) includes a preface by RB and EBB in EBB's hand and a note by RB on the MS suggesting an index: Robert Browning Settlement, *Browning Bulletin* [London, 1928], item 211. It and perhaps other copies were submitted about 1855 for publication. RB mentions his own help in submitting it in a letter, RB to RB Sr., [1855], *Browning Bulletin,* item 208. It is the subject, though ignored by the editors, of the letter, *NL,* p. 84, RB to Edward Chapman, [Dec. 5, 1855], where Browning speaks with quiet humor of "that notable Treatise on Bible-genealogies, for which all the Publishers were tearing each other to pieces just when I left London," and notes that he is sending an improved copy. RB Sr. refers frequently to it in the letters to RB, Fitzwilliam Museum, Cambridge.

60. The fullest sampling of his methods can be made in the Browning library collection at Baylor. See also A. F. Butler, *Robert Browning's Father—His way with a Book* (Ann Arbor, priv. prnt., 1969) for a study of one book of his at Baylor: John Landseer, *Lectures on the Art of Engraving* (London, 1807).

61. Dobell Catalog, *Browning Memorials,* item 283.

62. "Notebook with Index," MS, Humanities Research Center, Univ. of Texas.

63. Reuben Browning, MS Introductory Notes to a collection of RB Sr. sketches, in Kitton, "Robert Browning, the Elder, as a Caricaturist," p. 56.

64. Report of von Muller v. Browning, "Court of Queen's Bench," *Morning Chronicle,* July 2, 1852, p. 7 (copy at Boston Athenaeum).

65. *DI,* p. 87, RB to I. Blagden, Sept. 9, 1861; Henriette Corkran, *Celebrities,* p. 12. For an example, see Sotheby, item 127.

66. Alice Corkran, "Chapters," pp. 280-281.

67. Ibid., p. 284.

68. Griffin and Minchin, pp. 20-25. They suggest Wanley not only as a source for "The Pied Piper," "The Cardinal and the Dog," the story of Pope Stephen VII in "The Pope" (*The Ring and the Book*) and the Pambo story at the end of *Jocoseria,* but also as a possible inspiration for RB's interest in Agrippa (*Pauline*), Paracelsus, Sibrandus "Schafnaburgensis," and John of Halberstadt in "Transcendentalism." None of this proves RB read the work before about 1840, but altogether it suggest a deep and probably early familiarity.

69. Wanley, "Preface," *The Wonders of the Little World* (London, 1678).

70. RB to F. J. Furnivall, Feb. 4, 1883, MS, Huntington, FU 103.

71. RB to F. J. Furnivall, Oct. 8, 1884, MS, Huntington, FU 118. RB specifies the 1701 edition, 2 vols., which his father later gave him. It is not clear whether he also had the *Supplement* (1755). Collier's condensation of Fuller's famous account of Shakespeare and Jonson is used as a motto for *Ferishtah's Fancies* (1884).

72. Paracelsus is treated extensively and favorably and probably did serve to first interest RB. The Druses are discussed twice, as Druses and Druzes, the first mentioning their hopes

for a messiah and the second their tendency to incest, both likely to make some lasting impression on a casual reader.

73. RB to John Kenyon, [ca. 1844], MS, Baylor.

74. *LRB,* p. 98, RB to Robert Wiedeman Browning, [June 17, 1866].

75. *LRB,* p. 105, RB to Baron Seymour Kirkup, Feb. 19, 1867.

76. "The Christian Virtues," dated Paris, Oct. 10, 1858, MS, Baylor: based on Philippians 4.8.

77. Marginalia in Thomas Burnet, *A Treatise Concerning the State of Departed Souls, Before, and at, and after the Resurrection,* trans. Dennis, 2nd ed. (London, 1739), p. 367, copy at Baylor.

78. A translation by RB Sr. of the 124th Psalm, 8th verse, dated Oct. 10, 1830, celebrates the Lord "Whose power sun, moon and star display": see F. H. Stead, "Browning's Father," *Putnam's Magazine,* 7 (April 1910), 855; cf. the verses, first probably wrongly ascribed to Browning himself, "On Louvel's Reply" (see my "Correspondence," *TLS,* March 23, 1973, p. 325), which assert generally the patent justice of God. His annotations in Zachary Pearce, *The Miracles of Jesus Vindicated* (1749), Baylor copy, show great interest in the argument—made long before answers to Strauss and Renan were necessary—that the disciples' writings can be trusted because they were good men who would not deceive.

79. "Thomas Ingall Sketchbook," fol. 3.

80. Ibid., fol. 4.

81. Ibid., fol. 20.

82. RB Sr., "Scrapbook," Humanities Research Center, Univ. of Texas (No. 21, Appendix B).

83. RB Sr., "Caricature Drawings," MS, Victoria and Albert Museum, Forster Collection, 48.D.1, fol. 77.

84. "Thomas Ingall Sketchbook," fol. 41.

85. RB Sr., "One Hundred and Forty-Four Caricatures," MS, Baylor.

86. Ibid.

87. Kitton, "Robert Browning, the Elder, as a Caricaturist," p. 56. A slightly different version, "John Bull in a Quandary," is in "Bevan Scrapbook," Bank of England, Archives Section, fol. 84.

88. Ibid., fol. 49.

89. Ibid., fols. 22, 21. The "Bevan Scrapbook" contains more than fifty comments on the Reform Bill; there are a number of others in the Stephens "Scrapbook."

90. *Celebrities,* p. 12.

91. RB Sr., "Scrapbook," MS, Humanities Research Center, Univ. of Texas (No. 22, Appendix B).

92. Hallam Tennyson, *Alfred Lord Tennyson: A Memoir* (London, 1897), II, 364.

93. Domett's *Diary,* p. 73. Two other friends from school were Frank and William Channell. Frank died young. William (1804-1873) appears in RB's "Address Book," MS, Beinecke, Yale, at 12 Gower St., Bedford Sq. and 2 Mitre Court, Temple. Channell rose to be Sir William and a judge. See *DNB,* s.v. Channell.

94. Orr, p. 46. Appendix A, section IV summarizes the few facts known about the Silverthornes.

95. Sotheby, item 1080: see the discussion of RB's first reading of Shelley in chap. ix, section 1, below.

96. Furnivall, "Ancestors," p. 38.

97. See chap. ix, section 4, below.

98. *RBEBK,* I, 156 (letter 80), RB to EBB, [Aug. 15, 1845]. Kintner identifies the performance as probably that of May 18, 1832; certainly spring 1832.

99. *RBEBK,* I, 25 (letter 9), RB to EBB, [Feb. 26, 1845].

100. Griffin, "Early Friends," p. 440. Griffin's account is the fullest treatment of the set. His notes and correspondence were generously given to the BL by his family (Add. MSS. 45,558-45,564). My debt to Griffin's researches should be apparent throughout this history, but it is especially great in this discussion of the set.

101. Miss Emma Young to Emily Secretan, [ca. 1904], Hall Griffin Papers, BL, Add. MS. 45,564, fols. 66-68b.

102. *RBAD,* p. 132, J. Arnould to A. Domett, Nov. 30, 1846. The British Coffee House was at 27 Cockspur St., Charing Cross; J. Arnould to A. Domett, Nov. 24, 1845, Hall Griffin Papers, BL, Add. MS. 45,560, fol. 47.

103. Ibid.

104. *RBAD,* p. 122, RB to A. Domett, March 19, 1846.

105. J. Arnould to A. Domett, May 13, 1855, Hall Griffin Papers, BL, Add. MS. 45,560, fol. 61.

106. J. Arnould to A. Domett, July 16, 1847, Hall Griffin Papers, BL, Add. MS. 45,560, fol. 50; *RBAD,* p. 39, RB to A. Domett, July 13, 1842.

107. Griffin, "Early Friends," p. 440.

108. J. Arnould to A. Domett, Nov. 12, 1842, Hall Griffin Papers, BL, Add. MS. 45,560, fol. 31.

109. The family of Christopher Dowson, Sr. lived at Church Row, Limehouse. Christopher Dowson, Jr. (Jan. 1808-Sept. 1848) married Mary Domett, Alfred Domett's youngest sister, in 1836. Their address, noted in RB's "Address Book," MS, Beinecke, Yale, was 3 Albion Terrace, Commercial Road, Limehouse (see also Griffin, "Early Friends," p. 434). The younger Dowson family also had a cottage at Woodford, summers, 1837-1844. Chris had sisters, Eliza, Kate (Mrs. Baker), and Sarah. Joe Dowson died about 1857. Copies of Dowson family letters, mostly by Chris, are in the Hall Griffin Papers, BL, Add. MS. 45,562. Griffin, "Early Friends," prints some extracts.

110. Victor Plarr, *Ernest Dowson 1888-1897* (New York, Laurence J. Gomme, 1914), pp. 37-38, description from his own observation; his point is that the Bridge Dock hadn't changed since the early nineteenth century. The Dowsons had been on the Thames for generations, first at Richmond, then east of London Bridge, then, by 1804, at the Bridge Dock as Messrs. Christopher Dowson and Son: Desmond Flower and Henry Maas, eds., *The Letters of Ernest Dowson* (London, Cassell & Co., 1967), p. 5. There were at least two generations of Christophers before RB's friend. Chris's son Alfred, Domett's nephew, held the Dock in its slow decline, and it finally expired, as the arts flourished and wealth decayed, under Alfred's son Ernest. Chris had a daughter, Emily (Mrs. Holford Secretan), and other daughters who died young.

111. Sir Frederick Young K.C.M.G. (1817-1913) was a prolific propagandist and leader in the movement for Imperial Federation, a democratic federal plan for the British Empire. The father, George Frederick Young, was a member for Tynemouth, 1833-1837, and continued to represent the protectionist position for the shipping trade into the 1850s. The single publication of his other son, William Curling Young (1815-1842), is discussed below. The G. F. Young Papers, BL, Add. MS. 46,712-46,715, contain records of G. F. Young's father, Admiral William Young, and an early diary and letters of G. F. Young. W. C. Young is described by his father in letters to Arthur Wakefield, Nov. 13, 1842 and to the Court of Directors of the New Zealand Co., March 11, 1843, Add. MS. 46,715C, fols. 1, 12. A sometime member of the group was also William Young (1809-1882), brother G. F. Young, "an agreeable far travelled man of the world, well dressed," translator of Béranger (1847) and adaptor of Italian and French plays: J. Arnould to A. Domett, July 16, 1847, Hall Griffin Papers, BL, Add. MS. 45,560, fol. 50; the fullest record of his translations and adaptions is in the BL catalog.

112. Alfred's grandfather was customs officer at Lyme Regis where Alfred's father, Nathaniel (1764-1849) was born. The father entered the navy at age twelve, then left for the merchant service in 1781 and settled in The Grove, Camberwell, in 1801 on his marriage to Elizabeth Curling (?-1817), daughter of Robert Curling of Denmark Hill; they had 9 children. The Youngs of Limehouse were also related to the Curlings, hence the friendship of Youngs and Dometts. There was also a Domett and Son, Ship's Biscuit Baker, 7 Narrow Street, Limehouse, in 1823.

113. Domett's *Diary,* pp. 108-109.

114. *RBAD,* p. 32 f. A more realistic portrait, suggesting more of Domett's forceful temper, is reproduced in Domett's *Diary,* front.

115. Domett's *Diary,* p. 25.

116. Domett (May 20, 1811-1887) was educated at Stockwell Park House, Camberwell and St. John's College, Cambridge. His journey in the United States and Canada is recorded in *The Canadian Journal of Alfred Domett: 1833-1835,* ed. E. A. Horsman and Lillian Rea Benson (London, Canada, University of Ontario, 1955). He entered the Middle Temple in 1835 and was called to the bar in 1841. He had traveled to Venice in the late 1830s. On April 30, 1842 he emigrated to New Zealand where he became a journalist, an expert on land policy, a somewhat brutal if honest exponent of the settlers' rights (or pretended rights) against the native Maoris, a civil servant and government official, and, in 1862-1863, prime minister. He married a widow Mrs. George and had one child, Alfred, of his own as well as stepchildren. He returned to England in 1872; his *Diary* records some of his later life there. Domett also published poems in *Blackwood's* in the 1830s, one of which, "It was the calm and silent night," became a fairly popular Christmas poem in the United States. His *Flotsam and Jetsam: Rhymes Old and New* (London, 1877), dedicated to RB, included brief poems from 1834 on, some quite excellent. A revision of *Ranolf and Amohia* was published in 1883, 2 vols. E. A. Horsman, in the "Introduction" to Domett's *Diary,* notes a good deal of journalistic writing for the Nelson *Examiner* and a variety of petitions and New Zealand government documents. Horsman's account is the fullest one of Domett's life and career. See also *DNB,* s.v. Domett.

117. Domett's *Diary,* p. 74.

118. Emily Secretan to Griffin, [1904], Hall Griffin Papers, BL, Add. MS, 45,564, fols. 69-73b.

119. Ibid., and Emma Young to Emily Secretan, [ca. 1904], Hall Griffin Papers, BL, Add. MS. 45,564, fols. 66-68b. RB's "Address Book," MS, Beinecke, Yale, does not solve the mystery of Pritchard's address: RB wrote only his name. James Pritchard appears in the Camberwell rate book for 1813 without specific address. There was also a Thomas Pritchard, surgeon, living at Burlington Place, Camberwell in 1823. Pritchard died at 5, Oak Terrace, Battersea Bridge Road.

120. *LRB,* p. 1, RB to Christopher Dowson, Jr., [dated ca. 1830 by Hood and claimed as RB's earliest extant letter; however the date is no earlier than 1832, the watermark on the letter: BL, MS, Ashley 2542, fol. 11]. Pritchard left both Sarianna and Chris's daughter substantial gifts in his will (Griffin, "Early Friends," p. 440). The correspondence of 1859 at Baylor from Pritchard's executors (one being Bezer Blundell) indicates Sarianna was no relation but received both 1000 pounds and manuscripts, books, and papers; she also had a gold watch from him (Griffin, "Domett," p. 108). Pritchard evidently knew the entire Browning family and was in possession of some sketches by RB Sr.: Emma Young to Emily Secretan, [ca. 1904], Hall Griffin Papers, BL, Add. MS. 45,564, fols. 66-68b. That Pritchard was an old family friend is also suggested by RB's desire to have him serve with Silverthorne as witness at his wedding: *RBEBK,* II, 1066 (letter 559), RB to EBB, [Sept. 13, 1846].

121. This is the view of the introduction of RB to the set accepted by Griffin and Minchin, pp. 80, 84. Various evidence suggests RB's first acquaintance with Domett must have been earlier than the ca. 1840 they suggest. Inasmuch as *Sordello* was written over a period of 7 years, RB's statement that he would have included Domett in the tributes in the poem had he known him earlier does not establish a date. By contrast, Domett states explicitly that he heard RB speak of learning Hebrew "somewhere between 1835 and 1840": Domett's *Diary,* p. 249. A copy of *Paracelsus* with additional MS corrections by RB is inscribed to Domett with the date 1835: Humanities Research Center, Univ of Texas. Probably their acquaintance was not much before 1835. During the early 1830s Arnould was mainly at Oxford and Domett was traveling in the United States. Griffin is probably still right in arguing that their closer friendship began largely about 1840 (Griffin, "Domett," pp. 108-109).

122. *RBAD,* p. 115, RB to A. Domett, Nov. 23, 1845.

123. *RBAD,* p. 132, J. Arnould to A. Domett, Nov. 30, 1846. Blundell (1790-1878) took a degree in medicine at Edinburgh in 1813 and from 1814 to his retirement from Guy's Hospital in 1836 developed the most popular lectures on midwifery in London. He made 340,000 pounds in his profession but also did seminal work in abdominal surgery and wrote on physio-

logical research, obstetrics, and gynecology. His literary interests were serious enough to issue in a translation of *Four of Virgil's Pastorals* (London, 1838).

124. J. Arnould to A. Domett, July 16, 1847; Dec. 18, 1851, Hall Griffin Papers, BL, Add. MS. 45,560, fols. 50, 60. Bezer Blundell appears in RB's "Address Book," MS, Beinecke, Yale, at [3] Mitre Court, Temple. He became a prospering country lawyer but continued to speak out in print for court reform and against court fools. One satire, probably *The Wolverhampton Warbler: or County Court Christmas Carol* (London, [1852]), a satire on R. N. Clarke, judge of the County Court of Wolverhampton, ended him in jail (and for a while out of his rich uncle's will) when he refused to pay libel damages: see also Griffin, "Early Friends," p. 441.

125. Domett's *Diary,* p. 8, J. Arnould to A. Domett, Sept. 12, 1835.

126. J. Arnould to RB, July 20-21, 1847, MS, Alexander Turnbull Library, Wellington, New Zealand.

127. Arnould's letters, partly printed in *RBAD,* in Horsman's "Introduction" to Domett's *Diary,* and in Donald Smalley, "Joseph Arnould and Robert Browning: New Letters (1842-50) and a Verse Epistle," *PMLA,* 80 (March 1965), 90-101, are still widely scattered and deserve, for their literary merit as well as their associations, to be collected and well edited. There are copies of MS letters in the Hall Griffin Papers, BL, Add. MS. 45,560, and other originals at the Turnbull Library, and yet others evidently still in the possession of Domett's descendants (Domett's *Diary,* p. 43).

128. Published for the first time by Smalley, "Joseph Arnould and Robert Browning," pp. 92-93.

129. J. Arnould to A. Domett, July 28, 1844, Hall Griffin Papers, BL, Add. MS. 45,560, fols. 36-44.

130. J. Arnould to A. Domett, May 13, 1855, Hall Griffin Papers, BL, Add, MS. 45,560, fol. 61. Arnould's house was at 18 Victoria Sq., Lower Grosvenor Place, Pimlico; his chambers at 10 Ferrar's Building, Temple: both appear in RB's "Address Book," MS, Beinecke, Yale.

131. Arnould's father, also Joseph Arnould, owned property at White Cross near Wallingford that his son eventually inherited. Arnould, the eldest son, was born at Camberwell, Nov. 12, 1814, and died at Florence Feb. 16, 1866. Rate books, Newington District Library, have the family at Dowlas Common in 1813-1814 and thereafter in Camden Row (near the Silverthornes). Arnould was educated at Charterhouse and at Wadham College, Oxford, where his "The Hospice of St. Bernard" won the Newdigate Prize in 1834. He took a B.A. in 1836 with a first class; he was a fellow from 1838 and moderator of philosophy in 1840. In Nov., 1836, he entered the Middle Temple where he shared chambers with Domett. He was called to the bar Nov. 1841 and became a special pleader. In 1859-1869 he served on the supreme court of Bombay and the later high court of judicature; he was knighted in 1859. He married Maria Ridgeway in 1841 and Ann Pitcairn Carnegie in 1860. He wrote for Douglas Jerrold's *Weekly Newspaper* and for the *Daily News* in the 1840s. His *Treatise on the Law of Marine Insurance and Average,* first published in 1848, was in its 15th edition in 1961. *Verses, Collected and Reprinted as a Memento for Friends* (London, priv. prnt., 1859) brought together various periodical contributions and privately printed poems mostly on public themes, vigorous but mediocre. His *Memoir of Thomas, First Lord Denman, formerly Lord Chief Justice of England,* 2 vols. (London, 1873) is a product of his retirement leisure and a testimony to his liberal politics and humane legal interests. See *DNB Supplement,* XXII, s.v. Arnould and the "Obit," *Times,* Feb. 18, 1886, p. 10.

132. J. Arnould to RB, July 20-21, 1847, MS, Alexander Turnbull Library, Wellington, New Zealand, announces that the deed was executed "last Thursday week." RB to Reuben Browning, July 30, [1873], MS, Baylor, states that RB has seen Sir Joseph and has been advised to transfer the trusteeship to Sarianna. Arnould visited the Brownings and entertained Sarianna even after RB and EBB left for Italy. The letter of July 20-21, 1847 is written partly from Hatcham. He gave RB Sr. an old copy of Sir Thomas Browne's *Works* (Sotheby, item 422).

133. Emily Secretan to Griffin, March 9, 1905, Hall Griffin Papers, BL, Add. MS. 45,564, fols, 188-189b. Field (1815-1874) became a portraitist and landscape painter who exhibited regularly at the Royal Academy. He appears, probably as a relatively late (1840s) entry in RB's "Address Book," MS, Beinecke, Yale, at 70 Newman St., Oxford St.

134. Browning praises an exhibit by "Lance, your friend," *RBAD,* p. 53, RB to A. Domett, May 15, 1843. Lance knew Domett as early as 1836 when he did the romantic sketch of him: *RBAD,* p. 32 f. On Lance (1802-1864) see "George Lance," *Art Journal,* Oct. 1, 1857, pp. 305-307. Mrs. Lance also attended later reunions.

135. Griffin, "Early Friends," p. 441 asserts that Jowett was a member; Griffin and Minchin, p. 81 (no doubt Minchin) strongly questions this on the grounds that Jowett writes in 1865 of making a new friend in Browning. Also, there is no reference to old times in the Jowett letters to Browning at Baylor. But Griffin's early assertion was based on good authority, that of both Miss Emma Young and Frederick Young, from whom a great deal of the information about the set has been derived. See Emma Young to Emily Secretan, [ca. 1904]; Frederick Young to Griffin, Nov. 30, 1904, Hall Griffin Papers, BL, Add. MS. 45,564, fols. 66-68b, 108-110; Frederick Young recalled in addition that Jowett's father had offices below those of the Youngs and that Jowett came with one of the Blundells to the set. Griffin confirmed that Jowett's father was a close friend of Dr. Blundell who was remembered in Blundell's will: "Early Friends," p. 441. The Jowetts were also Camberwell residents.

136. J. Arnould to A. Domett, July 16, 1847, Hall Griffin Papers, BL, Add. MS. 45,560, fol. 50. The Oldfields were Edmund, Tom, and Emma; Champion Hill adjoined Camberwell Grove. The Bakers, apparently Kate (Dowson) and Robert, lived a few doors from the Dowsons in Church Row, Limehouse: Frederick Young to Griffin, Nov. 30, 1904, Hall Griffin Papers, BL, Add. MS. 45,564, fols. 108-110. Along with George Bidder sometimes came his younger brother, Harold F. Bidder who lived at 10 Queen's Gate Gardens, S. W.; George (1800-?) was president of the Institute of Civil Engineers, 1860-1861: see Griffin, "Early Friends," p. 442. Other peripheral members of the set were probably: Charles Walton, shipowner and ship and insurance broker, an early friend of Pritchard's and RB's: see *RBEBK,* II, 593 (letter 301), RB to EBB, [April 6, 1846]; a Barthwick, mentioned by Arnould as a member of the set but otherwise unidentified: J. Arnould to A. Domett, Feb. 26, 1848, Hall Griffin Papers, BL, Add. MS. 45,560, fol. 56. Very likely the Captain Lloyd who interrupted "The Flight of the Duchess" in the manner of Coleridge's farmhouse visitor was also a member of the set; his address, 8 Park Street, Greenwich, appears in RB's "Address Book," MS, Beinecke, Yale.

137. J. Arnould to A. Domett, Nov. 24, 1845, Hall Griffin Papers, BL, Add. MS. 45,560, fol. 47.

138. *RBAD,* p. 132, J. Arnould to A. Domett, Nov. 30, 1846: probably a recollection of an evening apart from the full set.

139. Emma Young to Emily Secretan, [ca. 1904], Hall Griffin Papers, BL, Add. MS. 45,564, fols. 66-68b.

140. Frederick Young to Hall Griffin, Feb. 11, 1905, Hall Griffin Papers, BL, Add. MS. 45,564, fols. 174-177b.

141. *The English in China* (London, 1840); first printed in the *Colonial Gazette,* No. 49 (1839). The copy of the book at Baylor is inscribed "Robert Browning Esqre with W. C. Y.'s best remembrances."

142. *RBAD,* p. 60, J. Arnould to A. Domett, [May ? 1843].

143. A. Domett to RB, Aug. 20, 1846, MS, Turnbull Library. Arnould speaks more objectively, but also critically, of Puseyism and of Newman: J. Arnould to RB, March 24, 1847, MS, Turnbull Library.

144. *NL,* p. 35, RB to F. O. Ward, Feb. 18, 1845.

145. See the portrait by Middleton, reproduced, *RBAD,* p. 60 f.

146. Domett's *Diary,* p. 4.

147. Smalley, "Joseph Arnould and Robert Browning," p. 96, J. Arnould to RB, Dec. 19, 1847.

148. J. Arnould to RB, July 20-21, 1847, MS, Turnbull Library. J. Arnould to A. Domett, July 28, 1844, Hall Griffin papers, BL, Add. MS, 45,560, fol. 36.

149. *LRB,* p. 1, RB to C. Dowson, [dated 1830 by Hood but from watermark not before 1832].

150. Domett's *Diary,* p. 13.

151. Griffin, "Early Friends," p. 440.

152. *RBAD,* p. 91, RB to A. Domett, Oct. 9, 1843; the letter of March 10, [1844], is published *LRB,* p. 9.

153. Griffin, "Early Friends," p. 439. Probably Chris had played some real parts in his day. Ernest Dowson "was wont to shake his head gloomily over a print or pencil sketch of an ancestor engaged in theatricals on a queer stage with spindling Corinthian columns in the period of George IV": Plarr, *Ernest Dowson,* p. 18.

154. Frederick Young to Emma Young, Oct. 23, 1904, Hall Griffin Papers, BL, Add. MS. 45,564, fols. 74-74b.

155. *RBAD,* p. 132, J. Arnould to A. Domett, Nov. 30, 1846.

156. Emily Secretan to Griffin, Jan. 5, 1905, Hall Griffin Papers, BL, Add. MS. 45,564, fols. 153-158b.

157. Frederick Young to Griffin, Feb. 11, 1905, Hall Griffin Papers, BL, Add. MS. 45,564, fols. 174-177b.

158. Domett's *Poems* (1833) are littered with references to Byron and Wordsworth as well as to Shelley. Chris and Joe Dowson were enthusiasts for Scott; Joe even wrote a poem on Scott's illness in 1832: Chris Dowson to Eliza Dowson, July 13, 1832, Hall Griffin Papers, BL, Add. MS. 45, 562, fols. 14-15.

159. A. Domett to RB, May 6, 1864, MS, Turnbull Library.

160. *The Trifler,* Nos. 1-2, (Jan.-Feb. 1835), pp. 1-20, Houghton, Harvard, 23443.75*.

161. Frederick Young to Griffin, Feb. 11, 1905, Hall Griffin Papers, BL, Add. MS. 45,564, fols. 174-177b.

162. The epigram is given in Appendix C with the other epigram on Ready for comparison.

163. The full article and the previous work on debt which it answers are given in Appendix C. About a fifth of Browning's article was published in Orr, pp. 63-64.

164. *Strafford* was sent to Pritchard May-Day 1837: Berg Collection, New York Public Library. A copy of *King Victor and King Charles* (1842) sent to Blundell is at Huntington, Hunt. 22900.

165. *RBAD,* p. 28, RB to A. Domett, [ca. March 25, 1840].

166. A. Domett to RB, May 6, 1864, MS, Turnbull Library; "Lines Sent to Robert Browning, 1841, On a Certain Critique on 'Pippa Passes,' " *Flotsam and Jetsam,* pp. 25-27.

167. See especially the copy of *Sordello* (1840) in the BL (Ashley 247) and *Paracelsus* (1835) in the Turnbull Library (the date of the copious comments is unclear). The *Paracelsus* (1835) and the *Bells and Pomegranates* (1841-1846) at the Humanities Research Center, Univ. of Texas, are less fully annotated but show signs of close attention. Domett's son recalled his father reading to the family from *Paracelsus* (A. N. Domett to Griffin, Aug. 11, 1904, Hall Griffin Papers, BL, Add. MS. 45,564, fols. 23-24). Domett's letters often allude to RB's poems and he did everything he could to make converts for his friend in New Zealand.

168. Donald Smalley, "Joseph Arnould and Robert Browning," p. 91, J. Arnould to RB, Nov. 27, 1842.

169. *RBAD,* p. 78, J. Arnould to A. Domett, [ca. Nov. 8, 1843].

170. A. Domett to RB, Jan. 30, 1846, MS, Wellesley.

171. *NL,* p. 72, RB to John Forster, April 2, 1854.

172. *DI,* p. 240, RB to Isa Blagden, June 20, 1866.

173. Reuben Browning, MS Introductory Notes to a collection of RB Sr. sketches, pub. in Kitton, "Robert Browning, the Elder," p. 56.

174. Mason, "Kinsfolk," p. 9.

175. Sotheby, item 1395. His name appears in RB's early "Address Book," MS, Beinecke,

Yale, at 15, rue Laffitte, Paris. RB speaks of his and Reuben's kindness in a letter, RB to Reuben Browning, Dec. 31, 1858, MS, Wellesley. The lack of surviving letters to or from William makes his relationship to RB less apparent than Reuben's. William's dates and publications are summarized in Appendix A, section IV.

176. Christiana Browning (daughter of Reuben) to F. J. Furnivall, [ca. 1890], MS, Huntington, FU 72; Robert Shergold Browning (son of William) to F. J. Furnivall, March 5, 1890, MS, Huntington, FU 159.

177. W. S. Browning, *Hoel Morvan* (London, 1845), I, 22.

178. The revised edition (1839 and later), carrying the story of persecution down to 1838, includes a long discussion of the more recent, and then still not fully acknowledged, religious persecution of 1830. The first edition (1829) was in the Browning library: Sotheby, item 526.

179. F. G. Kitton, "Robert Browning, the Elder," p. 55.

180. *NL,* p. 39, RB to E. F. Haworth, [1846?].

181. *Sordello* (1840), inscribed "William Browning from his nephew, RB" (copy at Houghton, Harvard). From William's poem it seems likely that *Strafford, Paracelsus,* and probably other works, were sent to him. The poem, *Leisure Hours,* p. 373, is 15 lines, beginning with an observation of a French picture of Strafford and moving on to RB's "British pen."

182. Mottoes to chaps. xxx, xli.

183. "Death of Reuben Browning," *Journal of Commerce,* Sept. 11, 1879 (from a copy in the possession of Mrs. Elaine Baly of East Barnet, England). Reuben's dates and publications are summarized in Appendix A, section IV.

184. Orr, p. 75.

185. Christiana Browning to F. J. Furnivall, [ca. 1890], MS, Huntington, FU 72.

186. Christiana Browning to F. J. Furnivall, [ca. 1890], MS, Huntington, FU 74.

187. Mason, "Kinsfolk," p. 86; RB to Michael Browning (son of Reuben), Dec. 29, 1860, MS, Wellesley.

188. Griffin and Minchin, p. 6, mentions the Smart volume. Epictetus, *Enchiridion* (Glasgow, 1748) is described Sotheby, item 652.

189. Mason, "Kinsfolk," p. 100. Orr denies that there was any financial debt to Reuben. The love letters mention only RB's taking a letter of credit from Rothschild's. However, some sense of special obligation seems to be implied in the contingent benefit RB gave to Reuben's children in his will.

190. There is an extensive correspondence, mostly unpublished, between RB and Reuben on business as well as family matters: partly published, *NL,* partly at Baylor and the Boston Public Library, and partly known only through a sale listed in Sotheby Sales Catalog, April 5, 1894, items 203-211. 2 other letters to Reuben in the State Library of Victoria, Melbourne, Australia, are given in facs. by Elaine Baly, "Talking of the Brownings—Robert's Relations," *Browning Society Notes,* 3 (Dec. 1973), 14-15. There is one other in the Berg Collection, New York Public Library.

191. *RBEBK,* I, 70 (letter 28), RB to EBB, [May 20, 1845]. Orr, p. 370, notes Reuben's deafness.

192. *RBEBK,* I, 307 (letter 168) RB to EBB, [Dec. 7, 1845]. The description is from a photo of Reuben in maturity in possession of Mrs. Elaine Baly.

193. Information kindly provided by Mrs. Baly, derived from her grandmother, Elizabeth Ann, daughter of Reuben.

194. RB to Reuben Browning, Dec. 31, 1858, MS, Wellesley.

195. Information from Mrs. Baly.

196. "Death of Reuben Browning."

197. For an account of Charles Mathews the elder (1766-1835) see *DNB,* s.v. Mathews, or the work by his wife, Anne Jackson Mathews, *Memoirs of Charles Mathews,* 4 vols. (London, 1838). Outline summaries of Mathews's "At Homes" were published in various pamphlet editions, now rare, under titles such as *Mr. Mathews' At Home* or *Mr. Mathews' New Entertainment for 1826* (copies, Harvard Theater Collection).

198. RB, marginal MS note, *Pauline* (1833), Mill copy, Victoria and Albert Museum, Forster Collection.

199. Reuben Browning, "Fictional Account of the Last Judgment," [ca. 1870s], MS, Baylor. RB to Reuben Browning, [ca. 1870s], MS, Baylor. RB also mentions the story of Cher but wonders if he was "worth powder & shot."

200. *NL,* p. 63, RB to Reuben Browning, July 18, 1853.

201. RB to Reuben Browning, Dec. 31, 1858, MS, Wellesley.

202. *Pauline,* inscribed by Reuben but location not identified, is on an Ann Arbor Microfilm (copy at Baylor); Houghton, Harvard, has copies of *King Victor and King Charles* (1842) and *Luria and a Soul's Tragedy* (1846) inscribed by RB to Reuben. A copy of *Men and Women* was sent Reuben through Chapman, *NL,* p. 81, RB to E. Chapman, Oct. 31, 1855. A copy of *Dramatis Personae* inscribed to Reuben was in the *Collection of Books and Letters of W. H. Arnold* (Jamaica, N.Y., 1901), item 32. *NL,* p. 215, RB to Reuben, April 27, 1873, promises to send his latest (*Red Cotton Night-Cap Country*). A letter, RB to Reuben, Nov. 6, 1875, MS, Boston Public Library, E.9.41, shows RB responding to a question from Reuben about well-known early poems.

203. *LEBB,* I, 387, EBB to Mrs. Martin, Dec. 3, 1848.

204. Copy in RB's hand, dated Aug. 10, 1884, MS, Baylor. The original entry was before March 8, 1864. George Montiero, "A 'Very Original Poem' by Robert Browning," *Notes and Queries,* 211 (Sept. 1966), 340, prints a copy made on that date by RB (now in the Massachusetts Historical Society). I prefer the later version, which has been revised and much improved. The later title (if this is the word) is "Economic Precept written more than twenty years ago in the first account book possessed by my son." It has a note on Lowndes similar to the earlier text: "Lowndes was a famous financier in Queen Anne's time."

205. *RBEBK,* I, 212 (letter 114), RB to EBB, [Sept. 25, 1845].

206. *RBEBK,* I, 197 (letter 104), RB to EBB, [Sept. 16, 1845].

207. *LRB,* p. 105, RB to Baron Seymour Kirkup, Feb. 19, 1867.

208. *LRB,* p. 27, RB to John Kenyon, July 29, 1850.

209. The only indication of RB's early study of Spanish is RB to Ripert-Monclar, Dec. 5, 1834, MS, Private Collection.

210. *NL,* p. 15, RB to E. F. Haworth, [April 1839].

211. *NL,* p. 28, RB to an unidentified correspondent, Sept. 3, [1842?], mentions a M. Desplace and his "clever article." DeVane and Knickerbocker suggest this is J. B. Desplace, editor with Capo de Feuillide of *Le Garde national* (Paris, 1848).

212. Professor Kintner presumed that the Roman friends mentioned in RB's letters, *RBEBK,* I, 161, 164, 164, 209 (letter 83, 85-86, 112), RB to EBB, [Aug. 18, 20, 21, Sept. 24, 1845], were the countess and her husband, whom he met at Rome.

213. William Shergold Browning to Reuben Browning, July 15, 1834, MS, Private Collection, introduces Monclar (along with a letter of introduction from one of the Rothschilds). Reuben Browning to Monclar, July 28, 1834, introduces RB to Monclar. Reuben had already spoken highly of his nephew when he returned Monclar's first call on July 23: "Voyage à Londres, 1834," MS, Private Collection. William thanks Fortia "(so justly esteemed among the literary circles of Paris)" for help in his *History of the Huguenots* (London, 1829), p. x.

214. Probably Monclar's grandfather or great-grandfather, François (1711-1773) was *procureur général* in the parliament of Provence; he worked and wrote against the Jesuits and in favor of Protestant liberties and was also an expert on financial and legislative affairs. See the entry in the *Biographie Universelle,* new ed., and an anonymous French newspaper clipping at Baylor (Meynell Collection). Orr, p. 68, suggests Monclar (1807-1871; full name, André Victor Amédée) later became Marquis. His son, by an English wife née Jerningham, François (1844-1921), also Marquis de Ripert-Monclar, wrote some minor historical and antiquarian studies. The family papers are in the Private Collection and include a brief account of Monclar by his son (letter to Henry cited below).

215. Monclar had been *procureur du roi,* hence his title *Ancien Magistrat.* He had joined an insurrection in the Vendée in 1832 and been released from prison under surveillance: Fran-

çois de Ripert-Monclar to Fernand Henry, Jan. 28, 1914, MS, Private Collection. Browning later speaks of his being occupied with "chancellerie." He wrote a memoir of his uncle, *Essai sur la vie et les ouvrages de M. le Marquis de Fortia d'Urban* (Paris, 1840); a popular treatise on finance, *Catéchisme financier* (Paris, 1848); a *Finances de l'Espagne* (Paris, 1850); and probably contributed often to periodicals such as the *Gazette de France*. François speaks of his writing for the *Nouveau Conservateur* and for other journals under pseudonyms: letter cited above.

216. Nothing in the journals, the letters, or the account of Monclar by his son indicates political activity in England. He did see his future in-laws, English who had served in France before 1830.

217. MS, Private Collection. Unless otherwise noted, information from Monclar's visit and quotations below are from this journal.

218. RB to Monclar, Aug. 9, 1837, MS, Private Collection.

219. 8 MS letters, one copy of a letter, and one separate envelope, RB to Monclar, are in the Private Collection. There are no letters extant from Monclar to Browning.

220. "Voyage à Londres en 1837," MS, Private Collection. Monclar arrived in London June 14, 1837. The journal breaks off Aug. 10, with Monclar still in London. He saw less of RB because he visited the rest of England and Ireland.

221. H. C. Minchin, "A Letter from Hanover Cottage," *Bookman,* 86 (April 1934), 6, RB to E. F. Haworth, [ca. Aug. 1, 1837].

222. By S. L. (Paris, 1833), copy at Baylor. Probably presented to RB on his call of Sept. 8, 1834: Monclar, "Voyage à Londres, 1834," MS, Private Collection.

223. Orr, p. 67.

224. The analysis is in the Private Collection. François' letter to Henry suggests that a review was planned.

225. Presentations of first editions of *Pauline, Paracelsus* (identified as Monclar's copy only by bookseller's provenance and uncut), *Strafford* (uncut), *Sordello,* and *The Return of the Druses* (inscription crossed out and presented instead to a Mrs. Wood) are at Beinecke, Yale; presentations of *Pippa Passes, Dramatic Lyrics,* and *King Victor and King Charles* (inscribed as a "souvenir of RB") are in the Private Collection.

226. Orr, p. 356, notes these drawings were still in Browning's possession in later years. Probably sometime in July, 1837, Monclar gave Browning an album with a lock in which to keep his drawings and lithographs. It is referred to in the letter RB to Haworth, [ca. Aug. 1, 1837], and its contents are described more fully in Dobell Catalog, *Browning Memorials,* item 1. Dobell claims it was given in 1838; but this is probably based on the earlier dating of the letter to Haworth as 1838 or 1839. It is now in the Private Collection and included a portrait of Monclar (see note below), drawings of a castle and of Hugo by Monclar, and other drawings by Haworth and Robert Wiedeman Browning.

227. RB to Monclar, Dec. 5, 1834, MS, Private Monclar Collection. RB admits he doesn't know Balzac well, RB to Monclar, July 30, 1835.

228. A review of Fortia's *Essai sur l'origine de l'écriture* (Paris, 1832), "Communicated by Comte A. de Ripert-Monclar, Ancien Magistrat," *Metropolitan Magazine,* 11 (Oct. 1834), 33-37: pub. by Saunders and Otley, the paid publishers of *Pauline.* RB had written the name of the magazine and the publishers at the top of a drawing of a dancing girl possibly by himself or by Monclar, dated Sept. 10, 1834, which he gave to Monclar as a souvenir when he left London in 1834, Private Collection. Very likely RB had played some part in polishing Monclar's English: his language is overblown but grammatical. Monclar's "Voyage à Londres, 1834" records writing the article and giving it to RB Aug. 20, 1834: MS, Private Collection. They originally planned it for Fox's *Monthly Repository.*

229. Three of the letters to Monclar speak with respect of Fortia's works. From the letter, RB to Monclar, Jan. 11, 1836, it is clear that RB knew at least the *Dissertation sur le passage du Rhône et des Alpes par Annibal* (in one of the many editions), the *Essai sur l'immortalité de l'âme* (Paris, 1835), and the *Examen d'un diplôme, attribué à Louis-le-Bègue, Roi de France*

(Paris, 1833); Monclar gave RB a copy of the work he reviewed in the *Metropolitan Magazine,* the *Essai sur l'origine de l'écriture,* on August 21, 1834: Dobell Catalog, *Browning Memorials,* item 147. There are 89 entries in the bibliography by de Hoffmanns attached to Monclar's memoir of his uncle; his histories survey mankind literally from China to Portugal, if not Peru, from primitive times to present France; he wrote, as well, on morals, literature and language, and on mathematics.

230. Later, probably after his marriage, Monclar appears next door to RB's Uncle William at 17 bis rue Laf[f]itte, Paris, "Address Book," MS, Beinecke, Yale. William was at No. 15.

231. Both Browning and Monclar are listed as members in the first list of Dec. 31, 1834: *Journal de l'Institut Historique,* 1 (Paris, 1834), 318; the Institut became the present Société des Études Historiques.

232. As Monclar emphasized in his memoir of Fortia, one of Fortia's major concerns was with the antiquity of the world. His major work, *Mémoires pour servir à l'histoire ancienne du globe terrestre,* 10 vols. (Paris, 1807-1811), attempts, in vol. X, the problem of reconciling Genesis with the evidence of early histories.

233. His *Chronologie de Jésus-Christ* was published Paris, 1830.

234. Monclar, Review of Fortia's *Essai sur l'origine de l'écriture,* p. 40.

235. Ibid., p. 37.

236. Orr, p. 67.

237. The portrait (a print) is still pasted in the Album in the Private Collection. There is a second copy in the collection as well as another more idealized portrait by the English portraitist, William Brockedon. François, letter cited above, speaks of his father at that time as "trés mondain."

238. Especially, RB to Monclar, Dec. 5, 1834; July 30, 1835; Jan. 11, 1836, MS, Private Collection.

239. He seems to imply that he had already been south; however, there is no evidence of any early trip to Spain or Italy.

240. François, letter cited above.

241. The pencil drawing is inscribed "Amedee de [or R] M. 7 juillet—37." Sittings were July 4 and 7. It was sold Sotheby, item 7 and reproduced among the illustrations at the end of the catalog. The same drawing is reproduced by Grace E. Wilson, *Robert Browning's Portraits, Photographs and Other Likenesses and their Makers* (Waco, Texas, Baylor University, 1943), p. 33 and by Jeanette Marks, *The Family of the Barrett* (New York, Macmillan, 1938), p. 554 f. Wilson's vague account claims her drawing is reproduced from an original at Baylor. There are records at Baylor, kindly searched for me by Dr. Herring, of the existence of a drawing described as a "copy" of the original in 1933. Even it, however, is now lost, and it may have been only a copy of the Sotheby illustration. The same may be true of Marks's illustration, which she identifies only as pasted into a copy of *Paracelsus* belonging to EBB without giving any location. Although we have only one version in these various reproductions, RB spoke of Monclar's doing at least two likenesses.

242. *RBEBK,* I, 228 (letter 126), RB to EBB, [Oct. 12, 1845].

243. *LRB,* p. 1, RB to E. F. Haworth, [July 24, 1838]. There seems to be no certainty in this dating and RB may actually have been longer in Europe. Miller, p. 71, notes the connection of RB's trip with Rothschild's.

244. The only record I have found explaining the embassy is a letter, Mr. Bligh, British Ambassador to Russia, to Palmerston, recorded in Palmerston's copy book, under dates March 28, 1834 (date of sending), BL. Add. MS. 48, 485, fol. 73: "Believes that Mr. Benkhausen has been sent relative to some business on the subject of the Loan entered into by Mr. Rothschild in 1822." An entry for Jan. 7, fol. 67b, had noted that Russia would need a foreign loan. The loan of 1822 was made in Oct. by Solomon Rothschild at the Congress of Verona. Since then the Rothschilds had become less friendly to Russia because of Russian treatment of Jews. George Benkhausen (not Orr's spelling, Benckhausen) is listed in RB's "Address Book,"

MS, Beinecke, Yale, at 9 Arglye St., Regent Sq. Benkhausen was Consul General for Russia in England under Ambassador Prince de Lieven, from 1828-1844 (see listings, *The Royal Kalendar*). The Argyle St. address is listed after 1839.

245. *The Holy Bible* (Cambridge, 1833), a small gold leaf edition now at Wellesley. It is inscribed to RB, Feb. 28, 1834. RB later used it to record family dates.

246. Griffin and Minchin plot out a route for RB through present Belgium and Aachen Germany (Aix-la-Chapelle) from mention of these places in later works: "How They Brought the Good News from Ghent to Aix" (1845), *Sordello,* and *Colombe's Birthday.* Possibly the journey out was the more southern one through Vienna which would have allowed this route but all evidence suggests only the more northern route through Berlin. RB mentions Tilsit in Prussia (now Russian Sovetsk) and his return visa, now at Baylor, was issued at St. Petersburg for passage through Livland and Kurland (Livonia and Courland, now part of the Soviet controlled Baltic states, Lithuania and Latvia) along the northern coast. RB passed the Aachen-Belgium area on his return from Italy in 1838 under more leisurely circumstances and the poetic reminiscences probably date from then ("How They Brought the Good News from Ghent to Aix" was probably not written until after the 1838 trip: see DeVane, *Handbook*, pp. 153-154). The total stay in Russia could not have been much more than two weeks. The exit visa, probably used soon after issue, is dated March 31, 1834.

247. *LRB,* p. 1, RB to E.F. Haworth, [July 24, 1838].

248. The drawing is described, "Notes for Bibliophiles," *Dial,* 63 (Aug. 16, 1917), 120; then in private hands.

249. *RBEBK,* I, 148 (letter 76), RB to EBB, [Aug. 10, 1845]. The play is not extant. Folk tunes he heard in Russia he remembered even in old age. See Katharine DeKay Bronson, "Browning in Venice," *Century Magazine,* 63 (Feb. 1902), 577.

250. *RBEBK,* I, 428 (letter 218), RB to EBB, [Jan. 31, 1846].

251. *RBEBK,* I, 148 (letter 76), RB to EBB [Aug. 10, 1845]. Wylie (1768-1854), a Scotsman, was physician to the imperial court at St. Petersburg from 1798 and a leading force in the development of medicine in Russia. See *DNB,* s.v. Wylie.

252. Griffin and Minchin, p. 63.

253. Orr, p. 61.

254. This is the view put forward by DeVane, *Handbook,* p. 12, now strengthened by information on the purpose of the mission. William did arrange the later offer to join the 1846 mission on which he planned to accompany RB: Mason, "Kinsfolk," p. 90. Nathan Meyer Rothschild was, of course, closely involved in international diplomacy and even served as London Consul for Austria in England. RB later was seriously tempted by M. D. Conway's suggestion that he join him on a trip to Russia: Sarianna Browning to M. D. Conway, June 18, [ca. 1868-1873], MS, Columbia University.

255. Orr, p. 61. Hall Griffin could obtain no affirmative evidence about RB's application. However, a letter, RB to Sarah Flower Adams, Feb. 4, [1836], MS, Humanities Research Center, Univ. of Texas, asserts somewhat defensively, that he isn't going to Persia, that it is too hot there anyway, and that Sir Henry Ellis, who presumably had turned him down, may go to an even hotter place for all he cares. Ellis (1777-1855) was a career diplomat (not the more famous Librarian at the British Museum); he had been appointed ambassador to Persia in July, 1835 but relinquished the appointment in Nov., 1836. See *DNB,* s.v. Ellis. There is also an entry for Christopher Hughes, American Minister to the Court of Stockholm, in RB's "Address Book," MS, Beinecke, Yale, perhaps another diplomatic contact. Hughes (1786-1849) was a career diplomat known for his wit and gregariousness. See *DAB,* s.v. Hughes.

256. Montefiore's mission is mentioned, *RBEBK,* letters 238-252. RB was to go with William.

257. T. Wemyss Reid, ed., *The Life, Letters, and Friendships of Richard Monckton Milnes* (London, 1890), I, 384, RB to R. M. Milnes, March 31, 1847.

258. Orr, p. 61.

259. E. Bridell-Fox, "Robert Browning," *Argosy,* 59 (Feb. 1890), 764.

260. Furnivall, "Ancestors," p. 32, ascribes this observation to a nephew, probably a son of William Shergold Browning.

261. *RBAD,* p. 143, J. Arnould to A. Domett, [after 1868].

262. See "Browning in Westminster Abbey," *Essays in London and Elsewhere* (New York, 1893), pp. 222-229. The article first appeared in the *Speaker* of Jan. 4, 1891.

263. RB to "Dear Friend," July 8, 1874, MS, Baylor.

Chapter VI   Art

1. *RBEBK,* I, 434 (letter 221), RB to EBB, [Feb. 4, 1846].

2. Richard and E. Garnett, *The Life of W. J. Fox* (London, John Lane, 1910), p. 194, fragment of E. Flower to Miss Bromley, [n.d.]. Dowden's comment is in a collection of letters, MS, Baylor. Browning *was* in the habit of speaking of head and heart and the need to join them, e.g., his comment on John Kenyon: "what goodness and intellect can do by combining to keep heart & head fresh & sound," RB to Mr. Ware, Jan. 11, 1849, MS, Baylor.

3. *RBEBK,* I, 25 (letter 9), RB to EBB, [Feb. 26, 1845]. A letter, RB to Mr. Courtney, March 30, 1876, MS, Baylor, lists some of the types of prints. Domett recalled RB Sr. as a connoisseur of engravings: Domett's *Diary,* p. 55.

4. RB praised Buchanan's "Capital Hendecasyllabics," *LRB,* p. 218, RB to Rev. J. D. Williams, April 17, 1883. He speaks of "poor dear Kirke White" in *RBEBK,* I, 25 (letter 9), RB to EBB, [Feb. 26, 1845]. There is a two-volume set of White's *Remains* (1808) in the Baylor Browning Collection, a gift to Sarianna. RB Sr. also refers to White as a contemporary poet (along with Moore) in a cartoon in the "Waltham Drawings," MS, Wellesley, fol. 50.

5. Orr, p. 378, RB to Mr. George Bainton, Oct. 6, 1887.

6. Kate Lemann to Hall Griffin, Nov. 8, 1904, Hall Griffin Papers, BL, Add. MS. 45,564, fols. 91-93b.

7. Griffin and Minchin, p. 12.

8. Reuben Browning, MS Introductory Notes to a collection of RB Sr. sketches, pub. in F. G. Kitton, "Robert Browning the Elder, as a Caricaturist," *Art Journal,* 3 (Feb. 1898), 56.

9. See n. 2, chap. v.

10. *DI,* p. 218, RB to I. Blagden, Aug. 19, 1865.

11. *RBEBK,* I, 509 (letter 255), RB to EBB, [March 3, 1846].

12. At a somewhat later period W. J. Linton, as an art student, studied at Dulwich "usually alone": *Memories* (London, 1895), p. 10.

13. Sarianna confirmed that RB was a very early and regular visitor to the gallery: Sarianna Browning to J. M. Campbell, July 14, 1899, MS, Humanities Research Center, Univ. of Texas.

14. Sharp, *Life,* p. 25—always a source of piquant, if somewhat dubious, anecdotes.

15. Jeanie Morison [Campbell], "Robert Browning and Elizabeth Barrett Browning," *Chamber's Cyclopaedia of English Literature* (Philadelphia, J. P. Lippincott, 1904), III, 551; Henriette Corkran, *Celebrities and I* (London, Hutchinson, 1902), p. 16, reports from Sarianna on her mother's musical competence.

16. *NL,* p. 340, RB to Miss Violet Paget, Jan. 31, 1887. RB speaks at length of his early pleasure in the "Grand March" in his "Parleying with Charles Avison" (1887) and prints it at the conclusion. RB's source for it was his father's notation. It appears identically in RB Sr.'s "Book of Music," MS, Wellesley. The only serious study of Avison, Norris Lynn Stephens, "Charles Avison, an Eighteenth-Century English Composer, Musician, and Writer," Diss. Univ. of Pittsburg, 1968, p. 189, finds the attribution of this work to Avison very dubious. It does not appear in any of his published or unpublished work; it does not seem stylistically similar to the one march, a "Marcia Andante" (Opus 8, No. 3), we have by him; possibly it is the work of Charles Avison, Jr. (1751-1795) and hence misattributed by RB's father. RB, however, believed that the "March" existed as a trio, and it is possible that a longer work by Avison which RB Sr. saw has been lost: H. E. Greene, "Browning's Knowledge of Music," *PMLA,* 62 (Dec. 1947), 1098, RB to Henry Spaulding, June 30, 1887.

17. *NL,* p. 340, RB to Miss Violet Paget, Jan. 31, 1887.

18. RB Sr., "Sketchbook," MS, Baylor (No. 10, Appendix B). References to music or musicians appear in many of RB Sr.'s various notebooks of cartoons.

19. *RBEBK,* I, 364 (letter 192), RB to EBB, [Jan. 6, 1846].

20. DeVane, *Handbook,* pp. 549-552, discusses the source of "Rephan." Vol. I of *The Contributions of Q. Q. to a Periodical Work: With Some Pieces Not Before Published* (London, 1824), now at Baylor, was given by RB's mother to his sister in 1827. "How it Strikes a Stranger" appeared in vol. II, probably part of the original gift; but RB would have been interested in it at a younger age and probably did know it in the earlier periodical publication.

21. Orr, p. 27. The anecdote seems at least a plausible indication of RB's response to children's tales. Samuel Croxall (?-1752) pub. his long standard translation in 1722.

22. *RBEBK,* I, 153 (letter 78), RB to EBB, [Aug. 12, 1845].

23. *NL,* p. 20, RB to W. C. Macready, [Aug. 23, 1840].

24. Orr, p. 22.

25. RB to Emily Harris, July 18, 1887, MS, Baylor.

26. Sotheby, item 675.

27. RB to Edward Twisleton, June 29, 1866, MS, Houghton, Harvard, Am 1408.43.

28. See n. 5, chap. i.

29. Orr, p. 378, RB to Mr. George Bainton, Oct. 6, 1887.

30. Records of these and other inscribed gift copies are found in Sotheby as well as in the series of resales by other booksellers and auction houses.

31. Sotheby, item 798.

32. Griffin and Minchin, p. 12.

33. The landscape is reproduced, *LRB,* p. 80 f. The portrait is in the "Scrapbook," MS, Humanities Research Center, Univ. of Texas (No. 22, Appendix B). There were also sketches and crayon portraits by her of RB and RB Sr. sold at Sotheby, items 90, 95, 95*.

34. Sidney R. Thompson, "Robert Browning, Teacher of Music," *Musical World,* 51 (May 11, 1889), 297.

35. RB to Ripert-Monclar, Aug. 9, 1837, MS, Private Collection.

36. Greene, "Browning's Knowledge of Music," p. 1098, RB to Henry Spaulding, June 30, 1887.

37. W. R. Benét, ed., *From Robert & Elizabeth Browning* (London, 1936), p. 44, EBB to Henrietta Barrett, Jan. 7, 1847. G. W. Curtis heard Browning play Gregorian chants and a hymn by Pergolesi in Italy; he played Rousseau's harpsichord at Les Charmettes on the voyage to Italy with EBB. R. W. S. Mendl, "Robert Browning, the Poet-Musician," *Music and Letters,* 42 (1961), 142-150, provides the fullest collation of references to the poet's interest in music throughout his life. To what he reports should be added the account by Henriette Corkran that RB had no difficulty playing "an intricate fugue by Bach, his favourite composer": *Celebrities,* p. 164.

38. [William Grove], "Browning as I Knew Him. By his Valet," *Sunday Express,* Dec. 4, 1927, p. 466 (copy at Baylor).

39. Greene, "Browning's Knowledge of Music," p. 1098, RB to Henry Spaulding, June 30, 1887.

40. RB, MS note, *Pauline* (1833), Mill copy, Victoria and Albert Museum, Forster Collection.

41. Griffin and Minchin, p. 16, quoting Mrs. Ireland from the *Manchester Examiner and Times,* Dec. 18, 1889.

42. RB has been criticized for having Vogler slide by semitones till he sinks to a minor, for making the answer to the dominant the octave, not the tonic, and for including a rare "diminished sixth" in "A Toccata of Galuppi's," and for using the phrase "mode Palestrina" in "Master Hugues of Saxe-Gotha." Yet even his fussiest critics grant that he makes no gross or obvious blunders; RB defended the use of Palestrina as an old designation; he certainly knew Palestrina and his works.

43. Charles Villiers Stanford, *Pages from an Unwritten Diary,* (London, Edward Arnold, 1914), p. 176, recalls RB in the company of musical betters such as Joachim, talking the most and knowing the least about Beethoven's last Quartets. On the other hand, Sir George Henschel, *Musings and Memories of a Musician* (London, Macmillan, 1918), p. 221, testifies

to the poet's love of music and interest in Handel; Sir Charles Halle stated that RB "knew the whole literature of music" and often directed him to neglected older pieces of interest: J. C. Hadden, "Robert Browning and Music," *Monthly Musical Record,* 42 (May 1912), 113-114.

44. Greene, "Browning's Knowledge of Music," p. 1098, RB to Henry Spaulding, June 30, 1887: RB was not speaking of the fugues of "the glorious Bach" but of one of his dry-as-dust imitators.

45. *NL,* p. 15, RB to E. F. Haworth, [April, 1839]: RB reproduces a song, perhaps taken down by ear, which he overheard children singing "arm over neck" at Venice.

46. Greene, "Browning's Knowledge of Music," p. 1098, RB to Henry Spaulding, June 30, 1887.

47. Domett's *Diary,* p. 145.

48. The even more fundamental influence of Eliza Flower's temperament and devotion to music is discussed in chap. viii, below.

49. *LRB,* p. 267, RB to F. J. Furnivall, Aug. 21, 1887. Abel would seem to be Johann Leopold Abel (1795-1871?), member of a family of German musicians, and not the younger Ludwig Abel (1834-1895) identified by Orr as a pupil of Ignatz Moscheles: *Grove's Dictionary of Music and Musicians* (1954), s.v. Abel. In RB's early "Address Book," MS, Beinecke, Yale, there is a John Abel at 19 Albion St., Hyde Park. At one time Abel evidently resided at Camberwell for he is listed among those who took lessons from RB's Italian teacher: Angelo Cerutti, *Vita* (Florence, 1846), I, 451: "un maestro di suono tedesco."

50. Accounts of Nathan's interesting personality and life are given in Olga Phillips, *Isaac Nathan, Friend of Byron* (London, Minerva, 1940); Catherine Mackerras, *The Hebrew Melodist; a life of Isaac Nathan* (Sydney, Currawong, 1963); Charles H. Bertie, *Isaac Nathan: Australia's First Composer* (Sydney, Australia, Angus and Robertson, 1922). Nathan's *An Essay on the History and Theory of Music; and on the Qualities, Capabilities, and Management of the Human Voice* (London, 1823) was reissued in 1836 under the better known title *Musurgia Vocalis.* He wrote memoirs of Byron and the opera singer Madame Malibran de Beriot. After his emigration to Australia in 1841 where he earned the sobriquet, father of Australian music, he published a mixed bag of music and essays, *The Southern Euphrosyne and Australian Miscellany* (1846). The most authoritative work on the *Hebrew Melodies* collaboration is Thomas L. Ashton, *Byron's Hebrew Melodies* (Austin, Univ. of Texas Press, 1972). Nathan's dates are 1790 (born Canterbury)-1864, not 1792-1864 as is often given. He was the student of Domenico Corri, the student of Porpora who was himself a student of Haydn. Nathan was twice married. A portrait of him appears as frontispiece in both Phillips and Bertie.

51. Nathan, *Essay on the History and Theory of Music,* p. viii, recommends "as familiar a style as possible."

52. *DI,* p. 324, RB to I. Blagden, Sept. 19, 1869. RB's statement, that he heard the story from Nathan "before I was twenty" suggests he took lessons in the middle or late 1820s.

53. Greene, "Browning's Knowledge of Music," p. 1098, RB to Henry Spaulding, June 30, 1887. Nathan's minimal relation to Jewish musical tradition is discussed in *The Jewish Encyclopedia,* s.v. Nathan.

54. There are no full studies of Relfe, who is today largely forgotten. F. T. Fétis, *Biographie universelle des musiciens et bibliographie générale de la musique* (Brussels, 1841), s.v. Relfe, is the fullest account. See also articles under his name in *Grove's Dictionary of Music and Musicians* (1954) and *La musica, dizionario* (Turin, 1971). Relfe (1763-1837?) was born at Greenwich, the son of Lupton Relfe, and trained under him and Keeble; he resided at Church Row, Camberwell. In addition to a number of musical works and pamphlets for instruction of students, he published *Guida Armonica* (London, 1798), reissued as *The Principles of Harmony* (1817), and *Lucidus Ordo: Comprising an Analytical Course of Studies on the Several Branches of Musical Science; with a New Order of Thorough Bass Designation* (London, 1821). (The *Remarks on the Present State of Musical Instruction* [London, 1819] is a prospectus for the later work.) RB once praised his new system of notation, but it was not adopted and was evidently based on some false premises. There is a "Prelude Petit Surprise" by Relfe in RB Sr.'s "Book of Music," MS, Wellesley. By the 1820s Relfe's charges bespoke his prominence

as an instructor: he advertises lessons at ten guineas entrance and ten guineas per quarter: *Lucidus Ordo,* end page.

55. Greene, "Browning's Knowledge of Music," p. 1098, RB to Henry Spaulding, June 30, 1887.

56. Thompson, "Robert Browning, Teacher of Music," p. 297.

57. Relfe, *Lucidus Ordo,* p. 61.

58. Fétis, s.v. "Relfe," notes that Relfe took his system from Vogler's books. DeVane, *Handbook,* pp. 290-291, implies that Relfe studied with Vogler; but his own discussion in *Browning's Parleyings, The Autobiography of a Mind* (New Haven, Yale University Press, 1927), pp. 254-256 is based on Fétis and makes no such claim. I have found no evidence that Relfe studied with Vogler, though he may well have met him.

59. *RBEBK,* I, 479 (letter 241), RB to EBB, [Feb. 20, 1846].

60. *NL,* p. 252, RB to William Black, June 6, 1879.

61. Robert Wiedeman Browning to Hall Griffin, March 12, 1904, Hall Griffin Papers, BL, Add. MS. 45,563, fols. 231-233b.

62. Robert Wiedeman Browning to Hall Griffin, Nov. 11, 1902, BL, Add. MS. 45,563, fols. 186-194.

63. RB Sr., "Sketch Book," MS, Baylor (No. 10, Appendix B).

64. Orr, p. 12; Sotheby, item 127, prints the example of the verses for his grandson. Henriette Corkran recalled similar verses.

65. "Verses on a Poet" (4 of 8 lines), "Thomas Ingall Sketchbook," MS, Boston Public Library, fol. 35.

66. "Thomas Ingall Sketchbook," fol. 6.

67. F. H. Stead, "Browning's Father," *Putnam's Magazine,* 7 (April 1910), 856: mentioned in Robert Wiedeman Browning to Hall Griffin, Nov. 11, 1902, Hall Griffin Papers, BL, Add. MS. 45,563, fols. 186-194. A copy is in the Bank of England, Archives Section, Misc. Acces. No. 107.

68. RB Sr., "Scrapbook," MS, Humanities Research Center, Univ. of Texas (No. 22, Appendix B).

69. Bertram Dobell Catalog, *Browning Memorials* (London, 1913), item 67, a "Sketch Book." Dobell cites another epigram "On a Poet." Besides the poems by RB Sr. discussed here there are his version of the Pied Piper Story and the political verses on the Reform Act discussed in chap. v above, and also a version of "Chatterton's Song" in RB Sr.'s "Book of Music," MS, Wellesley. The "Bevan Scrapbook," Bank of England, Archives Section, fols. 53, 76, has satirical "New Rhymes for the Nursery" and "Know all men by these presents." There is a parody of "The House that Jack Built," "Scrapbook of Cartoons," formerly property of Mrs. Stephens, also at the Bank, fol. 66. "On Louvel's Reply," first attributed to RB, is probably by RB Sr.: see my "Correspondence," *TLS,* March 23, 1973, p. 325, which should have noted DeVane's similar conjecture, *Handbook,* p. 572. There are occasional epigram couplets to sketches in the various collections; probably other poems will come to light.

70. RB Sr., "Book of Music," MS, Wellesley.

71. RB Sr., "Small Sketch Book," MS, Baylor.

72. "Bevan Scrapbook," fols. 85, 10-11; also a study from Hogarth, fol. 68. Cousin Mason reported having seen an entire series of parodies of Dutch old masters, Mason, "Kinsfolk," p. 93; cf. Dobell Catalog, *Browning Memorials,* item 68, drawings from Dutch originals. There is also a copy of a Teniers at Dulwich in the "Waltham Drawings," MS, Wellesley, fol. 2, as well as some burlesques of Raphael.

73. The *Fête Champêtre,* once thought to be by Watteau, is now ascribed to Lancret. See *A Brief Catalogue of the Pictures in the Dulwich College Picture Gallery* (London, 1953).

74. *RBEBK,* I, 509 (letter 255), RB to EBB, [March 3, 1846].

75. In later life, RB had a copy of Murillo's "Two Children, our Saviour and St. John, with a Lamb," now at Baylor.

76. RB's preference for the "Rinaldo and Armida" is confirmed by a picture, "Armide cherchant à se venger de Reynault," signed by him in pencil and dated Nov. 18, 1835, Sotheby,

item 89. (It is unclear whether this was a print of the Poussin or a copy by RB or RB Sr.)

77. What RB pointed out to EBB and J. R. Lowell: Frances Sim, *Robert Browning the Poet and the Man 1833-1846* (London, T. F. Unwin, Ltd., 1923), p. 27.

78. The frescoes, originally in the Casino del Bufalo are now (badly damaged) in the Museo di Roma. See Alessandro Marabottini, *Polidoro da Caravaggio* (Rome, Elefante, 1969), II, cxxxvi. The engraving by Johannes (Giovanni) Volpato (1733-1803) is entitled *Perseus et Andromede* (Rome, 1772), and identified as from Polidoro: in *Schola Italica Picturae, Piranesii Opere,* XXII (Paris, 1773), plate 13. This is the only engraving of this picture I have found; it is one RB Sr. would have been likely to have; it is very close to RB's rendition in feeling. Sutherland Orr, *A Handbook to the Works of Robert Browning* (London, 1886), p. 21, indicates that RB identified his engraving as from the Bufalo series.

79. Browning mentions it not only in the passage from *Pauline* but also in a letter to E. F. Haworth, *LRB,* p. 6, [Dec. 30, 1841], in which he speaks of his appreciation for Etty, "as well as Polidoro da Caravaggio," and in *RBEBK,* I, 25 (letter 9), RB to EBB, [Feb. 26, 1845], the letter in which he recalls how he found the painting. On RB's later use of the motif see W. C. DeVane's survey in "The Virgin and the Dragon," *Yale Review,* 37 (Autumn 1947), 33-46. In *The Ring and the Book* alone DeVane counts at least thirty allusions to the Perseus-Andromeda and related myths. The scene in *Pauline* is recreated in the "Parleying with Francis Furini."

80. Nathan, *Essay on the History and Theory of Music,* p. 13.

81. Avison, *An Essay on Musical Expression* (London, 1753), pp. 73-74. Avison's remarks on the tediousness of some fugues (p. 36) are also interesting in the light of "Master Hugues of Saxe-Gotha." There appears no need to postulate a source for Browning's musical ideas in Schopenhauer's parallel ideas on music and soul as does W. L. Phelps, "Browning, Schopenhauer, and Music," *North American Review,* 206 (Oct., 1917), 622-627. Of virtually a dozen studies of the music poems, George M. Ridenour, "Browning's Music Poems: Fancy and Fact," *PMLA,* 77 (1963), 369-377, gives the fullest and most interesting discussion of Browning's ideas on the aesthetics of music as they are presented in his poems.

82. RB to Ripert-Monclar, Aug. 9, 1837, MS, Private Collection. RB's return to music after his boyhood efforts in verse and Eliza Flower's influence on this change of emphasis are examined in chaps. vii and viii, below.

83. In the passage given, the "god wandering after beauty" (Apollo pursuing Daphne) and the "giant" (Atlas) are probably from Ovid, *Metamorphoses* I.452-567, IV. 631-662. The "hunter" (probably Peleus at his wedding to Thetis) would be from *Iliad* XXIV.55-64; the "chief" (Nestor or Odysseus as they leave Troy) is from *Odyssey* III.157-164. Browning probably read these in translation (the Homer in Pope) before he came to them in Latin and Greek.

84. RB to Ripert-Monclar, Aug. 9, 1837, Private Collection.

85. RB himself identified the plays he referred to in marginal notes in *Pauline* (1833), Mill copy, Victoria and Albert Museum, Forster Collection. He speaks of returning to these in his teens as to old delights. He could have read Aeschylus and Sophocles in the often reprinted, passable, if somewhat too Miltonic, late eighteenth-century verse translations of R. Potter, or Sophocles in the slightly earlier verse of Thomas Francklin. There is no evidence that these books were in the library of RB Sr., but with his interest in the classics it is unlikely that he would not have had some or all of these translations.

86. Cf. *Childe Harold's Pilgrimage,* Canto IV, CXXIII-CXXIV: "cure / Is bitterer still, as charm by charm unwinds / which robed our idols . . . / so are we doubly curst."

87. Browning's disillusionment with both these works has been intelligently treated by DeVane, *Browning's Parleyings,* chaps. vi-vii, to which this discussion is indebted.

88. Lairesse, *The Art of Painting in All its Branches,* trans. John Frederick Fritsch, 2 vols. (London, 1778); the first Dutch edition appeared in 1707; Fritsch's translation was first pub. 1738; Browning's copy is in Beinecke, Yale.

89. Ibid.; quoted Sotheby, item 807 and frequently elsewhere.

90. Of the three mentioned by DeVane, *Apollo and Daphne* (No. 176), and *Pan and Syrinx* (No. 179) are now ascribed to the Dutch G. Hoet, and the *Apollo Flaying Marsyas* to

the Roman Filippo Lauri. See, *A Brief Catalogue of the Pictures in Dulwich College Picture Gallery*. All three would have given Browning, nonetheless, a good idea of the practical results of Lairesse's theories.

91. "The Landscape of Browning's *Childe Roland,*" *PMLA,* 40 (June 1925), 426-432. DeVane's assertion that Lairesse's discussion of landscape was generally influential in RB's landscape poetry is less certain. From a reading of the whole of the poet's fine copy I was not persuaded, though the specific echoes of Lairesse he notes are plausible.

92. RB's idea of the ephemerality of musical style was influenced by at least two expressions of it which he came across in his reading: first, around 1830, the poem "Disappointment" by Henry Kirke White (1785-1806): see *LL,* p. 98, RB to Mrs. FitzGerald, Oct. 13, 1880; then, in 1846, the memoir of the French composer, Claude Le Jeune, once called phoenix of musicians, by then forgotten: see *RBEBK,* I, 522 (letter 261), RB to EBB, [March 7, 1846]. The importance of this idea of the relation of music to a *Zeitgeist* in poems like "A Toccata of Galuppi's" is discussed in DeVane, *Browning's Parleyings,* p. 267.

Chapter VII   Precocious Beginnings

1. Sharp, *Life,* p. 27.
2. Orr, p. 35.
3. Mrs. Nora Collings of Sevenoaks, Kent, granddaughter of Jemima, kindly reported the story. See Appendix A, section IV. RB's description of her is given, Orr, p. 74.
4. *RBEBK, I, 388* (letter 201), RB to EBB [Jan. 15, 1846].
5. RB to Ripert-Monclar, Aug. 9, 1837, MS, Private Collection.
6. Griffin and Minchin, p. 30.
7. Orr, p. 32, RB Sr. to Thomas Powell, March 11, 1843. These would seem to be distinct from the later "Incondita" verses.
8. "On Louvel's Reply," once ascribed to RB, is probably RB Sr.'s work: see my "Correspondence," *TLS,* March 23, 1973, p. 325. No other poems have been claimed as survivors from this very early period.
9. *RBAD,* p. 33, RB to A. Domett, [May 22, 1842].
10. "Poetical Contrasts," *New Quarterly Review; or, Home, Foreign, and Colonial Journal,* 8 (Jan. 1846), quoted *RBEBK,* I, 367. RB attributed the review to Powell and J. A. Heraud. The remark on RB's mechanical precocity fits the earlier work better; Powell was asked by RB Sr. not to tell RB he had seen the early poems which he sent to him.
11. RB to Monclar, Aug. 9, 1837, MS, Private Collection.
12. Sharp, *Life,* p. 26.
13. *RBAD,* p. 95, RB to A. Domett, Nov. 8, 1843.
14. Sharp, *Life,* p. 27.
15. *RBEBK,* I, 334 (letter 181), RB to EBB, [Dec. 21, 1845].
16. *RBEBK,* II, 998 (letter 520), RB to EBB, [Aug. 25, 1846].
17. Ibid.
18. Almost certainly, *Poems of Ossian . . . Containing the Poetical Works of James Macpherson, Esq., in Prose and Rhyme,* 2 vols. (Edinburgh, 1805).
19. *RBAD,* p. 109, RB to A. Domett, Feb. 23, 1845.
20. He may have had his attention called to the poem by Hazlitt's rather malicious allusion to it in "On the Living Poets," *Lectures on the English Poets* (1818). "Over the sea our galleys went" in *Paracelsus,* Part IV seems obviously inspired by *The Ancient Mariner.* I have not found other important echoes of Coleridge in RB's poetry.
21. *RBEBK,* II, 985 (letter 514), RB to EBB, [Aug. 22, 1846].
22. William Knight, *Retrospects* (New York, Scribner's, 1904), p. 75, RB to W. Knight, May 17, 1880. Despite his readiness to admit that he had captured only a distorted abstraction from Wordsworth in "The Lost Leader," RB also continued all his life to consider Wordsworth's change of politics "a sot" on his reputation: RB to James Freeman Clarke, May 6, 1884, MS, Houghton, Harvard, bMS Am 1596-7 (81). A memo headed "Wordsworth," Berg

Collection, New York Public Library, probably a fragment of a letter to R. H. Horne concerning mottoes for Horne's *New Spirit of the Age* (1844), shows real irritation with Wordsworth at that time. He proposed, then retracted as too biting, a quotation from *Paradise Lost,* x.441-454, implicitly comparing Wordsworth to Satan as he enters "In show Plebian Angel," then reveals himself in all his fallen "false glitter."

23. Knight, *Retrospects,* p. 88, RB to W. Knight, March 23, 1887.

24. Ibid. Similarly, to EBB it was the *Lyrical Ballads,* which he praised most highly: *RBEBK,* I, 463 (letter 233), RB to EBB, [Feb. 15, 1846].

25. RB to Charles Eliot Norton, Dec. 9, 1850, MS, Houghton, Harvard, bMS Am 1088 (711), acknowledges the gift of the poem; but RB, though respectful, is rather obtuse about its merits. "Transcendentalism" (1855) has a possible allusion to the "Immortality Ode" in the opening of heaven.

26. *RBEBK,* II, 985 (letter 514), RB to EBB, [Aug. 22, 1846].

27. Orr, p. 31: "Byron was his chief master in those early poetic days."

28. *RBEBK,* II, 985 (letter 514), RB to EBB, [Aug. 22, 1846].

29. Orr, p. 52, RB to W. J. Fox, [March 1833].

30. *LRB,* p. 19, RB to R. H. Horne, Dec. 3, 1848; RB to Monclar, Aug. 9, 1837, MS, Private Collection.

31. The ease with which he was imitated was one of the serious reasons for Byron's decline in popularity: Samuel C. Chew, *Byron in England: His Fame and After-Fame* (New York, Scribner's, 1924), p. 243.

32. Mentioned, but not given, in a note, Sarianna Browning to Robert Wiedeman Browning, June 25, 1888, MS, Balliol College Library, Oxford: probably an imitation of Byron's "Inscription on the Monument of a Newfoundland Dog."

33. RB knew the "Swan's one addled egg," *Childe Harold's Pilgrimage,* thoroughly. His comment, stanza LXVII, points out a solecism in "lay" for lie in *Childe Harold,* Canto IV, CLXXX. He also criticizes Byron's oceanic posturing in this passage and in Canto III, XII-XIII. The charge is repeated in the "Epilogue" to *Pacchiarotto,* stanza XX. RB also speaks of Byron as Childe Harold (the Pilgrim) in "At the Mermaid."

34. *RBEBK,* I, 74 (letter 31), RB to EBB, [May 24, 1845].

35. Sharp, *Life,* p. 29.

36. *Browning's Essay on Chatterton,* ed. Donald Smalley (Cambridge, Mass., Harvard University Press, 1948), p. 111: orig. pub., *Foreign Quarterly Review,* 29 (July, 1842), 465-483.

37. Ibid., p. 112.

38. Ibid., p. 111.

39. Ibid. Boyd Litzinger, "A Note on Browning's Defense of Chatterton," *Victorian Newsletter,* No. 19 (Spring 1961), pp. 17-19 notes the applicability of RB's ideas in the "Essay" to his early work generally.

40. First pub., Bertram Dobell, "The earliest Poems of Robert Browning," *Cornhill Magazine,* 36 (Jan. 1914), 1-9. The two poems were sent in a letter, Sarah Flower to W. J. Fox, May 31, [1827]: pub., ibid., pp. 3-4. See also *The Complete Poetical Works of Robert Browning,* ed. Augustine Birrell (New York, Macmillan, 1915), pp. 1327-1331. DeVane and Irvine and Honan, among others, have accepted Dobell's assumption that these verses were in the "Incondita." But Sarah explicitly gives RB's age in the letter as fourteen and speaks of " 'the boy' Browning" as now able, along with his verses, to speak for himself: that is, he is no longer the boy poet Fox had met earlier. All accounts of the "Incondita" date it at RB's age twelve or thirteen. (The letter to Monclar states specifically "in my thirteenth year.") There is nothing in Sarah's letter to identify these verses with the "Incondita" or to contradict RB's own report that the "Incondita" were shown to Fox by Eliza and that Fox met RB once thereafter. Rather, Sarah's letter assumes Fox already knows RB and would be interested in his verse. The details of the first meeting with Fox over the "Incondita" are given in the discussion of the Flowers below.

41. *RBEBK,* I, 270 (letter 151), RB to EBB, [Nov. 16, 1845].

42. RB to Monclar, Aug. 9, 1837, MS, Private Collection. *Pauline:* "I paused again."

43. *Browning's Essay on Chatterton,* ed. Smalley, p. 111.

44. RB's almost compulsive avoidance of any kind of simple imitation or extended work within one specific tradition is a commonplace. His slight interest in the sonnet, for instance, is explained by a comment made in a letter to J. S. Wood, March 12, 1884, MS, Baylor, that "writing a sonnet with Shakespeare in one's head, is a grave matter."

45. The vexed question of the relation between the first-person romantic poem (what M. H. Abrams calls the "greater Romantic lyric") and RB's dramatic monologues is most intelligently discussed by Robert Langbaum, *The Poetry of Experience* (New York, Random House, 1957), esp. chap. i.

46. W. W. Pratt, "Mr. Dalby and the Romantics," *University of Texas Studies in English* (Austin, University of Texas Press, 1947), p. 105, RB to John W. Dalby, Nov. 20, 1868.

47. RB's general sympathy with Burns as a Scots countryman of his mother (see n. 76, chap. iv) suggests but does not prove early reading. Burns receives favorable mention along with Shelley in "The Lost Leader." Family interest in Scott's historical novels is discussed in chap. xiv, below. There is no evidence that RB knew Blake in his youth. He does mention him in 1846: *RBEBK,* II, 860 (letter 449), RB to EBB, [July 9, 1846]; in 1848 EBB reports on his discussing both Blake's poems and drawings: EBB to M. R. Mitford, Feb. 22, 1848, Kenyon TS for *LEBB,* BL, Add. MS. 42,229, fol. 714.

48. *LRB,* p. 159, RB to A. E. Smith, [Aug.] 16, 1873.

49. J. Arnould to A. Domett, Sept. 15, 1867 and Jan. 28, 1873, Hall Griffin Papers, BL, Add. MS. 45,560, fols. 66, 72.

50. RB places the discovery of Shelley after this in the chronology in *Pauline.*

51. See n. 52, chap. vi. The story of the liaison with Augusta Leigh, which he heard before he was twenty, was confirmed by Murray's son, probably on RB's visit to him when he tried to get *Paracelsus* published: see Domett's *Diary,* p. 53 and the account of the visit to Murray's son, RB to S. F. Adams, [ca. 1835], MS, Humanities Research Center, Univ. of Texas.

Chapter VIII   A Sentimental Education

1. See the letter, Orr, p. 32, RB Sr. to Thomas Powell, March 11, 1843.

2. This account of the way in which Fox came to see the "Incondita" is that given by the earliest biographers, Orr and the less authoritative William Sharp. Their account is substantially confirmed by Browning's references in various letters: RB to Ripert-Monclar, Aug. 9, 1837, MS, Private Collection; Orr, p. 52, RB to W. J. Fox, Monday morning, [March 1833]; H. C. Minchin, "A Letter from Hanover Cottage," *Bookman,* 86 (April 1934), 6, RB to E. F. Haworth, [ca. Aug. 1, 1837]; *LRB,* p. 19, RB to R. H. Horne, Dec. 3, 1848; *LRB,* p. 263, RB to J. Dykes Campbell, March 30, 1887. The letter to Horne implies that Eliza saw the poems through a friend "to whom I confided the volume." It is thus possible that the idea of seeking a critical judgment and a publisher was an invention of the early biographers and that Eliza's reading and the subsequent closer acquaintance came purely by chance. But RB would have had good reasons for concealing his premature desire to publish and his interest in having Eliza and Fox see the work: therefore I have accepted the biographers' account. Eliza was possibly approached through a friend, perhaps their mutual friend Miss Sturtevant.

3. See the letter to Haworth and Monclar cited above.

4. Fox, rev. of *Men and Things,* by J. S. Boone, *Westminster Review,* 1 (Jan. 1824), 15.

5. RB's recollection: *LRB,* p. 19, RB to R. H. Horne, Dec. 3, 1848. The letter to Monclar suggests it was a personal interview.

6. Orr, p. 33.

7. Bertram Dobell, "The Earliest Poems of Robert Browning," *Cornhill Magazine,* 36 (Jan. 1914), p. 3, Sarah Flower to W. J. Fox, May 31, [1827]. As noted in chap. vii these poems appear to be clearly later works than the "Incondita."

8. *NL,* p. 15, RB to E. F. Haworth, [April 1839].

9. "I knew the Flowers when I was five or six years old,—earlier I do think": *LRB,* p.

19, RB to R. H. Horne, Dec. 3, 1848. Sarah speaks of knowing him as "a very little boy": E. Bridell-Fox, "Robert Browning," *Living Age,* 69 (March 22, 1890), 764. Eight would seem more likely in view of the Flowers' move to Dalston in 1820. Eliza's dates are April 19, 1803-Dec. 12, 1846; Sarah's, Feb. 22, 1805-Aug. 14, 1848.

10. Francis Sim, *Robert Browning the Poet and the Man 1833-1846* (London, T. F. Unwin, Ltd., 1923), p. 22: a positive assertion without any source.

11. The introduction through Sturtevant is the explanation given by Orr and Sharp and accepted by Richard and E. Garnett, *The Life of W. J. Fox* (London, John Lane, 1910), p. 107. Griffin and Minchin, p. 43, posit an introduction through a colleague of RB Sr.'s at the Bank, a Mr. Earles who lived at Hackney and knew the Rev. Robert Aspland, a friend of Fox. Their conclusion is based on L. Smallfield to Griffin, [ca. 1904], Hall Griffin Papers, BL, Add. MS. 45,564, fols. 63-64b. However, since all accounts show that it was through the Flowers that Fox was approached, the earlier version is more likely to be correct. A Charles Sturtevant is mentioned as a common acquaintance by Fox, Garnett, *Life of W. J. Fox,* p. 76, Fox to Eliza Flower, [ca. 1831]. A Miss Sturtevant, apparently *the* Miss Sturtevant, is mentioned twice as a common friend of his, of Fox's, and of the Flowers' by RB in letters to S. F. Adams, Wednesday Morning, [ca. 1835] and Feb. 4 [ca. 1836], MS, Humanities Research Center, Univ. of Texas. A Sturtevant appears in the Register of Burials, Locks Fields Walworth, Census Office, the Public Record Office, London. Probably the Brownings knew the Sturtevants through the church and both may have come to know the Flowers through Clayton's relation to them. Benjamin Flower, *A Statement of Facts* (Harlow, 1808), p. xxvii, specifically excludes George Clayton from the nasty quarrel between himself, his brother-in-law John Clayton (father of George) and two nephew Claytons, which had ended in a law suit. Clayton may have taken an interest in his younger cousins. Fox and the Flowers were neighbors at Dalston: J. C. Hadden, "Some Friends of Browning," *Macmillan's Magazine,* 77 (Jan. 1898), 198. They moved to Dalston in 1820, not 1827 as Griffin and Minchin assert: Francis E. Mineka, *The Dissidence of Dissent: the Monthly Repository, 1806-1838* (Chapel Hill, University of North Carolina Press, 1944), p. 190. Benjamin Flower lived 1755-1829.

12. That Eliza had given lessons at one time is suggested by a letter of Fox to her during a financially difficult time scolding her for talking of giving lessons: Garnett, *Life of W. J. Fox,* p. 222.

13. Ibid., p. 64.

14. P. 83. The identification of the characters was made by E. Bridell-Fox, Fox's daughter and someone in touch with family traditions. Not all of it is literal biography, however: the central incident of imprisonment abroad was probably drawn from a famous incident in which John Bowring was involved.

15. Miller, p. 30, quoting E. Bridell-Fox.

16. Sarah especially seems to have had a difficult time breaking free of his influence. Her letter to Fox about her loss of faith in the authenticity of the Bible explains that she doesn't dare bring up the subject with her father, a preaching layman and Arian dissenter. At his funeral she sobbed continuously. When she read the sentimental passages in her *Vivia Perpetua* where Vivia resists the temptation to return home to dependence on her strong father, Sarah broke down hysterically: see E. Bridell-Fox, "Memories," *Girl's Own Paper,* 11 (July 19, 1890), 659 and her "Memoir" of Sarah in *Vivia Perpetua* (priv. prnt., 1893), pp. vi-ix.

17. Garnett, *Life of W. J. Fox,* p. 66.

18. *Musical Illustrations of the Waverley Novels* (London, Joseph Novello, 1831). A second edition was published 1897. The "Songs of the Seasons" were published as front pages to the *Monthly Repository* (1834), with lyrics by Sarah Flower, Martineau, and others.

19. Her major work as a composer was published as *Hymns and Anthems* (London, 1842), 2 vols. Vol. 1 contains the sections "Adoration," "Aspiration," and "Belief"; vol. 2 was to have contained "Heaven Upon Earth" and "Life in Death." The only copies of this rare work I have seen, at South Place Ethical Society, Red Lion Sq., London, are pieced together in vol. 2, part printed, part TS. There are also the following other works with this name: an undated somewhat different published version of the above in 2 vols. (at South

Place); a MS in 2 vols. containing works from the 2 above and adaptions from other composers, probably a hymn book Eliza compiled for the Society (at South Place); a selection of poetry only (London, 1841); and a *Selections from Hymns and Anthems* (London, 1888). The hymns were original compositions with lyrics from poets such as Shelley, Wordsworth, and Goethe as well as from older English classics and the Bible. The most common themes chosen are of aspiration to light, to better hope, and to spiritual triumph through suffering.

20. "Obit: Sarah Flower Adams," *Westminster Review,* 50 (1849), 540.

21. E. Bridell-Fox, "Appendix ii," in M. D. Conway, *A Centenary History of the South Place Society* (London, 1894), p. 152; Garnett, *Life of W. J. Fox,* p. 195.

22. L. Hunt to Eliza Flower, Feb. 7, [n.y.], MS, Berg Collection, New York Public Library; E. Bridell-Fox in Conway, *Centenary History,* p. 153.

23. (N. Y., Bobbs-Merrill, 1957), p. 120: a pencil note by Helen Taylor on the MS identifies this as an allusion to Miss Flower.

24. E. Bridell-Fox, in Conway, *Centenary History,* p. 153. There is a drawing (print) of Eliza from memory by E. Bridell-Fox at Baylor, signed E. Fox (copy at South Place Ethical Society) and a portrait of Sarah by Margaret Gillies at the Society (apparently this is the original).

25. "Obit: Sarah Flower Adams," p. 540.

26. Garnett, *Life of W. J. Fox,* p. 233, notes that Macready also gave her informal encouragement.

27. Besides *Vivia Perpetua* (London, Charles Fox [W. J.'s brother], 1841), Sarah published eleven poems in the *Hymns and Anthems* (1841), including the two famous "Nearer, My God, to Thee" and "He Sendeth Sun, He Sendeth Shower." Fox printed two of her less worthy political songs in his, "On Living Poets; and their Services to the Cause of Political Freedom and Human Progress—No. 10. Miss Barrett and Mrs. Adams," *People's Journal,* 1 (March 7, 1846), 134. Fox implies that others were published anonymously and there is probably a good deal of her work scattered in Victorian periodicals. She deserves a collected edition or at least a bibliographical study. The closest thing to the latter is H. W. Stephenson, *The Author of Nearer, My God, to Thee* (London, Lindsey Press, 1922). She also wrote an attractive catechism for factory schools, *The Flock at the Fountain* (London, 1845), with poems by her.

28. Her 22 contributions to the *Monthly Repository* under the signature "S. Y." are listed in Mineka, *Dissidence of Dissent,* p. 401. These included some poems as well. Her most important prose works are probably the story, "The Actress" and the essay, "An Evening with Charles Lamb and Coleridge."

29. *LRB,* p. 19, RB to R. H. Horne, Dec. 3, 1848.

30. Orr, p. 35, There is no correlate to this assertion among any primary materials which I have seen; by contrast, RB never denies the implication that he had written Eliza poems directly at about age 13.

31. Henri-Léon Hovelaque, *La Jeunesse de Robert Browning* (Paris, Les Presses Modernes, 1932), p. 120, does just this in arguing the case for Sarah. We do know that Sarah tried to act as spiritual helper to young RB much in the role Pauline is given. In this one respect, she may indeed have suggested something of the imaginary persona's character. Hovelaque's biographical account is undependable and based entirely on secondary materials. Miller, p. 35, makes the same speculation. As Maizie Ward has noted, the two later letters from RB to Sarah, Wednesday Morning, [ca. 1835], and Feb. 4, [ca. 1836], MS, Humanities Research Center, Univ. of Texas, show a joking, friendly, and casual relationship—probably a good argument against the view that RB was ever more deeply attached to her.

32. Orr, p. 125, RB to Eliza Flower, Sunday, [1845].

33. Conway, *Centenary History,* p. 89.

34. *RBEBK,* I, 533 (letter 267), RB to EBB, [March 12, 1846]. RB begins to say something (unflattering) about Sarah and then stops himself: "no, I must be silent": a tantalizing allusion!

35. See n. 31, above.

36. For the full letter describing her crisis see M. D. Conway, *Autobiography, Memories and Experiences* (Boston, Houghton, Mifflin, 1904), II, 26, Sarah Flower to W. J. Fox, Nov. 23, 1827.

37. Dobell, "The Earliest Poems of Robert Browning," p. 3, Sarah Flower to W. J. Fox, May 31, [1827].

38. E. Bridell-Fox, "Memoir," p. x.

39. W. J. Linton, *Memories* (London, 1895), p. 25.

40. Ibid., pp. 25-26.

41. *Vivia Perpetua,* pp. 165-166.

42. Ibid., p. 65.

43. Conway, *Autobiography,* II, 26, Sarah Flower to W. J. Fox, Nov. 23, 1827.

44. E. Bridell-Fox, quoted in S. G. Ayres, "Sarah Flower Adams—One of the Early Friends of Browning," *Methodist Review,* 96 (Nov. 1914), 855.

45. Garnett, *Life of W. J. Fox,* p. 234.

46. The subject of most of the poems by her in the *Hymns and Anthems. The Flock at the Fountain* inculcates a faith that "children may see the signs of His goodness in the bright sky, and green fields and the lovely flowers": p. 41.

47. Eliza Flower to Walter Scott, March 7, 1828, with a letter, John Bowring to Scott, March 22, 1828, MS, National Library of Scotland.

48. Five lines from the end of Paracelsus' penultimate speech beginning "I stoop / Into a dark tremendous sea of cloud."

49. Garnett, *Life of W. J. Fox,* p. 219.

50. Ibid., p. 67.

51. Printed, Conway, *Centenary History,* pp. 155-159.

52. Sarah Flower, "Buy Images," *Monthly Repository,* 8 (1834), 756: quoted Mineka, *Dissidence of Dissent,* p. 339.

53. *Autobiography,* p. 119.

54. *LRB,* p. 263, RB to J. Dykes Campbell, March 30, 1887.

55. Stephenson, *The Author of Nearer, My God, to Thee,* p. 26, Sarah Flower to Celina Flower, June 1833.

56. *Pauline* (1833), Widener Collection, Harvard. See the full report on this copy in Appendix D.

57. Garnett, *Life of W. J. Fox,* p. 194.

58. Ibid.

59. Conway, *Autobiography,* II, 26.

60. *LRB,* p. 4, RB to E. Flower, March 9, [1840].

Chapter IX   Sun-Treader: First Flight

1. Sharp, *Life,* p. 30.

2. Benbow published *Miscellaneous and Posthumous Poems of Percy Bysshe Shelley* (1826), a combination of lyrics and some of the longer poems; a one-volume *Poetical Works of Percy Bysshe Shelley* (1826) consisting of *Rosalind and Helen* and *Alastor* (probably an adaption of the *Miscellaneous and Posthumous Poems,* copy in BL); and *The Cenci* (1827), as well as the edition RB had; there is no evidence that RB saw these others. Charles H. Taylor, Jr., *The Early Collected Editions of Shelley's Poems* (New Haven, Yale University Press, 1958), pp. 11-17, discusses Benbow's publications of Shelley and explains an anomaly that RB noted —that Benbow correctly prints two lines of "Stanzas Written in Dejection, near Naples" conflated in *Posthumous Poems*—as the result of Benbow's use of an errata sheet from *Posthumous Poems.*

3. The book, now in the Taylor Collection and on loan at the Firestone Library, Princeton, is fully described in Frederick Pottle, *Shelley and Browning: A Myth and Some Facts* (Chicago, Pembroke Press, 1923). A facsimile of RB's note is given, p. 24 f. On the basis of RB's statement, "probably as soon as published," Pottle dates the gift around 1826. Evidence

given below about the date of the later Shelley purchases that followed the gift would indicate a slightly later date, possibly 1827.

4. "Local Logic," *Monthly Repository*, 7 (June 1833), 421. Fox himself knew of Shelley as early as 1830 but had a higher opinion of the beauty of his widow than his verse. It is also possible that Isaac Nathan spoke of Shelley to RB. Olga Phillips, *Isaac Nathan* (London, Minerva, 1940), p. 67, asserts that Nathan did know Shelley. But RB nowhere connects Nathan and Shelley.

5. Orr, p. 52, RB to Fox, [March 1833]; cf. *LRB*, p. 263, RB to J. Dykes Campbell, March 30, 1887.

6. No. 566, p. 765. This is the only notice, 1826-1828, that fits RB's description: "from Hunt and Clarke, in consequence of a direction I obtained from the *Literary Gazette*," *LRB*, p. 246, RB to T. J. Wise, March 3, 1886. Correspondents usually used anonymous initials; this was not a common kind of correspondence and is unlikely to be a reply to someone else's similar inquiry. The date, later than Pottle suspected, is supported by RB's assertion that he had Keats's works "at least six years after his death [Feb. 1821]": *RBJW*, p. 112, RB to Julia Wedgwood, [Feb. 18, 1865]. RB speaks in this letter sending to Keats's publisher for his works, but it is unlikely that he would have known who they (Taylor and Hessey) were. In 1825 they had separated and turned over some of their publishing to Hunt and Clarke. RB's statement to Wise implies that the source for Keats and Shelley was the same and the purchase at the same time "nearly"; possibly he was directed by Hunt and Clarke to Taylor or Hessey at the time the Shelley purchase was made.

7. Pottle, *Shelley and Browning*, p. 25, speculates that Hunt and Clarke was a conflation in RB's memory of Hunt and the Clark who published *Queen Mab*. But Hunt and Clarke was a regular, if short-lived, publishing firm. In 1824, John Hunt, Leigh's brother, took his nephew Henry L. Hunt into the Tavistock St. firm. In the spring of 1825, John Hunt retired and Cowden Clarke, the old friend of Keats, took his place. Sometime thereafter the firm moved to nearby York Street, Covent Garden. They published Hazlitt, Leigh Hunt, and a distinguished series of autobiographies, but ended in financial disaster in 1829. See Richard D. Altick, *The Cowden Clarkes* (New York, Oxford University Press, 1948), esp. pp. 51-55, 62-64. Further confirmation is offered by another letter, RB to T. J. Wise, March 1, 1886, MS, Humanities Research Center, Univ. of Texas, which speaks of the purchase of the *Adonais* at Hunt's, Covent Garden.

8. *LRB*, p. 246, RB to T. J. Wise, March 3, 1886, mentions specifically obtaining the two Shelleys' *History of a Six Weeks' Tour* (1817); *Rosalind and Helen* (1819), lost by Eliza Flower; *The Cenci* (probably the 1821 edition); *Prometheus Unbound* (1820); *Adonais* (1821), borrowed and sold by Thomas Powell (see also RB to T. J. Wise, March 1, 1886, MS, Humanities Research Center, Univ. of Texas); *Posthumous Poems* (1824), sold Sotheby, item 1079. Wise recalled RB also said he had bought *Epipsychidion* (1821) and that it was given to Balliol College by RB, but it is not presently at Balliol and there is no record of its having been there. *The Revolt of Islam* (1818) was sold, Sotheby, item 1078, and was presumably among the original purchases. Griffin and Minchin, p. 53, add *Hellas* (1822) but there is no evidence for this nor have I found specific allusions to it by RB anywhere. There are no other Shelley first editions listed in the various other sales that fractionated Sotheby's lots.

9. Pottle, *Shelley and Browning*, p. 22, argues that Browning could only have been converted to vegetarianism by the long note in *Queen Mab*. He could, however, have learned of the master's dietary habits from other sources including Hunt's memoir in *Lord Byron and Some of his Contemporaries* (London, 1828), I, 323. Contrary to Pottle's argument, the reference to Clarke in Hunt and Clarke does not indicate RB's acquaintance with the name of Clark or his pirated edition of *Queen Mab*. As noted above, however, there may be a grain of truth in Sharp's account of RB happening upon *Queen Mab*. In the "Essay on Shelley," RB refers specifically to Shelley's early religious doubts.

10. See n. 6, above. *Endymion* (1818) was sold at Sotheby, item 799.

11. J. Arnould to A. Domett, Sept. 19, 1847, Hall Griffin Papers, BL, Add. MS. 45,560, fol. 54. RB's later opinion of Keats and the few specific reminiscences of his style (e.g., "Heap

Cassia" in *Paracelsus*) are discussed by George H. Ford, *Keats and the Victorians* (New Haven, Yale University Press, 1944). RB shows a detailed knowledge of *Lamia* in the memo headed "Wordsworth," [ca. 1844], Berg Collection, New York Public Library. He privately defended Keats against Mrs. Carlyle in 1845. As "Popularity" suggests, Keats was less a model for RB's own poetry than a personal inspiration as an artist with the courage to face unpopularity in pursuing his own vision and innovations.

12. Irvine and Honan, pp. 15-18 (Irvine), for instance, continue the focus begun by Sharp's inaccurate tale by a long account of the overwhelming effect of *Queen Mab* on RB.

13. William Raymond, "Browning and the Harriet Westbrook Shelley Letters," *The Infinite Moment and Other Essays in Browning,* rev. ed. (Toronto, University of Toronto Press, 1965), pp. 234-243, is still the most reliable treatment of the complicated dating of RB's changed views. An unpublished letter, RB to F. J. Furnivall, Jan. 5, 1886, MS, Huntington, FU 138, states that Peacock's memoirs in *Fraser's* in 1858 confirmed the view given him by Hookham, at least implying the correctness of the later dating against Miller's suggestion of 1852.

14. *LRB,* p. 222, RB to F. J. Furnivall, Sept. 29, 1883.

15. *LL,* p. 192, RB to Mrs. FitzGerald, Dec. 4, 1886. Richard C. Keenan, "Browning and Shelley," *Browning Institute Studies,* I, ed. William Peterson (Princeton, The Browning Institute, Inc., 1973), 119-145, provides a balanced brief survey of RB's changing later views on Shelley and the influence of Shelley on his work. He properly distinguishes, as other writers do not, between the large changes RB underwent in his views of Shelley as a man and the persistent influence on him of the poetry.

16. Pottle, *Shelley and Browning,* p. 78.

17. *LRB,* p. 47, RB to L. Hunt, Oct. 6, 1857.

18. Thomas Hutchinson, ed., *The Complete Poetical Works of Shelley* (Oxford, Oxford University Press, 1904), p. 616. RB suggested quotations from this poem to Horne as mottoes for chapters on Mary Shelley and EBB in his *New Spirit of the Age, NL,* p. 30, RB to R. H. Horne, [Autumn 1843].

19. Pottle, p. 24 f. The mispunctuation is RB's.

20. Shelley's manuscript at Harvard calls it "an Anacreontic." RB knew the work, then considered as actually by Anacreon, literally from infancy.

21. See the transcription in Appendix C. The poem to which he refers is given in RB's own translation in n. 111 to the Appendixes.

22. RB to Ripert-Monclar, Aug. 9, 1837, MS, Private Collection.

23. *NL,* p. 344, RB to F. Moscheles, May 26, 1887. RB also recommended passages from "The Witch of Atlas" to his son: "The Witch of Atlas," MS, Humanities Research Center, Univ. of Texas. He spoke of "The Sensitive Plant" to Monclar in a letter, Jan. 11, 1836, MS, Private Collection.

24. RB quoted easily from it in old age: *LL,* p. 96, RB to Mrs. FitzGerald, Sept. 3[0], 1880; his pleasure in the Lido was probably through the association with this old friend. It is also mentioned in the "Essay on Shelley."

25. The state of the volume, originally sold at Sotheby, is reported in Bernard Quaritch Catalog No. 326, *Rare and Valuable Books, Including Books of R. B. Browning, Most of Which Have Interesting Inscriptions* (London, June 1913), item 113. RB suggested a passage to Horne for a motto for Harriet Martineau: *NL,* p. 30, RB to R. H. Horne, [Autumn 1843].

26. Hiram Corson, "Robert Browning," *New York Evening Post,* Dec. 17, 1889 (clipping at Baylor).

27. RB quotes from memory a line and a half from stanza **xxxv** of *Adonais,* memo headed "Wordsworth" [1844]. Pottle, *Shelley and Browning,* pp. 44-64, offers very few parallels between these works and *Pauline* or *Paracelsus,* though the similar allusions to Christ and Cain in *Adonais* and *Paracelsus* are striking.

28. Felix Moscheles, *Fragments of an Autobiography* (London, 1899), pp. 327-329.

29. *RBEBK,* I, 220 (letter 119), RB to EBB, [Oct. 2, 1845].

30. *RBEBK,* I, 36 (letter 13), RB to EBB, [March 11, 1845].

31. *LRB*, p. 177, RB to H. Buxton Forman, March 27, 1877, recalls speaking of a note to Hunt, probably in the 1830s or 1840s. *LRB*, p. 47, RB to L. Hunt, Oct. 6, 1857, speaks of the same occasion as "years ago."

32. W. G. Kingsland, "Robert Browning: Some Personal Reminiscences," *The Baylor Bulletin,* 34 (July 1931), 31.

33. Reprinted in Hutchinson, ed., *Complete Poetical Works of Shelley* pp. xvi-xviii.

34. *DI*, p. 327, RB to I. Blagden, Jan. 19, 1870.

35. See *LRB,* p. 179, RB to H. B. Forman, July 2, 1877 and *LRB*, p. 146, RB to D. G. Rossetti, April 9, 1871; RB observes that the book was never reprinted and speaks of Hunt "in 1828" noting the loss of the line in the "Stanzas Written in Dejection, near Naples," which he later spoke to Hunt about when he met him. If RB had a copy, it has not survived. The one listed in some sales catalogs is EBB's.

36. Hunt, *Lord Byron,* I, 312, 320-321.

37. See *LRB,* p. 223, RB to Edward Dowden, Oct. 12, 1883; *LRB,* p. 371, n. 83, A. C. Swinburne to Rossetti, June 24, [1869].

38. Hunt, *Lord Byron,* I, 295-296.

39. *LRB*, p. 146, RB to D. G. Rossetti, April 9, 1871. The incident is not identified; Hunt's account of Shelley's warm efforts on a cold night to obtain help for a sick person among the cold Christian hearts of the Hampstead burghers seems a probable subject.

40. Domett's *Diary,* p. 53; Domett says it was given to RB by Mrs. Hunt herself. It is a reminiscent work, done after Shelley's death.

41. Masao Miyoshi, *The Divided Self: A Perspective on the Literature of the Victorians* (New York, New York University Press, 1969), pp. 124-130, in an interesting discussion of the poet's emerging resolution against self-consciousness, tends, for all his qualifications, to overstate the amount of direction in *Pauline.* The problem, as he recognizes, is that *Pauline* itself remains confused although we may conclude from it that young RB was clarifying his own mind in the process of writing it.

42. RB to Ripert-Monclar, Aug. 9, 1837, MS, Private Collection.

43. *Pauline* (1833), Mill copy, Victoria and Albert Museum, Forster Collection. A full transcription of the comments has recently been published by William S. Peterson and Fred L. Standley, "The J. S. Mill Marginalia in Robert Browning's *Pauline*: A History and Transcription," *Papers of the Bibliographical Society of America,* 66 (second quarter, 1972), 135-170. They read here "sword" for "award"—wrongly, I believe.

44. *LRB*, p. 181, RB to H. Buxton Forman, Dec. 27, 1877. See the "Memoir," *Athenaeum,* No. 252 (Aug. 25, 1832), p. 554.

45. *RBEBK,* I, 62 (letter 24), RB to EBB, [May 13, 1845]; "Memoir," *Athenaeum,* No. 251 (Aug. 18, 1832), p. 536.

46. In the "Essay on Shelley" RB shows his familiarity with this material.

47. Medwin, "Memoir," *Athenaeum,* No. 252 (Aug. 25, 1832), pp. 554-555.

48. Nos. 247-252 (July 21, 1832-Aug. 25, 1832), at pp. 472, 488, 502, 535, 554.

49. Sarianna explained that parts of the end of the poem were written while going to Richmond on that date to see Kean: see Robert Wiedeman Browning to Hall Griffin, Nov. 11, 1902, Hall Griffin Papers, BL, Add. MS. 45,563, fol. 186.

50. RB may also have been aware of two other recent recognitions of Shelley: Hogg's account of "Shelley at Oxford" in the *New Monthly Magazine* and the publication by Hunt of *The Masque of Anarchy,* both in 1832. RB refers to neither. He did know (though possibly only later) Medwin's earlier *Conversations of Lord Byron* (London, 1824), which also speaks very highly of Shelley in brief allusions to him throughout and which has a long footnote providing a "Memoir," really a factual synopsis of his life. But there is the same misleading reticence over Harriet.

51. "Robert Browning: A Reading of the Early Narratives," *ELH,* 26 (Dec. 1959), esp. 534-543. One of the best critical discussions of RB's early work.

52. Now at Wellesley; no date, but probably 1535. RB has reduced Agrippa's preface by more than half, with the effect of giving special stress to the excuse of youth and, it should be

said, omitting most of the references to magic. Pottle, *Shelley and Browning*, pp. 86-87, gives the entire Latin text.

53. Pottle, *Shelley and Browning*, p. 55, cites 5 parallels in Shelley to the Platonic conception of the cave of the mind.

54. See esp. ibid., pp. 36-55, a thorough collation of parallel passages and parallel forms and devices; also H. L. Hovelaque, *La Jeunesse de Robert Browning* (Paris, Les Presses Modernes, 1932), pp. 130-132, 139-141; also Park Honan, *Browning's Characters: A Study in Poetic Technique* (New York, Yale University Press, 1961), pp. 11-17. There are interesting general discussions of Shelley and *Pauline* in Thomas J. Collins, "Shelley and God in Browning's *Pauline*: Unresolved Problems," *Victorian Poetry*, 3 (Summer 1965), 151-160, in Miyoshi, *The Divided Self*, pp. 124-130, and, most recently, in Keenan, "Browning and Shelley," pp. 122-125.

55. "The Unpastured Sea: An Introduction to Shelley," *The Ringers in the Tower: Studies in Romantic Tradition* (Chicago, University of Chicago Press, 1971), p. 92.

56. Preyer "A Reading of the Early Narratives," p. 534, uses the term "spiritual confession" for this and RB's two other major early works; only *Pauline* is, strictly speaking, a confession.

57. See the suggestion of possible parallels to *Advice to a Young Christian* in the discussion above, chap. iv. section 2, p. 59.

58. Hovelaque, *Jeunesse de Robert Browning,* p. 126, suggests the influence of Rousseau and offers parallels to other continental Romantics. RB refers to Rousseau in the *Trifler* article (see Appendix C) and very likely knew him by 1832. See also n. 73, chap. x, below. Morse Peckham, "Browning and Romanticism," *Robert Browning,* ed. Isobel Armstrong (Athens, Ohio, Ohio University Press, 1975), pp. 47-76, suggests broad parallels between *Pauline* and international romanticism.

59. See above, chap. iv. section 3.

60. See Clément Marot, *Les Epigrammes,* ed. C. A. Mayer (London, University of London, 1970), p. 280: one of the "Epigrammes Diverses," sometimes published under the contrived title "De Soy mesme"; written ca. 1538-1542, first published 1542. Marot merely laments the passing of time; Browning's more Byronic use of the quotation probably arose from his previous acquaintance with Byron's versions of the epigram in *Childe Harold* (see n. 64, below). Browning quotes the two lines again in a letter to M. Le Chevalier de Chatelain, Feb. 16, 1866, MS, Humanities Research Center, Univ. of Texas. The lines should read:

Plus ne suis ce que j'ay esté,
et ne le sçaurois jamais estre;

61. W. S. Swisher, "A Psychoanalysis of Browning's *Pauline,*" *Psychoanalytic Review,* 7 (April 1920), 115-133; Preyer, "A Reading of the Early Narratives," p. 539.

62. Both Swisher, "A Psychoanalysis" and Keenan, "Browning and Shelley," pp. 123-124, have argued that the anxiety embodied in the dreams may be specifically about Shelley. Keenan persuasively sees young RB fearing that he may be himself a witch luring down and debasing a god. Swisher's article, a full-fledged attempt to put *Pauline* on the couch as a work of self-analysis intuitively performed by RB, shows many of the good and bad results of the interpretation of dreams in literature as if they were confession to an analyst. On very dubious biographical grounds (inferiority from the supposed touch of the tar brush) he posits that RB suffered from neurosis; then he does speculate interestingly on RB's possible fixation on his father and repressed hostility to his mother (embodied in the Orestes myth to which RB alludes in the poem). In Swisher's view, the love for Shelley is a transference of neurotic homo-erotic fixation on the father: a view parallel to my reading of his idealization of Shelley as a poet-model. To grow must be to move beyond this fixation and seek real fulfillment of desires in an Andromeda figure, who is to be rescued from the regressive libido (the snake). The dream imagery expresses his desire for rebirth (with the too predictable identification of swan's neck and phallus, cave and mother's womb). The general view of the poem is sensible: RB works to break

with his fixations on father and Shelley by exploring problems in dream symbolism; then he moves toward resolution of his problems in a quest for a real female and acceptance of a moral and religious vision of the world. It is less clear what firm biographical conclusions can be drawn from the symbolism alone. Certainly RB idealized his unworldly father and needed to break from him to a more healthy acceptance of reality in life and art. His mother's general influence on RB does not seem to me, as it did to Betty Miller, who follows some of Swisher's leads, to have been repressive and life denying. Freud tells us that all boys resent their mothers as forbidden sexual objects and certainly there was also a normal adolescent's revolt against the mother's restraining social position.

63. Miyoshi, *The Dived Self,* p. 130, concludes his interesting analysis of RB's movement from self to outside self with the unfounded further assertion: "For Browning, as for so many of his contemporaries, the will runs his life and his poetry too, art for its own sake being pushed back behind the moral statement."

64. *Childe Harold's Pilgrimage,* Canto IV, CLXXXV. Cf. Canto III, CXI: "We are not now what we have been." Probably echoes of Marot: see note 60 above.

65. Ibid., Canto III, VII.

66. See the fuller discussion of RB's reading in Shakespeare in chap. xiii, section 4, below.

67. RB to W. C. Macready, June 15, 1837, MS, Beinecke, Yale, speaks of seeing *Hamlet,* Oct. 21, 1830.

68. *Pauline* (1833), Mill copy, Victoria and Albert Museum, Forster Collection.

69. This is the date written with his signature on a blank sheet at the back of the Mill copy. Mill returned the copy to Fox on Oct. 10.

70. Masao Miyoshi, "Mill and 'Pauline': the Myth and Some Facts," *Victorian Studies,* 9 (Dec. 1965), 154-163, gives the fullest summary of the history of the comments and their impact on RB. O. P. Govil, "A Note on Mill and Browning's *Pauline,*" *Victorian Poetry,* 4 (Autumn 1966), 287-291, is correct in qualifying Miyoshi's attempt to refute the tradition that RB was stung by criticism of *Pauline* into a non-personal style: criticism probably added to a process of internal development; and RB may have been affected by Mill's criticism even if he wasn't badly hurt by it, and even if he was somewhat pleased by the attention. RB was developing toward a different poetry and view of the poet but had not fully arrived in *Pauline.*

71. RB to Monclar, Aug. 9, 1837, MS, Private Collection.

72. Michael Hancher has recently challenged DeVane's judgment, typical of most readings, that "Browning is the speaker hardly disguised": "The Dramatic Situation in Browning's *Pauline,*" *Yearbook of English Studies,* 1 (1971), 149-159. His approach, looking at the poem strictly as a dramatic monologue, serves only to point up RB's uncertainty about the character and age of his speaker. Hancher argues from the Marot quote, the passage on life waning, and the reference to a last state that this is the speech of an "old roué" on his deathbed (like St. Praxed's Bishop). Yet he honestly admits conflicting evidence: plans for personal improvement and talk about "this first stage" in life. He does not enough consider the overall boyish tone, which is what persuades most readers that this is the young author speaking. Nor does he acknowledge the correlations between the autobiography in the poem and RB's own life. Finally, the old-young poet, wearied not by age but by too intense living, is part of the romantic tradition in which RB is working. The failure to establish a clear dramatic character suggests that RB, like his romantic predecessors in similar poems, did not sufficiently distance his own concerns from those of his character to really conceive of a distinct persona.

73. Reported by Robert Wiedeman Browning to Hall Griffin, Nov. 11, 1902, Hall Griffin Papers, BL, Add. MS. 45,563, fol. 186. In the Harvard Theatre Collection there is a playbill for *Othello* for Oct. 29, 1832. The season ended Nov. 9; along with *Richard III, King Lear* and *Macbeth* had also been acted (Sept. 26 and Oct. 3). There are also a number of prints of the King's Theater, Richmond (London, T. Woodfall, Feb. 1, 1804).

74. *RBEBK,* I, 378 (letter 198), RB to EBB, [Jan. 11, 1846].

75. R. H. Shepherd's copy of *Pauline,* formerly in the Alexander Turnbull Library, Wellington, New Zealand, now lost. Reported in Johannes Andersen, *The Lure of New Zealand*

Book Collecting (Auckland, Whitcombe and Tombs, 1936), pp. 18-19. There is no evidence that this was Domett's copy. Possibly it is the same as the copy reported by Augustine Birrell, ed., *The Complete Poetical Works of Robert Browning* (New York, Macmillan, 1915), p. 1, as the Crampon copy. The entry was probably made at the time (1867) RB agreed to let Shepherd publish a few extracts from *Pauline* if he would remark that it was "purely dramatic and intended to head a series of 'Men and Women' such as I have afterwards introduced to the world under somewhat better auspices": DeVane, *Handbook*, p. 48, RB to R. H. Shepherd, Feb. 1, 1867. RB reported on *Pauline* to Monclar in similar language. Kintner guessed that RB's reference to his "Songs of the Poets—No. 1 M.P." is to *Pauline* as the work of *me poeta*, i.e., a first monologue of himself: *RBEBK,* I, 74 (letter 31), RB to EBB, [May 24, 1845].

76. F. W. Hawkins, *The Life of Edmund Kean* (London, 1869), II, 371, cites an account of his *Richard III* of June 4, 1832. Sergeant Talfourd in 1831 had focused more on Kean's debilities: H. N. Hillebrand, *Edmund Kean* (New York, Columbia University Press, 1933), p. 320. Talford adds, "Yet his last look at Richmond as he stands is fearful."

77. *RBEBK,* I, 74 (letter 31) RB to EBB, [May 24, 1845].

78. Orr, p. 65, RB to W. J. Fox, April 16, 1835.

79. In the performance of June 4, 1832 Kean was wildly applauded for his handling of the line: Hawkins, II, 371. The description is by Leigh Hunt, *Dramatic Essays,* ed. W. Archer and Lowe (London, 1894), p. 201.

80. Hawkins, I, 176; Hawkins, I, 154-177, cites a number of contemporary accounts of the part.

81. See the discussion *RBEBK,* I, 312, 314 (letters 170, 171), RB to EBB, [Dec. 9, 1845], EBB to RB, [Dec. 9, 1845].

82. See Pottle, *Shelley and Browning,* pp. 55-64. The lyrical scene with Aprile, especially the song, provides an opportunity for more echoes of Shelley than the more dramatic speeches of the rest would suggest.

83. Paracelsus himself, as Pottle notes, embodies some of the features of the Alastor figure; but RB obviously intends by him not a study of Shelley but only of some of his ideas and of the general theme of the quest.

84. RB to Monclar, Jan. 11, 1836 (copy of letter only), Private Collection.

85. Joseph Slater, *The Correspondence of Emerson and Carlyle* (New York, Columbia University Press, 1964), p. 329, T. Carlyle to Sterling, July 28, 1842.

86. *DI,* p. 127, RB to I. Blagden, Oct. 18, 1862.

87. Omitted again in 1863 and subsequently. Except for the important addition of an explicit suggestion of Christ as mediator, the changes in the text are not changes in direction so much as clarifications and expansions where RB felt he had left his intention vague. The addition of "peers" in the song of the poets and of the word "ring" in Paracelsus' description of them suggests striking parallels to Childe Roland's own end, where the theme is again, "Lost, lost."

88. DeVane, *Handbook*, p. 73, speculates, possibly correctly, that Shelley intrudes here because RB had invoked his aid in the earlier, less historical *Sordello* he had begun writing as early as 1833, then turned increasingly away from him as the poem developed. In its final form *Sordello* not only wishes Shelley away but even, in the caricature of Eglamor, a poet who "looped back the lingering veil / Which hid the holy place," pokes fun at some aspects of the Shelleyan poet.

89. *RBEBK,* I, 16 (letter 7), RB to EBB, [Feb. 11, 1845].

90. Ibid. RB's tower reappears as that of the objective poet in the "Essay on Shelley."

91. *RBEBK,* I, 142 (letter 72), RB to EBB, [Aug. 3, 1845].

92. Harold Bloom, "Browning's *Childe Roland:* All Things Deformed or Broken," *The Ringers in the Tower* (Chicago, University of Chicago Press, 1971), pp. 157-167. Bloom notes a probable echo of the image of the tower from "Julian and Maddalo," which RB knew well. Bloom's interpretation, like that of Miller before, and, to a somewhat lesser extent, Irvine and Honan after him, relies heavily on the assumptions: 1) that RB continued to feel a basic, self-abnegating guilt about his swerve from Shelley; 2) that, indeed, he should feel such guilt, for to

leave Shelley was to leave the work of the true artist. My argument obviously questions both assumptions. One might better read the poem as an answer to Shelley's own bleak, because hopeless, vision in "The Triumph of Life": an assertion of the force of life triumphant against its own most bitter vision of realities—bitter realities not, as Shelley would agree, merely existing in the eyes of the beholder. The parallel death of Aprile before his peers in *Paracelsus* implies that failure in the ultimate task need not be a source of guilt.

93. Park Honan, "Browning's Testimony on his Essay on Shelley in 'Shepherd v. Francis,'" *ELN,* 2 (Sept. 1964), 30.

94. [W. H. Grove], "Browning as I Knew Him. By his Valet," *Sunday Express,* Dec. 4, 1927, pp. 466-469 (clipping at Baylor). Grove became a prosperous photographer and is far from an illiterate source.

95. The importance of symbolic devices in Browning's mature poetry has not been sufficiently recognized in the criticism. Keenan, "Browning and Shelley," pp. 135-137, discusses the use of one symbol from Shelley, the white light of eternity broken into prismatic hues from the *Adonais.* The importance of one other Shelleyan image, the star, has been exhaustively illustrated in C. Willard Smith's classic *Browning's Star-Imagery: The Study of a Detail in Poetic Design* (Princeton, Princeton University Press, 1941). Smith concludes that the star image comes increasingly under intellectual or rhetorical control in RB's later poetry, in effect a slow waning of the more spontaneous and inspired Shelleyan symbol in the poems before *The Ring and the Book.*

Chapter X   Schooling and Society

1. Orr, p. 378, RB to Mr. George Bainton, Oct. 6, 1887.

2. Chesterton, *Robert Browning* (New York, Macmillan, 1903), pp. 12-13.

3. Despite the correction of this error in Griffin and Minchin, p. 47, Miller, p. 16 shows the same ignorance of the nature of public schools before Arnold as Orr, the first writer to suggest that Browning needed the more bracing training of the later nineteenth century.

4. In his *Liberal Education* (London, 1781), quoted in W. A. C. Stewart and W. P. McCann, *The Educational Innovators, 1750-1880* (New York, St. Martin's Press, 1967), p. 33.

5. Eldon's decision in the Leeds Grammar School case, 1805, against the use of endowed funds for purposes other than those ordained by the founder.

6. Thomas Wyse, quoted in Brian Simon, *Studies in the History of Education, 1780-1870* (London, Lawrence and Wishart, 1960), p. 100.

7. *Thoughts Concerning Education* (1692), quoted in S. J. Curtis, *History of Education in Great Britain* (London, London University Tutorial Press, 1967), pp. 114-115.

8. Quoted in John W. Adamson, *English Education 1789-1902* (Cambridge, England, Cambridge University Press, 1964), p. 61.

9. G. C. Lewis, "Public Schools of England—Eton," *Edinburgh Review,* 51 (April 1830), 69, 74. T. B. Macaulay had made much the same criticism of the university curriculum in 1826 in "The London University," *Edinburgh Review,* 43 (Feb. 1826), 315-341, esp. 329-336.

10. Quoted in Curtis, *History of Education,* p. 128.

11. Quoted in Adamson, *English Education,* p. 61, from the *Quarterly Journal of Education* (1834).

12. *Academic Errors; or Recollections of Youth by a Member of the University of Cambridge* (London, 1817).

13. Richard Edgeworth, *Practical Education* (London, 1801), II, 186.

14. *Academic Errors,* p. 158.

15. *Sartor Resartus,* Bk. II, chap. 3.

16. Mason, "Kinsfolk," pp. 14, 56-60. Mason suggests, but does not establish, that this Reuben was a schoolteacher (Mason was not aware of Reuben's connection with the Bank). He speaks vaguely of a "system" of education passed down from this Reuben to RB Sr. and from him to RB. But the system, as we shall see, was no scheme of education but merely a broad conception of the liberal arts.

17. On the varieties of educational alternatives in the eighteenth century see Nicholas Hans, *New Trends in Education in the Eighteenth Century* (London, Routledge, 1951). Stewart and McCann, *Educational Innovators,* are concerned especially with new educational practices.

18. The prevalence of home tutoring of varying kinds is discussed by Hans, *New Trends,* pp. 181-193.

19. Orr, p. 77.

20. See n. 17, chap. iii. The description is from the Advertisement for the school.

21. William Blanch, *Ye Parish of Camerwell* (London, 1875), pp. 452-455. On Camberwell schools in general see the listing in Douglas Allport, *Collections Illustrative of the Geology, History, Antiquities, and Associations, of Camberwell, and the Neighbourhood* (Camberwell, 1841), p. 211-238. Allport speaks of attempts to place Jephson's "upon a more efficient footing." RB's friend Domett went to a school at Stockwell; Arnould was sent to Charterhouse, not, as a letter, J. Arnould to A. Domett, Sept. 15, 1867, Hall Griffin Papers, BL, Add. MS. 45,560, fol. 65b, recalling old days "under the shadow of old Jephson's walnut trees" seems to imply, to Jephson's: see Domett's *Diary,* p. 1.

22. Orr, p. 26.

23. R. L. Archer, *Secondary Education in the Nineteenth Century* (Cambridge, England, Cambridge University Press, 1921), p. 98.

24. Quoted in Curtis, *History of Education,* p. 119, from Hoole's *A New Discovery of the Old Art of Teaching Schoole* (1660).

25. Archer, *Secondary Education,* p. 98.

26. Blanch, *Parish,* p. 263.

27. Orr, pp. 27-28.

28. There are allusions to Watts from childhood reading in *RBAD,* p. 95, RB to A. Domett, Nov. 8, 1843; *RBEBK,* I, 191 (letter 102), RB to EBB, [Sept. 13, 1845]; *RBEBK,* I, 282 (letter 155), RB to EBB, [Nov. 21, 1845].

29. Martin Ready is not listed among graduates of Oxford or Cambridge. Allport gives Ready's death as 1805. His name appears for Peckham in the rate books, Newington District Library, as late as 1804. Ann, probably his widow, succeeds him; then Thomas sometime between 1818 and 1825.

Thomas Martin Ready (?-1866) is listed as a ten-year man in the *Alumni Cantabrigienses:* admitted sizar at Queens College, 1816; migrated to St. Catharine's, Dec. 4, 1819; matriculated Michaelmas, 1828; LL.B. 1832. He was granted an Honorable M.A. from the University of Aberdeen, 1832. Very likely, after taking over the school at his father's death, he enrolled to complete his education as an older man, while continuing to run the school. A ten-year man was usually an older student who had only to reside for three terms during his last two years. The Stewards' Account Books at St Catharine's College, kindly searched for me by the Bursar, Dr. S. C. Aston, indicate that Ready was probably only a nominal student until matriculation in 1828. After 1828 he was at least occasionally in residence as a Fellow Commoner until Christmas 1831. In the civil law classes of 1831-1832 Ready appeared a none too impressive 9th out of 13. Ready must have taken orders before RB's schooling inasmuch as he is listed in the Cambridge University Calendar as "Rev." Apparently he gave up the school to become minister at St. James Episcopal Chapel, Kennington, ca. 1830? (Allport, *Collections of Camberwell,* p. 258). From 1841 till his death in 1866 he was Vicar of Mountnessing, Essex. He had one son, the Rev. Edward Martin Ready. I have not found his *Thoughts on the Divine Permission of Moral Evil* (1845). Blanch was apparently unaware that there were two Readys and gives a confused account. Between 1853 and 1855 he edited a number of translations of moral tales for young schoolchildren, most by the German writer for children, Johann Christoph Von Schmid: see the BL catalog.

30. Allport, *Collections of Camberwell,* p. 238.

31. Domett's *Diary,* p. 145. Alfred's brothers, but not Alfred, attended the school.

32. Blanch, *Parish,* p. 264. On Sir William Fry Channell (1804-1873) see *DNB,* s.v. Channell. Channell often lamented that he had been so ill taught. His brother Frank was also a schoolfellow, as was another judge, Baron Bramwell, though only for a short time.

33. Quoted in Hans, *New Trends,* p. 112. The school was run by the Rev. Nicholson.

34. H. J. Dyos, *Victorian Suburb: A Study of the Growth of Camberwell* (Leicester, Leicester University Press, 1961), p. 164, speaks of 10 pounds as a minimum for middle-class schools. But better classical boarding schools were generally even more: see Simon, *Studies,* p. 15 and Hans, *New Trends,* p. 11, for some fees for similar schools.

35. The site of the school was No. 77, Queen's Road, Peckham, opposite Rye Lane and Hanover Chapel. In 1855 the school was moved to Burchell Road on the Queen's Road. The exact history of the school remains somewhat unclear. There is no evidence except local tradition (see Domett's *Diary,* p. 74) to connect this school with Dr. Milner's where Oliver Goldsmith tried ushering. Both Blanch and Allport agree in giving the Rev. Martin Ready the honor of founding the school, not merely of taking it over. Allport's date for this, 1788, is probably more reliable than Blanch's vague suggestion of about 1770; Allport was closer in time. Milner had died much earlier, in 1757, and there is nothing to indicate any continuity to 1788. Possibly by coincidence the same building was used by Martin Ready. But by tradition the Goldsmith House in Goldsmith St. was the site of Milner's school (Blanch, *Parish,* p. 362). Although said to be too small for a school, the picture in Blanch, p. 360 f., shows quite a good-sized house.

36. Domett's *Diary,* pp. 73-74.

37. Ibid.

38. Ibid.

39. Sotheby, item 1047; Orr, p. 29.

40. Robert Wiedeman Browning to Hall Griffin, Nov. 11, 1902, Hall Griffin Papers, BL, Add. MS. 45,563, fols. 186-194.

41. Orr gives fourteen; the intermediate dates are conjectures from the usual term of the petty schools.

42. RB Sr.'s statement is in his letter to Thomas Coatts [sic], April 22, 1828, enrolling RB at The London University, MS, College Collection, D. M. S. Watson Library, University College London, pub. H. Hale Bellot, "Browning as an Undergraduate," *Times,* Dec. 17, 1926, p. 15. He means 6 years of intensive language work. An anecdote, *RBEBK,* I, 403 (letter 207), RB to EBB, [Jan. 19, 1846], indicates that RB had a good start on Greek before he began French at fourteen. It is possible, as the ages that can be deduced from the imaginary history of RB's Greek study in "Development" would suggest, that RB began Greek as early as age eight and was reading Homer by twelve. More likely, the Greek came somewhat later, with Latin begun at about eight or nine, Greek at about twelve, and French at fourteen. It is also possible that Greek was not offered at Ready's and that RB studied it only at home with his father, as "Development" seems to imply. Mason, "Kinsfolk," p. 98, also asserts that RB's father was his son's sole instructor in Greek. However, neither is good evidence. RB disliked his schooldays and wouldn't mention them in a poem. Mason had no firsthand experience of this period of RB's life and seems not even to have known that RB was at school for years, or that he later studied Greek at The London University. His bias, the desire to prove that RB was a homemade, hothouse poet, accounts for his emphasis on RB's home education.

43. The standard Eton curriculum: see Archer, *Secondary Education,* pp. 18-19.

44. Kensington Academy, with a far wider curriculum than Peckham, had classics from 7:00 to 9:00 and 10:00 to 12:00, translation from 12:00 to 1:00, and classics again from 3:00 to 5:00: Hans, *New Trends,* pp. 77-78.

45. Orr, p. 53, RB to W. J. Fox, [March 1833].

46. *Trifler,* No. 1 (Jan 1835), p. 12. On the attribution to RB see Appendix C.

47. Domett's *Diary,* p. 73: a transcription from RB's statement to Domett in 1873.

48. Ibid.

49. Orr, p. 29.

50. *RBEBK,* I, 428 (letter 218), RB to EBB, [Jan. 31, 1846].

51. The author of *Academic Errors,* p. 23, complains that his instructor did nothing to satisfy his literary curiosity: "Every current of fine and natural feeling had been frozen by the cold and cheerless atmosphere of this ill-regulated academy."

52. Simon, *Studies,* p. 84.

53. Quoted in Adamson, *English Education,* p. 48.

54. See above, chap. vi, section 1.

55. Orr, p. 41.

56. Mason, "Kinsfolk," p. 88.

57. Loradoux appears in RB's "Address Book," MS, Beinecke, Yale, but without address. His first name there is unclear; Ripert-Monclar records meeting "Augte. Loradoux" at dinner at the Brownings, "Voyage à Londres en 1837," MS, Private Collection. That such tutors of French were only too available in Camberwell is indicated by the report of the suicide of another Professeur de langues, a Horceau, in a state of extreme want in 1846: Blanch, *Parish,* p. 342.

58. *RBEBK,* I, 197 (letter 104), RB to EBB, [Sept. 16, 1845]. The text is *Le Gil Blas de la Jeunesse* (London, Whittaker & Co. and Wm. Pickering, 1835). The first 6 chapters (pp. 1-25) of the book have a very literal interlinear translation; pp. 26-40 then present parallel texts, English and French, on opposite pages. "Doing" the interlinear translation would be a credit only to RB's French. The separate pages of translation do have a vigorous and effective English style. LeRoy is identified in the work as Professeur au College de Camberwell—probably Jephson's School. What share RB had in this work has been disputed. Lionel Stevenson in "A French Text-Book by Browning," *MLN,* 42 (May 1927), 229-305, suggested RB probably did the English translation. Broughton, entry A178, asserts RB's part "could hardly have been great and may . . . have been almost nil." Yet surely RB's "did," with all allowance for bragging, means something: probably a good deal of translating, if not the entire work.

59. *RBEBK,* I, 403 (letter 207), RB to EBB, [Jan. 19, 1846].

60. *NL,* p. 28, RB to an unidentified correspondent, [Sept. 3, 1842].

61. *NL,* p. 377, RB to Robert Wiedeman Browning, June 19, 1889.

62. Griffin and Minchin, p. 47, quoting Robert Wiedeman Browning. RB's early facility in French is apparent from the Ripert-Monclar correspondence, frequently in French. RB's French was apparently better than Monclar's English and they probably conversed often in French.

63. *RBEBK,* I, 182 (letter 97), RB to EBB, [Sept. 5, 1845].

64. Rabelais is also mentioned familiarly in *RBEBK,* I, 44 (letter 15), RB to EBB, [March 31, 1845] and in *Pippa Passes,* part II. RB took great interest in an article by Arnould on Rabelais, *RBAD,* p. 109, RB to A. Domett, Feb. 23, 1845.

65. Orr, p. 144, EBB to M. R. Mitford, Feb. 8, [1847].

66. *DI,* p. 264, RB to I. Blagden, May 22, 1867.

67. See the discussion of Enlightenment historical attitudes in Mill's famous essay on "Coleridge," *Essays on Ethics, Religion, and Society,* ed. J. M. Robson (Toronto, University of Toronto Press, 1969), pp. 131-141, esp. pp. 139-141.

68. In RB's hand (1867 revisions) in the Frederick Locker-Lampson copy of *Pauline* (1833), Houghton, Harvard and in all later published editions in RB's lifetime.

69. *RBEBK,* I, 191 (letter 102), RB to EBB, [Sept. 13, 1845].

70. *The Political Ideas of the English Romanticists* (London, Oxford University Press, 1926), p. 235. Shelley's primarily ahistorical program for apocalyptic regeneration is analyzed in detail in Gerald McNiece, *Shelley and the Revolutionary Idea* (Cambridge, Mass., Harvard University Press, 1969) and in Carl Woodring, *Politics in English Romantic Poets* (Cambridge, Mass., Harvard University Press, 1970), pp. 230-325.

71. *RBEBK,* I, 36 (letter 13), RB to EBB, [March 11, 1845].

72. Orr, p. 30. How literally her "all the works of Voltaire" should be taken is a question.

73. It is not clear when RB first read Rousseau. He knew him certainly by the time of the *Trifler* article in early 1835. As noted in chap. ix, it is hard to read *Pauline,* without suspecting the *Confessions* are behind it. In later life, RB went out of his way twice to visit Rousseau's refuge at Chambéry (Oct. 1858 and Sept. 24, 1881) and he speaks of him with enthusiasm in *La Saisiaz.* Diderot is spoken of familiarly in letters to Elizabeth as an old, and by then not too highly respected, acquaintance. On Agrippa see n. 52, chap. ix.

74. Orr, p. 43.

75. Ibid.

Chapter XI   The London University

1. "State of the Nation," *Westminster Review,* 6 (Oct. 1826), 269; an article supporting the university. The standard work on University College is H. Hale Bellot, *University College London, 1826-1926* (London, University of London Press, 1929). I use the name The London University to distinguish the first university from its successors.

2. Bellot, *University College,* p. 62.

3. Bellot, *University College,* p. 80.

4. H. Hale Bellot, "Browning as an Undergraduate," *T.P.'s & Cassell's Weekly,* Feb. 26, 1927, p. 617; the Baptists at Hackney, where Fox lived, were the first Dissenter group to back the university. Nathan Rothschild was also an early subscriber.

5. MS, College Collection, D. M. S. Watson Library, University College London. The letter is pub. in H. Hale Bellot, "Browning as an Undergraduate: Entry and Withdrawal," *Times,* Dec. 17, 1926, p. 15. It is misaddressed to Coatts.

6. The register is cited, Griffin and Minchin, p. 48. It cannot now be located at University College. RB Sr. appears as a new proprietor in a university "Second Statement," "University College Documents and Notices," I, 1825-1829, College Collection, Watson Library. Bellot implies that the share gave full credit for tuition. A university "Classes for the Session 1828-9" speaks only of a one-and-one-half-pound reduction for those nominated by a shareholder: "University College Documents," I.

7. The name of the lodging-house keeper given by Sarianna to Griffin was Mr. Hughes: Robert Wiedeman Browning to Hall Griffin, Nov. 11, 1902, Hall Griffin Papers, BL, Add. MS. 45,563, fols. 186-194. Her information seems questionably detailed, especially since she is vague about the period of time. There are two Hugheses, a George of Wandsworth and a Christopher, American Minister to the Court of Stockholm, in RB, early "Address Book," MS, Beinecke, Yale. Orr, p. 44, presumably from RB's own recollection, asserts, probably correctly, that he remained only a week in lodgings. Why Griffin and Minchin, p. 48, concluded this was for the eight o'clock German class is unclear—possibly because they were not aware there was a later class. Bellot, "Browning as an Undergraduate," p. 617, notes that Browning paid the higher fee for the afternoon course of German (Tues., Thurs. 2:30-4:00). There is no evidence that Browning dropped any courses, including German, upon leaving Bedford Square. The records that Bellot saw cannot now be located at University College.

8. David Taylor, *The Godless Students of Gower Street* (London, Penguin, 1962), p. 14. No source for this remark is given: probably apocryphal. The building, designed by William Wilkins, was still being finished in 1828.

9. A. M. W. Stirling, *William De Morgan and his Wife* (London, T. Butterworth, 1922), p. 56.

10. Bellot, *University College,* p. 179.

11. Sir Joseph Prestwich, for instance, recalled walking "four miles daily to and from South Lambeth": Grace Prestwich, *The Life and Letters of Sir Joseph Prestwich* (Edinburgh, 1899), p. 20. Class hours were adjusted to the needs of "suburban sons."

12. "The London University," *Edinburgh Review,* 43 (Feb. 1826), 329-336.

13. Dale, "Lecture of October 24, 1828," in *Ten Introductory Lectures Delivered at the Opening of the University of London* (London, 1829), p. 7.

14. Ibid., p. 30.

15. The prospectus only is given, ibid., pp. 40-41. These were evening lectures meeting only twice a week—more like a set of lectures than a course.

16. Bellot, *University College,* p. 53.

17. Quoted in Adamson, *English Education,* p. 73, from a MS note of John Kemble in a copy of Connop Thirlwall's *Letter to the Revd. Thos. Turton on the Admission of Dissenters to Academical Degrees* (Cambridge, 1834).

18. Bellot, *University College,* p. 89.

19. Key, *A Latin Grammar on the System of Crude Forms* (London, 1844), pp. ix, 3; enclitics: "little words pronounced and sometimes even written with the word preceding."

20. Thomas Fitzhugh, ed., *The Letters of George Long* (Charlottesville, University Press of Virginia, 1917), gives the fullest account of Long (1800-1879). See also H. J. Mathews, "In Memoriam: George Long," *Brighton College Magazine* (1879). Key (1799-1875) had been professor of mathematics at Virginia.

21. The original two classes in both Greek and Latin were graded into three after the Christmas break. Classes included daily afternoon class exercises. There were forty-seven students in the senior Latin class, seventy-nine in the three Greek classes together: "University College Documents," I, Watson Library.

22. *RBEBK*, I, 36 (letter 13), RB to EBB, [March 11, 1845].

23. Sotheby, item 316: *Scholia in Aeschyli Tragoedias* (1820): I haven't been able to identify this edition.

24. Long speaks in his "An Introductory Lecture Delivered in the University of London, on Tuesday, November 4, 1828," *Ten Introductory Lectures*, p. 8, with praise of the "well directed labours of the German critics."

25. In "Marcus Aurelius," *Essays in Criticism* (1865).

26. In the "Introductory Lecture."

27. *RBEBK*, I, 36 (letter 13), RB to EBB, [March 11, 1845].

28. The "Supplement" is in "University College Documents," I, Watson Library. For his later more traditional pedagogy, see *Observations on the Study of the Latin and Greek Languages: an Introductory Lecture Delivered in the University of London November 1, 1830* (London, 1830) and "What are the Advantages of a Study of Antiquity at the Present Time?" *Central Society of Education Papers* (London, 1839), III, 184-234.

29. R. H. Hutton, quoted in Bellot, *University College*, p. 92.

30. Von Mühlenfels, "An Introductory Lecture Delivered in the University of London, on Thursday, October 30, 1828," *Ten Introductory Lectures*, p. 8. Information on von Mühlenfels is from Bellot, *University College*, p. 122. His appointment lists him as from the University of Heidelberg: College Collection, Watson Library.

31. Von Mühlenfels, "Introductory Lecture," pp. 13-14.

32. Von Mühlenfels, *An Introduction to a Course of German Literature; in Lectures to the Students of the University of London* (London, 1830), pp. 4-5.

33. Ibid., pp. 98-99.

34. See n. 7, above.

35. E.g., "Contrive a happy *anknupfen* [*sic*]," H. C. Minchin, ed., "A Letter from Hanover Cottage," *Bookman*, 85 (April 1934), 6, RB to E. F. Haworth, [ca. Aug. 1, 1837].

36. RB to Ripert-Monclar, Dec. 5, 1834, MS, Private Collection.

37. *RBAD*, p. 46, RB to A. Domett, Dec. 13, 1842. RB was apparently spurred to new exertions by his friendship with Carlyle and by the gift of G. M. Heilner, *A Grammar of the German Language* (London, 1842), from his Uncle Reuben, Dec. 18, 1841 (*sic*, copy at Baylor).

38. *RBAD*, p. 50, RB to A. Domett, March 5, 1843.

39. *LL*, p. 54, RB to Mrs. FitzGerald, Aug. 9, 1878.

40. W. J. Fox, whose religion was none too different from the Göttingen professor's, would not have suggested this portrait: he was a very persuasive speaker who could sway large political meetings.

41. Bellot, *University College*, p. 54.

42. Ibid., p. 143.

43. Quoted, ibid., p. 52.

44. Ibid., pp. 183-184, gives an example of the University Council discouraging students from a publication "tending to distract their attention from the prosecution of their prescribed studies."

45. Henry Solly, *"These Eighty Years" or the Story of an Unfinished Life* (London, 1893), I, 153; Richard Renton, *John Forster and his Friendships* (London, Chapman, Hall, 1912), p. 10; Bellot, *University College*, p. 188.

46. W. S., "Correspondence," *Times*, Dec. 14, 1889, p. 9.

47. Ibid.
48. Browning added the clarification, "learn for learning's sake," in editions after 1835.
49. Copies of exams are in "University College Documents," I, Watson Library. Exams in Greek and Latin were intelligent but demanded much factual detail, not just command of the language and quick wits.
50. This passage was added to *Pippa Passes* in 1849. The religious emphasis is typical of textual changes at this time. But the passage clarifies RB's portrait of Jules rather than changing it.
51. MS, College Collection, Watson Library, pub. in Bellot, "Browning as an Undergraduate," *Times,* Dec. 17, 1926, p. 15.
52. The recurrent statement that Browning left the university "after a little more than a term" (e.g., Miller, p. 18), is misleading and contributes to the impression that Browning had little or no regular education. Cf. Irvine and Honan (Irvine), p. 20: "within a few months." The year's prizes were given out July 9. Formal instruction probably ended sometime before. His name is not among the prize winners.
53. Apparently the share was never sold. RB was reported as a Life Governor of the university: "Contemporary Portraits: Robert Browning," *University Magazine,* 3 (March, 1879), 324.
54. Cf. Orr, p. 25 and Miller, pp. 14-15.
55. Orr, p. 48, speaks of the "idea of his father's that he should qualify himself for the Bar," by attendance at the university and by the "widening of the social horizon which his University College classes supplied."
56. *RBEBK,* I, 191 (letter 102), RB to EBB, [Sept. 13, 1845].
57. Ibid.
58. He is listed as Standing Counsel to the Bank in the *Royal Kalendar* (London, 1849), s.v. Bank of England.
59. *RBAD,* p. 109, RB to A. Domett, Feb. 22, 1845.
60. *LRB,* p. 286, RB to F. J. Furnivall, Feb. 12, 1888.
61. *RBAD,* p. 109, RB to A. Domett, Feb. 22, 1845.
62. Quoted in Elvan Kintner's perceptive "Introduction" to *RBEBK,* I, xli-xlii, from an 1842 review.
63. *RBEBK,* I, 197 (letter 104), RB to EBB, [Sept. 16, 1845].
64. *RBEBK,* I, 191 (letter 102), RB to EBB, [Sept. 13, 1845].
65. *RBEBK,* I, 203 (letter 106), EBB to RB, [Sept. 17, 1845].

Chapter XII   Rededication: Toward Humanity and the Human Past

1. Orr, p. 77. On Blundell, see n. 123, chap. v.
2. Miller's view of Browning. Cf. Irvine and Honan (Irvine), p. 292: "Dependence, conformity, and reverence assumed the feminine image first of his mother, whom he had preferred to Shelley as a spiritual guide."

Chapter XIII   A Poet's Education: Tradition as Found

1. *BAF,* p. 82, RB to Mr. & Mrs. W. W. Story, Nov. 10, 1861. Cf. EBB: "I hate public schools, & so, happily, does my husband": EBB to Mrs. T. B. Fell, June 30, [1858], MS, Huntington HM 20071. *BAF,* p. 93, RB to Mr. & Mrs. W. W. Story, Jan. 21, 1862; *BAF,* p. 132, RB to Mrs. W. W. Story, Nov. 26, 1863.
2. H. C. Minchin, "A Letter from Hanover Cottage," *Bookman,* 86 (April 1934), 6, RB to E. F. Haworth, [ca. Aug. 1, 1837]; *NL,* p. 20, RB to W. C. Macready, [Aug. 23, 1840].
3. *LRB,* p. 8, RB to R. H. Horne, [ca. Dec., 1842].
4. *NL,* p. 20, RB to W. C. Macready, [Aug. 23, 1840].
5. *LRB,* p. 8, RB to R. H. Horne, [ca. Dec. 1842].

6. *RBEBK,* I, 10 (letter 5), RB to EBB, [Jan. 27, 1845].

7. *RBEBK,* I, 191 (letter 102), RB to EBB, [Sept. 13, 1845].

8. Carlyle, who later, in fact, borrowed books from RB, sought just this kind of library in founding the London Library.

9. Orr, p. 50.

10. *RBEBK,* I, 74 (letter 31), RB to EBB, [May 24, 1845].

11. Most of the out-of-the-way reading is discussed extensively in Griffin and Minchin, pp. 20-26: see also chap. v, section 2, above, on childhood reading in Wanley, Melander, and Collier's adaption of Moreri's *Grand Dictionnaire historique.*

12. S. W. Holmes, "Browning: Semantic Stutterer," *PMLA,* 60 (March 1945), 250.

13. As noted in chap. i, DeVane's generally fine study of the *Parleyings,* subtitled *The Autobiography of a Mind* (New Haven, Yale University Press, 1927), has been too influential here. Mandeville and Lairesse did have some importance in RB's overall education. Smart was significant, but only for a single poem, and less important to RB than many other poets. Avison, as we have seen, played some part in RB's musical education, but the focus in the *Parleyings* is on Avison's music. RB had little respect for Bartoli, a low opinion of Dodington, and knew Furini only after 1846. The *Parleyings,* as DeVane shows, explain many ideas important to RB throughout his life. But the works discussed, it should be emphasized, are themselves far from central in RB's education. John Woolford, "Sources and Resources in Browning's Early Reading," *Robert Browning,* ed. Isobel Armstrong (Athens, Ohio, Ohio University Press, 1975), pp. 1-46, speculates interestingly on some of RB's early reading in relation to his mature work. Despite his awareness of the problem, he doesn't fully escape the limitations imposed by heavy reliance on the works indicated in the *Parleyings.*

14. *RBEBK,* I, 484 (letter 243), RB to EBB, [Feb. 21, 1846].

15. Katharine deKay Bronson, "Browning in Venice," *Century Magazine,* 63 (Feb. 1902), 574-575.

16. *LL,* p. 155, RB to Mrs. FitzGerald, March 17, 1883.

17. *RBEBK,* I, 161 (letter 84), EBB to RB, [Aug. 19, 1845].

18. RB to J. Churton Collins, June 8, 1886, MS, Humanities Research Center, Univ. of Texas.

19. *Pauline* (1833), Mill copy, pp. 40-41, Victoria and Albert Museum, Forster Collection.

20. For references in letters see: *RBAD,* p. 28, RB to A. Domett, [March 25, 1840]; *RBEBK,* I, 443 (letter 227), RB to EBB, [Feb. 8, 1846]; RB to Monclar, Dec. 5, 1834, MS, Private Collection. The *Hippolytus* was RB's starting point for a play he planned, from which "Artemis Prologuizes" remains a fragment. Echoes in the poems are thoroughly catalogued by classical authors in the two standard works on RB's classical sources to which the discussion below is indebted: Thurman L. Hood, "Browning's Ancient Classical Sources," *Harvard Studies in Classical Philology,* 33 (1922), 79-180; Robert Spindler, *Robert Browning und die Antike* (Leipzig, Bernard Tauchnitz, 1930), esp. II, 77-159. For Horace see also Mary R. Thayer, *The Influence of Horace on the Chief English Poets of the 19th Century* (New Haven, Yale University Press, 1916), pp. 102-110. RB's general attitudes toward the ancients are discussed by W. C. DeVane, "Browning and the Spirit of Greece," in *Nineteenth-Century Studies,* ed. H. Davis (Ithaca, Cornell University Press, 1940), pp. 179-198.

21. See chap. vii above. The authority is the dubious one of Sharp. Thayer, *The Influence of Horace,* finds an echo of Horace even in *Pauline:* "not die utterly"; "non omnis moriar": *Carmina* 3.30.6.

22. Sotheby, items 652, 1160, 995.

23. *NL,* p. 15, RB to E. F. Haworth, [April 1839].

24. "Some Strictures on a Late Article in the 'Trifler,' " *Trifler,* No. 2 (Feb. 1835), p. 17. See Appendix C.

25. W. R. Benét, ed., *From Robert & Elizabeth Browning* (London, John Murray, 1936), p. 22, EBB to Arabel and Henrietta Barrett, Oct. 2, 1846.

26. E.g., he was rereading Homer and the Greek Bible as late as the 1880s: see RB to Mrs. Smalley, Sept. 17, 1880, MS, Baylor and RB's copy of a *Greek Testament* (Oxford, 1881), at Houghton, Harvard.

27. Esp. RB to Monclar, Dec. 5, 1834, March 2, 1835, July 30, 1835, MS, Private Collection.

28. *RBEBK,* II, 657 (letter 332), RB to EBB, [April 27, 1846], speaks of letting "this reading drop some ten years ago."

29. *RBEBK,* I, 156 (letter 80), RB to EBB, [Aug. 15, 1845].

30. *RBEBK,* II, 880 (letter 460), RB to EBB, [July 16, 1846].

31. *RBEBK,* II, 657 (letter 332), RB to EBB, [April 27, 1846].

32. RB knew *Lucrèce Borgia* (1833, see n. 63, below) and in 1834 mentioned *Notre-Dame* (1831), *Le Roi s'amuse* (1832) and *Les Feuilles d'automne* (1831), the last with levity, in a letter, RB to Monclar, Dec. 5, 1834, Private Collection.

33. *RBEBK,* II, 890 (letter 466), RB to EBB, [July 20, 1846]. There was still a picture of Hugo by Monclar in the Picture Album he gave RB when it came into the Private Collection.

34. *RBAD,* p. 33, RB to A. Domett, May 22, 1842.

35. RB to Monclar, Dec. 5, 1834, July 30, 1835, MS, Private Collection. The second letter, admitting he doesn't know Balzac well, probably discredits the theory of Henri-Léon Hovelaque, *La Jeunesse de Robert Browning* (Paris, Les Presses Modernes, 1932), pp. 121-125, that RB imitated Balzac's *Louis Lambert* in *Pauline.*

36. *RBEBK,* II, 657 (letter 332), RB to EBB, [April 27, 1846].

37. Ibid.

38. *NL,* p. 15, RB to E. F. Haworth, [April, 1839].

39. *LRB,* p. 105, RB to Seymour Kirkup, Feb. 19, 1867. EBB to Mrs. Martin, Dec. 29, [1859], Kenyon TS for *LEBB,* BL, Add. MS. 42, 231, fol. 248, speaks of Balzac as "one of our gods"; Flaubert would also become one of RB's favorites in the 1850s.

40. *RBEBK,* II, 657 (letter 332), RB to EBB, [April 27, 1846].

41. Griffin and Minchin, p. 90, imply that he started tutoring in Italian while at London, thus dropping plans to take the Italian course there. It would seem more likely that German was taken instead of Italian; then, in his dissatisfaction with London, he came back to Italian at home in 1829. Italian had originally been entered on the university books, then scratched out and replaced by German.

42. He thanks a merchant from Camberwell named Thomas Griffin in his autobiography, *Vita* (Florence, 1846), I, 275, for helping him settle in London and find students.

43. Ibid., I, 332.

44. Ibid., I, 451.

45. Both RB and his sister are listed as subscribers, as Griffin and Minchin, p. 20, note.

46. By 1834 RB certainly was familiar enough with Italian to pepper his letters to Monclar, MS, Private Collection, liberally with Italian phrases and to translate Italian at sight (see text below and n. 62).

47. *Vita,* I, 332.

48. *RBEBK,* I, 449 (letter 229), RB to EBB, [Feb. 11, 1846]. The exercise does appear in *A New Italian Grammar* (London, 1828), p. 330.

49. Preface, *Italian Grammar.*

50. Ibid.

51. *Vita,* I, 220.

52. Ibid., I, 143.

53. RB to Edward Twisleton, June 12, 1867, MS, Houghton, Harvard, bMS Am 1408(46). RB's copy of Bartoli is now at Balliol College, Oxford. DeVane, *Handbook,* pp. 153-154, 165, is probably correct in arguing that both poems were written in the 1844 voyage; RB also took Bartoli with him in 1838.

54. *RBEBK,* I, 518 (letter 259), RB to EBB, [March 6, 1846].

55. DeVane, *Browning's Parleyings,* pp. 56-57, identifies Bartoli as a specific source for

details in "The Bishop Orders his Tomb at St. Praxed's Church" and information on the Athenian theater in *Balaustion's Adventure* and *Aristophanes' Apology*.

56. Griffin and Minchin, p. 90.

57. He was rereading the *Purgatorio* in 1845: *RBEBK,* I, 53 (letter 20), RB to EBB, [May 3, 1845].

58. *Il decameron . . . testo poggiali . . . rincorretto dal professore A. Cerutti* (London, 1829). There is a copy at the BL.

59. Richard Henry Wilde, *Conjectures and Researches Concerning the Love Madness and Imprisonment of Torquato Tasso,* 2 vols. (New York, 1842), was the first work discussed in RB's review, the so-called "Essay on Chatterton."

60. *RBEBK,* I, 49 (letter 18), RB to EBB, [April 30, 1845].

61. RB's early study of Spanish and the ability to read some Calderón is indicated only by the letter, RB to Monclar, Dec. 5, 1834, MS, Private Collection. Speaking of learning Spanish with a grammar, *LL,* p. 54, RB to Mrs. FitzGerald, Aug. 9, 1878, RB vaguely alludes to earlier, unsystematic attempts at Spanish. *RBEBK,* I, 62 (letter 24), RB to EBB, [May 13, 1845], speaks of the play Shelley dreamed about, *El embozado, O el encapotado,* as one he knew. Lawrence Poston, Jr., "A Possible Echo of Calderón in Browning," *Browning Society Notes,* 4 (Dec. 1974), 26, offers interesting parallels between *La Vida es Sueño* and "The Bishop Orders his Tomb at St. Praxed's Church." On RB's study of German see chap. xi, section 1.

62. Diary of Catherine (Katie) Bromley, entry for ca. Nov. 1, 1833, reported at Old Battersea House, Battersea, and quoted A. M. W. Stirling, *The Merry Wives of Battersea and Gossip of Three Centuries* (London, Robert Hale, 1956), p. 120, entry ca. Nov. 1, 1833. Katie lived at Stamford Grove, Upper Clapton, and went to Fox's chapel. She and her husband were both artists. I have not been able to locate the Diary to confirm this report. There were manuscripts at Old Battersea House, Battersea, London, but the House has changed hands and many of the possessions have been sold.

63. Ibid., p. 121, entry for Nov. 8, 1833.

64. Ibid., p. 122, source not identified.

65. *RBEBK,* I, 239 (letter 133), EBB to RB, [Oct. 17, 1845].

66. See above, chap. vi, section 1 and n. 25.

67. Melvill (1798-1871), the son of an army officer, was educated at St. John's and St. Peter's Colleges, Cambridge, and was a fellow and tutor at St. Peter's until 1832. He was minister at Camden Chapel, 1829-1843, principal of the East India College, Haileybury, 1843-1857; Golden lecturer at St. Margaret's, Lothbury, 1850-1856; Canon of St. Paul's, 1856-1871: see *DNB,* s.v. Melvill. He published many of his sermons (see the far from definitive list of main collected editions, *DNB*) but he was most famous for his great popularity as a rhetorical preacher.

68. On the history of the chapel see Douglas Allport, *Collections Illustrative of the Geology, History, Antiquities, and Associations, of Camberwell, and the Neighbourhood* (Camberwell, 1841), p. 192. The Chapel itself was built in 1797 on the Peckham Road just west of the entry to Southampton St. near the Silverthorne's brewery and was described in 1823 as "a very neat edifice of brick, handsomely ornamented with brown stone . . . neat pilasters, surmounted by a cupola": Pigot and Co., *London & Provincial New Commercial Directory* (London, 1823), p. 10. It was expanded once in the 1830s and then further enlarged by G. G. Scott with the advice of Ruskin in 1854. There are 1825 views of interior and exterior by G. Yates at the Minet Public Library. Ministers before Melvill had been Dissenters, but when he became minister it was registered as an Episcopal chapel. Clayton had refused the ministry in 1804, disapproving of the middle plan.

69. Frederick Rogers, *The Early Environment of Robert Browning* (London, priv. prnt., 1904), p. 15; Allport, *Collections of Camberwell,* p. 224n.

70. Sarianna Browning to Fannie C. Browning, April 27, 1888 (a note to RB's letter of the same), MS, Balliol College, Oxford, MS. 393 in the catalog of Balliol College MSS. A copy

of Melvill's *Sermons* (London, 1833), is in the Meynell Collection, Baylor: it is probably the Browning family copy, though it is not signed; some chapters are checked in pencil and there are marginal markings by some passages. Two other works by Melvill were in the Browning library: *Sermons Preached at Cambridge* (London, 1840) and *A Selection from the Lectures Delivered at St. Margaret's* (London, 1858): Bertram Dobell Catalog, *Browning Memorials* (London, 1913), items 292-293.

71. RB's letters to A. Domett, 1842-1845, *RBAD,* repeatedly mention seeing Domett's father at Camden Chapel.

72. Sarianna Browning to Fannie C. Browning, letter of April 27, 1888.

73. See *The Diaries of John Ruskin,* ed. Joan Evans and John Howard Whitehouse (Oxford, Clarendon Press, 1956), esp. I, 238, 240-241, 243, 246; Ruskin's profile of Melvill in *Praeterita* (New York, 1887), II, 278-282, reflects his rebellion against the ethos of evangelical Christianity; though he notes that Melvill argued "the inexplicable into the plausible," his satire is mostly against his smug listeners; his opinion of Melvill remains quite high. Cf. *Diaries,* III, 1001. Melvill's qualities are apparent in the portrait by J. J. Williams (Day and Haghe, [ca. 1832]), Newington District Library.

74. William H. Blanch, *Ye Parish of Camerwell* (London, 1875), p. 209, citing a contemporary observer.

75. Melvill, see esp. "The Doctrine of the Resurrection Viewed in Connection with that of the Soul's Immortality," *Sermons,* pp. 139-145; the Baylor copy is marked in the margin in this sermon and the sermon is checked off in the Contents.

76. Ibid., p. 212.

77. Ibid.

78. Anyone who reads the sermons in the Browning family copy would be tempted to say more about Melvill's influence, though biographical evidence is lacking. Melvill often speaks directly to young people misled by the "sceptical writings" and "voluptuous poetry" (pp. 123-125) of the age and, from the position not of an uncouth zealot but of one who has known "the choicest assemblies of the literary youth of our land," calls his young parishioners to take their professed religion seriously. Whether or not Browning heard such remarks and heard them as addressed particularly to him, he clearly must have found Melvill important as a mediator between his own early religious belief and his later adolescent freethinking as he attempted to synthesize them in the 1830s.

79. Ruskin, *Praeterita,* pp. 281-282. The *Diaries* often remark on the persuasiveness of his exegeses.

80. *RBEBK,* I, 16 (letter 7), RB to EBB, [Feb. 11, 1845]: Isaiah 38.5.

81. *RBEBK,* I, 142 (letter 72), RB to EBB, [Aug. 3, 1845]: Matthew 23.23.

82. Minnie G. Machen, *The Bible in Browning with Particular Reference to The Ring and the Book* (New York, Macmillan, 1903), tabulates the use of the Bible in *The Ring and the Book.* The discussion below is indebted to her useful general observations, esp. pp. 1-33.

83. *RBEBK,* I, 287 (letter 157), RB to EBB, [Nov. 23, 1845]. Browning's Hebrew study —especially in the 1880s not the mere amusement it has been taken for—is discussed in Judith Berlin-Lieberman, *Robert Browning and Hebraism* (Jerusalem, [Azriel Press], 1934), esp. pp. 10-13.

84. W. S. Landor to John Forster, Aug. 10, 1836, MS, Baylor: trans. Kintner, *RBEBK,* I, 286 (letter 156), from Proverbs 15.30. EBB mentions the Hebrew, *RBEBK,* I, 285 (letter 156), EBB to RB, [Nov. 22, 1845].

85. Domett's *Diary,* p. 249.

86. Boyd Litzinger, *Robert Browning and the Babylonian Woman,* Baylor Browning Interests, No. 19 (Waco, Texas, Baylor University, 1962), discusses RB's attitude to Catholicism. RB was almost always critical of the religion, but this general impression needs to be balanced by recognition of his affection for Italian institutions and his ability to portray positive Church figures, in whom Christian goodness is stressed above the particular creed, e.g., Caponsacchi and the Pope in *The Ring and the Book.*

87. Moncure D. Conway, *Autobiography, Memories and Experiences* (Boston, Hough-

ton, Mifflin, 1904), II, 24. Berlin-Lieberman's thorough *Browning and Hebraism* discusses RB's extensive and sympathetic, if neither too deep or scholarly, acquaintance with rabbinical literature and the use that he makes of it in his poems. Although he especially turned to themes of Jewish tradition in the 1880s, there is every reason to suppose that RB became interested in Hebrew writings apart from the Bible when he took up Hebrew. The poems on Ben Ezra and Karshook are, of course, earlier than the 1880s, as well. Even earlier, he spoke to EBB of the *Travels of Rabbi Benjamin, Son of Jonah of Tudela,* trans. R. Gerrans (London, 1784): *RBEBK,* I, 147 (letter 75), EBB to RB, [Aug. 8, 1845]: the book had his grandfather's name as subscriber.

88. On Collier's work, see n. 72, chap. v. DeVane, *Handbook,* p. 134, cites the latter two as sources.

89. RB quoted the article above the poem when he first published it, *Monthly Repository,* 10 (Jan. 1836), p. 45. See DeVane, *Handbook,* p. 123.

90. The family's copy of Isaac Watts, [*Psalms and Hymns*] (London, n.d.) with the autograph of RB Sr., and the *Hymns and Spiritual Songs in Three Books: Collected from the Scriptures* (London, 1813) are at Baylor: bound with George Burden, *A Collection of Hymns from Various Authors Intended as a Supplement to Dr. Watts's Psalms and Hymns,* 13th ed. (London, 1812).

91. *RBEBK,* II, 978 (letter 510), RB to EBB, [Aug. 19, 1846].

92. Ibid. Orr, p. 30, reports that RB read often in his father's volume of the *Emblems*— actually probably his grandfather's copy: *Emblems, Divine and Moral: Together with Hieroglyphics of the Life of Man,* 2 vols. (1777), with engraved plates and stamp of RB's grandfather: Bernard Quaritch Catalog, No. 326, *Rare and Valuable Books, Including Books of R. B. Browning, Most of which Have Interesting Inscriptions* (London, June 1913), item 104. The poem is identified by Kintner as *Emblems* V.6. The town is actually Finchfield (Finchingfield). The plate can be seen in R. P. T. Coffin and A. M. Witherspoon, eds., *Seventeenth Century Prose and Poetry* (New York, Harcourt, Brace, 1929), p. 95 (poetry section). RB read the *Divine Fancies,* to which he also refers in the letters to EBB, in his mother's edition: *Divine Fancies, digested into Epigrams, Meditations, and Observations* (London, 1723): autograph of "Sarah Anna Browning" and also by RB: "Nov. 19, 1837." See Anderson Galleries, *Catalog* (W. H. Arnold Sale), No. 4107 (New York, May 2-3, 1924): now in a private collection. Sarah Anna might also be RB's sister. Quarles was then still a popular book among the middle class and the Dissenters.

93. RB Sr., "Scrapbook," MS, Humanities Research Center, Univ. of Texas (No. 22, Appendix B); partly reproduced, Alice Corkran, "Chapters from the Story of My Girlhood," *Girl's Realm,* Nov. 1904, pp. 282-283.

94. *NL,* p. 251, RB to W. H. White, May 2, 1879.

95. *NL,* p. 30, RB to R. H. Horne, [Autumn 1843].

96. Sothby, items 925, 922, 926, 927, 921. The lock of hair referred to below is listed Sotheby, item 1370, and was probably not given until Hunt's death. See Griffin and Minchin, p. 77*n.*

97. *Pauline* (1833), Mill copy, Victoria and Albert Museum, Forster Collection.

98. *NL,* p. 30, RB to R. H. Horne, [Autumn 1843]. Although there are no clear borrowings or allusions, it seems likely that *Paracelsus* was consciously or unconsciously modeled on the inner drama of Samson. Like Samson's, Paracelsus' development is strangely undramatic and unrelated to the dramatic dialogue, which serves only to illuminate issues to the reader. Both heroes wait for, and eventually receive, a rousing spirit that restores them at their end to something like their early promise and that proclaims the validity of God's plan. At the least such similarities demonstrate a kinship in temperament between the two poets.

99. RB received Smart's translation of Horace's *Odes* (1767?) from his Uncle Reuben in 1824 and may have known Smart's works from his father's library. He speaks in the "Parleying with Christopher Smart" (1887) of reading "At length" Smart's song. If he did read other works, his enthusiasm for Smart was based almost entirely, as he explains in the "Parleying," on the "Song to David," which he saw in the "small paperbound book," *A Song to David,* ed.

John Rodwell and B. J. Holsworth (1827); RB told Furnivall he bought it "at the time [i.e., probably before 1829 or 1830] and received the impression I still retain." The book was then lent to a friend who never returned it. RB could have and very likely did see the Rodwell edition advertised in the *Literary Gazette,* No. 536 (April 28, 1827), p. 272: It was to the *Gazette* that RB turned later the same year to obtain information regarding Shelley's works (see n. 6, chap. ix).

RB saw the "Song" again "for but a few minutes," about 1844 or 1845, reprinted in *Chambers' Cyclopaedia.* This information, from a letter, RB to F. J. Furnivall, March 2, 1887, MS, Huntington, FU 149, corrects the view that RB only appreciated the work when he saw it in 1845. Rather, it influenced him at the same time Shelley's lyrical influence was most strong, though possibly the rereading stimulated the writing of "Saul." Cf. DeVane, *Handbook,* pp. 506-507, *Browning's Parleyings,* pp. 102-106. *LRB,* p. 262, RB to F. J. Furnivall, March 4, 1887, corrects RB's "*Chalmers*" for "*Chambers*" in the 1st letter. But the "nearly fifty years" ago must be a slip for sixty. There is an allusion to Smart in *Paracelsus,* I. There is also an allusion to the "Song" in *Browning's Essay on Chatterton,* ed. Donald Smalley (Cambridge, Mass., Harvard University Press, 1948), p. 112. Claude W. Sumerlin, "Christopher Smart's *A Song to David:* Its Influence on Robert Browning," *Costerus,* 2 (1972), 185-196, suggests Smart as inspiration for Aprile and some of the study of young Sordello, but the connection is vague. Anon, "Reminiscences of Mr. Browning, By a Friend," newspaper clipping, [1890?], Huntington, T. Martin Scrapbook, recalls RB recited the entire poem by heart.

100. Orr, p. 31.

101. Ibid., p. 30.

102. On the general development of literary history in the eighteenth century, see esp. René Wellek, *The Rise of English Literary History* (Chapel Hill, University of North Carolina Press, 1941). Eighteenth-century relations to the Elizabethans are discussed by Earl R. Wasserman, *Elizabethan Poetry in the Eighteenth Century,* Illinois Studies in Language and Literature, vol. 32 (Urbana, University of Illinois Press, 1947).

103. *RBEBK,* I, 328 (letter 178), RB to EBB, [Dec. 19, 1845].

104. He speaks of an article by Lamb in the *London Magazine* of 1825: *RBEBK,* I, 434 (letter 221), RB to EBB, [Feb. 4, 1846]. There is a reference to Hazlitt's essays in a letter, Orr, p. 54, RB to W. J. Fox, March 31, 1833. He almost certainly read at least Hunt's *Lord Byron and Some of his Contemporaries:* see my discussion, chap. ix, section 2.

105. *RBEBK,* I, 428 (letter 218), RB to EBB, [Jan. 31, 1846]; *RBEBK,* I, 413 (letter 211), RB to EBB, [Jan. 23, 1846]. RB told Hiram Corson that he had read all of Chaucer in youth but never afterwards: "A Few Reminiscences of Robert Browning," *Browning Institute Studies,* 3 (1975), p. 65; rpt. from the *Cornell Era* (1908).

106. *NL,* p. 20, RB to W. C. Macready, [Aug. 23, 1840]; *RBAD,* p. 46, RB to A. Domett, Dec. 13, 1842.

107. *Paracelsus,* n. 5, quotes *Volpone* on Paracelsus' sword. The dedication of *Luria* to W. S. Landor echoes Webster's compliment to Shakespeare, Heywood, and Dekker in the Preface to *The White Devil. NL,* p. 30, RB to R. H. Horne, [Autumn 1843]; *LRB,* p. 1, RB to E. F. Haworth, [July 24, 1838]; *RBEBK,* II, 724 (letter 372), RB to EBB, [May 24, 1846]; *LRB,* p. 301, RB to F. J. Furnivall, Feb. 23, 1889.

108. Minchin, "A Letter from Hanover Cottage," p. 7, RB to E. F. Haworth, [ca. Aug. 1, 1837]. See DeVane, *Handbook,* p. 132.

109. Orr, p. 258, quoting the diary of Mr. Thomas Richmond. RB's many reverent allusions to Shakespeare are collected in G. R. Elliott, "Shakespeare's Significance for Browning," *Anglia,* 32 (Jan.-Apr., 1909), 90-162, an early but interesting essay.

110. RB to W. C. Macready, June 15, 1837, MS, Beinecke, Yale, speaks of seeing Hamlet Oct. 21, 1830.

111. Sotheby, item 1074: inscribed as a gift, "Miss Barrett from R. B." Victoria and Albert Museum, Forster Collection, Forster Book 7952. RB inscribed the book in turn, "(to J. Forster) / R*B*."

112. *NL,* p. 20, RB to W. C. Macready, [Aug. 23, 1840].

113. "Character Versus Action in Shakespeare," *The Poetry of Experience* (New York, Random House, 1957), pp. 160-181. Elliott, "Shakespeare's Significance for Browning," makes a similar and also interesting argument, tracing the origin of RB's dramatic monologues in part to a one-sided concentration on one element in a Shakespearian drama, in practice usually character divorced from action.

114. Orr, p. 31.

115. [G. S.?] Smalley, quoted in "Memoirs of Robert Browning," *Pall Mall Budget,* Dec. 19, 1889, p. 1621.

116. A reference to *The Faerie Queene* is made in *NL,* p. 11, RB to W. C. Macready, May 28, 1836, and probably in *NL,* p. 20, RB to W. C. Macready, [Aug. 23, 1840].

117. *RBAD,* p. 28, RB to A. Domett, [ca. March 25, 1840]. Sidney speaks of lawyers using hypothetical names, "John of the Stile and John of the Nokes."

118. The Powell gift is Sotheby, item 634, *Poems on Several Occasions* (London, 1719). Geoffrey Keynes, *A Bibliography of Dr. John Donne,* 3rd. ed. (Cambridge, Cambridge University Press, 1958), pp. 166-167, 176-177, lists collected and selected works of Donne, including Chalmers', Campbell's, and Southey's. The following discussion of Browning's reading in Donne is indebted throughout to Joseph E. Duncan's model study "The Intellectual Kinship of John Donne and Robert Browning," *Studies in Philology,* 50 (Jan. 1953), 81-100, reprnt. in his *The Revival of Metaphysical Poetry: The History of a Style, 1800 to the Present* (Minneapolis, University of Minnesota Press, 1959), pp. 50-69. Duncan's account provides a continuation of the series of articles by A. H. Nethercot on the critical fortunes of Metaphysical poetry after the time of Donne: see Douglas Bush, *English Literature in the Earlier Seventeenth Century: 1600-1660,* rev. ed. (Oxford, Clarendon Press, 1962), p. 474.

119. *RBEBK,* I, 139 (letter 71), EBB to RB, [July 31, 1845]; *RBEBK,* II, 666 (letter 337), EBB to RB, [May 1, 1846].

120. Orr, p. 41.

121. "Some Strictures on a Late Article in the 'Trifler,' " *Trifler,* No. 2 (Feb. 1835), p. 16: Harvard, Houghton 23443.75*. The quotation (see Appendix C) is from the epistle to *The Progresse of the Soule.*

122. *RBJW,* p. 85, RB to Julia Wedgwood, Oct. 17, 1864.

123. See the summary of references to Donne in Duncan, "The Intellectual Kinship of John Donne and Robert Browning," pp. 83-85. RB often mentions Donne in the letters to EBB. The "Metempsychosis" referred to by William Michael Rossetti as a favorite of RB's is not identified by Duncan. Probably it is *The Progresse of the Soule.*

124. It is also referred to in *Letters of the Brownings to George Barrett,* ed. Paul Landis (Urbana, University of Illinois, 1958), p. 317, RB to George Barrett, Dec. 21, 1888; RB knew it as early as the *Trifler* article (see n. 121, above).

125. *RBEBK,* I, 25 (letter 9), RB to EBB, [Feb. 26, 1845].

126. Orr, p. 30, notes early reading in Walpole. RB speaks of Chesterfield in *RBEBK,* I, 509 (letter 255), RB to EBB, [March 3, 1846]. Walpole's unfortunate relations with Chatterton would later make him anathema to RB.

127. Minchin, "A Letter from Hanover Cottage," p. 6, RB to E. F. Haworth, [ca. Aug. 1, 1837]. The play, identifiable from RB's reference to Richard and the "fair Elizabeth," is Cibber's *The Tragical History of King Richard III Altered from Shakespeare,* one still sometimes acted in RB's day, very probably by Richardson. *The Royal Convert* is listed, Sotheby, item 1047.

128. Sotheby, items 868, 409.

129. *Hudibras* is referred to twice, both times affectionately, in the letters to Elizabeth: *RBEBK,* I, 16 (letter 7), RB to EBB, [Feb. 11, 1845]; *RBEBK,* I, 545 (letter 274), RB to EBB, [March 18, 1846]. In his n. 4 to *Paracelsus,* RB quotes Butler on Bumbastus' (Paracelsus') sword.

130. Sotheby, item 898. I have inspected it in a private collection. The edition is London, 1795. It is inscribed on the front endpaper: "from Robt Browning to [hand of RB] R Browning 1833 Feb. 1. Friday [hand of RB Sr.]." There are the usual notes and corrections by RB Sr.

131. Smalley, "Special Pleading in the Laboratory, "*Browning's Essay on Chatterton,* pp. 78-101.

132. Orr, p. 53, RB to W. J. Fox, [postmark March 29, 1833].

133. "Some Strictures," p. 18. RB alludes generally to the title and subject of the prose "Inquiry into the Origin of Moral Virtue" in the *Fable*. See the text of RB's article in Appendix C.

134. *Bacchae* 480. A similar quote from the *Medea* appears on the endpaper signed by RB and dated June 15, 1874.

135. DeVane, *Handbook,* p. 498 and *Browning's Parleyings,* chap. i, again reads the *Parleyings* too literally as intellectual autobiography: there is no indication that RB saw "God and truth" in Mandeville when he read him in 1833.

136. Report of RB's comments on Mandeville, Sutherland Orr, *A Handbook to the Works of Robert Browning* (London, 1886), p. 345.

137. "Some Strictures," pp. 17-18: an allusion, not quite accurate, to the first chapter: see the text of the article in Appendix C.

138. RB quotes from the "Epistle to Dr. Arbuthnot" in *RBEBK,* II, 764 (letter 396), RB to EBB, [June 7, 1846]; the one allusion to Johnson, to the "Life of Dryden," in the love letters was apparently a misremembrance: *RBEBK,* I, 328 (letter 178), RB to EBB, [Dec. 19, 1845].

139. Mandeville, discussion in the "Fifth Dialogue," *The Fable of the Bees.*

Chapter XIV   A Poet's Education: Limits and Promise

1. *RBEBK,* I, 378 (letter 198), RB to EBB, [Jan. 11, 1846].

2. Edward Berdoe, *Browning's Message to his Time* (New York, 1891), p. 55. Berdoe's weak and overworked justifications for this opinion from RB's poetry are rightly criticized by Lionel Stevenson, *Darwin Among the Poets* (Chicago, University of Chicago Press, 1932), p. 121.

3. Quoted in William S. Peterson, *Interrogating the Oracle* (Athens, Ohio, Ohio University Press, 1969), p. 62.

4. RB's views on evolution and Darwinism are competently discussed in Stevenson, *Darwin Among the Poets,* pp. 117-182 and in Georg Roppen, *Evolution and Poetic Belief: A Study in Some Victorian and Modern Writers,* Oslo Studies in English, No. 5 (Oslo, Oslo University Press, 1956), pp. 112-174.

5. Thomas P. Harrison, "Birds in the Poetry of Browning," *Review of English Studies,* n.s. 7 (1956), 393.

6. There is no evidence that he knew these or the newer work of Charles Lyell in geology, though it is likely that he had run across ideas of evolution in his reading. In his father's text of physiognomy, for instance, he would have found a lyrical description of Erasmus Darwin's speculations: "when we hoist the sails of philosophy, and launch forth into the wide ocean of time, where fleeting ages, and centuries, and epochs, are gliding along in full sail, then can we discern the progressive motion of nature;—then can we see life gradually rising from its modest beginnings; minerals gradually spreading out into vegetables; vegetables as if tired of their future, packing up to travel forth under the character of animals; the immense system of living beings, moving onwards towards perfection with various and varying speed, like one vast host, with man at their head": John Cross, *An Attempt to Establish Physiognomy upon Scientific Principles* (Glasgow, Andrew and John M. Duncan, 1817), p. 9: the work quoted by RB Sr. in a study in "Fifty Pen, Pencil, and Watercolor Sketches," MS, Beinecke, Yale. Cross mentions Darwin, p. 10.

7. Both are referred to affectionately in letters to EBB, e.g., *RBEBK,* II, 745 (letter 385), RB to EBB, [May 31, 1846]; *RBEBK,* I, 355 (letter 189), RB to EBB, [Jan. 4, 1846].

8. The later references to evolutionary theory are summarized in the discussions of RB in Stevenson, *Darwin Among the Poets,* and Roppen, *Evolution and Poetic Belief.* The "Parleying with Francis Furini" confronts Darwinism, if not Darwin, directly.

9. *LRB,* p. 198, RB to F. J. Furnivall, Oct. 11, 1881.

10. Ibid. A reference to an observation in *The Descent of Man* in the "Parleying with George Bubb Dodington" shows RB had at least looked into Darwin: see Harrison, "Birds in Browning," p. 400.

11. To William Allingham, quoted in Stevenson, *Darwin Among the Poets,* p. 180.

12. Berdoe, *Browning's Message to his Time,* p. 99, RB to E. Berdoe, June 11, 1885.

13. RB to Ripert-Monclar, Dec. 5, 1834; March 2, 1835, MS, Private Collection.

14. Orr, p. 42, makes just this charge.

15. The amount of pure invention in RB's account, as well as the "apparent erudition" of his notes, is discussed at length by Griffin and Minchin, pp. 66-72. See also DeVane, *Handbook,* pp. 52-55.

16. "He said his (own) father had studied the question of the authorship fully": Domett's *Diary,* pp. 72-73. The essay "Junius," 6 pp., MS, Fitzwilliam Museum, Cambridge, is that of a connoisseur of the subject. There are also detailed discussions of the issues in two of his letters to RB, Dec. 15, 1863 and [n.d.], MS, Fitzwilliam. Ripert-Monclar remarks to his journal that RB Sr. showed him a collection of all the works of Junius: "Voyage à Londres, 1834," MS, Private Collection.

17. Orr, p. 30.

18. *RBEBK,* II, 724 (letter 372), RB to EBB, [May 24, 1846].

19. Sotheby, item 1030: inscribed, "Robt. Browning, from my Father, 12 March, 1833."

20. RB Sr., "Waltham Drawings," MS, Wellesley, fols. 12, 16. One character puns (badly) on the "Art of Mid Loathey"; another expresses the view that all young people should read the novels of Mr. Scott. A cartoon, "Scrapbook of Cartoons," formerly property of Mrs. Stephens, Bank of England, Archives Section, fol. 1 laughs at a lord visiting the Bank who has never heard of Scott.

21. See discussion, chap. v, section 4; William's publications are listed in Appendix A, section IV; mottoes from his master Scott are used for chapter headings in *Hoel Morvan.*

22. His preface introduces the prose "tales founded on fact" as a new kind of literature. They are colorful incidents from history told well—something on the line of his nephew's later more garrulous poetic tales from history.

23. In *Leisure Hours.* There are also reviews of Vigny's *Othello* and Lucien Arnault's *Gustavus Adolphus.* Perhaps the same interest led him to overvalue his nephew's *Strafford.*

24. In view of the family interest in him, it is hard to imagine that RB would not have known Scott's novels. However, I have found no positive evidence of early reading in Scott. RB gave his son an entire collection of the Waverley novels: Sotheby, item 1059. RB, and no doubt his uncle too, also had the model of Hugo for historical fiction. Scott was also a favorite topic of Chris and Joe Dowson: see n. 158, chap. v.

25. *Leisure Hours,* pp. 225-231.

26. There is no adequate study of Browning's relation to history and the historical thought of his time. Two insightful and suggestive essays are J. Hillis Miller's chapter on Browning in *The Disappearance of God: Five Nineteenth Century Writers* (Cambridge, Mass., Harvard University Press, 1963), pp. 99-109 esp., and Morse Peckham, "Historiography and *The Ring and the Book,*" *Victorian Poetry,* 6 (Autumn-Winter 1968), 243-257. See also the recent essay by Roger Sharrock, "Browning and History," *Robert Browning,* ed. Isobel Armstrong (Athens, Ohio, Ohio University Press, 1975), pp. 77-103.

27. The original membership is given in the *Journal de l'Institut Historique,* 1 (1834), 318. RB and C. W. Dilke of the Athenaeum were the only corresponding members from England in the *troisième classe.* His correspondence with Monclar shows that RB did owe his membership to Monclar: RB to Monclar, Dec. 5, 1834; July 30, 1835; Jan. 11, 1836, MS, Private Collection.

28. RB's letter to Monclar of Dec. 5, 1834 asserts that he hopes to make substantial contributions to the work of the Institut: I have found nothing that seems to be his in the *Journal de l'Institut Historique.*

29. *RBAD,* p. 28, RB to A. Domett, [ca. March 25, 1840].
30. *RBEBK,* I, 121 (letter 61), RB to EBB, [July 13, 1845].
31. *RBEBK,* I, 161 (letter 84), EBB to RB, [Aug. 19, 1845].
32. *RBEBK,* I, 507 (letter 254), EBB to RB, [March 2, 1846]. The "somebody" is identi-fied as Alexander Kinglake by Griffin and Minchin, p. 26. Cf. the comment on the learning of the mature RB by a Mr. [G. S.?] Smalley: "Mr. Browning is a mine of knowledge, knows with minute accuracy the history of literature, of art, of music, of many other things": "Memoirs of Robert Browning," *Pall Mall Budget,* Dec. 19, 1889, p. 1621.
33. *RBAD,* p. 78, J. Arnould to A. Domett, [ca. Nov. 8, 1843].
34. *Browning's Essay on Chatterton,* ed. Donald Smalley (Cambridge, Mass., Harvard University Press, 1948), p. 116.

Notes to the Appendixes

1. Entries in an "old Biographical Dictionary" reported by Robert Shergold Browning (son of Uncle W. S. Browning) to F. J. Furnivall, May 1, 1890, MS, Huntington FU 164. "W. Hon" could be any number of places, including West Holme near Corfe Castle. The abbrevia-tion is too vague for positive identification and the handwriting allows other interpretations, i.e., "W. Hun[dred]." Furnivall considered the place to be in Gloucestershire: letter to H. G. Bowen, Feb. 25, 1890, MS, Bank of England, Archives Section, Misc. Acces. No. 107.
2. For the family legends, see chap. iii.
3. Browning entries in the parish register, now at the Dorset Record Office, and in other local records are given in Furnivall, "Ancestors," pp. 28-29; they were confirmed by Anthony J. Lane, "The Brownings at Woodyates," TS, Baylor: see also his "The Brownings at Woodyates and Pentridge," *Dorset: The County Magazine,* No. 28 (Winter 1972), pp. 50-59.
4. Sotheby, item 371: a copy of L. Bayly, *The Practice of Pietie* (Delff, 1648), with autograph of Elizabeth Pethebridge, a pedigree, and note by RB: "(who was therefore the Great-Great-Grandmother of RB.)" Her will of Oct. 23, 1754 is given in Furnivall, "Ances-tors," p. 41; it was proved in 1759.
5. Christiana Browning (daughter of Uncle Reuben Browning) to F. J. Furnivall, [ca. 1890], reporting her cousin Ellen Browning (d. of Uncle W. S. Browning), MS, Huntington, FU 74.
6. Furnivall's information ("Ancestors," p. 26) was based on a written statement of a descendent, Robert Browning of Morley's Hotel (d. July 18, 1866). Sir Vincent Baddeley, "The Ancestry of Robert Browning, The Poet," *Genealogist's Magazine,* 8 (March 1938), 4-6, points out that Corfe Castle was destroyed and a Sir John Bankes died in 1644. Contrary to Baddeley's implication ("Correspondence," *TLS,* April 17, 1948, p. 219), Furnivall did have an authentic statement from Robert Browning of Morley's Hotel: sent to Robert Shergold Browning as indicated in Robert Shergold Browning to F. J. Furnivall, March 17, 1890, MS, Huntington, FU 161 (hence Baddeley was questioning not Furnivall's word, but that of his own grandfather, Robert of Morley's). Corfe Castle is a place as well as a castle, so there may be some truth in the original statement.
7. Lane, "Brownings at Woodyates and Pentridge," p. 53, citing the account book of the Overseers of the Poor.
8. Henry Symonds, "The Manor, Hundred and Priory Courts of Cranborne, 1725-35," *Proceedings of the Dorset Natural History and Antiquarian Field Club,* 32 (Dorchester, 1911), 55-60. On Oct. 25, 1725 he also appeared on a roll of inhabitants and on Oct. 14, 1733 a "recitements" tax is recorded as paid by him. Mrs. Elaine Baly of East Barnet, Herts, kindly called my attention to this information.
9. He gave his birth date (as opposed to date of baptism) in a book, William Martyn, *The Historie, and Lives, of Twentie Kings of England* (London, 1615): "The [*sic,* for Tho.]

Browning Woodyates July 19th: 1970 Born Sept. 30th: 1721." (Copy at Baylor; it has the signatures of five generations of Brownings.) W. S. Browning's entry, "1723," in the "old Biographical Dictionary" is incorrect.

10. He had taken a temporary position as master's mate; he drowned in English Harbour, not St. John's Harbour as the tombstone indicates. Lane, "Brownings at Woodyates and Pentridge," p. 55, cites the muster book of the *Sybil* at the Public Records Office, London. Lane also gives a clear photograph of the tombstone.

11. Furnivall, "Ancestors," pp. 26-27, citing documents from the Shaftesbury estate muniment-room, 1733, Oct. 29, 1760, May 6, 1779. The landlord was the fourth earl (1713-1771). Although Furnivall asserted the footman ancestry and the mulatto strain in the Tittles on insufficient evidence, he was not guilty of forgery nor imprecise in his research and citations. Contrary to Mason's assertion that the Brownings were not at Woodyates Inn, a book of Robert Browning, grandfather, *Precious Remedies Against Satan's Devices* (see the books of Robert Browning, grandfather, below) has the entries: "Robin Browning, son of Thos. Browning, was born July 26th anno Dom. 1749, Woodyats [*sic*] Inn, in the County of Dorset, Anno Lapo [*sic*] 5766" (p. 313, probably by Thomas) and "Robert *alias* Robin Browning his Book, anno Dom. Nov. 16, 1766, Anno Mund. 5776—Woodyates Inn, Dorset" (last fly, probably Robert, grandfather). The connection to the Inn has been confirmed by a letter among family papers of Mrs. Nora Collings of Sevenoaks, Kent, granddaughter of RB's Aunt Jemima, that speaks of a small piece of land not sold with the Inn: "Research Notes," *Browning Society Notes,* 4 (March 1974), 23, Thomas Browning to Robert Browning (grandfather of the poet), Feb. 25, 1779.

12. "Brownings at Woodyates and Pentridge," p. 51. Local tradition confirms what seems obvious enough from the name. For Lane's source see John Hutchins (1698-1773), *The History and Antiquities of the County of Dorset* (London, 1774), II, 158. The inn is also mentioned in the 2nd. ed., rev. Richard Gough (London, 1813), III, 194. The "noted inn on the London Road" was close to East Woodyates on the edge of the county. There was a West Woodyates; the Village of Woodyates proper was Pentridge where the parish church still is. Lane gives a photograph of the inn before its demolition in this century. Even without the huge stables added by William Day, a nineteenth-century proprietor, it is an impressive holding. Furnivall, "Ancestors," p. 27, notes that it ceased to be an inn only about 1870, though even then a pub was maintained. He also notes that Michael Browning, son of RB's Uncle Reuben, still possessed some of the inn accounts.

13. Lane, "Brownings at Woodyates and Pentridge," p. 53; Furnivall, "Ancestors," p. 29. Furnivall notes he was fined once for failing in his duties as overseer.

14. Lane, p. 55, cites records from the Overseers of the Poor of special services rendered.

15. "Research Notes," letter cited above. A Mr. Longman is mentioned in the letter— possibly lending credence to Mason's claim that the family knew the publisher.

16. Mrs. Collings still possesses some of his furniture.

17. Mason, "Kinsfolk," p. 13. Furnivall concluded that the Reuben Browning who served as churchwarden at Pentridge in 1781 was the earlier brother of Thomas. Reuben was still at home at the time of Thomas's letter of 1779, cited above. Other page references here are to Mason, "Kinsfolk."

18. The rate books, Newington District Library, have a "Jn." Browning for 1813-1815 on Edmund St. very near the poet's Southampton St. I found no Reuben.

19. H. G. Bowen to Robert Shergold Browning, Dec. 27, 1889, MS, Bank of England, Archives Section, Misc. Acces. No. 107. In reply Dec. 29, 1889, Robert Shergold Browning, son of William Shergold Browning, said he had never heard of Reuben—a fact to balance against Mason's claims.

20. Substantiated by a "Methodist" magazine Mason inherited, the gift of Reuben to his stepdaughter-in-law, Jane Eliza, RB's half-aunt. (The York Street baptism is noted below under Jane Eliza, section IV, 2.) Mason's claim that the widow Mason married the poet's

Great-Uncle Reuben, not a Thomas Browning, son of William, as Furnivall asserted ("Ancestors," p. 45), has obvious authority. In light of this, I cannot certainly place this Thomas Browning who kept the New Inn at Old Bailey, 1834.

21. Furnivall, "Ancestors," p. 30; J. A. Giuseppe, "Families of Long Service at the Bank of England," *The Genealogist's Magazine,* 10 (Sept. 1949), 403, confirms Furnivall's figures and supplies other dates.

22. A "Release" of Oct. 21, 1771; a Bond of 1784 for £120, MS, Baylor.

23. A record by RB Sr. of the tombstone of his brother and mother gives his death as Dec. 12, 1784: on the fly of his copy of J. G. Raymond, *The Life of Thomas Dermody* (London, 1806), 2 vols. in 1: Bertram Dobell Catalog, *Browning Memorials* (London, 1913), item 357. William Blanch, *Ye Parish of Camerwell* (London, 1875), p. 182, cites his burial on Dec. 16, 1784, from the parish register. Robert Browning appears in the Camberwell rate books for 1784 and 1785: Newington District Library.

24. "Memorandum of an Agreement" with Catherine Abbott for rental of a house, April 3, 1794, MS, Baylor. The W. S. Browning "old Biographical Dictionary" notes his own birth in 1797 at Chelsea.

25. Islington developed early into a suburb for prosperous Londoners. Colebrook Row was built along the New River in 1768: John Summerson, *Georgian London* (London, Pleiades Books, 1945), p. 261; it was a distinguished address, with literary associations from the Lambs' residence there in the 1820s. The date of the move to Islington is established by Mason's association of his mother's courtship with it. Furnivall has the death of Robert Browning, grandfather, at 2 Camden St., but this was probably not a new residence: Camden St. was across the New River from Colebrook Row. The number is 13 Camden St. in Ripert-Monclar's "Voyage à Londres, 1834," MS, Private Collection: this is, again, probably the same place.

26. Furnivall, "Ancestors," pp. 39-40, prints the will and codicils in full. The mourning ring is described, Sotheby, item 1378.

27. Abbreviations used here are those explained at the beginning of the notes.

28. *The Family of the Barrett: A Colonial Romance* (New York, Macmillan, 1938), esp. pp. 102-153.

29. Marks, *Family,* p. 112.

30. John Tittle was not mentioned in his mother's will of Oct. 25, 1743 (Marks, *Family,* p. 133) nor in that of his sister Ann of ca. 1846 (p. 130); yet in his own will of July 1, 1748 (p. 146) he spoke of his "loving sisters" and left them a considerable gift and he made his brother heir to his estates if he died without issue or, if not, left him also a large sum of money. John may have been the son of a previous liaison by his father (a Rachell Hartshorne, wholesale dealer of Port Royal, mysteriously favored the family of John Tittle in her will, see p. 130), or a son of a previous marriage, or merely estranged at the time of his mother's will, or even so well-to-do that he was left out of wills of his relatives. None of this would lend any particular credence to Furnivall's belief, which was mere speculation; John's education and social position would imply greater tolerance for mulattos in St. Kitts and London than was likely at the time.

31. Marks, *Family,* p. 152. John Tittle died in Kingston and was buried Nov., 1758 in the parish church.

32. The correspondence, among the Missionary Papers at Fulham Palace, London, is fully discussed by Marks. Her primary research is exemplary, her interpretations less so.

33. The likelihood was he went back to Jamaica in his last sickness and used the mortgage to raise money quickly. This was a very large sum.

34. Marks, *Family,* pp. 138-139. His parish records for St. George, St. Peter Basseterre, and St. Mary Cayou Parish are in the Board of Trade Papers, Public Record Office, London.

35. In Raymond, *Life of Thomas Dermody:* see n. 23 above. Her burial date is given in Blanch, *Parish,* p. 182, as April 21, 1789.

36. Furnivall, "Ancestors," p. 39.

37. This Uncle Tittle was evidently not killed on St. Kitts, though Browning repeatedly misremembered the story about him, once when he told it to EBB and again in a report arising from an attempt of a psychic to read the significance of the studs (RB, "Notes in Correction,"

MS, Baylor; J. T. K[nowles], "Brain-Waves.—A Theory," *Spectator,* 42 [Jan. 30, 1869], 134-137, quoted Orr, p. 213: the latter gives a rough date for the death of this Uncle Tittle: contrary to Marks's assertions, a good deal before RB Sr. was in St. Kitts). RB corrected what he told EBB after speaking to his father. His uncle was killed on the Guinea coast: *RBEBK,* I, 557 (letter 282), RB to EBB, [March 25, 1846]. This may be the uncle vaguely recorded by Orr, p. 9, as an African explorer; or Guinea may be a mistake for Guiana on the coast of South America where the Tittles might have had a plantation and slaves. RB spoke of an estate, which does not suggest African exploration. The links are probably the gold ones initialed "R. B.," sold Sotheby, item 1366. There was also a gold watch and other items of the great-uncle given to RB's grandfather.

38. A crown piece of William III with the engraving *"Mrs. Sarah Mill, 31 Augt. 1791, and R. B. "* was sold Sotheby, item 1364.

39. It is reproduced in the full Sotheby catalog, item 63, illus., and also in Marks, *Family,* 131 f. (present location unknown).

40. Robert Shergold Browning, son of William Shergold Browning, confirmed the family story that Margaret Tittle had a plantation in St. Kitts: letter to H. G. Bowen, Dec. 29, 1889, MS, Bank of England, Archives Section, Misc. Acces. No. 107. The amount inherited by RB Sr. is suggested by the will of Robert Browning, grandfather: "a much greater proportion" than he could leave any of his children from his second marriage—i.e., a sizable amount, though not by any means a fortune. He gave Jane Eliza, probably partly as an expression of disapproval, only two hundred pounds (one hundred in dowry, one hundred after her mother's death); presumably other children might have expected a good deal more than this. The small legacy inherited by RB Sr.'s sister Margaret Morris Browning (see below), apparently just enough for her to live on, probably suggests how much RB Sr. had from aunt and uncle.

41. Daniel Hipwell, "Robert Browning's Maternal Ancestors," *Notes and Queries,* 8th ser., 11 (April 3, 1897), 261. Wiedemann is twice described as a sugar refiner in the Register of Sasines (property ownership). Hipwell concludes his Dutch origin from the general presence of Dutchmen in the refinery. There seems no substantiation for the Hamburg origin (Sharp, *Life,* p. 18n, muddled by Orr, p. 18) to oppose this supposition. Hipwell has been accused of republishing information collected by H. H. Millar, but Millar's information, as reprinted by Furnivall, "Ancestors," pp. 32-33n, is less complete and partly wrong. Millar originally published his findings in the *Dundee Advertiser,* March 8, 1890. An unsigned article, "Robert Browning's Mother: New Facts Regarding Her Parentage," *Pall Mall Gazette,* Dec. 28, 1896, p. 3, contains much the same information as Hipwell's and probably is by Hipwell.

42. Purchase of June 27 is listed in the Register of Sasines, Burgh Charter Room, Dundee: cited Hipwell, "Maternal Ancestors," p. 261. It was on the corner of Sea-Gait and Trades Lane (not now existing).

43. Ibid.

44. Ibid., in his sasine in 1787. RB's mother had an uncle, but it is unclear whether he came from the Wiedemann or Revell side.

45. Ibid., citing Register of Burials, Dundee Charter Room.

46. Millar (cited Furnivall, "Ancestors," p. 33) based his conjecture on the sasine of 1787. But this was done not as an act of coming of age but as a formality preparatory to sale. RB's mother's birth in 1772 carries authority.

47. Hipwell, "Maternal Ancestors," p. 261, thus explains the title. His mother's share in a Merchant Company would substantiate this, as it would obviously fall to the son.

48. Ibid., p. 262: record kept by John Small and seen by Hipwell at the Register House, Edinburgh. This entry has been confirmed for me by the General Register Office, New Register House, Edinburgh. The mother's name is given as Sarah Revell and the father's name misspelled and Anglicized as Weideman.

49. Rate books, Newington District Library.

50. Sotheby, item 301: see the discussion in chap. iii, above.

51. Basic information on RB's closest relations, his mother, father, and sister, is given in the text and notes to chap. iii.

52. Robert Shergold Browning, son of William Shergold Browning, noted that she had a

small income, apparently just enough to support her, from the old Long Annuities. Family jokes turned on whether she or the annuities would expire first: letter to H. G. Bowen, Dec. 29, 1889, MS, Bank of England, Archives Section, Misc. Acces. No. 107. Elaine Baly, "Talking of the Brownings—Robert's Relations," *Browning Society Notes,* 3 (Dec., 1973), p. 5, speaks of her living with the poet's family. If this were the case there probably would have been other allusions to her presence in the household.

53. Mason, "Kinsfolk," p. 124.

54. Ibid., p. 12.

55. See n. 23, above.

56. Furnivall, "Ancestors," p. 30*n*.

57. Mason, "Kinsfolk," pp. 98-99.

58. Sarianna Browning to J. M. Campbell, [July 4, 1899], MS, Humanities Research Center, Univ. of Texas, confirmed that she had been jealous of the children from her husband's first marriage.

59. Mason, "Kinsfolk," p. 99.

60. Ibid., p. 92.

61. Furnivall, "Ancestors," pp. 34, 45, quoting William's son, Robert Shergold Browning. He must have been in Paris until 1846 (not 1845 as asserted) because RB speaks in a letter to EBB, *RBEBK,* p. 819 (letter 426), [June 27, 1846], of entertaining his daughter, Louisa Jane, then over from Paris.

62. RB, "Address Book," MS, Beinecke, Yale; RB and EBB, "Address Book" (1848), MS, Humanities Research Center, Univ. of Texas. William was buried at Nunhead Cemetery, near the poet's mother.

63. For RB's relation with William see the discussion in chap. v. section 4.

64. An "Autograph Book" of his daughter Elizabeth Ann, now belonging to Nora Collings, of Sevenoaks, Kent, granddaughter of Jemima Browning, shows the family traveled widely in Italy and Spain as well as in France.

65. Furnivall, "Ancestors," p. 39.

66. The birth and baptism of a daughter Mary Ann appears in the Register of Baptisms, Locks Fields Walworth, p. 56b, Census Office, the Public Record Office, London. The Masons were then at St. Mary Newington Butts.

67. Mason, "Kinsfolk," pp. 72, 74. Elaine Baly, "Talking of the Brownings," p. 5, also mentions some time spent in South Africa.

68. Ibid., pp. 81, 85-86.

69. Ibid., pp. v, vii: Turner cites correspondence of Mrs. Barbara Scarlett, granddaughter of Cyrus, MS, Baylor. Mr. Turner kindly provided Mason's dates and occupation from his death certificate. Mason went to Australia about 1852.

70. Ibid., p. 69.

71. Mrs. Elaine Baly, great-granddaughter of Reuben, recalls that her grandmother Elizabeth made the "constant assertion" that there was much friction and jealousy between the Masons and Reuben's household. Mrs. Collings also recalls many disagreements between different wings of the family.

72. His relation with RB and his literary and intellectual interests are discussed in chap. v, section 4.

73. Information from Mrs. Baly.

74. RB and EBB, "Address Book" (1848), MS, Humanities Research Center, Univ. of Texas. Obit of Reuben Browning, *Times,* Sept. 9, 1879, p. 1. Reuben was buried in the family vault at Shirley near Croydon. His will of Nov. 22, 1871 was sworn under at a modest two thousand pounds: Furnivall, "Ancestors," p. 37.

75. Furnivall, "Ancestors," p. 37. There is a cordial letter, RB and EBB to Michael Browning, Dec. 29, 1860, MS, Wellesley. In later letters to Reuben RB sends best wishes to the entire circle at Croydon.

76. Information on Christiana from Mrs. Baly. She provides further notes on Reuben's

family and a sample of the music in her "Talking of the Brownings," pp. 8-9, 18-19. One of the three photos in her possession, about 1872, is repro. p. 17.

77. "Death of Reuben Browning," *Journal of Commerce,* Sept. 11, 1879 (from a copy in possession of Mrs. Baly).

78. F. W. Gunsaulus, *The Higher Ministries of Recent English Poetry* (New York, F. H. Revell, 1907), front., RB to Louisa and Sarah Browning, Nov. 11, 1864 (incorrectly described, Broughton, entry D808, p. 357).

79. Furnivall, "Ancestors," p. 40.

80. Arnold Sales Catalog, *Books and Letters Collected by William Harris Arnold* (Jamaica, N.Y., 1901), item 50, RB to Louisa Browning, Aug. 1, 1863, regretting a visit; see the letter about Mary, above.

81. Mason, "Kinsfolk," pp. 76-78.

82. Christiana Browning (daughter of Reuben) to F. J. Furnivall, [ca. 1890], MS, Huntington FU 72. She says 1827 but Bank records give his period of service as July 27, 1826-Nov. 4, 1829: H. G. Bowen to Robert Shergold Browning, Dec. 27, 1889, MS, Bank of England, Archives Section, Misc. Acces. No. 107.

83. Mrs. Nora Collings of Sevenoaks, Kent (granddaughter of Jemima) kindly informed me of the family tradition which, as an oral tradition, is, of course, a vague one; it is somewhat supported by RB's admiring description of her: Orr, p. 74. Baly, "Talking of the Brownings," pp. 6-7, supports the tradition from memory of her own grandmother's recollections as well as from similar correspondence with Mrs. Collings.

84. Mason, "Kinsfolk," p. 6.

85. Furnivall incorrectly identified him as John Silverthorne from Directories of 1809-1811. Pigot and Co., *London and Provincial New Con.mercial Directory* (London, 1823) gives Wm. Silverthorne. William took over the Brewhouse from a Nathaniel Silverthorne, a father or other relative (probably married to an Elizabeth: see Blanch, *Parish,* p. 174). Nathaniel first appears in the rate books, Newington District Library, for the Brewhouse in 1784; he paid rates until April 29, 1819, when his name was crossed out and William's written in; William appeared previously as a Peckham resident, though he probably already worked at the Brewhouse. Nathaniel had resided at The Terrace (south side of the Peckham Road), then, as early as 1813, at Camden Row, a terrace row at the corner of Southampton St. and the Peckham Road. In 1819 William also took over this residence. James, however, died at North Terrace, indicating that the family had moved, probably much earlier, west on the Peckham Road opposite the parish church. The brewery, a block west of Southampton St. on the Peckham Road at Portland Place, ceased to operate in 1853 and was apparently succeeded by Jenner and Mills North Surrey Brewery in 1857 (see Blanch, *Parish,* p. 152), later T. O. Pugh and Co. North Surrey Brewery (1896), finally New Phoenix Ltd. (1902). There is a twentieth-century watercolor by Guy Miller of the Peckham Road New Phoenix Brewery in the South London Art Gallery, Camberwell. The succeeding corporations are listed in the *London Post Office Directory* at North Terrace (later 37 Peckham Road) not at Portland Place. Possibly the brewery pictured remained while the offices were shifted to the former family residence of the Silverthornes in North Terrace; or the picture is of the North Terrace office (building not now existing).

86. *LRB,* p. 10, RB to F. O. Ward, July 1844. William's death at 71, of decay of nature, attended by S. A. Browning, is entered in the Camberwell District registry, No. 111. His address there is Peckham Road.

87. *LRB,* p. 23, RB to Sarianna Browning, July 2, 1849. Orr, p. 51, records the gift to publish *Pauline.*

88. Silverthorne (first name illeg., but identified as son of John) to Hall Griffin, Jan. 22, 1903, Hall Griffin Papers, BL, Add. MS. 45,563, fols. 204-206. The writer speaks of her leaving the country without a word of kindness from Browning about 1856 (date of birth of Napoleon III's son). *NL,* p. 67, RB to Sarianna Browning, Dec. 19, 1853, speaks of her leaving the old house. Of course, RB was in Italy most of the 1850s.

89. Births and baptisms of James and his brothers were recorded by Clayton in the Register of Baptisms, Locks Fields Walworth, pp. 3, 6b, 10b, 14b, Census Office, the Public Record Office, London.

90. For RB's relation with him see chap. v, section 3.

91. Furnivall, "Ancestors," p. 38: Furnivall's evidence is not given: possibly only his death destroyed the family business.

92. *NL*, p. 67, RB to Sarianna Browning, Dec. 19, 1853. Jane would almost certainly be Jane Silverthorne. James's death by chronic inflammation of the lungs is entered in the Camberwell District registry, No. 383, as May 19, 1852. The family residence there is North Terrace. The age of death given, forty, is incorrect. The birth entry is clearly 1809.

93. *LRB*, p. 23, RB to Sarianna Browning, July 2, 1849, sends love to "Aunt and James." Cf. *LEBB*, I, 322, EBB to Sarianna Browning, [ca. Feb. 1847], regretting an illness of James's.

94. Sotheby and Co., *Catalogue of the Papers of Lt.-Col. Harry Peyton Moulton-Barrett* (London, May 10, 1937), lot 6, EBB to Arabel Barrett, May [1852].

95. See n. 88, above. A "[Mary] Buchanan Album" of photos, MS, Baylor, has photos of some Silverthornes, probably later second cousins of the poet: one is labeled James, another G. C. The "Album" contains some family photos of the Brownings, but is largely unlabeled. There is also an unidentified Silverthorne, "E. Silverthorne. High R[oad] Croydon," entered in RB and EBB, "Address Book" (1848), MS, Humanities Research Center, Univ. of Texas.

96. Most of the sketchbooks and notebooks have no formal titles and are necessarily vaguely cataloged in MS collections. Two works provide fuller descriptions for some items than I have attempted to give in this finding checklist: Jack Herring, *Browning's Old Schoolfellow: the Artistic Relationship of Two Robert Brownings* (Pittsburg, Beta Phi Mu, 1972), pp. 74-76; Joseph C. Carson, "A Collection of Books from the Brownings' Personal Library," unpub. M.A. Diss. Baylor, 1970: for the Baylor collection. References are to items in their descriptions.

97. Herring, V., C, reports a "Commonplace Book" at Wellesley; though it is possible the book came from RB Sr., I found no internal evidence that it was his; many of the clippings are from as late as 1890; it may have been Robert Wiedeman Browning's or given to him by a friend.

98. Because published descriptions are often vague, some of these may repeat MS listings above; I note likely duplicates; descriptions of MSS clearly in one of the collections above are noted there only.

99. Houghton 23443.75*. The inscription is at the top of the front cover to No. 1, with printed title *"The Trifler."* Below in an unidentified hand is written, "The contribution signed Z is by Browning, whose copy this was. 1835 [date of pamphlet, not of the second hand]." Orr, pp. 63-64, quotes about one-fifth of RB's "Strictures," probably from this copy, probably then in the Browning family library. The Harvard copy came into the library Nov. 18, 1920 as a library purchase from the Samuel Shapleigh Fund. There are no records of its provenance nor is it listed in any sales catalog I have seen. A fragment of a seller's label stuck onto the back of the front cover reads "[fr]om ND SHOP." RB used the signature Z again in 1836 for his contributions to the *Monthly Repository*. The contents of the two editions are:

No. 1, January 1835:
1. "Pleased with a trifle," editor's essay, signed E., p. 3.
2. Untitled Essay on Debt, signed C., p. 6.
3. Travers Templeton to Horace Seymour, Esq., epistolary story, signed L, p. 7.
4. To a Lady Who Had Worked Me a Watch Chain, poem, signed O., p. 12.
5. Epigram, probably by RB (see text below), no signature, p. 12.

No. 2, February 1835:
1. "Pleased with a trifle," editor's essay, signed J., p. 13.
2. Some Strictures on a Late Article in the "Trifler," by RB, signed Z, p. 16.
3. The Rhone. Written on its banks in the autumn of 1833, signed E., p. 19.

100. John Donne, Epistle to *The Progresse of the Soule* (written 1601); on RB's reading in Donne see chap. xiii, section 4.

101. Sir Charles Manners-Sutton, Speaker of the House of Commons since 1817 and a Tory, had been ousted by the new Whig Parliament on Feb. 19, 1835 after strong debate.

102. "Oh idler," or "trifler."

103. Not identified.

104. Francis Quarles, "On the Life of Man," *Divine Fancies* iii . lxix.5-6.

105. RB quotes the end of the Essay on Debt.

106. "A Voyage to Lilliput," chap. i: not quite an accurate recollection of Gulliver's plight.

107. Jean-Jacques Rousseau, *Le Contrat social* (1762). On RB's interest in Rousseau see chap. x, n. 73.

108. Bernard de Mandeville, "An Inquiry into the Origin of Moral Virtue," *The Fable of the Bees* (1714). On RB's reading of Mandeville see chap. xiii, section 5.

109. Probably an allusion not to the Duke of Wellington but to his brother, Richard Colley, the Marquis of Wellesley (1760-1842) who had been prominent 1832-1834 as the Lord-Lieutenant of Ireland and who was often criticized for his conciliatory policy on Ireland as well as for his autocratic manner.

110. "As the countless sand"; adapted from Horace, *Carmina* i .xxviii.1. The extra *r* in *carrentes* has been struck out in the Harvard copy.

111. Anacreon: RB refers to one of the Anacreontics, once thought to be Anacreon's poems, now considered the work of later imitators. The poem, usually numbered ode 19, on the need of drinking, was translated by RB himself ("Translations from Greek Poets," MS, Houghton, Harvard, MS Eng 865):

> The earth drinks herself dark with the fast falling rain,
> And the roots of the trees drink her moisture again.
> And the sea drinks the wind, till she welters aloud—
> And the sun drinks the sea, till he sets in a cloud.
> And the moon drinks the sun, till her circle is plain.
> Then O wherefore my friend, are ye angry & curst
> Because *I* too would drink, while the world is athirst?

112. Shelley, whose poem "Love's Philosophy" (1819) imitates Anacreon's strategy for recommending drink. It was published with the subtitle "An Imitation from the French" in the Benbow *Miscellaneous Poems* (1826), p. 2, where RB first read it; in his copy he crossed out "the French" and wrote in "Anacreon ode." Shelley's MS in the Harvard Notebook has the heading, "An Anacreontic."

113. Leonz Füglistaller (1768-1840) was not, as might be imagined, from Teufelsdröckh's Weissnichtwo but from real German Switzerland. He was a Germanic philologist who amused himself and his friends with Latin translations of Schiller. His version of *Das Lied von der Glocke* was published as *Schillers Lied von der Glocke in gereimten lateinischen Rhythmen* (Lucern, Joh. Martin Anich, 1821) and was often republished: see Edward Studer, *Leonz Füglistaller 1768-1840: Leben und Germanistische Arbeiten* (Freiburg, Switzerland, Paulus-druckerei, 1952), esp. p. 165n. RB still recalled Füglistaller's (as Fuglichstaller's) translation in 1883: RB to the Rev. J. D. Williams, July 26, 1883, MS, Humanities Research Center, Univ. of Texas: Schiller's lines for the Latin RB quotes are:

> So laßt uns jetzt mit Fleiß betrachten,
> Was durch die schwache Kraft entspringt;
> Den schlechten Mann muß man verachten,
> Der nie bedacht, was er vollbringt. (13-16)

114. The bailiffs, trying to serve the author with his debts.
115. Orr, p. 53, RB to W. J. Fox, [March 1833].
116. E. Bridell-Fox, "Memories," *Girl's Own Paper,* 11 (July 19, 1890), 658.
117. Wilfred Partington, *Thomas J. Wise in the Original Cloth* (London, Robert Hale, 1946), p. 277, notes that the sale of Slater's work at Hodgson's, Feb. 22, 23, 1945, exhibited the finest collection of Wise's forgeries in existence. Widener's personal records of receipts for purchases show he bought the volume not from Slater or Wise but from the reputable Dodd & Livingston, Aug., 1911, for $2250. A letter from L. S. Livingston to H. E. Widener, June 30, 1911, MS, Widener Collection Archives, acknowledges that the marginalia are not authenticated.

Index

Titles throughout are indexed under author. References given in italic type are to illustrations.

Abel, Johann Leopold, 140, 141-142, 304

Academic Errors, 245

Adams, Sarah Flower, 164, 265, 308, 429n16; letters of, 3; letter of crisis of faith, 60, 181, 186, 261; portrait, *178,* 430n24; sends RB's poems to Fox, 181, 186; first acquaintance with RB, 181; Martineau on, 183; temperament, 183, 186, 187-190; as writer, 184; "Nearer, My God, to Thee," 184; occasional articles, 184; *Vivia Perpetua,* 184, 188; other publications, 189, 430nn27, 28, 431n46; actress and monologist, 184, 187, 221; admires RB's early verse, 186; supposed lover of RB, 186; later relation to RB, 186, 191-192; religion, 186, 188; on RB's appearance, 191; marginalia in her copy of *Pauline,* 191-192, 383-385 (transcription); dates, 428n9

Adams, William Bridges, 184

Aelian, 339

Aeschylus: *Agamemnon,* 154-155, 273, 300; *Choephori,* 154, 300; in Long's course, 271-272; *Prometheus Bound,* 271-272; *Scholia,* 272; *Clytemnestra,* 300; *Eumenides,* 300; in *Sordello,* 300

Aesop, *see* Croxall, Samuel

Agrippa, Cornelius, 260; *De Scientiis,* 86; *De Occulta Philosophia,* 210, 219, 434n52

Albert Terrace, 115, 361, 364, 396n29, 399n61

Albion Terrace, 411n109

Alciphron, 302

Alcott, Bronson, 230

Alfieri, Vittorio, 306, 307

Alleyn's College, 247

Ampère, J.-J., 347

Anacreon, 109, 138; Anacreontics, 202, 381; allusions in RB's poems, 301

Andromeda, 150-151, 155, *160-161,* 425n78, 435n62

Antinomianism, 56

Apostles (Cambridge Conversazione Society), 270, 349

Ariosto, Lodovico, 307

Aristotle, 116

Armstrong, Dr., 92

Armytage, James Charles, engraving of RB, *iii,* 6, 392n13

Arnault, Lucien, *Gustavus Adolphus,* 453n23

Arnold, Matthew, 18, 59, 207, 272, 279, 301, 308, 333, 336

Arnold, Thomas, 244, 265, 272

Arnold, Tom, 100

Arnould, Ann Pitcairn Carnegie, 413n131

Arnould, Dr. Joseph, 16, 413n131

Arnould, Joseph, 97, 98, 104, 413n131; law career, 17, 101; relation to RB's family, 35, 47; member of the set, 98; literary taste, 99; character, 101; education, 101; poetry and articles by, 101-102, 413n131; later life,

Browning, Thomas (of New Inn, Old Bailey), 456n20

Browning, Thomas Pethebridge, 356, 369

Browning, William, great-uncle of RB, 356, 369

Browning, William, uncle of RB, 357, 361, 370

Browning, William Shergold, half-uncle of RB, 127, 128, 372, 374, 420n256; relation to RB Sr., 40; career, 113; publications, 113, 362; *History of the Huguenots,* 113, 343, 362, 416n178; *Hoel Morvan,* 114-115, 362, 453n21; *Leisure Hours,* 115, 345, 362; *The Provost of Paris,* 362; relation to RB, 114-115; scholarship, 114-115; French connections, 114; praises *Strafford* and *Paracelsus,* 115; introduces Monclar to RB, 121; historical novels, 345; on Sir Walter Scott, 345; biographical sketch, 362; children, 362, 375

Browning family: distant ancestors, 19, 294nn2,3; motto, 20; pride, 20; family autographs in books, *22,* 420n245, 454nn1, 9, 455n11, 456nn23,24; RB's relation to, 40-41, 363-364, 364-365; business connections, 113-114; genealogy, 355-358; theories of racial origin, 359, 394n1

Brownrigg, Elizabeth, 23

Brutus Brittanicus, *see* Browning, Reuben, half-uncle of RB

Buchanan, George, 134

Bunyan, John, 139, 153; *Pilgrim's Progress,* 134, 315; *Life and Death of Mr. Badman,* 315; RB Sr. on, 378

Burke, Edmund, 293

Burnet, Thomas, *A Treatise Concerning the State of Departed Souls,* 410n77

Burns, Robert, 62, 175, 428n47

Burton, Mrs., 405n56

Bush, Douglas, 274

Butler, Samuel, *Hudibras,* 329-330

Butler, Samuel (of Shrewsbury), 244

Byron, George Gordon, Lord, 45, 50, 66, 99, 115, 131, 157, 304; *Childe Harold's Pilgrimage,* 70, 99, 214, 435nn60,64; RB's early imitation of *Childe Harold,* 170; relation of *Childe Harold* to *Pauline,* 219-220; Arnould on, 107; *Hebrew Melodies,* 140; and Nathan, 142; relation to RB's "The First-Born of Egypt," 172; continuing influence on RB and RB's refusal to follow entirely, 175-178; life, 177; in Eliza Flower's hymn book, 189; Leigh Hunt on, 206; RB on, in "At the Mermaid," 220; on Kean, 226; compared to RB in *Paracelsus*

and *Sordello,* 228-229; as political influence, 257; Domett on, 415n158

Byronism, 170

Cabinet Dictionary, 86

Caesar, 250

Caldara, *see* Caravaggio, Polidoro da

Calderón, 307; *El Embozado, O el encapotado,* 447n61; *La Vida es Sueño,* 447n61

Calvinism, 53, 56, 188

Camberwell, 13-18, 20, 357, 363; location, 9; Dewhirst map, *10-11,* 398n58; "View of London from Camberwell," *12;* 1763 map of, 13; rural character, 13; growth, 14, 17; architecture, 15; churches, 15, 19; schools, 16, 247, 439n21; subject to mediocrity, 18; prudishness, 18, 82; residence of RB's grandfather, 21; residences of RB's family, 33, 398nn58,61; repressive forces, 39, 82; limitations, 42; churches, 53, 309; wild animals, 64; countryside and woods, 64; sexual mores, 81-82; folk rituals, 81-83; elections, 83-84; poor laborers, 84; relation to London, 113; local histories, 393n1

Camberwell Fair, *78,* 82-83

Camberwell Grove, 13, 67-68

Cambridge University, 264, 265, 270

Camden Chapel, 15, 51, 309, 447n68; views of, by G. Yates, *311*

Camden Row, 413n131, 459n85

Camden Street (Islington), 456n25

Camoëns, 139, 307

Campbell, Miss, 344

Campbell, Thomas, 265, 278

Caravaggio, Polidoro da, *Perseus and Andromeda* (Casino del Bufalo), 133, 150-151, 155, *160-161,* 219, 425n78

Carducci, Count and Countess, 121

Caricatures, by RB, 80-81. *See also* Browning, Robert, father of RB, art by

Carlyle, Jane Welsh, 433n11

Carlyle, Thomas, 130, 230, 260, 274, 346; first meeting with RB, 7, 129; "Signs of the Times," 45; on Sarah Anna Browning, 47; discussed by the set, 107; *Sartor Resartus* on education, 245; on history, 257; relation to The London University, 270

Carnegie, Ann Pitcairn, *see* Arnould, Ann

Carroll, Lewis, *Alice in Wonderland,* 341

Casino del Bufalo, 425n78

Catholicism, 54, 313

Cerutti, Angelo, 423n49; on Sarianna Browning, 35; *Vita,* 304, 305; *Grammatica filosofica,* 304; life and works, 304-305; *A New Italian Grammar,* 305; teacher of Ital-

Silverthorne family, 365-366; photos, 460n95
Slater, Walter B., 383
Smalley, Donald, 331
Smalley, G. S., 453n32
Smart, Christopher, 45, 298; translation of Horace's *Odes,* 116, 317; "A Song to David," 317-319, 449n99; influence as religious visionary on RB, 318; date of influence on RB, 449n99; Rodwell and Holsworth edition of "A Song to David," 450n99
Smith, Adam, 257, 333
Smith, James, 361, 372
Smith, Jane, *see* Browning, Jane Smith
Snellgrove, Anthony (the younger, 33, 377, 378, 394n1, 400n74
Snow, C. P., 337
Société des Études Historiques, *see* Institut Historique
Sophocles, 271; *Ajax,* 154, 300; *Antigone,* 154; *Oedipus at Colonus,* 300
Southampton Street (now Row), 33, 361, 365, 398n58
Southey, Robert, 169, 288
South Place Chapel, 183
Spenser, Edmund, *The Faerie Queene,* 324
Spiritual Gleanings, 57
Staël, Madame de, 255
Steen, Jan, 75
Stevenson, Robert Louis, 130
Stillman, W. J., 402n24
Stockwell Park House, 412n116
Strachan, George, 359, 370
Strachan, Margaret, *see* Tittle, Margaret Strachan
Strauss, David, 88, 309
Sturtevant, Miss, 182, 428n2, 429n11
Sturtevant, Charles, 429n11
Suburban, as descriptive term, 15
Suburbs of London, *see* Camberwell: Dulwich; Islington; Limehouse; New Cross; Peckham; Walworth
Sue, Eugène, 302, 347
Suetonius, 86
Surrey Canal, *1,* 15
Surrey Zoological Gardens, 81
Swift, Jonathan, 329; *Gulliver's Travels,* 109, 333, 381
Swisher, W. S., 435n62

Talfourd, Field, 102, 413n133
Talfourd, Sir Thomas Noon, 102, 284, 437n76
Tasso, Torquato, 139, 307

Taylor, Harriet, 183
Taylor, Jane, 422n20; "How It Strikes a Stranger," *Youth's Magazine,* 136-137
Telegraph Hill, 33, 67
Teniers the Younger, David, 75
Ten Introductory Lectures Delivered at the Opening of the University of London, 272
Tennyson, Alfred, 49, 55, 72, 349; on historical poetry, 95; discussed by the set, 107; alienation of, 130; *The Devil and the Lady,* 260; at Cambridge, 270; *In Memoriam,* 291-292; on science and evolution, 338; "Locksley Hall Sixty Years After," 341
Terence, 250, 302
Terraces, development, 14
Thackeray, W. M., 284
Theater: John Richardson's, 82; RB attends with James Silverthorne, 97, 221; Chris Dowson on, 107; Reuben Browning and, 117; Charles Mathews in, 117-118; RB and Monclar see Macready, 124; Sarah Flower Adams as actress, 184, 187; RB sees Kean in *Richard III,* 221, 223; RB's school acting, 251; Elizabethan and Jacobean drama, 321; Restoration and eighteenth-century drama, 329
Theophrastus, 139; *Characters,* 79, 302
Thierry, Augustin, 125
Thomson, James, 23; *The Seasons,* 360
Thornton, John, 404n52
Thucydides, 302
Thurlow, Lord, 13
Tieck, Ludwig, Shakespeare translations, 277
Times, The, 34
Titian, 135
Tittle, great-uncle of RB, 360, 370, 395n15, 456n37; story of death and cuff links, 41
Tittle, Ann, great-great-aunt of RB, 370
Tittle, Edward, great-great-grandfather of RB, 358-359, 370
Tittle, Edward, great-great-uncle of RB, 358, 370
Tittle, the Rev. John, great-grandfather of RB, 359, 370; will, 456n30
Tittle, Lucy (Lucia) Molison (or Mollison), great-great-grandmother of RB, 358-359, 370
Tittle, Margaret, *see* Browning, Margaret Tittle
Tittle, Margaret Strachan, great-grandmother of RB, 359, 370
Tittle, Mary, great-great-aunt of RB, 371
Tittle, Sarah, *see* Mill, Sarah Tittle
Tittle family, 19, 358-361; plantation, 23, 359